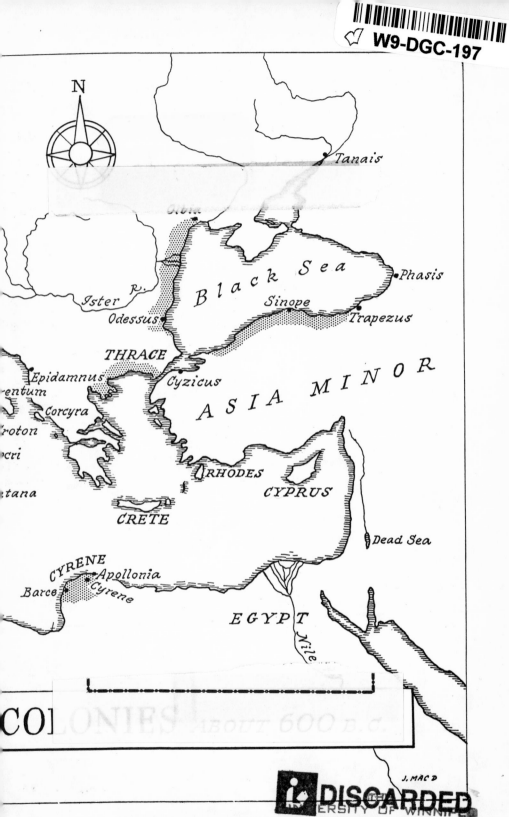

N

Tanais

Olbia

Black Sea

Phasis

Ister R.

Sinope

Odessus

Trapezus

THRACE

ASIA MINOR

Epidamnus

Cyzicus

entum

Corcyra

roton

cri

RHODES

tana

CYPRUS

CRETE

Dead Sea

CYRENE

Apollonia

Barce

Cyrene

EGYPT

Nile

COLONIES *ABOUT 600 B.C.*

J. MAC D

The Ancient World

THE
ANCIENT
WORLD

RICHARD MANSFIELD HAYWOOD

Professor of Classics

New York University

id McKay Company, Inc.

York

THE ANCIENT WORLD

To my brother Charles

PREFACE

In this history of the ancient world I have taken especial care with the beginning and the ending. The achievements of the early peoples in Egypt and in the Near and Middle East need to be carefully presented, since these peoples invented and developed so much of civilization before the brilliant era of the Greeks. The period of the so-called decline and fall of the Roman Empire also needs to be carefully dealt with so that the student will not have the idea that all was lost then and that civilization had departed. In the body of the book I have tried to show all sides of the civilizations and how they succeeded one another. I have also tried to write entirely for the reader without regard to the possible criticism of the specialist that this or that has been slighted.

My chief obligation, as usual, is to my wife, for her encouragement, for her criticism of the manuscript, and for doing most of the work on the index.

New York University   Richard M. Haywood

CONTENTS

ILLUSTRATIONS

xi

The Ancient World

CHAPTER

1

INTRODUCTION

The Scope of Ancient History

Ancient history begins with the rise in southern Mesopotamia of systems of living of a certain complexity. Although scholars offer different definitions of a civilization, they do agree that some thousands of years before Christ the people of the southern part of the region between the Tigris and Euphrates rivers were civilized and that shortly thereafter Egypt was civilized. Soon afterward there was a civilization in the Indus Valley in what is now Pakistan, and by late in the third millennium before Christ there was also a civilization in the Yellow River Valley in China. The New World civilizations of the Aztecs, the Mayas, and the Incas are a little younger.

Most important for us are the civilizations of Mesopotamia and of Egypt, where great advances were made in the mastery of physical things and in the organization of human society, and those of Greece and Rome, from which the civilization of the modern West descended directly. The achievements of the peoples of India and China will occupy us less. Interesting as it is for us to know the great cultures of the modern East, their ancient history contains less independent achievement, and we know less interesting detail of them than of the others. The history of the early civilizations of the Americas is a story by itself.

By about 3000 B.C., the civilizations of southern Mesopotamia and of Egypt were in full swing. Presently the movement spread more widely over the Middle and Near East, and for two thousand years or so this part of the world was the chief civilized area. We know a great deal in detail of what these people did and achieved, of the ups and downs of nations, the spread and disappearance of languages, and the varying popularity of gods. Through all the change we can see the rise of a more or less common background of ideas and superstitions, practices in government and trade, and techniques, whether in agriculture, metalwork, or weaving. At the same time some of this knowledge was being communicated to nearby peoples to whom traders went and from whom certain natural products were sought. This happened even at distant places like Afghanistan or Spain, around the tin mines of Bohemia, or where the amber was gathered on the Baltic coast. In two of the areas to which this influence spread there was brilliant success: Crete and Mycenae. In Crete there was a civilization of considerable originality and charm which was fully developed shortly after 2000 B.C. and lasted until some unknown force cut it off around 1400 B.C. On the mainland of Greece the civilization that seemed to center on Mycenae flourished from perhaps 1600 or 1500 B.C. until it, too, was cut off a little before 1100, probably by the movement southward of people from northern Greece. Crete never again developed any intensity of culture; on the mainland of Greece, life again began to be more intense around 800 B.C. Thereafter followed the great age of Greece.

The Greeks were the first of the moderns. They were a people of mixed blood who developed a style of their own, the beginning of the style of the West. For some reason they began early to generalize and analyze, trying to see all experience as parts of a related whole that made sense (the earlier peoples probably would have thought it silly to imagine that it could make sense) and trying to analyze everything that presented itself to them, from the movements of the heavenly bodies to the fascinating behavior of man. The earlier peoples, for all their great achievements, had a different style; they were not so given to generalization and analysis. Probably this new attitude, so like our own, is largely responsible for the great appeal of Greek literature and art to Western man since the Renaissance.

As they began again after about 800 B.C. to have an intense and strenuous culture, the Greeks slowly spread over a great deal of the Mediterranean world and up to the shores of the Black Sea. The conquests of Alexander the Great, who died in 323 B.C., led to the formation of Greek kingdoms in Egypt and the Near East, and many Greeks from the older regions went to them to participate in administration or business or to serve in the armies. Thus the culture of the Mediterranean world of Italy came to be strongly Greek, although in Egypt and the Near and Middle East the local cultures still were strong. During the eighth and seventh centuries, Greeks had emigrated to South Italy, Sicily, and southern France, and their culture strongly influenced the Etruscans of northern Italy and later the Romans.

The Celts of the European continent, the Etruscans, and the Carthaginians of North Africa all developed to a degree worthy of respect, as we shall see, but all in turn were conquered by the Romans, who by 200 B.C. were the dominant power in the West. They then began to gain power slowly in the East, and in 30 B.C., Octavian, the grandnephew of Julius Caesar, took the kingdom of Egypt from Cleopatra and completed the conquest of the great kingdoms of the Mediterranean world. A few years later Octavian was to be known as Augustus Caesar. Under the pretense of restoring the old Roman Republic, he founded what soon was plainly a monarchy and began the process of rounding out its boundaries. The Roman Empire soon included Spain, France, the Low Countries, Britain, a strip of Germany, Switzerland, the countries south of the Danube, Asia Minor, Syria and Palestine, Egypt, and a strip across North Africa from Tunisia to Morocco. A Greco-Roman culture was created. Now the civilized world was, under the control of one government, as nearly one world as it has yet been.

The energetic and able managers of the Christians slowly made great changes during the second, third, and fourth centuries that led toward the Western culture of the Middle Ages. The Empire had considerable military and economic difficulties and was frequently strained by the energy with which the people from outside attacked or raided it. By the latter part of the fifth century a new age was clearly beginning; the West was slipping from the control of the Romans and into the hands of Germanic kings; the East, with its capital at Byzantium, was to go on for a thousand years more.

How Ancient History Is Written

Scholars all over the world contribute to the development of our knowledge of ancient times. Many of them work on the history of their own areas, especially those who are archaeologists. Some of these, like the members of some other branches of scholarship, have no formal connections with universities. Some are part-time amateur scholars; some are members of museums and governmental organizations designed for the study and preservation of local antiquities. The professor, the local enthusiast, and the government expert work together.

Some scholars work on chronology. The establishment of a sound chronology is indispensable to the proper firmness of any history. Naturally it is desirable to establish an absolute chronology whenever we can, like the one that is reckoned by years before Christ and after Christ or the Jewish chronology reckoned from Abraham until the present. If we cannot do this, it is some help to have established a relative chronology between events that appear to have some connection, or to have established a temporal sequence of styles of pottery or of some other artifact; archaeologists working on excavations in the Middle and Near East use this system for dating materials. It is easier to fix dates absolutely when we get to the Greeks and the Romans, where we often have reliable written accounts; some, like the letters of Cicero, even give a day-by-day story of some series of events that covers several days.

Often the excavators in the Near East find a fragment of something from a chancellery—a decree, a proclamation, a letter to a fellow sovereign or to the governor of a province—that has a date with a day and a month and a year of the king's reign. The officials of the chancellery needed some way of dating what had happened and what had been done for their records, and the obvious method was to date by the years of the king's reign, thus making his reign an era of sorts. The kings in Asia after Alexander the Great (generally referred to as the Seleucid Kingdom) made the beginning of the reign of Seleucus I, the founder of the dynasty, the beginning of an era, rather than make a separate era for each new king in the line.

A Greek of Elis, where the Olympic Games were celebrated, originated the idea of dating by Olympiads, the four-year periods at the end of which the games were held, and it was agreed that the first meeting should be dated in the year that we know as 776 B.C., so that an era was created that began in a certain year. One could locate a date, for example, as being in the third year of the ninetieth Olympiad. The Romans were to develop a comparable system, but they dated by years after the founding of the city (*ab urbe condita*). "The city" was Rome, and its founding was assigned to our year 753 B.C.

There are also literary sources for ancient history. The literary sources get better as we go along, and when we come to the Greeks and Romans they are often excellent. There are some good historians; orators often published their speeches, although these must be used with care; there are some biographies. Philosophers and writers on government give us some understanding of speculative thought. Even the poets, when subjected to the industry of the scholar, will yield some useful facts, for scattered through them, as through the other writers, are facts about the origin of natural products, about winds, the names and locations of public buildings, odd facts about individuals, facts of the organization of society, or preferences in food, all of which are noted and used in the appropriate place.

Papyri, pieces of paper made of narrow strips from the papyrus plant pasted together to make sheets, have been found in great numbers in modern Egypt, generally deep down in ancient dumps where the freedom from moisture and the protection of the sand preserve them. Many scholars have made papyrology their chief interest. Some of the papyri come from the older days of Egypt, as far back as 2000 B.C. Many were religious; some are formulas for passage into the other world. Others give examples of the working of arithmetical processes, and others show us something of medical knowledge. More of the papyri come from the days after the death of Alexander, when Egypt was the kingdom of the Ptolemies, the descendants of Alexander's general Ptolemy, and even more come from the time of the Roman dominion, after 30 B.C. From the Greek and Roman periods we get many fragments of the works of Greek authors on papyri, some several pages long, and of these some offer us writings that otherwise were not preserved for modern times.

Most papyri contain small pieces of practical information that are useful in reconstructing the history of the times, like contracts, receipts for payments, business and private letters, and official papers of various kinds that illuminate the government's management of the fertile soil of the Nile Valley—the assignment of quotas for crops, the collection of the government's share, checking it in at the government granaries, and so on. We get a vivid picture of the despair of a town council during the troubling days of the third Christian century, when it was faced with an added exaction ordered by the Roman imperial government; we can read certificates issued during persecutions of the Christians showing that so-and-so has come before a magistrate and performed the ritual acts of loyalty to the empire, which Christianity forbade because such acts seemed impious.

Collections of papyri are found in many universities and institutes. Scholars who are interested in them correspond with one another, meet at congresses, and support international publications in which the results of their researches are recorded, and these results are eagerly used by other scholars in ancient history.

Cuneiform tablets made of clay were used in the Middle and Near East. They are called cuneiform (*cuneus* is the Latin for "wedge") because the wedge-shaped end of a stylus was used to impress wedge-shaped marks on them. The meaning of such writing resulted from the combinations of these marks. The tablets were often baked to harden and preserve them. Sometimes the tablet was wrapped in a clay envelope, which was marked with identifying signs as a paper envelope would be nowadays, and they were baked together. The only way to use a document filed by this system was to break the clay envelope.

The cuneiform tablets are much like the papyri in that most of them contain data never intended as the material of formal history. They carry the records of business houses, the correspondence of chancelleries, private letters, lists of words to serve as partial dictionaries, and astronomical facts. They are written in several languages and date from a little before 3000 B.C. to the first century of the Christian era. The decipherment and study of these tablets is so forbidding a task that the few scholars who choose this as their specialty have not yet been able to treat thoroughly the large number of tablets already found in excavations. Yet, as we shall see, the information that scholarship has gained from the cuneiform tablets has thrown floods of light onto parts of history that in the early nineteenth century were almost entirely dark.

The inscriptions and the coins of the ancient world were meant to be seen and pondered and are a useful source of information. Often the inscription carries some statement that the government wished to propagate, as when the kings of Egypt ordered inscriptions in the temples to provide accounts of their military campaigns, with pictures to accompany parts of the story, or a successful claimant to the throne of the Roman Empire recorded on a triumphal arch that he had restored order and freed the commonwealth from its enemies.

The Roman Empire was the heyday of the inscription, and thousands of them have been preserved. Men set up inscriptions recording their careers—their success stories—from which the epigrapher can deduce the typical course of careers in the imperial civil service. The careers of the emperors are illustrated by many inscriptions, some on milestones, some on public buildings, some on the bases of statues. Epitaphs, too, yield much information to the historian.

The numismatist may regard his coins as works of art or as documents of economic history or as evidence of government propaganda. They often are very beautiful and may be taken seriously as works of art. As documents of economic history the coins well repay the arduous work of analyzing their metal content, establishing their dates and sequences of issue, and studying the extent of their circulation. The Roman government especially used coins to express the government's message—that peace has been reestablished, that everything is under control, that the new emperor is devoted to the public interest.

But why is it that ancient history was not completely written long ago, leaving nothing for the modern scholar to do? The first reason is that new material appears steadily. Often it appears by accident. The building of roads or foundations of new buildings often discloses significant remains from ancient times. During World War II both bombing and aerial photographs taken for military purposes disclosed the presence of ancient materials. In addition the purposive search for new materials goes on continuously. For example, the scholars interested in manuscripts can still make an occasional find in a monastery, sometimes by disclosing that a manuscript is a palimpsest, that is, that the original writing, which may have been something by a classical author, was erased so that the piece of parchment on which it was written could be used for writing something else of a later time. Methods of reading the original writing have been devised.

The most spectacular and popular method of getting new evidence from the ancient world is archaeology. The public is impressed and excited by the recovery of important things long lost to sight. Little is written for popular consumption about the difficulties and dangers of such a project: the personnel may get shot at; their chances of suffering from the local diseases are excellent; much of the work is boring, for there is a great deal of unavoidable routine and many days when nothing interesting happens; and the living conditions are often uncomfortable, for these are usually primitive places, and it is usually high summer.

Little is said, too, about the desk work of the archaeologist, the long hours that he must spend studying materials that do not yield their secrets at once. Perhaps he has a great many fragments of pottery. Nothing in the lot is beautiful or striking, but this stuff can, with hard work, be made to yield a story of manufacture and of trade relations that will be helpful in reconstructing one small part of ancient history.

In addition to the new material that accidentally comes to light or is purposively brought to light, there are new ideas and new energy involved in the writing of ancient history. Now scholars ask questions that the scholars of two hundred years ago would not have thought to ask—questions about economic motivations, for example, or about the location of power in a society. Furthermore, the appearance of new material often leads to a reappraisal of old material. As we come to know more about the people of the Near East, we make more effort to see how their ideas and practices may have been transmitted to the Greeks and Romans. The number of active scholars is also greater than it used to be; the more minds at work on a subject, the more shades of ideas will be explored.

THE OLD STONE AGE

Earliest man seems to have had nothing except potentialities to distinguish him from the other creatures. He had not learned to use tools of any kind or to make fire. He had no organization of any kind and lived only on what food he could gather, since he had not learned to produce food. He did, however, enjoy a body and brain that were capable of developing. When he came down to the ground and began to use his hands as hands, not as feet, his brain was forced to develop its coordination of sight and of the movements of the hands. The parts of the human brain that retain and combine information are better developed than in other creatures, so that man can profit by past things to avoid dangers and to conceive new things that will not exist until he causes them to exist, the simplest example being to make a tool and then to make tools with which to make tools. Now, in our time, he can see better than the keenest-eyed animal with his helps to vision, can wield tremendous weapons although physically he is no match for many animals, and can take the wings of the morning and fly far beyond the uttermost parts of the earth, leaving the birds earthbound.

The Old Stone Age, or Palaeolithic Age, began a half million or so years ago, when men began to make simple stone tools. Excavations and finds in Europe, North Africa, and Asia indicate that men in many parts of those three continents learned the new techniques. Simple as these techniques were and slowly as they came, they represent tremendous advances. Man learned to make fire and to use it for cooking, for warmth, and apparently for artificial light. His simple tools were made of horn, bone, and ivory, as well as flint. Simple clothing of skins was sewn with bone needles. As the centuries went by, the simple tools became somewhat specialized throughout the large area where men roamed.

It is amazing to see the paintings done by men of the late Stone Age. Caves have been found in Spain and France whose roofs were painted with wonderful pictures of animals perhaps 20,000 years ago. Possibly the pictures were intended to bring success in the hunt by sympathetic magic, since many of the animals are portrayed as pierced by lances. The artists had a keen eye for the essential and made lively and charming pictures that catch the characteristic features of each animal. Iron and manganese oxide gave red and black paint; there were also blue-black and dark brown manganese oxides; soot was used for black. The colors were applied with the fingertip or with a pointed stick dipped in paint or with a crude brush such as one might make by chewing the end of a twig.

The cave at Altamira, in northern Spain, was discovered in 1868 by a hunter whose dog had fallen through the small opening of the cave and could not get out. On the floor of the cave were the bones and teeth of horses, stags, and bisons, oyster shells, flint knives, bone awls and needles, things that the archaeologists were used to seeing in geological surroundings plainly dating from the Old Stone Age, but for many years no one would accept the paintings as belonging to the Stone Age. Once they were so accepted, a search for more caves disclosed many with similar paintings. One of the best, that of Lascaux in France, was discovered by a similar accident with a dog. Arrangements were made to admit the public to view the paintings, but it turned out that the paintings, like people, suffer from the noxious gases of modern civilization, and some of the caves have had to be closed to the public. The Archaeological Museum of Madrid has met the problem by digging a large hole in its front lawn and creating an underground room with replicas of some of the Altamira paintings on the ceiling, dim lights, and comfortable reclining seats for viewing the ceiling.

THE NEW STONE AGE

In the Neolithic (New Stone) Age men began to make more refined tools; they are more carefully shaped, better smoothed, completely finished, and the comparative crudity of the tools of the Old Stone Age is obvious. It is questionable, however, whether these tools were so much of an improvement that their appearance in itself would mark a genuinely new age.

The domestication of plants and animals was a far greater achievement of the men of this age (which began about 10,000 to 9000 B.C.). It was a far more revolutionary advance and did much to bring about a radically new way of life among mankind, comparable to the new ways brought by the Industrial Revolution, so that we may properly speak of the "Neolithic Revolution."

It seems probable that it was in the Near East that man first became a food producer rather than a food gatherer, and the first garden plots were probably in clearings in the forests rather than out in the open spaces where trees were rare. Grains of wheat and barley in recognizable condition have been found during the excavation of Neolithic sites in the Near East. The first animals to live with man were those that in the wild state had led a social life with leaders—the dog, the goat, the cow, and the horse—and at some stage or other the cat strolled in and made himself at home. Few people nowadays have any experience of what it is to acquire such assistance as the animals can give—for example, to struggle by hand with a garden in heavy soil and then to have the help of a horse and harrow.

Some very shrewd examination of the material traces that remain from this time and some very shrewd theorizing have given us plausible reconstructions of the growth of the new kind of life, and to these we may add the idea of a revolution in man's attitude toward the world. Now must have come the dawn of the idea that man can shape the world to his ends instead of merely accepting it as he finds it, the beginnings, faint and far away, of our own aggressive manipulation of nature. The new possibilities in nutrition must have increased life expectancy, producing a number of old gentlemen of thirty-five or even of forty, whose greater experience and longer memories may well have helped people in general to plan their lives and deal with their environment.

We may suppose, too, that the new possibility of having enough food regularly and even of having a surplus gave rise to new virtues, such as steady application to work and thrift, that no one would have thought of before. The fact that people stayed in the same place, at least for a few years at a time, would lead to new thought on how groups of people could live together in an orderly way. Excavations in the Near East have shown that villages began to grow up and that there were separate houses; in the ruins of the earliest ones there was no pottery, but pottery was discovered or invented during early Neolithic times, probably about 6500 B.C. The ruins of the houses also yield traces of simple looms, the evidence that people had learned that they could appropriate the clothing of the sheep or goat as they had learned to appropriate the milk of the cow. The house, the loom, the pot to store food, the possible surplus of food, the rude tools that scratched the ground and reaped the wheat and barley—all these were property and must have given rise to ideas about property that had not existed before. Property in animals was most useful, and the idea of capturing people and making property of them to work for a master as the animals did must have arisen fairly early.

The domestication of plants and of animals appears to have spread rapidly. Possibly the two techniques were invented independently in several places. The variety of plants in different places is interesting, for the Indian corn, squash, and potatoes of the New World apparently were grown by the early peoples there, while the rice of southeastern Asia and the wheat and barley of the Near East seem to have been there from the beginning of agriculture. A group of botanists have interested themselves in the study of the grains of cereal and fragments of other vegetable foods that have been found in the remains of early villages of the Near and Middle East and have shown that the transition from the wild to the domesticated variety of these plants can be traced by the analysis of the grains and other remains. They call themselves palaeoethnobotanists.

Since the Second World War the archaeologists have searched systematically for evidence of the very first steps of the domestication of plants and animals and the formation of villages and cities. There is evidence that the domestication of animals began in the tenth millennium before Christ, that is, earlier than 9000 B.C. (The carbon-14 test, on which such early dates depend, will be described at the end of the chapter.) The remains of the plants are not found (so far) in deposits dating from the ninth and eighth millennia, but in at least three areas of the Near East the use of the grains seems to have been regular by 7000 B.C., and the palaeoethnobotanists can tell us that by that time the grains were standardized enough to imply a considerable amount of conscious management of them by the farmers. There are also discoveries of the tools used in connection with grain: grinding stones have been found, as well as sickles and pits that showed traces of having been used for the storage of grain. The argument has reasonably been advanced that the original domestication of plants and animals took place in the Near East, since only there was to be found the combination of the animals—sheep, goats, cattle, and pigs—and of the wild ancestors of the plants—wheat, barley, peas, and lentils—that man brought under his control. Egypt, it is argued, did not naturally have all these elements and must have borrowed them from the Near East, as did many other areas.

The evidence discovered by the search for early sites in the Near and Middle East suggests that the earliest settlements were in the highland zones there rather than down by the rivers in Mesopotamia and by the Nile in Egypt. The earliest date for settlements by the rivers in Mesopotamia that our evidence will justify is 5800 B.C., and the earliest evidence for attempts at irrigation is a few hundred years later than that. We may not suppose that somehow the possibility of great, unified irrigation systems was discovered and exploited all at once; irrigation is not one thing, but many things, and was organized gradually. We have also learned that there were many cases of attempts, either in the highlands or later down by the rivers, to gather a group of people for settled agriculture which were abandoned, after which the people presumably reverted to nomadism or the old food-gathering culture.

THE URBAN REVOLUTION

Probably the organization of a village should be regarded as a remarkable feat; the organization of the city is hardly more so. Historians differ somewhat in their definition of the city. We can start by saying that a village is not a city. We can also say that in a village all the people do much the same things, like hunting or farming. The city is surely larger than the village, even if no one can say precisely where the dividing point may be. It is much more important that in the city the functions of people began to be differentiated and that some were able to persuade the others to contribute to their support so that they could pursue such specialized functions as soldiering or being priests or coppersmiths. Once some people are relieved of the necessity of having to produce their own food and are free to do other specialized things, life gains in intensity and complexity. Some people can turn their attention to things other than the daily struggle for food, and it becomes possible for the organization as a whole to do things that were not possible before, for instance, the building of temples and elaboration of ritual to improve relations with the Unseen, the organization of an army to deal with troublesome neighbors, or the development of a publicly managed irrigation system.

Some historians object to the terms "urban revolution" and "Neolithic revolution," saying that these were rather evolutions. It is true that it is good, especially in the last third of the twentieth century, to be careful in using the term "revolution," and it may well be left to the individual to decide whether or not these two great movements were truly revolutions. There has been objection, too, to the idea that there is a period that may properly be called "Neolithic," or "new stone," since the change in the manufacture of stone tools was not really significant, and the term has outlived its original usefulness as a rough description that would make the long history of early man a little easier to describe. The idea of what constitutes a historical period, like the idea of what constitutes a revolution, is an interesting and important one and will come up several times in the course of our narrative.

Zawi Chemi in northern Iraq will serve as an example of a very early village; the date of material from its lowest level established by the radiocarbon (carbon-14) test is 9217 plus or minus 300. Although tools for the handling of food (sickles and grinders) have been found, there is nothing to prove that the people produced food rather than gathered what grew wild. The huge deposits of bones seem to suggest that their chief occupation was hunting. The site measures only 215 by 275 meters; it was not walled; there are remains of huts roughly built of stone, but no traces of cooking arrangements. Stone and bone tools were found there. There was no pottery and no trace of weaving. In the upper levels evidence was found that sheep had been domesticated.

The village of Jarmo in Iraq probably was organized by 6750 B.C., a date that depends on several carbon-14 tests. It was a real agricultural village, where cereals were grown, not merely gathered, and where there were domesticated animals. The site covered three or four acres and had twenty or twenty-five houses and perhaps 150 people. The houses were rectangular rather than round and had several rooms and arrangements for cooking. The tools were more sophisticated than those found at Zawi Chemi, and in the later levels (those found nearer the surface of the ground by the excavators) pottery was present. The village was probably abandoned around the year 6000.

The site of Jericho in Palestine seems to provide evidence for a transition from a hunting village like Zawi Chemi to an agricultural village like Jarmo, whereas those two villages are not connected by any intermediate stage. There are traces of the presence of early hunters around the great spring there. The hunters built a rude wooden structure by the spring; it burned and left charcoal that in turn yielded a date 7800 B.C. plus or minus 210 by the carbon-14 test. The excavations conducted on the site have shown that during the next thousand years the spring resorted to by hunters was succeeded by a settled agricultural village that even had fortifications. Again a fire left charcoal, the analysis of which gave the date 6850 B.C. plus or minus 210.

It is generally believed that real cities arose between 3500 and 2500 B.C. among the Sumerians of lower Mesopotamia (we shall discuss them in detail in the next chapter). These cities had priests who organized temples that took shares of the produce of everyone and acted as a sort of government. It may well be that priests came before kings as specialists supported by the surplus, but soon there were kings, too. We can easily imagine how a man might distinguish himself by leadership in a struggle with neighbors and gain the place of king, as Saul later did among the Hebrews.

In the temple (or the palace) there was a group of specialist artisans. Metallurgy had been invented in the fourth millennium, and the smith naturally was important among the few specialists. Writing, too, was invented for the purpose of keeping track of the supplies, and the scribe became another important specialist. The building of the god's house, the daily or periodic services to the god—feeding him, washing him, entertaining him, adorning his house and his statue—was done by a corps of people.

Naturally the great inventions of the domestication of plants and animals spread quickly and widely, but the more complex way of life centering in the cities also spread, if more slowly. The new and more complex organization reached out for raw materials and brought in luxuries, too. Some of the records of Sumerian businessmen that have been preserved on baked clay tablets show us explicitly that they had caravans which had to pay protection money here and there as they journeyed out into the Arabian desert or up into the hill country. For an enterprising local brigand to organize the levying of protection money on passing caravans was in itself a marked advance in the complexity of society in those early days, and if the people far out on the fringes gathered raw materials of some sort for trade—ivory or gold dust or turquoise or slaves—their own society became more complex as they organized to make the transaction.

The spreading of culture on a large scale will be very important in our story. The Egyptian influence on Crete is an example. The Egyptians taught the Cretans much and made them more prosperous by paying them for their raw materials, like fruits, hides, meat, and timber. The Cretans became steadily more prosperous and more sophisticated, modeling their civilization on the Egyptian, but in their best days producing works and a way of life unmistakably their own, in spite of their debt to Egypt. The Cretans in turn passed on much of what they knew to the Greeks of the mainland while trading with them, and these Greeks, as they became more sophisticated, in turn developed a way of life and a group of products from their workshops that were their own even as they showed a clear indebtedness to the Cretans.

It is an interesting fact that while some of the peoples on the periphery of the great powers were drawn as groups into the high civilization of the ancient world, with its cities and other complex features, other peoples sturdily resisted, much as some peoples in modern times have resisted the civilization of the West. The Scythians of south Russia, for instance, were organized as nomads. Some few of them, as individuals, were drawn into the high civilization of the Greeks and later into that of the Romans, but as a group they resisted. Their simpler civilization was so stable and so satisfactory that it could hold its members against what was evidently the very strong attraction of the Greeks and Romans. The early Germans were organized in more sedentary groups than the Scythians, but they too were without city life. Many of their members, as individuals, went over to the Romans, but again the community refused to adopt the more complex and fragile organization and generally managed to hold its members against the new attractions.

Carbon-14 and Other Tests

The archaeologists are increasingly helped by the natural scientists in extracting information from the things that they find. The approximate age of objects of an organic nature is revealed by the carbon-14 (radiocarbon) test. Cosmic rays create carbon 14, or radiocarbon, in the upper atmosphere, whence it slowly comes down and is mixed into our atmosphere and into the sea water. Plants eat carbon 14; we eat plants and the flesh of animals who feed on plants; thus we become radioactive with carbon 14. When we die, ingestion of carbon 14 ends, and all radioactive materials in us transform and disintegrate and very slowly disappear. The disappearance of the beta particles, unstable in the nucleus of carbon 14, causes the carbon 14 to change to nitrogen; in 5700 years half of the beta particles will be gone, and after another 5700 years a half of those that remained will be gone. The age of the material under examination is determined by counting the number of the fleeing particles within a given unit of time compared with what the number would be if the organism had that instant died. The age of materials from the ancient world, thus calculated, has to be expressed as a number of years plus or minus 150 to 300, since accuracy is impossible.

Wood is susceptible of other tests. We all know the idea of counting the rings in a tree when it is cut down to calculate its age; this idea has naturally been greatly refined. There are many ways of analyzing the structure of wood, and these can often be used for the analysis of very old specimens. Also the pollen of trees survives well, and all the types have been catalogued, so that it is possible to tell what kinds of trees were in a place or near it at different times, even to the point of telling how the trees varied as the ice ages came on and retreated.

A surprising array of tests for pottery has been developed. Sometimes the clay can be identified, although naturally there might be scores of different clays within an area of moderate size. One method of analyzing pottery is to give additional firing to pieces of different pots under completely controlled conditions of temperature, time, and kiln atmosphere to see what changes will take place in them. The glazes and pigments of the ornamentation may also be analyzed. The x-ray fluorescence spectrometer does wonders in the analysis of the chemical composition of materials. There is continual progress in this aspect of archaeology, for natural scientists seem pleased to apply their new knowledge to it.

CHAPTER

2

EARLY BABYLONIA AND EARLY
EGYPT; EARLY INDIA AND CHINA

Mesopotamia—the land of the two rivers—was the scene of the first great step beyond the Neolithic culture described in the preceding chapter. The Sumerians, who lived in the southern part, where the two rivers come close to each other and empty into the Persian Gulf, made a brilliant cultural advance during the fourth millennium. Their achievements may well have inspired the Egyptians to a new intensity of culture, although the specialists in Egyptian history are somewhat loath to give up the idea that Egyptian civilization arose independently. Probably the culture of the Indus Valley in India also drew its inspiration from the culture of Mesopotamia.

The full presence of many striking new elements must be considered to mark the arrival of a new period in history, even though their development obviously was slow and uneven, and we cannot give an exact date for the beginning of the period. We probably can say, however, that by 3500 B.C. the new way of life was firmly established. Since the arrival of writing implies the possibility of our having histories to use as sources, the new period has often been spoken of as the historical period in contrast to the prehistory that preceded it. This contrasting terminology is not satisfactory, difficult as it is to think of something better. In the first place, the invention of writing may have led to the creation of materials that we can use for historical purposes, but the writing of historical accounts was not to come for a long time. In the second place, the advances of archaeology have so improved our knowledge of the period

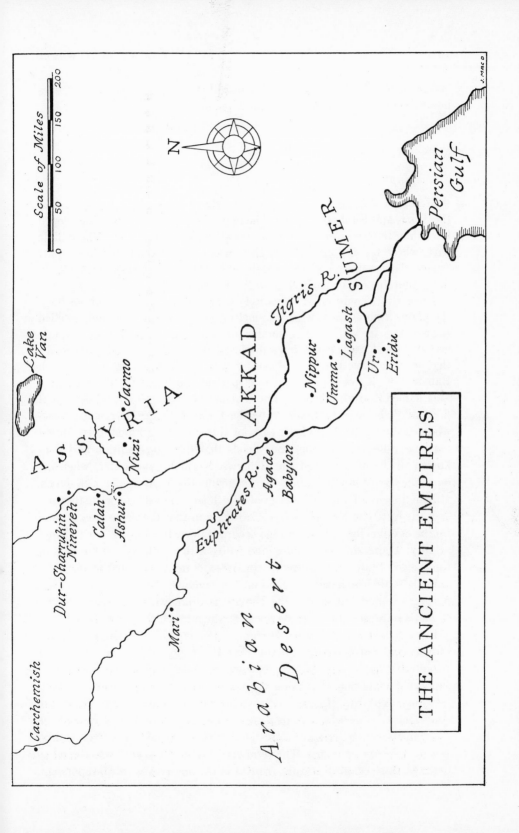

THE ANCIENT EMPIRES

before the invention of writing that to call that period "prehistoric" does less than justice to the present knowledge of it.

MESOPOTAMIA

Geography

Mesopotamia, "the region between the rivers," is the land lying between the Tigris and Euphrates rivers. The upper part, Assyria, which developed later than the lower and middle parts, will be discussed later. The middle part, where lay the city of Babylon, was called Akkad, the lower part Sumer. Together we call them Babylonia. The two rivers, which rise in the mountains of Armenia, flow to the Persian Gulf.

These rivers could never be entirely tamed so that they would not flood the plains around them when the melting snows of the highlands swelled their waters in March. In a number of places in southern Mesopotamia archaeological excavations have disclosed strata of pure water-borne silt that seem to have been laid down by floods. One of these, in the south Babylonian city of Shuruppak, may perhaps be dated to the reign of a king named Ziusudra, whose name is attached to a local legend of a great flood and who may be taken to be the Biblical Noah. He reigned somewhere around 2900 B.C. Whether or not this was "the" Flood, there surely must have been some monstrous floods that lived in tradition and were known to the ancestors of the Hebrews. Normally the water, when led onto the farms by irrigation works, made the earth yield rich crops, although some of the soil was gradually made too saline for further use and was lost. The Egyptians were fortunate in that the depositing of mud by the overflowing Nile each year occurred in such a way as not to cause salinity. The grains, vegetables, and fruits with which we are familiar in the United States can be grown in Mesopotamia, as can the domestic animals with which we are familiar. In summer the region is hot, but not very humid; in winter the climate is mild, with infrequent frosts. A year's rainfall is likely to be about six inches, which is very scanty.

East of the two rivers were Media and Persia, whose territory is mountainous and not infertile. To the west lies the Arabian Desert, a vast region that is largely barren, but whose oases and sparse vegetation supported some nomads. Along the upper reaches of the rivers the land was high and the climate cooler than farther south. Here lived the Assyrians, who were later to be a great imperial people. To the west of the Arabian Desert lie Syria and Palestine, which are more fertile than Arabia, less so than Mesopotamia. The term "the Fertile Crescent" was coined to describe this region of mostly fruitful land; one end is in Mesopotamia, then the crescent curves above Arabia and descends through Syria and Palestine, as it were, to plant its other end in Egypt.

The Source Materials

These Near Eastern lands were long a place of mystery to Westerners. From the time of its conquest by the Turks in the thirteenth and fourteenth centuries until well into the nineteenth century, travelers from the West almost never went there. There was little to be learned about the most ancient Near East from Greek and Roman authors. The cuneiform writing developed by the Sumerians and used by many other nearby peoples had not generally been understood by the ancient peoples to the West (e.g., the Greeks) and was not understood by the moderns either. Except for some information in the Bible, no sources for this part of history were available in early modern times.

The recovery of masses of evidence for the history of Mesopotamia is one of the most exciting feats of modern scholarship. The languages were deciphered by the use of the trilingual inscription on the great Behistun Rock. Five hundred feet up on a cliff in western Iran are carved figures and an inscription in three languages—Persian, Babylonian, and Elamite. The figures and the inscription record the deeds of King Darius I of Persia (521–486 B.C.), and the inscription is written in cuneiform. A good copy of the inaccessible inscription was made in the 1840s by the daring Henry Rawlinson, and little by little the Persian part was deciphered, as was the Elamite part. Elamite, spoken in the southern part of the Persian realm, is of far less importance for us than the other two. The combined efforts of many scholars finally achieved the decipherment of the Babylonian part and with it the understanding of the ancient Babylonian-Assyrian language, now generally called Akkadian. This led in turn to the recovery of the ability to read Sumerian. There were other languages used in the Near East, most of which are now well understood. The excavations in the Near East have brought to light so many inscribed clay tablets that the small group of scholars specializing in this field has not yet been able to give adequate attention to all of them.

The other great source of information is, of course, the objects that excavation has brought to light. The early excavators were bold men. Even to enter Mesopotamia was a bold thing for a European to do, but they persevered. Their excavations disclosed the ruins of ancient cities under the mounds, or tells, that dot the landscape. Many of the ancient cities were first built on clay platforms to raise them above the high water of the river. The houses of unbaked brick would crumble after a while and their remains would be tamped down and new ones built above them. A thousand years or so of this would create a considerable hill composed of the ruins of houses. Shrewdness in dealing with the stratification of their excavations was forced upon the archaeologists. They learned to distinguish levels and to keep precise records showing at what level each object was found and what objects were found together. They learned, too, to work out sequences of styles in pottery, following the slow and conservative changes of styles of the ancient peoples. This is easier if some pottery is found unbroken, but can be done even if it all is found in fragments. The pottery, which is fairly easy to break but almost impossible to destroy, has proved a great help in establishing relative chronologies and also trade routes, for nowadays the well-trained archaeological eye can tell almost at a glance where a pot or a piece of pottery found in an excavation came from and where it belongs in the sequence of pottery made in its place of origin. Great efforts have been made to coordinate these sequences of pottery (and other finds too, of course) with firm dates, so that often the archaeologist can give a date as well for the ware from somewhere else which suddenly appears in his excavation.

The earliest archaeological expeditions were financed by governments, museums, and art dealers and conducted with the idea of finding museum pieces and without any idea of studying everything found to see what it would contribute to our knowledge of history. Nowadays, "treasure hunt" is the ultimate term of contempt when applied to an archaeological campaign, since it implies that the purpose of the campaign is to find spectacular pieces rather than to investigate the site scientifically. But the idea of archaeology as a science grew rapidly. Archaeological institutes were organized; governments became interested in the serious study of the subject; universities created professorships; museums began to organize serious collections for study, and a number of new museums were founded to handle such materials. It has now become difficult to find space to store or display the great numbers of significant objects that have been found.

THE KINGDOMS OF EARLY MESOPOTAMIA

The Sumerians

The Sumerians, who lived in the southernmost part of Mesopotamia (where the two rivers are closer together than above and pour into the Persian Gulf and where in those days there were great lagoons and a slowly extending delta) were the first to intensify the widespread Neolithic civilization. The archaeological evidence does not show clearly whether the Sumerians came into an empty region and developed it or whether the earliest settlements there, which seem to have been brisk late-Neolithic organizations, were developed by other people with whom the

Sumerians joined. The important fact for us is that a new kind of life was developed in this region, and that by about 3200 B.C. a group known as the Sumerians had developed a civilization of cities there with many tremendously important inventions: advanced metallurgy, writing, a more complex and sophisticated art, the wheel, the sail, and so on.[1] Some of these were new things, while some were striking improvements of things already known, like irrigation or communal life in villages. The Sumerians were the first of the strenuous national groups, energetic and ambitious people who enjoyed competition. They seem to have made a genuine leap forward, since there is no evidence of gradual advances beforehand in most of the directions that they took. Why the Sumerians were as they were we naturally do not know.

They had a dozen cities, each with its surrounding hamlets. Eridu was farthest south, down among the lagoons. Ur, which was the birthplace of Abraham, has been given prominence by the excavations there conducted by Sir Leonard Woolley, especially that which brought to light royal burials accompanied by striking works of art. Uruk, too, appears in the Bible, but as Erech; it now is called Warka. Lagash and Umma, still a little farther north, have yielded many tablets, especially those that throw light on the economic organization of the temple at Lagash. Nippur and Kish, the latter almost as far north as Babylon, are informative ruins and have yielded tablets that are useful. Attempts at calculating the population have led to reasonable figures of 100,000 for Lagash and 200,-000 for Ur at perhaps 2500 B.C.—a contrast indeed to the villages of the time before this sharp advance in the complexity of civilization.

We must suppose that careful exploitation of the possibilities of irrigation greatly increased the food supply and was thus the most important factor in the advance in population, just as the advance in the food supply made by the domestication of plants and animals must have led to an increase in population. To make a swift advance in the production of things other than food was less easy, although the production of sheep would give both food and wool for clothing. Southern Mesopotamia does not have metals nor timber nor stone; in fact, its only plentiful natural product is mud, and this the Sumerians learned to use to make brick that would last for three or four decades at a time. Some importation was forced upon them, and especially the importation of metals, since they could manage after a fashion without stone or timber. Gold and silver were desirable for objects of art, and copper, to be alloyed with tin to make bronze, was a necessity for tools and weapons. Their own manufactured objects could be exported.

[1] Samuel N. Kramer's *History Begins at Sumer* (see the bibliography) has an interesting list of "firsts" to be credited to the Sumerians.

The cities must have been monotonous in appearance, since they consisted of houses of one story, occasionally two, that had few windows opening onto the narrow and crooked streets. The chief feature of every city was the *ziggurat,* the great mound of rammed clay faced with brick on the top of which stood the temple and around the bottom of which were the storerooms and workshops of the temple and the living quarters of the temple personnel.

It used to be thought that all the land of the city was the property of the local god and was administered by the officials of the temple, but further examination of the evidence has given us good reason to believe that the temple owned only a part of the land, which was farmed for it on shares by free men. The temple also had, beside the priests and attendants who served the god, a staff of workmen who presumably were chiefly busy supplying the needs of the people of the temple.

The land not owned by the temple was owned partly by the king, partly by the nobles, and partly by freeholders of small parcels. There is good reason to suppose that kings came into existence only after a complex society had existed for some time and in response to the pressure exerted by the cities on one another. There apparently were standing armies, which doubtless arose for the same reason, and they seem to have been equipped with body armor, to have fought in a phalanx, and to have had chariots as a part of their offense. Although a very gifted commander might be made permanent head of the armed forces, given the title of king (or what we choose to translate by that word), and endowed with land and a palace that would enhance his dignity, it does not necessarily follow that all the citizens gave themselves over to him entirely, for the nobles also were people of consequence with large holdings of land and humbler people as clients. Beside the humbler free people who farmed the land of the temple, the king, and the nobles, there were the free smallholders, and beside them there was a class of professional men—physicians and scribes—and of artisans. There seems to have been an explicit legal system, something rather more than a few principles of customary law, to regulate the relations of man to man and to guide the adjustment of conflicting interests, and there were courts.

The scribes, the people who had mastered the difficult system of writing, were generally the sons of people of good social position and received their training in formal schools. We may suppose that their art stirred them to more intellectual activity than the general public indulged in, and obviously certain kinds of knowledge depended largely on them. The idea of the priests as the chief intellectuals of the community and the repository of all kinds of important knowledge is no longer held by the scholars who work in this field.

Written allusions to struggles between the Sumerian cities and to occasional combinations of them under a single overlord exist. In the early third millennium the Sumerians as a group were dominant all over southern Mesopotamia. Sometimes we get interesting details. The records of an early king of Lagash, for example, tell of the raising of temples and the digging of canals. Those of his grandson tell of victories over several neighboring cities. This early imperialist was celebrated on a famous work of art, "the Stele of the Vultures," a stone column (Greek *stele*) decorated with a lively scene in which his phalanx is shown advancing, while vultures are already feasting on the enemy warriors who have fallen before it. A few generations later a scribe of Lagash describes, in a work that has come down to us, a disgraceful time of corruption in the city. King Urukagina, who must have been an administrator of some talent, managed to reform this situation and give honest government. But Lagash fell shortly thereafter to an old rival, the city of Umma, whose king, Lugalzaggisi, was an able imperialist. We hear that under him Umma dominated Uruk and Ur and that his armies even went as far as the shores of the Mediterranean.

The Early Akkadian Empire (ca. 2390–ca. 2180 B.C.)

But the Sumerians sometimes had to bow to the energy of other people of Mesopotamia. Sargon the First came to power about 2360 B.C. in the city of Agade, the Biblical Akkad. He is one of the earliest great men who is a little more than a mere name to us. He rose from humble station to be king. He conquered Lugalzaggisi, established himself as ruler of all Mesopotamia, and campaigned in other lands, even asserting his power in Syria and Anatolia. Enough examples have been found of the inscriptions that he set up to show that he had the idea of using them to glorify his own regime and suggest its efficiency and care of the people, to speak of his victories in war and the correctness and generosity of his behavior in the nation's behalf toward the gods. If he lived for many centuries in the imagination of the people, it was presumably because he thoroughly understood the art of presenting himself as a monarch in a favorable light; we have learned to speak of this as the efficient creation of an image.

Among the other kings of the hundred years or so of Akkadian domination of Mesopotamia, Naram-Sin, grandson of Sargon, is especially known because of his conquests and the discovery of the striking stele that portrays his victory in a mountain campaign: the troops are light armed and the king leads them in person up a mountain; as in "the Stele of the Vultures," a number of fallen enemies are shown.

The Sumerian Revival (2070–1960 B.C.)

Between the Akkadian Empire of the descendants of Sargon and the revival of Sumerian control there was an interlude of about a century (2180–2070 B.C.) when Mesopotamia was dominated by the Gutians, a people from the mountains to the east. We know very little about them, but it is certain that the Sumerians hated them as barbarians and that they were slack about keeping up the canal system.

There is a surprising lack of information about the political history of this period. A king of Uruk drove out the Gutians, but the leadership of the cities soon passed to Ur, and the rest of the period of the Sumerian revival is often spoken of as the Third Dynasty of Ur. A man named Gudea, a governor of Lagash rather than a king, is known to us by several statues that, although stylized, portray a calm and forceful person, and there is some little evidence that he restored irrigation and trade and was thought of as a careful shepherd of the people.

One of the kings of the Third Dynasty—his name is not known, but it has been suggested that we may speak of him as Shulgi until someday a tablet is found that gives us the full form of his name—extended the control of Ur over many places in Mesopotamia and waged frequent war out on the boundaries, some four hundred miles from Ur, against the peoples from outside. It may well be that the Gutians were not ready to give up to the Sumerians and go away, and there are mentions of other peoples who were difficult; the situation is an anticipation of the conditions in the later Roman Empire, when the Romans struggled to hold off the barbarians who wished either to raid the prosperous territories of the Empire or to be admitted and given land in return for which they would render military service. In the end a combination of the outsiders conquered and sacked Ur thoroughly. It never was great again.

This same King Shulgi seems to have had the soul of a bookkeeper as well as the force of a conqueror, for there is a flood of evidence on government bookkeeping during his reign, in spite of the paucity of evidence about the general affairs of the government. There are beautifully written tablets from several centers of the kingdom that show us the administration of temple and royal properties. This king plainly took a lively interest in such affairs. We sense the presence of the managers of the temple workshops, the stewards of the temples, and the governors of the cities. Income and outgo are carefully noted, and there are even summaries of the figures for periods of some time. Shulgi also rearranged the calendar, provided for an official set of standards, and made an official set of weights.

Apparently the first proclamation of a king as a god came during his reign. Perhaps popular superstition had a little to do with it, but it was an obviously administrative move that was justified by the usefulness of having the king august enough to act as he willed in all the affairs of the realm. The evidence indicates that henceforth the kings actually built temples for themselves and had their images tended as were those of older gods.

The Babylonians

There now was a period of some confusion from which a new state emerged with its capital at Babylon; it was controlled by Amorites or "Westerners" who had come from up the Euphrates. This Semitic people had drifted slowly into Babylonia and had made themselves at home there without being much noticed at first. Their dynasty of kings at Babylon lasted from about 1830 to about 1530 B.C., when it was quietly superseded by a dynasty founded by an Iranian people called Kassites. Kassites appear in Babylonian documents for some time before 1530 as ordinary working people; they rose to power, however, and for more than five hundred years they dominated Mesopotamia. They were not a creative or an imperialistic people and apparently were content to keep the realm going and to let its inherited culture lose some of its quality.

The sixth of the Babylonian kings, Hammurabi, has long had a great reputation as conqueror and gifted administrator, which some of the new evidence has tended to dim. His reign used to be placed as early as 2300 B.C. Now it is generally dated at 1728 to 1686 B.C.; another way of stating it is that his reign began in 1750 B.C. plus or minus fifty years. This reduction of chronology resulted largely from excavations at Mari, a brilliant city on the Euphrates well above Babylon that had begun long before as an outpost of the Sumerian civilization. Twenty thousand clay tablets and fragments were found in the palace archives. Some letters are originals of the king's correspondence with Hammurabi. Others show that the king was contemporary with an Assyrian king, Shamshi-Adad, whose dates can be established by other lines of evidence.

Hammurabi did come to dominate the area generally known as Sumer and Akkad after many years of only holding his own among the rival nations, but was not the great conqueror that he once was supposed to be. The royal correspondence that has been found shows him as a somewhat nervous and timid king, not always sure of his authority, rather than as a genius at management. Further, the glamor of his code of laws—which was found in 1901, inscribed in the Akkadian language on a stone stele seven and a half feet high—has been lessened by the discovery of earlier Sumerian codes and of some contemporary codes from other jurisdictions.

ACHIEVEMENT DOWN TO 1500 B.C. IN MESOPOTAMIA

The Management of Nature

The attempts of the peoples of Sumer and Akkad to manage the Tigris and Euphrates rivers for irrigation constitute a first step, although a very small step, toward our aggressive attitude toward nature; in other matters they were not at all aggressively disposed toward nature. Naturally our archaeological information about irrigation is scanty and hard to interpret, since the soil of the region so easily shifts and obscures or obliterates such artificial features as canals and dikes. Irrigation is mentioned now and then in the written sources, however; we find that during the Third Dynasty of Ur each temple had an official who watched over the distribution of water, and the kings often repeat that they had had work done on the canals as part of their constant assertion that they were the shepherds of the people.

Scholars used to assume that large units of government arose in response to the need for an agency that could control large units of irrigation. This assumption has been abandoned, and many attempts have been made to find archaeological evidence of how irrigation arose and grew; the people who work on the written sources carefully note whatever is found on this point. It seems plain that small units of irrigation were practical in Mesopotamia as well as large ones.

The official practice of religion such as we find it in early Mesopotamia was actually a way of managing nature, for the gods were regarded as forces of nature who had no special fondness for man and were likely to crush him or knock him about if they were not made aware of his presence and propitiated. There seems to be a religious edifice of some sort in the earliest villages and cities, and the priest seems to have been one of the first specialists who was relieved from the labor of providing his own sustenance so that he could devote himself to an activity that was thought to benefit the public at large.

As we look at Mesopotamian religion, we can see that the Sumerians evolved a cosmology (an explanation of the origin of the world) and a theology which were adopted by most of the peoples of the Near East. Their story of the Creation is not unlike that of the Bible, beginning with an inchoate watery mass upon which form was imposed so as to create earth and sky as separate realms, to stud the heavens with the celestial bodies, and to separate the lands and the waters upon the earth, after which the plants, the animals, and man were created to people the great home that had been prepared for them. The whole and every part thereof was believed to be controlled by the gods, who were living beings, invisible, necessarily immortal. The company of gods was not all of the same rank, since the god whose sphere was the creeping things of the earth could hardly be thought equal to the god who controlled the sun, and a few of the gods were thought of as being able to create, whereas the others could only manage what the superior ones had created. The great gods of the heaven, earth, sea, and air were the chief creative ones. The development of an explanation of the origin of the world seems to satisfy some need in the simplest of peoples.

Rituals and a system of tendance of the gods were developed. Ordinarily every locality had a chief god to whom the people were most attentive and for whom they built a house in which his image lived. A corps of priests fed the god (nothing was said about the mystery of how the god was nourished by this food) and bathed him and dressed him and entertained him and took him for an occasional promenade. There was a daily ritual of prayer and sacrifice, and a system of special festivals was worked out, partly with an eye to amusing the public and giving it a good view of the ingenuity and pomp with which the priests were making the god friendly to the community.

Throughout the history of the ancient world, that is, until the end of the Roman Empire, the state religion was conducted by the priests of the state, and the individual had no part in it. There was nothing like going to church.

The strangest part to us of the religious practices of the state is the practice of divination, or the attempt to learn the will of the gods or get advice from the gods by the observation of signs and omens. The Sumerians and the Babylonians tried very hard to work up a science of omens, especially of those that might be gained from inspection of the livers of animals killed for sacrifice. There is evidence that the commanders of armies in the field would allow themselves to be guided by such omens and that the men in charge of major policies of government were likewise swayed. In general scholars have abandoned the idea that the priests were literate and learned and controlled the whole tradition of specialized knowledge; that function is now thought to have belonged rather to the scribes, who alone were literate. Models of livers have been found that plainly were meant to show how the formation of the liver of a victim should be interpreted.

The Sumerians also developed a lively mythology, as we learn from the cuneiform tablets. The conjecture has been made that these myths were first thought of by illiterate bards like those of early Greece, of whom we shall hear later. In these myths the gods had adventures, love affairs, and struggles with one another. Enlil, the air god, a benevolent and creative force, is an important character in these stories. He used to be thought of as a wild and destructive god because some of the tablets that were first deciphered told of his carrying out punitive decrees of other gods with the force of a whirlwind. Tablets discovered later tell of the other side of his nature. An, the heaven god, apparently was conceived of as the chief of the gods in early Sumerian times, but lost that position and became simply one of the major gods. Enki was a managing type of god who constructed the earth following suggestions from Enlil; one of the myths tells of his establishing the physical background and the dispositions in man that were necessary as a basis for civilization. Ninhursag was regarded as the mother of all living things. The sun god, the moon goddess, and the goddess of love were rather more important than other deities.

The Management of People

Monarchy soon became the normal form of government among the Sumerians and the other peoples of Mesopotamia, and the role of the king was early developed. His care for his people as their shepherd is often mentioned. It is plain, too, that some thought went into devising titles and other symbols of royal power, such as the building of impressive royal residences and the creation of works of art that would project the message of the king's majesty and power.

The art of writing was an important by-product of the development of the art of government; it apparently was invented as a device for keeping track of the supplies that were brought in (first to the temple, and later to the palace) to support the government. In later times we shall find writing used exclusively for governmental records at Cnossus in Crete and at Pylos and Mycenae in Greece. There were schools for scribes that attracted students of good social position; the graduates held positions ranging from that of clerk without responsibility to that of major administrator. They were the learned class; priests, judges, and administrators were usually illiterate. The scribes expanded the art of writing until it was used for business and legal matters, for historical records, for hymns (addressed to kings as well as to gods), for inscriptions set up by kings to help form their royal "image," and for myths. It has been said that in all the writings of the Sumerians we find very little trace of the abstract and generalized thought that was to be the great contribution of the Greeks after 600 B.C. and that is so characteristic of our own culture. The schools, for example, had discussions of grammar, word forms, and usage, but no general rules in these matters. There are court records and codes or collections of law, but no rules or principles of law are found.

The tablets offer us a great deal of evidence that the kingdoms of early Mesopotamia developed bureaucracies, that is, responsible bodies of officials. Organized armies, too, were developed, and we have bas-reliefs showing soldiers in a tight phalanx, protected by helmets and shields and using swords, lances, and bows as offensive weapons. Techniques of fortifying cities and of assaulting fortified cities were known.

The so-called Code of Hammurabi and others of the sort are somewhat puzzling in that scholars do not believe that they guided the work of the courts as a modern code would do; the evidence of the tablets suggests that in the courts illiterate judges judged according to the customary law. Perhaps, then, we should speak of these as collections of laws rather than as codes. Yet these collections depict an interestingly advanced state of society and of law, no matter what we think about their purpose and the extent to which they were used. The fact that agriculture was the basis of society is clearly reflected, of course, by rules about using one's share of the irrigation system so as to protect the interests of all in the land and the water, by rules about the selling, renting, and bequeathing of private real estate, and by rules about the use of animals. A special and important case is that of soldiers who hold land from the crown and owe military duty in return.

It is plain that business and trade were active. Manufacturing, for example weaving, was still actively carried on in the temples, as was providing everything else that the god and the temple staff needed, and it is reasonable to suppose that often a surplus overflowed into the open market. Many kinds of free artisans are mentioned along with slave artisans and those attached to temples, who probably also were slaves. There is precise regulation of wages, rents, commissions, and damages either for nonperformance or for negligence. All agreements had to be written and witnessed.

Business practices included partnerships and agencies, but not limited-liability corporations. The practice of lending at interest was common; gold, silver, copper, and bronze were lent, for money in the strict sense of metal whose weight and fineness were guaranteed by a government stamp did not yet exist. There are records of the fairly complicated financing of long caravan journeys by merchants.

We can see some of the working of a stratified society, with responsibilities as well as privileges for the nobles. The commoner who struck a noble was punished more severely than for striking another commoner. Slavery was recognized, but the slave enjoyed some protection from ill-treatment. A woman was expected to be under the protection of a man, and marriages were arranged with a view to the solidity and strength of the family. Dowries and family property were carefully watched by the eye of the law.

The Use of Materials

Wood and stone were rare in Mesopotamia. Little wood was used for building, but there are traces of skillfully made furniture. There are records of its importation, and one of the great temples was far ahead of its time in having a tree farm and thus being a producer of wood instead of merely gathering it. There is very little evidence that stone was used in building. Most building employed mud brick, and we can sometimes see notable technical skill in the use of asphalt (a natural product of Mesopotamia) and mortar. The Sumerian builder was familiar with the arch and the vault, both of which were formerly considered later inventions.

Cylinder seals that came into use early among the Sumerians showed artistic skill, too. A design was cut into a little cylinder of hard stone, so that when the cylinder was rolled with some pressure on moist clay, the owner's seal came out in relief—a personal seal that could hardly be counterfeited. Pottery passed quickly beyond mere utility to something of beauty. Eventually the manufacture of metal vessels so surpassed that of pottery that the potters lost interest and produced mechanical work for a long time until they realized that they could imitate the fine work done in metal and began again to work with artistic interest.

In the use of metals we find both the artist's concern with rightness of form and considerable technical skill in production. These artists cast copper and bronze, knew how to solder and rivet, and engraved and inlaid metals beautifully. Their managers had access to supplies of gold, silver, copper, and bronze (copper alloyed with tin).

The workmen had many other skills. Not only could they weave cloth; they could also bleach it, dye it, and soften it. They had learned how to prepare leather. The idea and the use of cosmetics had been developed, as had perfume and incense. It was understood that certain substances, which we now class as drugs, had specific effects on the human system. A number of wonderful tools were invented, first of which was the plow. Others were the solid wheel, the sail, and the potter's wheel. The basic idea of standard measurements appeared. Another of the great inventions was a number system; it was sexagesimal, like the system by which we keep time, and had a place notation, with an equivalent for zero.

EGYPT

The Nile

The great river Nile starts as the White Nile in the lake country of equatorial Africa and the Blue Nile in the highlands of Abyssinia. After they join, these two rivers receive the waters of a third, the Atbara, and then run 1700 miles northward to the Mediterranean. In several places along its early course the river runs across rock so hard that the water wears it down extremely slowly and runs in cataracts through narrow channels. After passing Assuan it runs through a wider channel that it has cut over countless years in a plateau of sandstone, then of limestone. Finally it runs through a goodly stretch of flatter country, much of which is composed of the rich alluvium washed down and deposited by the river. This is called the Delta (north of Cairo; see the map), since it forms a triangle like the Greek letter *delta*.

The annual flooding is caused by the spring rains and the melting snow in Abyssinia. The rise does not reach the main part of Egypt until July and does not come to its peak until the beginning of September. In modern times before the building of the dam at Assuan a normal rise was about twenty-five feet. A rise of only twenty feet meant a dangerous shortage of food for the next year, twenty-three would mean an uncomfortable shortage, while thirty might mean damage to dams and dikes and perhaps some loss of soil rather than the usual increment of rich new soil from the settling of the silt brought down by the river. Presumably conditions in ancient times were more or less analogous.

The Egyptians spoke of their country as "the Two Lands." It is both one and two. It is one in that all its life is related to the river and all its usable territory lies close on either side of the river; just beyond on both sides is the desert. Egypt does not have the cloudy and rainy weather that occurs normally in many parts of the world, and day after day is bright and cloudless. The rain does not fall at all except for insignificant sprinklings in the Delta. Water comes only from the river, and there is a visible line on either side where the effect of the water from the river stops and the cultivated soil marches with the dry and unirrigated desert. To the virtual absence of rain and the dryness of the atmosphere, as well as to the hermetical sealing effect of the desert sands, we owe the preservation of many records of ancient Egypt written on papyrus. These would not have survived in a moister climate.

Egypt is also two lands. Upper Egypt, along the southern or upper course of the river, lies in a narrow valley held in by cliffs on either side, with the desert beyond. Lower Egypt, the northern part of the country, widens out into the Delta because there are no longer the restraining limestone cliffs. Here the flat, marshy land stretches farther on either side before it is bounded by the desert. In early times the two parts were separate kingdoms whose people spoke different dialects and regarded themselves as having different habits of thought.

Outside the fertile area provided by the river, Egypt is entirely desert. To the west of the Nile the desert stretches away to the Sahara, dotted by a few oases, some of which were important in ancient times. About

RHODES

Mediterranean Sea

CYPRUS

Ras Shamra (UGARIT)

Orontes R.

SYRIA

Byblos
Qargar
Sidon
Damascus
PHOENICIA
Tyre
Kadesh
Sea of Galilee

Megiddo
Samaria
Jericho
Jerusalem

PHILISTINES

Alexandria

Gaza
Dead Sea

Naucratis
Tanis

Cairo

Gizeh
Memphis
Sakkara

N

PENINSULA OF SINAI

Gulf of Aqabah

Nile R.

Fayum

Red Sea

Abydos
Thebes

Karnak
Luxor

EGYPT
AND
PALESTINE

Assuan

J. MAC D

fifty miles south of Cairo is the one really green spot away from the river in all Egypt: the Fayum, a large oasis with an ancient canal that connects its lake with the river and makes a lane of cultivated land. East of the Nile are only desert and rocky hills, so that the journey to Palestine was made through a most inhospitable country.

The Earliest Times

In the Palaeolithic Age, when northern Africa still had rainfall, the Nile was wider than it is now. A series of terraces above the present level suggests that the river cut itself a somewhat narrower and deeper channel, then another and another, as over thousands of years the climate became drier. At the same time the land on either side of the river became less and less hospitable; the Sahara Desert was created by the gradual cessation of rainfall. Some of the people went elsewhere, while others descended to make the river valley their home, bringing with them animals, as the deposits of bones show.

The earliest villages seem to go back to about 5000 B.C. A cemetery of this period has been found at Deir Tasa in Middle Egypt, the graves of which contain the remains of food, as well as ornaments and Neolithic tools. A few hundred years later copper had been introduced, so that the culture can be called Chalcolithic. The people were agricultural and pastoral. They made good pottery, the even firing of which shows that they had kilns. They had a taste for jewelry, some of which was made by boring and shaping rather hard stones. In the next period there was a sudden flowering of the ability and inclination to draw. Slate palettes on which to grind cosmetics also appeared and persisted. On such a slate one would grind a little malachite with a pebble and make green eye paint of a sort still used in Africa; it is germicidal, very helpful in keeping flies away from the eyes, and probably useful in lessening the glare of the sun. These palettes were often carefully shaped, and their ornamentation became increasingly elaborate as time went on.

Even in prehistoric times Lower Egypt, the northern part, seems to have had more contact with other parts of the world than the southern part did. The style of some of its clay jars suggests a Palestinian origin. Lapis lazuli, which originated in India, probably came to Egypt from Mesopotamia, and obsidian came from Arabia, Abyssinia, or the islands near Sicily. There is archaeological evidence from near the end of the prehistoric period, perhaps around 3500 B.C., of a sizable and continued immigration of new people who probably were Mesopotamian in origin. This discovery of new physical types in the graves of this time, combined with the appearance of new cultural traits of Mesopotamian style, seems to indicate a strong new influence upon Egypt by immigrants. Pretty examples of cylinder seals appear, and in architecture there begin to be decorative panels of brickwork, and there are new artistic motifs: balanced groups in composition, sometimes strange animals, sometimes a hero or divinity with flanking animals. From this time on civilization in Egypt seems to have advanced rapidly, both appropriating many cultural traits from Mesopotamia and developing new ones of its own. Egypt was always to be different from Mesopotamia in many ways in spite of its taking over cultural traits from Mesopotamia at this time and in spite of sending influences in the other direction later. To the archaeologists and art historians objects from the two cultures are instantly distinguishable.

By about 3400 B.C. the two kingdoms of Upper Egypt and Lower Egypt had been organized. For three centuries the two lived independently and more or less peaceably. Then, about 3100, Menes (also called Narmer), king of the southern kingdom, was able to gain control of all the northern region, and a union of Egypt was effected that essentially has lasted until the present day. A capital city was built at Memphis, just south of the Delta at the natural junction of the two parts of Egypt.

THE EARLY HISTORICAL PERIOD: 3100 TO 2686 B.C.

The Sources

In addition to our regular system of dating, scholars customarily use the system of dynasties of Egypt that we owe to Manetho, a Greek-speaking Egyptian priest of the third century before Christ. His purpose may well have been to remind the Greeks who then ruled Egypt of the ancient glories of his people. He had access to the native source materials and could read them. Unfortunately his work survives only in the form of more or less extensive quotations by Greek and Roman authors interested in chronology. He had tried to make his book more usable by arranging his material according to the families of kings, or dynasties, and even today it is convenient to use these middle-sized temporal units. Thus, the early historical (or archaic) period may also be spoken of as "the first two dynasties." There will be other periods when the use of the dynastic system seems to make references more meaningful; the Eighteenth Dynasty, a golden period from 1567 to 1320 B.C., is one.

The sources are scanty until the later periods, but there are lists of kings and events. The Turin Papyrus, written in the Nineteenth Dynasty, contains the remains of a complete list of all the kings from Menes, at the beginning of the First Dynasty in 3100 B.C., down to the time when it was written. The Palermo Stone, so called because it is in the museum of Palermo, Sicily, offers what seem to be authentic records of Egypt up to the Fifth Dynasty, not in terms of wars or conquests, but rather in terms of the height of the Nile from year to year, the consecration of temples, the arrival of forty-nine ships with cedar wood from Lebanon, and the return of an expedition sent to the South bringing back gold and incense.

The Egyptian language could be written in the pictorial signs that are known as hieroglyphs or with cursive forms of the signs in the style known as hieratic. Presently a system was devised to write it as an alphabetic language, with at least one character understood as expressing each of its twenty-four consonantal sounds. The vowels, which were not written, can often be guessed by comparison with the way in which Egyptian words are written in Babylonian or Greek and especially in Coptic, the later popular form of the early Egyptian language.

Just as the study of the Near Eastern languages was greatly helped by Rawlinson's providing a good copy of the almost inaccessible inscription on the Behistun Rock, so the study of the Egyptian language was helped by the discovery of the Rosetta Stone (named for the place of finding) in 1799 by a member of Napoleon's expedition to Egypt. This black stone slab, now to be seen in the British Museum, contained a decree of the priests of Memphis in honor of Ptolemy the Fifth, one of the Macedonian kings of later Egypt, written in hieroglyphic characters in one section, in the very rapid form of hieratic known as demotic in another, and in Greek characters in the third. The Rosetta Stone, helpful as it was, did not alone make possible the decipherment of the Egyptian language. The gathering and comparison and analysis of many Egyptian texts by many scholars also led to that end. As in the Near East, we have many inscriptions of kings that furnish useful information, and information of different kinds comes (now that we know the language) from the many papyri that correspond to the cuneiform tablets.

Napoleon, like Alexander the Great long before him, took men of learning with him on his expedition. Although the British brought about the failure of the expedition, which was intended to go all the way to India, the savants performed useful scientific studies of Egypt and prepared a description of Egyptian antiquities that was later published in many illustrated volumes. This admirable beginning of Egyptian archaeology was followed by alternations of shameless treasure hunts and careful archaeological studies until at last, well toward the end of the nineteenth century, the situation was gotten fairly well in hand; since then a great deal of very useful archaeological investigation has been done.

The Achievement of the First Two Dynasties (3100–2686 B.C.)

The four hundred years of the early historical period, the period of the first two dynasties, was a time of great progress in Egypt. Although de-

tails are often lacking, we can at least point to the results that we know
were achieved by the end of the period. The unified government of the
Two Lands, Upper and Lower Egypt, was well established. The court was
organized and the army and the civil service were responsive to the will
of the monarch. The irrigation system and the cultivation of the dispos-
able land were well advanced, even though some pictures belonging to
the period show hunting scenes in uncultivated areas along the river bank.
The idea that the one kingdom was composed of two kingdoms had such
vitality that the king had to wear a double crown to symbolize it, and
because he was buried in Lower Egypt, there had to be a cenotaph in
Upper Egypt to symbolize his burial there. The government was an absolute monarchy based on the idea that the king was a living god. This
idea was so generally accepted that service to the king, in this life and
the next, was the most important of all activities.

Goods were sought in many places and carried—even heavy stone—
for surprising distances. For example, the materials found at Sakkara in
Lower Egypt—alabaster, basalt, diorite, and other stones—come not only
from nearby, but also from the eastern and western deserts, from the
Fayum, and from Nubia, south of Egypt. Finds of pottery show that
the products of certain shops were widely distributed. Sinai sent turquoise, malachite, and copper. The woods of Lebanon were imported in
some quantity. Ebony came from the South, far up the river, as did ivory
and resin. In Egypt the river was the one great highway: heavy loads
traveling short distances on land went by sledge, since the wheel was
not suited to the sandy soil.

Tools were chiefly of copper. We have examples of fine work in wood
preserved in the dry climate, and fine ivory fittings, like feet for tables.
The people of this period made good ordinary pottery, but seemed to put
their greater effort on elegant stone vessels. They learned to make gold
jewelry and to shape hard and precious stones. After a good many unim-
pressive efforts they began to shape free-standing sculptures of some merit.

Remains have been found of simple houses of sun-dried brick; reeds,
too, were used, especially the papyrus reed. When, in the First Dynasty,
some stone began to be used, the design appropriate to the earlier materials was often reproduced in stone; for example, stone walls were
carved to look like walls of reed matting. The Greeks, too, did this when
they began to use stone, and we ourselves often copy the forms of old
materials in new materials. Sun-dried brick, or mud brick, however, remained the chief material in such structures as the royal tombs at Sakkara, not far south of modern Cairo, on the Nile near Memphis.

These tombs could be as large as 200 by 100 feet, with several rooms
around the central chamber, and are thought to imitate the structure of
the palaces. Some have been found unplundered, and they show what was

thought to be needed for the life beyond the grave. In the storerooms are food and drink, of course, in impressive variety and quantity. There is furniture of wood inlaid with ivory and plates and cups to set on it. There are tools and weapons of every kind. In a pit beside each royal tomb was buried a boat in which the spirit of the monarch was to travel with the sun god on his daily trip. There is evidence, as in Sumeria, that attendants were killed so that they could serve the king in the other world.

Another great achievement of the age was the calendar year of 365 days. There were three seasons, each of four thirty-day months, and at the end of the third season were five days to fill out the number of 365. The first season, which began toward the end of July, was named for the flooding of the Nile, the second was named for the growth of the crops, and the third for the harvest. Since 365 days is not the true length of the year, the calendar would gradually get out of order and after four years would be wrong by one day, as it is with us, but they did not correct the calendar in leap year, as we do; we are not sure what adjustments they made.

THE OLD KINGDOM

The period of Egyptian history known as the Old Kingdom lasted from 2686 to 2181 B.C. and included the Third, Fourth, Fifth, and Sixth Dynasties. What used to be the last centuries of the Old Kingdom are now often regarded as the First Intermediate Period and include dynasties seven through ten, from 2181 to about 2040 B.C. The distinction between these periods is based on the firmness of the power of the central government at Memphis during the Old Kingdom, the inability of the dynasties trying to rule from Thebes and Herakleopolis to do more than exercise a very limited control over the rulers of the nomes (the smaller governmental units) during the First Intermediate Period, and the restoration of control over all Egypt by the Theban rulers, which marks the beginning of the Middle Kingdom about 2040 B.C.

The Royal Government

The society of the Old Kingdom was admirably organized. At its head was the absolute monarch, the king, who was also a god. The people regarded him as the source of all law and the owner of all land and other material property in the country. A class of nobles managed his contact with affairs and with the common people. The most important offices of the realm were filled by members of his family. The vizier, or vice-king, administered justice, the grain supply, the treasury, army, public works, and the priesthoods of the state gods. The king had managed to gain enough power to be able to appoint rotating governors for the forty-odd nomes, which formerly had been independent. On some of the borders, however, he seems to have tolerated permanent wardens of the marches, especially in the South.

The king's divinity was such an awful thing as to make him untouchable and unapproachable. It lent authority to his will, supported his assertion of the ownership of all Egypt, and, perhaps most important, was thought to continue after death and improve the chance of his subjects' survival after the close of this life. Yet a time was to come when the king had to struggle for power with the priests of the great state cults and with the governors of the nomes, who succeeded in exacting permanent and hereditary standing from him. Even without enough evidence to follow the process in detail, we can see that power relations shifted from time to time and that they depended, not on arrangements once made nor on written formulas, but on the people involved in them and the forces operative at a given time.

Although life could surely not have gone on without a goodly amount of small-scale barter between individuals, all formal trade seems to have been conducted by the king and his officials. His expeditions went to Byblos on the coast of Palestine to get the cedar and other woods of the mountains behind, woods that are generally spoken of simply as "the cedar of Lebanon." The exploitation of the turquoise and copper mines of Sinai was managed by royal officials and guarded against raids by detachments of the army. The tomb of a First Dynasty king at Sakkara has yielded a rich collection of copper tools and weapons, together with a great reserve supply of copper; it must have been plentiful. The government regularly conducted a census of resources and exacted taxes in kind. Those holding some of the grain-bearing land paid in grain, and those holding grazing land paid in either animals or hides.

The king could also exact labor for the irrigation works and for other public projects, the most spectacular of which were the pyramids. It was said that 100,000 men worked for twenty years to build the Great Pyramid, but perhaps only a smaller corps of men, chiefly the expert workers in stone, was on duty all the year, and the many unskilled peasants were gathered to furnish the power of their muscles during the season of high Nile, when the farm work would be at a virtual standstill and the great blocks of cut stone could be floated to the spot and hauled into position.

The great efforts expended on these tombs were expected to benefit everyone. The king himself was to continue to rule in the next world. The writings put in the chambers of the pyramids and known today as the Pyramid Texts offer an astounding variety of religious, ritual, and magic attempts to ensure the eternal life and the eternal status of the dead king. Possibly the most inconsistent feature of this mixture, from the modern point of view, is that it represents the king both as the humble servant and the irresistible lord of the gods. The noblemen hoped to benefit in the next world by having their tombs grouped around the pyramid of their sovereign, and presumably the common people, too, hoped for a share in the immortality of the king.

The first king known to have had a pyramid was Djoser, founder of the Third Dynasty, who began his rule about 2686 B.C. His gifted vizier, I-em-hotep, planned and built an elaborate mortuary complex of the local white limestone at Sakkara. A pyramid rose in six unequal stages to a height of about two hundred feet and was surrounded by the tombs of nobles, altars, shrines, and storehouses. This gifted and original architect still made these stone structures imitate the appearance of earlier structures of light wood, reeds, and brick.

The Fourth Dynasty was the great age of pyramid building. The first king, Snefru, built a pair of pyramids, only one of which was of true pyramidal shape. The second, third, and fourth rulers of this dynasty built the best-known of the pyramids at Gizeh, by the river, a few miles below the modern Cairo. Khuf-wy, whom the Greeks were later to call Cheops, built the Great Pyramid around the year 2590 B.C.

The Great Pyramid is the largest single building ever constructed. Its base covers thirteen acres and is virtually square, the longest side, 756.08 feet, being only 7.9 inches longer than the shortest. The sides almost exactly face the points of the compass, and the corners are almost exact right angles. It was 481.4 feet high, but the top thirty-one feet are now missing, for in a later age the Arab conquerors of Egypt stripped off the white limestone blocks that formed the outer surface and the peak. The core of the pyramid consists of about 2,300,000 large blocks of a less fine yellow limestone. Inside are corridors and chambers. Nearby there are small pyramids for the king's three queens and a group of tombs for other members of the family and noble officials. The complex includes a mortuary temple, where prayers for the king were to be said, a processional causeway that leads almost to the edge of the river, and a modest temple at the end of the causeway. This arrangement came to be standard.

Here design and execution alike are mature. The Great Pyramid is built with great skill, and the accompanying structures are well designed and well grouped. A great many statues formed part of the equipment of the complex. In addition the tomb, found unviolated, of Queen Hetep-hras, Cheops' mother, has yielded furniture that is classic in design and perfectly executed. Never again, however, was a king to build his tomb with such an expenditure of effort. The pyramids of Cheops' son Kha-ef-Re (Chephren) and of his grandson Men-ku-Re (Mycerinus) are smaller, and thereafter the size of the pyramids declined steadily. The last one of classic dimensions was built by Pepy II at the end of the Sixth Dynasty, about 2180 B.C.

The maintenance of the power of the central government is one of those persistent problems of government that must be worked on steadily and can never be permanently solved. Truly it was a tremendous achievement for the government to have maintained its sway over all Egypt from the union of 3100 B.C. to about 2181, when the First Intermediate Period began, yet somehow it was possible for local rulers to assert themselves against the power of the central government for the two hundred years that that period lasted; we do not know how the authority of the central government was reestablished.

Although the power of the god Re increased greatly during the Fourth Dynasty and after it, the evidence does not allow us to conclude that the rising power of the priests shook the power of the central government. Re had at first belonged to the city of Heliopolis as its local deity, but the fact that he was thought of as the sun brought him more than local worship, for his cult was suited to be associated with and to support the royal power. In the Fifth Dynasty the pyramids began to be accompanied by an obelisk and a temple of Re. Nevertheless, we do not know that the priests of Re could either challenge the king or exert a quiet control over him.

In the Fourth and Fifth Dynasties the kings had perhaps increased the power of the nobles by granting them lands in order to provide the services of food and prayer for the royal tombs, and in the Fourth Dynasty they had conceded the permanent tenure of the governorships of the nomes, which until then had been held by nobles in turn at the king's pleasure. We still do not know why it was that with the Sixth Dynasty, about 2181 B.C., the central government became unable to exert control over all the land. Only then did the First Intermediate Period—two centuries of control by local dynasts—begin.

Religion

Re was only one of a bewildering number of Egyptian gods. Each locality and district early developed its own deities, which represented the forces of nature. The gods were thought to have a variety of forms, especially the forms of plants and animals, and might be conceived of as the friendly, useful cow, the fearsome lion, the despised jackal, or lowly snake, or as some tree or plant—although the modern mind may have trouble comprehending a tree or plant divinity. Since these were nature gods, they often were thought to die and be reborn with the cycle of the year, a cycle accompanied by ceremonies, prayers, and festivals.

Some gods were widely recognized from an early time because they were thought of as cosmic forces. Re was the sun, Ya'h the moon, Nut the sky, and Geb the earth. Osiris, originally a local god of the type who died and was reborn, achieved national status as a dying and returning god because the story of his vicissitudes had great appeal to all classes of society, apparently because the priests of his cult polished up the story; other dying and returning gods remained local rather than national.

Some attained national recognition because as their worshipers became prominent they brought the divinity forward with them. The god Horus, for example, was the local god of a small place who became god of the nome, then of his part of the Delta, then of the whole kingdom of Lower Egypt, then of both kingdoms, and then, when Menes united the two kingdoms, of the united kingdom of the Two Lands. Much later, with the rise of the Thebans in the Middle Kingdom and in the Eighteenth Dynasty, the god Amun of Thebes was carried up in power with the new rulers to such a position as no Egyptian god had ever before enjoyed.

THE MIDDLE KINGDOM

The restoration of unity and of the effective power of the central government in about 2040 B.C. marks the end of the First Intermediate Period and the beginning of a new period, the Middle Kingdom, which continued until about 1780 B.C. There is no clear reason to be given why the rulers of Thebes, which was not a mighty city, were able after eighty years or so of struggle to prevail over their chief rivals, the rulers of Herakleopolis, and reunify the country and begin the Middle Kingdom. The new central government went along fairly steadily until about 1780, when Egypt was invaded gradually by groups of the Asiatic chariot people, known as the Hyksos, who controlled the country until about 1570 B.C. The time of their control is often called the Second Intermediate Period, a time that we shall discuss later.

The Government of the Middle Kingdom

The new regime of the Middle Kingdom resumed the activities that had been beyond the reach of the local governments. They sent an expedition across to the Red Sea, where it built ships and sailed down to Punt, the land of myrrh, at the bottom of that sea. The exploitation of the mines of the Sinai Peninsula was renewed, and commerce was reestablished with Nubia for the stone that was desirable for the royal statues. Trade with Byblos and the interior of the Near East began again.

The kings were able to exercise firm control over the realm, although local power and interests could command their respect. They were regarded as gods, like their predecessors of the Old Kingdom. To give proper divine support to their enterprises they brought forward Amun, the local god of Thebes, to take a leading place in the pantheon with Ptah of Memphis, Re of Heliopolis, and Osiris of Abydos. Amun, "the hidden one," was also combined with the sun god Re.

The burial customs of the age suggest something of the relation between the kings and the nobles. At times like the end of the Old Kingdom when the nobles seemed to be gaining in power, their tombs became larger and those of the kings less ambitious. In the Middle Kingdom the tombs of the kings are plainly grander than those of the nobles. Yet the nobles, as shown by the finds in their tombs, could use the same spells and prayers and rituals as those used by the king to achieve beatitude in the next world.

Since they felt that some material form was required to house the personality in the life after death, the Egyptians had early developed the process of mummification to preserve bodies. Because it was still possible that the body might decay, figures or paintings were also put in the tomb as substitutes for the actual body. Careful mummification was expensive and was for kings and nobles rather than for the common man, who at best could afford only a less thorough attempt at preservation, perhaps backed up by a very simple image of himself.

A New Time of Troubles: The Second Intermediate Period

Renewed internal struggles around 1780 B.C. made it easier for the Hyksos to infiltrate Egypt in such numbers that by about 1720 they were in control of the Delta, where they lived in great fortress camps for over a hundred years more. They dominated Lower Egypt and compelled Upper Egypt to accept their leadership.

Although the Hyksos "ruled without Re," as the Egyptians put it, and were not highly respectful of Egyptian culture, they were not utter barbarians, but were typical of the peoples who, terrible with their horses and their chariots, appeared in many places in the early second millennium, dominated others, and ruled efficiently. Their distinctive traits, which the Egyptians borrowed from them, were the use of the horse and the battle chariot, the compound bow, which was more powerful than the simple bow, body armor, and some elements of design in clothes and jewelry. Perhaps their greatest influence on Egyptian life lay in the fact that they toughened the Egyptians and changed their attitudes, as those who practice continued coercion of other people are likely to do. The Egyptians finally drove out the Hyksos about 1570 B.C. The brilliant period that followed will be described in the next chapter.

EGYPTIAN CIVILIZATION OF THE OLD AND MIDDLE KINGDOMS

Agriculture

The government assisted agriculture by setting up, far to the South, the Nilometer, a gauge that gave some indication of what the year's rise would be early enough to allow for any special preparations, especially the strengthening of the dikes that kept villages and gardens from being flooded and that constituted the walls of the basins that held the flood water while its silt was deposited. The all-important cereal crop—wheat, barley, and emmer—was planted as soon as the land was again dry enough to be worked, probably late September or October. The harvest came in the spring.

There were many vegetables: onions, radishes, beans, lentils, and others. All kinds of melons grew well, and the date palm and other fruit trees were highly prized. Olive oil, a most important food in the ancient world, had to be largely imported, since the olive does not grow well in Egypt. Oil for food, lighting, and the base of medicines and toilet preparations was extracted from the castor-oil plant, sesame seeds, and the seeds of a number of other plants. The Egyptians enjoyed native wines and a brewed drink like beer.

Flax and papyrus grew in the marshes. A few surviving pieces of linen cloth are very finely woven and attractively dyed. Paper was made by preparing thin strips of papyrus that could be pounded together in a lengthwise and crosswise pattern. The writing was done with reed pens and with ink that is still legible today. Papyrus was strong enough for sails for river boats and to be woven into cables.

The well attested love of the Egyptians for flowers, as for many other aspects of nature, is part of the ample proof that they loved and enjoyed this world; their thoughts were not all of death and a different life. They relished this life and firmly believed that it continued beyond the grave. We get glimpses in paintings of pleasure in Egyptian gardens where there are pools, flowers, and fruit trees. Flowers were used at private feasts and public festivals. The floral motif appeared in such architectural forms as stone columns imitating the stems of plants, with capitals representing the flowering heads. Their successful use of the floral motif in ornamentation of many kinds had an influence on Syrian, Assyrian, and Persian art, and then on the art of the Greeks.

The ox and the cow were the chief large animals. There was little place for the horse in Egypt except to draw the chariots that were used after the Hyksos had introduced them. One or two attempts to introduce the camel apparently did not succeed, and the donkey continued to do the carrying. The goat, as everywhere, was the poor man's animal. Sheep were raised, and in the Delta, where the soil is generally moister, pigs were kept. Fowl were part of every household.

Materials and Craftsmanship

The Egyptians were superb handlers of wood, although their native woods were scarce and of an inferior sort. Large pieces of wood with a good grain had to be obtained from Asia Minor through Byblos and other ports. The more exotic woods, like ebony and the fragrant woods, came from the lands south of Egypt. There was elaborate woodwork inside the pyramids and the temples of the Old Kingdom. The Egyptian cabinetmaker was a master; rare and fine woods were often used, and inlaying was common.

Egypt was better supplied with gold (from the mines of the South) than were the nations of the Near East. Some silver came from Egyptian mines. The craftsman worked these metals with sure taste. In addition, the desert east of Egypt yielded a variety of stones that were made into attractive jewelry: garnet, onyx, chalcedony, jasper, turquoise, carnelian. The blue lapis lazuli was brought from Asia even in very early times, and the purple amethyst came from Nubia. All these materials were skillfully worked.

Copper was the most important working metal of the Old Kingdom. Some came from the mines of Sinai; some was imported from Asia. There are samples of true bronze from the New Kingdom; the source of the tin is not known. Probably long copper saws and abrasive powdered stone were used to cut stone for building.

Many kinds of stone were used. A good limestone from nearby covered the Great Pyramid; the core was of a plainer stone. Much granite of various colors was used, the most famous quarry being at Assuan, in the South. Alabaster was used for statues and parts of buildings as well as for small ointment jars and other little vessels, and one great quarry can still be seen. Another quarry produced the very hard dark yellow quartzite much used for the sarcophagi of the kings. Two blocks from this quarry are known to weigh over a hundred tons apiece.

Many of the products of Egyptian workmen that have come down to us so satisfy our aesthetic sense that we refer to them as works of art, and Egyptian art has its champions who insist that the art of the fifth century before Christ in Greece is not the only classic art, as is often asserted or implied. Egypt, they maintain, had more than one period of truly classical art and in more than one department of art. From beads to pyramids, Egyptian objects often show a truly classical beauty.

The Handling of Ideas

Although they made careful astronomical observations and devised a superior calendar, the Egyptians did not work out any body of theory on such matters. Although they were competent in the practical geometry of surveying land and building large structures, they showed little interest in theoretical geometry. But such statements are made from the point of view of modern Western civilization, which admires the Greeks for their pioneering in generalized and abstract thought. If it is true that the Egyptians, like the other peoples before the Greeks, did not excel in this area, the fact does not detract from the most important thing about their work in science, which is that they did a good deal of basic work that enabled the Greeks and the modern world to start farther ahead than might otherwise have been the case.

It seems possible to discern what in their religion was spontaneous sentiment and what was the product of priestly agents of the government. The determination to use every means of prayer, ritual, and magic to make this life continue after death seems spontaneous, even if the means may have been partly devised by priestly managers. The early worship of local nature gods in every region seems the natural product of people in general, as does the strong feeling for the sun as the source of all good things. On the other hand, we can see that the priests did some effective work on the elaboration of cult and ritual and on the shaping of the stories about the gods and their relations as a means of governmental control of the people.

There was only a modest amount of literature. People sometimes gave accounts of themselves in the form of instructions to their descendants. In the First Intermediate Period such instructions had often breathed a strong spirit of self-reliance and independence, whereas in the Middle Kingdom they are more likely to suggest that the king is the source of all profit and advancement.

A rather sprightlier piece is the three-hundred-line "Tale of Sinuhe," the story of a noble of the Middle Kingdom who, having an uneasy political conscience, thought it politic to remove himself from the jurisdiction at the accession of a new king. After spending many a year as the valued helper of a minor king in Palestine, he was moved as the twilight of his life drew on to ask the king of Egypt whether he might return to what still seemed home to him. A slightly amused monarch assured him that Egypt was always open to him, and he settled down for his old age, the story tells us, in the only country that an Egyptian could love.

The spells intended to help people in the other world are a fairly important part of literature. Those of the Old Kingdom, found in the chambers of the pyramids, are referred to as "Pyramid Texts," while in the

Middle Kingdom they are known as "Coffin Texts," since they were written on the coffins of prominent private persons who arrogated to themselves the use of these charms, formerly reserved for the king.

EARLY INDIA AND CHINA

The influence of Sumerian civilization on the civilization of the Indus
Valley (once in India, now in the new state of Pakistan) seems plain to
the archaeologists who have been working in Pakistan and India; the
question of how the influence was transmitted is difficult.[2] The Indus
civilization has two very important cities, Mohenjo-Daro and Harappa,
which are almost four hundred miles apart, and a number of lesser cities.
The role played in the culture by the two major cities is not known. They
have religious centers like the Sumerian cities, although the style is
different. They differ sharply from the Sumerian cities, however, in being
laid out on a consistent rectangular plan that contrasts strongly with the
irregular Sumerian streets and also suggests an official foundation. Both
have areas of about a square mile. Many of the houses were arranged as
multiple dwellings. The streets have brick sewers.

Although seals have been found on which there is pictographic writing,
the writing still cannot be read, so that our information is only archaeological. Only in the last few decades have serious attempts been made
to explore the great extent of the Indian subcontinent archaeologically,
and one can see the work there bringing more and more results as it continues with modern methods and standards. We know something of the
crops—wheat, six-rowed barley (for such distinctions can now be made
when a few surviving grains are found), peas, melons, sesame, dates, and
history's first cotton. It is easy to identify the bones of cattle, camels,
buffaloes, asses, and horses. The traces of workshops suggest that there
were specialized workers. There was trade with Afghanistan, Iran, Mesopotamia, and south India. As has already been said, finds at Akkad in the
time of Sargon (24th century) clearly establish a connection, and it seems
reasonable to suppose that ships of the Sumerians went down the Persian
Gulf and over as far as the mouth of the Indus River and perhaps up
the river.

In the Indus Valley, then, there are strong likenesses to the civilization
of Sumer, consisting of the complexity of the cities, the trade with places
at a distance, the well organized agriculture, the specialized manufacture, and the ceremonial centers, but we must remember that the Indus
civilization had its own style. Egypt likewise had these things, but in its
own style.

[2] Glyn Daniel, in *The First Civilizations,* discusses at length and interestingly the possible relations between the group of earliest civilizations.

Certainly the civilization of the Indus Valley cannot be regarded as a colonial offshoot of the Sumerian civilization. The archaeological investigations seem to show that around 2500 B.C. advanced civilization arose rather suddenly from the village civilization of the region, which was not unlike the simpler cultures that we saw in earlier Mesopotamia. There are traces of attempts that failed to establish cities in the Indus Valley, presumably because the waters of the river, which floods every year, are difficult to deal with and because city life is more strenuous and demanding than village life. Then, the evidence seems to say, a far more determined effort was made which led to the successful establishment of cities and city civilization of a sort rather reminiscent of Sumer. The reasonable theory is offered that many of the people of the Indus region had been to Sumer, had seen how life was lived there, and had decided to try to live in somewhat the same way at home. Travel by water between the two regions is possible, and the people could have gone to Sumer on Sumerian ships if they did not yet have any of their own.

Although the region has not yet been investigated with anything like the intensity of archaeological exploration in the Middle and Near East and the Greek and Roman world, it has clearly shown that the Indus civilization covered an area larger than that of any other until the Roman. How intense it was outside the cities will not be known until the exploratory work in many places continues systematically to uncover whole sites. Perhaps we soon shall be able to read the writing, although there is as yet nowhere near as much of it as in Mesopotamia and Egypt.

The remains do seem to indicate that as the generations went by the inhabitants of Mohenjo-Daro had increasing difficulty in keeping up the works that protected them from the river. Whatever the natural difficulties may have been, somewhere around 1600 B.C. an invasion, probably of the people known as the Aryans (the word has been misused in Western contexts), ended the life of Mohenjo-Daro and of Harappa, leaving the bodies of the fallen to be found by the modern archaeologist. The life of other cities, especially those in the South, did not end, as archaeology shows, although until fairly recently the view still prevailed that there was a Dark Age until about 500 B.C. There is now reason to believe that in many places life went on through the millennium after the invasion in a modest but barbaric way. The energy needed, however, to restore the intenser life of Mohenjo-Daro and Harappa could not be found. We shall find a situation very like this one when we come to the destruction of the cities of Mycenaean Greece by the invasion of the Dorians and to a Dark Age that archaeology has shown much less dark.

Our knowledge of the Shang civilization on the Yellow River in China is even more recent than our knowledge of the Indus civilization, since the first excavation on the Yellow River was in 1921. The first signs of an intense civilization in China seem to date from about 2100 B.C., and the archaeologists are equally sure that this was not a colonial offshoot of one of the more western civilizations. There is not even a basis for arguing that the pattern of city life as opposed to village life may have been inspired by the Sumerians or the Egyptians, as seems possible in the case of the Indus civilization. The rich finds of bronze, however, do seem to have some western motifs, although the style is the local style, and it is supposed that the techniques of handling bronze were indeed brought from the West.

The present evidence seems to indicate that the earliest period of the Shang culture, as it has come to be called, is still Neolithic and is dated 2500 to 2100 B.C. Three other stages, called Early, Middle, and Late Shang, take us down to 1100 B.C. Apparently this civilization covered an area as large as those of Mesopotamia and Egypt and has analogous characteristics, but in its own style. The cities were on the bank of a great river. On rich plains the people grew cereals; they had oxen, sheep, pigs, and dogs. The artisans could handle gold and could cast copper, lead, and bronze. They worked stone, including jade, ivory, bone, and shell, could do fine inlaying, and had a range of pottery. Some of the work was fine in its detail. Their writing was a combination of the pictographic and the phonetic and seems to have been developed for the keeping of records, as it was elsewhere. There is a huge collection, however, of questions and answers put to oracles, the variety of which makes them useful as historical documents, and one of the tasks of contemporary Chinese scholars is the digesting of this mass of material.

3

THE NEW KINGDOM IN EGYPT;
PALESTINE; ASSYRIA

Recovery and the Building of a New Egypt

The period of Egyptian history that is sometimes called the Empire and sometimes the New Kingdom followed the domination of the Hyksos. It may well be that the gathering of their energies to expel the foreigners stirred the Egyptians to a new strenuousness that first led them to a thorough overhauling and improvement of their territories in Africa, then, after three generations, to conquests in Asia such as they had never before attempted.

Thebes was the center of resistance to the Hyksos, just as it had been the locus of the central power that gained strength and brought the Middle Kingdom into being out of an age of self-assertion by local powers. Ahmose I of Thebes, founder of the great Eighteenth Dynasty, assumed dominance in 1570 B.C., drove the Hyksos from their main camp at Avaris in northern Egypt in 1567, pursued them from the country, and captured their chief fort in southern Palestine. He then achieved the reconquest of Nubia, a useful part of the Egyptian domain, especially because of its gold. After some fighting against minor leaders not ready to acknowledge his authority, Ahmose I settled down to reconstitute the national government. For the next three hundred years, a highly successful time, we hear nothing of centrifugal tendencies, that is, the national government exerted a firm control over local governors and other officials.

Amenhotep I, son of Ahmose I, ruled from 1546 to 1526, spending most of his time on the internal affairs of the kingdom. Thutmose I, however, who ruled from 1526 to 1508, extended his sway far to the South. In Asia Minor his army went far into northern Syria, to the great bend of the Euphrates, where he set up a triumphal column on the bank of the river. Such a parade of military strength would do much to establish prestige and make peaceable trade possible.

The next king, Thutmose II, died in his early thirties. He and his half sister Hatshepsut had been married for eighteen years when he died about 1504 B.C. He had already proclaimed as his successor Thutmose III, his young son by a concubine. For a year or so Hatshepsut seemed content to be dowager queen, but she must have been consolidating power behind the scenes, for soon she had herself proclaimed king with all the royal titles of a male king. Strong-minded women were not unknown in the Egyptian royal family, for the grandmother and mother of Ahmose I, as well as his wife (who may have been his sister or half sister), are recorded to have furnished some of the energy and resolution needed to free Egypt from the Hyksos and start reconstruction.

Our evidence is full enough to allow us to trace Hatshepsut's use of some of the great officials and her propaganda for her unusual position. Hers was a peaceful reign; she boasted of her trade expeditions down the Red Sea to Punt for incense, ivory, and rare woods, and down the Nile to get gold and fine woods, and of her care for the Sinai mines. She also erected some buildings, especially to the greater glory of Amun, as part of tending her image. There can be no doubt that she retained her power against the young king's will, even while allowing him a position as co-regent, and that he fiercely resented her, for when he finally was able (1482 B.C.) to remove her, he had her name removed from many monuments where it had appeared. The Roman emperors were later to call this process *damnatio memoriae* when they did it. We know that some of her collaborators among the high officials fell before she did and that Thutmose was so able a soldier that he could probably get the help of the army, but we do not have the complete story of this struggle for power.

Formidable as the lady was at home, the petty princes of Palestine and Syria had become sure that she would not move an army against them and gathered in force to assert themselves. Almost as soon as Thutmose III had asserted his power, he set out and met them at Megiddo in Palestine and smote them; thereafter he could count on their remaining quiet while he fought against the little kingdom of Kadesh, north of Palestine, and against the rather larger kingdom of Mitanni, farther north and across the Euphrates, which was encroaching on Syria. The domination of Palestine and Syria was profitable for Egypt, since trade there was lively. Thutmose III reigned until 1450 B.C. and was succeeded by two men who successively cared well for their empire without doing anything spectacular. With the accession to power of Amenhotep III in 1417 B.C., we come to what may be called the Golden Age of Egypt.

THE WORLD OF AMENHOTEP III (1417–1379 B.C.)

The power of Egypt extended southward as far as the Fourth Cataract, about a thousand miles upriver. Caravans of donkeys (rather than camels, which were introduced later) came there from the Sudan and Central Africa, bringing gold dust, ostrich plumes and eggs, and slaves. To the West there was mostly desert, punctuated by a few oases. Near the Mediterranean lived uncultured people who rarely made the Egyptians any trouble and had nothing to offer them, for in this age the people of Africa outside Egypt were not in the mainstream of civilization.

Palestine and Syria were well under Egyptian control. The Hebrews had not yet arrived in Palestine. The Canaanites had come out of the desert, however, and the Aramaeans (still another people whom we shall discuss later) had come to northern Palestine. There were groups of Hyksos here and there. The petty principalities of the area were often prosperous and could offer desirable products made by their craftsmen, especially chariots, inlaid wood furniture, and rich stuffs for clothes.

From the other side of the Euphrates three peoples of Mesopotamia looked toward the Egyptians with respect. The old kingdom of Babylonia had been under the control of the Kassites for some time when Amenhotep came to the throne. Farther north in Mesopotamia were the Assyrians, who were later to be the most important people of the Near East for a while. In the great bend of the Euphrates, which is nearest Syria, was the kingdom of Mitanni. The people of Mitanni were a part of the Hurrians, the Biblical Horites, who were also found in other parts of the Near East, but who were less powerfully organized elsewhere.

The rulers of these three kingdoms and several of the petty princes of Palestine appear in the Amarna Letters, a cache of clay tablets found at Amarna, a city built by Amenhotep IV, or Akh-en-Aten, just after the time of Amenhotep III. The tablets were a part of the royal correspondence of the time, and the situation they portray may certainly be projected back into the time of Amenhotep III. The letters are in cuneiform writing and most are in Akkadian, a language of international intercourse formerly used in Mesopotamia. Although her firm power extended only up into Syria, Egypt's sphere of influence plainly included the Kassites, the Assyrians, and Mitanni, for the rulers of all three repeatedly requested gifts of gold from Egypt, and we get the impression that the use of cash payments in international affairs was familiar. The others in turn sent the Egyptians expensive gifts of furniture, clothes, and jewels. There is also talk of treaties and royal marriages and of the other things normal in diplomatic exchanges.

In addition the correspondence found at Amarna illustrates the relations of Egypt with still a fourth power, found north of Syria in what is now Turkish territory—the Hittite kingdom. This kingdom, which was very important during the reigns of Amenhotep and his immediate successors, was formed shortly after 2000 B.C. and was to last until its destruction in the great migratory movement of 1200 B.C. Our present knowledge of the Hittites is another triumph of modern research. The excavation of their former capital, near an otherwise unimportant place in Turkey called Boghaz-Keui, disclosed remains of buildings and brought to light about ten thousand cuneiform tablets. Some of them threw light on matters already known from the Amarna Letters. Although some were written in Akkadian, most were in Hittite (four other languages were also found). These finds were made early in this century, and since then a great deal of excavation has thrown light on many sites in the Hittite realm.

A period of strength that is known as the Hittite Old Kingdom had begun in about 1650. The Hittite hold on the center of Asia Minor was strengthened and an advance was made into Syria, which was always a bone of contention between the great powers because of its central position among them and the advantages in trade that came from controlling it. The opposition of the kingdom of Mitanni, combined with troubles about the succession to the throne and the general difficulties of maintaining an empire, caused the Hittites to draw back for some time from Syria. Thutmose III of Egypt had been able to dominate Syria from about 1471 to 1450 and perhaps a decade longer; if the Hittites could not then control Syria, they probably were glad to have Egypt help contain the kings of Mitanni.

In 1380 B.C. the great king Suppiluliumas came to the Hittite throne and almost at once secured the boundaries near home and began a career of conquest. The period from 1380 to 1200 is known as the Hittite Empire, for his successors, too, were able men who kept most of what he gained. His reign came at the time of Egypt's greatest weakness, when the monotheist king Akh-en-Aten was neglecting everything but religion, so that the Hittites moved down into Syria successfully. A major episode in their continuing struggle with the Egyptians was the battle at Kadesh in 1300, in which they caught the Egyptian Rameses II with his army strung out on the march and inflicted heavy losses, although he rallied the troops and prevented disaster. In 1284 the two powers made a treaty of peace and nonaggression; we are in the unusual position of having copies of it in both languages. The end of Hittite greatness came around 1200 B.C.; the country was overrun by the peoples who were on the move at that time.

The Hittite kings of the Empire had made themselves absolute monarchs whose power descended by inheritance, whereas the earlier kings acquired and maintained their power as best they could. The queen seems to have had a separate set of functions and to have inherited her power separately. A feudal system had grown up with a large class of what later would be called knights, men who fought with horses and light chariots and were supported by grants of land so that they would be available for military service. The governors of the provinces were in complete control, but had to swear allegiance to the king, do him homage, and honor his requests for armed forces. The religion of the country was so intensely conservative that the cults of the various people who were fused into the kingdom were managed in the old languages and gods who obviously were the same remained carefully distinguished.

The world of Amenhotep III and of the rest of the 1300s and of the 1200s, down to the disasters of the end of that century, was unusually well-unified. The Egyptians, the Hittites, and the peoples of Mesopotamia could understand each other in the literal sense because of the international language and the international writing that were in use. There was also, to a certain extent, an international set of ideas, of religious practices, and of motifs and methods in art, even while each area was distinct in style from the others.

If we return to our survey of the lands upon which Egypt looked out at this time, we shall see that Egyptian influence extended to the islands of Cyprus and Crete. Cyprus had long been a source of copper and timber; its name means "Copper land." At one time the Hittites made an effort to control it. Crete, as we shall see, had slowly developed a brilliant civilization, largely under Egyptian influence, and at the time of Amenhotep III it had just been enjoying its greatest period. Crete had great influence on the mainland of southern Greece, where there were several small and brilliant kingdoms just coming to their most successful time.

Beyond these lay other less civilized places, sometimes sources of raw materials for the great empires, that were reached by land and by sea. Presumably Egyptian ships went no farther than Crete, but the sea rovers of Mycenae in Greece may well have gone as far as the Baltic, and an occasional ship based in northern lands like Sweden may well have come down into the Mediterranean to call at Egyptian or other ports. The land routes connected with the amber regions of the Baltic and the tin mines of Bohemia.

The Egyptians liked to say that tribute came to Pharaoh from all the world around Egypt,[1] although the fact seems to be that tribute or im-

---

[1] The word "Pharaoh" means "The Great House," as in our expression, "the White House announces...." The first certain use of it known to us occurs in a letter to King Akh-en-Aten in the Eighteenth Dynasty.

posts came only from Palestine or Syria. But Nubia and the Sudan yielded no mean amount of gold, the fertility of the soil remained, and trade with other lands was lively, so that Egypt was now richer than any country had ever been. The internal affairs of the realm seem to have been competently administered. If there was some friction between the great priesthoods and the civil officials, it was only natural. In foreign affairs, however, the king seems not to have been disposed to keep a firm grip on Palestine and Syria, which gave the Hittites an opportunity to advance in those areas; the long-term result, if we look forward to the treaty of 1284, was only that Egypt and the Hittites reached a reasonable compromise.

The Art of the Golden Age

These years included the third classical period of Egyptian art; the first was the time of the great pyramids of the Old Kingdom and the second was during the Twelfth Dynasty in the Middle Kingdom. The workmen of this third period did everything from great temples to fine jewelry with skill and taste. One curious feature is that the architects of all ages in Egypt plundered earlier buildings for material in spite of the wealth of the country and the plentiful labor supply. The architects of this age dismantled some earlier buildings to get dressed stone for their own buildings, and their buildings were in turn plundered on a large scale by the architects of Rameses II a hundred years or so later.

The palace of Amenhotep III in Thebes was built largely of mud brick, with some painted wood and a little stone. The remains of walls were waist-high, and the excavators found a surprising number of small objects in the ruins. Unearthed were traces of gay and attractive paintings such as were found in Crete. Faïence tiles were set into the walls, and faïence friezes ran around the rooms.

Amenhotep III had several series of commemorative scarabs prepared and sent around the kingdom; they were generally oval, a little over three inches long and finely made. They carried hieroglyphic inscriptions. The first series let it be known that he had married the commoner Teye, who was to be a strong partner to him in all respects. Another series tells of his exploits in a wild bull hunt and another of his shooting lions. From another we learn of his marrying a princess of Mitanni who arrived with a retinue of 317 ladies. We shall later find the Roman emperors using coins for this same purpose of emphasizing certain events and ideas.

In the cemetery at Thebes there are some ninety private chapels of the golden time of the fifteenth and fourteenth centuries B.C. The paintings on the walls display clear and fresh colors—blue, yellow, pink, brick-red

—and are rich and sophisticated in composition and execution. On other walls there are reliefs of the same classical perfection.

The skill of the Egyptian artist and the corresponding good taste of the consumer of art showed itself in innumerable small items and practical things. Not only was the jewelry of the noble lady beautiful, so too were things for the table that cannot have been very expensive. Vases, bowls, and spoons are generally well designed. The decoration is inspired by plants or flowers of the Nile Valley or by the animals and birds. For some reason Egyptian pottery was never as highly developed as in other countries, but glass was made from early times. In the Eighteenth Dynasty the manufacture of faïence reached a high point with pleasing shapes and designs and with bright colors in the applied glaze.

Literature

The spells intended to benefit the dead form a large part of the literature, as was the case in earlier periods. In the New Kingdom the spells were written on papyrus rolls and are somewhat misleadingly called "The Book of the Dead," since there was no one book or place where all the known spells were collected. Perhaps there was somewhat the same intent of helping the dead in the victory hymn addressed to Thutmose III, in which the god Amun-Re is represented as praising the king for his great victories and expressing his satisfaction at the king's devoutness, his temples, and his offerings.

From the tomb of Amenhotep III, just before his son's promotion of Aten as the one god, comes a lofty hymn to the sun that has a certain spirit of monotheism. The sun is addressed as the great source of all life and light and also as a god who is everything, sees everything, and does everything. The greatest of all hymns to Aten was composed in the next reign, a majestic address that is better poetry than the earlier hymn and has a more consistent tone of monotheism. Although comparison of this hymn to Psalm 104 is not unjust, there is probably no direct connection between the two. Two excellent lyric poems come from another tomb dating from the Eighteenth Dynasty. On one wall of the tomb a fine "Praise of Death" was inscribed; on the other wall was "The Harper's Song," a sweetly melancholy exhortation to a pleasant indulgence during this brief existence.

From the New Kingdom also come tales of marvelous adventure—one, for example, of a younger son forced to leave home by the advances of his older brother's wife—which suggest *The Arabian Nights*. Another such tale is about the capture of Joppa by an ingenious ruse that introduced Egyptian soldiers into the city in baskets said to be full of booty. The

Greek historian Herodotus later recounted stories of the kings of Egypt that have this same flavor, which to us suggests the Near East.

THE MONOTHEISTIC INTERLUDE

Amenhotep IV ruled from 1379 to 1362. His mind seems to have been almost entirely devoted to religion, and especially to the worship of Aten, the sun's disk, to the exclusion of all the older gods. The worship of Aten seems to have begun only about a century before. The worship of Re as the god of the sun was intensified and specialized as the worship of Aten, the visible form of the sun's disk, regarded as a universal god.

The young king's fervor toward Aten was such that he officially turned his back on the other gods, their priesthoods, and the needs of their worshipers; the power and prestige of the throne were such that for a while he was able to do so. He changed his own name, "Amun-is-content," to Akh-en-Aten, "he-who-is-serviceable-to-Aten," (often given as "Ikhnaton"), and built himself a new city, Akh-et-Aten, "Horizon of Aten." Here he retired with his family and a group of courtiers who had supported him in making this break with tradition. He went so far as to forbid the worship of the old divinities. He and his family worshiped Aten directly; he was himself regarded as the embodiment of Aten, and the nobility were expected to worship him directly. The people apparently were expected to acquiesce in the disappearance of such other religious support as they had previously known.

The new city was a spacious and beautiful place on the Nile about halfway between Memphis and Thebes. The modern name of the site is Tell el Amarna; the Amarna Letters are named from the fact that they were found there. Archaeology gives us the picture of it as a charming place in which to live, and for the archaeologist it has the special charm of having been inhabited only until 1362, so that anything found there presumably was put there no later than that date and probably was not made much earlier, which helps greatly in the problem of establishing dates for things found in excavations.

Akh-en-Aten appointed one of the younger members of his family as coregent, and after a few years he seems to have made overtures through this coregent toward a reconciliation with some of the priests by permitting the re-establishment of the worship of Amun at Thebes. But he died in 1362 B.C., and the coregent died soon after, leaving the throne to his younger brother, Tut-ankh-Aten, who ruled at Amarna only for a short time. Thereafter the exclusive worship of Aten was apparently abandoned, and the king moved to Thebes, changing his name to Tut-ankh-

Amun. The excavation of his unplundered tomb in 1922 caused great excitement because of the extraordinary wealth of its furnishings. Upon his death in 1352 B.C. he left no male heir in the Thutmosid line, and his queen attempted to hold the power by writing to the great Hittite king Suppiluliumas, asking for a prince to marry her and be king of Egypt. The Hittite king moved cautiously, and the queen sent a second letter; both have been found in the Hittite archives. But others were fishing in these troubled waters, and the Hittite prince was murdered on the way to Egypt.

We can now follow, on the surface, at least, what was done by practical-minded people to set things in order and give the government firm control once more. Probably the most powerful man in Egypt was Horemheb, commander of the army and a man who had served the pharaoh well for a long time. Very likely it was he who intercepted the Hittite prince. Then what power the queen had was neutralized by his marrying her to her aged grandfather, Ay, a high official of long service, one whose blood was obviously good enough for the royal position. The old gentleman died soon, and Horemheb took the throne, having doubtless spent the interval in assuring his own power. When he came to the throne, Horemheb completely restored the worship of Amun, returned the priests to their posts, gave back the confiscated endowments, and repaired temples everywhere. He punished men in the civil government who had taken advantage of the inexperience and inattention of the recent rulers to abuse the power of their offices. He tried to efface every reminder of the Atenist pharaohs by leveling the city of Akh-et-Aten (Amarna) and by chiseling their names off monuments elsewhere. Their names were dropped from the official records and the succession was reckoned from Amenhotep III to Horemheb.

It is difficult to see what good there can have been in the Atenist movement. It was not a forerunner of Judaism and Christianity. It had no ethical content and promised no benefits to anyone. The rulers who practiced it seem to have had no sense of their responsibilities to the nation at large and of their duty to provide, or not to impede, some means of religious satisfaction. Probably the damage was successfully repaired; if there was some loss of territory in the long contest with the Hittites in Asia, little real harm was done.

It has been conjectured that Akh-en-Aten was attempting to break the influence of the priests of Amun. The god's wealth in land, animals, stores of grain, slaves, and gold was immense; Amun was the senior partner in all the imperial ventures of Egypt and received the better share of the yield. At about this time he was getting several hundred pounds of gold a year from the mines of Nubia and the Sudan. Yet it was within the king's power to dismiss the priests and confiscate their endowments, and he did so. A more worldly king might have reduced or broken the power of Amun for good reasons, but he would surely have seen to it that there was a form of religion acceptable to the people to replace it. It is not clear, however, that the power of Amun did harm to the realm at this time either by any actions of the priests or by the concentration of wealth. The great temple estates may well have served a useful purpose as units of society.

THE LATER CENTURIES

The Nineteenth Dynasty (1320–1200 B.C.)

Presumably it was because Horemheb had no son that the throne again had to pass to someone of a different family. He made a succession arrangement something like that by which he had come to the throne, where a most respectable elderly man took the throne and soon passed it to a vigorous younger man. His old friend Pa-Rameses (who is known as Rameses I) had a long and honorable career behind him and a grown son who already was vizier of Upper Egypt. Their joint prestige, together with Horemheb's, assured the succession without trouble. Rameses I died after a little more than a year, and his son Sethi succeeded him.

Sethi (1318–1304 B.C.), an experienced and vigorous soldier, immediately reestablished the power of Egypt in Palestine and checked the Hittites in Syria. He also took the practical step of moving the administrative and military center of Egypt to a place near Tanis in the Delta, nearer to the sea and to other countries, building a whole new government city.

Rameses II (1304–1237 B.C.) came to the throne at the age of twenty and was soon tested by a full-scale movement of the Hittites against the Egyptian possessions near them. In 1300 Rameses took the field and met the enemy at Kadesh, as we have seen, and probably averted a disaster by his courage and skill and was able to keep the Hittites from taking Palestine. But our knowledge of the affair cannot be gained by the version inscribed in text and pictures on his mortuary temple at Thebes, at Karnak, farther south at Abydos, or even in the great temple that he cut out of the rock of the valley wall far down in Nubia at Abu Simbel. In 1284 B.C., as we have seen, the long struggle between Hittites and Egyptians was ended by a defensive alliance and an agreement that the Hittites should have northern Syria, while the Egyptians took southern Syria and Palestine.

The buildings and monuments of Rameses II are found everywhere in

Egypt. The chief feature of his building at Karnak is a hall so vast that it could contain the cathedral of Notre Dame in Paris. He seems never to have lost his taste for covering wall surfaces or columns with partly spurious accounts of his prowess.

As the thirteenth century drew toward its close, a great movement began among peoples who had not been much heard of in the civilized world. Some moved by land, and some had learned to be rovers of the sea. More than one group of the sea people had established bases in Africa west of Egypt. In 1232 they invaded the Delta and there were struck down by the Egyptians, although this was not the end of their attacks. It is difficult to be precise about these migrant and troublesome people, for we have references to the strangers only when they attacked the established peoples.

The Twentieth Dynasty (1195–1080 B.C.)

The Nineteenth Dynasty ended with a confused and difficult period because of the migrations and troubles with the succession. Finally the orderly succession to the throne was reestablished with the accession of the vigorous Rameses III (1198–1166 B.C.). The great crisis of Egypt in this dynasty began with a new joint attack by the Libyans and the sea peoples, who were again defeated. There was no other great attack from the West, but from the East came a great wave of people migrating by land, whom Rameses III defeated as they reached the boundary of Egypt. They had already defeated the Hittite Empire, which dissolved into separate kingdoms and was never again of great weight internationally. At the same time the Egyptians also won a great naval victory against sea people who moved against them, apparently intending to take and hold Egypt rather than merely to raid it.

Egypt was not to end its history by being so conquered. Through the more than one hundred years of the Twentieth Dynasty it remained powerful enough to discourage attacks from outside, although the Asiatic possessions had been lost in the great invasion that was repelled at the border. The domestic agricultural wealth of the nation remained unimpaired, as did the supply of gold from the South. The chief difficulty of the twelfth century B.C. seems to have been the failure of the royal management, for which there is no ready explanation. In general, the authority of the central government was not well maintained. Not only some local officials, but the priests of Amun, too, seem to have been able now and then to challenge the authority of the king. The priesthoods, especially Amun's, constituted very considerable nuclei of power and might even be compared to the local powers that opposed the central government toward the end of the Old Kingdom. Furthermore, the army was composed of foreign mercenaries and often proved very difficult to control.

The end of the Egyptian Empire (or New Kingdom) may be said to have come about 1085, when the kingdom was separated again into the North and South, with the priests playing a very important part. The great days were over, and for the next four hundred years there was very little worthy of remark. Egypt had not fallen, in one sense, although in another sense she had, for she was controlled by dynasties of Nubians and Ethiopians. Life went on at a lower level of intensity. What was lacking was not a government or a way of life, but the intensity and efficiency and extra achievement, the artistic and literary successes, that in the past had raised Egypt above the level of commonplace and routine social organization.

SYRIA AND PALESTINE

The region of Syria and Palestine was open both to invasion and to peaceful infiltration with the resulting introduction of new ideas and practices that might come from Mesopotamia, the Hittite country, Egypt, or the desert. The broken and uneven character of the country made it difficult to build up political units of any size there. In a rough way the land is divided into four strips, which run north and south. The western strip is the plain that runs along the shore of the Mediterranean. Next comes a series of rugged hills. The third zone is that of the Jordan Valley, where the Jordan River, which is amply fed, flows through a lower and lower channel until it goes through the Lake of Galilee, about seven hundred feet below sea level, and ends in the Dead Sea, about 1300 feet below sea level. The fourth strip is a range of barren hills beyond the valley of the Jordan.

The older name of the whole region was Canaan, a name found in the Bible, in the records of Egypt, and in the Amarna Letters. The name of Palestine for the southern part of it comes from the Philistines, who were settled on the coast by the Egyptians in the late thirteenth century. Part of the Canaanites, who lived about halfway up the coast, more or less in modern Lebanon, came to be known as Phoenicians and their territory as Phoenicia. The northern part of Canaan was known as Syria, as it still is.

Earlier History

Archaeology has brought a startling increase in our knowledge of this region, as it has for other parts of the Near East. Often we find that archaeological discoveries enable us to make more exact translations of passages of the Bible. The most significant advances in the archaeology of Syria and Palestine have come not from spectacular finds, but from the careful study by fine scholars of the unspectacular materials that come to light and the interpretation of them to give chronological data and trace the movements of peoples. The types and sequences of pottery have been classified by arduous and brilliant efforts, and dates have been established for the destructions and rebuildings of many of the cities. For example, it seems possible to date some remains of destroyed towns to the time of the campaigns of Joshua and others to the time of the campaigns of the Chaldaean king, Nebuchadnezzar, thus giving corroborative evidence to our scanty accounts of the two campaigns. The study of unspectacular objects has also added depth to our knowledge of religious practices, craftsmanship, and trade routes.[2]

Syria and Palestine (and Anatolia, too) were part of the area where the domestication of plants and animals began. The excavations at Jericho seem to indicate that this was the earliest settled community yet discovered. By the great spring that still serves the city of Jericho, the hunters of the Stone Age apparently built a little wooden shrine. As if in anticipation of the coming of the carbon-14 test, the shrine burned and the charred remains of the wood were left there, then covered with the remains of new levels of occupation. When subjected to the radiocarbon test, they gave a date of 7800 B.C. plus or minus 210 years. Since it is believed that these hunters were also experimenting with agriculture, we may have here an approximate date for the transition in this area from food gathering to food production. The excavations of the site show that it became more and more of a town, with well-built houses and fortifications, and another deposit of charcoal from a burned house amid this better developed town gives a date about a thousand years later, 6850 plus or minus 210, which was remarkable progress at that stage, no matter how long a thousand years may seem to us.

In the region that later became Canaan, the Chalcolithic period, or the time when both stone and copper were used, seems to have begun at about 4500 B.C., and the Early Bronze Age began just before 3000 B.C. and lasted for perhaps a thousand years. At the end of the Early Bronze Age, toward 2000 B.C., there was an influx (which even washed the shores of Egypt) into Canaan of the nomadic Amorites whom we have already encountered in Mesopotamia. The archaeological evidence suggests that many towns of Canaan were destroyed at this time and remained un-

---

[2] William F. Albright, one of the leaders in such studies, explains clearly and in detail in his *The Archaeology of Palestine* how the pottery is dated, how the general chronology is worked out, and how the objects found in excavations are made to yield information.

inhabited for several generations; there thus was a definite break in the cultural tradition of the region.

The period from 2000 to 1500 is called the Middle Bronze Age, and one of its chief features was the arrival of the Hyksos and their domination of the land. From perhaps 1750 to 1500 they were in control, and it was a prosperous time. The migration of Abraham from Ur, in southern Mesopotamia, to Canaan also falls in this period. During his time the Bible speaks of Amorites and Hittites as being in the region that later became Palestine.

The Late Bronze Age in this region is reckoned at about 1500 to 1200 B.C.—the time of the greatest power of the Egyptian Empire and a time when the people of Palestine were thoroughly exploited by the Egyptians. After about 1200 B.C. comes the Iron Age and with it the phenomenon of most interest to us in this region—ancient Israel. Let us note that it was also a time when the great powers ceased troubling the area. The Hittites and the Egyptians were not in a position to trouble each other or the lands in between them. The power of Assyria was not yet felt, although later it played an important part in the history of Israel.

The Hebrews and the Origin of Judaism

Between the twentieth and the twelfth centuries before Christ, documents of Mesopotamia, Asia Minor, Syria, Palestine, and Egypt mention groups whom they call Habiru, people who wandered about, sometimes living off animals in the nomad style and sometimes working as musicians or smiths or practitioners of other crafts; they also appear as brigands, mercenary soldiers, and slaves. It may well be that some of the people referred to in these documents were the Biblical Hebrews, because many of the names and activities and localities of the two are similar.

The Hebrews of the Bible, as a probable part of the Habiru, were many separate groups. There came a time, however, when some groups of the Habiru, the Biblical ones among them, became associated with certain territories by conquering them or being absorbed into their people. In such cases they took on national names. The Hebrews of the Bible settled in Canaan and became known as Israelites, whereas other groups of the Habiru became Moabites, Ammonites, Edomites, and Midianites. At this point both the Bible and the other documents cease to speak of any group as Habiru or Hebrews.

Abraham and his group came to the hilly strip of Canaan that lies between the coastal plain and the Jordan Valley. In these hills, which are hardly fit for agriculture, they lived the life of seminomads with their sheep and goats. The Biblical account of their life gives a fine picture of the tribal and family organization of a society. Now that we know something of the earlier literature of Mesopotamia we can see where these people got their ideas of the world. The Creation, the Garden of Eden and the Fall, the Flood and the Ark, and the Tower of Babel were all Mesopotamian stories.

The religion of the Hebrews in these earlier days, however, was not the polytheism common in the ancient world, but a working monotheism. The patriarch, the head of the tribe, would make an agreement that he and his people would worship one god exclusively. It was understood that the god, in turn, was to take this one tribe under his protection under a bilateral covenant that was to be binding on both parties forever. These people did not deny the existence of other gods, for to have done so would have been an idea that could not have occurred to anyone at this time.

Soon a considerable group of Hebrews went down into Egypt, perhaps in company with the Hyksos, which would make more plausible the story that some of them rose to positions of power. If the captivity in Egypt began when the Hyksos were expelled, it lasted a long time, for it was probably in the thirteenth century that Moses, of the tribe of Levi, led the group of state slaves who made the break for freedom. There must have been considerable cohesiveness among the Hebrews for them to have preserved some sense of being a group all this time, and this feeling probably furnished the unity needed for the organization of the exodus from Egypt.

The traditional forty years of wandering ascribed to this group may be regarded as one generation or a little more. They made their way into the peninsula of Sinai, where a new covenant was made in the name of the whole group, which was far larger than any of those family groups who in former times had made their covenants through the patriarchs. Now Israel came into being as a nation by virtue of the covenant that it made as a whole, and the god of Moses and of Israel came to be known as Yahweh or Jehovah. After the Babylonian Exile of the sixth century these people came to be known as Judeans and Jews, but in the late thirteenth century it was Israel, or the Children of Israel, who came out of the wilderness to the land of Canaan. That is, they came up from the desert of Sinai to the coastal strip of Canaan, which was then inhabited by a mixed people who may be called the Canaanites.

Moses died before the Promised Land was reached, and Joshua led the people into Canaan. He apparently won some swift and brilliant victories—recent excavations seem to show traces of the destruction and rebuilding of some of the cities in question at about this time—and there was also a long period of Israelite conquest, Canaanite recapture, reconquest, and distressing disunion among the Israelites that lasted long beyond the death of Joshua.

The Civilization of Canaan

Naturally the Israelites, after their stay in Egypt in an inferior status and their wandering in the wilderness for a generation, were not abreast of the ideas and techniques of their day as the Canaanites were and had a great deal to learn from the people that they had conquered. Canaanite pottery and jewelry was far superior to that of their conquerors, and they also built better towns and fortifications. A number of them were literate; there were people who could write Akkadian cuneiform or Egyptian hieroglyphs or their own alphabet, which was to give rise to the Phoenician alphabet, which in turn gave rise to the Greek alphabet and eventually to ours.

The Canaanites had also achieved the other part of literacy—a literature. It was especially strong in religious and mythological pieces, many of them the stories that circulated through the Near and Middle East and that used to be thought of as exclusively Bible stories, like those of the Creation and the Flood. The style was the figurative and balanced style that we have come to think of as the style of the Bible, and even the vocabulary and syntax of the Hebrew language were much influenced by the language of the Canaanites. It is now believed that the Canaanites, like the Sumerians and some other peoples, had illiterate bards, or what have come to be called "oral poets" by the scholars who study them, and that many of the tales of the gods were the products of these bards rather than of priests trying to manufacture a body of theological tales. Baal, the god of the Canaanites who in the Bible got the worst of it in a contest with Yahweh, was a god of rain, the god who made everything happen in the agricultural world. He was represented as being done to death every year by Mot, who represented drought and thus the death of all vegetation and of all life, and at the coming of the autumn rains there was a great celebration of his rebirth. Canaanite divinities as well as Canaanite tales had an unfortunate attraction for the Children of Israel, and it was not always easy to recall the wandering children to a purer and more austere form of worship. It is thought that the idea of prophecy in the Biblical sense came from the same source, where it could properly be called religious raving, and when it passed to the Hebrews was raised to the lofty prophecy of Samuel, or Elijah, or Amos, or Isaiah.

The Kingdom of Saul, David, and Solomon

The Peleset, or Philistines, had been settled by the Egyptians on the coast not far from Egypt, and the land came to be called Palestine from their name, which has come to signify people of little cultivation or sensitivity, although the Philistines were more cultivated than the people of Israel. They also had a good political organization, and somewhere they had picked up the secret of making iron, which they managed for some time to keep out of the hands of their neighbors. They were acquainted with commercial practices and had ships.

These factors led them, in about 1050 B.C., to attempt expansion at the expense of Israel. Here at last was a force sufficient to drive Israel to the creation of a central political authority. In fact she had had neither political nor religious unity. There was no national government as we know it, no central capital nor shrine. Each tribe had complete autonomy. The emergencies of the twelfth and eleventh centuries called forth local leaders known as judges, but none of them seemed very near to becoming king.

But now Saul, of the tribe of Benjamin, was chosen to be king and to lead the opposition to the Philistines. The ineffective opposition of the priest and prophet Samuel showed the particularistic spirit that must have done much to prevent the earlier rise of a king or a strong central government. Saul was chosen king about 1020 B.C. He had a stormy career. Although he won some significant victories, he always had to contend with the conservative element led by Samuel. He found it hard to give due credit to his helpers, he was subject to fits of dark depression, he sometimes flew into frantic rages, and he was too pleased with minor soothsayers and witches.

Saul's military problems and his problems of public relations were much helped by the appearance on the scene of David, a young professional soldier who had already made his reputation somewhere. He was neither so young nor so modest as the story of his victory over Goliath would suggest. His exploits raised Saul's jealousy to such an extent, however, that David finally had to flee to the Philistines to escape him. Saul died in 1005 B.C. after his troops had been badly defeated by the Philistines.

David returned and was made king, not without some violent incidents. He led Israel to a new unity of action and to a series of military successes that made her the leading nation of western Asia. He took Jerusalem from the Jebusites, so punished the Philistines in a number of engagements that they never threatened Israel again, made Israel's force respected beyond the Jordan, and overcame some of the Aramaeans of Palestine. Israel now controlled the territories lying between Kadesh in the North and the head of the Gulf of Aqabah in the South. It must be remembered, of course, that the great powers were temporarily in eclipse and that when they recovered Israel was not strong enough to hold her own against them.

David exerted himself to make Israel a nation. Jerusalem was made the political and religious capital; there had been no capital city up to this time. A part of the city, to be known thereafter as "The City of David," was adorned to add to its dignity. Jerusalem, not being within the jurisdiction of any tribe, made a good symbol of national government. Plans were made, too, for the building of the temple that should be the center of the worship of the God of Israel, and David appointed priests from among his adherents.

The Bible describes other measures taken to make a national government out of a loose organization. The boundaries of some of the tribes were altered, apparently to weaken the tribes, and royal officials instead of the heads of families and tribes were appointed to represent the new units at the capital. The army was made a professional and national group rather than a tribal militia and was under the authority of the king, not under that of the several tribes. Naturally plans for national taxation were made, and a new civil service was built up, many of whose members were not Israelites, but had been trained elsewhere.

Solomon, one of David's sons, became king in 965 B.C. and ruled until 925. One of his tasks was the completion of the organization that David had so well begun. Another, especially important, was the completion of the temple, for which he could draw both craftsmen and materials from that group of inhabitants of Canaan who had come to be known as Phoenicians. They lived about halfway up the coast, had three good ports, and controlled the hills that yielded the various excellent woods that the Egyptians called "the cedar of Lebanon." Their political power was never great, and now they found it politic to do what they could for the king of Israel. The great temple was built in the Canaanite style, with vestibule, holy place, and holy of holies. The excavations have disclosed that at the Solomonic level there was much Phoenician influence in the walls and gates of the towns as well as in the small material remains.

Solomon was a shrewd merchant. The trade in horses and chariots that he conducted fitted in well with his use of chariots as a specialty of his armed forces so that he could cope with the forces of any of his neighbors. Like David, he charged transit taxes for the use of the great caravan routes that ran through his territory. One important route ran from Egypt up to Gaza, on the coast of Palestine, then northward through the Phoenician territory. A connecting route ran eastward from Gaza to meet the route that came up from southern Arabia and went east of the

Jordan River to Damascus and thence to northern Syria and Asia Minor or eastward toward Mesopotamia. The profit from these routes had often been the prize of military and diplomatic maneuvers and perhaps had compelled a certain amount of international comity at times. The visit of the queen of Sheba, a part of southwestern Arabia, must have had something to do with the caravan trade.

Solomon also had trading ships that sailed from a port at the head of the Gulf of Aqabah. We hear of their going to Ophir, which probably was southern Arabia, for gold and silver and precious stones and rare woods. Perhaps the ships could carry out copper and iron, for traces have been discovered of foundries for copper and iron and of deposits of those metals.

Inevitably foreign influence crept in, for Israel could not live entirely to herself in these circumstances. Her people needed to travel for commercial and diplomatic reasons, and strangers came into the kingdom for those purposes or to serve the government. Intermarriage with foreigners was not unknown. The later historians were to feel that Solomon was responsible for weakening the religion of Israel, although basically that religion did not change, even with the introduction of some foreign religious elements.

The prosperity of the regime of Solomon was not shared by all the people. Taxes were high, drafts of labor for the government's projects were frequent, and there was corruption in government. Furthermore, the northern tribes were galled by Judah's assumption of superiority. Under Solomon's son the kingdom could not hold together. The leaders in the northern part apparently wanted to throw off what seemed to them the domination of the South, and they wished to continue religious life in the old-fashioned way. There was no objection to monarchy, if that monarchy did not seem to favor the southern regions of the kingdom. With the violent refusal of the people of the North to pay taxes, the kingdom was permanently divided. The northern kingdom was to be known as Israel and the southern as Judah, and we shall presently discuss their later history against the background of the Assyrian Empire.

The Phoenicians

The Phoenicians had a far wider outlook on the world than did most of the small peoples with whom Israel came into contact. They lived on the coast and had three good harbors: Tyre, Sidon, and Byblos. Even in the Old Kingdom the ships of Egypt had come here, and the local people must have been mariners themselves, at least in a modest way. For some time the Egyptians dominated the nearby sea, but later, from perhaps

2200 to about 1400 B.C., the ships of the great commercial people of Crete patrolled the waters to put down piracy and were very likely to destroy the vessels of rival traders. During the last two centuries or so of Cretan power, the Mycenaeans of southern Greece must also have ranged widely through both the eastern and the western Mediterranean. During this time the Phoenicians presumably were doing some modest local shipping. The great movement of peoples on sea and land that did so much damage around 1200 B.C. harmed the Phoenicians, too, but they slowly restored themselves.

There was apparently a time, perhaps after 1100 B.C., when the seas were more or less open to enterprising people like the Phoenicians. Little by little their ships began to venture farther through the waters of the Mediterranean. The trip to Greece through the islands was no great feat of navigation. Their visits to Greece during the Dark Age that followed the fall of the Mycenaeans were, as we shall see later, useful in restoring to the Greeks a knowledge of Near Eastern culture. Perhaps the most important cultural item thus transferred from East to West was the alphabet, toward 800 B.C.

We do not know when the Phoenicians pushed into the western Mediterranean; perhaps it was as late as the 700s. It has been thought that they founded Carthage on virtually the same site as that of the modern Tunis just before 800, but this dating is traditional, and some studies of the pottery found there would put the date nearer 700 B.C.; Utica, near Carthage, claimed that she was an earlier foundation. The Carthaginians then founded colonies and trading posts all along the coasts of what are now Tunisia, Algeria, and Morocco. The places seem generally to have been twenty-odd miles apart, or a day's sail. Since the early ships were not well pitched and calked, it was beneficial to draw them out of the water every night at one of these stations to give their hulls a chance to dry. Phoenician colonies and stations were later established in western Sicily, in the Balearic Islands, and in southern Spain, and their ships are thought to have gone down the Atlantic coast for some distance and up it as far as Cornwall.

Around 800 B.C. the Greeks began to come out of their Dark Age, and before long their ships were seen in many places. They managed to drive the Phoenicians from the trade along the northern shores of the Mediterranean. Greek settlers in the eastern half of Sicily struggled with the Phoenicians over several centuries. Carthage became the leader of all the Phoenicians of the West and the mistress of a considerable empire. Except for the coasts of southern France and northeastern Spain, she managed to keep the Mediterranean west of Sicily a closed sea patrolled by her warships, which forthrightly sank interlopers. Finally, in the third and second centuries before Christ, she fought a series of three wars with the Romans that are known by their Roman name, the Punic Wars, and was destroyed by the Romans in 146 B.C. at the end of the third war. This was to be the end, far away in the West and far in the future, of the Phoenician expansion upon the sea, which was well under way in the days of David and of Solomon.

The Aramaeans

The Aramaeans deserve special mention among the numerous smaller peoples of the Near East who are known to us at least by name. During the reign of David they were organizing a kingdom in upper Transjordan, and in the reign of Solomon they were prospering. Presently they established a strong kingdom at Damascus, and somewhat later we find them even farther north, on the edges of Assyrian territory.

The Aramaeans played a role in inland trade analogous to that of the Phoenicians on the sea, although they never built up an empire like that of Carthage. They were the managers of the caravans that traveled about the Near East, sometimes making connections with overseas trade at the ports. Their language came to be so widely used that probably more people in Palestine at the time of Christ spoke it than spoke Hebrew. At one time it was the language of diplomacy throughout western Asia, and some of our historical source materials are written in Aramaic.

ASSYRIA

Assyria was located on the upper Tigris in a territory about three hundred and fifty miles long and nearly three hundred miles wide, or about the area of a fair-sized American state. The western part, a little too dry for agriculture, was suitable for grazing, whereas the eastern part was more fertile. The climate can be very hot in the summer, although the nearness of the mountains is a help; in winter there is occasional snow. The country is fairly well supplied with building stone, and many interesting stone remains have survived from ancient times. The names of the chief god, the principal city of the early period, and the nation as a whole were the same—Ashur; we call the country Assyria. It often appeared as part of the name of the king, too, as in Ashur-uballit, "Ashur-has-given-life." In the same way we have seen "Amun" or "Aten" as part of the names of Egyptian kings.

The Assyrians were on the scene as an organized nation during most of the long period that we have been considering, so that we can set them in some relation to almost every group that we have discussed. By the middle of the third millennium, Ashur was a city and was especially under Sumerian influence. It gained in power very slowly, but played some part in the history of the Akkadian, Amorite, and Kassite kingdoms down the river. On their western side the Assyrians were in frequent contact, both friendly and hostile, with the Hittites, with Mitanni, with the people of Syria, and with Egypt. Thutmose III seems to have had Assyria as an ally in the rear of Mitanni during his Asiatic campaigns and parades. He speaks of tribute from Assyria—lapis lazuli, horses, wagons, and valuable woods—although probably it would have been more accurate to speak of reciprocal gifts. In the time of Amenhotep III, however, Assyria apparently fell under the power of Mitanni, then enjoying its strongest period. Very shortly afterward Ashur-uballit was able to throw off its domination. This king appears in the Amarna Letters asking his brother monarch of Egypt to send him gold. Although the Assyrians were a little out of the path of the migrations that occurred around 1200, they felt some of their force, but were able to survive and remain a nation, as they had survived many shocks before.

The reign of Tiglath-Pileser, who ruled from about 1114 to about 1076 B.C., is probably typical of Assyria in the centuries just after the great migrations and before her real rise to power. We happen to have the annals of this reign, from which we learn of the king's campaign against minor peoples who had taken over part of the Assyrian territory in the northwest, of his subjugation the next year of a confederacy of twenty-three princes near Lake Van in the North, and of a campaign somewhat later that crossed the Euphrates and went into Phoenicia. The king, whose earlier annals told of his hunting elephants and wild bulls, as a monarch of those times was expected to do, now showed true sporting blood by going out upon the sea with the Phoenicians and killing a great fish; he was the first of the Assyrian monarchs ever to see the Mediterranean. The Phoenician cities of the coast paid him tribute, partly in the prized woods of Lebanon. We hear, too, of repeated invasions of Aramaeans and of a Babylonian invasion that was avenged conclusively.

The Assyrian Empire

Ashur-nasir-pal II (885–860 B.C.) should probably be regarded as the first real empire builder among the Assyrian kings. The bas-reliefs of the palace in his new city of Calah show us something of his army and its exploits. By now the army had weapons of iron (strictly speaking, wrought steel). The heavy infantry, made up of native Assyrians (the cavalry came from the allies, as was later to be the practice of the Romans) and armed with weapons of the new and superior metal, was an extremely formidable force. One of the bas-reliefs suggests that the camps of the army, like those of the Romans, were very carefully and thoroughly made. We can also see battering rams, sheds to protect the sappers as they tried to undermine the walls, towers from which to shoot at the defenders on the walls, and a technique of concerted action in assaulting fortified places.

The kingdom of Urartu in the rough country east of Assyria was able to repel this king's attempts to subdue it, and he left them to themselves while he campaigned in the West. Urartu did not play any large role, but excavations have shown that it shared in the civilization of the time, for its workmen were competent in both large and small things. Their temples were planned differently from those of the Assyrians. Fine masonry has been found in the remains as well as wall paintings, sculptures, and good small pieces worked from ivory and metal.

We have the list of the booty exacted from a minor Aramaean king whose city Ashur-nasir-pal took. There were horses with chariots, cattle, and sheep. Although only two talents of gold and two of silver (a talent weighed about sixty pounds) were on the list, there were a hundred talents of lead, two hundred of bronze, and three hundred of iron. Evidently the Aramaeans were already becoming a manufacturing people, for they were also required to give a great many bronze vessels and gold and ivory couches. Those Aramaeans who were conquered by the Assyrians established themselves within the Syrian territory and, as time went on, became the trading class of Assyria.

The Phoenicians, who saw the prospect of good trading in any region organized by this energetic king, sent him rich gifts—things made of precious metals, cloths of Tyrian purple, furniture of boxwood, ebony, and ivory, and a collection of wild animals from gazelles to lions, which the king put in his zoological collection in Calah.

The palace at Calah is famous in archaeology, for here the Englishman Layard began his pioneer excavations in 1845. He found that the king had surrounded his new city with walls and moats and had brought an ample water supply from the Tigris. The palace and the adjacent temples were partly of mud-brick and partly of stone, and figures of winged animals, often with human faces, were prominent. The wall reliefs are precious documentation of the time as well as major works of art, showing us, for example, the weapons and techniques of the army. The reliefs and the annals inscribed on great stone slabs also show us that the king was a master of "calculated frightfulness"; he boasts that he made great piles of the heads of the conquered or impaled their bodies or that he flayed them alive.

His son Shalmaneser III (858–824 B.C.) boasted that he defeated a

coalition of twelve Syrian kings in 853 B.C. at Qarqar on the Orontes
River; whether he did or not the Assyrians now gained control of practically all Syria and Palestine and retained it for two centuries, that is,
until the downfall of their nation. Hadadezer of Damascus was named
first among the Syrian leaders in the inscription describing the battle.
Damascus, or Aram Damascus, was one of the most important of the
several Aramaean principalities in Palestine. Third was Ahab of Israel,
who ruled a prosperous kingdom from the new capital of Samaria. He
was in close association with the Phoenicians and had married the Phoenician princess Jezebel, that Jezebel who won herself an immortality of
dishonor by procuring the death of Naboth, the neighbor who would not
sell his ancestral vineyard to the king. Ahab must have been a powerful
king for his time and place, because the Assyrian inscription ascribes two
thousand chariots and ten thousand men to him at the great battle (which
is not mentioned in the Bible).

Tiglath-Pileser III (744–727 B.C.) is of interest for his management of
the Assyrian realm. He proclaimed himself king of Babylon as well as of
Assyria, presumably to try to gain more loyalty from the Babylonians.
The kings of Israel and Damascus planned a revolt and tried to force
the king of Judah to join, but he appealed to the Assyrians and brought
Tiglath-Pileser down upon the other two nations. The deportation of
many of the inhabitants of Israel is described in the Assyrian annals.
This shifting of population to break up whatever loyalties and constellations of power existed was a regular Assyrian method of dealing with
conquered territories. As the Romans were to do later, they began to regard conquered territories as provinces and to put their own governors
over them instead of leaving them under the original government, obliged merely to pay tribute. The governors were compelled to submit frequent reports and were closely watched and rotated from province to
province so that they could not muster the economic or military forces
to oppose the king or to revolt.

In 722 B.C. a rebellion against the son of Tiglath-Pileser brought about
the destruction of Samaria, the capital of Israel, and the dispersal of the
inhabitants. The city was then rebuilt and furnished with an adequate
number of new residents brought from elsewhere. This move marked the
end of Israel as a sovereign nation.

Assyria at its Height (721–633 B.C.)

Sargon II (721–705 B.C.) established a standing army instead of the occasional levies that had been the rule. Although many of the soldiers were
foreigners, we do not hear of any difficulty in managing the army or

keeping it in its place politically. He established a new capital, Dur-Sharrukin or Sargonsburg, which was not a real city, but a great palace with the necessary background. Formerly Sargon's name was known only from the reference in the Bible to his taking the city of Ashdod, but since the excavation of his palace in the middle of the nineteenth century we have found letters discussing the building of the palace and its setting, reliefs from the palace showing the king and his court at their various activities, and the royal annals, which were inscribed on stone slabs and displayed in the palace.

Sennacherib (704–681 b.c.) is known for the mysterious misfortune of his army before Jerusalem. Perhaps, as the Bible says, the army was smitten by a plague from God as they were besieging the city. The annals of the king claim no more than that he shut up Hezekiah, the rebellious king of Judah, in his city and reduced the other places of his kingdom. In the East and Northeast Sennacherib's frontiers were under pressure from the Medes, Cimmerians, and Scythians, pastoral or nomadic peoples of Indo-European stock. We learn something of this danger from the surviving records of the king's consultations of the sun god and the answers to his questions given by the priests from their inspection of the livers of the sacrificial victims, for the Assyrians were given to this practice, as were the Sumerians and Babylonians.

With such pressures on the kingdom from the eastern peoples it was folly for Sennacherib's son Esarhaddon (680–669 b.c.) to make the effort to conquer Egypt, which for several hundred years had been under dynasties from Libya and Nubia and often had been unable to hold herself together as a nation. Her products had appeared in the trading records and the tribute lists of the Assyrians, and now, in 670, Assyria took the country, but held it only until 662. The Egyptians were able to drive out the Assyrians as they had driven out the Hyksos long before, but much more quickly. Psamtik, or Psammetichus, used Greek mercenaries as part of the forces with which he recovered Egypt's freedom.

Ashur-bani-pal (668–633 b.c.) was the last of the great kings of Assyria. Although he scored no spectacular success either in politics or in warfare, he was successful in maintaining the power and prosperity of his country, a task that never allowed any room for slackness or complacency. His real distinction was that he was a learned prince, with a touch of the antiquarian about him. He learned the dead Babylonian language of a thousand years before his time and the Sumerian of two thousand years before. There were beginners' books and grammars and dictionaries, of course, just as there are nowadays for the study of languages.

He formed a great royal library at Nineveh, much of which survived to be found by excavators. Some of the tablets that his agents brought

in contained omens; Assyrian scholars made a great and serious effort to
see whether the study of omens and of their supposed connection with
occurrences could be made into a science. Other tablets contained the old
legends of Mesopotamia. Many tablets contained historical information,
sometimes sober, sometimes a purple patchwork, sometimes edited to
bring out official truth. The mathematical and astronomical knowledge of
Babylon was inscribed on others. The great library also contained dis-
patches and archives of the royal government. Research shows that the
Assyrians really understood the works that they gathered and copied,
for we find that they edited, and commented on, and combined them.
We find also that there was a sound system of instruction in the necessary languages for the scribes. It may be said that the Assyrians were
forerunners of the Romans in their appropriation of the intellectual
achievements of more original and more brilliant people.

Assyrian art, too, was at its height, as the reliefs in the king's palace
show. Scenes of the king's lion hunts were especially favored. One large
hall still shows a hunt something like a modern rodeo. In the first scene
a wooden enclosure is about to be opened, with a great square of soldiers
around it. From it issues, not a calf to be pursued and roped, but a group
of lions, which the king pursues in his chariot and kills. There have been
few finer representations of animals than these. The artist must have
studied many lions in motion, and his technique was adequate to portray
what he saw.

The Fall of Assyria

Occasionally during the reign of Ashur-bani-pal and even oftener in
the two decades after his death, the Assyrian Empire had difficulty in
performing all the tasks involved in warding off the enemy on the outside
and keeping a firm hand on the restless elements within. Then the Chaldaeans of Babylon decided to make an alliance with the Medes. Nabopolassar of Babylon and Cyaxares the Mede joined to assault Nineveh
in the year 612. They took and destroyed the city. A group of the Assyrians escaped and maintained a minor Assyrian kingdom until 608, but
with no real effect. Assyria was divided between the Chaldaeans and the
Medes.

In spite of the rejoicings of the Hebrew prophets we are not entitled
to conclude that Assyria fell because her imperialism and her cruelty had
earned her the bitter hatred of mankind. Her conduct had been no better and no worse than that of most imperialist nations throughout history. The attack of the Chaldaeans and Medes should be regarded as a
normal piece of international business.

Nor is it possible to draw up a scheme of events that led Assyria inevitably to her fall. As Carthage, wealthy and spirited, was to be utterly cut off by the Romans in 146 B.C., so Assyria fell when she might conceivably have prospered for centuries more. The serious student of history must recognize the fact that there have been declines without falls and falls without declines and thus fortify himself against the meretricious persuasiveness of the phrase "decline and fall."

CHAPTER

4

THE CULTURE OF THE NEAR EAST
AND EGYPT; THE PERSIAN EMPIRE

The time had now come for Persia's emergence as a great imperial power in control of all the regions that we have been considering. Since the rise of Persia combines all the life of Egypt and the Near East under one great government and since the new element of the Greeks and their confrontation with Persia must be introduced, it will be helpful to give a summary of the achievements of the peoples whom we have been discussing and to make clear to the reader how laudable their achievements were.

Government

By the time of Persia's rise the techniques of governing were well developed. Psychological methods of supporting the government were understood. The person and the office of the king were supported by such dignities and attributed characteristics as the aura of divinity and the role of the shepherd of his people. Statesmen had a sense for ensuring the loyalty of the people, perhaps partly by refined terrorism, partly by the connection of religion with government, partly by the furnishing of protection against raids from the outside and oppression from fellow citizens. Several nations had had successful civil services. Egypt, especially, had learned to manage its closed and unified territory so as to extract all possible revenue from agriculture, industry, and commerce. Incidentally, but usefully for us, there was a remarkable amount of governmental record keeping.

If we consider the troubles afflicting governments, we find ourselves scantily informed except for certain recurring patterns. It was always difficult for those in power to avoid murder by their nearest and dearest. Again and again rulers were assassinated by members of their own families who hoped to usurp the throne. Attacks by foreign powers were always a danger, too, for predatory imperialism was an accepted and even honorable means for kings to employ in retaining the respect of restless elements.

We should probably be justified in saying that church and state were intimately connected all through the period and that it would never have occurred to anyone that the two should be separate. The conditions of society and the religious attitudes that could lead a man to think of his religion as something intimate and personal still lay far in the future. The managers of religion set up a cosmogony, or theory of the creation of the universe. The stories of the Creation gave satisfaction from the time of the Sumerians onward. The nature of the gods and their relations among themselves tended to be rather alike among all peoples. The sky god or father of the gods, the storm god, the god of the sea, and the god of the underworld, the goddess of love—all are known in many places. All seem to have been suggested by the powers of nature, and the common conception of a god who dies and is reborn seems to have grown out of her cycles. The god of the Hebrews, however, even before their religion attained the austere elevation of its later period, was the lord of nature rather than merely a part of nature. Everywhere the idea of a single god above others, a national rather than a local god, helped to cement society. Sets of festivals were worked up in all the countries. These gave a comforting rhythm to life, helped to relieve the boredom of toil and sameness, and promoted unity of feeling.

Technological Achievement

The peoples of lower Mesopotamia made the best of the fact that stone was not readily available by working out techniques for making mud bricks, or clay bricks, which when reinforced with the bitumen that was a natural product became extremely strong. The Assyrians had stone at their command, and their monumental stone figures and such engineering works as the great stone canal of Sennacherib show their mastery of the material. At the beginning of the Pyramid Age the Egyptians suddenly overcame the problem of working in stone and became very skillful. They learned to quarry and dress it and they worked out means of transporting huge pieces on the Nile. Although their early stone work showed too much influence of other materials that they had been used to, the designers soon learned to think in terms of the stone they were now using.

Wood seems never to have been used for buildings of any importance, but the examples of furniture preserved by the dry climate of Egypt show how skillfully the ancient artisans dealt with it. They used hammers, saws, chisels, drills, awls, files, and rasps. They were fond of inlays of ivory, a material that they handled with skill and assurance, or of fine woods, and they also used inlays of glass and sometimes semiprecious stones. Their adhesive was a casein glue.

Painting of all kinds was known. Paint has been found applied to many materials—wood, pottery, plaster, canvas, papyrus, and ivory. Some of the paints can be analyzed, like the crimson cochineal, which comes from an insect, or madder (red) from a root and henna from a conifer, yellow from saffron or turmeric, and blue from indigo. Wall plaster was known and paint was sometimes applied to it, but frescoing, or the application of paint to fresh wet plaster, seems to have been practiced only in Crete.

Clothing was made chiefly of wool and linen. Although it was known in India, cotton was rare or unknown in the West, and silk was not yet being imported from China. Time has spared not only some of the fabrics, but also pictures of the looms, the nature of which is intelligible to the modern expert. The most striking find of fabrics was linen cloth in the tomb of King Tut-ankh-amun woven so fine as to have 280 by 80 threads to the inch.

Man by this time had come a long way from being a mere gatherer of food. We can tell by the study of seeds found on ancient sites as well as by mention in documents what vegetables and fruits had been domesticated. Wheat, millet, and other cereals were of prime importance, and rye would push its way into use whenever conditions were difficult for wheat. Ovens were developed early; an Egyptian papyrus has recipes for over thirty forms of bread and cake. There were peas and beans, artichokes, cucumbers, leeks, onions, garlic, beets, lettuce, and radishes. Among the fruits were dates, figs, pomegranates, and watermelons. Wine was common. Oil was made from olives and many other materials, such as almonds, linseed, radish seed, and sesame. Honey served for sweetening, and there were flavorings of almond, aniseed, cinnamon, and ginger. Beef, veal, lamb, pork, fowl, and fish were eaten.

The wheel, the greatest of all inventions in transportation, was invented in the period that we have studied. There were only the simplest beginnings of the complementary invention, the paved road for the wheel to run on, although the Assyrian army had a corps to clear roads, and the Persians were soon to have a system of royal roads that seems to have been partly paved. Yoked oxen were first used to pull wheeled vehicles. The shoulders of the horse and of others of his kind are not shaped properly for yokes, and the ancient world never developed a harness that allowed a horse to exert his full strength.

Boats of every kind had been developed. On rivers and lakes there were small affairs of skin and reed; on the Nile there were boats or rafts that could carry huge blocks of stone. Boats were propelled by sails, generally square-rigged, and by oars. Navigation on the sea was generally confined to the less stormy months from spring to autumn. The ancient mariners sailed to Britain and beyond, and it is plain that on some runs, like that from Egypt to Crete, they must have gone well out of sight of land.

The development of metallurgy was a long and complicated process. Although it is easy to imagine some man seeing beads of copper shining where he had built a fire on copper-bearing rock, the actual situation was far more difficult. Somehow the idea had to be grasped that certain raw materials could be made to yield metals, and then appropriate means of applying heat had to be devised for each metal. For example, the simplest class of copper ores—carbonates and oxides—can be reduced to copper by heating them in a crucible with charcoal. Here, with the use of small crucibles, true metallurgy may be said to begin.

Iron ores—compounds of iron and sulphur—must be put through a more complicated process of roastings and smeltings. Iron is much more difficult to handle than copper, and the processes that bring success are not obvious even to the man who has learned to handle copper. Iron must be smelted with a good heat, and the bloom, or mass, that comes from the smelting must be hammered to remove impurities and produce wrought iron. This is only the first product, the second and final being wrought steel. The old-fashioned production of wrought steel from wrought iron had two parts. First, the metal was heated in contact with charcoal, then hammered, a process that added a carbon content to the metal and began its transformation to steel. The second part was to heat and hammer the metal, then cool it suddenly by immersion in water (quenching) to maintain the desirable inner structure that the metal had when it was hot. The smith could, if he wished, heat his metal slowly and cool it slowly to make it tougher and less brittle, although he sacrificed some of its hardness by doing so. Little by little, over a number of centuries, this art was learned. By perhaps 1500 B.C. there were smiths who were masters of it all and who could with fair consistency combine these techniques to produce usable steel weapons and tools. For many an age thereafter the smith was one of the most respected of all workmen.

Nonmaterial Achievements

Writing, which began as a means of governmental record keeping, obviously had tremendous influence. The governments learned to use it as a device for enhancing their prestige—for example, by inscribing highly tendentious accounts of military successes on stone on temple or palace walls and floors. The use of writing for belles lettres was slight compared to what it was to be in Greek and Roman times and later.

The two earliest writing systems, the Sumerian and the Egyptian, developed from pictographs. The Egyptian was ordinarily written with pen and ink on papyrus, the Sumerian and its successors in Mesopotamia on clay tablets with a stylus. Syria and Palestine were the scene of the liveliest inventiveness in this field. Some people there could write Akkadian, the international language of 1500 to 1200 B.C. or thereabouts, in cuneiform. A well trained man could also handle Egyptian hieroglyphics and demotic and the cuneiform alphabet of Ugarit, which has become known to us through the excavations at Ras Shamra, on the coast of Syria. More important, after 1500 B.C. some people knew an alphabet from which Hebrew, Syriac, Arabic, and other oriental languages developed their form of writing. From this alphabet, too, the Phoenicians developed the system that they were later to teach the Greeks and that eventually became the alphabet of the Western world.

Cuneiform writing gradually gave way to alphabetic writing in antiquity; the latest known cuneiform tablet can be dated A.D. 75. Well before this time people in general had switched to the use of the alphabet. Not only did the form change, but the material used changed also. People had written on everything—stone, wood, leather, cloth, pottery—but papyrus and the clay tablet were used most. Parchment appeared during the reign of Tiglath-Pileser III. Cuneiform and the clay tablet finally yielded to the combination of the alphabet, papyrus, and parchment toward the beginning of the Christian era.

Another outstanding achievement of these centuries was the development of the processes of business. Techniques of measuring had been worked out, and standards of measurement for areas of land and for volume and weight of all kinds of goods had come into use. The idea that the government could serve its citizens by regulating and guaranteeing such measures had arisen. There were laws to regulate all the arrangements having to do with the production and exchange of goods. Principles of contract had been devised and partnerships were known. The principles of financing industrial and commercial transactions were far beyond a primitive stage. Sensible practices had been set up for the acquisition, ownership, alienation, lease, use, and inheritance of land.

The achievements of these ancients in what we should call science are less impressive. Nevertheless, if we add to them the mathematical and astronomical work of the Babylonians in the next few centuries—say between 400 B.C. and A.D. 100—we see that a very respectable start was made in the abstract sciences by the peoples of the Near East. The Babylonians developed a sexagesimal numeration; we use their circle of 360 degrees and in a way we use the sexagesimal system when we say "one twenty-three" instead of "twenty-three minutes past one," for the "one" represents an hour, a unit with sixty parts, and the "twenty-three" the twenty-three parts of a second unit. The figures used had varying values according to their places (what is called "positional notation") just as they do in the decimal system.

Some of the Babylonian clay tablets that have been found give tables for such arithmetical operations as squaring and cubing. Many tablets include problems and their simple algebraic solutions. These tablets show that among the Babylonians an interest arose in mathematics in the proper sense of the word. Their mathematics and astronomy were closely connected, and if we again go a little ahead of our period, we find them going beyond the observations of the heavenly bodies made for religious purposes by the priests and beginning true astronomy with attempts to theorize.

Professional physicians had arisen in both Mesopotamia and Egypt. Part of their ideas and practices depended on the supernatural, for it was felt that disease might be sent by the gods and could be removed by them. As a result spells and incantations were freely used. They had some genuine knowledge of drugs, although some substances that they administered seem to us to be without efficacy. The physician had learned to examine his patient by questions, by ocular examination, and by palpation, and to record and compare symptoms. The so-called Edwin Smith Papyrus shows an Egyptian attempt to consolidate the knowledge of the treatment of wounds resulting from war or accident. The Ebers Papyrus discusses physiological matters; in spite of its rational attitude it naturally suffers from lack of physiological knowledge.

Conclusion

The purpose of this summary of ancient culture to about 600 B.C. has been to emphasize the enormous progress made by the peoples of the Near East and of Egypt. Not only the brilliance of the Greeks, but also the congeniality of the Greek style and ours have tended to obscure somewhat the achievement of those who came before. In the twentieth century the peoples of Egypt and the Near East have frankly acknowledged the superiority of the West in power and in technical matters, and Westerners have as frankly thought of them as backward. Such attitudes are sometimes applied to earlier times in such a way as to cause an unduly high estimate of the contributions of the Greeks to Western civilization and an unduly low estimate of the contributions of their predecessors. The fact is that the Greeks and Romans made very few improvements on the technology of the Near East and Egypt; here and there they even regressed. Although it may not be the primary task of the historian to make judgments, it seems that here a comparison must be made for the sake of counteracting a somewhat unfair and widely disseminated opinion.

THE WORLD OF THE SIXTH CENTURY
AND THE PERSIAN EMPIRE

By the sixth century the Greeks had become a people of marked characteristics and by the year 500 B.C. they stood on the threshold of their greatest age, an age at which the world has wondered ever since. In the next chapter we shall move backward in time to the Minoan civilization of Crete and the early civilization of Greece. This Mycenaean civilization, as it was called, was followed by a Dark Age among the Greeks, from which they began to emerge in the ninth century B.C. In the meantime some of them had emigrated to the coast of Asia Minor and in the eighth and seventh centuries some emigrated to Thrace and to the northern and southern coasts of the Black Sea, so that there were Greeks in the sixth-century scene in the Near East. In Italy the Etruscans dominated the northern part of the peninsula and some of it below Rome; by the year 500 the Romans were ready to throw off Etruscan domination and start their slow advance to the control of Italy and later of the whole Mediterranean world. The Carthaginians of the sixth century were rich and powerful; their story will be told in connection with the history of Rome. A number of loosely grouped peoples known as the Celts were found in many parts of Europe. They were fearsome fighters on the one hand, and possessed an interesting taste in art on the other hand. They, too, will play a part in the later history of which Rome was the center.

But before we turn our full attention to the Greeks and then to the Romans, we must consider the situation in Egypt after the fall of Assyria, the situation in Asia Minor after the fall of the Hittites, and the brief history of the Chaldaean or New Babylonian Empire, which controlled Mesopotamia after the fall of Assyria. All three regions—all the Near East, that is—came under the control of the empire of the Persians, which suddenly rose to power late in the sixth century. When we turn to the Greeks, we shall have to describe a long conflict with the Persians which ended with the campaigns of Alexander the Great from 334 to 323 B.C. and his conquest of the Persian Empire. Thereafter the Near East appears in our history as subject to those Greeks who became kings there after Alexander and then as provinces of the Roman Empire.

It must be remembered that during a large part of the most brilliant history of Greece many of the most civilized Greeks, those of Asia Minor, were under Persian control, and that the Persians dominated the rest of the Near East, a region of old and intense civilization. The Greek kingdoms of the successors of Alexander in Egypt and in the Near East were highly successful. Although later they were not able to resist the Roman armies, these regions were still populous, rich, and civilized. Indeed, the Roman Empire in the West probably never equaled the Empire to the East in wealth and civilization. When, in the fifth century of the Christian era, the West finally slipped away into the hands of German kings, the peoples of the East were able to maintain themselves as Romans. While the West was struggling through a long attempt to regain some intensity of civilization, the peoples of the Near East, under the leadership of Byzantium, perpetuated their brilliant culture.

Egypt in the Sixth Century

Esarhaddon's overextension of Assyrian power by the conquest of Egypt in 669 B.C. did not last out the decade, for by 662 the Egyptian Psamtik (663–610 B.C.), whom the Greeks called Psammetichus, had become king and had ousted the Assyrians. Psamtik had been much helped in his rise to power by Greek mercenaries from the Greek cities of Asia Minor. In 650 B.C. or even earlier a group of Greeks had established a trading place on one of the branches of the Nile in the Delta of Egypt, calling it "The Fort of the Milesians," Miletus being perhaps the most active and enterprising of the cities on the coast of Asia Minor. The question of how much these early Greeks learned from the Egyptians in the intercourse that now became frequent is a disputed one. We must believe that they learned something, yet it is very hard to establish that either the mechanic arts or the fine arts of Greece owed much to Egypt. The intellectual life of the Egyptians was too magic-ridden and too confused by their inability to discard anything once believed to have appealed to the Greeks or taught them much.

Necho II, the Egyptian king from 609 to 595 B.C., tried to play the old game of international affairs by helping the Assyrians against the Babylonian and Median alliance. At least he tried without success to help the remnant of the Assyrians after the fall of Nineveh. In 605 he was defeated at Carchemish, at the great upper bend of the Euphrates, by Nebuchadnezzar, crown prince of Babylon. This defeat ended any hopes of regained Egyptian power in the region.

Although her political and military strength no longer sufficed for empire, Egypt was still able to prosper by virtue of her production of wheat and oil, her manufactures, and the gold from the regions of the South. Necho built (or repaired) a canal from the Nile to the Red Sea. He sent out an expedition of Phoenician sailors to circumnavigate Africa, which they apparently succeeded in doing. He encouraged Greek merchants.

The archaizing movement of this period was designed to restore public morale. In art the style of the Old Kingdom was revived, sometimes illogically, as when an old funerary motif was copied on a small box having nothing to do with matters funerary. The "new" style was apparent in many branches of art, from scarabs to larger architectural decorations and statuary. Old Kingdom priesthoods, titles, and ranks were revived. This movement seems to have been a conscious attempt to provide a new set of ideals and aims and thus a new source of energy for a society bruised in spirit by the consciousness that it had been through a period of weakness and disorganization. We of the twentieth century have seen much of attempts, some very successful, to enliven and encourage nations by recalling a glorious past or by creating new and attractive aspirations.

Amasis, who ruled Egypt from 569 to 527 B.C., began as the opponent of the Greeks in Egypt, for the recent patriotic movement had raised feeling against foreigners, and this attitude seemed politic. Gradually, however, Amasis turned to the practical course of using the Greeks. He had a garrison of Greek mercenaries at Memphis to protect the capital. In about 565 he gathered all the resident Greek merchants into a new extraterritorial city at Naucratis, in the Delta, presumably to keep them from being too much in the public eye in several places. Their trading brought wealth to Egypt, they helped him to keep in touch with affairs in the world outside, and they also kept him in touch with sources of mercenary soldiers. It is interesting that he sent gifts to the Delphic Oracle, in Greece, of which we shall hear more later, presumably because the priests at Delphi had become well-informed about international affairs by learning what they could from the many people who went there for consultation.

When Amasis became king, the New Babylonian Empire under Nebuchadnezzar probably seemed the chief power of the world and a real threat to Egypt, since it claimed all the domain of Assyria. But the vigorous Nebuchadnezzar died in 562 and was replaced by a less aggressive king. Before long, however, Cyrus the Persian gained control of the Medes and showed the world that he was an active imperialist. The Egyptians, Babylonians, and Lydians made an alliance against him. In 547 Croesus of Lydia was conquered by Cyrus, and in 539 Babylon fell to him. Then Cyrus was succeeded by Cambyses, who conquered Egypt in 525 B.C.

Egypt was under the control of the Persians until its conquest by Alexander the Great in 332 B.C., although it more than once threw off Persian control temporarily. After the death of Alexander his general Ptolemy became king of Egypt, and the Ptolemies governed the country with some success until 30 B.C., when the Ptolemaic queen Cleopatra died and her kingdom was taken by the Roman Octavian, soon to be known as Caesar Augustus. The Romans then ruled Egypt until the end of the ancient world. In the seventh century the Moslems took Egypt as they moved across North Africa toward Spain, and ancient Egypt became medieval Egypt.

The New Babylonian (Chaldaean) Empire

After Cyaxares the Mede and Nabopolassar, the Chaldaean king of Babylonia, had defeated the Assyrians, Babylonia's share of the territories of Assyria was Mesopotamia, Syria, and theoretically Egypt, while the Medes took the part that lay north and east of the Tigris. Nabopolassar was succeeded in 605 B.C. by his son Nebuchadnezzar, a very able soldier and administrator who was to rule until 562. The excavations have shown that his capital of Babylon was a large and gorgeous city. We also have an enthusiastic description of it by the Greek historian Herodotus, a native of the subject city of Halicarnassus on the coast of Asia Minor, who visited Babylon about the middle of the fifth century. The walls of mud brick were often covered with brilliantly colored tiles. One entered the city through the great double gate named for Ishtar, the goddess of love, and decorated with fine representations of dragons and bulls in colored enamel. From the gate one could go down the great processional street whose name reflected the fact that it was the route of the annual procession in honor of the god Marduk. The walls flanking the street were decorated with enameled pictures of lions and of imaginary beasts; most of the larger museums of the Western world have one of these pictures.

In 600 B.C. Nebuchadnezzar marched to take possession of Egypt, theoretically his after the defeat of the Assyrians, but was turned back in a battle near the border and returned to Babylon. Perhaps this event encouraged Jehoiachim, king of Judah, to declare his freedom from Babylon. The frantic warnings of the prophet Jeremiah went unheeded, and the Babylonian king returned in 598 to besiege Jerusalem and take it in March 597. The king was taken off to Babylon with great numbers of his people, and a puppet king, Zedekiah, was put on the throne. Unfortunately the Jewish people were led into revolt again shortly afterward. In 586 Jerusalem fell, and Nebuchadnezzar, determined to have done with such annoyances, ravaged the land. All over the region archaeologists have found signs of fierce destruction that can be dated to this period.

The Babylonian Captivity

Presumably some of the Jews who were taken off to Babylon led a life of slavery. Others who were not enslaved became Babylonians of whatever station was possible for them, often a reasonably comfortable one. A group of the more important people, able to live well in Babylon and always in touch with one another, were resolved to keep alive their Jewish faith and practices and looked forward to the day of their restoration. The writings of the prophet Ezekiel and of the prophet known as Deutero-Isaiah belong to this group and period. The day of their deliverance came in a mere forty-odd years with the capture of Babylon in 539 by Cyrus the Persian.

Cyrus soon issued an edict of toleration that made it possible for the Jews to return to Judea, as their territory should now be called. A rather small number went back, and restoration was a slow business. After some painful vicissitudes the faithful few succeeded, about 516 B.C., in rebuilding the Temple, but the Jewish community was small and could not draw to itself many of those who should have been its members.

The scribe Ezra and the administrator Nehemiah succeeded in reinvigorating their people somewhere around the last half of the fifth century and the beginning of the fourth—the closest that we can come to their dates. The Persian king had authorized Ezra, an important man among the Jews of Babylon, to return to Judaea and reorganize his people there. He brought back the early sacred writings that were to be formed into the Pentateuch (the first five books of the Bible) and expounded them to the people, causing a great revival of religious feeling and a wave of desire for restoration of the old ways.

Nehemiah, who also figured in this restoration, was a cupbearer of the Persian king. He asked to be sent to Jerusalem with extraordinary powers, chiefly because a movement to rebuild the walls had been denounced to the king as a preliminary to rebellion. Nehemiah, although he defended the restoration of the walls, was, like Ezra, appreciative of the sober and tolerant Persian government and intended to be loyal to it. He set up a theocratic administration in Judea under the Persian government that lasted until the Hellenistic period, which followed the death of Alexander the Great in 323 B.C. The high priest governed under the Persian government and under the law of Moses. Below him were both a civil administration and a temple administration. Naturally the two branches were jealous of each other and managed to create trouble, but not enough to keep the government from functioning successfully.

Thus Ezra supplied a new devotion to an old way of life and Nehemiah supplied an administrative system that worked. These two, with the group who had stayed loyal to the faith of their fathers, may be said to have saved the Jewish people as a society from the real danger of disintegration, in the exact sense of that word.

The Phrygians

The Phrygian kingdom was another of those, like Mitanni or the Kassites in Babylon, that arose and flourished for several hundred years and vanished without leaving more than a few ripples on the surface of history. The Phrygians apparently came from Thrace and northern Macedonia and were a part of the great movement of peoples that destroyed the Hittite Empire and swept on to the border of Egypt around 1200 B.C. They cannot be said to have appropriated all that the Hittites had had, either in territory or in culture, but they settled in the middle of Asia Minor and little by little formed a powerful kingdom and learned the more civilized ways of people in this part of the world.

The Phrygian capital was Gordium (or Gordion, to spell it more nearly in the Greek than in the Latinized style), about seventy miles southwest of the modern Ankara. A number of their kings seem to have been named Midas, as in the familiar tale of the Midas to whom the god granted that everything he touched should turn to gold. Beside the gold mines there, this part of Asia Minor is good for agriculture, and in those days it was strategically situated for trade, so that the Phrygians prospered mightily.

In recent decades the city of Gordium, like many sites of Asia Minor, has been explored by the archaeologists, whose discoveries show that for about fifty years the Phrygian kingdom enjoyed a Golden Age. But there are plain traces, too, of the disaster that then overwhelmed Gordium and presumably the whole kingdom. The Phrygians were overrun in 696 B.C. by the Cimmerians, a people of the rough and ready type that they themselves had been more than five hundred years before. Although we shall hear again of Cimmerian incursions into Asia Minor, it is impossible to say with any assurance who they were and where they generally were settled.

The Lydians

After the great disaster of the Phrygians the ascendancy in Asia Minor passed to the Lydians, whose capital was at Sardis, not far from the coast. By now we are concerned with a part of history recorded by Herodotus, the fascinating Greek of Halicarnassus, who tells us about early events in Asia Minor as a preliminary to his account of the great struggle between the Persians and the Greeks of the mainland. Gyges was the first of the line of Lydian kings described by Herodotus; he acquired the throne about 685 B.C. by a more than dubious piece of dealing, and it is interesting that he sent to Greece to consult the Delphic Oracle about the whole matter.

The kingdom of Lydia grew rapidly in wealth and power in spite of one or two damaging raids by the Cimmerians. It now controlled the gold and silver deposits, the rich agricultural country, and the trade routes from the coast into Asia Minor. The Greek coastal cities came more or

less contentedly under Lydian control, for they thus had access to the
wool and woven goods and other manufactures of the interior and continued to send their ships to Egypt, to Greece proper, and to the territories that produced grain, fish, timber, and wrought steel on the shores
of the Black Sea.

Croesus of Lydia, like Midas of Phrygia, still symbolizes the wealthy
king. He could see Cyrus, the aggressive new king of the Persians, as a
menace. After some thought and inquiry, including, according to Herodotus, several consultations with the Delphic Oracle, he decided to move
across the Halys River toward Cyrus. In 585 B.C. the Medes and the
Lydians had decided to terminate their territorial dispute by putting their
common boundary at the Halys, which flows northward through Asia
Minor to the Black Sea. As we shall see, Cyrus learned that Croesus had
crossed the river and was trying to establish a hold on that piece of
Median land, all of which Cyrus believed now to be his (see following).
The Persians conquered the Lydians in 547 B.C., and Asia Minor, including the Greek cities of the coast, was to remain in their possession until
they were defeated by Alexander, a little more than two hundred years
later. There is every indication that it was a peaceful time in general
and a time of great prosperity for the whole region.

THE RISE OF PERSIA

Early Times

The peoples from whom the Persian Empire was to develop probably
drifted in from farther east about 1500 B.C., occupying the Iranian plateau, which stretches eastward from Mesopotamia to the Indus River.
They called themselves Aryans and their language Aryan; the country
was called "Land of the Aryans," or Iran, as it is nowadays.

The Medes and the Persians were the most important of these new
peoples. For a long time the Medes played the largest role, and their
king ruled over a loose federation from his capital in the North, which
was later to be known as Ecbatana, one of the capitals of the Persian
Empire. The Persians were settled in the South, near where the kingdom
of Elam had been, to the east of lower Mesopotamia. Elam appears often
in the history of Assyria, for her kings often incited the Babylonians to
resist the Assyrians until, in the seventh century, the Assyrians destroyed
it as a kingdom. The Persians had occupied some of the former Elamite
territory. The Medes and the Persians lived a simple life, largely pastoral.

It was Cyaxares the Mede who joined with Nabopolassar of Babylon to
destroy Nineveh in 612 and end the empire of the Assyrians, and he took
the Assyrian territory on his side of the Tigris. Median leadership of the

group continued until the rise of Cyrus, who became king of Persia in 549, owing fealty to the king of the Medes. Two years later he had reversed their position; Persia was now the suzerain of the Medes. People still spoke, however, of the Medes and the Persians.

The Medes and Persians belong to a large and loose group of people whom we call Indo-Europeans. The basic resemblance between their languages points to a common origin or at least to residence near each other at an early stage in the formation of language. We can be sure of the affinity of the languages; we cannot be sure of the affinity of the people. Such common words as "father" and "mother" and the verb "to be" tend to be alike in these languages. One group of Indo-European languages belongs to India and others to peoples found in the Near East: Hittites, Medes, and Persians. The branches of the Greek language form another group in this linguistic system, as do the Italic, Slavic, Germanic, and Celtic. The Semitic languages also form a group with strong similarities to one another; Akkadian and Assyrian were the great Semitic languages of Mesopotamia, while Canaanite, Hebrew, and Aramaean were the chief Semitic languages of Palestine and Assyria. The Egyptian language belonged to still another group, the Hamitic.

Persia Becomes an Empire

Cyrus set out from his Median capital of Ecbatana in 547 B.C. on a great tour of conquest and organization in the Northwest. He secured the territory of Assyria proper, then moved to Asia Minor, where the smaller kingdoms of Cilicia and Cappadocia prudently put themselves under his protection, then conquered Croesus and annexed his kingdom. At the same time the Armenians acknowledged the power of Persia and were made into a satrapy, or province.

Cyrus offered a reasonable arrangement to the Greeks of the coast. Miletus alone accepted it at once. The people of Phocaea decided to emigrate and sailed away to the West one night. Some of them lost their nerve and returned to be Persian subjects, but the rest settled at last in Italy, where we shall see them again. The rest of the Greek cities refused Cyrus' offer, whereupon he took them by force, his task being made easier by their failure to combine for resistance. The cities prospered under the Persians as they had during their nominal subjection to the Lydians.

Now Cyrus turned to the subjection of his Iranian relatives to the East and made a swing through lands of Asia that still have a romantic sound to Western ears. Sogdiana lay between the Oxus and the Jaxartes Rivers, and its capital, Maracanda, was later to be the golden storied city, Samarkand. Cyrus moved across the plateaus and the rivers and the rich oases of this region as far as the boundary of India. Bactria was the easternmost province; it was to be a notable outpost of Western influence after Alexander the Great took over the Persian Empire and brought many Greeks into it.

Cyrus then turned his attention to Babylon, the greatest fortress of the world. There is room for suspicion that it was the powerful priests of Babylon who really saw the handwriting on the wall and read it as meaning that Cyrus was certain to be king of Babylon soon. His armies were able to enter the city without striking a blow. The priests were confirmed in all their properties and privileges, possibly as a reward for disloyalty rather than as a result of religious tolerance. Such tolerance was the Persian policy, however, strikingly manifested in connection with the Jews. In 538 B.C. an edict was published in Aramaic (the official language of the Persians for business in the western satrapies) decreeing that the Temple in Jerusalem should be re-established. Despite this policy, as we have seen, the restoration of the Jewish people required more than simply a Persian royal decree.

In 530 B.C. Cambyses succeeded his father on the throne. His great project was to conquer Egypt; by 525 the conquest was complete. The Greeks of Cyrene, to the West on the African coast, submitted to his power, and he thought of taking Carthage. The Phoenicians, who had yielded to the Persians with their usual indifference to the notion of sovereignty and their usual interest in commercial possibilities, for once showed a stubborn side by refusing to transport the troops in their ships to subdue their fellow Phoenicians in Carthage.

Darius the Great and His Empire

The spectacular story of the rise of Darius the Great illustrates one difficulty of orderly government in the Near East. As has been said, the persistent problem of regulating the succession to the throne was very difficult for these people. When Cambyses died in 522 B.C. on the way home from his conquest of Egypt, there had undoubtedly been foul play. We cannot be sure now whether Cambyses had secretly killed his brother Bardiya before he left for Egypt, as one tradition has it, and whether it was a pretender or Bardiya himself who now, in the spring of 522, proclaimed his rule as Bardiya. Whoever the man was, he gathered enough support to make himself king in fact of Media and Persia.

Darius was twenty-eight at this time and had been in the entourage of Cambyses in Egypt. Although his family belonged to the nonruling branch of the royal house, in the most practical sense he was born to rule, for he was the sort of person who by nature manages other people and administers affairs. Within a few months and with the aid of six noble

Persians he had slain the usurper of Cambyses' throne and gained control of the government. Then he had to face a series of revolts in the eastern part of the empire; before he was through he even had to face a revolt in Persia itself. Fortunately he was able to handle these outbreaks in succession and did not have to struggle with any combination of those who opposed him. The personal ambitions of the satraps may have had much to do with the revolts, but they were not the only cause. There was a feeling in Media that the old supremacy of the Medes should be re-established. The Armenians may have been aiming at complete independence. The Babylonians seem to have wished to set up a king of their old line and be independent. The Lydians and the Egyptians, however, made no attempt to throw off their new yoke, and to the Phoenicians it probably seemed a good protective arrangement rather than a burden. In the next year, 521, Darius had the whole Persian Empire in hand again. It was he who put on the Behistun Rock the story of his rise to power, which was discussed earlier.

The Organization of the Persian Empire

Darius ruled from 521 until 486 B.C. During this time he perfected an organization that was already well begun. At the head was the king, a hereditary monarch who ruled by the grace of the Persian god Ahurah-Mazda or, in other lands, by the grace of Amun, Marduk, or whatever divinity was thought to dispense grace to monarchs. The king's word was law, but only within the framework of what his men of law told him was "the law of the Medes and Persians, which changeth not," or the custom of the country, or the law or the custom of one of the countries that had been made a part of the Persian Empire.

The Persians were tolerant of differences of every kind except those that might break the peace or lead to rebellion. They did not allow the local rulers to continue as client kings. Deposed sovereigns were treated with the respect due their station, but were firmly kept away from their people. We must not attribute too much mildness and humanity to the Persians, however; punishment—mutilation or impalement, for example—was inhumane in the extreme.

Persia stood firmly at the center of the whole governmental organization. She was not taxable. Efforts were made to preserve the rugged breed of Persian citizen soldiers who, with the Medes, still made up the solid part of the army. Many of the soldiers whom the subject peoples had to provide were of good quality, but others were mere rabble. There was an attempt, too, to preserve the slightly unsophisticated virtues of the nobility, on whom the government had to rely to staff important positions in the army and the civil service. Herodotus tells us that the essentials of their education were learning to ride, to shoot with the bow, and to speak the truth.

The royal roads were an essential part of imperial management. About every twelve or thirteen miles there was a station with horses, sometimes with an inn. Whereas the ordinary traveler might take ninety days to get from the coast at Ephesus to the royal city of Susa, the imperial post could probably do it in a week.

There were twenty subdivisions of the government called satrapies and governed by satraps, a word that means "protector of the realm." The twenty satraps were at first chosen from among the noble Persians, but their office seems to have become hereditary, as did the office of nomarch in Egypt. The central government was able to exert sufficient control over the satraps to keep the empire together, even though it allowed them the surprising privilege of making war on one another.

The satrap was almost independent. His state was elevated, and he might revel in pomp. Always, however, he must have been conscious that he had a secretary and a local military commander who were independent of him and whose duty it was to make regular reports to the king. He also received periodic visits from the king's "eyes and ears," traveling inspectors whom presumably the satrap could not coerce or bribe. The satrap's duty was to keep the peace, administer justice, and get the taxes in. He could use his discretion, but was expected not to outrage local feelings or customs and not to oppress the people financially or otherwise.

The Religion of Zoroaster

The religion of the Persians was based on recognizing and placating the forces of nature, as was customary among ancient peoples. As usual there was a chief god, called Ahurah. Mithras, who was conceived as the sun, was worshiped for a long time and was still a religious factor much later when Christianity was about to triumph. In this milieu, somewhere between 1000 and 600 B.C., the great mystic Zoroaster worked. He did not transform the milieu. Although his *Gathas,* the verses that contain his visions and his teaching, came to form part of the *Avesta,* the sacred book of the Persians, Zoroaster was never honored as a prophet, as for example Mohammed was, and his teachings never met with popular or official acceptance.

Zoroaster refused to recognize the manifold divinities of nature, asserting that there is only the lord Ahurah-Mazda, god of all the universe, who represented the principle of light and Goodness. This god had an entourage of ten vaguely conceived attributes, including Righteousness, Good Thought, Piety, Salvation, Obedience, and Fire. This grouping of abstractions often occurred in religions of the Near East and was to continue even in early Christianity.

Zoroaster dismissed the other gods of common belief as *daevas,* or demons. Naturally he could not claim that they did not exist. The Christians were to have the same difficulty later with their assertion of monotheism. Any suggestion that nature gods of the Persians or the gods worshiped when the Romans came to power did not exist was countered by the believer with the simple answer that everyone knew that they did exist. Easier than denying them was asserting that what seemed to be gods were demons, or spirits, who had no powers comparable to the powers of God, yet could be active for evil.

Zoroaster apparently was the first to assert that there is a principle of evil that makes itself felt in the world. He called it Ahriman. Between it and the lord Ahurah-Mazda there could be only a fight to the finish, a finish that in this theology was foreordained: the victory of Light over Darkness. Zoroaster believed that no man can escape making the great moral choice, that he must march under one banner or the other and in the end suffer judgment for his life and receive his reward or his punishment.

INDIA AND CHINA

The farthest satrapy of the Persian Empire reached to somewhere near the Indus River, and the influence of the Persians was felt beyond the river in the kingdoms of northern India. After the breaking up, apparently about 1600 B.C., of the old Indus civilization, which is symbolized for us by the impressive ruins of Mohenjo-Daro and Harappa (see Chapter 2), there was a long period in India, perhaps to about 1000 B.C., in which men must have lived in some kind of organization without attaining anything near the complexity and intensity of the former civilization. The slow advance of archaeology in India has revealed something of some large cities dating from after 1000 B.C. in northern India, but the work has hardly gone beyond the recognition of their outlines and the sinking of vertical shafts here and there to gain some idea of their stratigraphy and thus of the bare outlines of their cultural phases and dates. The impression gained is that after 1000 B.C. these cities grew and prospered and were energetic rivals of one another in a spacious region of rich soil and ready communications by river. The use of iron came late to India, perhaps about 500 B.C., and may well have come from Persia. The use of coins probably came from Persia at about the same time, and archaeology suggests that Persia may also have inspired the people of India to a more complex trade than they had before.

The distinctive civilization that grew up in India in the first millennium before Christ persisted with little change into modern times. We find all the basic traits of the civilized peoples of antiquity: the Neolithic domestication of plants and animals, the use of metals and writing, and true city life (some powerful nomadic peoples like the Scythians and agricultural peoples like the Germans did not live in cities in ancient times). The cities were not as large and complex as those of some other countries, nor were industry and trade as intense.

The Indian civilization was literate in the larger sense of having a literature rather than in the sense of using writing only for a few practical purposes, as was the case with the Persians and many other peoples. The literature developed about as far as those of the Near and Middle Eastern civilizations that we have discussed, having some epic, some law, a great number of hymns, and other religious literature. There was no real historical writing nor exploration of the feelings and relations of people. The limitations were what we should expect in a literature dominated by a priestly class.

Hinduism, the religion that to this day is most influential in India, was clearly formulated in the first millennium, at least in the teachings of the Brahmans, who made an elevated and somewhat abstract system of it. We may suppose that the common man's version of it was less elevated and less consistent. The caste system of India, which has persisted into modern times, apparently was developed as part of the teachings of the Brahmans, whose chief idea seems to have been to construct a closed and static society with themselves in the chief role.

The chief event in the intellectual life of early India was the opposition offered to Brahmanism around 500 B.C. by Prince Gautama Siddhartha, "the Buddha," and by the Jains, an opposition in both cases to the rigidity and to the superior attitude of the Brahmans. The life of the Buddha, "the enlightened one," fell in almost exactly the same years as the life of Darius I of Persia, and his years of teaching were almost exactly those of Darius' reign, 521 to 486 B.C. He preached to all men and was opposed to the caste system. His message was a simple one of sweet reasonableness and attempts to live well and to gain release from the endless cycle of rebirth. Nothing could be more alien to the strenuousness that, beginning with the Greeks, was to be the chief trait of Western man. After his death his disciples reduced his teaching to a system, and Buddhism spread through India to Burma, Ceylon, and China, where it still exists, although after more than a thousand years it was reabsorbed by Brahmanism in India. Jainism, too, opposed Brahmanism, but by setting up a remarkably rigid system of such appeal that until now it has always had a sufficient number of adherents to continue and has not changed its original tenets at all.

The civilization of China in the first millennium B.C. had many of the same traits as those just listed for India, although naturally its style was different. Its literature was limited, like that of India, but did include some genuine historical writing. The Shang Dynasty of northern China, which was mentioned in Chapter 2, was replaced in 1027 B.C. by the first king of the Chou Dynasty, which ruled until 56 B.C. The records of China are such that we know more of this modest empire than we do of the political life of India. For example, we can see that during the first part of the millennium the central government was strong, as was the Old Kingdom of Egypt, and that eventually a period came when the kings had great difficulty, as in Egypt, in managing the nobles to whom they had made concessions and granted power. The Chinese were more energetic than the Indians and more of this world. They improved their agricultural methods and built irrigation and flood-control works, learned to make silk, became skillful in working bronze and iron, promoted trade, and developed the fine arts. A class of scholars appeared who both taught the young and advised princes, as has recently come to be the case with Western man.

Like India, China had a great philosopher whose teachings on the simple life were widely influential. Confucius (551–479 B.C.), as we know him in a Latinized form, or Kung Fu-tze, or Master Kung, preached the simple and good life, as did the Buddha. However, he also resembles Socrates, who was to be born in Greece a few years after Confucius died, in his teaching that the good is desirable in itself, once a man comes to know it. If China was less static in its culture than India, its history still lacks the change, variety, and self-consciousness that we find in the history of the nations that were the founders of Western culture.

CHAPTER

5

THE GREEKS AND THE AEGAEAN
AREA IN EARLY TIMES

lthough as we look back we tend to identify the Greeks with the Aegaean area—Greece proper, the islands, the European shore north of the Aegaean, and the shore of Asia Minor east of it—it is good to remember that the Greeks were so vigorous and bred so well that all through ancient times they spread out around the Mediterranean world. After the fall of Mycenae, as we shall see, a goodly number of them emigrated to Asia Minor. In the eighth and seventh centuries B.C. there was a great emigration to the north and south shores of the Black Sea and westward to Sicily and south Italy. There were Greek mercenary soldiers and Greek merchants in the Persian Empire before Alexander conquered it, but after his death in 323 there was a large flow of Greeks to the Greek kingdoms organized in the former Persian territory that he had conquered, since there were great opportunities for soldiers, administrators, and businessmen. The last great Greek emigration of ancient times was to Rome from about 200 B.C. through perhaps A.D. 200.

All these places around the Mediterranean were somewhat similar in climate; naturally the Black Sea region was cooler and the interior of Egypt or the Near and Middle East was hotter. The Mediterranean climate is subtropical. There is snow in the mountains, but it is not common at sea level. The heat of summer is often tempered by breezes. Winter weather is brighter than in England, most of Europe, or most of the United States, and at any time of year the clearer air and sharper outlines of the Mediterranean landscape are most agreeable to those who come from other places.

96

The Drift to the West

The persistent attempts of the archaeologists since aboout the middle of this century to find and study prehistoric sites have revealed that in Greece and the islands there were many Palaeolithic and Neolithic settlements, the latter yielding plain evidence that agriculture and the herding of animals were practiced. These sites are architecturally less sophisticated than the Neolithic sites of the Near East, and the assemblages of materials are simpler.

Some of the archaeological investigations have yielded evidence that in about 3000 B.C. men whose culture was in the early bronze stage drifted westward from Asia Minor, Syria, and Palestine to the smaller islands of the Aegaean, to Cyprus, Rhodes, and Crete, and to the mainland of Greece. Others moved along the same routes at later times.

The evidence again is archaeological for what is regarded as the last significant movement of new people into the circle of the Aegaean world. A new kind of pottery, the so-called Minyan ware, is thought to have appeared in Greece around 1900 B.C., or even a little earlier. The same kind of ware appears at Troy at about the same time and in several other places in the part of Asia Minor where Troy is; perhaps there was a movement from somewhere in Anatolia or from farther east, some members of which stopped at Troy and around that area, while the others went on to Greece. Few scholars now hold to the older view that all the people entered Greece from the north and by land.

Obviously the Greeks were a somewhat mixed people. It is an important fact, however, that they themselves in later times felt able to say that some people were Greeks and some were not; the question arose more than once—when people whose Greekness was in doubt offered to compete in the Olympic Games, for example. To us, looking back, it must seem that there was a unity that we call "the Greeks," whose achievements we admire and whose analytical approach to the world, so different from that of the earlier peoples of the ancient world and so like ours, made them the first of the moderns. The formation of this people during the second millennium before Christ is the most important part of the early history of the Aegaean area. From here on "the Greeks" will be a part of our story. We must remember that those who lived outside Greece proper—perhaps far away on the French Riviera or the fertile soil of south Russia at the edge of the Black Sea—still were real Greeks. We must also remember that the Greek character was not cast in only one mold; it will be better to tell of the fascinating and highly differing things that they did for better or for worse, than to try to describe "the Greek character."

THE GREAT CENTERS

The history of three great cities—Troy, Cnossus, and Mycenae—is the most important part of the history of the Aegaean area in the third and second millennia B.C., that is, from about 3000 B.C. to the little understood time of troubles and destruction around 1200 B.C.; none of the three cities survived this period. All were excavated by giants of archaeology in the late nineteenth and the twentieth century; for all three we have very little or no written evidence and must depend largely on archaeology. The excavation of hundreds of unspectacular sites in the Aegaean area has been tremendously important for the establishment of the sequence of pottery and other artifacts and in general for our archaeological knowledge of the period, but while we use this mass of evidence, we cannot find any one of the sites that will serve our account as do the great centers.

Troy

Troy was in the northwest corner of Asia Minor, four miles from the Aegaean and from the Dardanelles, where it was safe from casual raids of pirates, but could exercise some control over the passage of the Dardanelles or the crossing of it between the Asiatic and European sides. Heinrich Schliemann went there in 1870 to vindicate his belief that Homer had sung of the real conquest of a real city, and in 1872 announced that he had found the city of the *Iliad*. Schliemann thus opened the study of the prehistory of the Aegaean, a study that has replaced the old notion of the Greeks as springing suddenly to miraculous achievements with a more realistic and more interesting view of their development. In the 1930s a University of Cincinnati expedition headed by Carl Blegen resumed the work and brought it to completion.

At Troy the problem of establishing levels is especially important because we want to know, once we accept that this site probably is ancient Troy, which level represents the Troy of Homer. The first level, that is, the bottom level, the oldest level, gives evidence that from about 3000 to 2500 there was a small stone fortress, that copper tools had been introduced, and stone tools had not yet gone out, and that a great fire destroyed the city. There was no evidence of trade with other places. The second level, or Troy II in the modern terminology, apparently was what Schliemann called Homeric Troy, but we cannot be sure because in the early work his reporting was not careful by modern standards. (His techniques improved with amazing speed as he went along.) There had been a fire, and people had fled and left bronze weapons, jewelry, and vessels of gold, copper, and bronze lying about. Troy III, IV, and V take us to about 1900 B.C. with no signs of a new culture, but at about that time the

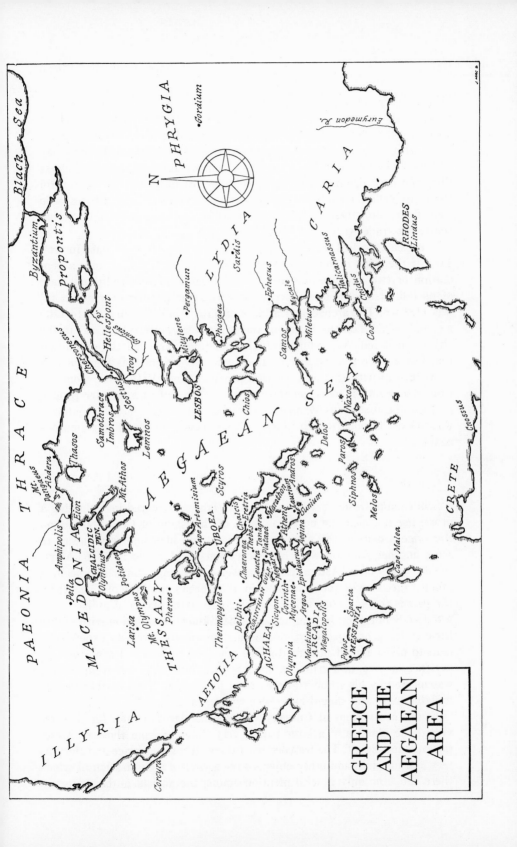

GREECE
AND THE
AEGAEAN
AREA

Minyan ware appears in Troy VI, suggesting the arrival of a new people, some of whom went on with their distinctive pottery to Greece. Troy VI lasted until about 1300 B.C. Several hundred Mycenaean vases prove a trade with Mycenae; the Trojans may well have exported horses (they had good grazing lands) and textiles (loom weights in the ruins suggest this) and may also have had an invisible export in their power to control the Dardanelles. There is no sign that they traded with the Hittites, who were flourishing then, or with the cities of the Palestinian and Syrian coast, but trade with Cyprus was important.

The archaeological remains would indicate that Troy VIIa was Homer's Troy if the Troy of song and story existed at all. It lasted only a generation or two and was destroyed by a great fire. The traditional date of its fall, arrived at later by counting back the number of generations, was 1183 B.C. The archaeological date of Troy's fall is from 1250 to 1200 B.C. and is based on the dating of the Mycenaean pottery that was in the city when it fell. Agamemnon of Mycenae may have led the expedition that brought Troy down; we do not know. No writing was found in the ruins to help with this or any other problem. Troy VIIb arose from the ruins and went on for a generation or so, then fell to a simpler people, perhaps the dangerous wanderers of around 1200 B.C. Troy (or Ilium) was to exist through Roman times, but was never important or glamorous again.

Cnossus

Schliemann, fresh from his triumph at Troy, considered investigating a promising site near the northern shore of the island of Crete, but found the price asked by the owner of the land too high and went away to score another triumph with his excavation at Mycenae in 1876. About twenty years later, Arthur Evans, a well-to-do Englishman approaching middle age, bought the land, and in 1900 began the first of five yearly campaigns there. Evans, who passes for one of the giants of archaeology, was like Schliemann in coming to his best-known excavation with rather little training or experience, but he had prudently hired an experienced man to assist him. Unfortunately he was less willing to learn from experience, advice, and criticism than Schliemann was, so that his career was marred by his stubborn defenses of ideas about Cnossus that he formulated early and should have been willing to modify.

Evans' excavations at Cnossus were spectacular, however, for they revealed the remains of a large palace very different from those of Mesopotamia and Egypt. The frescoes from the walls of the palace and the pottery and figurines and other objects gave a view of a civilization of which there had been only general mention among the ancient authors (for instance, in Homer's phrase, "Crete of the hundred cities"), but which now emerged on archaeological evidence as a rich and refined civilization, cheerful and elegant. Cnossus and the many other sites on Crete that have been excavated since Evans began and are now being excavated have revealed far more through archaeological evidence than the bare story of successively larger cities and occasional disasters which the ruins of Troy can tell us.

The age of metal on Crete began about 3000 B.C., and after a millennium without distinction the culture of Crete seems suddenly to have advanced around 2000, at least partly because of the influence of Egypt. Egyptian jewelry of this time has been found in Crete, and an Egyptian note becomes discernible in Cretan work. Sequences can be worked out in the materials found at the successive palaces whose ruins can be identified at Cnossus and elsewhere on Crete. The major palaces, those at Cnossus and at Phaestus and Mallia in the south of the island, the rich finds of pottery, and smaller objects like seals all show traceable developments of style. Evans' early classification of Early, Middle, and Late Minoan (from Minos, a frequent name of the kings) has come to seem unsatisfactory, but is still much used beside such other systems as calling 2000 to 1600 B.C. the maturity or the Early Palace Period and 1600 to 1400 B.C. the zenith or the Late Palace Period.

The archaeological evidence tells us much about the charming and brilliant culture of the so-called maturity, or the Early Palace period, in spite of the gaps that only written evidence could fill. There was writing, to be sure, the so-called Linear A writing found in the palace storerooms at Cnossus, but it has not yet been deciphered. The palace, a few miles from the sea, had no fortifications, and scholars (with some exceptions) have concluded that the Cretans did control the sea at this time, as the later Greeks believed.

The palace at Cnossus was large and complex; there were living quarters and rooms of state and many service rooms and storerooms. One can see how the legend of a labyrinth in Crete may have originated. The palace was decorated with charming frescoes; it was four stories high, with broad stairs and light wells, and was well supplied with running water. The architect sees in it a building built outward from an inner court and open to its surroundings, whether for views outward to the surrounding hills or for a person approaching it to see entrances that seemed to lead easily inside, and the houses (probably those of nobles of the court) that surround the palace are built on the same plan, in direct contrast to palaces and houses of the Near and Middle East, which hid themselves behind an impenetrable and concealing outer wall.

The cheerful and luxurious life of the Cretans is suggested by frescoes, reliefs, statuettes, and jewelry. We see a representation on a fresco of a small sports arena, which may have been the palace courtyard, and male and female athletes are shown who meet a charging bull, grasp his horns as he lowers his head, and vault over onto his back as he raises his head to toss them. They were slim and graceful people who dressed so as to show off their bodies without the glum modesty of people farther east; the women wore graceful skirts and bodices cut low enough to show the breasts. The bull was sacrificed by the Cretans and therefore can hardly have been worshiped, yet it is a dark legend that tells that seven Athenian boys and seven girls were sent each year to Cnossus to be eaten in a labyrinth by a creature that was half bull and half man. Archaeology can uncover the pervasive symbolism of the bull, but cannot explain its significance.

There seems to have been a female goddess, whose occasional epiphanies, or appearances, seem from the pictures to have been the great moments of the religious experience; she was winsome rather than grim and fearsome. In the palaces and around the countryside were little crypts where apparently votive offerings were left; there were no images there of the divinity.

The artists of the Early Palace Period, the period called the maturity of the Minoan civilization, had mastered their techniques and were pleasantly inspired. The architects, as we have seen, had a new and rich conception of what a palace could be. The makers of pottery, whose work survives abundantly, were devoted to ornamentation of curved lines, which developed into representations of fish or of leaves, blossoms, and plants. They could make pottery of eggshell thinness, the so-called Kamares ware, and ornament it beautifully. The cutting on stones of pictures for seals reached a high point in this period.

The finds show that the Cretans sent their pottery to the Near East by way of Cyprus; there is evidence that it went even as far as Mari, on the Euphrates. A little of their pottery went to Egypt, and it may be conjectured that they supplied timber and hides and textiles to the Egyptians. The ships of the Minoan merchants also sailed westward to Malta and Sicily and southern Italy and farther west. Not least important were the exports to the Greek mainland of pottery and other manufactured objects and of ideas. The Minoans put the mainland Greeks in touch with the larger civilized world of Egypt and the Near East, with which they themselves were by now familiar, and in this way were largely responsible for the great cultural advance of the mainland Greeks toward the middle of the second millennium.

In the Late Palace Period, or the zenith of Minoan culture, the palace was destroyed, as had happened before; this time it probably was shaken down by the great volcanic eruption that is thought to have blown away part of the nearby island of Thera, the modern Santorini, around 1500 B.C.

The new palace was marked by luxury hitherto unknown. Some scholars attribute to it a sophisticated use of space and light as architectural components and say that by its very richness and complexity it achieved a monumental quality more impressive than the rather squat and heavy monumentality of the Near Eastern palaces; others find this opinion fanciful.

Perhaps more important than the changes in the styles of pottery and gem cutting and the excellence of the frescoes that are apparent in this period is the question of who controlled Cnossus. The writing used on the tablets in the palace storerooms, known by Evans' designation of Linear A, was succeeded by a modification that Evans called Linear B. After many scholars had attempted to decipher both scripts, more Linear B was found in Greece at Pylos in the Southwest, at Mycenae, and elsewhere, and in 1953 Linear B yielded to the cryptographic methods used by Michael Ventris, an architect who had learned cryptography in the British service in World War II. The language was Greek. Since Linear B was found in Crete only at Cnossus, it would seem likely that Greeks of the mainland gained control of Cnossus a good many years before the final destruction of the palace, which seems to have taken place around 1400 B.C. There would have been no great hurry to devise a new system under which the palace staff could write the records of the storerooms in Greek rather than in the old language, whatever it was. If we may reasonably conclude that Greeks were in control of Cnossus through most of the fifteenth century (and there are changes in artistic style after the destruction of the palace that took place around 1500 that could mean the presence of a new people), we still must wonder who destroyed the palace about 1400. It would hardly have been Greeks from the mainland if they were already in control; perhaps it was a raid from the sea, perhaps a rising of the local people against those who still seemed to be foreign invaders on their soil. Life in Crete went on after the destruction of the palace at Cnossus, but in a commonplace way.

Mycenae

Schliemann's excavation at Mycenae opened up a new view of the prehistory of the Aegaean. The site had always been visible, of course; it is a hill below a much larger range of hills—always a good place for underground water supplies, if one is thinking of constructing a fortress—in the upper Peloponnesus, only a few miles from the eastern coast, and looks out over a green and pleasant plain. The strong walls, the imposing gate with its huge slabs of stone and its twin lionesses on their hind legs with their forepaws on a column between them, which probably symbolizes the royal power, and the remains of structures inside the walls, as well as the tombs outside—all this had never been covered and was known as the remains of Mycenae. Schliemann dug here, too, with the intention of vindicating the accuracy of Homer, who spoke of the wealth of Mycenae. The Greek government, having heard of the slashing attack he made on the remains of Troy in his earliest digging, laid severe restrictions on him as to the number of men he could use at one time and sent a member of the Archaeological Commission to watch him.

He startled the world again by finding five multiple graves (a sixth was found later) which now are known as the Shaft Graves of Circle A. For such graves a rectangular pit was dug into the soft rock to a depth of as much as twelve feet, and artificial walls were built inside it to perhaps shoulder height. The dead person was lowered into it and his gifts put beside him, beams were put across the tops of the walls to form a ceiling, and the hole above the beams was filled in with earth. At the time of the next burial (for the shaft was made large enough to be used for more than one) all the covering had to be removed.

The graves of Circle A had not been robbed; the richness of the objects in them, which may now be seen in the National Museum in Athens, is almost incredible. The grave to which the number IV was given, for example, contained gold masks, gold crowns, gold diadems or headbands; there were twenty-seven swords and sixteen ivory sword pommels, five daggers and sixteen knives; there were vases of gold, silver, bronze, alabaster, and faïence, and pitchers and rings of gold and silver. From the clothes of the ladies came 683 gold discs and ornaments, and there were 1290 beads of Baltic amber that may have been sewn onto a dress as ornament. The workmanship and the obvious cost of the things are most impressive. Two of the daggers are famous ones with inlaid scenes; the sword pommels are beautifully ornamented; the gold and silver cups have fine ornamentation. There are precious international materials beside: ostrich eggs from Nubia, lapis lazuli from Mesopotamia, raw ivory from Syria, silver from Anatolia.

The graves of Circle A are on the boundary between the Middle and Late Helladic periods, to use the terminology worked out for this area; this means that the earliest burials were around 1550 B.C. and the latest after 1500. In these graves there are things of many origins and many styles and many degrees of excellence. Along with the fine and mature things there are some styles not yet fully worked out, some that are primitive in style, and differing styles like the naturalistic and the abstract. The whole effect, however, is that of the beginning of a lively and wealthy period when the leaders of Mycenae could reach far and pay what they had to for the good things of the world.

Since the excavation of Circle A our knowledge of the styles and sequences of the artifacts has improved greatly. Many Bronze Age graves and sites have been excavated, especially by Blegen and the Englishman Alan J. B. Wace; these two studied especially the rather unspectacular finds that have been the foundation of our improved knowledge when studied as a whole.

The so-called tholos tombs of Mycenae, those shaped like old-fashioned beehives, are thought to belong to the same time as the shaft graves and are thought to be, like the shaft graves, evidence of the arrival of a small number of powerful people, since there are no archaeological antecedents elsewhere for these two kinds of tombs and there is no evidence of a major migration. The legends of early Greece are suggestive: they tell of the arrival in Greece at different times of several important people, like Cadmus, Danaus, Pelops, and Perseus, from Egypt, the Near East, and Asia Minor. Perhaps a couple of the Hyksos kings came from Egypt with their retainers at a time when the Theban kings were pressing the Hyksos hard in the 1500s; this would explain some of the Egyptian things in the shaft graves. All these men are figures of what is sometimes called the First Heroic Age of Greece, before the Trojan War.

At about 1450 a great period of prosperity and expansion began that was to last until the difficulties of about 1200. Palaces were built at Mycenae, Tiryns, and Thebes. The great citadel of Mycenae is thought to have replaced a simpler early fortification of the hill in about 1350, and soon thereafter the palace was rebuilt on a larger scale, as was the case at Tiryns, Pylos, and Thebes, as well. A great citadel and palace were also built at Athens. After a time of prosperity and brilliant achievement during the thirteenth century, the whole area suffered the same mysterious invasions and assaults that were common all around the Mediterranean at about 1200. The palace at Pylos was destroyed then. There was widespread destruction and abandonment of centers on the mainland, and many people seem to have moved to the islands, which apparently continued in peace during the twelfth century. At about 1120, however, came the final destruction of Mycenae and Tiryns, presumably because of a great invasion of the Dorian Greeks from northern Greece. Here the Mycenaean Age ends.

Sir Arthur Evans maintained stubbornly that the culture of the mainland was only a colonial offshoot of the Cretan and that the Cretans dominated the mainland politically. Although we may now say that there is no evidence of such political domination, our wealth of archaeological information does not show the shifts of power. Plainly the Minoan cultural influence was strong on the mainland in the 1500s, but the evidence also seems to indicate that at that time princes or powerful men arrived in Greece from somewhere in the East—not from Crete. Did the mainlanders ever dominate Crete? The evidence in Crete of the development of the Linear B script and of a new general style in art seems to point that way, but we do not know any details.

The culture of the mainland has much interesting detail even though it cannot equal the cheerful elegance of Minoan culture. It lagged behind Crete in the construction of both palaces and houses; the palaces start in perhaps 1450, long after Crete had elaborate and beautiful ones. The mainland palaces are citadels, which is natural; the Cretan palaces were exceptional in not being fortified. Kings generally chose sites with good water supplies and had some good engineers to build tunnels from the springs to underground reservoirs for sieges. At Pylos there are traces of an aqueduct leading into terracotta pipes in the palace and of drains to carry the waste water away. Some of the kings had roads built in the neighborhood of the palace—a most unusual thing in those days.

The evidence for the industrial and economic aspect of the palace is a little better than it is in Crete. The excavations at Pylos disclosed rooms filled with pottery as if this part of the palace were a warehouse; it is amusing to think of old King Nestor who entertained Telemachus so graciously in the *Odyssey* as a shrewd manager of the industry in kitchenware and other necessities. The excavations both here and at Mycenae disclose that there was a large industrial area of the palace where smiths and carpenters were busy, as well as chariot makers and makers of horse furniture, armorers, masons, and decorators. The Linear B tablets also give us the names of many kinds of workmen. We can imagine the palace as a tremendously busy place. The quarters of the king were spacious and well decorated with frescoes, with a busy area nearby for those who prepared the food and the clothing for the palace. The industrial area must have rung with noises and reeked with smells. Everything except a few fine and small importations like vases or ornamented daggers was made there, since there was no other place for the things to come from.

The Lion Gate of Mycenae is about the only example of monumental sculpture either in Crete or on the mainland; in both places people seemed to have preferred small and fine things. The artists of the mainland were highly competent, but their work is less interesting than that from Crete. They carved gems, made jewelry, and worked in metal. They made good pottery. In ivory carving they were especially competent. The business side of the art industry was able to send its products far and wide, especially after the fall of Cnossus removed a very able competitor. Mycenaean products went beyond the areas of Greek population; some can be dated precisely from being found in the ruins of Amarna, which lasted only from 1379 to 1362. Others have been found in the ruins of places in the Near East. Cyprus seems to have been an important intermediate point for this as for other kinds of trade, and it even looks as if the technique as well as the pots had been exported there, since remains have been found there of establishments making ware of Mycenaean style. Mycenaean pottery has been found, too, in Sicily and Malta and on the island of Ischia off Naples.

It is possible that mainland Greece was the land that the Hittites respectfully referred to as Ahhiyawa, although it may have been Rhodes. Ahhiyawa seems to have been Greek, whatever place it was, and the manner in which the Hittites spoke of it shows that the Greeks of the Late Bronze Age, the fourteenth and thirteenth centuries, were a power to be reckoned with and treated with respect.

THE TIME BETWEEN

The time between the ending of the Mycenaean civilization and the beginning of the classical civilization of the Greeks lasted about three hundred years, from about 1100 B.C. to about 800 B.C. To call it "the Dark Age" seems less appropriate now than it did before archaeology revealed that civilization did not cease then nor did the people disappear in the territories inhabited by the Greeks, but that there was rather a time when people lived in the simpler manner common before the formation of the kingdoms and centers of the Mycenaean Age.

We know from the archaeological evidence that in the century after about 1200 B.C.—the twelfth century, that is—the quality of life as betrayed by material remains had fallen off somewhat. Presumably the troubles of the late thirteenth century had made communications less easy, beside harming cities and causing the building of more fortifications; the result was less uniformity of material things that people used. Not only did more purely local styles grow up, but, as time went on, things were of poorer quality and seemed to show less artistic merit.

After about 1100 B.C. the great centers were gone. Mycenae, Tiryns, Pylos, Thebes, and other centers had been stormed and destroyed by the Dorians and their allies around 1100 B.C. No new center had replaced Cnossus after its fall around 1400, and even the more remote influence of Egypt was in abeyance because of a period of weakness there. Troy, too, was gone. Although communication with the more civilized world of the Near East had not ceased, the disappearance of all the centers of strenuous and concentrated commercial and artistic activity must have caused life around the Aegaean to be lived in a quieter and more parochial style.

The Athenians of the great age liked to speak of themselves as sprung from the soil of their country and as having lived there always without interruption, and indeed archaeology seems to show that Athens suffered no disaster at the end of the Mycenaean period. The quality of its pottery did fall off for many generations, but toward the end of three quiet centuries there was a stir of life there, and a local style having a certain keenness and good taste emerged that was to become the best form of Geometric Pottery (so called because its ornaments are geometric figures).

Greek tradition has many stories from this period of the movements of peoples and of the acts and adventures of kings and great men. The authors of classical Greece, both historians and others, took these stories seriously as information from the period before written history. Modern historians, perhaps under the influence of the great movement of the nineteenth century to make history scientific, have long been inclined to regard such stories as suspect, but more and more the tendency is to suppose that they contain a considerable amount of truth. Although such stories were handed down orally until in the sixth or fifth centuries they found a place in the written treatments of an earlier Greece, they were stories of great events among a people used to relying on their memories. Since the Greeks were very careful about genealogies (although they doubtless improved them sometimes with a little editing) it is likely that they got the names straight in telling these stories and that the main events were often substantially correct.

Although to the Greeks the movements of many tribes or peoples were interesting, for us the Dorians and Ionians seem most important. The Dorians and their allies had been in northern Greece for some centuries before they began to move southward in force, first causing difficulties for Mycenae and other centers and then, around 1100, destroying them. They then went into southern Greece, below the Gulf of Corinth; this part of Greece probably began then to be called "Peloponnesus," or "Island of Pelops," the name it still has. At this time, too, the terms "Hellas" for all Greece and "Hellenes" for all the Greek people, terms that are still in use, seem to have originated. These names, and "Dorians" as well, are not found in Homer's poems. From now on the Spartans, the most prominent group of the Dorians, lived in the Peloponnesus, while others went to Crete, to many of the islands, even as far as Rhodes, and to a few places on the mainland of Asia Minor. By the Classical Age of Greece, the Dorians were still thought of as a recognizable group and as the most powerful one among the Greeks.

The Ionians, a less belligerent group, migrated from Greece to the coast of Asia Minor in many modest-sized groups during the century from 1000 to 900 B.C., to judge by the archaeological evidence, and were able to take or gain possession of some fine city locations on the coast and the two desirable islands of Samos and Chios. Although other Greeks went to this region, it was generally thought of as an Ionian place, as the Peloponnesus was thought of as a Dorian place. None of the cities, however, was ever able to expand inland to any extent or to become a land power of any significance, although many of them became great seafaring centers and founders of overseas colonies.

Thus the whole circuit of the Aegaean Sea—mainland Greece, Crete and the smaller islands, Rhodes and Cyprus, the coast of Asia Minor, and the islands near it—except Thrace, which constituted the northern shore of that sea, had come to be inhabited by Greeks who had some sense of likeness to one another, and through the rest of ancient history this was to be a Greek region. The Greek language came to be spoken through the entire area. There were a number of different dialects, but a man could generally make himself understood by another Greek.

THE HOMERIC POEMS

Iliad, Odyssey, Epic Cycle

Two great epic poems, the *Iliad* and the *Odyssey,* arose somewhere in Ionian Asia Minor between 850 and 750 B.C. and are ascribed to Homer. The *Iliad* is some 16,000 lines long and would take several long sessions (over thirty hours) to recite; the *Odyssey* is somewhat shorter. The *Iliad* describes an intense incident of the war at Troy (it does not tell of the fall of Troy), while the *Odyssey* is a tale of adventure in the western seas, the story of Odysseus on his way home from Troy. Some critics find such difference in the tone of the two poems that one man can hardly have written both—a dangerous argument!—and there are internal inconsistencies that suggest that each poem was somehow built up from other poems. In the *Iliad,* for example, the great Greek warriors Achilles and Diomedes never appear together in the fighting, which would suggest that two stories, one about Achilles and one about Diomedes, had been mechanically combined. Because nothing at all was known of Homer's life even in antiquity, questions about him and his poems have been raised and discussed: Was there any such man? Are the poems compilations made by one man or perhaps by a group? Are the two poems a pair or were they produced by different people at different times? All these doubts constitute the Homeric Question.

A group of poems called the *Epic Cycle,* written by many authors, told the whole story of the Trojan War from the earliest events that led to the abduction of Queen Helen by the Trojan prince, Paris, through all the details of the war and through the homecomings of all the heroes. Although the authors of the *Epic Cycle* were so overshadowed by Homer that their works failed to be copied in late antiquity and therefore did not survive to modern times, we know the content of their poems because they are so often referred to by Greek and Roman authors who have survived.

The Oral Poet

It has long been known that the Greeks had bards who sang for the entertainment of others; recently it has become the custom among scholars to refer to them as "oral poets." A small group of scholars has investigated the methods of modern oral poets, especially those of the south Slavic poets. These poets are illiterate; they sing in metrical lines, as Homer did, although their line is shorter and easier than his. They rely on memory to an extent that often surprises us. They learn by starting as youngsters to imitate the oral poets whom they hear; they build up huge armories of phrases and parts of lines and whole lines, from which they further build armories of themes, or units of narrative, such units as banquet scenes, scenes of heroes arming themselves for battle, challenges, fights, stripping the armor from a fallen enemy, departures, arrivals, sunrises, or storms. They gradually build up a repertory of these basic materials, constantly practicing the combination of the materials for the production of songs for which there is, of course, no written text. Originality is not prized. They frankly draw on traditional material or on any song that they may hear sung, changing and adapting as they please. The best performers sing songs very like those of the other men, but manage to give them more life and more polish.

The oral poets of ancient Greece worked this way, if we may judge by the *Iliad* and the *Odyssey*. The main characters have standing epithets, such as "Achilles swift of foot" and "flashing-eyed Athena," which occur again and again. Many whole lines occur several times in exactly the same form, for example, "And Odysseus, ready in counsel, answered him, saying. . . ." Sometimes a group of several lines recurs in exactly the same form, as does one that describes the hospitable offering of food to a newly arrived stranger. When Agamemnon, in the *Iliad,* is ready to offer restitution to Achilles for affronting him, he gives a long description of the gifts that he is prepared to give him. The description is repeated word for word by the envoys whom he sends to Achilles. This repetition of phrases, lines, and passages, which would seem strange in other Greek works, apparently is evidence that the two Homeric poems were composed in the tradition of the oral poets and were offered to audiences familiar with their manner. There are other signs: again and again there are swift recapitulations of earlier action or repeated explanations of the same fact, as if the poem were meant to be intelligible when presented in parts or on several different occasions.

If the *Iliad* and the *Odyssey* were produced by a man or by two men trained in the tradition of the oral poets, the Homeric Question is not to the point. A man so trained naturally composed a large story by using a number of smaller traditional stories, and it is not surprising that the joints are discernible here and there. For example, the story of Odysseus's relations with the princess Nausicaa sounds like the story of a princess who would have none of her suitors, then lost her heart to a dashing stranger shipwrecked on the coast of the kingdom. The natural end of the story could not be used, for Odysseus was going home to his wife, but the first part of it serves very well for his arrival in the kingdom of Phaeacia, where he told the long and fascinating tale of his adventures, after which a Phaeacian ship took him home to Ithaca. Any awkwardness of this sort in the structure weighs nothing against the great unities of either poem—the fine basic structure that discloses itself to examination, the unity of tone, the unity of characterization of the major figures. The poems, with their manifold excellences, would be within the powers of a very great practitioner in the tradition of the oral poets.

How did Homer's poetry come to written form? Probably it was dictated, for it seems that the Greeks were beginning to write in an adaptation of the Phoenician alphabet at about the time when Homer was active (the use of Linear B did not survive the troubles of the late twelfth century). Scholars have persuaded the modern south Slavic oral poets to present their best songs slowly so that they can be written down or recorded on tape. The singers have generally felt that the version of the song produced this way is superior to what they do when they sing at normal speed to an audience.

The activity of the oral poets for many generations before Homer will explain why works of such excellence as the *Iliad* and the *Odyssey* appeared at the very beginning of Greek literature. They were not produced from nothing by a miracle. Homer inherited the results of the careful practices and performances that had gone on for probably three or four hundred years.

Homer as Evidence

The two poems must contain some elements of fact from the Bronze Age during which Troy was destroyed, from the Early Iron Age during which the civilization of Greece was quiescent, and from the beginnings of the new age of Greece in which Homer lived. It seems very likely that a great assault on Troy did take place and that the great men of this event and of others mentioned by the way are known to us by their right names, since a people so interested in genealogies probably would not have accepted a tale with fictitious heroes in the first place, or at any time.

The catalogue of the Greek chiefs and their contingents fits the Mycenaean Age and no later age; apparently it was passed down in the same form through all the time between. Homer also knows (as do the

poets of the *Epic Cycle*) many stories of great and grim events from all
the Mycenaean centers. The stories of Oedipus the Theban, the stories of
Hercules, which have Tiryns as a center, the basing of the legend of the
Argonauts at Orchomenus, and the great stories of Mycenae itself suggest
that all the great and lasting tales arose in Mycenaean times. There is no
reliable evidence as to when the race of oral poets arose; the Mycenaean
society may well have enjoyed such entertainments. Many traits of the
poems suggest that the poetic tradition must have arisen at least soon
after the fall of Mycenae; we shall remember, of course, that information
was also preserved by the prose tradition.

The most striking evidence for discontinuity in the tradition is the fact
that Homer knew nothing of the complicated arrangements disclosed to
us by the finds of Linear B tablets at Pylos and at Mycenae which com-
plement the evidence of excavation. In spite of one or two facts about
weapons that would fit the weapons of the earlier age as archaeology has
shown them to us, Homer's weapons are often wrongly described. He gets
mixed up between throwing spears and the thrusting spears of the earlier
age and, most of all, he does not understand how chariots are used in
warfare; for him the chariot is something like a sports car in which one
might drive to the polo field to play.

Homer is unimpeachable evidence for one fact far more important than
anything connected with the Mycenaean Age: he shows us what the
Greeks of his time, the later Greeks, and the Romans regarded as the true
stuff of life. Homer can hardly have learned through the tradition anything of the feelings of men in the Mycenaean Age or of their view of life
or of the structure of society; he gives us what to his own age and a few
generations before it, at least, must have seemed a true picture of the
hearts and minds of men and of their practices in the good old days.

Those good old days were a Heroic Age, that is, an age that glorified
the hero, or the leading man of warlike qualities. At the top of the society
was the king, either a great king like Agamemnon of Mycenae, or a minor
king like Odysseus, who was hardly more than the first among equals on
a remote and poor island. The power of the king was hereditary, but had
to be maintained by his own ability; Telemachus, son of Odysseus, was
recognized as rightful king, but amidst the general belief that his father
had perished on the way home from Troy the suitors of his mother hoped
that one of them could shoulder him aside, marry her, and make himself
king. Kingship, once gained, was not an assured and comfortable position,
and some of the most famous stories from the early days were about
struggles for royal power, for romantic love was not yet known as a
subject, and few other activities except warfare had much dramatic quality. Both the oral poets and the general tradition kept such stories alive
from generation to generation, and many of them were finally made im-

perishable by the Athenian writers of tragedy who reworked them to bring out their deeper significance.

Warfare was the best sphere for the assertion of royal leadership, although the disclosures of the Linear B tablets at Pylos and Mycenae suggest that in such a realm the brisk businessman might sit even more firmly on the throne than the mighty man of muscle. The routine problems of government that are dealt with by the administrators of a modern state hardly existed in so simple and highly traditional a society. Even the administration of justice hardly existed, for the rise of problems of justice was prevented by the weight of tradition, or those that did arise were dealt with by the heads of families, clans, or in extreme cases, by a meeting of all the men who could bear arms.

The nobles were below the king and were linked to him by bonds of mutual obligation something like those that existed during the Middle Ages in France and England. Naturally the duty to support the king in war was most important. Both the king and the nobles had land, which was the chief source of wealth. There was a real gap between the landowning king and nobles and those who had no land or had only tiny subsistence plots. It was not possible to make money and buy land with it. There was free land available in many places to which a group of people could go as a community, fully organized with government and gods. The Ionian Greeks who crossed to Asia Minor and found new land did so in this manner, as did the Greeks of another great colonizing movement in the eighth and seventh centuries. Probably very few Greeks ever even thought of separating themselves from their communities to go out alone and face both the dangers and the isolation of starting a new frontier farm.

Indeed the ordinary man probably never thought of going anywhere, for he was one of the members of an estate, or *oikos* (a "manor" in later times), which was an economic and social unit where everyone worked, was supported by the products, and had his place, whether he was the pig man, like the admirable Eumaeus of the *Odyssey,* or the carpenter, smith, or the head of the organization. In ordinary times there was nowhere else for a member of an *oikos* to go to or to visit. Perhaps a very few workmen were itinerant, like smiths, but generally a fair-sized estate would have men to do all the skilled work. It is tempting to conjecture that the oral poets, with their peculiar skill, were the first workmen regularly to move about freely and offer their services here and there.

Probably the slaves were mostly women, because in warfare the men of the losing side were likely to be butchered. There was plenty of work for everyone to do, and the children that the women bore were useful and could be second-class citizens without bearing a painful stigma because of their illegitimacy. The slave had to work hard, as did the free

people, but could count on food, clothing, and shelter and the same treatment that would be given to a free person of humble status. The real
unfortunates were often the *thetes,* free men who had no land or only
a tiny plot and could have no economic security nor sense of belonging as
all the members of an *oikos* could.

This was a closed society, one which worked by tradition and authority.
Groups like the *oikos* and the family grouping were the important rallying points for loyalties and the important sources of status. Such connections mattered in regard to status and loyalty to a degree that we can
hardly imagine nowadays. The authority of the group also determined and
restrained the actions of the individual member to a degree that is strange
to us. It may well be that the ordinary man, unlike us, did not think
of himself as an individual with highly personal aims and preferences
and problems. Likewise the individual had no doubts and probably even
no thoughts as to where he belonged in society; also he had neither doubts
nor thoughts about his code of behavior, which he had acquired without
realizing that he was doing so. Later we shall describe the process of the
loosening of these social bonds and the growth of individualism. Some of
the best things in later Greek literature came from the attempts of the
Greeks to work out a rational way of living in the open society to replace the traditional way that had prevailed in the earlier closed society.

Religion in Homer

Homer practically ignores the chthonic gods—the gods of the earth
—which were worshiped by the simpler people. Such worship is bound to
be much concerned with fertility on the one hand and with the uncanny,
monstrous, and formidable powers of the underworld on the other hand.
There was a real division in Greece between the worship of the chthonic
powers and the worship of the other gods who have come to be known
as the Olympians because Homer placed their home and their councils
on Mount Olympus.

Zeus and his entourage had come to power by hard fighting against
earlier divinities who were gross and crude. The struggle is rarely mentioned in Homer; his emphasis is on the refinement and excellence of
the gods who now reigned. Zeus presided over a court of mighty gods
who recognized his superiority in power. They had their alliances, intrigues, loyalties, jealousies, and love affairs. Although they lost their
power to inspire fear or awe even in Greek times, these gods did not lose
their power to inspire the literary man and the plastic artist, and they
have not yet lost it. Zeus was the king of the gods; Hera was his wife,
one of whose chief activities was resenting his amorous adventures. His
younger brother Poseidon ruled the sea, and Pluto or Hades, another

brother, ruled the underworld. Pallas Athena, patroness of Athens and of all the civilized arts, was the virgin goddess who sprang from the forehead of Zeus. Aphrodite, the goddess of love, was known to every ancient people under some name, for she symbolized all the forces of attraction and union in human affairs. Ares, the god of war, was the symbol of the opposite tendency, that of strife and opposition. Homer represents Ares and Aphrodite as lovers, a natural piece of symbolism.

Apollo, in the first book of the *Iliad*, rained his disease-bringing arrows on the Greeks for their insult to his priest. He was god of medicine. Later he became very important through his oracle at Delphi, which stood for everything wholesome and elevated in religion. He was also god of the sun; his twin sister Artemis was the moon goddess and in later ages was known as a virgin goddess who loved the forest and the hunt. Hermes was the messenger of the gods; it was he who journeyed to Calypso's island with the unwelcome message that she must let Odysseus return to the world of men. Hestia was the goddess of the hearth, the center of the home. Demeter represented the earth and its fruits. Last came the grubby god Hephaestus, the smith, whose skill at the forge was truly godlike, but who looked like a workman. It is not clear why he should have been the husband of Aphrodite, the symbol of every man's desire.

Zeus was not a just god; he sent the good or the bad to man as suited his notion of the moment. We shall see that in the Classical Age of Greece the idea of Zeus was refined somewhat, a process that is often referred to as "the moral education of Zeus." Men did not revere, worship, or love the gods, but made offerings to them as one might send off dues to some remote feudal lord, hoping for nothing so much in return as to be left strictly alone. There was no sense of sin; one might sin against the unspoken code of his group, but not against the gods. If he swore falsely by a god, this was an injury to the god for which he might well be forced to make amends.

The Influence of Homer

Homer is the fountainhead of European literature. He has inspired authors from his own time to this, beside being in the popular consciousness all that time. If there is any one secret to his influence, it is that his vision of life has given satisfaction to generation after generation. His narrative skill, the charm of his language, the richness of his meters add to his appeal, but the essence of his greatness is that his characters and their relation to one another appeal to all generations as a satisfactory statement of human life (although in both ancient and modern times there have been short periods of reaction). That the Greeks of Homer's own time found his view of life satisfying is a fact about them worth recording. The later Greeks and the Romans had an equally high opinion of him. Even the dissent is significant. If the Greek philosophers wished to argue a new view of the powers of the universe, they said that the Homeric point of view—not merely general opinion—was wrong. The Athenian Plato, who wished to construct a carefully controlled society, stated emphatically and specifically that there would be no place in it for Homer or other poets of his kind.

CHAPTER

6

THE NEW AGE OF GREECE;
800 TO 500 B.C.

Up From the Dark Age

We do not know why life among the Greeks became somewhat livelier around 800 B.C., after about three hundred years in which they had lived rather quietly and had not regained the intensity of the My-cenaean Age that had been ended by the Dorian invasions. The evidence of renewed vitality is archaeological and scanty: the Greeks seem to have started to do more trading among themselves and with Phoenicia, Palestine, and Egypt, and their pottery and other possessions improved in quality.

The contact by sea with the old world of the Near East and Egypt involved Cyprus (which had kept up its old culture better than other Greek places), Rhodes, Crete, and southern Greece, and the merchants of these places set up a trading station at a place now called Al Mina at the mouth of the Orontes River in Syria and took pottery there to offer in exchange for textiles, jewelry, and articles of ivory and bronze. The lively colors and patterns of Near Eastern decoration freed the Greek potters from their austere tradition of geometric decoration. The archaeologist finds traces of this new influence first in Crete, then in Corinth and Laconia (the Spartan territory in the Peloponnesus, or southern part of Greece), then in Athens, and finally among the Ionians of Asia Minor.

The Ionians, who had migrated to Asia Minor in the tenth century and established themselves on the coast, were late in being stirred to new life. By 700 B.C. their merchants were trading in Cyprus and northern

Syria, yet it was not until about 650 that they made one of those sudden surges such as we saw on the Greek mainland around 1500 B.C., appropriated the techniques that many other Greeks had known for well over a century, and took the lead among the Greeks in both artistic and intellectual life.

The Greeks probably thought of themselves as a recognizable group well before 800 B.C.; they knew that some people were Greeks and others were not. This feeling depended partly on the fact that the dialects of Greek were mutually intelligible; probably the difference was no greater than that between the speech of Maine and of Georgia a hundred years ago. Beside the unity of blood and language there was substantial unity of religion. The Greeks worshiped the same gods, even though different gods were favored in different places, and some after the beginning of the new age this unity was heightened by the institution of the Olympic Games in honor of Zeus and the rise of the influence of the Delphic Oracle, the oracle of the god Apollo at Delphi, just above the Corinthian Gulf. The games were believed to have been founded in 776 B.C.; not very long afterward the Pythian Games were instituted at Delphi, the Isthmian at Corinth, and the Nemaean at Argos. The Olympics came every fourth year, as the modern ones do, and the others were rotated so that every summer there was one of these great meetings of people from all over the Greek world. The Delphic Oracle also became an institution for all the Greeks and was consulted by foreigners, too, as we have seen.

The beginning of writing among the Greeks (of course, the use of Linear B for keeping records had long been forgotten) was an important factor in the slow raising of the cultural level among the Greeks in general. The Phoenician alphabet began to be used for the writing of Greek about 800 B.C. If certain letters were added—*phi* (ph), *chi* (ch), *psi* (ps), and *xi* (x)—which were not needed in Phoenician, since there were no such sounds, the alphabet was adequate for Greek, and within a century it was established among all the Greeks. Alphabetic writing is far easier to master than cuneiform, for example, and can be used by people in general rather than only by professional scribes, with the result that the use of writing for the keeping of records and for other purposes became fairly common.

Another important feature of the new age, but not a borrowing from other people, was the beginning of what is known as the polis, or city-state. These poleis (the plural of polis) were genuine cities and were also sovereign states of very modest size, sometimes incredibly tiny by our standards. Historians have generally spoken of them as city-states; lately the useful custom has grown up of using the word polis without translating it.

COLONIZATION

The great movement of colonization began around 750 B.C. and continued actively until after 650. The migrations of the age before, especially that of the Ionians to Asia Minor, may be regarded as the first Greek colonizing movement. This was the second; the third was to the kingdoms of the successors of Alexander the Great in Egypt and the Near East, and the fourth was to the Roman West. Obviously Greece could readily become overcrowded, since it was neither large nor fertile, but in attempting to explain these great migrations we should give due weight also to the factor of the new opportunities that became evident abroad.

Neither individuals nor very small groups of people went out to colonize under their own auspices, as so many did in the early days of the United States. The Greek colonists went as communities, ready to set themselves up in working order. The project was always under the auspices of some polis, which was called the metropolis, or mother city. The colony generally retained a sentimental tie, but little more, with the founding city.

At the outset an *oecist,* or founder, was chosen to be in charge. He generally went to Delphi to ask the oracle about the religious life of the new community and generally got a rather conventional answer that the worship should be of Apollo and the greater Olympian gods. He might also get a suggestion as to where the colony should be, for the priests of Apollo were great collectors of information from their visitors and were as well informed as any chancellery about the affairs of the Mediterranean world. The *oecist* would also have information from the reports of merchants about sites offering agricultural or commercial advantages and having a reasonable climate and neighbors who, if not disposed to be friendly, would not be too powerful. We may suppose that by 750 Greek merchants traveled all over the Mediterranean, even in the West where the Carthaginians were trying to maintain a closed sea. We may also suppose that the colonists often had to fight, wherever they went, and that they did so with resolution and skill and with no little profit from the experience that many Greeks had had as mercenaries in the service of the kings farther east, where they had learned both formation fighting and the use of wrought steel weapons and armor.

Although no detail on the gathering and dispatching of colonists has been preserved, it is plain that some cities acted as agents for the founding of colonies. Megara, a commercial city at the northern end of the Isthmus of Corinth, sent out many colonies. Her reason surely was not overpopulation, but the serving of her own commercial interest by gathering groups of people to go out and exploit opportunities or create opportunities. Miletus, another active commercial city, also sent out many colonies and presumably for the same purpose.

The Range of Colonization: The East

Let us begin with the colonies at the eastern end of the Greek world even though they were not the first. As we have seen, the Ionians were slow in joining the more active style of Greek life after 800 B.C., and it was only after 700 B.C. that they joined the colonizing movement, and then for a long time their efforts to extend their territories inland had no success. Their first colonies seem to have been founded with the idea of getting more agricultural territory rather than more trade. They began by trying to establish agricultural colonies in eastern Thrace (now Turkey in Europe) and in the Propontis (now the Gallipoli Peninsula).

Only three colonies succeeded in Thrace. One, Abdera, was twice wiped out by its neighbors, but was successful when the whole people of Teus packed up and went there in 547 B.C. to escape the victorious Persians, just as the people of Phocaea went to the West. During the rest of antiquity Thrace was to be a strategic region of considerable natural wealth, not a place of cultural activity. Its good soil, its timber, its minerals, and its location made it an object of interest to the Persians, who made it a part of their empire in the late 500s. Later the Macedonian king, Philip II, saw its value when he was trying to build up his own weak country in the fourth century B.C. and went to some pains to acquire and hold it. Under the Romans it was of great strategic importance as part of the land route between West and East and produced men along with its other products.

Colonies were founded by the Ionians on both the north and the south shores of the Propontis, both as agricultural communities and as way stations for the Black Sea trade. Trade with the Black Sea was difficult because of the difficulty of getting through the Bosporus, the strait through which one finally enters the Black Sea after going through the Dardanelles and the Sea of Marmora and past Istanbul, the modern city on the site of Byzantium. During the sailing season the ship heading for the Black Sea would have to sail into the prevailing northwest winds and in addition fight the current coming from the Black Sea through the strait. But the sailors of the Ionian city of Miletus discovered that in the spring one could catch southwesterly winds, that a good skipper might learn to use more favorable currents near the shore, and that at night in the summer one might even get a favorable wind. Thus new opportunities were created by energy and enterprise.

The Black Sea region was a magnificent source of raw materials. There was some gold. From inner Asia, south of the Black Sea coast, came wrought steel. Flax and hemp were both produced. The waters were rich in fish. Timber was available. Perhaps the prize product was the cereal yield of the lands on the north shore, what is now southern Russia.

Many of the cities founded by the Ionian Greeks prospered here, but none became famous or produced a famous man unless he went to Greece and became famous there. They rubbed elbows with people who often were rough and wild, they took on sometimes the rough ways of the frontier, but it would be a mistake to shape our ideas of the Greeks so narrowly on the Athenian—and, it sometimes seems, a somewhat idealized and ethereal Athenian, too—as to assert that these energetic people were not typical Greeks. There is room for a great deal of variety and inconsistency among the Greeks of different places and different centuries whom we shall discuss.

Eretria and Chalcis in Euboea specialized in the colonizing of the three-pronged peninsula of Chalcidice and the region around it in western Thrace; their cities were only on the coast and had little hold on any territory inland. Another colony that may be regarded as being in the eastern Mediterranean was Cyrene, in North Africa, in that well watered and fertile coastal section between Egypt and Tripolitania that is still known as Cyrenaica. The people of Cyrene were noted for their addiction to pleasure, which was possible in a land noted for its grain, its wine, its roses, its horses, and a peculiar plant called *silphium*, which has been equated with asafetida and was in demand for seasoning and medicinal purposes; it is beautifully portrayed on the coins of Cyrene.

Obviously it was generally not possible to found colonies in the old established countries. Greek traders were invited to organize the commercial colony of Naucratis, in Egypt, however, and the one at Al Mina on the Orontes, known then as Poseidium. There was a goodly number of reasons for colonies; beside those reasons we have already mentioned, some colonies were sent out with the simple purpose of practicing piracy from a base on shore, and others were as frankly sent out to rid a polis of perhaps a tenth of its citizens whom the majority regarded as undesirable.

The Range of Colonization: The West

Corinth led in Western colonization. Her position on her isthmus gave her a great advantage in trade, for she could ship or receive goods either at her harbor on the eastern side of the isthmus for the Aegaean trade or at her other harbor three miles away on the western side of the isthmus for the trade to the West. Sending goods through the Gulf of Corinth was advantageous in two ways: it was a short route to western Greece, southern Italy, and Sicily, and it avoided the difficult and dangerous rounding of Cape Malea, the southern tip of Greece. It was well worth while to have the goods carted across the Isthmus of Corinth to another ship.

Corinth had colonies on the west coast of Greece, the chief of which was Corcyra. Her most important colony, however, was Syracuse, founded in 735, where the fine harbor and the rich Sicilian hinterland made an excellent combination. The colonial foundations in Italy avoided the coast closer to Greece, the east coast, which is made inhospitable by the fact that the central mountains of Italy come much nearer to the sea here than in the West. Cities were founded on the coast at the bottom of Italy and on the western coast up as far as the north shore of the Bay of Naples.

Sicily and southern Italy may be called the "America of Greece," the richer and more open place in the West where the Greeks went in search of new opportunities. Because there was no new nation there to claim their allegiance, they remained Greeks in thought and feeling and were regarded as still eligible to compete in the Olympic Games, which were open only to Greeks.

Acragas in Sicily and Poseidonia in Italy are two Greek cities of the West whose remains are still admired. Acragas (called Agrigentum by the Romans) was on the southern coast. We hear of the luxury of its citizens, their artificial lake, and their enjoyment of their festivals. They built temples that would be large by any standard and are surprising as the products of a city of this size; their remains are a great attraction for tourists in Sicily. Poseidonia was on the west coast of Italy, some sixty miles south of Naples. The great temples that attract modern tourists to this site were built in the fifth century B.C., a little earlier than the Parthenon at Athens, and show all the refinements such as the subtle curves to correct optical illusions that are so admired in the Parthenon. Like Acragas, Poseidonia has a Roman name: Paestum.

The most civilized peoples whom the Greeks met in the West were the Carthaginians and the Etruscans. The former had trading stations in western Sicily. The Etruscans were established on the coast of western Italy above Rome; we shall discuss later the interesting question of their origin. Both these peoples taught the Greeks a few things of no great importance. The Greeks taught the Carthaginians little; much Greek ware has been found at Carthage, for example, but it seems to have done nothing to refine the local product. On the other hand, the Etruscans took from the Greeks many details of the manufacture of pottery and of metal wares, as well as some more abstract ideas. Because they controlled the city of Rome, the Etruscans were the first great teachers of the Romans, and their indirect Greek influence on the Romans came earlier than the direct Greek influence from south Italy and Sicily. The long-term result was the combined Greco-Roman culture that has formed a most important part of the modern culture of Europe and the United States. But we must return to the Greeks themselves during the period of colonization.

The Phocaeans had the honor of going farthest west. In about 600 B.C. they worked up a route to Tartessus, in Spain, where silver and tin were to be had, and used packs of *penteconters,* or fifty-oared warships, which even the Phoenicians might shrink from attacking. Such ships, on the other hand, could not carry a heavy load and could be used only on a run where precious metals formed a cargo that was valuable without being bulky. The Phocaeans planted colonies along their route—on the island of Ischia near Naples, in the Balearic Islands near Spain, and on the east coast of Spain—where their ships could refit and provision. They founded Massilia, the modern Marseilles, through which a steady stream of Greek influence was to go to the people of Gaul, the modern France. When in the middle of the sixth century they left their home on the coast of Asia Minor to avoid the rule of the Persians, the Phocaeans went to Corsica, which was so good a place that the Carthaginians and Etruscans felt that they must combine to drive the Phocaeans out of it. The Phocaeans finally yielded in the late 500s to their joint aggression by moving to the mainland below Naples.

The Carthaginians pressed their attacks on the Greek colonies until the situation evolved that essentially was to endure until the Romans became masters of the West. By 500 B.C. Carthage controlled the Strait of Gibraltar and the metal trade from Spain, the whole coast of North Africa from Cyrene to Morocco, the Balearic Islands, Sardinia and Corsica, and the western end of Sicily. The Greeks controlled the coasts of South Italy, a large part of Sicily, and the northern shores of the Mediterranean of eastern Spain, France, and the Italian Riviera.

The Effects of Colonization

It seems, although it cannot be proved, that the movement of colonization must have greatly increased the total number of the Greeks. The removal of many people to lands that were far more fertile than the old and the removal of others to fine sites for commerce, combined with the new and energetic spirit of the time, would logically promote a growth in numbers.

The colonizing movement must also have promoted changes in the social alignment of the Greeks. Many an energetic man must have found himself a weightier member of the community than he had been as the third son of a poor farmer at home. Many shrewd people must have improved their status by making their way into the lively new industry and trade instead of remaining in marginal agriculture. We must remember that the well-to-do as well as the poor could perceive and seize the new opportunities.

The new distribution of the Greek people endured for several centuries. When the brilliant culture of Athens is described in some of the following chapters, or the struggles of Athens with Sparta, we shall do well to remember that at that same time other Greeks were going their own way all over the Mediterranean world without doing anything distinctive enough to be mentioned. Nevertheless, if these Greeks never achieved the intensity of Athenian life, they spread to other people at scores of points something of a culture that these people would otherwise not have known.

COMMERCE AND INDUSTRY

The early Greek ships were small and capable of being drawn up on shore. They were rigged with a single square sail and had oars for use at certain times, as in rounding difficult headlands, where a little auxiliary power would be of great use. Early in our period—probably by 800 B.C.— some ships were made into warships by being fitted with bronze rams at the water line. Naturally the builders of warships, led by those of Corinth, learned to design slimmer and faster ships that also carried more oarsmen for motive power. In the most advanced design there were three banks of oarsmen. One would sit with his legs almost touching the back of the man just before and below him; the head of the man in the middle row would be about on the level of the stomach of the man in the top row, and the man in the bottom row would be in the same relative position. The upper men pulled slightly longer oars. The men were highly trained to get the ship into position, to deliver a crisp blow with the ram on the side of another ship, then back off to clear the ram.

Miletus was probably the greatest of the Greek commercial cities at the eastern end of the Mediterranean, although Phocaea and the island cities of Samos and Chios were close behind her. Many communities were famous for special products, like the woolen products of Miletus and the wine of Chios. Miletus was strong in the Black Sea trade where many of the colonies were of her founding. The agents of Milesian firms may well have been given preference in buying cargoes of the steel, wheat, fish, furs, timber, flax, and hemp produced in the colonies.

From the middle 600s on, Egypt was receptive to Greek merchants and used Greek mercenary soldiers; the Assyrians had used Greek mercenaries even earlier. The services sold by the mercenaries should not be overlooked when we consider Greek trade. Some left their bones on foreign fields, to be sure, but others returned with fortunes made from their generous pay and their booty and with many ideas gained in the older lands.

Corinth was probably more powerful and wealthy even than Miletus. Trade tended to come to the Isthmus of Corinth, whether it came from the East across the Aegaean or from the West and through the Gulf of Corinth. The traffic between east and west was so lively that it finally seemed worth the expense to make a ship railroad across the Isthmus to link the two harbors. It was about three miles long and was paved with marble slabs in which grooves had been cut. The ships were drawn out of the water in a wheeled cradle and were hauled along this road by oxen.

Corinthian shipwrights gained a great reputation for merchant ships and ships of war, which led to a lively business in building both for other cities. Her merchants profited from being at the crossing of the water route from east to west and a land route that went south into Laconia and north into central Greece either by land or first through the Gulf of Corinth to the north shore of the gulf and then by land. The chief manufacture of Corinth was a fine pottery of what is known as the orientalizing style, the more lively style that under Eastern influence replaced the more austere Geometric after about 750 B.C. This pottery was very popular everywhere and often was sold as a container already filled with another product. Perfume from the East, for example, packaged in such containers, must have been very popular in the West. Corinthian bronze work, especially armor, was acceptable everywhere.

Toward 550 B.C. the pottery of Athens became far more important in trade than before and was sent almost everywhere that Greek trade went, even to the places where Corinthian ware had formerly dominated. Many beautiful Athenian pieces of every type are found in the museums of Italy that display the finds from Etruscan sites. Since the Etruscans controlled iron deposits on the mainland of Italy and on the island of Elba and were good smiths, they probably paid for their imports from Athens in iron or wrought steel.

Many other cities prospered on the lively trade around the Isthmus of Corinth. The island of Aegina, just below Athens, was prosperous and important. Megara, on the Isthmus, prospered, but was well behind Corinth. Sicyon, on the southern coast of the Gulf of Corinth, also prospered.

Corcyra was the chief of the colonies on the west side of Greece, dominating with her island city the trade that went up the Adriatic Sea to a region inhabited by intractable people with whom it was possible to trade if precautions were taken, but who remained outside civilization. Syracuse was undoubtedly the greatest colony in the West. Goods carried there would often be redistributed, going to other cities of Sicily, up the west coast of Italy to the Greek cities and to the Etruscans farther north, or even southward to Carthage, Massilia had no near rivals for the trade with the rich territory of Gaul.

Among the ideas and cultural traits that came to the Greeks along with new goods and new processes in this age of increased intercourse between peoples, the use of the alphabet and the use of coinage were very important. As we have seen, the alphabet spread rapidly and was passed on to other peoples, including eventually ourselves. The use of coinage, as was said, began with the Lydian kings and spread from Lydia to the Ionian cities. Miletus and Ephesus were very active in coining, producing handsome coins of electrum, a natural mixture of gold and silver found in

Lydia. Two other systems of Greek coinage soon joined the Ionian. Aegina showed its enterprising spirit and its commercial importance by devising a system of silver coinage that became known as the Aeginetan standard and was used in Athens for some time, in Megara, in the Peloponnesus, and in some of the southern and eastern islands as far away as Rhodes. The third system, the Euboic, began in Euboea and had Corinth as its most influential user. In 593 Athens changed from the Aeginetan system to the Euboic. The development of the silver mines of Spain facilitated the wide use of silver coinage. Croesus of Lydia minted some coins of pure gold; the Persians followed with a famous gold coin, the daric, and much later Philip II of Macedon minted very beautiful gold coins, the first gold coinage of Europe; however, gold coinage remained rare.

Naturally the introduction of coinage, beside facilitating the exchange of goods in intercity trade, could intensify the social effect in a city by its having some trade along with the former static agricultural economy. A certain amount of intercity trade by barter would probably have little effect in stratifying the population, whereas the introduction of trade by money would create a monied class sharply separated from those who had no money or could not learn readily to manipulate money. The Cretans and the Spartans and the Byzantines resisted the introduction of coinage, being conservative people who were worried by the social changes that they could see going on in other cities and perhaps beginning in their own.

THE RISE OF THE POLIS

Another important feature of this age among the Greeks, but not a borrowing from other people, was the rise of the polis, or city-state. The Ionians of Asia Minor had rid themselves of their kings by 800 B.C. and had partly replaced their attachment to their tribes and clans by loyalty to a state, which had a visible center with temples, other buildings, and ceremonies which served the purposes of the state. The kings apparently lost their positions all over the Hellenic world, but not violently; their heads did not roll. Instead of being first among equals, the king now became one nobleman among equals. Sometimes he retained the hereditary position of high priest because the king had traditionally dealt with the gods on behalf of the people.

The Dorians who had conquered Crete and the Peloponnesus during the Dorian invasion also discarded their kings and organized themselves into poleis, but generally without much of a visible center or a citadel. Their unity was clearly functional, for they had subject populations to hold down. If a group of villages combined into a polis, the move combined the forces of the dominant Dorians into groups strong enough to assure their control of the people whom they had subjected. The essence of the new Dorian polis was that it could produce a body of men trained and toughened in the practice of arms and raised in the tradition of an aristocracy that expected to maintain its privileged position by force whenever need arose.

Sparta was, of course, the most important Dorian polis. The kingship did not disappear there, changing instead into a double kingship. The Athenian historian Thucydides was to remark at the end of the fifth century that no one in some later time, seeing the ruins of Sparta as he knew it, would think them appropriate to the power of the Sparta of his time. Five villages were combined into the polis, as if it were in the state of Maine and the township of Sparta contained the towns of North Sparta, East Sparta, Sparta Falls, Sparta Corners, and Sparta Center.

Like the Spartans, the Corinthians were Dorians, but theirs was to be the greatest commercial city in Greece during most of this period and therefore had a busy and built-up focus.

Athens will serve as the type of polis that had a good citadel. We do not know precisely how the people of Attica, which had a thousand square miles and many small centers of population, came to make a center of their territory around the Acropolis of Athens, nor how the people of many other poleis did, although the main outlines of such a development must be always the same.

The Aristocracy

The life of the Greek and Roman world was dominated by the aristocracies, in spite of the fact that the democracy of Athens is in the foreground of much recent writing. If, in fact, we look at the whole course of history up to modern times, the occasional appearance of democracies may seem to be no more than an interesting eccentricity.

In the period from 800 to 500 B.C. the aristocrats gained in power, wealth, and spirit at the expense of both the kings and the common people. It was they rather than the common people who could force the king to retire to the position of merely another aristocrat and the leader of one clan. In many cases an official was chosen to hold the title of king and take charge of sacrifices and of relations with the gods in general, often for one year at a time, although at the beginning it might be for life or for ten years.

In a number of places there is evidence that the aristocrats chose some of the older men to sit on a council. They were likely to be past military age, which might mean either forty-five or sixty, to be chosen for life, which meant that vacancies came from deaths, and to be accountable to no one for their acts in office. There is also evidence that there were magistrates to preside over the rudimentary business of the polis, sometimes for a term of one year and sometimes for ten. These men were likely to be held accountable, that is, they had to undergo a formal review of their acts at the end of their term of office and answer for what they had done. They were, of course, aristocrats chosen by their peers, not by the people at large.

If this is a dim and faraway beginning of what we think of as democracy, it still is a beginning. For a fairly tight group of aristocrats to elect one of their number every year to be chairman and handle routine business in a simple polis was a new idea. Presently there was to be a group of such officers with more work to do, and the time was to come, at least in Athens and in some other poleis, when a large number of citizens were to have a voice in the choice of officers, and it can be said that there were democratic elections.

The Bacchiadae of Corinth are said to have ousted the king in 747 B.C. and ruled as a clan for ninety years. Earlier there had been a notable king of Corinth named Bacchis, and the Bacchiadae were the clan who claimed descent from him. It has been estimated that there were over two hundred men more than fifty years old in the clan. Because no firm rule of succession among the descendants of the king had been worked out, there were struggles among those who claimed to be in the proper relation to succeed to the throne, leading at least once to murder and usurpation. Finally the whole clan took control of the situation. They deposed the men who then claimed kingship, made a formal council the chief body, began to elect one of their number each year as magistrate to preside and made him eponymous (that is, the year was named for him), and occasionally called an assembly of those who could fight in the armed forces to inform them of matters that needed to be widely known or to ask for their ratification of some proposal for action. We may assume that by 747 Corinth was well into the new surge of commerce and that the chief people were resolved not to be interfered with either by useless struggles for power or by any king who did not understand that the times were changing or who might try to pre-empt for himself all the profit from the new opportunities. Other poleis, too, were dominated by one clan rather than by the whole aristocracy. The Aleuadae dominated Larissa in the rich plains of Thessaly; the Penthilidae controlled the city of Mitylene on the island of Lesbos in the Aegaean; the Neleidae were the chief clan of Miletus; the Alcmaeonidae were the most important clan of Athens. All these names end in -dae, a patronymic, or word ending meaning "the children of" or "the descendants of." It was common practice for clans to group themselves, as the Bacchiadae did, around the memory of a distinguished earlier member by calling themselves his descendants.

The aristocracy gained in wealth and power during the period of colonial enterprises and rising industry and commerce. The better land at home was generally in their hands, and they were best able to find resources for trading ventures. They organized and led the new colonies that gave new opportunities to the common man as well. As time went on the new state of things slowly gave rise to a considerable group of able men who had gained some property and who wished to be heard in matters of government and resented the assumption of the aristocracy that government was their prerogative. In the early part of our period, however, the aristocracy led and managed and were able often to encroach on the land of the ordinary man. We shall see that around 600 B.C. in Athens the misery and resentment of the common people was such that there was fear of revolution.

The aristocrats could also base their power on their claim to be the repositories of all knowledge of how to deal with the gods. No one would have thought, at least in the early part of our period, of challenging the necessity and efficacy of the customary addresses and gifts to the gods, and the idea that it had to be done in certain ways that not everyone would know seemed natural. The aristocrats could also claim a monopoly of the rudimentary courts, for the polis had not as yet taken over the administration of justice. The poet Hesiod, whom we shall discuss later, complained bitterly of the rapacity and venality of those who sat to arbitrate the claims of others. There was at first no written law.

Early Law Codes

The formulation and publication of the early law codes was not caused, as we might suppose, by the demands of the ordinary man that the laws be codified and published so that the aristocracy could not manipulate them for its own advantage, but rather to protect the interests of the whole polis, in which the aristocracy played a very important part. Zaleucus of Locris, a rich colony in southern Italy, is said to have published the first of the Greek law codes in 663 B.C. and to have based his code largely on the customary rules of Crete, Sparta, and Athens.

Vengeance for murder and other deeds of violence had been the duty of the clan and had, of course, given rise to feuds. Now Zaleucus and legislators in other places declared that the polis would protect its interests, especially its interest in avoiding repeated religious pollution by bloodshed, by acting against the guilty party. Undoubtedly some of the old-fashioned people saw this change as an unwarranted intrusion of the government into what were essentially the private affairs of citizens and clans.

Another object of the legislators was to protect the noble families, who to them were the essence of the polis, by protecting their estates. The alienation of the estate, already tacitly forbidden, was specifically forbidden in the code. The Greek lawgivers also provided that a man without sons might adopt sons, and they threw safeguards around heiresses so that their property might not be lost for want of a protecting man. Because civil rights depended on property, the loss of an estate, beside weakening that family group, cost the chief of the family his citizenship and thereby cost the polis a citizen.

A third object of the legislators was the one that to us seems most natural and important, that of establishing courts other than those courts of arbitration (if they can be called courts) that were generally held informally by the nobles. To bring disputes before the magistrate who presided over the whole polis or in some cases to bring them to the council or the assembly of all full citizens might insure fairer settlements for the aristocrat as well as for the common man and prevent the rise of resentments that might prove hard to control.

A generation or so after Zaleucus, one Charondas drew up a code for Catania, in Sicily, which resembled that of Zaleucus. He framed his code in verse for ready memorization, and it was widely copied throughout the Greek world. These codes were far simpler than those of Mesopotamia, which were published a thousand years earlier. Not all peoples desired such complex and specific bodies of law. The Egyptians, who must have known the Mesopotamian codes, preferred to continue with their system of the dispensation of a customary and unpublished law under the control of the vizier. The Greeks were to develop laws rather than the law during the next few centuries, for this was one field in which their passion for analysis and system did not operate strongly. The Romans, who were the chief appropriators of Greek culture, adopted many Greek laws as part of a great legal system, which is one of their bequests to the modern world. There were other peoples who came in contact with the Greeks or Romans who still preferred to operate with only customary and unwritten law, as did the Scythians, or with very simple systems of law that were finally put into writing, as did the Germans.

The Physical Structure of the Polis

Some idea of the appearance of a typical polis at this stage is possible. Perhaps the territory around it consisted of fifty to a hundred square miles, although Athens had a thousand and many had less than fifty. Those outside Greece proper, which had been founded as colonies, naturally had more room. There was ordinarily a citadel, a high and defensible place with a water supply. Houses were tightly packed inside its defenses. Below the citadel was an open place for meetings, whether an assembly of the people, a market, or the informal gathering that is a necessary ingredient of life around the Mediterranean. Then, as the town grew, more houses were built in the lower town outside the defenses, and in time there might be a new wall enclosing much additional space. Houses and temples were likely to be of timber and mud brick in a style something like that of the modern house of timber and stucco.

THE TYRANTS

In the century from about 650 B.C. to about 550 B.C. many tyrants arose in all parts of the Greek world. The word is applied to a man who achieved sole power in his polis by illegal means, not by inheritance or by popular demand, as a proper king would. They all arose more or less at the same time, the late seventh and early sixth centuries. They were usually aristocrats; often they used high office as their means of becoming tyrants. None of them was able to establish an enduring monarchy, although in one or two cases the family stayed in power for a hundred years. Most frequently the sons of the tyrant lost power after a period of oppressive and unpopular rule.

The tyrants had in common the fact that they arose in cities of a commercial cast, where it was easier for factions to exist. Conversely, the places that never had tyrants were those, like Sparta, that were out of the stream of commercial life and had carefully planned aristocracies. The tyrants differed, however, in their reasons for aspiring to power and in the character of the support they commanded. Although some seem to have supported the desires of the common people, we should be cautious about supposing that any of them were genuine champions of the downtrodden. The chief tyrants of Greece in this period were those of Corinth, Sicyon, Megara, and Epidaurus. The slightly later tyranny of Peisistratus at Athens will be discussed later.

In Corinth the tyrant Cypselus seized power just before 650 B.C., using his position as commander of the army to drive out the ruling clan of the Bacchiadae. His son Periander was tyrant from about 627 to 586. While Periander maintained his own power with an iron hand, he did his best to encourage the general prosperity, partly because such a policy would lessen discontent with his rule and partly because he needed money to support his position. Like most of the tyrants, he improved the physical appearance of the city. He made rich offerings at Delphi and Olympia and instituted the Isthmian Games, which were among the most important, although they were never so brilliant as those at Olympia. The duties on trade gave him a considerable revenue. He cared for the security of the landowners by prohibiting the movement of people from the country to the city and for the common people by prohibiting the purchase of slaves, who would have furnished competition for the free poor man on the farm and in the shop. It was he who made the ship road across the Isthmus and he even spoke of cutting a canal. In his later years he became most odiously tyrannical in the modern sense of the word. An oligarchy followed the end of the tyranny when Periander's successor was murdered about 582.

Orthagoras became tyrant of Sicyon about 650 B.C. and founded a dynasty that lasted for a century. These tyrants, too, became oppressive to all, but like those of Corinth they encouraged trade, attracted competent artists, and built distinguished buildings to beautify their city. Cleisthenes, who ruled from about 600 to 570, was an oppressive and a brilliant ruler. He made a ruling that serfs could not even come into the city; the masses were to be kept down strictly. On the other hand, it was he who was chiefly responsible for attracting artists to Sicyon. After the Olympics of 576 he invited suitors for his daughter to come to Sicyon, where he spent a year entertaining them and assaying them. Finally he chose an Athenian, Megacles. Cleisthenes of Athens, a notable statesman, was the son of this marriage, and the great Pericles was a great-grandson.

If they sometimes confiscated the lands of aristocrats and gave them to landless men, the tyrants were trying not to help the masses, but to remove the power of their opponents by taking their land and bestowing it upon people who would thereby be made adherents of the tyrant, knowing that he could revoke the gift. Another method used by the tyrants to increase their own power and lessen that of their opponents was to force reorganization of tribes or other social units so as to break up old sentiments of solidarity and build up new sentiments more favorable to the regime. Still another was to replace old cults with the cults of new gods, with friends of the tyrant as priests and with observances and festivals that would support the popularity and influence of the regime.

CHAPTER

7

SPARTA AND ATHENS
IN THE NEW AGE

The Spartans were among the Dorians who moved into the Peloponnesus to end the Mycenaean Age, and while many others went on, this group remained there. At the outset their new polis was plagued with strife arising from the former rivalries of the tribes and clans and from the social and economic pretensions of some of the more powerful citizens. This situation was ameliorated by the reform attributed to Lycurgus, the first notable event in the history of the Spartan state and possibly the greatest event.

The reform of Lycurgus probably came between 825 and 800 B.C., although the evidence is contradictory and scholars have urged widely differing dates. We cannot even be sure that there was a man named Lycurgus who pushed through the reform. The essential thing is that somewhere in the earlier history of Sparta, before the days of her greatness and preparatory to them, there was made a new arrangement of her people and government that removed the old causes of internal strife.

The three old tribes found almost everywhere among the Dorians were superseded by five new tribes, one for each of the villages. The power of the clans was neutralized, as was that of the old tribes; they remained, but only as framework for the registry of citizens and for the performance of some religious duties, not as centers of loyalty or power. The two kings of the Spartans had chiefly the religious function in Sparta itself, but they were also the commanders of the army when it was in the field. They acted like true kings, however, in the administration of the territories that Sparta presently came to dominate in Laconia around her.

Presumably the heads of the kinship groups had been the counselors of the king. The reform now provided that the twenty-eight regular members of the council, of which the two kings were *ex officio* members, should be elected from the men over the age of sixty by vote of all the men who had achieved citizenship. They were to hold office for life. The council was generally called the Gerousia, or Council of Elders. This reform also helped to neutralize the power of the kinship groups, for the members of the Gerousia represented the whole people, and if any one of them felt his own kinship group to be highly important, he would be unlikely to find much support among the others for settling anything on such a basis.

The men who had full citizen rights—the Equals—made up the Assembly, which met at certain times to hear the proposals that had been framed for it by the Gerousia. Although the system had a strong democratic tinge as it concerned those who had full status, it was not democratic enough to allow the Assembly the initiative in legislation.

The polis had triumphed, too, in the fact that among the Equals there were no distinctions arising from the old racial division of the tribes and from kinship divisions of family and clan or from differences in economic status. Every man who could achieve the grade of Equal was to fight in the army and participate in the Assembly. No basis was left for struggles arising from racial, kinship, and economic groupings. Other poleis were stirred and riven by problems caused by these other loyalties and consequently found themselves in the hands of tyrants, but Sparta never had a tyrant, since the loyalty of her citizens was so strongly directed toward the polis that there was no issue by which an aspirant to tyranny could attract support and no disaffected group to which he could appeal.

The final support of the rights and interests of the citizenry was the board of Ephors, or overseers, five men who were elected by the Assembly for one-year terms. They were also to supervise the working of the system that molded the people; two specific functions within that framework were to watch over the condition of the boys and to judge cases of disobedience. A time was to come when the power of the Ephors grew so that they were almost a presiding group.

In the three generations or so following the organization of Sparta attributed to Lycurgus, the Spartans conquered the Dorian villages around them in the district of the Peloponnesus called Laconia, from which comes the word "laconic," which we use to describe the brief Spartan form of speech. Lacedaemon is another name for the region about Sparta, which is a pleasant and fertile one. The conquered people, to whom the Spartans now referred as *perioeci*, or "dwellers around," now acknowledged the suzerainty of Sparta by accepting resident Spartan agents to watch over the self-government of their villages, by paying some tribute to the Spartans, and by allowing themselves to be conscripted for military service with the Spartans. They had no political rights at Sparta. In the long run, however, they seem to have found their relationship reasonably comfortable.

The Spartans next conquered, between 740 and 720 B.C., the rich territory of Messenia, west of them, and made the inhabitants serfs, calling them Helots and binding them to cultivate the land for half the produce, paying the other half to whatever Spartan was now master of that piece of land. Villages of *perioeci* were established here and there in Messenia. The Spartans now had greater resources in land and men than any other polis in all eighth-century Greece. They apparently felt little pressure to colonize, for they sent out only one colony, Taras (the Latin Tarentum and Italian Taranto), near the heel of Italy.

The culture of Sparta in the late eighth century and the first half of the seventh century was not what we think of today as Spartan, being neither grim nor austere. The Spartans were a landed aristocracy supported by the toil of serfs on deep-soiled fields. They themselves were free of menial duties, confident in their superior position and their equality with other full citizens, owing no more than a proper respect to the Gerousia and the kings. They took great pleasure in their sports and their hunting and their race horses, as would be expected of landed aristocrats. Their entries in the Olympic Games always did well. They also took pleasure in handsome and spirited girls and women. The girls were not secluded, but were trained to a vigorous health, as were the boys, and to a modest and becoming frankness and freedom.

Although the Spartans did not have luxurious houses—the five villages were unwalled and the houses were made only with axe and saw, something like our log houses—they did have some luxurious personal possessions. They were friends with the people of Samos, who were great traders and must have called often at Spartan ports on their way to the West with the products from the East. The Spartan lady could have things of ivory or bronze made either abroad or by the workmen in Sparta, and in either case they showed the fashionable orientalizing motifs. Sparta had its own makers and painters of pottery who developed a style of their own that was still recognizably in the orientalizing stream, as was the work, too, of the Corinthian and Athenian craftsmen.

Although Sparta and Corinth were consistently on friendly terms, Argos more than once defied or defeated Sparta. The Arcadians, who were in the north central Peloponnesus, were able to discourage Spartan interference with members of their group. Sparta's greatest difficulty was caused by the revolt of the Messenians, which lasted from about 640 to 620 B.C. and was supported by some of the other peoples. Twenty years of struggle for what seemed her very existence must have made Sparta feel that stricter measures for security must be taken.

One measure was the creation of a system of alliances to insure the safety of Sparta against her serfs or outside attack. As the largest and most stable of the poleis she was generally able to take the lead, and in time her system of alliances became solid and influential. In a number of cases the Spartans gave others assistance in getting rid of their tyrants, so often indeed that their hostility to tyrants came to be taken for granted.

The other measure for security was the heightening of her own conservatism. After the suppression of the revolt of Messenia, every part of the system seems to have become more rigid. Although the system was admirably calculated before to produce the specialized Spartan type, it was now made more difficult for a Spartiate, or full citizen, to have any thought of business and trade or for a middle class to grow up. The best way to gain this end seemed to be to reject the new invention of coinage. The Spartans were to have no silver coinage. The old iron money was to be used, money that could serve for nothing except a few simple internal transactions and that was of no use in the new world of silver coinage and of fairly large denominations meant for use in international trade.

The suspicion arises that the Spartans were worried about far more than the revolt of the Messenians. They were enough in touch with the world to form an estimate of the new forces abroad. New possibilities, new horizons, and a new spirit had combined with the old loyalties and animosities based on race and kinship to give the more enterprising of the downtrodden a hope that they might rise, to give the group in general a new sense of opportunity for those who were bold and vigorous, and to cause bitter factional struggles and the rise of tyrannies in many poleis. To the Spartans none of this seemed good. They had committed themselves to an economy based on agriculture and realized how upsetting it might be to their system to have a lively trade develop. They had no desire to allow a strong commercial class like that of Corinth to arise, to allow the downtrodden to improve their position, or to reintroduce any of the causes of factional or class struggle or tyranny that they had forestalled by devising their conservative constitution.

Sparta's desire to stand apart from the international trade of the day was made easier of fulfillment by the fact that she had some iron in her territory and had learned how to handle it. As in the earlier Homeric days, metals usually were the one thing not available for self-sufficiency. Iron and wrought steel had long been important items of international trade, and now silver bullion and silver coinage were important. If they could get along without silver and could produce enough wrought steel for weapons and for tools, the Spartans could have much better success with their program of living largely to themselves and avoiding such involvements with other people as might cause breaches in their unity.

The Spartan System

After Lycurgus's reform the interference of the state in the affairs of the Spartan began at his birth. He was presented for approval not to his father alone, as with the other Greeks, but also to a board of elders who had the power to order that a deformed or sickly baby be exposed out in the mountains to die. Once through this exacting *rite de passage,* the Spartan boy had six years of living with his mother, and the idea of the stern Spartan mother is part of the idea of Sparta.

At the age of seven he was called by his draft board. From then until he was thirty he lived in barracks, and all his training looked toward his attachment to the larger unit of the state rather than to any small units like the immediate family or a larger kinship group. The little boys were organized into troops that were led by older boys and supervised by men. The responsibility of training the young was taken very seriously by all the men. The boy went barefoot winter and summer and wore one simple garment. His bed was of rushes, which he pulled with his own hands along the banks of the Eurotas River. His food was simple and well-spiced with appetite.

The boys were hardened by physical and military exercise as well as by this cheerless way of living. Discipline was strict. The spirit of competition was fostered by games of various kinds. At the age of eighteen the youngster became what might be called a junior member of the armed forces for two years. He received intensive military training and was also employed in the force known as the Crypteia, or secret police, which was charged with watching the Helots.

At thirty a man's education was over. His final examination came with his nomination to one of the messes, or dining societies. One blackball kept him out. If he was elected, he became an Equal; if he was blackballed, he became an Inferior, a definite position that left him without a vote in the Assembly and without full civil rights. It is hard to imagine a better way of forcing a man to shape himself to the standards and ideals current in his society. The average Spartan probably could read only a little; he was not musically nor artistically trained. He had little idea of the amenities of life as they came to exist among the other peoples of Greece, notably the Athenians. He might readily be called uneducated, and the word would apply if our system or that of the Athenians were a universal model. Education, however, is what a society wants the young to learn. Probably few societies have had so good a method as the Spartans for teaching the young what they wanted the grown man to know. He was trained to put the whole society, or the state, before any part of it in his loyalties. He was given the attitude that it was the right of the Spartan to be master and to live on other people's work and that it was his duty to protect and support this system in every way and at any cost. He was taught to be a skilled soldier and to feel himself one with his comrades at home and in the field. He was protected from the distractions of knowing overmuch about the pains and pleasures of other ways of living.

Comment on the training of the boy has tended to emphasize the brutal side. At one festival the older boys underwent hard whippings. Cakes were set out on the altar, and the successful boy was the one who approached the most times through a gantlet of men (those who laid on the whips), took a cake, and withdrew through another gantlet. It was not unknown for a boy to die of bruises and loss of blood.

The boys were taught to steal, too. This idea should be regarded with some common sense, for it is hard to believe that they were encouraged to roam up and down alleys and try to raid backyard gardens. Much more probably they received careful training in slipping unseen through the farming country as part of their work with the secret police who watched the Helots. They would need to live off the country without being noticed, and anyone who called attention to himself had bungled and was punished.

The more positive side of the training of the young has been less noticed. The Spartan boy was taught good manners. The men made it their business to watch the young at their exercises and games and to commend honorable and brave conduct. They also taught them to take part in serious and agreeable conversation. The boy was not allowed to be a boor who paid no attention to his elders or to people whom he did not know well. He was taught to pay respect to age; other people were aware of Spartan success in this respect.

The man of thirty who had succeeded in winning full acceptance into society by being elected a member of a mess and thus becoming an Equal expected to be a member of the army until he was sixty. Now that he was an Equal, he was a full voting member of the Assembly. He was allowed to marry at twenty, but for the ten years between twenty and thirty he was expected to live in barracks and visit his wife by stealth. It has been suggested that the brief notices on this custom refer to a secret trial marriage that did not become fully effective unless and until it turned out that the couple were capable of producing the children who were so important. After he reached thirty he could set up a household, but had to take one meal a day with his mess. The Helot who worked his land supplied him with plain fare for his meals at home and in the mess. Legally he could alienate the piece of land that the state assigned to the upkeep of himself and his family, but it was regarded as dishonorable to do so, and the man who could no longer make his contribution to the mess could no longer belong to it. We are not properly informed about those who were blackballed and failed of election to the company of Equals or about those who somehow lost their land. Both groups were doubtless treated with condescension and both groups doubtless found practical consolations for not being able to take part in the narrow and strenuous life of the full citizens.

Although they were of Dorian blood like the Spartans, the *perioeci* were kept in an inferior position. But they had their land, their dues were moderate, and they enjoyed the protection of the Spartans. Many a time they distinguished themselves on the battlefield as part of the Spartan army. They were free to engage in trade, but the trade can hardly have amounted to much. Yet some of them were well-to-do. They perhaps did not grieve that they could not be Spartan Equals.

For the Helots life was grimmer. They were not slaves who had lost every freedom, but serfs, who had lost the right to move. The Helot was attached to the holding of a full Spartan citizen and obliged to give him half the produce of the land. It was good land, and a man could live well on half the produce of it; the rate could not be raised.

Helots campaigned with the army, sometimes to fight, but mostly in menial capacities. Now and then one would strike a blow with such courage that he would find himself promoted to a second-class citizenship, and it even became possible to have a section of the army composed of these "new people." But in general there was war between Spartans and Helots, not only in the loose sense of opposition of interest, but in the strict sense that every year the Ephors declared war on them so that it would be legal to attack them at any time.

The Symbolism of Sparta

Sparta has served wonderfully as a source of symbols in history. Spartan simplicity, Spartan courage, and the Spartan mother are ideas that have long been useful to the orator and the statesman who wished to put certain ideals of communal life in concrete terms. There are other and more complex ways, however, in which Sparta has been used as a symbol of historical ideas.

One of these is to make Sparta symbolize the excessively militaristic nation that has abandoned higher values in pursuit of power and that pays the penalty in the end by so brutalizing its citizens that, in addition to losing the higher things, they can no longer perform their civic and military duties properly. It is not true, however, that the Spartans brutalized themselves, that they banished all higher values or that they ruined themselves.

The Greeks themselves were very interested in Sparta, most of all as an example of a polis with a stable constitution. Sparta avoided factional struggles once she had her constitution, had avoided tyrants in the age when tyrants were found everywhere, and had avoided the struggle of the few and the many—the oligarchs and the democrats—of which we shall presently hear a great deal. Many theorists offered explanations of how it was done and tried to show that Sparta was the great example of one thing or another. Perhaps the most influential of these theories was that Sparta was the great example of the mixed constitution, or the threefold form of government.

In the threefold scheme the kings represented monarchy, of course, the Gerousia represented aristocracy, and the Assembly represented democracy. No one in ancient times was troubled by the unmentioned presence of the slaves, serfs, and inferior citizens. The fact that there were three elements rather than two (oligarchs and democrats) was thought to encourage compromises and second thoughts instead of resorting to force in civil disagreements. From another point of view, that of the Greek theorists, the kings represented the executive, the Gerousia the legislative, and the people the judicial, because the people were the fount of authority and the court of last resort.

This symbolic view of Sparta was widely discussed by the Greeks, was taken up and discussed by the Romans, was known to the Italian Machiavelli and the Frenchman Montesquieu, and was a part of the intellectual equipment of the men who framed our own constitution. Thus the theory of the mixed form of government, the tripartite form, in which Sparta was made to symbolize the ideal, had a definite influence on the formation of our constitution.

ATHENS IN THE NEW AGE

Athens Before Solon

Although they had survived the shocks of the Dark Age after the fall of Mycenae and other great centers, the Athenians were slow to unfold their capabilities and to gain in intensity of living and performance in the new age. Perhaps the reason is that they were relatively late in developing their polis; it does seem that this more concentrated political and social form often led to a new spirit and heightened performance. We do not know exactly when it was that Attica was unified by bringing the dozen or so little kingdoms in that region into alliance with Athens. The Athenians were slow, also, to take the next step, that of concentrating many of their people in a center where the stimuli of life together and of exchange with other lively centers could act on them. Athens, the great sea power of the future, was behind Corinth, Megara, and Aegina on the sea and behind the Spartans in the development of a heavy infantry. She had not sent out colonies when the others did and had not developed industries at home.

The aristocrats of Athens, like those of the other poleis, took the king's power from him early. As was usual an aristocrat was given the title of king for the purpose of attending to religious affairs; this title for this purpose persisted even in the days of the full democracy in Athens. We see this "king" sitting in judgment on cases of impiety, presiding over the council when it dealt with murder (which was regarded as essentially a matter of pollution by bloodshed and therefore a religious matter), and performing a rite that we have already heard of in the Near East: the sexual intercourse of priest and priestess, in this case man and wife, a symbolic act to bring fertility to their people.

The first new office to be created was that of archon. This word is the counterpart of our "regent," which is derived from Latin. The archon was at first an officer for life, although the office was not hereditary, then for a term of ten years, then for one year. This last arrangement may have begun in 683 B.C.; at least the listing of one-year archons began at that time. A polemarch, or general, was created sometime after the development of the new-style king and the archon. In times when Athens had more wars to fight it would not perhaps have been so easy to take away the king's function of leadership in war and hand it over to one of the aristocracy. Next a group of six lesser archons was created, the *thesmothetae;* they were concerned with the law.

It is difficult for us to realize how little government a Greek polis needed at this time. The religious functions of the man called the king can hardly have occupied him for more than a dozen days a year. The archon was not like the head of a nation or even the mayor of a city, for there were almost no functions of government to occupy him. Orphans were his wards, for the aristocrats of Athens, too, thought it beneficial to protect families from the loss of their land if possible, at least to the extent of not allowing orphan minors to lose it.

The conspiracy of Cylon in 632 B.C. was for Athens the most exciting single event of these centuries. This young man had the glamor of a victory at Olympia, but it was rather more useful to him that he had married the daughter of the tyrant of Megara. Cylon had some soldiers from Megara to assist the people on whom he could count because of his family connections, some of them relatives and some retainers, when he seized the Acropolis in Athens. Megacles, the archon, who was of the great Alcmaeonid clan, sent around Attica and soon had a force of men to blockade the Acropolis. Ordinary men supported the archon because they were not ready to desert the loose government of the great families for anything that they might be led to expect from the promises of a tyrant. Cylon escaped. Although they took sanctuary, his supporters were massacred by order of Megacles. Such ruthlessness among citizens shocked everyone, and the conviction grew that the polis had been so polluted by this shedding of blood that some purification was necessary. The details of the story are not quite convincing, yet it seems that a special court of aristocrats did pass some sentence on the whole clan of the Alcmaeonids, who were exiled for a long time thereafter.

About 620 B.C. the laws were published by a commissioner named Draco, whose name has become synonymous with severity. We do not know why the Athenians wanted a code published at this time; it probably was the reason that led to the codes of Zaleucus and Charondas. We know very little of the code. For one thing, it was possible to sell an insolvent debtor and his dependents into slavery. In homicide trials the question of intent came up; if the killing was not intentional, the killer had to go into exile for life unless unanimously pardoned by the kin of the slain man. This looks not so much like ridding the polis of the guilt of bloodshed as like getting a guarantee that the kin of the slain man would not repay unintentional bloodshed with intentional bloodshed.

The Reforms of Solon

Solon was chosen archon for the year 594 with the idea that he would devise some changes to remedy an unhappy situation that had arisen. He was chosen, as the archons were at that time, by the aristocrats of the council, the governing body of the polis. Athens was still very much under the control of the clans, although in other cities the central government had taken away much of their power. Even though industry and commerce were undeveloped, the foremost people had acquired a taste for imported luxuries, and the rivalry among the great clans had extended itself to movable wealth. In their greed many people had taken too great advantage of the weakness of the poor.

Probably the leading men realized that they had pushed the common people to the point of revolution. In the beginning the possessors of the best land were the leading people. The small farmer on the hillier and poorer land was always at a disadvantage and often must have had to appeal to his more powerful neighbor for help. The beginning of the use of money made the situation worse because the management of money, even in a simple way, is done better by some people than by others. Many poor men had got into debt, and some of them had been seized for debt and sold into slavery with their families. Some were probably working their own farms as agents for people to whom they were hopelessly in debt. Many a man had of course bettered himself by going off to a colony; the men of whom we speak are the poor who had stayed at home.

Naturally the more able individual could not be expected to refrain from attempts to prosper further, and the less energetic and able man might seem to have paid the natural penalty for his own deficiencies. Yet the time came when the aristocracy collectively stood back and decided that it must find a way to protect the weaker men. Very likely there was also some sentiment for giving the middle class more voice in government and for putting Athens more in touch with the modern world of industry and trade. Solon would hardly have dared to make the changes that he did, nor would he have thought of them, had they not been favorably discussed beforehand by some of his contemporaries.

Solon himself was from one of the lesser families of the Athenian aristocracy. He had been engaged in trade and had traveled widely. He had proved his leadership by stirring up the Athenians to drive the Megarians out of the island of Salamis, which lies very close to the Greek coast and very near to Athens. In a sense Solon was a one-man constitutional convention, yet the matters he dealt with must all have been discussed again and again. If it had the political wisdom to allow a change, the aristocracy must have had some collective wisdom to offer him on the nature of the change.

Although no one was thoroughly pleased with Solon's reforms, the council and the assembly of the arms-bearing men had sworn to accept what he offered, and they did. He disappointed the hopes of the poor by not redistributing the land and disappointed the rich by canceling all debts that involved land or persons. In addition he forbade any further enslavement for debt and the use of one's person as security for debt. The polis now sought out and ransomed many citizens who were in slavery at home or who had been sold into slavery abroad. A bill of amnesty restored citizenship to those who had lost it, except those who had been guilty of violence against individuals or the polis. We shall hear of wise acts of amnesty in Athens later.

Solon went to the root of the troubles of the poorer citizens by his measures to change Attic agriculture from cereal growing to a preponderance of olive growing and to encourage industry and commerce. These moves were the beginning, after centuries of quiet agricultural life, of the brilliance of Athens as an industrial and commercial city, the intellectual as well as the commercial center of the Mediterranean world.

First Solon prohibited the export of cereals. The soil of Attica is not well suited to them, and what was grown was needed at home. For olives, however, the composition of the soil is good, and olives can be grown on slanting hillsides on scattered patches of ground that will not grow cereals. The roots of the olive strike deep and tap moisture well below the ground. Olive trees take a few years to mature and bear fruit, however, and are thus better for the man who has a little capital or does not need an immediate return because he has other products.

Although some cereals were always grown in Attica, a goodly part of the required cereals was henceforth imported. Solon boldly aimed at the conversion of Athens to an olive-growing, cereal-importing, and industrial and commercial polis, and his plan succeeded. He provided that every father see to it that his son was equipped with a trade. He also provided that citizenship be granted to skilled workmen who would come to Athens with their families and stay.

Another aspect of his sweeping economic policy was to desert the Aeginetan system of coinage and shift to the Euboic. This meant that the silver content and the weight of the coinage of Athens was changed slightly; the effect was to make it readily acceptable in a different set of places, although a soundly based coinage could pass anywhere with some calculations and adjustments.

The landowning class suffered somewhat from his measures, for many of them must have had heavy losses from the cancellation of debts, but they also were the chief producers of olives and had some capital for trading, so that they would be among the first to profit by the new economic structure. Those Athenians who had trades or who soon learned them would also be among the first to profit.

Pottery came to be one of the great specialties of the Athenians. Not long after Solon's enactments Athens was again at the front of the industry as she had been in the days of Geometric ware. Now her ware was made of a fine local clay with a little imported red color added to it to make a product that looked much like the reddish soil of Attica. These vessels were painted with black designs and are referred to today as "black-figured ware." Presently it became the style to use the black as the background, leaving the red to show through as the pictures. This style is called "red-figured." Here, as so often, we must stop to reflect that what we speak of as "Greek art" is the product of men who were straightforwardly producing for the commercial market and produced very fine work. Greek vases were meant to be used. Today they appeal to us for their grace of line and for the clean and lively drawing of the pictures on them, often scenes from Greek myth and legend. The discovery of them in excavations, whole or in fragments, shows us that Athens had now developed a lively trade with the West, with Etruscans and Carthaginians as well as with the western Greeks. The Corinthian ware had become a little mechanical and careless and did not stand up well to the competition of the new Athenian product.

Although in later days at Athens, when there was much argument about political origins, Solon was claimed as the founder of Greek democracy, he probably would have preferred himself to say that he had given recognition in government to all elements of the citizen body. His govern-

Bison and wild boar from the cave of Altamira, Spain
Courtesy of the American Museum of Natural History

Panel of enameled brick from the Procession Street of the Babylon of Nebuchadnezzar II (605–562 B.C.)   *Ny Carlsberg Glyptotek, Copenhagen*

Wall panel of winged being pollinating the sacred tree from the Palace of Ashur-nasir-apal II (885–860 B.C.), King of Assyria, at Kalhu, modern Nimrud
The Metropolitan Museum of Art, Gift of John D. Rockefeller, Jr., 1931

Old Akkadian cuneiform inscription, c. 2200
B.C. Contract for the purchase of a house.
Courtesy of The Metropolitan Museum of Art

Akkadian seal, 24–2200 B.C.
Courtesy of The Metropolitan Museum of Art

Impression of the seal.
Courtesy of The Metropolitan Museum of Art

Assyrian ivory inlay for furniture, c. 710 B.C.
The Metropolitan Museum of Art, Fletcher Fund, 1958

The ziggurat at Ur   *Courtesy of the Trustees of the British Museum,*
University Museum Expedition to Ur.

The Sphinx, Gizeh   *Courtesy of Trans World Airlines, Inc.*

The royal official Methethy, late 5th
Dynasty about 2420 B.C.
Courtesy of the Brooklyn Museum

Bronze Mirror, Egypt, 18th Dynasty
Courtesy of the Brooklyn Museum

Queen Hat-shepsut, c. 1490–80 B.C., from Thebes: Deir el Bahri
The Metropolitan Museum of Art,
Rogers Fund and Contributions from Edward S. Harkness, 1929

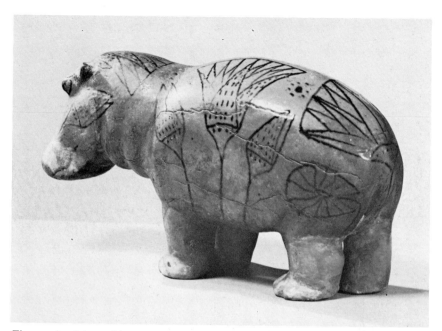

Figure of a faience hippopotamus from the Tomb of Senbi, at Meir
The Metropolitan Museum of Art, Gift of Edward S. Harkness, 1917

Columns of the temple of Amun at Karnak, 14th Century B.C.
Courtesy of Trans World Airlines, Inc.

King Akh-en-Aton and Queen Nefert-iti standing with offerings for the sun-god Aton, from the balustrade at Armana

Palace at Persepolis; north stairway of the audience hall begun by Darius I (521–486 B.C.)

ment seemed conservative in practice even to those who later claimed him as the founder of democracy; they did no more than assert that he had taken the first steps. He divided the free citizens into four classes according to income in terms of farm produce. Those of the first class were called *pentacosiomedimnoi,* or five-hundred-bushel men. The second class were known as *hippeis,* or knights, or three-hundred-bushel men. The name of the third class was *zeugitae;* there is no English equivalent, but we do know that they were two-hundred-bushel men. The fourth class, the *thetes,* were laborers who had no land and no specified income. Probably money from trade could be calculated on this scale of income so that the economic status of a new trading group could be recognized. Implicitly the former qualification of birth was dropped.

The assembly of the people was now open to citizens of all four classes. The Assembly had the privilege of electing the archon, and all four classes could vote. The uses of the new classification become clearer when we see that only the first two classes were eligible for the archonship, as doubtless seemed right and proper to the two lower classes, little as we should like such a distinction nowadays. But for the first time the archonship was open to people of the first two classes whether or not they belonged to the group of the Eupatrids, or nobles (those people who had owned the good land for several generations). This modification may well have given a chance at the archonship to some people who had risen in the economic scale and could now show the proper amount of income. Possibly it promised more opportunity for some strong clans who came from the outskirts of Attica and had never been able to gain admission to the inner group that passed the archonship and the consequent membership in the council among its members.

The men of the highest class were distinguished by alone being eligible for the office of state treasurer. Perhaps it was felt that the men of most property had the most financial ability and that their property would assure their responsibility. The members of the third class were eligible for certain minor offices, and the members of the fourth class were not eligible for any.

In modern terms the assets even of the top class represent only a very modest property. If we reckon the yield of ten bushels of wheat to the acre, the five hundred bushels would come from fifty acres. A man would be likely to have more land than that, some of it in wheat, some in vines or olive trees. There would be a house of mud and timber, a yoke of oxen, some sheep and goats, poultry, and a horse for the head of the family.

Under the new arrangement the archons passed into the council, as before, after their term of office. The council now came to be known as the Council of the Areopagus, from the place where it met. This council, like those of most of the Greek states, had general supervisory powers. Being composed usually of the heads of important families, it wielded a certain amount of power and controlled the polis in much the same way that the clan heads ruled their own little areas by dealing sensibly or firmly with anything or anyone who threatened to disturb the peace or upset the existing order.

Solon introduced a new council, to be known as the *Boule* (pronounced boo-lay′), or simply "the Council"; it is often spoken of, too, as the Senate of Athens. Its composition could hardly have been more different from that of the Council of the Areopagus. It had four hundred members, a hundred from each of the four tribes that were traditional among the Ionians (to whom Athens belonged); they were chosen by lot from those who came forward and served for only a year. We shall hear more of the practice of choosing men by lot for offices; to the Athenians it seemed the most democratic way. The use of the lot made it impossible to organize a group beforehand to dominate the Council of a given year, and it would be hard to organize such a party after the drawing of lots, since the term was only for one year. The function of the *Boule* was to keep a general watch on the affairs of Athens and to prepare proposals for each meeting of the Assembly. It plainly took away something from the power of those who had been used to directing the state, for the old council had been able to manage the Assembly, assuming administrative authority themselves and only occasionally offering the Assembly a carefully timed and carefully phrased proposal for its approval. It must be noted that some modern scholars do not believe that the *Boule* was created by Solon and date it a hundred years later.

Solon gave the Assembly a new power, the judicial power. Those people who qualified for the Assembly were felt to be the final source of justice, and thus it was not uncommon among the Greeks to regard them as the judicial element among the constitutional powers and to bring cases before them as a court. When the Assembly constituted itself a court, it was called the *Heliaea*. This court had one piece of business not common among the other Greeks—the examination of the accounts and the acts of the outgoing magistrates, for the ex-magistrate did not get his place in the Council of the Areopagus unless he passed this scrutiny. When the *Heliaea* sat as a court in other matters, it divided itself into panels of five hundred.

We are not as well informed about the reforms of Solon as it might seem from the foregoing account. We can put together an outline of them that is fairly certain and that seems to make good sense, but for the motives and the details we have little evidence and are driven to conjecture and to argument by analogy from what we know of other poleis. There can be no doubt that after him the government of Athens was more broadly based and that Athens took her place among the leading industrial and commercial states.

THE TYRANNY OF PEISISTRATUS

The sworn agreement to observe the laws of Solon for ten years was kept, although he was besieged with complaints and abuse from all classes. There was no explosion when the ten years were over, but there was an unsuccessful attempt at tyranny by one Damasias, who was elected archon and was then unwilling to lay down his power and had to be dislodged by force. After Damasias was removed, a group of ten archons was elected of whom five were Eupatrids or nobles, three were small farmers, and two were craftsmen from the town. We may be sure that before Solon the small farmers and the craftsmen would not have been able to gain such recognition. There were also two occasions during the ten years when the strife of factions was such that it was not possible to choose a group of magistrates.

Slowly the chief interests in the polis crystalized into two political parties. The main group of the Eupatrids, who were great landowners, came to be known as the Party of the Plain, because their holdings were chiefly in the flatter and better land of Attica. Their opponents were mostly the group who had supported Solon's reform in the first place and were unwilling to allow reaction against it and nullification of it now; they were known as the Party of the Coast or the Shore; it is tempting to suppose that many among them were deeply involved in commerce. The rise after some time of a third party, that of the Hills, is connected with the great name of Peisistratus, who was soon to be tyrant. If the third party can be assigned a definite program, it may be said to have favored a stronger central government with more control over the local grandees and the encouragement of a large class of holders of moderate-sized farms who could be relied upon as heavy infantry. These two measures were practiced in many other poleis. The three parties were combinations of local groupings and class groupings and groups supporting the interests of the great families. Their actions cannot be so analyzed as to be ascribed in each case to specific and isolated motives.

Peisistratus had distinguished himself as a general in some engagements against the Megarians. He appeared one day with wounds bleeding and asked the Assembly for a bodyguard on the ground that his enemies had tried to murder him; his enemies, of course, could tell no other story than that he had wounded himself. The Assembly found his story convincing and provided the bodyguards. Fifty citizens armed with clubs were thought to be enough, for these were the machinations of local great men in a city of modest size. In 561 B.C., with the help of his bodyguard, he was able to seize the Acropolis and make himself tyrant. Soon the parties of the Plain and the Shore, which could have prevented him in the first place had they combined against him, did finally unite, and their show of force was enough to make him give in and leave town. Presently they fell out again, and the leader of the Party of the Plain, Megacles the Alcmaeonid, made a plan with Peisistratus that brought him back to the city as tyrant. He married the daughter of Megacles, but because he already had sons, he did not consummate the marriage, not wishing to complicate his plans with further children. After a while the bride went home, and her father, thoroughly alienated from Peisistratus, forced him to withdraw again.

Peisistratus now began a long period of preparation. He and his supporters moved to the north shore of the Aegaean, where they made a settlement and in ten years had acquired both money and allies, the money from the timber and precious metals of the region and the allies from the neighbors of Athens who were not friendly to her; he was able to hire a thousand mercenaries from Argos. In 546 B.C. he marched on Athens and once again made himself tyrant, this time with little trouble. To use mercenaries and foreign support to gain a tyranny was a new method. Even this probably would not have worked if Athens had had a strong and united government.

Between his first usurpation in 561 and his death in 527, Peisistratus was in power for nineteen years and out of power for fourteen. Once firmly established by force in 546, he settled down to a consistent policy. Although he confiscated the estates of a few of his enemies, notably the Alcmaeonids, he respected the property of others who withdrew to exile. He distributed some of the confiscated land to make new small farmers who would owe their position to him. He sent traveling justices of the peace around Attica to hear cases for two reasons: to undermine the traditional jurisdiction of the chiefs of the clans and to help the farmers by not taking them away from their work for court sittings in the city. Probably, too, even an enlightened tyrant would prefer not to have the country people more in touch with politics through visits to the city. With the income from his mines in Thrace he could make loans to farmers on easy terms for improvements and equipment. He made himself accessible and agreeable to all, since an executive of any kind, and especially a tyrant, must try to keep himself from being shut off from the flow of information about how the organization is going.

Although he maintained the constitution as it had been (he himself held no office), Peisistratus's men were elected or appointed to every vital post. As ex-archons they little by little filled the Council of the Areopagus. The *Heliaea* was composed of the people in general, who were largely favorable to him. In a trial of naked force he would have had all the advantage, for he had disarmed the citizens and had his own mercenary force. He controlled the official revenues and the unofficial ones that he had developed for himself in Thrace. Meanwhile the Alcmaeonids had settled at Delphi and made themselves respected and influential. More than once they tried to return to Athens by force, but were foiled each time.

Beside favoring the common man somewhat against the nobles at home and making alliances for Athens abroad, Peisistratus pursued an enlightened commercial and cultural policy like that of many other tyrants. Although we cannot point to specific measures to help trade, we do know that the Attic pottery, the reliable index of Athenian trade, spread during this period as far as Spain in the West and all over the Aegean and up to southern Russia on the Black Sea. Peisistratus had the good sense to pay for such popular public works as a new water supply. A number of Ionians now migrated to Athens at the tyrant's invitation and from distaste for the new Persian rule of the coastal cities of Asia Minor; such new members would enliven cultural life, for Ionia had been feeling the stirrings of new cultural life for two or three generations. A most important innovation was the beginning, in about 535, of the performance of plays at the festival of Dionysus. From this came Attic tragedy, the great literary glory of Athens. The festival began to be built up as an attraction for visitors to the city—the first example of the glorification of a local festival for economic purposes and to stimulate local pride.

Peisistratus died in 527 B.C., the tyranny passing smoothly to his sons who were well trained in governing and continued all his policies. In 514 a curious event occurred that according to popular song and legend was the cause of the fall of the dynasty. Two young men, Harmodius and Aristogeiton, assassinated Hipparchus, one of the sons of Peisistratus, because of a personal grievance having nothing to do with the government. Nevertheless these two came to be known as "the tyrannicides." Statues of them with daggers raised to strike were made, and drinking songs honoring them as the authors of freedom became popular.

The expulsion of the tyrants actually came about through the assistance of the Spartans, which for a long time had been sought by the exiled Alcmaeonids. Hippias, Peisistratus's remaining son, repelled the first Spartan attack, but another attack in greater force drove its way into Athens, and the tyrant and his mercenaries were blockaded on the Acropolis. As fate would have it, the Spartans captured the children of the family as Hippias tried to smuggle them out, whereupon terms were made under which he and the others of the family of Peisistratus withdrew from Athens. Hippias went to his son-in-law, one of the tyrants of the Greek cities of Asia Minor under the Persians, who introduced him to the protection of the Great King, as the Greeks called the king of Persia.

The Reform of Cleisthenes

The Spartans had hardly withdrawn from Athens when the nobles began a violent struggle for primacy in the new government. Cleisthenes, the
current leader of the Alcmaeonids, was the moving spirit in gaining Spartan help and organizing the nobles to do their part in their own restoration, yet his rival Isagoras, a friend of the Spartan king, was elected
archon in 508 B.C. Cleisthenes, unwilling to accept the election, spread the
word that he would welcome the support of the humbler people whose
position had been improved by Peisistratus and who could now expect
much less favorable treatment from a government of nobles, promising
that in return he would formally improve their constitutional position.

Isagoras tried to nip this movement in the bud by calling the Spartans
back. The Spartan king sent a herald ordering the Alcmaeonids to withdraw from Athens because of the old pollution that they had incurred by
their massacre of the supporters of Cylon in 632 B.C. Cleisthenes had as
yet no force to oppose the Spartans, so he withdrew, and the Spartan
king came to Athens with troops and began to banish those people who
seemed dangerous to Isagoras; the king also ordered the dissolution of the
Council of the Areopagus, which he planned to replace with a small oligarchic council favorable to Isagoras. But the Council rallied the citizenry
and blockaded the king, his troops, and Isagoras on the Acropolis, although
finally they were allowed to withdraw. Cleisthenes and the others came
back, and he was given the opportunity to make the changes that he had
promised.

Cleisthenes intended to create a new basis of participation in the affairs of the polis that would leave no free citizen under a disability as a
newcomer or as a descendant of a poor and unprivileged family. The basic
unit of the new system was the already existing deme, which was somewhat analogous to the little settlements about Attica or to the neighbor-
hoods into which every modern city divides itself in the sentiment of its
inhabitants. In Athens there were several, and in all Attica there may
have been 170; each citizen belonged to one and kept his membership in
it even if he moved to another. The demes served as the basic units in
elections. In the registration of new members there were no distinctions
such as those that had worked against the old poor and the new craftsmen.
The new equality, which we might be tempted to call democracy, was
called *isonomia,* or equality before the law. The demes had a sufficient
number of functions to seem real units of the polis, but were small enough
to allow a certain intimacy among their members. Casual references to
them in later literature all assume that membership in the deme was a
real bond.

Starting from the fact that the people were used to being members of the four tribes traditional among Ionians, Cleisthenes boldly reorganized the people into ten new tribes and succeeded in breathing life into them, borrowing the idea of a tribe but making no further political use of the four old ones. He used an old category called a *trittys,* or third, but took away the geographical character that it had formerly possessed. Each of the ten tribes had three of these thirds, and each of the thirds was made up, not of a piece of territory, but of a group of demes from one of the three working divisions of Attica: the city and its suburbs, the coastal region, and the agricultural interior. Thus each tribe had elements from each of the three main elements of the polis, and no tribe was so solidly constituted that any clan, group, or economic or social interest could dominate it. The tribe, like the deme, was endowed with functions and emotional components that enabled it to work, for it had an electoral function, its own finances and religious observances, and was also the basis of military organization.

All the old organizations remained, just as the Council of the Areopagus remained when Solon created the new council, the *Boule.* The old organization of the four tribes, the clans, and the old priesthoods remained, but only to perform their old religious functions. In modern life we hardly notice that we, too, have such survivals of institutions. For example, in some heavily populated areas of the United States the county has largely been superseded by other political units, yet the courts are likely still to be organized by counties.

The new system worked very neatly in the matter of forming the *Boule.* The demes elected a number of men who were over thirty and at least of the third class in property. Then each tribe chose fifty men from those whom its demes had proposed; the choice was made by lot from men already guaranteed, as it were, by election. The five hundred members of the *Boule* were separated into ten *prytanies* of fifty men each. The *prytanies* took turns being on full duty for a tenth of the year, living in the council hall and being on call twenty-four hours a day. A chairman was elected by lot for each day. Thus one man every day had the experience of being at the head of the group that was guiding the polis. Because a man could be on the council only twice and be chairman only once, a very large part of the eligible citizens must have served on the council and so acquired an intimate knowledge of how affairs of state were managed.

Ostracism

The procedure of ostracism was perhaps devised by Cleisthenes, although it seems more likely that someone else invented it about the time it was first used in 487 B.C. The essence of the procedure was that the Assembly was asked whether it wished to have an ostracism. If it voted in favor, another meeting was held at which, without discussion, the voter could write on a piece of broken pottery, an *ostracon,* the name of anyone whom he wished to see sent for ten years into honorable exile, his property being publicly preserved inviolate. Whoever received most votes (presumably with some minimum number necessary) had to retire for ten years. This was one way of dealing with great issues in the state; the people could vote that the chief proponent of one point of view must go away for a while. The several men ostracized in the 480s were either of the Peisistratids or closely connected with them, and it is possible that they represented the idea of submission to Persia; it may be said that the people chose Themistocles to lead them by removing the opponents of his policy from the scene.

Excavations have uncovered many *ostraca* scratched with names. One find had the same name written in the same hand on each fragment. Apparently someone's chief opponent intended to come to the voting prepared to furnish anyone who wished it with an *ostracon* ready to use against him.

RELIGION, PHILOSOPHY, ART, AND LITERATURE IN THE NEW AGE

RELIGION

In general the poleis established cults of the major gods whom we met when discussing Homer. Zeus was worshiped everywhere. Some other god, however, was likely to be the favorite of a polis, as Athena was thought to be especially devoted to the interests of Athens. Hera was a favorite with women as a help in childbirth. Probably Apollo was most popular of all; his temples were everywhere. There was never a precise and unified body of dogma about the nature of the gods. Each was likely to have several aspects, as Apollo was god of the sun, disease and medicine, and prophecy. A god could be worshiped in different aspects and under different names in various places. Pythian Apollo of Delphi was a god of prophecy,[1] while Delian Apollo was patron and protector of the holy island of Delos, his birthplace.

The cult of the hero is strange to us. These were local cults, centered on the graves of great men of earlier times, whose remains were thought to have some power. In some colonies, for instance, rites and sacrifices were offered at the grave of the *oecist,* the founder of the colony. Such hero cults were common all over the Greek world.

Before the rise of the polis the clans and family groups had necessarily had their own religious observances, because it was always felt that the Unseen must somehow be dealt with. In Athens at the height of the enlightenment of the fifth century a citizen could not become a member of

[1] See p. 157 for the explanation of the word "Pythian."

the Council unless he could prove that he performed the acts required by the family cult.

Religious feeling became connected with many places. It was thought that in some spots the gods spoke to men. There were many such spots, in all parts of the Greek world. In innumerable minor places, too, the power of some god was believed to have manifested itself. Offerings were brought there and prayers were said.

The temple might be called an afterthought. The holiness of the place was established first, and the rites and observances did not require a temple. Someone—a tyrant or the polis—would decide to build one. The temple was always located in the holy place, for the Greeks would have seen no point in choosing any available site and building on it, as we do with our churches. Furthermore, the temple was for the god, not for the people. The interior usually contained a room for the cult statue and perhaps a storeroom or treasury. Admission might even be forbidden to all except priests or attendants on the ground that the temple was too holy a place for others. The adjective "profane" originally applied (in Latin) to those ordinary persons whose approaching a ceremony too closely or entering the temple violated this taboo.

The Great Games

The athletic competitions of the Greeks were likely to be connected with regular religious gatherings. The Olympic Games were the first to become national rather than local, and the other three leading sets of games were founded in the early sixth century in frank imitation of them and all in honor of divinities. The Isthmian Games were at Corinth, the Nemean near Argos, and the Pythian at Delphi.

The most famous of all Greek festivals was the Olympic Games, closely followed by the great (nonathletic) festival of Dionysus at Athens. Athletic festivals were common in Greece, although we find no trace of such contests among the earlier peoples whom we have considered. Hunting was always a favorite sport of the kings and nobles of the earlier peoples, and they seem to have found that danger spiced their enjoyment, but contests between man and man did not suit them.

Olympia is in the western Peloponnesus. The festival there was in honor of Zeus, and the accepted date for the first meeting was 776 B.C. The period of four years from one meeting to another came to be known as an Olympiad, and dating by Olympiads and intermediate years ("in the second year of the fifty-first Olympiad") became an accepted system. The last meeting was 1168 years later, in 393 A.D. The games retained their religious character to the last, and they were shut down for this reason by an edict of the Christian emperor Theodosius I, who forbade public worship of pagan divinities. An interval of 1503 years followed until the modern Olympics began at Athens in 1896.

The original games took place at the August full moon, a time when the grain was in and there was a lull before the harvest of the grapes and olives. Heralds went far and wide through the Greek world to announce the sacred truce that protected the occasion. All freeborn Greeks were eligible to compete. The athletes and the spectators came from all over the Greek world. The Greeks of the region of the Black Sea and of Asia Minor and the islands came by water, not in passenger ships (for there were none), but in fishing smacks or freight ships. The emigrés of the prosperous poleis of South Italy and Sicily, who were still thought of as Greeks, also came by ship. The Greeks of Greece walked. It was a hundred and twenty-odd miles from Athens, not an unreasonable walk for a party of Greeks of those days.

Olympia itself was not a polis, but a place for the sanctuary of Zeus and the celebration of the games, under the management of the people of nearby Elis. They had no place to shelter the visitors, but the season was mild and there were fields and pine groves in which to sleep out. Merchants might well summon their agents to a meeting here; friends and relatives from different poleis could meet, and many a man must have recognized a smiling face that he had last seen scowling at him over the rim of a shield in the front lines of a battle. All sorts of men came in the hope of some gain—jugglers and tightrope walkers, men who had portable and fine merchandise, like jewelry, to sell, or men who wanted to air a theory or a point of view. The historian Herodotus is said to have introduced his history of the Persian wars to the public by giving readings from it at the Olympics.

First the contestants, who had done the last month of their training at Elis, stood before the altar of Zeus with their trainers and their fathers and swore to contest fairly. Then they paraded to the stadium, where the heralds introduced each man by proclaiming his name, his father's name, and his city. The games began with races of four-horse chariots and of riding horses. The contests of the athletes began with the pentathlon, the five parts of which were the dash, the broad jump, the discus, the javelin, and wrestling. Great importance was attached to good form in the jumping and throwing events, and they were customarily performed to the music of the flute. The winner was nevertheless picked on distance, not on form. The winning distance was not measured and there was no mania for keeping records and seeing them broken. The jumper used weights that looked like dumbbells. He would swing them forward sharply as he left the take-off, then swing them back sharply and let them go. These weights have been found in excavations, and pictures of their use have been found on pottery. Similar ones were used in the first few meetings of the modern Olympics.

The day of the full moon had no contests, for it was the day of the sacrifice to Zeus, the original cause of the meeting at Olympia. Perhaps fifty or sixty thousand people would gather about the great altar. There was a parade of the officials, the athletes, the horses, and the delegates bringing the offerings of the poleis to the god. Because the best artists worked on these gifts of the cities to the god and on the victory offerings as well, Olympia became a great repository of art.

The next morning there were three races. The stadium did not have an oval track, but twenty-one straight lanes almost two hundred meters long. The starting line was a marble slab with double grooves into which the runners could set their bare feet for the start. One cannot set a foot very firmly into the grooves (the slab is still there to be seen and tried out), and they are a little close together for the modern idea of starting holes. The Greek word for them was *gramma,* or "scratch," whence the modern word "scratch" for the starting line.

The first race was one length of the stadium. The second was the double dash, down and back. Twenty runners ran in the twenty-one lanes, and each man turned round a post set in the marble slab at the far end and came back in the lane to the left of the one he went down in. Obviously the race was slower than a straightaway race or one around a curve, but the race was the thing, not an attempt to get the time down. The third race was about three miles.

In the afternoon there were the boxing, wrestling, and *pancration,* or general contest. The boxers wore strips of soft leather around their hands, there were no rounds, and the fight ended when one man signified that he had enough. In the wrestling it was not necessary to pin the opponent's shoulders to the ground, but only to make some part of his body above the knee touch the ground, and two out of three falls gave the victory. The *pancration* may seem brutal to modern taste because, along with wrestling holds and striking with the fists, kicking and choking were allowed. This does not mean kicking with boots on, however, but kicking with the bare foot, which requires much skill and is open to disastrous countermoves, as is choking.

The winner of each event was called to the judges' table of ivory and gold, itself a famous work of art, and given a simple wreath of olive leaves as the herald announced his name. On the evening of the day after the meet, as the crowd was on its way home on its little ships or trudging over the hills and far away, the managers of the games gave a banquet for the victors. Often statues were commissioned in honor of a victory, either by the winner or by his polis, and set up at Olympia. Famous poets, of whom

Pindar's name is best known, were commissioned to write victory odes. The city, too, honored the victor on his return home. The other point of view—the scornful criticism of the cult of athletic glory—was also represented in literature.

It is customary to say that Greek unity was promoted by the Olympics and by the other great games as well as by the common language and religion. We cannot be sure, of course, how much the games did to promote a genuine unity of the Greeks. It was surely something to go every summer (for some set of games was held every year) to a great meeting of people all of whom considered themselves Greeks. Ideas and news could circulate thus among people who had no other regular means of communication. Many disputes between cities were arbitrated at the games and many treaties were made; copies of treaties were often deposited in the temple of Zeus at Olympia.

The Delphic Oracle

The story of Pythian Apollo, the god of prophecy at Delphi, begins with the combat in which he vanquished the great serpent Python. Zeus himself had a similar combat with the monster Typhon, and the myths of the ancient world are full of these struggles in which gods and heroes destroy giants and monsters. When the age of colonization began, people began to consult the oracle of Apollo about the proper forms of religious observance in the prospective colonies. The priests were shrewd about learning whatever could be learned from their patrons, who generally had to stay in Delphi a little while awaiting the days when the priestess was sitting. These men of religion learned so much about the geography of outlying regions that they could give good advice on possible sites for new colonies. In addition, they were not above asserting in retrospect that they had given advice when they had not or that their advice had been better than was really the case. Be that as it may, Pythian Apollo acquired great prestige and influence as an adviser on colonization.

Many a delegation was sent to Delphi to inquire what could be done about religious pollution; the answer, of course, was always that certain religious observances must be offered to the gods. The Greeks were much concerned about pollution. A whole clan might become polluted, as the Alcmaeonids did by the massacre of the supporters of Cylon. A whole community could be polluted by a murder or by an accidental homicide. Many an individual had doubts and fears to which the oracle could minister. Some, for instance, believing that they lay under an ancestral curse, would be willing to pay for ceremonies of exorcism.

The beautiful site of Delphi lies a few miles north of the Gulf of Corinth so that some people could come there by ship, while most walked. The post of priestess was held by a succession of local women. They are said to have raved when possessed by the god; the board of priests reduced what was said to respectable verse—no one used prose then for serious matters— and gave it in writing to the inquirer. The theory that the priestess was influenced by gases arising from a chasm has been given up for lack of evidence.

Dionysus

The modern idea of the division of life into the Apollonian—the sober, steady, and orderly way—and the Dionysiac—the impulsive and emotional —is suggestive if used with care. The mention of Dionysus in Homer, suggesting his worship in early times, is now supported by mention of him in the Linear B tablets. There is one persistent tradition, however, that the worship of Dionysus came from Thrace, and another tradition would have it come from Asia Minor, in both cases in the new age. It may well be that all are true, and that Dionysus was worshiped in early Greece as a god of vegetation, whereas the aspect of him most familiar to us, that of the god of wine, was a later importation both from Thrace and from Asia Minor.

Dionysus was readily received in Greece, whatever his origin. The people were ready for a religion that offered joy and ecstasy. The word *ekstasis* means a "standing apart from," and one benefit that the god offered was the faculty of standing apart from one's self, away from that more individualistic self that had recently been discovered and must have seemed to many people tiresome to have always around. In the old days one could lose oneself in the clan, with no need to be so conscious of the individual self and new, individual responsibilities. Under the influence of the wine that went with the festivals of Dionysus and as one of an excited crowd one might occasionally give one's self the slip, so to speak, and have a few minutes of freedom from individuality.

But more is involved in doing justice to Dionysus. He was concerned with vegetation and wine. He must somehow have been connected with fertility, for a model of a phallus—often a huge one—was invariably carried in his processions. The Greeks were not self-conscious as we are about human reproduction, and to exalt and promote the powers of reproduction by carrying model phalluses in parades seemed only logical.

The Eleusinian Mysteries

The Eleusinian Mysteries developed from the cult of Demeter and Persephone at Eleusis, near Athens. The pretty tale is that Persephone, daughter of Demeter, the goddess of the grain, was carried off to the underworld by Hades, the god of that realm. Her mother wandered in search of her and finally found her there and got Zeus's permission to take her back. Because Persephone had eaten something while in Hades, however, there had to be a compromise that allowed her to spend half her time on earth and half in the world below. All this is described in a beautiful poem of the seventh century, the *Hymn to Demeter*.

There were two great developments in the cult attached to the Mysteries. First the performance of the ritual that symbolized the idea of the death and return of the vegetation somehow turned into a mystery play, accompanied by the belief that there ought to be certain initiated people who would see this play and thereby gain immortality, while all others were barred. The second development occurred when Eleusis became part of Athens and the whole cult was subjected to the Athenian flair for dramatizing and publicizing everything Athenian. There are many references in ancient literature to the Mysteries, but the actual performance was secret, and we can only guess that it repeated the chief story of the cult.

There were other mysteries that we know very little about. The island of Samothrace, for instance, was the seat of a considerable cult. Recent excavations have shown us something about this cult and its buildings. After the end of the fourth century the famous Winged Victory, now in the Louvre, stood in the basin of a fountain on the hillside overlooking the precinct where these mysteries were celebrated.

PHILOSOPHY

In science, as in many other fields, the Greeks were the first of the moderns. They stood upon the shoulders of the Near Eastern peoples and the Egyptians, whose first steps in science are coming to be rated more and more highly by scholars. If we cannot give the Greeks credit for starting from nothing, as they were thought to have done when our knowledge of the earlier peoples was still scanty and vague, we can give them credit for cultivating scientific studies more intensively, organizing the knowledge into systems of general laws in the modern style, and trying to explain everything without ascribing it to the caprice of divinities. The style of Greek science, as of almost everything the Greeks did, is the beginning of the modern Western style and is in contrast to the more ancient Near Eastern and Egyptian style.

Science and philosophy were one and the same thing at their beginning, which took place somewhere around the year 600 B.C. among the Ionian Greeks of the coast of Asia Minor. Until about that time the ancient mythological and religious explanations of the nature of the world suffered no serious challenge. It would not have occurred to these Ionian Greeks to

call themselves either scientists or philosophers, for neither of these words
had yet been invented. After a century or so the word "philosophy" (*philo-
sophia*) came into use; it was applied to the whole process of understanding
what life and the world are, and science was a major part of it.

Thales of Miletus

Thales is the first man to whose name we can attach any definite philosophical ideas. His lifetime fell somewhere between 640 and 545 B.C. He
presumably was a lively and able merchant and traveled widely in business. He is said to have been a good astronomer and especially interested
in navigation. Thales said that water is the primary substance, or substrate,
from which all other substances are derived. Whatever one may think of
this statement as a piece of science, it clearly took a new frame of mind
to raise the point at all. He was probably influenced by the fact that we
can see water in three states—liquid, solid, and vaporous—and can follow
the change between states. It would seem a reasonable conjecture that
water might undergo many other changes not so easily followed.

The Ionian School

The Greeks who later wrote about these early philosophers obviously
knew little about them. They did know the name of Anaximander, who
lived in Miletus the generation after Thales, and the name of Anaximenes,
the leader in the next generation. Probably a number of people were interested in this sort of study and speculation, but there is no reason to
suppose that they spent all their time this way. They were more likely
to be merchants who had lively minds. Although they were, and are, people of considerable importance in intellectual history, accurate information
about them must have been hard to get two or three hundred years later
when attempts were first made to describe the beginnings of philosophy.

Anaximander of Miletus is called the pupil of Thales; this probably
means only that he was a younger man who profited by discussions with
Thales. He was in the prime of life in about 560 B.C., and probably wrote
a book. He struggled with the problem of the primary element, or substrate. In the place of water, which Thales had put forward, Anaximander
spoke of the *apeiron,* or the Unlimited. Earth, air, fire, and water seemed
to him to be the most handy gross classifications of matter, as they did to
many other Greeks. He divided these four elements into pairs of opposite
qualities: hot-cold and wet-dry. It seemed inappropriate that water, only
one of these elements, should be primary. The more generalized conception
of the Unlimited allowed these four to be derived from it and to be mixed

together in it. The Unlimited itself was neutral in quality, not limited (that is, not limited by definite qualities) and was not itself subject to changes, as water is.

The third leader of this sort of activity in Miletus was Anaximenes, who was said by later writers to have been a pupil of Anaximander. For us the noteworthy part of his scantily recorded contribution is his assertion that air is the primary element. From air, he said, all things are created by condensation and rarefaction.

Heracleitus of Ephesus was the last of the great philosophers of the Ionian school. He was probably in the prime of life about 500 B.C. Like the others, he was deeply interested in the constitution of the physical world. He nominated fire to be the substrate and tried to work out a cycle of change from fire to air to earth to water and back to fire. He was much impressed by the prevalence and importance of change, for him best represented by the nature of fire, which is constantly moving and shifting, yet continues to be fire even as it changes. We are to imagine that beside the fascinating visible movement of fire there are two other movements: the struggle within it of the opposites hot-cold and the larger movement in the cycle of change into air, earth, and water. The river, too, is a convenient symbol of sameness with change. One cannot step twice into the same river, as Heracleitus puts it. The water is different the second time, yet it remains the same river, for it has a form that persists through the change of the water. "Everything is in flux," he said, by which he meant that behind the apparent sameness of solid things there is a change like that of the water in the river.

None of these men intended to allow his philosophy to end in nihilism; Heracleitus found a basic principle, an unchanging reality that could be relied upon, in what he called the Logos. This difficult word means a law or principle; in an orderly way it unites the substrate and the process that changes it. The Logos is not a material thing, and Heracleitus does not try to explain where it comes from. Here we have come upon a more abstract way of thought than we found among the early Ionians, and we can see the development of a contrast between a Form which in itself is something and has existence and the Matter that fills in that form.

Heracleitus was suffused with a consciousness of his own intellectual superiority. Among the fragments of his works that later Greeks preserved for us by quoting him there are a number expressing a lofty contempt for the stupidity of people in general. He declares Homer and other authors to be inadequate as guides to life. He sourly disapproves of all emotional forms of religion. In human affairs, he said, one's own character is one's destiny. Such a statement shows that individualism and consciousness of self were advancing.

The Pythagoreans

Pythagoras of Samos flourished in the latter part of the sixth century; possibly he lived from about 560 to 480 B.C. He left Samos in early life for Croton, in southern Italy, where he founded an order or brotherhood of which the chief purpose was the purification of the soul and its eventual release by the usual methods of mystic ritual acts, abstinences that we should call taboos, and ceremonial purgations. There is no plain reason why the Pythagoreans were interested in science. Probably Pythagoras himself originated their two great concepts: number as a first principle and the importance of groups of opposites. Pythagorean discoveries in the realm of musical tones as related to the length of the vibrating string seem straightforward enough. We are less satisfied when we try to understand the mystic properties of numbers, but this idea had vitality until the time of Dante and beyond. They spoke of perfect numbers, which are equal to the sum of their factors, including one, as six equals one plus two plus three. Ten also was called perfect, but for different reasons. Aristotle reports that they found void, proportion, and other qualities in ten. Another writer speaks of ten as containing the linear, plane, and solid types, for one, he says, is a dot, two is a line, three is a triangle, and four is a pyramid, and all add up to ten.

One of their most brilliant ideas was that of incommensurable numbers, those which cannot be expressed as the quotients of integers. This arises from the so-called Pythagorean theorem that the square of the hypotenuse of a right triangle is equal to the sum of the squares of the other two sides. If the other two sides are one, the square of each is one, and the sum of their squares is two, and the square of the hypotenuse is two, so that the hypotenuse is equal to the square root of two. To recognize this as a numerical entity expressible only as the square root of two was a leap in mathematics.

ART

Changes Brought by the Restoration of Contact

When significant contact was restored between Greece and the Near East, the workmen of some places were more alert than those of others to study the new products from overseas. We have already noted that the Ionians were slow to accept the new influences, then suddenly bounded to the fore in both intellectual and artistic life. Athens and Corinth were quick to make a change in their Geometric pottery that may symbolize the new influence; the straight lines of the geometric decoration were replaced by curving lines in the patterns and by flower designs borrowed from the older civilization. The Geometric had had some schematized and angular figures of men and animals. Now these figures were filled out with curves, and a whole zoo of monsters and imaginary creatures was brought from the East to join them. The Greek was soon joyously adding fauna of his own devising to the traditional creatures of the East on his pottery. Archaeologists have also found bronze bowls, shields, and small figures that show the same spread of influence to the Greeks, and there are little ivory reliefs that tell the same story. Doubtless the same would prove true of fabrics if specimens survived. Now the period of local styles during the "time between" and the period of the new age characterized by borrowing of Near Eastern techniques was succeeded by a time when Greek workmen of every kind knew what was being done in the world and were able to create with inspiration from, but without undue dependence on, the work of others and without shortcomings in their own technique.

Jewelry and Other Small Things

The technique of making jewelry and other small, fine things was developed early among the Sumerians and continued to flourish thereafter. Those few scholars who have worked comprehensively with the great number of such objects preserved from ancient times are inclined to believe that there was little fluctuation in this type of art. After the great early surge that brought it to a high level of excellence it went on and on in most civilized countries with little change in quality and with few new discoveries. During the new age the Greeks became competent in this field and continued to be so.

We can reconstruct the activities of some of the great artists who made small items during the age from 800 to 500 B.C. By the third of these three centuries the industry—or the art, if we should call it that—was firmly established throughout the Greek world, and certain men had founded businesses that continued after them. We know of such enterprises in Asia Minor, in the islands, in Laconia, and in Athens. The master did small pieces himself and handled larger pieces with the assistance of his sons and of others whom he was training. The references to such establishments are reminiscent of what Benvenuto Cellini tells us about his work first in the service of older masters and then as an independent producer.

Such masters and the men with whom they had surrounded themselves produced a great variety of things in gold, silver, bronze, hard stone, ivory, the combination of gold and ivory known as chryselephantine, marble, and wood. They made jewelry of every imaginable sort, ornamental fittings for daggers or for the bridles and bits of horses, and small things for use in houses: gold bowls, bronze figurines, plaques of gold, silver, and bronze ornamented with everything from geometric designs to sphinxes and griffins. There was almost nothing for which they could not design some small and beautiful part. The person of refined and imaginative taste was able to surround himself with some very beautiful things.

Sculpture

In the latter part of the seventh century the Greeks began to make sizable statues of limestone and marble. Although it is generally supposed that they got the idea from their contacts with Egypt, it is agreed that the surviving statues from the earliest period are decidedly not imitations of those that they could have seen in Egypt. Probably the cost of statues was moderate, whether they were in limestone, which was easy to work, or in marble, which was more difficult to work but could be given a very satisfactory surface texture and clearness of line. These statues should be regarded as fine commercial products in order to avoid the mysticism so often attached to discussions of art.

Statuary was very desirable for religious purposes; since religion was the affair of the polis, the statue would presumably be publicly commissioned. An establishment might take an order for the construction of a bronze statue of a god to be put in a temple or a holy place and send a team to the site to stay there for some weeks, build a little foundry, cast the statue on the spot from a design made by the master of the whole enterprise, then dismantle the foundry and depart. It is possible that some stone statues were made in somewhat the same way, that is, a fairly skilled stonecutter would shape a block of good stone according to a design made by the master. There is evidence that successful statues were often reproduced many times by the work of such assistants.

Many examples of male figures called *kouroi* (young men) and female figures called *korai* (girls) have been preserved. Both males and females followed a closely defined type, and it was not until after 500 B.C. that the conventions of the type were relaxed and there existed real freedom and variety in these statues. The *kouros* is naked, stands with his left leg slightly advanced, is upright, and looks straight ahead. The female figure is clothed, but follows the same rigid pattern as the male. There is disagreement among art historians as to why this highly stylized and somewhat archaic type persisted for so long among the Greeks. There are those who feel that the sculptors were slow to learn and that what we see in these figures is an early stage of development of taste and skill. The other point of view is that the stiff, conventional, and unchanging quality of the *kouroi* and *korai* is due to the strength of convention, not to the artist's inability to do what he wished to do, because the other works of this period—relief sculptures, for example—show that the artist had technique sufficient for other demands.

Another contested point is the use of color on Greek statues and buildings. Many people long refused to believe the plain evidence of the traces of paint remaining on many stone statues and on many buildings. The Greeks did use color. Bright red, blue, brown, and gold were favorites. Garments were gaily painted; flesh was painted red or red-brown, and sometimes the details of faces were brought out by emphasizing eyes, lips, and hair with an effect like that of modern women's make-up. The details of buildings could be brought out in the same way. Scholars now all agree that paint was used.

Painting

Painting progressed rapidly during the new age. Because so much of it has been lost, a somewhat wrong impression is created by the fact that a great part of what has survived is the painting done on pottery, which offers a restricted and curved surface. There is evidence, however, that painting was done on larger surfaces as well, as in the public porticoes. The interesting frescoes in the tombs of the Etruscans in Italy give some idea of what the Greeks could do on walls. The influence of Greek painting is plain in Etruria, and perhaps some of the tombs were done by Greek workmen.

Although painted pottery was produced in Ionia, the islands, Laconia, and Corinth, and during the eighth and seventh centuries the Corinthian dominated the market, the Athenians improved their product by the later years of the seventh century and by the middle of the sixth century they had almost achieved a monopoly of the export trade in pottery.

Architecture

The temples of the Greeks were their most important buildings. Their houses usually looked in on a courtyard and were not interesting to look at from the outside. They probably were cramped and uncomfortable, as one would expect in a country where people live mostly outdoors or in a courtyard. There were no large buildings like ours for business or like those that the Romans built, and the government buildings did not amount to much. In Egypt and the Near East there had been palaces for the kings and temples for the gods. In Crete and Mycenae there were no temples, since the gods lived in the king's house or in holy outdoor places. In this Greece of the new age there were no kings and no palaces, but it began to seem a good idea to build houses for the gods. The first ones were fairly crude structures of wood and mud brick, perhaps not even so large and imposing as the houses of some of the leading citizens. With the development of stone buildings, however, a new architectural elaborateness appeared.

Two chief styles of architecture developed, with thought and experiment and even theoretical discussion: the Doric in mainland Greece and among the Greeks of Italy and Sicily, and the Ionic among the more eastern Greeks. The Ionic also appeared in Attica, which was the only place where both Doric and Ionic seemed at home. The two orders differ chiefly in columns and friezes and in the generally lighter effect of the Ionic. The Doric column has no base; the Ionic has a round base. The Doric column seems sturdier, the Ionic more slender. The Doric capital is square, whereas the Ionic is turned over into volutes. The Doric frieze is an alternation of metopes, or squares sculptured in relief (or sometimes left plain), and triglyphs, or squares marked with two deep vertical grooves, while the Ionic is a running frieze, an uninterrupted series of relief sculptures. The Parthenon is the perfect embodiment of the Doric order, and the temple of Nike on the Acropolis is a good example of the Ionic. In the Corinthian order, which was not popular until after the Classical Age of Greece, the capitals of the columns are ornately carved with acanthus leaves. Otherwise this order is essentially Ionic.

LITERATURE

Hesiod

The earliest of the Greek authors of the new age was Hesiod, who lived at about the end of the eighth century. He tells us that he was the son of a Greek of Asia Minor who had emigrated back to Greece and come to the little town of Ascra, in Boeotia, to become a small farmer. Hesiod himself evidently knew the farmer's life. Yet he must somehow have learned the art of the oral poet, for his language is a stiffer and less graceful version of the language of Homer. His interest is in the way of life of his own time and especially in how a man of the small farming class can get along in the world. In his *Works and Days* he discusses the difficulties of the farmer's life on a small and not very fertile farm.

Hesiod gives many homely precepts for farming. In contrast he discusses the life of the seagoing merchant, a life from which he shrinks as difficult, dangerous, and dishonest. Another part of the work lets us know that when he and his brother disagreed about the division of his father's farm, his brother corrupted the arbitrator, one of those local grandees whose legal jurisdiction the rising polis was to supersede, and thus cheated Hesiod out of his share. *Works and Days* is an essay on life in the new age that cries loudly for justice for the common man.

In *Theogony*, or *The Family History of the Gods*, he struggles to expound a larger conception of justice. He tells of the crude early generations of the gods and makes Zeus a great improvement upon his predecessors in refinement and justice, but one who needs still to improve. That later Greeks had a very high opinion of Hesiod is puzzling if one thinks of him only as a purveyor of tales about the family tree of the gods or a chronicler of the life of the small farmer, but understandable if he is regarded as one of the earliest Greek reflective thinkers. He was apparently the originator of what is sometimes called "the moral education of Zeus," the process of refining Greek thought about the divine nature.

Elegy and Iambic Poetry

By about 700 B.C. the development of more personal forms of poetry had begun. The new poems, or elegies, were short, not narratives, but exhortations to valor, songs of sorrow, songs of love, and expressions of personality. The language of elegy still borrowed much from epic, however, despite the changes in form and content. The old expressions and turns of phrase were ready at hand, and the workers in the new field naturally used some of them. The meter was modified by changing every second line. The epic had had a succession of dactylic hexameters, with no setting off of stanzas or strophes. In elegy the hexameter was followed by a pentameter—as it were, by a hexameter that had had a piece dropped out of its middle and another piece dropped off its end, so that it was a little shorter and the rhythm was changed in an agreeable way. A hexameter followed by a pentameter was called an elegiac couplet; an elegy was composed of a succession of elegiac couplets. Elegy was sung to the accompaniment of the flute.

The first distinguishable elegiac poet is Tyrtaeus, who worked in Sparta. What little we have of his elegies is fine, straightforward, martial poetry, urging the Spartans to reflect on the disadvantages of being worsted and to stand bravely and fight for all that was dearest to them. The Spartan spirit is also found in his elegy called *Eunomia,* a word that to the Spartan signified the well ordered condition of his state. The martial elegies were learned and sung by the Spartans for hundreds of years afterward.

Mimnermus of Colophon, an Ionian, lived at about the same time as Tyrtaeus, in the late 600s. In contrast to the martial note of Tyrtaeus, he sang of love and the fleeting quality of youth. His elegies were popular as solo pieces to be sung to languorous melodies and accompanied by the flute. The following is an example of his poetry:

What living, what delight is there without Aphrodite the golden? May I die off when these things no longer can move me—love taken in secret, sweet gifts, the bed—the things that are the bright flower of youth for both men and women. But when painful old age comes on, age that takes away a man's attractiveness and strength, unpleasant worries wear continually upon his mind. He can take no pleasure in regarding the light of the sun; he is disagreeable to boys, unhonored by women. Thus have the gods laid evil old age on us.

Elegy was used rather differently by the statesman Solon, the first literary man of Athens. Elegy was essentially a personal address to other people. The addresses of Solon, whether to his fellow Athenians or to the world in general, reflect his varied interests. One of his liveliest elegies, that on the necessity of recovering the island of Salamis from the Megarians, was delivered in the agora, or market place, presumably because the presentation of formal proposals about Salamis in the Assembly had been forbidden. The poem is said to have stirred the Athenians to effective action. Others deal with the unhappy state of affairs that led to his being elected archon for the year 594 and describe and defend the remedial measures that he devised. These elegies show some poetic quality. In addition they illustrate the fact that elegy was used for a variety of subjects on which the author wanted to expound his views, but most forcibly they illustrate the fact that prose writing did not grow up among the Greeks until after men had written in verse for a long time.

Archilochus of Paros, who probably flourished just before the middle of the seventh century, was said by the Greeks to have invented the iambic meter, meaning that he was the first man who wrote polished and effective iambic lines. The iamb consists of a short syllable followed by a long syllable. The iambic trimeter, or line with three pairs of iambs, came to be the normal line of the speeches of Greek and Latin plays; its easy conversational quality, as well as tradition, recommended it to the earlier writers of plays in the modern languages.

With Archilochus purely personal expression makes a dramatic appearance on a scene previously peopled only with Homer, some lesser men who were producing the *Epic Cycle,* Hesiod, and the elegiac writers. He was the son of an aristocrat of Paros and a slave woman. Possibly the fact that he was without a settled place in society, although he was a man of force and ability, caused him to take the unusual step of writing frankly and vividly about his own situation, adventures, and feelings. In any age the settled aristocrat rarely writes; had he had a place like his father's in that highly conservative society, Archilochus might well not have been impelled to write and to set the precedent of personal expression in poetry. As it was, he attached to iambic poetry its connotation of bitter attacks on Fate and persons.

As a young man Archilochus had an opportunity to make a new start by going out as a member of a colony that the Parians sent to the island of Thasos. The young man complained in his verses of the dullness of the place. But when life was enlivened by some military action, he wrote of this, too, in his cross-grained manner, telling how he had thrown away his shield and run. But he had saved himself, he said, and he could get another shield better than that one. Presumably this is scoffing at the standards of society by one who resented the fact that he did not have a proper place in society; cowardice in battle was of necessity very seriously regarded. He finally became a mercenary soldier, as many a disgruntled man has done, and met his death in battle in early middle age.

The ancients, who had all his work, regarded him highly. He was a poet of great ability in spite of his continual disappointment with life. In his iambics he was a master of form and had wit and spirit that raised his satirical and critical observations far above the level of mere dreary complaining.

Lyric Poetry

Alcaeus and Sappho, two poets of Mitylene, the chief city of the island of Lesbos, both lived in the latter part of the seventh century and the early part of the sixth. Both wrote lyric poetry in the original sense, poetry meant to be sung to the accompaniment of the lyre.

The poetry of Alcaeus has many reflections of the political struggles of his age, for example, attempts by the clans of the nobility to take away the ascendancy of a single clan that had ruled since the bygone days of the kings. He apparently was the first to use the figure of the ship of state in poetry; the Roman Horace, a student of Alcaeus's work, used this figure effectively, and in modern times it has become common. Alcaeus wrote hymns to the gods—Apollo, Hermes, Hephaestus, Artemis, Eros— that appear to have been intended not for public use but for social gatherings. Pleasant in tone, they seem more the expression of a poetic imagination than an uplifting of the spirit toward the god. He often sang the pleasures of wine and sociability. In one short extant passage he speaks of trying to make tolerable the blazing heat of midsummer; in another, later echoed by Horace, he gives a charming picture of indoor joys about the fire in winter.

Sappho is one of the small circle of lyric poets of the first rank whom the West has produced. Hers is personal poetry, indeed, a compelling statement of the ecstasy and the pain that can come from the fierce attraction of one human being to another. The beauty, charm, and power of her verses need not be lessened by the recognition that the objects of her passion and desire were women. Mere respectability has had its revenge by destroying perhaps ninety-five percent of her bequest to us, an example of which follows:

Deathless Aphrodite, gorgeously enthroned, Zeus's child, contriver of wiles:
Lady, I pray you not to crush my spirit with heartaches and with anguish,

but come to me if ever in the past you have heard my cries and your heart
was moved and you left your father's house and came,

yoking your golden chariot. Your pretty swift swallows brought you from
heaven through the middle air and over the dark earth with many a quick
stroke of their wings,

coming promptly to me. And you, blessed lady, with a smile on your divine
face, asked me what my sufferings were this time and why I called on you
this time,

and what my heart most desired to have. "Whom am I to persuade this
time to be your dearest one? Sappho, who is treating you badly?

For if she flees now, she soon shall pursue you. If she disdains your gifts,
she yet shall give. And if she does not love, soon she shall, and even against
her will."

Come to me this time, too, and free me from my bitter pangs. Do all the
things my heart would do. Fight, you yourself, on my side.

The form of this famous poem, which was preserved only because a
later critic quoted it in full, is essentially a prayer, yet the suggestion is
plain that all this has happened before, and the detachment and humor
contribute no little to the charm of the poem.

Anacreon, who came from Teus on the coast of Asia Minor, lived perhaps a generation later than Alcaeus and Sappho. Like them, he sang of
the pleasures of love and wine and sociability, but always in a lighter
vein than theirs. He was invited to the court of Polycrates, the brilliant
tyrant of the island of Samos, and after the death of Polycrates he was
invited to the court of Hippias and Hipparchus, the sons of Peisistratus.
The grimmer atmosphere after the murder of Hipparchus was uncon-
genial to him, and he spent his last years in the less glamorous court of
the Aleuadae in Thessaly.

Simonides of Ceos (556–467 B.C.) was another Ionian who made the
rounds of the courts of the tyrants. Finally he settled in Athens, by then
a democracy, and sang her glories and the especial glory of the great
resistance to the Persians. His *threnoi,* or laments, were highly esteemed;
they were meant to be sung to the flute at funeral ceremonies. He also
gained many commissions for the *epinikion,* or triumphal ode for a victor
in one of the great games. He may be said to have raised both the lament
and the poem of victory to the status of literary types.

9

THE FIRST HALF OF THE
FIFTH CENTURY AND THE
EARLY FLOWERING OF ATHENS

I t is good that the communities of Greeks were not seriously attacked by larger powers until they had had time to absorb the cultures of more advanced peoples and to develop the culture of their own which has been so important to the West. Such attacks finally came, beginning about 550 B.C. The Lydians and then the Persians laid a heavy hand upon the Asiatic Greeks. Later the Persians attacked Greece itself, and they did so at the very time that the Greeks of the West had to fight against the Carthaginians and, less dangerously, against the Etruscans.

The high tide of Persian attack was rolled back at Salamis in 480, as was the Carthaginian at Himera in Sicily in the same year. After the Persian defeat at Plataea in 479, the Persian land forces withdrew from Greece. In 474 a great naval battle in Italian waters broke the sea power of the Etruscans. The Greeks were largely free of interference for the rest of the fifth century and through most of the fourth century, until the time of Alexander the Great. We are not entitled to assert that political freedom was a necessary condition for the flowering of Athens and for the fine achievements of Greeks from many other cities. The fact is that freedom from outside interference enabled the Athenians and others to engage in some very interesting political experiments that were not the least part of the activities of this brilliant time.

The Persians and the Asiatic Greeks

The Greek coastal cities, which in 547 B.C. had rejected the suggestion of Cyrus the Persian that they desert the Lydians and come over to him, were subjected by the Persians soon after Croesus fell. The Persians required tribute and soldiers from them, as they did from everyone. They did not try to enforce cultural uniformity. There was no pressure on the Greeks to speak the Persian language or to adopt Persian customs or the Persian religion. Their membership in the Persian Empire may have been an economic advantage, yet it is difficult to see precisely how. Their old water routes could hardly be protected for them by the Persians; they had already had profitable trade with the interior of Asia Minor under the Lydians; possibly they were now able to draw some profit from being free to trade with Babylonia and Persia, although there they would find very strong competition from old, established manufacturers and merchants.

Did the Greeks resent the political situation? The Persians appointed some leading local man as governor (or tyrant, as the Greeks chose to call him) of each city. Although this move should have been thoroughly distasteful to the Greeks, we have no explicit evidence that it was. Indeed, the local tyrants may well have been very acceptable, since the Persians naturally did not allow them to commit excesses against their fellow citizens.

Greek loyalty to the Persians was tested when in the year 513 Darius the Persian attacked the Scythians. His army crossed the Bosporus on a pontoon bridge, marched to the Danube and crossed that, too, on a pontoon bridge built by the Greeks of his fleet and guarded by them in his absence. He pursued the Scythians, who retreated before him, having no cities to defend, until he decided that it was not possible to bring them to an engagement. The Greeks who were guarding the bridge were urged by the Scythians to break it down, but they refused to do so. Although Darius had failed to win the submission of the Scythians, whom he thought of as causing pressures on his northern boundaries, he left an army in Thrace that subdued the Thracians as far west as the Strymon River and induced the Macedonian king Amyntas to submit to the Persians.

Yet the Ionian Greeks did revolt against the Persians in 499 B.C., forty-odd years after they first became Persian subjects. The historian Herodotus gives the personal ambitions of certain Milesians as the cause of the revolt. The upper classes proclaimed *isonomia,* or equality of rights, to win the adherence of the lower classes, and the revolt spread through all the cities. From our evidence we can find no better reason for this unpromising and dangerous revolt than a somewhat impractical desire for complete independence.

The leaders of the revolt petitioned Sparta for aid. The Spartans refused, correctly fearing what nowadays is known as a land war in Asia. The Athenians, who had already refused Persia's demand that they reinstate the Athenian tyrant Hippias, decided to send twenty ships, and Eretria, on the island of Euboea, sent five. In 498 the Ionians, thus reinforced, took their troops by sea to Ephesus and marched to Sardis. They could not capture the citadel, but the city was burned.

The rebels did not put forth their full force on the sea, however, nor were they willing to cooperate fully with each other, and Athens and Eretria presently thought it best to withdraw their forces. The other cities carried on the war, the Persians having the advantage by land and the Greeks by sea, until the naval battle of Lade in 495, where the flight of some of the Greeks led to a decisive Persian victory. By 493 the Persians had reduced the last of the rebellious cities.

The Milesians were severely punished. Their city was destroyed, their men killed, and their women and children enslaved. The Persians were not unduly severe on others. Indeed, they reviewed the taxes to make sure that they were not provocatively harsh, made the cities enter into mutual nonaggression treaties, and replaced the tyrants with democracies. The modern scholar living in a democracy is tempted to regard this last move as a sign of growing enlightenment among the Persians: it is rather more likely that the Persians felt that democratic governments in the Greek states would be less able to agree on any move against Persia than the former governments had been.

It has been suggested that the establishment of Persian control over the Greeks of Asia Minor in 547 B.C. stopped the activity of the lyric poets and the philosophers there. It is true that the activity of both poets and philosophers seemed to trail off in Ionia at this time. It is not necessarily true, however, that intellectual activities do not flourish under imperial control, for poetry and philosophy are highly individual enterprises.

THE PERSIAN INVASIONS OF GREECE

Darius's Expedition to Greece: Marathon

The Persians now moved to strengthen their hold on their other western possessions. In 492 an expedition to the Thracian satrapy soundly defeated the one tribe that showed fight and reasserted Persian sovereignty over all the peoples, including the Macedonians, who had submitted to the Persians before the Ionian revolt. The next move was against the Greeks. Herodotus has a story that King Darius, enraged by the burning of Sardis, had a slave say to him at dinner every day, "Master, remember the Athenians." Doubtless he felt special annoyance at the Athenians and the Eretrians. The main consideration was, however, that if Greece were subdued, the whole complex of western Asia Minor, the Bosporus, Propontis, and Chersonesus, Thrace, and Macedonia would be quiet. The first expedition was probably sent out to secure the islands, to punish Athens and Eretria, and to lead up to the subjugation of all Greece.

In the summer of 491 Darius gave orders to his maritime subjects to prepare warships and transports. Envoys demanded tokens of submission in the usual form, "earth and water," from the islanders of the Aegaean and from the mainland states of Greece. Most of the islanders submitted. Aegina, which was in a state of undeclared war with Athens, gave the tokens of submission. Although they were not on the best of terms with the Spartans, the Athenians knew that the Spartans had always been opposed to any advance by the Persians, and they now complained that Aegina was deserting her obligations to the Spartan alliance and was acting against the common interest of the Greeks. The Spartan king, Cleomenes, gave an example of Spartan control of her alliance by arresting the oligarchic leaders of Aegina, who had favored medizing, or taking the Persian side.

Demaratus, the other Spartan king, was himself inclined to medize. Indeed, he was at odds with Cleomenes on almost every issue. Cleomenes claimed that Demaratus was illegitimate and at last succeeded in making him leave the country. Demaratus went to the Persian king, as did so many exiled Greeks of high rank. He later (in 480) accompanied the next king, Xerxes, on his invasion of Greece, and some of the best passages in Herodotus's account of the war are those in which Xerxes asks Demaratus from time to time what to expect from the Spartans and Demaratus tries to explain to an Oriental despot what Westerners will probably do.

In the early summer of 490 the Persian fleet moved through the islands, which had submitted, took Eretria, which after a week of attacks was betrayed by two of its own citizens, and landed on the mainland at Marathon above Athens. They presumably were advised by Hippias, the exiled Athenian tyrant whom they had brought with them, planning to reinstate him at Athens. Hippias had long ago defeated a Spartan force trying to land at Phalerum below Athens, and his father had landed successfully at Marathon when he returned from his long exile.

The Athenians intended to fight. They sent a runner to Sparta to call for help. He covered about a hundred and forty miles in about two days. The Spartans answered that they were in the midst of a festival and could not go out to war until the full moon, six days away; apparently such religious scruples were genuine. The Athenian assembly decided to send their ten thousand hoplites, or heavy infantry, out to Marathon to meet the enemy. The cavalry and light-armed troops, who could hardly have faced their much superior Persian counterparts, stayed at home.

At this point in the gallant operation of the Athenian people a single man exerted a decisive influence. He was Miltiades, the third of his name, the grandson of a man who under Peisistratus was invited to be king of the Dolonci of the Thracian Chersonesus. All three had ruled there while remaining Athenian citizens and had had experience of Persian military methods. This Miltiades had given up when Persia tightened her control of the territories north of the Dardanelles and had returned to Athens. He was in this year one of the ten generals who commanded the contingents of the ten tribes, and he had been important in persuading the Athenians to send the troops out to Marathon. Now, when the ten generals were evenly divided as to whether to fight or return to defend the city, he influenced Callimachus, the polemarch, to vote for fighting. The generals customarily commanded the whole force in turn, but the influential Aristides and three others yielded their days of command to Miltiades.

As luck would have it, the great day was his own day of command in the regular rotation. One of the Ionians serving with the Persians stole across before dawn to tell the Greeks that the Persian cavalry was away —we do not know why or where. With the dawn the Greeks moved across the plain of Marathon, their line thinned out to strengthen the wings, and they finally charged the Persians on the run. The Persians broke through the center and pursued, but the Greek wings wheeled to encircle. At last it became a Persian retreat to the shore and a battle around the ships that they were trying to board in order to get away. The Persians, who may well have planned to embark that day anyway, left six thousand dead on the field to the Athenian 192 and sailed away with the loss of seven ships. As the defeated enemy departed late in the morning, the Athenians saw a signal from some point near Athens as the sunlight was reflected from a polished shield.

What the signal meant has never been established. Knowing all too well, however, that treachery was possible, the army set out on the march of eight or nine hours to the city. When the Persian forces sailed up to the beach at Phalerum next morning, they saw that the Athenian army had arrived and was ready to defend the city. Further, the approach by sea was now formidable, thanks to the foresight of Themistocles, who as archon in 493 had persuaded the city to begin the fortification of Peiraeus, which was a complex of three harbors. Without further ado the Persians gave up their attempt on Athens and began their journey home. The Spartan advance guard of two thousand men arrived, heard of the victory, went on to Marathon to study the field and the Persian weapons, returned to congratulate the Athenians, and set out to march another hundred and forty miles home.

A Breathing Space

After Darius had spent three years preparing for a great new invasion of Greece, Egypt revolted, giving him a check, and in 486 he died. His son Xerxes, who succeeded him, completed the reduction of Egypt in 485, then turned his attention to the preparations for the invasion of Greece, the most spectacular of which was the cutting by forced labor of a mile-and-a-half canal across the peninsula of Mount Athos, on the point of which a Persian fleet had been wrecked by a storm in the campaign of 492. Although some scholars of the nineteenth century doubted the statement of Herodotus that the canal was dug, the place where it was, now filled in, shows up plainly in airplane photographs.

In Greece meanwhile there was a lively struggle during the decade of the 480s about policies. Themistocles was the leading figure in advocating an active policy of building up naval power to resist the inevitable attack by Persia. During the decade a number of men were ostracized, all of them Alcmaeonids, and their ostracism seems to mean that Themistocles and the group who favored breaking the power of the great clans, on the one hand, and preparing actively for resistance to Persia, on the other hand, were in the ascendant. Themistocles' policy gave Athens great naval strength and led her into the naval league that became the Athenian Empire, which in its turn was to give the common man employment and political significance, thus furthering democracy at Athens. The historian Thucydides later praised Themistocles as one who, better than any man of his time, could foresee the developments likely to result from a policy. Prescient as he was, Themistocles could hardly have foreseen all these results.

In 487 another change was made that lessened the power of the great clans and favored democracy: the archons were henceforth to be chosen by lot from a panel of five hundred elected by the demes. They were still to be drawn only from the first two classes in the state, and they still had to be able to command votes in the first stage of the process, but since they were chosen by lot in the second stage, the influence of the clans or any other group was undermined, and the system was thereby made more democratic. It followed naturally that the archonship became less important politically and that the office of general, which remained entirely elective, became more important politically, because a general gained his office only by being able to command votes.

In 483 the discovery of an excellent new vein of silver in the state mines gave rise to a high political controversy. Themistocles wished the city to use it for new warships instead of distributing it among the citizens as a windfall, as had been done before. Aristides, who opposed Themistocles, was ostracized, and it is interesting that he retired to Aegina, that great enemy of Athens, where the upper class dominated. Class lines could thus be more important than national lines. Although full democracy was yet to come to Athens, the events of this decade represent a strengthening of the polis in general as against the clans and a definite move toward democracy.

The two hundred new ships that the Athenians provided for their navy were triremes. The ship was perhaps one hundred and twenty feet long and fewer than twenty in the beam. It had one hundred and seventy oarsmen, a small group of officers and petty officers, and an armed group of fourteen spearmen and four archers. Its square sail was generally left ashore when battle was imminent. The ship was used chiefly to ram opposing warships; the armed personnel were to prevent boarding. Ramming was a skilled operation and required a highly trained crew. For the two hundred triremes 34,000 oarsmen were needed. Obviously a polis that wished to be a naval power had to have some money at its disposal, as well as a large pool of citizens and allies; this was not work for slaves. Such a polis was also bound to feel some immediate political effect from the participation of so many citizens in the armed forces.

By late 481 Xerxes was at Sardis and making ready to move his vast forces toward Greece. Heralds came to demand the submission of all the Greek states except Athens and Sparta. About a third of the Greeks gave their submission, chiefly the islanders and the people of northern Greece, all of whom felt farthest from any protection that Sparta and Athens might give. The Delphic Oracle, which had been known before to show a rather distressing worldly practicality, counseled against resisting the might of the Mede.

The poleis who were willing to resist, thirty-one in number, met at ·Sparta late in 480. A new league was formed, called simply "The Greeks" (although modern scholars generally call it "The Hellenic League"); it included the members of Sparta's league but was distinct from it. The leadership was Sparta's, but by decision of the members rather than by Sparta's demand. There was a congress with wide powers in every field; Sparta, as leader, could appoint the military and naval commanders. The Greeks were at least capable of imagining a federal organization and making it work for a short time; to make it work for a long time proved impossible.

The Great Invasion

The ponderous forces of the Persians, which may well have numbered about 500,000 although Herodotus would make them number 1,700,-000 active combatants, crossed the Hellespont on a pontoon bridge and slowly made their way across Thrace and Macedonia, drinking the rivers dry and eating the country bare, as it seemed to those inhabitants who were ordered to contribute to their supplies. They made their way down through Thessaly, whose people joined them of necessity, not having the strength to oppose them.

The first Greek resistance was offered at Thermopylae, where the road for the Persian land forces was narrow, flanked by the sea and by steep cliffs, and where the supporting fleet had to come through the narrow waters at the northern tip of the island of Euboea if it was to land troops in the rear of the Greeks without making the long trip around Euboea. The prayers of the Greeks to Poseidon and the winds were answered by gales that first damaged the main Persian fleet, then wrecked a detachment that had been sent around Euboea to close the southern entrance to the strait and bottle up the part of the Greek fleet that was between the island and the mainland.

On the shore one of the classic scenes of human history was enacted as the best troops of the Persians, in this narrow space where it was a fair fight of man against man, were repulsed again and again by a small Greek band, the core of which was three hundred Spartans under King Leonidas. At this point a traitor appeared, one Ephialtes, whose contemptible deed deserves to be kept green in memory because it was done in conjunction with the immortal bravery of the Spartans. He led the Persians around by a mountain path to take the Spartans in the rear. The Spartans died there, obedient to their orders.

Probably the desire for money caused Ephialtes' treacherous deed. The motive of those Eretrians who betrayed their city to the Persians in the invasion of 490 was perhaps different, for they may have thought that they could thus escape the dire fate that awaited all the citizens when the city was taken. From now on in Greek history treason was frequent. Perhaps in the earlier days there had been less of it because there was less opportunity. Perhaps, too, in the earlier days it was less easy to imagine one's self as separate from the rest of the community and capable of profiting individually from treason. In the earlier days there would have been no place for the traitor to live during his remaining years. But in the Classical Age of Greece, treason was frequent, not only the treason of individuals, but the treason of a faction in the polis—whether the rich or the poor—willing to betray the whole polis in the hope of getting the advantage over the other faction. Treason was almost unknown among the Spartans, however.

After the battle at Thermopylae the Persians came down to Athens and burned the city. The men of Athens were in the armed forces, and the women and children had been sent to safety in friendly cities. According to plan, the Greek fleet was to make a stand as the Persians came down toward the Isthmus of Corinth and the Peloponnesus, but now the Peloponnesian naval forces wished to retire without a struggle, intending instead to build a wall across the Isthmus in plain defiance of the fact that the Persian fleet, if not opposed, could land men anywhere it wished below the fortifications. Themistocles, who was in charge of the two hundred Athenian ships, was able to prevent his colleagues from withdrawing before the Persians. In a stormy session he threatened that the whole Athenian people would sail away to the West and found a new Athens there. He also sent a message to the Persian king, who apparently found it perfectly natural to receive what seemed to be a treasonous message from a leading Greek, telling him that the Greek fleet was about to retire and could be confined in the Bay of Salamis if Xerxes acted promptly. Themistocles hoped that such action by the Persians would both keep the Greeks from retiring and draw the Persians into an engagement in an unfavorable place.

The Persians took the bait and sent a force that closed the western entrance to the bay. On the morning of September 23, 480, they advanced in a long line into the eastern entrance. Themistocles had thus drawn them into a spot where their broadsides were exposed to the Greeks waiting for them and where not all their ships could be used. The Greeks let them get a little way into the passage, then appeared in formation and backed water until the head of the Persian line was opposite them and directly under the hill where Xerxes had stationed himself to watch the destruction of the Greeks. When the morning onshore breeze sprang up, as the Greeks had expected, and made a quartering swell that rocked the Persians out of formation and spoiled their coordination, the Greeks attacked. The maneuver, like the modern one of "crossing the enemy's T," brought the full Greek force to bear on the head of the enemy line, with the rear unable to help. The Persians lost about two hundred ships out of perhaps a thousand. The rest withdrew from the bay.

The Persian fleet was not destroyed, but this defeat was severe enough to make Xerxes change his plans. The ships and the king returned to Asia, with the Greeks following, but at a respectful distance, not in hot pursuit. The Persian army withdrew to northern Greece, whence part was sent home to Asia and part left to continue the war.

In the spring of 479 the Persian commander tried to separate the Greek forces that might be opposed to him by offering the Athenians their independence and an alliance with Persia if they would desert the league and cease to resist. The Athenians, whose eyes were fixed on the risen star of their destiny, refused. Again the Persians occupied Athens, and again the Athenians withdrew from their city. Again he made his offer, and again they rejected it, but this time they sent a furious protest to the Peloponnesians, who had done nothing, and at last the loyal forces of Greece moved. A hundred thousand men took the field to engage the Persians in Boeotia. This unusually large army showed cohesion and steadiness for the few weeks needed to defeat the enemy. The final battle was fought in 479 near Plataea after the armies had been in each other's presence for some time. The bravery and skill of the Spartan hoplites was the deciding factor. Only a remnant of the Persian army survived.

The Ionian Greeks, meanwhile, seeing an opportunity to be free of Persia, joined the Greek naval force. The Greek fleet had crossed the Aegaean and sought out the Persian fleet. In a decisive battle at Mycale, near Miletus, the Greeks defeated the Persians on land and destroyed their beached ships. This success induced many more Greeks to revolt from the Persians.

Although the league's fleet now went home, the Athenian commanders remained and conducted a siege of Sestus, the Persian naval base in the Chersonesus. They took it in the early spring of 478, then sailed home. Herodotus ends his history at this point, a logical point for him if one reflects that much of his story revolves around the startling defeat of King Xerxes. It was not the end of the war, however. For another ten years or so the Persians maintained garrisons on the European side of the Hellespont. Naval warfare went on, always with the possibility of a new Persian naval offensive against Greece, until 448. In 478 the threat from Persia still seemed great, and for this reason some Greek states took the fateful step of making a new organization for naval warfare in the Aegaean, the Delian League, which we shall discuss later.

The Western Greeks in the Early Fifth Century

In the early fifth century a brilliant cavalry officer named Gelon made himself tyrant, first of Gela, then of Syracuse. Leaving his brother Hiero to rule Gela, he made Syracuse his own center of operations. Thither he brought some people from Gela and the upper classes from some towns that he conquered. So far was he from being a champion of the oppressed or caring about the harmony of the few and the many that he sold the ordinary people of these conquered poleis into slavery. He made Syracuse probably the best fortified city in the world and developed an army of some 20,000 hoplites with a fine cavalry force and a navy of two hundred ships. He allied himself by marriage with Theron, the tyrant of Acragas.

Gelon was visited in the 480s by envoys of the Greeks who asked him for help against the threatened new invasion of the Persians. He felt strong enough to offer some troops, but on condition that he have the supreme command. Since the Spartans would not agree, he asked for command of the fleets, but to this the Athenians would not agree. Gelon therefore remained outside the conflict, taking only the practical step of sending an envoy to Delphi to wait there and give the Persians, if they were victorious, some money as well as the earth and water that signified submission.

The Carthaginians probably saw that the alliance of Gelon and Theron could cause them trouble in the western part of Sicily, which they considered their own. Having made elaborate preparations, they descended on the Greeks of eastern Sicily in 480, intending to conquer the whole island, but were so dreadfully defeated at a battle fought near Himera that they even feared a Greek attempt at invasion of the Punic territory in North Africa and were glad to make a treaty to end hostilities.

It was seventy years before the Carthaginians again tried to get control of the whole island, during which time Syracuse and the other cities prospered exceedingly. The alliances and the common action of the tyrants made them too strong for Carthaginian attack and fostered a prosperous trade; the tyrants also tried to promote culture in the old tradition.

The Greeks of South Italy preserved the Greek spirit of separatism in their dealings with one another. Some were overcome and destroyed by their Greek neighbors; some were overcome by the Italian peoples of the region; none of them ever grew very strong, as did Syracuse. Their pressure on the Etruscans, however, helped the Romans to rid themselves of their Etruscan kings in 509 B.C., and in 474 the people of Cumae, near Naples, having called the Syracusan fleet to their aid against the Etruscan fleet, defeated the Etruscans so thoroughly off Cumae that Etruscan naval power never again was formidable.

GREEK CULTURE IN THE EARLY FIFTH CENTURY

In more than one field of Greek culture the early fifth century was a time of rapid progress and of achievements full of power and promise, yet distinguishable from the fully matured products of the middle and latter part of the century.

Architecture

In Sicily and southern Italy some grandiose temples were built during the early fifth century. Theron of Acragas used part of the spoils from the Carthaginians to build a huge (173 by 361 feet) temple to Olympian Zeus in his rather modest polis. The temple of Zeus at Selinus, in Sicily, was almost as large. The fine temples of Poseidonia, the Roman Paestum, in southern Italy, were built not long after the Persian Wars. These temples were all of the Doric order.

The temple of Zeus at Olympia, probably built between 470 and 460, is a typical Doric temple. Although little of it remains standing, we know a great deal about it from excavations and from ancient descriptions. It was rectangular, 91 by 210 feet, made of rather poor local stone, since the expense of transporting marble to this out-of-the-way place would have been tremendous. It stood on a stone platform. A row of columns ran across each end and along each side, six on the ends and thirteen on the sides. There was a little space between the columns and the inner structure, making a porch on each end and a sort of side aisle down each length. The columns were of the style that characterizes the Doric order.

The Doric column is not raised on a base. It has a slight *entasis*, or convexity, near its middle, in order to correct the optical illusion of concavity that would be given by a row of straight columns. There are vertical grooves in the column, called flutings. The column is made of fair-sized drums of stone piled one on another. Each drum has a hole in the middle of the top and bottom surfaces. A plug of wood, often reinforced with an iron rod, fits down into the top hole of the drum below and up into the bottom hole of the drum above. The flutings are cut after the column has been all built up; they help to emphasize the vertical lift of the column. At the top is a swelling called the *echinus,* above which is a square capital.

A plain beam, called the architrave, rests on the capitals of the columns. Above the architrave is the frieze, a band of alternating triglyphs and metopes. The triglyph, a square piece with two deep vertical grooves, is above the head of a column and represents the end of a crossbeam in the older wooden structures that these stone temples suggest; we have already seen in Egypt this reproduction of wood when stone began to be used. The metopes are square pieces in between, which merely filled spaces, and they were usually ornamented. Above the frieze begins a pitched roof that is generally tiled. At the ends of it are triangular spaces called pediments. It was becoming the custom to fill them with figures at the time when the temple of Zeus was built; a problem in composition was set by the triangularity of the working surface. Inside the temple was the *cella,* or chamber, which in the temple at Olympia contained the greatest of all chryselephantine statues, the Zeus of the great sculptor Phidias. It stood forty feet high and was viewed from a gallery within the temple.

The architect was a local man who did a good conservative job and produced a standard Doric temple. The sculptor Phidias was an Athenian. Two of his associates did the pediments, one of which represented the beginnings of a legendary chariot race, the other the fight of the centaurs and the Thessalian tribe of the Lapithae, a wild, swirling composition.

Sculpture and Painting

During the fifth century there was a movement in sculpture away from the conventionality typified by the *kouroi* to a more literal and perhaps prosaic art. Here again we meet a difference of opinion among the experts. There is none to deny the excellence of the sculpture of the late fifth century, but some feel that art portraying faithfully what everyone can see is a little inferior to art in which the artist portrays what he himself sees according to a poetic convention. For the layman the profit of such discussions probably lies in the suggestion that he look with care and sympathy at the more conventional late archaic art of Greece as he encounters it in pictures or in museums.

A number of *kouroi* of the early fifth century suggest the change, for it is plain that their makers had been doing very careful studies in anatomy and had moved somewhat toward representing the body with its real structure. Although our perception tends to be pleased by this change, it is not necessarily an artistic advance. Rather it is the beginning of a shift in the attitude of the artists of the time that culminated in the production of many statues full of realistic action, like the well known discus thrower, the Discobolus.

The Discobolus is a marble copy of Myron's bronze original and probably dates from a little after 480, when realism was displacing the late archaic style. It has been suggested that all copies of Greek statues were made for rich and vulgar Romans in later ages. In fact the Greeks themselves often bought copies of statues.

The ancients thought of Polygnotus, a painter of this period, as a distinguished early painter. Pausanias, who wrote a Baedeker-like handbook in the second century of our era, gave a carefully detailed description of the pictures, now no longer extant, with which Polygnotus decorated the treasury of the Cnidians at Delphi. He made murals so large that they allowed many figures of nearly life size. "After the Fall of Troy" was a subject that permitted him to concentrate on character and emotion rather than action. "Odysseus in the Underworld" allowed a careful study of the shades in Hades reacting to a visit from a living man.

Literature: Lyric Poetry

Pindar (521–441 B.C.) of Thebes was the greatest of the writers of choral lyric. His first commission to write a victory ode is said to have come when he was only twenty years old, a commission to celebrate the victory of a young Thessalian noble in the footrace in the Pythian Games at Delphi. In later years he spent some time at the courts of Syracuse and Acragas. He received commissions from other tyrants and kings— those of Cyrene and Macedonia, for instance.

We have forty-four victory odes, or *epinicia*, that Pindar wrote for victories in the four great sets of games. The handling of language and meters combines with splendor and elevation of thought to make these poems masterpieces of their kind. The construction of such odes offered something of a problem, for all one had to start with was the fact that one's patron, his horses, or his son or nephew, had won a victory at one of the great meetings. Pindar had great success at choosing a myth that he could somehow connect with the victory or person he was to extol. The language was bold, elevated, and brilliant. Pindar uses metaphors frequently, often daring ones and often concerned with light. His own inclination, as well as the tastes of his patrons, led him to glorify all that was old-fashioned and aristocratic.

The Beginnings of the Tragic Drama

The history of the early drama is not clear. We do know that choral lyric had been developed to a real art form by the middle of the sixth century. We know also that tragedy was always connected with the worship of Dionysus and that somehow the choral lyrics in honor of Dionysus developed into a series of exchanges between the chorus and its leader. Thespis of Athens was said to have done something in 535 B.C.—we do not know what—that contributed largely to the rise of tragedy. By about 500 the choral lyric had developed into a series of exchanges between the chorus, its leader, called the *tragodos,* and another man who was known as "the answerer," or *hypokrites. Hypokrites* came to be the Greek word for "actor," and from it comes hypocrite, "one who plays a part."

The tragedy of the fifth century was always presented as a religious ceremony in honor of Dionysus. In Athens there were three such festivals, the Rural Dionysia in December, which was celebrated in the separate demes of Attica, the Lenaea in January, and the Great Dionysia or City Dionysia in March, which became much more important in the sixth century and was the prototype of all festivals organized for effect and for profit. In the fifth century the festival gained in fame as the fortunes of Athens rose and the dramatic part of the program developed. By March the sea was open again after the dangerous storms of winter, and visitors from all parts of the Greek world came to Athens, often to combine attendance at the great festival with business or diplomatic affairs. Athens had its Honors Day then, when honors were proclaimed for citizens or foreigners who had deserved well of Athens. It was a natural time for the arrival of ambassadors, and after Athens had turned the Delian League into the Athenian Empire, it was the time when her subject states made their monetary contributions, which were carried in one of the parades.

First came a ceremonial re-entry of the god Dionysus into Athens, escorted by a torchlight procession. The next morning there was a great parade that took sacrifices and gifts to his temple. That afternoon there was a choral contest among the entries of the ten tribes, and at night there was a *komos,* or revel, at which there was a good deal of drinking and riotous gaiety.

The other days were given over to the performance of tragedies and comedies in the Theater of Dionysus. The priest of Dionysus, flanked by other priests, sat in his special seat in the front row. Authors who wished to present plays submitted them to an official chosen to select the plays. Three of the writers would be told that the official would "give them a chorus." The expense of the chorus (costumes, for example) was borne by some rich man as a liturgy.[1] The author would train the chorus himself, at least in the early days; later there were professional trainers. The writer himself in the early days took the part of *tragodos,* the person who led the chorus and talked with it.

Aeschylus

Aeschylus, the first of the three great writers of tragedy whose works are partly preserved, was born in 525 B.C. at Eleusis, on the shore of Attica near Salamis, and died in 456. He had a vein of poetry and a sense of the spectacular, but he was not a deep or original thinker. Of the eighty or more tragedies that he wrote, we have seven. Aeschylus was a tremendous innovator. It was he who introduced the first actor, the *hypokrites,* or "answerer," who with the *tragodos,* or leader of the chorus, carried on the first dramatic conversations. Soon he added another answerer, who completed the canonical number of three on the stage who had speaking parts. He made the corresponding innovation of cutting down the lines spoken by the chorus so that the dialogue might have first importance. He is said to have given great attention to every detail of the production of his works, from the music and dances of the chorus to the masks and costumes and background. It has been suggested that the realism of European drama—as contrasted with the quality of Chinese or Sanskrit drama, for example—is essentially due to the influence exercised by Aeschylus on both the matter and the staging of the incipient Greek tragedy.

Each playwright customarily presented a group of three tragedies, called a trilogy, and a satyr play, which was a light and farcical piece. The *Oresteia* of Aeschylus is the only surviving trilogy. Its three plays form a connected story, which was not always the case. *Agamemnon* tells of the return of the great king after the fall of Troy and of his murder by the queen and her lover, who was his cousin. *Choephoroe* (Libation Bearers) tells of the return of Orestes, the son of Agamemnon, who was away from home when his father was murdered, and of his killing of the queen, his mother, and her lover in obedience to the command of the god

[1] The system of liturgies will be explained in the next chapter.

Apollo. At the end of the play he sees the dread figures of the Erinyes, or Furies, the old spirits of vengeance for the shedding of blood, rising to pursue him for the killing of his mother. The third play is *Eumenides,* or "The Kindly Ones." In the play the Furies pursue Orestes to Athens, whither Apollo told him to go as a suppliant. There the Court of the Areopagus is set up to hear his as its first case. Apollo and the Furies present their cases, the vote is tied, and Athena casts the vote that frees Orestes. Then, as the Furies complain that their ancient nature has been outraged, Athena urges them to put off their gory nature, become goddesses of Athens, honored by the greatest city of the world, and assume a kindlier nature suitable to the new age and the enlightenment of Athens. Finally they are persuaded by her talk—as fine a piece of nationalistic glorification as was ever written—and agree to become the kindly modern spirits of the modern city and assume the new name of the Eumenides, or Kindly Ones.

The playwright Phrynichus, a contemporary of Aeschylus, wrote a play (not extant) on the sack of Miletus by the Persians toward the end of the Ionian revolt. The assembly held at the end of that festival is said to have fined him for reminding them of the misfortunes of their kinsmen. He later produced a play (also not extant) on the battle of Salamis with no less a person than Themistocles, the hero of Salamis, as *choregus,* or furnisher of the chorus. Aeschylus's *Persians,* also about this battle, was produced in 472, with Pericles, who was to become so famous as a statesman, as *choregus.* These three plays are the only ventures into contemporary subjects of which we have any word.

Aeschylus's *Persians* is an Athenian glorification of the great battle at Salamis. The possible consequences (from the gods) of open and straightforward gloating are avoided by placing the action at the Persian court and making the play a story of Persian defeat, the consequence of Persian *hubris,* which may perhaps be defined as "a haughty spirit before a fall." The play gains in grandeur from the pomp of the Persian court, from its remoteness from Athens, and from the rolling, sonorous lists of Persian names. There is little or no dramatic conflict; the play comes close to being an elevated and interesting tale of how Persian power became *hubris* and how the nemesis that naturally followed brought the Persians low at Salamis.

Aeschylus's famous *Prometheus Bound* was one of a trilogy of which the others, *Prometheus Unbound* and *Prometheus the Fire-Bringer,* have been lost. The Titan Prometheus had helped Zeus to gain the mastery among the gods. Zeus represented the triumph of intelligence over the older powers, which were only brute force, and one of the first reforms planned by him was the eradication of man, a brutish creature. Prometheus went counter to Zeus's plan by giving man fire and thus, by implication, all the mechanic arts, which began his rise above the beasts. The play begins with the fastening of Prometheus to a great crag in the Caucasus mountains by the command of Zeus. The playwright has him visited there by a procession of people and divinities whose conversation with him brings out several aspects of the situation. The fact that Zeus's power is new is strongly emphasized. Zeus is a little uncertain, Zeus tends to be hasty and cruel, Zeus forgets what is due to older ideas of propriety and right. Apparently the trilogy ended in a reconciliation, Zeus abating his tyrannical wrath and Prometheus his stubbornly disobedient spirit. The insistence on the attitudes of one whose power is new could perhaps have some reference to the fact that the power of the Athenian democracy was relatively new, although it is rash to be too ready to see parallels and allusions of this sort. Zeus has his problem, too. Any executive faced with so reckless a rebel as Prometheus within his organization may find it difficult to assert his own authority and maintain order and efficiency without destroying good feeling.

In spite of the fact that we often cannot say precisely what problem or what contemporary interest a Greek play was meant to deal with, we can be sure that Aeschylus and after him Sophocles and Euripides were dealing with matters of intense concern to their audiences. The work of other men has been lost or survives only in isolated quotations or fragments. If we had even a quarter of the two thousand or so tragedies (the estimated number written), we could make interesting comparisons of the subjects handled. We know, generally speaking, that in the fifth century there was furious discussion of all sorts of human relations that in earlier times had been governed by strict tradition and had not therefore arisen as matters of discussion. The fact that the Greeks discussed those matters that present themselves to people coming out of a closed and traditional society into a more open society, where decisions are made on many social and moral matters after thought and discussion, has made them interesting to Europeans going through the same process in the last few centuries. It has even been said that the Theater of Dionysus was a great philosophical forum. To discuss these matters only on the tragic stage, rather than in prose discussions, seems strange, yet the problems, the interested audience, and a potential art form were there, and men of genius brought that art form to its height as they offered treatments of matters in which everyone was interested. Then, at the end of the fifth century, tragedy suddenly went into eclipse just as a new form of discussion, the philosophical discussion in prose, sprang suddenly to vigorous life.

BETWEEN THE WARS: 479 TO 445 B.C.

The period between the end of the Persian invasions (479 B.C.) and the outbreak of the Peloponnesian War (431), or the war between Athens and her allies and Sparta and her allies, is sometimes known as the *Pentakontaetia,* or "The Fifty Years." This name is also applied to that part of Thucydides' history of the Peloponnesian War that discusses this period. We shall now discuss the first part of that time, from 479 to 445, during which the rise of Athenian power led to conflicts between Athens and Sparta that ceased temporarily under a truce, the Thirty Years' Peace, made in the year 445. Full-scale war between the two powers and their allies, what we know as the Peloponnesian War, broke out in 431, before the Thirty Years' Peace had run half its course.

Athenian energy, exuberance, and achievement are the chief phenomena of all the first part of the fifth century. If we look farther back, we can see that Athens had been shaping herself for greatness during the preceding century. The policies associated with the names of Solon, Peisistratus, and Cleisthenes gave the masses of the Athenian people more dignity and freedom and prosperity and sense of participation in a commonwealth than the common people of other Greek states could have. The small farmer, the small tradesman, and the workman enjoyed a feeling of worth and responsibility as they participated in the work of the Assembly or of the *Heliaea.* The political reorganization of Cleisthenes had helped to create a sense that men were members of Athens more than of clans or of sectional groupings, so that Athens wasted less energy on factional feeling or struggles than many poleis did. The glorious success of the city in the wars with the Persians had added to the feeling that the Athenians formed a polis of special ability and of a great future.

A New Phase in the Struggle with Persia

The Greek defense against the Persian invasions had been conducted by the Hellenic League under the formal leadership of Sparta. The victory at Mycale in 479 B.C. was the last operation conducted by the league with the membership that it had during the invasions and almost the last conducted under Spartan leadership. After the victory at Salamis, when the Ionians wanted to join the league, Sparta was unwilling to incur the obligation of defending them.

While the Athenian forces were trying to reduce Sestus in 479, the government at home began to reconstruct the fortifications and the people as individuals began to rebuild their homes and reconstitute their farms. The Spartans sent an embassy to urge that neither Athens nor any city outside the Peloponnesus be fortified lest the Persians, returning, find

such cities useful as secure bases of operations. Themistocles urged that
the ambassadors be sent home at once with the message that Athenian
ambassadors would follow them soon to discuss the matter. He himself
went to Sparta as the forerunner of the embassy. At home the whole population—men, women, and children—worked furiously on the walls, while
at Sparta Themistocles led the Spartans along from day to day with
flattery and promises. Hearing that the walls were rising, the Spartans
protested, whereupon Themistocles urged them to send another embassy
to Athens and sent secret instructions that the embassy was to be de-
tained there.

At last the word came to him that Athens had her walls, walls high
enough to be defended, and he came out openly and told the Spartans
that Athens had fortified herself adequately and was no longer receptive
to Spartan suggestions that did not suit her own interests. It is plain that
for the Athenians this was a great moment; they were so used to accepting the leadership of Sparta that they felt this to be a very bold move.
When he proposed a little later to improve and further fortify the harbor
of Peiraeus, Themistocles was able to persuade the Spartans beforehand
that the new fortification was necessary to secure Peiraeus as a naval
base against further naval action by the Persians.

Athens was soon to have further recognition of her new spirit and her
new position. In the summer of 478 the Hellenic League sent out another
expedition, under the command of the Spartan Pausanias, which captured
most of Cyprus, one of the Persian naval bases, and then captured Byzantium from the Persians. The latter was an important achievement, for
it opened the grain route from the Black Sea and closed the best Persian
route to Europe. Pausanias behaved in such an arbitrary and dictatorial
manner, however, that some of the Greeks of Asia proposed to the Athenians that the representatives of Athens should assume control of the
enterprise.

Pausanias's government had already become very sensitive about un-
Spartan behavior by its commanders in the field. Further, he was said to
have engaged in treasonable correspondence with the Persians. He was
recalled, put on trial, and relieved of his command, although no severer
measures were taken against him. Meanwhile all the naval forces of the
league except the Spartans had placed themselves under the command
of the Athenians. The officer whom the Spartans sent out found that
the forces were unwilling to accept him as their new commander and
withdrew.

His government did not insist that he return and be recognized by the
others. They felt that they were not needed for the prosecution of the
present type of operation against Persia, which also seemed likely to involve more than had been planned, since the Greeks of Asia Minor were

seeking to assert their freedom from Persia. The Spartans felt, therefore, that they preferred to withdraw and might properly do so. The other people involved wished the Athenians to lead them, and the Athenians were willing, so a new league was formed.

The First Phase of the Athenian Alliance

The new league did not supersede the league that had fought the Persians in Greece, for the need that had given rise to that league was not felt to be past, and Athens and the rest had committed themselves to the alliance. It was by the terms of the old league that some years later Sparta called on Athens and others for help in her serious domestic troubles. Although the detailed arrangement of the new alliance apparently was never set down in a single document, its nature was fairly plain. Athens by herself was named as one partner; all the others were the other partner. The council had two parts, the Athenians on one side and the synod of the other members on the other side. The treasury was at Delos, the island sacred to Apollo and his twin sister Artemis, who were born there. The synod met at Delos, as well; hence the new organization was known as the Delian League.

The members agreed to have the same friends and enemies and to remain in alliance permanently. It was agreed that some members should furnish ships and men for the campaigns and some should furnish money. Aristides, who happened to be in command of the Athenian fleet in 478, the year when the league was set up, decided upon the amounts that were to be contributed and added to his reputation for fair and equitable dealing, acquiring his nickname "the Just."

During the first ten years the league freed many Greeks from Persia. The Athenians provided a great deal of energy and direction and in so doing they made such desirable acquisitions for themselves as Eion on the Strymon River in Thrace and the pirate island of Scyros, whose troublesome inhabitants they sold into slavery, taking their land for distribution among Athenian *cleruchs,* or colonists, whose land was given to them by lot and carried the obligation of military service to defend it. Carystus, in Euboea, was forced to join the alliance, and Naxos, which had seceded, was forced to return to it. On the other hand, the league had good success in drawing in new members along the coast of Asia Minor.

The climax of the league's operations in this theater was a great victory over the Persians at the Eurymedon River in 467 B.C. The enemy had gathered a sizable fleet, evidently intending to take strong action against the Greeks. Cimon, the brilliant Athenian aristocrat who commanded the joint fleet and a son of Miltiades, boldly took his ships into the river mouth on the shore of which the Persian base was situated.

There they had room for a formal naval action. The Athenians drove the Persian ships ashore and followed with a sharp attack on the Persian soldiers who came to cover the landing of the survivors. The base was taken. Then Cimon surprised and destroyed the other coastal squadron of the enemy. For the present the league, with Athens furnishing both leadership and more than her share of the men, had driven the Persians out of Europe and had freed many of the Greeks of Asia Minor.

Sparta's Troubles

In the struggle with Persia Sparta's men had had to be away from home and in contact with other people far more than was thought desirable. It had been especially unfortunate for the *perioeci* and the Helots in the armed forces to see so much of the other Greeks and above all to catch the new mood of the Athenians. There had been booty to divide, which put new strains on the Spartan system. The captains and the kings had great difficulty in retaining their virtue when faced with the temptations of the great world outside Sparta, for the holding of commands away from the constant inspection and repression of the Spartan elders could cause a certain wildness of spirit, far removed from the Spartan ideal of service to the state and repression of individualism.

To retire to their old, quiet ways as soon as possible was obviously desirable for the Spartans. This they did in the year 478, when they refused to go farther with the admission of the Ionians to the Hellenic League, which had fought the Persians, and would not take the responsibility for freeing the Greeks of Asia from Persian control. They made no objection, however, to Athens' organizing the new Delian League. At home they conscientiously moved to return to their former quietness of life, repression of individualism, and avoidance of contacts with the world around them. The supervision of the Ephors and of the Gerousia was tightened.

The successes of the new league under the control of Athens were such, however, that a few years later, possibly in 475, a debate took place among the Spartans as to whether they should wage a preventive war against Athens and assume her place as leader of the Greeks on the sea. They seem to have decided that the project was undesirable and probably impossible. That is, they had decided that Athens had become too strong and vigorous for Sparta to be able to dictate to her and keep her in a subordinate position.

In 469 the Messenians revolted from Sparta and were not reconquered until 460. The fact that Sparta was deeply involved with the suppression of this revolt and then in addition shaken by earthquakes caused restlessness among the Peloponnesian members of Sparta's alliance, and a certain amount of force had to be used to keep the unruly members from withdrawing. The maintenance of the Spartan system in the Peloponnesus was a fairly difficult task, and Sparta chose wisely in not challenging Athenian leadership on the sea.

Policies and Personalities at Athens

The great success of the Eurymedon brought Cimon to the peak of his career. He was a handsome, straightforward, soldierly man who believed in war with Persia and cooperation with Sparta, both of which policies he pressed frankly. As commander of the fleet he was efficient and popular.

Themistocles, too, had a great naval success to his credit; Salamis was his masterpiece. His talent for assessing a situation and for making tenable decisions showed best, however, in the wide and difficult field of state policy. The development of the Athenian navy and of the policy of strength on the sea was due to him. It was a difficult and strenuous policy, but one that was in accord with the times and with the temper of Athens, and one that, if directed with wisdom and skill, promised prosperity and greatness to Athens for a long time.

The great admiration that the Athenians felt for Themistocles was mixed with uneasiness caused by his moral unreliability. Again and again he had given rise to suspicions that he was trying to be a member of both sides at once. Yet we do not know exactly why he was ostracized, somewhere around 472 B.C. Perhaps it was in a trial of strength as to whether his aggressive policy toward Sparta should be followed to the extreme or a more friendly policy adopted, like that of Cimon.

True to himself, he was compromised again just after his ostracism, for he was believed to have been engaged in sympathetic correspondence with the Spartan king, Pausanias. After Pausanias had had to be recalled in 478 from his command of the fleet of the Hellenic League's fleet in Asiatic waters, he had, incredible as it seems, gone to Byzantium, somehow set himself up as tyrant there, and renewed his overtures to the Persian king. Again he was called back to Sparta. When the Ephors finally got proof of what he had been doing, he fled to a temple for sanctuary, and there they let him starve, only allowing him to come out to die.

Themistocles, who had settled in Argos for his period of ostracism, escaped from the agents of both Sparta and Athens who were closing in on him there because of his involvement with Pausanias and went to the court of the Persian king, as was usual in such circumstances. A series of adventures and escapades marked his irregular progress thither. Finally he contrived to have himself presented to the king, who was inclined to allow him to give an account of himself. Themistocles asked for a year, learned the Persian language, and so impressed the king that he was made a royal pensioner. More than ten years later, when the Athenians had encouraged Egypt to revolt, the king is said to have demanded that he contrive some measure to damage and check the Athenians. Then, as the account goes, Themistocles decided that he had lived long enough.

The leadership of the progressive group earlier exercised by Themistocles and Aristides (about Aristides' career after the organization of the Delian League hardly anything is known) passed after 470 to Ephialtes (not to be confused with the traitor at Thermopylae) and to that Pericles who was soon to become the great leader of Athens. Ephialtes was apparently the stronger and more influential of the two men at first. The Athenians took the money which Cimon had persuaded some of the weaker members of the Delian League to contribute instead of ships and men, built ships in their own yards, and manned them with their own men, thus increasing the prosperity and skill of their shipbuilding industry and giving employment to those who manned the ships while increasing their skill, too. This increased their own naval strength while it lessened that of the allies. It is hardly surprising that naval imperialism appealed to the common people as well as to others.

In 465 Athens sent ten thousand citizens and allies to colonize a place in Thrace called Nine Roads. This move, plainly an attempt to control some part of the rich natural resources of Thrace, raised up a concerted Thracian effort the next year that inflicted a great defeat on the forces of the colony and prevented it from continuing. In the same year the rich island of Thasos withdrew from the league, but the Athenians replied by defeating the thirty-odd ships that Thasos could muster and began a siege of the city, for they could tolerate no withdrawals from what was turning into their empire rather than a league of mutual help. The people of Thasos in desperation asked Sparta to help them raise the siege, and later it came out that Sparta intended to answer the call by invading Attica. But to these elements of power politics was added a pure historical contingency—a major earthquake that destroyed Sparta and killed more than 20,000 people. Many of the Helots rose in revolt to join the Messenians who had been holding out since 469.

The Spartans turned to Athens for help in their extremity. Ephialtes urged that Sparta be allowed to fall, but Cimon, in his straightforward way, urged that Athens support Sparta as her partner and yokefellow, as he put it. The more generous policy prevailed, and he was sent at the head of the Athenian troops. Other states, too, rallied around, and Sparta was able to fight off this most critical danger and presently to take the offensive against the rebels.

From Sparta Cimon returned to the siege of Thasos, which capitulated in the summer of 462. Its fleet was confiscated and its walls torn down. Its gold mines were ceded to Athens and its contributions to the league were henceforward to be in money, for it was to have no armed forces. In other words, Thasos was to be a dependent of Athens. But when Cimon returned from Thasos, he was prosecuted by Pericles for mishandling of funds, for the rising democratic faction regarded him as an obstacle, and in recent years it had had some success with prosecuting members of the more conservative group and thus removing them from active political life or undermining their influence. But Cimon was notoriously incorruptible, and he was acquitted. Then another appeal for help came from Sparta, which was besieging the rebels in their stronghold and hoping to crush them. Again Cimon was sent to Sparta with troops.

While he was away with a good-sized force of hoplites, composed of propertied men of conservative political views, Ephialtes and Pericles brought forward a measure that they had been planning for some time, a measure to limit the powers of the Council of the Areopagus, which were thought to stand in the way of a properly democratic government. They carried their measure, which may properly be called revolutionary in that it removed a conservative check on the power of the democratic majority. The bitterness aroused by the move is shown by the fact that the conservatives soon procured the murder of Ephialtes.

Perhaps the Spartans heard of this, and they may have grown mistrustful of the Athenians or of their influence among the other peoples assembled for the siege of the rebel stronghold, for they brusquely invited the Athenians to go home. Cimon did so and there tried to have the vote that had been taken when he and the soldiers were absent reconsidered. But the people at home were infuriated by the Spartan slight; in the end the legislation stood, and in the spring of 461 Cimon was ostracized. This was the end of good feeling between Athens and Sparta.

The Council of the Areopagus, composed of ex-archons, had had wide powers, both of a general supervisory kind and of a definitely judicial nature. The conservatives called these powers traditional, while the democrats were more likely to speak of them as usurped. Although the Council had probably lost vigor since the introduction of the lot for choosing archons in 487 and because some of its members had been successfully prosecuted or discredited by the attacks of the democrats, it still included a good many men of notable families and still had its traditions. As ex-archons the members had to belong to the two highest property classes. The new legislation stripped the Areopagus of all its powers except that of hearing prosecutions with a religious element—for example, cases of murder or of willful damage to the sacred olive trees. Its political powers gone, it could not serve as the check on the people that it had been before. The people was now fully sovereign; it had become the radical democracy of Athens, able to do what it wished, even to changing the whole form of the government.

The Council of Five Hundred (the *Boule*) was given the power to hold the magistrates accountable, make arrests, judge, and execute judgment in cases that had belonged to the Areopagus. It was felt that the summary exercise of such powers by a body not responsible to the people was not consistent with democracy. Indeed, the exercise of similar powers by the Board of Ephors at Sparta was of cardinal importance in the maintenance of conservative society. In the next century the Athenian teacher and essayist Isocrates, in his *Areopagiticus*, was to call for a restoration of the power of the Areopagus to deal in a general way with the health of the body politic. John Milton chose to call an essay arguing against similar authority *Areopagitica* in order to challenge Isocrates' point of view by his very title. Such far-reaching and unspecified powers as the Areopagus had are hardly imaginable to those who live in democracies of long standing and of Anglo-Saxon traditions.

Open Hostilities with the Spartan Alliance

The naval alliance, which by now was completely under Athenian control, continued its war against the Persians. But a new possibility presented itself: in 460 B.C. Inaros, a Libyan king, raised a revolt in Lower Egypt, apparently not without Athenian encouragement, and promised extravagant rewards to the Athenians for assistance. The fleet broke off operations against the Persians, sailed up the Nile, and won a victory, but not a decisive one. The Persians and the loyal Egyptians held out, and for several years this ill-advised and overambitious operation diverted some Athenian power from other theaters.

It was not only the slight given to Cimon and his soldiers in the year 462 that ended good feeling between Athens and Sparta. The Athenians also learned that Sparta had been planning to intervene on behalf of Thasos, and they probably knew that Sparta had discussed the possibility of a preventive war against them in about the year 475. A sterner attitude toward Sparta began to seem desirable.

Athens seems at about this time formally to have ended her membership in the Hellenic League, which had been formed to fight the Persians. When the rebels in Messenia capitulated to Sparta in 460, their right to leave the country unharmed was one article of the agreement. Athens received them and finally settled them at Naupactus, a good site on the north shore of the Gulf of Corinth—a move in rivalry of Corinth and of her trade with the West. Then in 459 Megara, on the Isthmus of Corinth, left the Spartan alliance and made a treaty with Athens because she found the pressure of her near neighbor Corinth hard to bear. The Athenians helped the people of Megara to build walls from their city to their port of Nisaea, on the Gulf of Corinth, and sent a garrison to help in the defense of Megara. Athens thus gained the use of a port on the route to the West and a strong point on the Isthmus to oppose Spartan marches into northern Greece. She was also deliberately affronting both Corinth and Sparta at a point close to home.

In the year 458 these Athenian advances led to war with Corinth, and at the same time war broke out with the old rival Aegina. The Athenians defeated the Aeginetans in a naval battle and laid siege to their city. Corinth sent help to Aegina and prepared to take advantage of Athens' commitment at Aegina to get her out of Megara, but the Athenians boldly and successfully defended Megara with their reserve troops, the old and the youngsters, against the main Corinthian force.

In the next year, 457 B.C., the Spartans sent an army of her alliance, with a modest number of heavy-armed Spartans and some ten thousand allies, into Boeotia to settle a dispute between Doris and Phocis. The army went north without incident, but while it was in Boeotia the Athenians assumed a hostile posture by sending a fleet around the Peloponnesus and into the Gulf of Corinth to prevent the army from being ferried back across the Gulf, while at the same time they put troops into position to contest the return of the Spartans by land along the Isthmus of Corinth and past Megara. As he weighed the situation, the Spartan commander was approached by members of the oligarchic faction at Athens, which did not slumber all through this century, no matter how outnumbered it was or how hopeless a return to a conservative form of society might seem. These men hoped that the Spartan might be induced to use his army to overthrow the democratic government at Athens. Now was an especially good time to strike, for Aegina might soon fall and free a number of Athenian troops, and the long walls from Athens to Peiraeus would soon be completed, making Athens, Peiraeus, and the space between the walls all one great fortress. Further, the Spartans must be aware of the new spirit of active hostility in Athens toward Sparta and her allies.

The Athenians had prepared themselves for a possible Spartan attack by gathering a respectable army of their own hoplites and troops from their allies, although the members of the naval alliance felt no little irritation at being required to cooperate in ventures such as this. A battle was fought at Tanagra, in Boeotia, which the Spartans won, although with losses far heavier than they could afford; losses were also heavy on the Athenian side. The Spartan army, too depleted by the battle to remain an effective instrument of policy against Athens, went home, since the Athenians were no longer able to blockade the Isthmus.

About two months later another Athenian army went to Boeotia, defeated the army of the Boeotian League, expelled the oligarchic leaders of the cities whose position Sparta favored, and set up democracies.

Athens was now in control of central Greece and remained so for several years. Before the end of 457 the long walls were finished, making her position slightly stronger, and Aegina surrendered. Athens took away Aegina's fleet, razed her walls, and forced her to join the naval alliance as a dependent of Athens. In the next few years Athenian power in Greece was supported by constant demonstrations of sea power, some of which damaged the fleets of Corinth and Sparta so much that they were well below their former modest strength. On land she forced the establishment of democracies in many places, supporting them with the threat of armed intervention. The point at issue in the constant tension between the few and the many in the Greek poleis was always who or how many men should have full voting rights so as to control the essential policies of the polis.

In 454 B.C. the Athenians and their allies suffered a disastrous defeat in Egypt that put a sorry end to their adventure there. In this same year and probably because of this reverse, the Athenians took all the money of the Delian League, which was deposited at Delos, and transferred it to the protection of Athena at Athens. This was a forthright declaration, if one was needed, that Athens regarded herself as the mistress of the alliance and regarded all its resources as being at her disposal.

For some years now Pericles had been the leading man in Athens. Although he was elected general of his tribe every year, it was his character and his abilities rather than his office that made him the most important person in the city. In 457 he had asked the people to rescind the ostracism of Cimon, who had then returned and resumed command of the naval forces. There is no record of any great activity in the rivalry between Sparta and Athens during the three or four years after the disaster in Egypt, and in 451 Cimon brought about a truce between them that was to last for five years. He also conducted successful operations against the Persian fleet in the Aegaean that brought about a peace between Athens and Persia, although he died without seeing it. The peace, concluded in 448 and known as the Peace of Callias, provided that the Greek cities in Asia should be autonomous and settled the long quarrel between the Greeks and Persians with a reasonable definition of the sphere of each and a guarantee of peaceful trading on the sea.

The Thirty Years' Truce

Late in the year 447 the tide suddenly began to turn against the Athenians. The oligarchs whom they had driven out of Boeotia returned and managed to gain control of several cities. A small force of Athenians, backed by troops of the allies, went to Boeotia, captured Chaeronea, and placed a garrison there, sending off the men of the city to be sold into slavery. A strong force of the oligarchic exiles then attacked the Athenians and defeated them with heavy losses, and the Athenians agreed to evacuate Boeotia to gain the release of those men who had been captured. The oligarchs at once regained complete control.

At this point Euboea revolted, and on the other side Megara revolted with the assistance of Corinth, and word came that the Peloponnesian forces were on the march. The Spartan king invaded Attica, but suddenly withdrew, and the word went around that Pericles had bribed him. Then Pericles took a strong force to Euboea and brought the whole island back under Athenian control.

Negotiations with Sparta during the winter resulted, early in 445, in the conclusion of the Thirty Years' Peace. Peace between the two powers and their allies was now to rest upon an explicit agreement, backed by what seemed necessity rather than by good will. It was agreed that neither party would attack the other for thirty years. Because the question of influence was important, it was provided that any state not allied at the time of the treaty to one or the other might make an alliance with either. The Thirty Years' Peace was observed by both sides until 431; it gave them both a respite from the losses and waste of their struggle, a respite that made them more powerful and prosperous than they had been before. The Athenian Empire was now at its height, and its guiding spirit was Pericles.

CHAPTER

10

THE AGE OF PERICLES

PERICLEAN DEMOCRACY

It was an advantage to Pericles that his family was one of the most distinguished in Athens; on his mother's side he was of the great Alcmaeonid clan, and his father's family was also prominent. The demoratic Athenian voter consistently preferred the genuine aristocrat, and Pericles' attitudes were so thoroughly favorable to democracy that no one could accuse him of oligarchic sympathies because of his family connections. His character was also helpful to his career, for he was above any suspicion of peculation or of shaping policies for his personal advantage.

Pericles and Ephialtes had come to the fore together in the late 60s as the leaders of the democratic element. When Ephialtes was assassinated, the leadership devolved upon Pericles. The manner in which he guided the Athenian polis during the next thirty years was very much out of the ordinary. During that time he was regularly elected general of his tribe. The office of general, which by now was the position of military leader of one of Cleisthenes' ten tribes, was the only important office in Athens to which a man could be elected. Scholarly attempts to find some way in which Pericles, as general, enjoyed a constitutional position superior to that of the other nine generals have not been successful; there was no such position. Further, the board of the ten generals did not constitute a government or an informal ruling group. There was no tradition of their banding together to promote policies.

Pericles was able to commend his views and measures to the Assembly over this long period because of his character and dependability, his incorruptibility, his sound if not spectacular ability as a military man, his skill as an orator and political manager, the essential harmony of his views with the wishes and the temper of the people, and his great skill in analyzing and predicting in the sphere of government. Of course he was not always in the forefront of affairs. Most of the speeches and proposals came from his friends and lieutenants while Pericles saved himself for the more important occasions when strong influence was necessary. The Athenian people was a great, restless, wrathful beast that might at any time turn on its leaders and rend them. Pericles led it, shaped it, and controlled it. It turned on him once at the end of his career, just after the beginning of the great Peloponnesian War in 431. Even so, the people repented and restored him to favor and office before his death in 429 B.C.

Thucydides, in his history of the Peloponnesian War, gives an account of the funeral speech that Pericles had been chosen to deliver over the Athenian dead in the first year of that war. Their ashes lay in state for three days, during which times relatives made their offerings to the dead. Then the ashes were put into ten cypress coffins, one for each tribe, and carried on wagons to the place where they were given the honor of a public burial and where Pericles spoke from a platform built for the occasion. The speech is interesting as a demonstration of the persuasiveness of Pericles and as the first known attempt to convey to a people a picture of their ideal type, something the Romans of the Republic were to do with great success in their presentation of the portrait of the old Roman.

He began, not with the bereavement and grief of his hearers, but with the valor and constancy of earlier Athenians who had made Athens the only Greek city free and continuously inhabited from earliest times. Then he turned to praise of the Athenian system, contrasting it with the Spartan system in which only a few could really participate, and skillfully describing its pleasures and its excellences. "Our city," he said, "shows the Greeks what a polis can be, and the individual Athenian can show himself the complete man, ready to present whatever facet of himself the occasion demands."

Here Pericles turned to words of direct consolation to the bereaved, having portrayed the unrivaled worth of the polis for which the sacrifice was made. Not only must his hearers have gone home feeling a sober joy at the sacrifice, but they must also have felt themselves reinforced in the idea that Athens herself was the supreme value in life and that to be an Athenian was worth every effort.

Some Events of the Period

Pericles carried through a number of measures that to the conservatives seemed reprehensible, one of which provided that the state should pay jurors for their days of attendance in court. The business of the courts was increased by the business of all the members of the Delian League, who were obliged to bring it to Athens. The original purpose of this provision had doubtless been to make sure that the courts of the other poleis of the league should not be the means of attacks on the pro-Athenian element anywhere, for the Greeks early realized that formal prosecutions could be an effective way of removing or discrediting political opponents. The trial of these cases in Athens gave an opportunity to spread some of the profits of empire, especially among elderly Athenian citizens who were past rowing in the fleet or similar active occupations and who could use the sum paid for jury duty, even though no man with a family could live on this as a daily wage.

Pericles also began, after 454, to use the funds of the league to rebuild temples in Athens and to build new ones. Here was more work. He continued the system of sending out *cleruchies,* or military colonies, something that the Romans were also to do. Some of them went to places where land had been confiscated because of opposition to Athens, as was done in Euboea in 445 because of the struggle just before the peace treaty in that year. Many other *cleruchies* were placed on land that had been peaceably acquired, but that still might need to be defended by its new owners, for during all the fourteen years of the peace, from 445 to 431, the Athenians were always on the watch for new alliances with which to strengthen themselves or for new points of economic contact in such places as Thrace or the region of the Black Sea.

Thucydides, the son of Melesias (not the historian of the Peloponnesian War, who was a generation younger and was the son of Olorus), was a relative of Cimon and expressed the conservative view with the same straightforward honesty that Cimon had shown. He surrounded himself in the Assembly with a group of sober and influential men who signified by their mere presence their approval of his able speeches against the measures of Pericles, which to them seemed bribery of the people, dishonest use of the funds of the Delian League, and likely to corrupt the polis. It was Thucydides who compared the building of the beautiful structures on the Acropolis out of the funds of the league to a prostitute's decking herself out in expensive finery.

The conservatives were easily able to point out the less admirable side of the democratic system, just as a democrat could have pointed out the less admirable side of the conservative systems of the day, and neither party was willing to admit the truth of the arguments made by the other.

Pericles answered that the tribute money belonged to Athens because she furnished the security for which the others were paying. The furnishing of employment to the citizens or the granting of land to them as *cleruchs,* the beautification of the city, and the new splendor of the festivals were the rewards of their efforts and dangers. The real question was which of the two men could command more support, for there was no way of their coming to any compromise or accommodation of views. The conservatives tried once to ostracize Pericles and failed. Then, in 443, Thucydides was ostracized.

The revolt of Samos in the year 440 was a spectacular incident in the life of the Delian League. Samos and Miletus came to blows over a territorial question, and Miletus, worsted, appealed to Athens. Athens had no right to interfere, for by the treaty of alliance in 478 the members were declared to be autonomous with the right to make war among themselves, but she had no intention of allowing them to go their own way in such matters and ordered Samos to cease her hostile action and submit the question to Athens for arbitration. Samos refused, knowing that Athens as arbiter would not be impartial. It was with great difficulty that Athens finally reduced Samos and made her a dependency.

Shortly after the making of the Thirty Years' Peace the people of Sybaris, in southern Italy, asked the Athenians and the Spartans to help them in refounding their city, which had been destroyed by the neighboring city of Croton. The Spartans refused; the Athenians accepted and supervised the gathering of volunteers from the Peloponnesus as well as from other places. Before long there was friction, and the original Sybarites were driven out; in 443 there was a new formal founding with a new name, Thurii, under the auspices of Athens. This was Athens' first colonial foundation (*cleruchies* were not new poleis), and it was done in the grand style. Hippodamus of Miletus, the eminent city planner, laid out the new city. Lampon of Athens, an expert on religious matters, was one of the two official founders. Protagoras of Abdera, a leading Sophist, whom we shall discuss later, devised a new and doubtless very up-to-date code of laws. Despite all this the city did not become distinguished among the poleis of southern Italy.

The Periclean System: Citizenship

Most Greek states did not readily bestow their citizenship on outsiders, although Sparta sometimes granted the citizenship as a reward to *perioeci* and to Helots. The Athenians, too, were very slow to bestow citizenship on outsiders. They even took it away from some who had been thought to have it when, in the time of Pericles (451 B.C.), they passed a law that no one should be an Athenian citizen except those whose parents were both Athenian citizens; an unwillingness to share the profits of empire made men willing to inflict this blow on some few of their number. Naturally the children of noncitizens did not acquire citizenship merely by being born in Attica.

The Athenians were ingenious in using the great value of citizenship as a lever by making the entire or partial loss of citizenship the penalty for various offenses, both civil and criminal. They were like us in making it possible for the state to confiscate property to pay fines or judgments or to make good embezzled moneys, but in Athens, if he thus lost his property, the citizen also lost his civil rights. There was a long list of offenses for which a man might lose the right of speaking in the Assembly or bringing actions in the courts. For some heinous offenses he might lose all his civil rights; such offenses were the avoidance of military service or cowardice when in service, embezzlement, bribery, or mistreatment of parents.

The Demes

Athenian citizenship was based on membership in the demes. The new father enrolled his new son in his own deme, and later the youngster was received into manhood as a member of that deme. A man's official name was a single name, the name of his father, and the name of his deme. If a man moved to another part of Attica, he kept his membership in his hereditary deme and enrolled his children there, not in the deme where he now lived. Not all demes were the same size or contained the same number of citizens, but it is a fair guess that the average deme had in it several hundred families of citizens. It had a definite territory and generally a modest official building. It also had financial and religious functions.

The Tribes

Cleisthenes' creation of the ten new tribes had been a stroke of genius, for a unit of government was needed at about this level. The new tribes performed a function intermediate between those of deme and polis. They could evoke loyalty and spirit in more than one way. Since the army was organized by tribes, the men served together in training and in the field. When for a tenth of each year its representatives in the *Boule* were the responsible government on full-time duty, the tribe must have been especially conscious of itself as an entity. Other activities, too, promoted tribal spirit; for example, at the Great, or City, Dionysia in March the tribes entered choruses to sing in a formal contest.

Membership in the new tribes was hereditary and permanent, as in the demes. The tribe kept records of its members and of its formal acts and had a place for the performance of its regular religious acts. Its important electoral function was the election of its general, one of the ten who commanded the ten tribal contingents of the army.

The Assembly

Every young man who had reached his eighteenth birthday and was in possession of full citizen rights was entitled to participate in the work of the *Ecclesia,* or Assembly. After the time of Cleisthenes he did not need to own land. At the end of the fifth century, pay for attendance at the Assembly was introduced, as pay for jury duty was introduced by Pericles; at this time, however, any citizen whose income depended on his own day-to-day efforts had to resign himself to losing a day's work and income if he chose to attend the Assembly.

The Assembly was sovereign in Athens, not only in theory but also in fact. No official or group could dictate to it, check it, review, or revise its actions, as the Areopagus had been able to do before 462 B.C. There was no unofficial group that by shrewdness and experience could manage it behind the scenes, although the example of Pericles shows that an exceptional man might openly lead it, but not dominate it. There were no powers of finance or of aristocratic privilege that could dictate policies or quietly exert decisive influence on the Assembly. There was no written constitution that might have been difficult to change.

One of the four scheduled meetings in each prytany (this word can be used to mean both the period of time—a tenth of the year—and the group of members of the *Boule* who were on full-time duty during the time) was a major meeting in which certain standing questions had to be raised. The conduct of the magistrates had to be reviewed. The matter of the food supply had to be reviewed. The general state of the army and navy was another standing question. Other matters were brought up at a specified meeting once a year.

Business other than that prescribed for certain meetings was brought before the Assembly only by the *Boule.* It was not allowed to propose a a new subject of discussion in the Assembly; the proposal must be drafted and presented by the *Boule.* This provision offered some check on hasty action. If it did not like the preliminary proposal, the Assembly could reject it, amend it, send it back to be amended, or even offer a new one. All that was needed was that the *Boule* should have initiated discussion of the subject.

The sovereign people attended to all the government of Athens and her empire. The officials, whom we shall discuss, were regarded as agents of the people and not sufficiently independent to initiate policies. They certainly were not legislative leaders, as the President of the United States or the governor of a state is expected to be. The Assembly scrutinized their actions ten times a year, and they had to render account on leaving office. There were many administrative boards, too, as closely watched and controlled as the officials were.

It is not certain how many people were present at meetings of the Assembly. A quorum for the major meetings of each prytany seems to have been six thousand. Although theoretically every citizen had the right of addressing the Assembly, in practice this group of people was not readily approachable. The unpracticed orator who ventured to address them, the man who had no weight of personality, or one who seemed to be wasting their time might even be hooted down. Naturally a group of men arose, known simply as "the rhetors" or "the speakers," who customarily took part in the debates in the Assembly and were listened to out of respect for the proven worth of their judgments. A man who had some property to provide his support might make a career out of being such an unofficial adviser of the people. Having made himself a real authority on the affairs of Athens, domestic or foreign, he would spend much time in discussion or in the execution of tasks delegated to him by the people, perhaps serving on some of the many boards and commissions, embassies, or military and naval commands. He was likely to find his income augmented by allied states or by foreigners who wished to gain influence with the Assembly. By custom these payments were regarded as gifts rather than bribes.

The Offices

The office of general was not usually combined with great political influence; Pericles was exceptional in this. The generals could approach the *Boule* directly, however, and ask it to make proposals to the Assembly. As officials of their tribes they had a certain prestige.

After the reform of 487 the archons were chosen by lot from lists of men sent up by the demes. By the time of Pericles both the third and the fourth property classes were eligible for the archonship. Although they did not perhaps require as much ability as those of the generals, the functions of the archons still were not so simple that any ordinary man could perform them. We find that a good many Greek (and Roman) officials availed themselves of assessors in such situations. Literally the word means people who sat by them; that is, one could ask a more experienced friend to help. Many an official must have been helped and comforted by the slender permanent staff of his office, who generally were slaves and who naturally were familiar with all the routine work.

"The" archon—he had no further title—who had originally been in charge of the government now had jurisdiction over legal cases that involved family relations. It is not certain what other functions he still had. The archon *basileus,* or king archon, was the general supervisor of religion and was in charge of all the cults of the polis. The polemarch had by this time yielded his military jurisdiction to the generals and was now in charge of all legal dealings between citizens and noncitizens. The *thesmothetae,* the six junior archons, were still in charge of the whole body of the laws. The nine archons never formed a college that worked as one or exerted influence as a group.

There were about seven hundred officials in all, and virtually all were selected by lot. All were paid, as was the *Boule.* It was characteristic of oligarchies that no one was paid for such public services. There were more boards and committees than seem necessary to get the work done; perhaps the idea was partly to distribute responsibility and partly to reduce opportunities for peculation. In naval matters, for example, the Assembly decided whether any new ships were to be built during a year and settled on the number. The *Boule* was in charge of the building of the ships, but worked through a board of ten. Another board of ten was in charge of the yards. There was a surprising array of magistrates and boards to manage financial affairs. The income of the polis was received from taxes, rents, and fines, plus the large tribute from the Delian League. At every stage there were two or three boards or commissions through whose hands the money had to pass, each watching the others and signing receipts for one another.

An interesting feature of the system was the *leitourgiae,* or liturgies, services requisitioned by the polis from the richer citizens. The richer citizen was required to give extra money, but he was also in charge of spending it. One such requisition or liturgy was the trierarchy. The trierarchs were each responsible for outfitting a trireme, for outfitting and training the crew, and for commanding the ship, even in time of war. Another rather satisfying liturgy was the providing of choruses for the singing contests of the tribes and the choruses for the tragedies and comedies at the City Dionysia. Here, as in naval affairs, the Athenians were keen and expert. The rich man who undertook to provide a chorus could find a great many good performers of every kind and men who were expert at coaching them. There were prizes for the best plays, and modern Athens still can show some of the "choregic" monuments erected by the men who acted as *choregi* for prize-winning plays.

The Two Councils

The Council of the Areopagus had given over most of its power to try religious cases to the courts, keeping only cases of deliberate homicide.

Its other jurisdiction, such as that over magistrates derelict in their duty, was transferred to the *Boule.* The third power and the most important, that of general supervision and summary action, was dropped. Seemingly the Areopagus had been able to inflict fines and take other punitive or repressive action without even stating a reason. Such authority is the kind that the heads of the clans had probably been used to exercising in the old days, the kind most natural and useful to an oligarch and most distasteful to a democrat.

The *Boule* was extremely useful in that it served to link all other agencies of the polis. Any event of significance was reported to it and all agencies of the government reported to it. It proposed action to the Assembly when action seemed appropriate. If they had served for life, as Roman senators did, the members of the *Boule* would have been in practical control of the government because of their monopoly of detailed information and their increasing skill in making judgments and handling affairs. But they held office only for one year and could not count on ever being chosen again. Because they were chosen by lot from the list of those elected by the demes, it was hardly possible to plan on becoming a member. On the other hand there must have been a very large number of men who had gained some governmental experience by being members of the *Boule* for one year.

The Courts

Cleisthenes did not alter the *Heliaea,* the single court of the people that was instituted by Solon, but toward the middle of the fifth century it was broken into a number of divisions called dicasteries, usually of 201 or 501 jurors, or dicasts. These juries, so large according to our notions, were thought of as divisions of the whole people. They were presided over by a magistrate who acted only as chairman, having none of the powers of the modern judge except that of directing the whole course of the trial. Since the jurors represented the whole people, their decision was final; there was no other power or agency to which appeal might properly be made. Every year the *thesmothetae* chose six thousand jurors from those who volunteered for the task, divided them into panels of 201 for civil cases and 501 for criminal cases, and attended to paying them. Pericles instituted the daily pay for jurors to make jury service possible for men of limited means, or, as the conservatives put it, as another way of using the people's money to bribe the people.

In civil matters only the injured party or those in fairly close relationship could bring suit. In criminal matters Solon had ruled that anyone could prosecute, a rule that made it possible for a powerful patron to act on behalf of a humble man who had been injured and did not himself dare to bring suit. A prosecution was begun by summoning the defendant before the magistrate in charge. When the case came on, both parties had to represent themselves. They could interrogate each other and each other's witnesses. They could appeal to the jury with the *argumentum ad hominem,* or frank appeal to prejudice, the successful use of which would cause a case to be retried today. The jury was flattered to have a defendant appeal to it for mercy. To bring in one's wife and small children was a standard piece of stage setting. Exchanging personal abuse of the most indecent kind was customary.

The *graphe paranomon,* or writ of unconstitutionality, often served as the basis for a purely political prosecution. Once the *Boule* had introduced a subject in the Assembly, any citizen could offer a new law or measure or proposal for action as a way of dealing with it. If what he offered was accepted by the Assembly, any other citizen could prosecute him, alleging that the new measure was improper or was in conflict with existing law. Any active statesman continually made proposals that the Assembly accepted, and because any one of them might lead to such prosecution, an active man might face several such suits in a year.

The so-called sycophants also made use of the courts for their own advantage. Because anyone was allowed to initiate a criminal prosecution, these men brought suits against the wealthy, hoping to extort money in return for dropping the prosecution. We can see, of course, that the wealthy man detected in some small irregularity might regard a prosecution as a form of blackmail, whereas others might regard the same prosecution as the performance of a patriotic duty. It seems established, however, that there was a class of those who prosecuted only as a kind of blackmail, and as a result it became customary for prosecutors to protest their personal enmity to the defendant in order to avoid the suggestion of sycophancy. Forthright and professed attempts to injure one's personal enemies were a recognized feature of Greek life.

Still another activity of the courts, strange to us, was the continued scrutiny of officials. The new members of the *Boule* and the new archons were examined by the *Boule* before they took office, but all other officials underwent scrutiny, or *dokimasia,* in the courts. Certain persons were excluded from office; those, for example, who had suffered partial or complete loss of citizenship or those who had not yet rendered account for some other office. The man who had no such disabilities had to prove to the *Boule* or to the court that he was of the third generation of citizens, that he had performed all his filial and military duties, that he had a family tomb, and that he had performed his duties to certain religious cults, those of "ancestral Apollo" and "Zeus of the family." If no one successfully cast doubts on his character, he was certified to hold the office to which he had been elected or chosen by lot.

The Old Oligarch's Treatise on Government

Criticism of Athenian democracy was not welcome, for frank talk about things that really matter is never gracefully tolerated. The Athenians liked to talk about the *parrhesia,* or freedom of speech, that could be enjoyed in Athens. The work of the comic poet Aristophanes is often cited as an example of the freedom with which one could poke fun and criticize in Athens, but it is worth noting that, despite his obviously conservative sympathies, he does not make direct attacks on or criticisms of the principle of democracy.

Nevertheless an adverse judgment on Athenian democracy was offered by a writer of the late fifth century. His name is not known, but he has been happily christened "The Old Oligarch," a nickname that fits him well, for he is a real hard-shelled opponent of the people. His brief essay opens briskly with the assertion that he has no praise for the governmental system of Athens, which gives the poor and the bad pre-eminence over the rich and the good. Then he shrewdly analyzes the system from the hostile oligarchic point of view, continually pointing out that it is well designed to cater to the many and to assure the rule of Athens over her allies of the naval league. He is frankly contemptuous of the people at large; they are untutored, undisciplined, bad. That such people should be allowed to speak in the Assembly or to cast votes would be inconceivable in a well ordered polis, where they would be strictly controlled by people of the better sort. The participation of superior people in government obviously benefits the many, however.

How did oligarchy differ from democracy? We may note that the Old Oligarch would not allow the common man to speak in the Assembly or vote on public affairs. He says plainly that the Athenian populace realizes that under a government of the best people they would soon be reduced to a state of servitude. Presumably he does not mean literal slavery, although the Greek word he uses, *douleuein,* can mean that, but that the many would be completely controlled by the few, and that will serve as a simple description of oligarchy at Sparta and at Thebes. What the oligarchs of Athens really did when they saw their opportunity we shall describe later.

ART, LITERATURE, AND SCIENCE

The Acropolis of Athens

The Acropolis of Athens, the most brilliant of all the Greek sanctuaries, assumed its final form during the age of Pericles and just after. It was in accordance with Pericles' program of building up the pride and self-consciousness of the Athenians, as well as with his program of improving the economic position of the many," to persuade the people that they should use some of the funds of the Delian League to finish the temple of Athena, the Parthenon, which had been started fifty years or so before. Work was resumed in 447, and the temple was completed in 438. Ictinus deserves to be remembered as the main architect, and Phidias was the maker of the great chryselephantine statue of the goddess for the chamber of the temple.

The Parthenon is the most important Doric building. Large for a Greek temple, 101 by 228 feet, it was built throughout of the gleaming white Pentelic marble that came from a mountain not far from Athens. We must not think of the temple as all snowy whiteness, however, for the Greeks painted their temples as they did their statues. Bronze and gold were also used for parts and ornaments of the roofs, adding both utility and satisfying color.

"The sculptures of the Parthenon are the perfection of the style of the fifth century, which had dropped some of the conventions of the sculpture of the century before and had thus become more realistic." On one of the pediments the birth of Athena from the forehead of Zeus was shown, and on the other the great contest between Athena and Poseidon to see whose gifts would win the favor and worship of the Athenians. The outer frieze is Doric, with alternating triglyphs and metopes. On the metopes are carved scenes from the early history of gods and men, wherein the gods struggle with the uncouth monsters who challenged them in earliest times. The inner frieze is of the Ionic type, a running frieze of continuous figures not interrupted by triglyphs and going around the wall of the cella, or inner building, whereas the Doric frieze was on the outer surface above the columns that surround the building. The inner frieze was a portrayal of the procession that came up to the Acropolis to give offerings to Athena at the Panathenaic festival celebrating the union of Attica. There were officials, women and girls with offerings, and young men on horses. Over five hundred feet of frieze was done with the greatest care; there was no formal repetition, but rather a wonderful variety in the figures and their poses.

The beautiful marble of the Parthenon lent itself to sharpness of outline and necessitated subtlety. Not only did the columns have the swelling known as *entasis,* which is necessary to keep the columns from looking thinner in the middle, but they also leaned inward a little to correct another optical illusion. The whole platform on which the temple is built rises from each corner to a high point in the middle. The rise can just be seen if one sights with care along the long side; it amounts to about four inches there. A slight upward bend of the same sort keeps the architrave from being a straight horizontal. The effect of these and certain other deviations from geometrical rigidity is not only to correct optical allusions, but also to give the building a certain life and charm and likewise a certain restfulness to the eye. It is possible, as has been maintained, that some of these slight deviations were due to accident or clumsiness, but it is not likely, since similar ones appear in more than one building and passing references in later classical authors show that some were discussed in the lost theoretical treatises on architecture.

The Acropolis was also given a large and beautiful entrance building, the Propylaea, like those given some other sanctuaries a century before. It was an irregular and complex building on the one side of the hill that can be fairly easily climbed. On one of the corners of the hill, by the end of one wing of the Propylaea, was the dainty little Ionic temple of Nike, or Victory. The Erechtheum, another Ionic structure, is on the other side of the hill from the Parthenon and on lower ground, where it balances the Parthenon nicely without challenging it or distracting attention from its effect. Its chief feature is the Porch of the Maidens, the roof of which is supported by caryatids, beautifully conceived figures of women that serve as columns and carry the weight of the architrave with grace. This building was begun in 421 and finished in 405. Another feature of the Acropolis was the great bronze statue of Athena, Queen of Battle, near the Erechtheum.

Sophocles (496–406 B.C.)

Sophocles, like the other two masters of Greek tragedy, Aeschylus and Euripides, was an Athenian. He was born to high social position and a comfortable economic condition. It is recorded of him, as of many Greeks, that he retained his powers through a long old age. Clearly his tragedies were highly esteemed, for he won twenty-four first prizes. Of the more than a hundred and twenty plays that he wrote, only seven tragedies and one satyr play survive.

Sophocles' play *Oedipus Tyrannus,* "Oedipus the King," is known also as *Oedipus Rex.* The Greek audience did not know the background of the play as the well-read modern knows it. The modern belief that the ordinary Athenian was a walking handbook of mythology and legend and that the playwrights worked on this assumption is quite untrue. The texts of the plays show clearly that the playwright expected to have to inform his audience about the myth or the legend or the version or section of it with which he was dealing, and the sophisticated reader or playgoer may derive pleasure from observing with what skill Sophocles imparts the necessary information to his audience a little at a time as it is needed. Indeed, everything is skillfully done; the characters, too, are revealed in a sure and economical way, and we are shown as much of them as we need to understand why they act as they do.

Of the other plays, *Antigone* comes nearest to *Oedipus Tyrannus* in suitability to the modern stage or the modern reader. This play and one other, *Oedipus at Colonus*, also dealt with Oedipus and his family; the three did not form a trilogy, however, but were written years apart. Apparently the subject was one that was continually present in the mind of Sophocles. *Antigone* has two chief characters, Oedipus's daughter, Antigone, and her uncle, Creon, the brother of Jocasta, mother and wife of Oedipus. The Creon of this play, incidentally, is of a very different character from the Creon of *Oedipus Tyrannus*. The Greek playwright felt no need to be consistent in such matters, for there was no accepted version of these legendary stories from which he could never depart. The Creon of *Antigone* is not the reasonable man of the other play, but is a new power on the throne, something like Zeus of *Prometheus Bound*, and exercises his new authority with a somewhat uncertain touch, like Zeus, inclining too much to harshness.

It is generally hard to show that any play of Sophocles has a single, clear-cut, abstract thesis. Some critics have asserted that *Antigone* does have such a simple thesis—the superiority of "the higher law" to man-made law. Such an idea is certainly present, and it had much to do with the popularity of the version of the play done by the French playwright Jean Anouilh during the German occupation of France. But prominent, too, are the questions of the relative importance of the individual and the group and the deportment of those newly in power. There is no need to find a single and simple message in these plays, for they are plays about people and richly filled with the questions about people that to moderns, at least, seem to be universal questions.

Herodotus and History

It is necessary to remind ourselves sometimes that during this most brilliant period of Athenian history there were substantial achievements of every sort made by Greeks from the rest of the Greek world. Many of these men were drawn to live a part of their lives in Athens, while others cultivated their talents in a wide variety of places.

The rise of prose writing is a noteworthy feature of the age. The use of verse continued to seem natural in fields where we should not think of employing it, as in the drama; not a single line of Greek drama is written in prose. Prose made its way in the newer fields of activity—in the writing of history, in philosophy, some of which had been written in verse, and in natural science.

During the late sixth and early fifth centuries there grew up in the

Ionian cities of Asia Minor a tradition of writing both the legends and the histories of the poleis in prose using the Ionian dialect. We must remember that what we should call legend was the traditional version of great events and was taken seriously. These early attempts at recounting the past were serious work in that they attempted to give accurate versions of what had happened insofar as oral tradition or the very scanty written records of the cities could serve as sources.

Herodotus, a native of Halicarnassus on the coast of southern Asia Minor, was born in 484 B.C. The fact that he was born a Persian subject, knew many Persians and Greeks who had been among the Persians, and had himself traveled in Persian territory, gave him a breadth of view not possible for every Greek. He was a traveler; he had been to Egypt and got some distance up the Nile. He went into the Persian Empire, probably as far as Mesopotamia. He had been in the Black Sea region in ships and knew something of the coastal regions of that sea, and, in the other direction, had been to Cyrene. He spent time in Athens and other places in Greece and was for some time a member of the Athenian colony of Thurii in southern Italy.

He represents the life and interests of the whole Greek world, not, like many writers, only the narrower Athenian interest. He knows the feelings of those Greeks around the Mediterranean who lived the broader Greek life and constantly rubbed elbows with non-Greeks. His world of the spirit is a wider world than that of Athenian rationalism, for it is full of the older spirit of uncritical piety existing side by side with the newer rationalism. To him we owe many stories of the Delphic Oracle and of other religious agencies. Facts of geography, commerce, local customs, and systematic anthropology enliven his story.

His story was, in a way, the tale of the Persian Wars, but it may well be that in his mind the center of it was the incredible reverse suffered by the Persians under Xerxes when they finally made a major effort to chastise the Greeks. He told of the formation of the kingdom of Lydia, its conquest of the Greek coastal cities of Asia Minor, its fall before Cyrus the Persian, and the Persian appropriation of the Greek cities. There is a description of the earlier history of Persia, which leads to a description of Egypt, a country of great interest to the Greeks. Persian invasion leads also to an account of the Scythians, the nomads of the territory above the Black Sea; here Herodotus shines as anthropologist. With the revolt of the Ionian cities he comes to the Persian decision to "regulate the Greek question," and the story of their invasion and repulse is told, but from the point of view of the Persian king, not that of a Greek.

Herodotus's book, in English translation, fills some seven hundred pages. It has a very carefully planned and elaborate structure. If the book has weaknesses, such as a certain lack of understanding of military affairs, we must remember the physical and mental energy involved in the construction of such an edifice of thought, which had no model in previous writing, and the wide range of intellectual power required to dominate information obtained mostly from oral informants and covering a huge mass of facts on everything from colonists in Cyrene to nomads in Scythia and from Persian monarchs to tiny Greek democracies.

Science

The study of medicine had reached a high point in Egypt in the seventeenth century before Christ, but continued in later ages with less brilliance. The Greeks, on their emergence from the "time between," had a normal mixture of treating disease by superstitious means, such as reciting charms, and by rational means. In the fifth century the rational physicians had two chief schools, those of Cnidus and Cos, two islands off Caria in Asia Minor and not far apart. The school of Cnidus apparently devoted itself to the diagnosis and treatment of individual diseases, a worthy proceeding but ahead of its time because not enough of the necessary preliminary work had been done. The school of Cos, to which the great name of Hippocrates belongs, gave its attention more to the human body and its ailments in general.

We know little of Hippocrates, although his name is attached to the *Hippocratic Corpus* (and to the Hippocratic Oath taken by physicians at the beginning of their careers), a collection of writings, perhaps put together at the end of the pre-Christian era, that represents the beginning of scientific medicine as we know it. Many authors, schools, and types of treatise are represented. Although they do not have names attached to them, the studies plainly were written by many men. Some of the books are introductions to medicine. There are general reference books for practicing physicians, special books, as on the diseases of women, collections of case histories, and books of theory. The authors would probably not regret having retired into an immortality of anonymity, their work well done. *Ars longa, vita brevis* represents a saying of theirs: short as one physician's life is, the art of healing goes on.

The careful observation and recording of cases was the basis of their method. The reports in the *Corpus* are scientific, that is, they describe the disease exactly and unemotionally. The onset of the disease is described, with such features as fever, coughing, sweating, appearance of the skin, discharges, and then the course of the disease. Unfortunately the practice of writing up and collecting case reports later fell into long disuse.

The physician's knowledge of internal anatomy left much to be desired. Even on Cos a certain amount of theoretical system appeared where knowledge failed, as in the theory of the humors of the body and their relations. Fevers were carefully and subtly observed, but the concomitant phenomenon of the pulse rate seems hardly to have been noticed. Many important diseases—smallpox, measles, scarlet fever, diphtheria, bubonic plague—are not mentioned. The physicians of the Hippocratic school were aware of the importance of treating the whole man. They recognized the *vis medicatrix naturae,* "the healing force of nature," and took account of it in their treatment.

PHILOSOPHY

Parmenides of Elea in southern Italy was in his prime about 475 B.C. and his first impulse toward philosophy is said to have come from some members of the Pythagorean group. The system that he worked out is much concerned with the idea of being. Parmenides says that only those things that are thinkable exist; what the mind cannot conceive does not exist. The mind cannot conceive nothing, or not-being; therefore not-being does not exist. It follows from this that being does not come into existence, does not cease to exist, is whole, and is motionless. It does not come into being because there is nothing else for it to come from, and it does not cease to be because there is nowhere for it to go.

The development of his thought along these lines led to the assertion that all apparent change is a delusion. Logically all the world is one and unchanging; apparently only our hallucinations change. Such a view seems to outrage common sense, yet has a certain logic. Parmenides' pupil Zeno defended it by the method of dialectic that Socrates was soon to manage with such skill. He examines the consequences of the usual pluralistic view and finds severe difficulties in what seems to be the view of common sense.

Anaxagoras (500–428 B.C.) of Clazomenae, a Greek city of Asia Minor, proposed the view that the seeds of everything are present in everything. It is possible, therefore, for any particle of matter to change into anything. The chief interest of the life and teachings of Anaxagoras lies, however, in the fact that he came from his home in Asia Minor to Athens, apparently at the invitation of Pericles, and was for some thirty years a friend of the great man. He was prosecuted for his religious views, however, for he taught that the heavenly bodies are not gods, but material things. Such theories seemed dangerous, for they denied gods who might retaliate upon the city of Athens.

Leucippus, who flourished in the middle of the fifth century, and his pupil Democritus were concerned with the nature of matter and came to the conclusion that the substrate, or primary stuff of the world, is broken up into innumerable bodies too small to be divided farther and for that reason called "atoms," which means "undivided." These atoms can be of different sizes and shapes, but apparently have no other properties. They are uncreated and indestructible and infinite in number. We shall see how Epicurus of Athens borrowed all this later as a part of his own philosophy.

The series of philosophers that begins with Thales [1] and ends with Democritus is known as the pre-Socratic philosophers in recognition of the fact that late in the fifth century Socrates of Athens gave a new direction to philosophy, although if full justice were done, the Sophists, whom we are about to discuss, would share the credit with Socrates. The philosophic achievement of the pre-Socratics is impressive. They asked many questions and showed along what lines some answers may be given. They discussed such matters as whether reality is one or many, whether we may perceive it by the senses or by reason or not at all, whether there are realities like the Logos of Heraclitus that are not material but may have an effect on matter, the nature of the human mind and its relation to the body, and how human values are determined.

The Sophists

Although one would expect the pre-Socratic philosophers to be followed immediately by Socrates, the Sophists must come first, for the earliest of them were nearly a generation ahead of Socrates in giving a new direction to philosophy. They perceived, first, that the philosophers had practically argued themselves to a standstill. Firm knowledge and comprehension of the world had come to seem impossible. Secondly, the Sophists felt that the new freedom of the individual in the less rigid system of the polis as opposed to the old rigid system of the clans was the great subject of the time. They therefore turned away from the interests of the former philosophers and devoted themselves to the study of man in society. This is exactly the line of activity that Socrates is said to have initiated. One reason for the tradition is that the great Plato, Socrates' devoted friend, in a number of brilliantly effective dialogues so denigrated the Sophists that their achievements were not properly respected until late in the nineteenth century.

The work of the Sophists had two main aspects. The first was that they attempted to analyze, as the philosophers did, but directed their attention to man and his activities and problems. The second was that they professed to be able, on the basis of their analyses, to teach men how to excel in certain activities, especially effective speech and government. Many people were glad to pay their fees. The conservatives disapproved of advising other men for pay, and they disapproved of any means of get-

---

[1] See Chapter 8 for a discussion of the earliest pre-Socratics.

ting ahead in the world that might bring forward people or groups who had hitherto been in subordinate positions.

Corax of Syracuse made himself a reputation as a teacher of convincing oratory in the 460s. He analyzed successful speeches and claimed to be able to show the difference between a speech that would convince and one that would not. Protagoras of Abdera in Thrace went a step farther and devised and taught methods of making an argument appear stronger than it really is—the sort of thing that is still called "sophistry." He would offer paired arguments on an interesting question, one for and one against, and this setting up of arguments on both sides of a question became very popular in Athens and was often presented in the tragedies. Euripides, for example, had a debate between Jason and Medea in his *Medea*.

ECONOMIC AND SOCIAL LIFE

Although our evidence of Greek economic and social life is not nearly so rich as that at our disposal for the study of any modern country, it is varied and full enough to give us what is probably an adequate and reasonably correct picture. There are only scraps of official records. Yet we can learn a great deal by putting together the incidental remarks of writers on various subjects. The comedies of Aristophanes are especially rich in sidelights on Greek life. Archaeology, too, has uncovered much evidence.

Production and Consumption

Food production was the chief business of the entire ancient world from beginning to end. It is probably true that industry never amounted to more than five percent of the economic activity. We must remember that a great many articles were manufactured on the farm, as they continued to be until almost the end of the nineteenth century. The farmer built his own simple house (his few iron tools would have to be purchased somehow) and shelters for his animals, fowls, and bees. He made harness or pack saddles for the animals. The wood on his land or perhaps a small deposit of suitable clay provided materials for dishes, pails, and other utensils. He made his olive press of wood, perhaps with some stone parts. He either pressed or trampled his grapes, and the containers, like those for the oil, were made of clay. The tendency for the subsistence farm to disappear from modern countries of the West makes it all the more necessary to insist upon its former pervasiveness and its dissimilarity to the large modern commercial farm.

Cereal was the most important food, and barley was generally the chief cereal. Wheat, rye, millet, and spelt were also raised. A variety of vegetables was grown. Oil was pressed from a number of seeds—radish, for example, or poppy. Meat was expensive and was a rarity on the tables of ordinary people.

The region of the Mediterranean as the Greeks knew it had widely differing capabilities for producing food, as it did for producing other things. The region of the Black Sea was fertile, especially the northern side, which produced cereals and exported them to Athens. The control of this trade route was often threatened, and the Athenians made great efforts to keep it open, because their economy required imported cereals. Dried fish was an important product of the Black Sea region. Egypt was a great producer of cereals. In 445 B.C. the Egyptian government was able to send a gift of nearly 50,000 bushels of grain to Athens. Many such gifts are recorded as part of the diplomacy of the ancient world. In Greece itself the soil was somewhat thin for cereals. Greece in the West— southern Italy and Sicily—had flatter and deeper soil and did much better in cereal production. Sicily, like Egypt and North Africa, was an important source of cereals for the Romans in later times.

Plain oil and plain wine could be procured in many places around the Mediterranean, but then, as now, certain oils and wines were favored. The differences were due partly to fortunate combinations of soils and climates with the strains of trees and vines and partly to superior skill in producing and marketing the oil and wine. The selective breeding of trees and vines as well as of animals was beginning to be understood by the fifth century.

The olive was eaten green or ripe, as it is now, or was preserved, sometimes by pickling. The best method of preserving it was to make it into oil, which could be stored and used for food. Until the later invention of soap, olive oil was rubbed on the body, then scraped off, as a method of cleaning. It was also burned for light in simple lamps, often mere dishes with a wick hanging over the edge. Since these gave only poor light, people tried to do their living during the daylight as much as possible.

Greek clothing was simple. The basic garment was the *chiton,* a rectangular piece of cloth with a hole for the left arm. It was put on and pinned at the right shoulder and down the right side to form a sleeveless tunic that fell almost to the knee and could be belted at the waist. Women wore longer ones, for the Greek girl or woman, if respectable, was not encouraged to display her physical charms. Another garment, a mantle or cape called the *himation,* was thrown over the *chiton* by those who dressed with any care. It was of fine wool, and the cut and drape of it could be matters of some concern. Trousers seem to have been worn only by the Persians and some peoples of Gaul; they often seemed odd enough to provoke the mirth of those who saw them on strangers. Many people did not wear shoes at all and many others wore them only occasionally. Sandals were known, however, and shoes that covered the ankle, and boots. Most people did not wear coverings for their heads.

Houses, too, were simple. They generally were built of adobe, or sun-dried brick, a material that is both stronger and more resistant to the weather than is generally supposed. A coat of stucco and an overhanging roof, whether tiled, or of wood, can do a great deal to protect walls of adobe from rain. The house looked inward to a court rather than outward to a street. It was ordinarily square or rectangular. The group of ancient Greek houses most useful for study was found in the excavation of Olynthus on the Chalcidic Peninsula, a small city that was destroyed by Philip II of Macedon in 348 B.C. and never inhabited again enough to disturb the remains. It is unusual in having a regular network of streets and houses all of regular shape. The houses generally have five to seven rooms, some of which were on a second floor. The existence of these upper rooms is proved by the remains of an inner stairway, which must have led to a second floor, because the remains show that the roofs were tiled and pitched and therefore not used as living space. In some houses at Olynthus the room used as kitchen is distinguished by remains of a hearth and a flue to carry off the smoke. Some houses had a bathroom near the kitchen; warm water had to be carried to the bathroom from wherever it was heated. Terracotta bathtubs were found, made in such a way that the bather could sit in the upper part and put his feet in the lower part, while presumably someone else poured water over him. The courtyard saw more living, presumably, than any other area of the house. All the rooms opened onto it for light, even those having windows toward the outer side. In a country with a fairly warm climate it would be possible to live with some comfort in the colder seasons by occasionally taking the chill off the rooms with a brazier of charcoal and spending as much time as possible in the outer air of the courtyard, where the sun could be felt and the winds were somewhat warded off.

Although the three basic products that we have discussed—food, clothing, and houses—must largely have been produced by the users, there is interesting evidence of commercial and professional activity in producing them. There must have been much professionalism in the breeding of plants and animals and in the preparation of certain articles of food, especially wine and oil. We have written evidence of real professionalism in cooking, for a great household might even have a group of specialist cooks—one for meats, one for sauces, one for pastry—and some famous cooks are known to have written cookbooks, but none have survived.

The first professional in the line of clothing manufacture was the man who bred sheep to produce better wool. Making the fabric could involve much skill and equipment. There were towns and whole regions (as in Asia Minor) where there was a tradition of fine work in fabrics for the market. Naturally many people possessed of such skills went to the larger cities, where some dealt with the fabrics and some with the design and production of the garments. Some specialized in dyeing and some in fulling, the ancient method of cleaning by chemicals and powdered earth and water. Some were specialists in shoes, from the tanners to the people who fashioned stout and dainty shoes.

The simplest house could be very simple, and professional production had no part in it. The ordinary farmer could build himself an adobe house with only a few pieces of timber to stiffen it here and there. The house of a rich man, however, might include a fair amount of stone construction, which was expensive, or it might be built entirely of wood, which was ostentatious even for a rich man. We know that there were master builders and carpenters who tended to specialize and who were equipped with an impressive range of tools for working wood. It was possible, too, to buy fine furniture of wood or wrought iron or partly of ivory.

In the matter of production it is surprising to realize that the Greeks were not so inventive and ingenious as some of the peoples who had flourished earlier. Many Greek craftsmen had fine technique and wonderful ability in design and ornamentation, but they were not strong in improving technical procedures or inventing new ones.

In the matter of consumption there were great differences. The Greeks had not heard of the Puritan way of life that Americans associate with old New England. They were not devoted to plain living (except for the Spartan Equals) and high thinking. Those who could be comfortable or luxurious were glad to be so, and ostentatious luxury seems to have been common among the well-to-do. As for high thinking, we have seen that it was a small minority who did the glorious high and deep thinking of the Greeks and that they often were mistrusted and opposed by the majority.

Labor

Although slavery was pervasive in Greece, free people always had a great deal to do. A careful housekeeper with one maid kept herself rather busy, and a farmer with one slave to help him would work hard, as would a shopkeeper who manufactured and sold something and had one slave to work with him. Slaves had a hand in every kind of work, and the free man who hired himself out to work was a rarity on the farm or in the shop. Large concentrations of slaves were unusual, however. A factory employing twenty slaves was large, although one is known to have had a hundred and twenty. On the other hand, the Athenian Nicias (late fifth century) is said to have owned a thousand slaves and to have leased them out to work in the state silver mines at Laurium; such leasing out of one's slaves was common among both Greeks and Romans.

The absolute number of slaves in the Greek world cannot be determined or even accurately guessed. Thucydides tells us that when the Spartans, late in the Peloponnesian War, fortified the position of Decelea not far from Athens, 20,000 Athenian slaves deserted to them, many of them valuable artisans. This figure at least gives us something to which to add the artisan slaves, the agricultural slaves, and the domestic slaves who did not desert, and we might arrive at a goodly number of slaves for Athens at this prosperous time. A less industrialized city would have fewer slaves in proportion to the free men. It is plain, at least, that slavery was accepted and was found everywhere and in every activity of life, but that there were not troops of slaves standing at the beck and call of every Greek. He could not have fed and clothed them.

Apparently the existence of slave labor did not depress the wage or the income of free workmen. The free artisans and owners of shops could not be harmed by slave competition because acquiring or training a skilled slave and giving him adequate incentives to produce was so expensive that the slave's product cost as much as the free man's. The records of the building of the Erechtheum, some of which happen to have been preserved, show that the same wages were paid to free men and to slaves for the same work; apparently there was no attempt to make the slave worker take less pay for the same performance. The wage was a drachma a day, a fairly typical wage. The drachma was the monetary unit of ordinary daily use, like the shilling or franc. It has been calculated that a man and a wife could live, but barely, on about two hundred drachmas a year.

As we have no record of complaints from free labor of being injured by slave labor, so we do not hear of slave revolts. There was in general no sense of a class, slave or free, called "labor."

People became slaves in several ways beside the obvious one of being born to slave mothers. If Greeks fighting against Greeks took captives, they generally got a good ransom for the men instead of selling them into slavery, but they usually sold the non-Greeks into slavery. Kidnappers were active on land and sea; they, too, might hold their victims for ransom or sell them into slavery. Any Greek, of any level of society, could fall into slavery through war or kidnapping. Many non-Greek slaves were netted by raids across the border. The chief outside sources of slaves for Greece were Phrygia, Lydia, Caria, Thrace, Illyria, and Scythia.

Another source of slaves was the abandonment or sale of infants or young children. It was not illegal in many Greek states to expose (that is, to abandon) unwanted babies. A slave dealer might take such a child and raise him. There were risks: if the child had been born a slave, the dealer might lose him on proof of ownership being offered. If he was a citizen, proof of his citizen birth had the same result. Illness and death took others. A youngster bought from the Thracians, who regularly sold their children, or from another outside source, might of course also be lost by death.

The rougher and more intractable slaves were suitable only to be leased for work in the quarries or the silver mines. Other untrained slaves were used in agriculture, as domestics, or as porters, and the females were domestics or routine prostitutes.

But many slaves were intelligent and highly trained, some before falling into slavery, others at the expense of dealers or private owners. The more able man in agriculture became the overseer. A carefully trained girl might become an entertainer or a high-class prostitute. A trained slave might be a shoemaker, a stonecutter, or an accountant for a banker. Yet probably the profit was no greater in owning trained slaves, since their superior productivity was balanced by the cost of purchase or training and the necessity of offering them incentives. One group of slaves, the so-called "dwellers apart," were even allowed to have separate establishments and work entirely under their own supervision.

The scanty data available suggest that two hundred drachmas was the usual price for a trained slave in the fifth and fourth centuries. Prices ran as high as three hundred drachmas for slaves with special qualifications and as low as fifty for children, who were a risky long-term investment. The slave was a piece of property; he could be bought, sold, mortgaged, or rented out. The children of slave mothers were slaves. Slaves could not contract legal marriage or own property. Masters could inflict corporal punishment on them, although in some places the law did protect them from inhumane treatment. Probably the worst fate for a slave was to be sent to the silver mines, yet the slave of a small shopkeeper making a precarious living must have had a miserable life.

Many slaves were allowed to buy their freedom. It is not clear, however, that all of them felt that the effort was worthwhile. One who was allowed to was given a fictitious ownership of part of his earnings until he could meet the stipulated price. The owner's purpose was to stimulate the slave's efforts so that he could get back his original investment and make sure that premature death would not cause him loss. The freed slave could still be profitable to his former owner if he worked with facilities belonging to him, as in managing a small shop belonging to him. At Athens freed slaves became metics, or resident aliens; their former slavery did not make them of a lower social class than the other metics.

Resident Aliens in Greek Communities

Any theory about what caused the great surge of energy and achievement in Periclean Athens must take into account the fact that Athens, like Sparta and many other poleis, relied in many ways on the free non-citizens residing within her borders. "Metic" is the customary way of Anglicizing the Greek word *metoikos* which the Athenians applied to these people, calling them "dwellers with," while the Spartans called them *perioeci,* or "dwellers around." There is every reason to suppose that they, like the Athenian citizens, were an unusually energetic group, since they had uprooted themselves from their native places and come to Athens, often by invitation because of their special skills, or were slaves who had found the energy to work their way out of slavery. There must have been at least as many metics as citizens at Athens. Other cities, too, had such resident aliens.

Since they were not citizens, there were things the metics could not do and things they could not have. They could not perform any of the civil functions of the citizen, such as holding office, speaking or voting in the Assembly, or sitting on juries. They could not perform the functions of the citizen in court, whether as plaintiff or defendant, but had to have citizens represent them. They could not hold land, because the possession of land was connected with citizen status.

They were compelled to do a few things. They had to serve in the armed forces, both as hoplites and as peltasts, or light-armed troops. They were liable to special taxes. Although they were not subject to the liturgies or extra duties of the rich, they often performed them voluntarily. At the great procession of the Panathenaic festival the metics marched in scarlet gowns.

The usual reason for their presence in Athens and in other cities was to engage in trade of every kind. Further, the metic could be a philosopher (Anaxagoras) or a distinguished writer of speeches for other men to use in the courts (Lysias), or, in the feminine gender, a woman of distinguished personality and cultivation and a professional companion to men (Aspasia, the mistress and then the wife of Pericles). Metics were artists and physicians. Although some came from the outsiders whom the Greeks liked to call barbarians, probably most of them were Greek citizens of one polis who lived and worked in Athens or some other polis not their own. It is plain that they were welcome to the good livings made by many of them, for if it had so wished, the citizen body could have reserved for its own members every lucrative occupation.

Public Finance

Athens's income from her lively commercial empire was considerable. After she took control of the Delian League's treasury away from the congress of the league in 454 and moved the treasury from Delos to Athens, the Athenian *Boule* was in control of this great fund. Eight thousand talents were brought from Delos to the Acropolis in 454; the tribute from the allies in the following years was generally something over four hundred talents a year.

We may here remind ourselves that a talent was sixty minas, a mina was one hundred drachmas, and the drachma was the ordinary coin corresponding to our quarter, shilling, franc, or mark. There seems little use in trying to equate the talent with a number of dollars. Since a drachma was an ordinary day's wage, the talent was six thousand days' wages. A talent is known to have purchased the hull of a warship in 483 B.C., and apparently a few decades later three talents would buy a completely fitted warship. We know that 2012 talents were spent on the adornment of the Acropolis during one period. When the Peloponnesian War began, the reserve was six thousand talents; at one time it had reached 9700 talents.

The *Boule* fixed the amount of tribute to be paid annually (after 454) by four-year periods on the basis of the supposed resources of each member state, ally, or subject, as we may choose to call them. An appeal from this assessment could be made and would be heard in an Athenian court, as would any case whatsoever arising from the relation of Athens to the allies. If any allies failed to pay, they were visited during the summer by Athenian naval units that collected the money. A sixtieth of the tribute, or a mina from each talent, was formally set aside as Athena's share and paid into the treasury of the goddess, which was administered by a board of temple treasurers.

There was income from the empire other than the tribute. Athens profited indirectly from the requirement that all law cases of persons in the member states be tried at Athens. Sometimes there were spoils of war from the operations of the empire, and rents came in from some of its properties. The preference or monopoly in trade that she could insist on in many areas because of her imperial position was profitable. Her prosperity naturally drew to her the goods of the whole world, so that she profited greatly even from the port tax on goods that came to Athens for distribution.

There was no direct tax on the Athenian citizens. The state drew in perhaps four hundred talents a year from the silver mines at Laurium, from scattered public lands, from taxes for the use of the port of Peiraeus, and from a few minor taxes. How much was contributed to the state by the rich men who performed liturgies is not readily calculable.

Expenditures were high, but during times of peace the empire yielded a profit. During peacetime an active fleet of sixty triremes was maintained. The ships had to be steadily replaced, a few every year, because they neither endured storms nor accidents well nor stood up under ordinary service. About ten thousand citizens were employed by the state as rowers for eight months or so of every year. The state paid many people for official service. Under Pericles six thousand dicasts, or jurymen, were paid two obols a day and had their pay raised to three obols a day a little later. This was supplementary income rather than a living wage, for three obols was only half a drachma. The five hundred members of the *Boule* were paid, as were some seven hundred other officials. The state also supported a number of slaves, some of them highly expert, like the permanent helpers in the offices of the government. Although all this could easily be paid for in peace time, the extra expense of the army and navy in time of war caused expenditures to rise far above income. Yet Athens sustained the burden of the Peloponnesian War for a long time in spite of the huge cost of the Sicilian expedition, and she might even have won had not the Persians subsidized a Spartan fleet at the end.[2]

Education

We should think of Greek education as a process of teaching the young what society wanted them to know rather than as a system of schools. Nowadays a great deal of educating is done outside the schools at all ages and levels. Even more was done in Greece. Because all Greek societies were more conservative than ours and changed less from generation to generation, there were seldom new conditions that the young understood and welcomed and to which their elders found it hard to adjust, thus creating constant tension between the generations. Nevertheless such times did occur in Greece, and the Periclean Age was one of them. Certain new ideas were abroad at this time, even though the age was a conservative one by our standards. To many people the idea of democracy was still radically new. Many new ideas were presented on the tragic stage and by the Sophists. None of these new ideas was presented in what we should

[2] See Chapter 11.

call a school, although the paid instruction offered by the Sophists was somewhat of this kind.

If we start with the young male Athenian of a rich family, we shall have to count the influence of nurses and other servants. Eventually the little boy would go to school, usually under the supervision of a *paida-gogos,* a "child leader" or pedagogue, an elderly and responsible slave. Generally the child went to more than one school, for he must learn the three *R*'s from one master and music from another, and soon he would have a master in athletic exercises. None of this instruction was paid for by the state.

We are poorly informed about Greek music. We do know that there were differing modes, or scales with differing intervals. The flute and the lyre were popular instruments. We do not know where the line was drawn between the amateur playing suitable for a gentleman and the professional playing more suitable for a slave. Certainly no leading Athenian family could have endured the thought that one of their sons might become a professional musician, but not to be able to play at all stamped a man as an oaf lacking advantages.

The athletic training took place on an outdoor exercise ground, the gymnasium, as it was called. Such places were meant to provide a combination of manly exercising and passing time. The older men regularly went there for sociability. Sometimes the youngsters exercised in armor and with weapons, but their more usual exercises were those of the Olympic and other games—the dash and the longer run, broad jumping, throwing the discus and javelin, wrestling, and boxing. The nominal purpose of the exercises was to prepare the citizen for military service by developing his body.

Probably at about fifteen or sixteen the young Greek began to have a slightly older man as a lover. This practice needs to be made quite clear. It was homosexual love, in the sense that it was love between men—members of the same sex. It does not carry any implication that the older man who initiated the relation was unable to achieve a proper heterosexual life. The word "love" is not ordinarily applied to such a relation today because our idea of the relation between men and women (which would have seemed strange to the Greeks) has made love a forbidden word in connection with members of the same sex in most parts of the West. The emotion that we call love, blended of admiration and sexual attraction, seems to have been genuinely felt in these affairs of Greek men with one another, or those of Greek women, if we may believe Sappho. The relation between the Greek lover and his male beloved did plainly become at times an active physical sexual relationship. The Greeks explicitly say so and as explicitly say that this was a most regrettable form of what was usually a lofty and educational relation. The good that a young man of perhaps twenty-two to twenty-five can do in molding a boy of fifteen to nineteen hardly needs to be described in detail; few influences, for good or for evil, in the life of a boy can be compared to that of a young man whom he whole-heartedly admires. Such a relation was a very important and highly approved educational force among the Greeks; its other form was just as highly disapproved.

At the age of eighteen the young man became liable to two years of military service as a cadet. Little is known exactly about the terms of his service. It is to be presumed that he was given a certain amount of instruction in military matters. It is to be presumed also that there was much comparing of information, misinformation, and attitudes when the group was away from home together on service. We must remember, too, that the education of the Athenian continued during his manhood, as is often the case with us. Attendance at the Assembly was a most educational activity, as was attendance at the plays during the festivals. There was constant discussion everywhere the Greek man went, for he was a great talker, and in the time of Pericles especially there were new ideas in the air that the middle-aged man knew about, even if he was less ready than the young to accept them.

Upper-class women were not entirely secluded. Although the Athenian girl did not have occupations outside the home and was not schooled as her brother was, it would be a mistake to regard her as living the life of an animal chained in a kennel. She may well have received more practical education from her mother than the boy did from his father, for the father was in many cases too occupied to take a hand in his son's training. An intelligent Athenian girl brought up by an intelligent mother must have received a good education for the kind of life she was going to live. If the domestic scene was to be most of her life, we need not feel sorry for her or regard her as an unfulfilled person. If she did not receive romantic love, we need not think of her as emotionally starved.

The less prosperous classes of society got a different and livelier kind of education, as the less prosperous classes do everywhere. There were ways of learning the three R's other than going to school, and there were other skills, often not quite respectable ones, for which the more prosperous family would not have known how to find a teacher. Naturally the females of the poorer classes were not so much sheltered as the more prosperous and were more aware of what went on. The poor men learned, as did the rich, from meetings of the Assembly or from the plays or from the endless discussion and argument that swirled through the life of the Athenian. The metic and the slave, too, usually got an informal education. If he was wealthy, the metic might send his son to school, but the youngster would be destined for a career in business, and this he would learn in practice, not in school.

THE AGE OF PERICLES REVIEWED

The Age of Pericles is the first of those few periods in Western history which have so impressed us that we ordinarily use the capital *A* and designate it by the name of a leading person. There was an Age of Augustus in Rome, and in modern times Elizabeth I and Victoria of England lent their names to their times. The Age of Pericles was extraordinary in the strict sense of the word: it was a time that had something more, something above and beyond the regular course of life and affairs. It will be worth our while to pause to see if it is possible to summarize the qualities of this extraordinary period in a sober and factual way.

In one way it is easy to define: it was the stretch of about thirty years when Pericles was regularly elected general by his tribe, from about 465 B.C., or a year or two later, until his death in 429 from a plague. Perhaps the beginning of this period should be put in 461, when Pericles and Ephialtes together carried through the changes that made Athens more democratic. Although Cleisthenes had moved far toward democracy, the Age of Pericles was the beginning of complete and radical democracy. The period is defined with unusual sharpness at its ending as well as at its beginning, for the combination of the Peloponnesian War and, just at the beginning of the war, the terrible plague [3] and the death of Pericles brought a great change in the life of Athens after 429 B.C. It is of course true that many of the tendencies of the Age of Pericles continued or first came to full flower in later years. Socrates was formed in this age, as was the historian Thucydides, and the activity of the Sophists began. Yet the changes that the war, the plague, and the loss of Pericles wrought in the political and military power of Athens, in the spirit of the Athenian people, and in the spirit of the Athenian government were so great that after the death of Pericles Athens rapidly began to become a different place; an epoch had ended.

The brilliance and the successes of the Athenians in the Age of Pericles may be called one of the great triumphs of the polis. The historian must, of course, perch far enough above the bustle and the conflict to be able to perceive that there were other and different triumphs for the polis—the long, sober, and steady course of Sparta, the brilliance of Corinth, or the humdrum and obscure existence of hundreds of tiny poleis that did nothing more than attend to their own affairs and allow their citizens, under

[3] For a discussion of the nature of the plague see p. 235.

the law, to lead a quiet life and occasionally attend the great games or the festival of Dionysus at Athens.

The unity and the energy of the Athenians at this time are a notable phenomenon and seemed such to their contemporaries. Whatever they undertook, privately or publicly, they pursued with great energy. The manufacturer, the trader, the soldier, and the sailor drove hard toward their goals. As a society they were ready to attempt great things, to run the necessary risks, and to make the necessary sacrifices. Their goals were not always disinterested, for they were forthright imperialists, taking advantage of their former allies, now their subjects, and ready to punish ruthlessly any assertion of independence among them. The pursuit of their commercial and military interests in other directions was forthright, vigorous, and often brutal.

The members of some modern societies would not approve of the restless energy of the Athenians, for it is the antithesis of the ideal of quietism of these societies. The strenuous life suits the taste of the modern West, however, and we may see in the Athens of the Age of Pericles a remarkable example of a society that was so organized as to produce great amounts of energy both individually and collectively. When we attempt to explain how it was done, we are on unsure ground, as there is little study or understanding of the decline and the building up of communal energy among other peoples. Certainly we cannot say without further explanation that democracy was the cause. Perhaps the mass of the people felt more enthusiasm for fighting and striving because they could vote in the Assembly. There is no way of proving such a thesis, however, and experience has shown that men will also drive hard under the leadership of privileged aristocracies or strong monarchies. It seems likely that the personality of Pericles was one cause; his skill in proposing both material and ideal goals and in suggesting ways of realizing them must have aroused a good deal of energy.

This was a period of high achievement in the arts. The artists of Athens and of Greece in general were working along sound lines and with ample patronage. Earlier in the century some of the conventions that had ruled in sculpture had been put aside, giving a freer and more realistic style. There had been a good deal of theorizing and experimentation. The general judgment has been that the Greek art of this century and especially of the Age of Pericles is unsurpassed. It is going too far, however, as was said in connection with the classical periods of Egyptian art, to claim the work of this period in Greece as the only truly classical art and to deduce all the laws of art from it, as some critics of art have attempted to do.

In thought and in literature the period was extremely lively. The only type of literature in which Athens excelled at this time was the drama, but here she had the masters of both tragedy and comedy—Aeschylus, Sophocles, Euripides, Aristophanes, and others, which perhaps is as much as might be expected of one city. She never had a great lyric poet, although the writers of tragedy and comedy could write very fine poetry (lyrics to us, but not lyric poetry by the Greek definition) in the choruses of their plays. Socrates and Thucydides were in their early maturity. Attic oratory was yet to be developed, as was the philosophy of Plato and others, later to be one of the distinctive products of Greece.

CHAPTER

11

THE PELOPONNESIAN WAR AND
THE END OF THE FIFTH CENTURY

The Peloponnesian War may be said to have lasted from 431 B.C. until the capitulation of Athens in 404, even though technically there was a period of several years of peace after 421. There is no evidence that the conditions of the fourteen years of peace from 445 to 431 were felt to bear hardly or unfairly on either the Athenians or the Spartans. What, then, were the circumstances of the resumption of warfare in 431?

The Quarrel of Corinth and Corcyra

The quarrel that eventually brought on the conflict started in western Greece. Corinth had founded a colony, Corcyra, on an island off the west coast. Corcyra in turn had sent out a colony, Epidamnus, and the mother city of Corinth had shared in the auspices of the new city, as was often done. Now in Epidamnus the few (the oligarchs) and the many (the democrats) were at swords' points, and the many had got the better of it and exiled a group of the few. The exiled few had enlisted the help of the neighboring barbarians and were pressing the many hard. The many now appealed to Corcyra for help and were refused; then they appealed to Corinth and were promised help, whereupon Corcyra espoused the cause of the few and decided to take an active part in the siege of Epidamnus.

Corinth and her colony of Corcyra, then, were in active disagreement because they supported different sides in a class struggle that had come to the fighting point in Epidamnus. Corinth called for volunteers favor-

able to the cause of the many to join in the defense of Epidamnus, and
several small states from western Greece who were friendly to her did so.
In the summer of 435 a naval battle was decisively won by the Corcyreans, and on that day they also captured Epidamnus. Corcyra now exploited her victory by acts of senseless cruelty.

Corinth set to work to build a larger fleet to return to the struggle,
which for her involved important issues of prestige and trade routes.
Corcyra began to cast about for allies and shrewdly turned to Athens,
hoping that other considerations would be more powerful than Athens'
consistent support of the many. The Corinthians sent an embassy to urge
Athens to refuse, and this momentous issue was debated before the sovereign people of Athens. Athens could grant Corcyra a defensive alliance
and still be within the terms of the Thirty Years' Peace; an offensive alliance would seem to be directed against Corinth, a member of the Spartan alliance, and would contravene the agreement. The Athenians at first
refused Corcyra's request for a treaty, but on the second day, at the
urging of Pericles, they made a defensive alliance with Corcyra.

Pericles must take some responsibility, it seems, for the war that followed. He had always been a strong advocate of resistance to Sparta's
claims, pretensions, and pressures, and therefore to those of Corinth and
Sparta's other allies. He included in his admirable program a dash of
calculated hostility to another nation as a device to increase his popularity. Such devices sometimes do not leave a man free to choose the best
course, and so it was with Pericles. It may well be, too, that he considered
it a good idea to attach Corcyra to Athens with the thought that an ally
on the way to the West might be useful.

In the early autumn of 433 the battle between the Corinthians and the
Corcyreans was observed by ten Athenian ships, which came between the
combatants when it seemed that all was lost for Corcyra. The Corinthians
withdrew when the Athenians told them that they would defend the
Corcyreans. The Athenians had now gained a useful ally in Corcyra, the
only naval power in the western waters of Greece. The Athenians had
acted with full knowledge that the move was contrary to the spirit of
their treaty with the Spartans, but their professed view was that war
would come anyway. The Spartans did not move in retaliation, apparently not intending a war and therefore not proclaiming the inevitability
of one.

In the next year (432) the Athenians made two more provocative
moves. One was to exclude the Megarians (allies of Corinth) from all
ports and markets of the Athenian Empire, a deadly blow to a commercial
city like Megara. The other was to begin bullying Potidaea, a Corinthian
colony in the north near Macedonia, ordering it to tear down its walls
on the seaward side, to give hostages to Athens, and to notify the Corin-

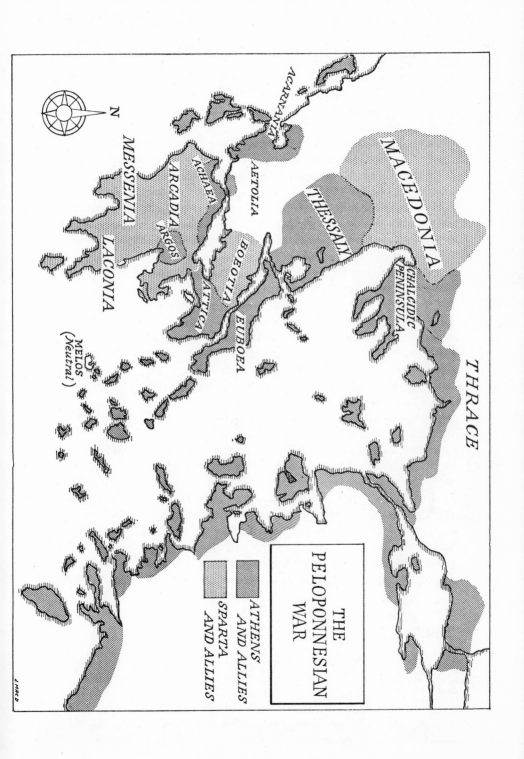

THE PELOPONNESIAN WAR

ATHENS
AND ALLIES

SPARTA
AND ALLIES

MACEDONIA

THESSALY

THRACE

CHALCIDIC PENINSULA

ACARNANIA

AETOLIA

MESSENIA

ARCADIA

ACHAEA

ARGOS

LACONIA

BOEOTIA

ATTICA

EUBOEA

MELOS
(Neutral)

N

thians that it would no longer receive the yearly magistrates customarily sent to Potidaea by Corinth, its mother city. The Potidaeans appealed to Corinth and Sparta and got a promise that if Athens attacked Potidaea, Sparta would invade Attica. The Athenians began a siege of Potidaea late in the summer of 432.

In the early autumn of 432, because the Spartans had made no move, the Corinthians went and complained to them that the Athenians had violated the treaty by their aggression. The Spartans called an assembly of the alliance, at which complaints against Athens were made by the Corinthians, the Megarians, and others. The assembly was also addressed by some Athenians who had been sent there on other business and who reminded the company of the formidable qualities of Athens. They urged the Spartans to submit any disputes to arbitration.

The assembly finally voted for war. Now it was necessary for the whole alliance to consider the matter, and presently they, too, voted for war, with the Corinthians actively stirring up sentiment as best they could. Sparta first demanded that Athens rescind her decree against Megara, leave Potidaea alone, and restore to Aegina the autonomy that had been taken from her twenty-five years before. There was a small minority at Athens that favored the strict observance of the peace treaty with Sparta made in 445 B.C. Pericles spoke for war, using the disingenuous argument that Athens should not yield to Spartan threats of force. The answer was put in the form that Athens would not yield to demands, but would follow the procedure of arbitration provided in the treaty.

Still nothing happened until, in March, 431, a Plataean opened the gates of his town one night to a force of three hundred hoplites from Thebes, whose errand was to force Plataea to join the Boeotian League, headed by Thebes. The Plataeans moved in the Athenian, or democratic, orbit and the Thebans in the Spartan, or conservative. Before the night was over the Plataeans had killed many of the Thebans and had captured the rest, had told a larger Theban force to withdraw or the prisoners would be killed, but, after it had withdrawn, murdered them anyway. This double display of treachery apparently seemed to both sides an opening of hostilities.

The First Stage, or The Archidamian War (431–421 B.C.)

The aim of the Spartan alliance was to defeat the Athenians in a pitched battle if they could be induced to risk one. If not, they would have to ravage Athenian territory and hope thus to force a battle, since they were not strong enough for a naval offensive. The Athenians, knowing that they were not strong enough to meet their adversaries on land, adopted the strategy proposed by Pericles of moving the citizens of Attica and their animals inside the city and the Long Walls. Even the wood-work of some of the buildings was moved in, suggesting the prevalence of adobe construction reinforced with wood in farmhouses. The vines and the fruit trees had to be left and were cut down by the invading Spartan army. The reserve hoplites were to guard the walls that surrounded Athens and Peiraeus and connected city and port. The first-line hoplites were to be out with the navy conducting the Athenian offensive, which would strike at Sparta and her allies, now here, now there, making sudden raids on the shore and cutting off trade and food supplies on the sea. Pericles assured the Athenians that if they could find the patience to endure being shut up in Athens while the Spartans ravaged their land and insulted them, they could eventually force the Spartans to end the war by the steady damage that they could inflict on them without ever risking a great battle on land. Athens could easily import food and other necessities. Some were impatient at this proposal, notably Cleon, who was to be heard from later, but Pericles persuaded the people to endorse it.

In May of 431 the Spartan king, Archidamus (from whose name the first part of the war is sometimes called "the Archidamian War"), led a mighty army into Attica. Although many of the Athenians complained bitterly as the enemy paraded before them and spread destruction through Attica, Pericles would allow no discussion of an attack on them. Before the enemy had left Attica, however, the ships of Athens were out carrying the Athenian offensive to many points in the Peloponnesus. Two Corinthian stations in western Greece were captured.

In 430 the Peloponnesians again invaded Attica and spread destruction for several weeks. In this year the plague came from the East. Modern physicians have often puzzled over Thucydides' careful description of the symptoms. Typhus and measles have been thought to be the most plausible suggestions. There may also be merit in the suggestion that germ strains have changed since then so that no disease that we now know is exactly like the plague of ancient times.

The plague raced through the crowded city. Men sickened and, after a few days of misery, died. Some few, including Thucydides, survived and were immune thereafter. The scanty water supplies were soon infected; prompt and proper disposal of the bodies was impossible. The city and the space between the Long Walls were crowded and uncomfortable enough at best with the country population added to those who normally lived in the city. Now fear stalked everywhere, and for a little while the Athenians degenerated. Extravagant and lawless behavior became common as men waited for a horrible death.

Pericles called his people back to courage, but fear had made them sullen and resentful. They deposed him from his office and fined him. The next year, however, he was re-elected and again put in charge of the war. But in 429 the plague was still present, and in the autumn Pericles died of it. The plague did not disappear until 426.

In the summer of 428 Mitylene, the most important city on the island of Lesbos, revolted from the Athenians, the propertied class having inspired the move. They asked for help from Sparta; had they been able to act with promptness, the Spartans might have helped Mitylene break free and might have gained strong recruits for their own side. The Athenians, as usual, did act with promptness; they besieged the city. For a moment we see the relation between the few and the many in more detail than usual. The few were urged by a Spartan adviser to arm the many in order to drive off the Athenian besiegers. The many, finding themselves armed with real weapons and defensive armor, turned on the few and forced them to surrender the city.

Now a famous debate took place in the Athenian Assembly, the substance of which is reported by Thucydides. Cleon, a vigorous man who had prospered as a tanner, proposed that every adult male in Mitylene—those of the friendly many as well as the hostile few—be put to death and that the rest of the people be sold into slavery. The resolution was carried and a message sent off to the Athenian commander in Lesbos. But Athens was a radical democracy and what it had done on the spot one day it could undo the next day without serving notice or waiting for committee reports. Next day the Assembly, a little awed by its own action, heard more discussion, knowing all the while that its message of the day before was on its way to Lesbos.

Diodotus, whose decree was to be carried this time, argued that the decree of the day before should be repealed because it was unwise. Such severity, he argued, would not prevent further revolts, which to the Greek mind seemed inevitable; it would only embitter and alienate the democratic majority in the cities of the Delian League, the element that favored Athens. Cleon persisted in his belief that exemplary severity was necessary to prevent further trouble. Diodotus managed to have the decree rescinded by a narrow margin, and another ship set out on a spectacular race to overtake the first. The new message arrived just as the Athenian commander in Lesbos was preparing to carry out the first order. The walls of Mitylene were dismantled and its fleet confiscated, for it was one of the few allies that still had a fleet. The land was parceled out to Athenian settlers for whom the natives had to work. In addition Cleon persuaded the Athenians to execute a thousand of the leaders of the revolt.

The Mitylenean Debate, as it often is called, has sometimes been taken as a hardening of sentiment among the Athenians as the war went on, especially since Diodotus's arguments for mercy were put on such severely practical grounds. Probably the calculations of the Athenian Empire had all been made on hard-headed and unsentimental grounds; such practical views can hardly have been a new development.

The unnecessary brutality shown by both sides in the war was, however, something new. Wars in Greece had been conducted on reasonably humane lines up to this time. They were generally settled by pitched battles, which were not followed by pursuit and slaughter of the vanquished. Prisoners ordinarily were not butchered, but were treated with decency until they could be exchanged or ransomed. At this time, though, there was a notable increase of man's inhumanity to man in the conduct of war. There seems to have been an increase of brutality in the struggles of the few and the many in individual cities, too, although some evidence suggests that these struggles had often been marked by bitterness and cruelty. Perhaps the fact that they involved people more closely connected to one another tended to embitter and degrade them, as often happens. Many factional struggles at this time were connected with the war. The affairs of Corinth, Corycra, and Epidamnus before the war, the episode of the Theban attempt on Plataea, and the revolt of Mitylene were all episodes of the continual struggle between the few and the many.

In 427 Corcyra suffered another factional struggle that is described in detail by Thucydides and is notable even among similar contests of the time for the depths to which the participants descended. Corcyra had been on the oligarchic side in the earlier affair of Epidamnus, while Corinth had favored the democrats. Now the democrats were in control in Corcyra, presumably because Athens had assisted them. But the oligarchs, made desperate by the fact that the democrats had imposed confiscatory fines on several of them, attacked the democratic council while it was in session, killed many members, and seized control of the city.

A hideous civil war began. The Athenians were bound by their power politics to favor the democrats; in the end they found themselves standing by while a massacre of the few was perpetrated by the many. Emotions ran so high and cruelty became so riotous that some of the oligarchs were said to have committed suicide rather than trust to the mercies of the democrats when they saw that capture was inevitable. It did not go unnoticed that certain personal projects were advanced in the general confusion; old enmities were liquidated, and sons assisted their fathers to pay their overdue debt to nature.

During the years between 431 and 428 the Spartans had not succeeded in winning any signal victory over the Athenians, who fought the war as a sea power (with one notable exception) according to Pericles' plan and advice. Their energetic general, Demosthenes, conceived a plan for general land operations in central Greece. He apparently expected to overcome the Aetolians, who lived just north of the Corinthian Gulf in western Greece, and finally to invade and conquer Boeotia in the East. The expected allies refused to cooperate, however, or did so tardily and ineffectively. Furthermore, the Athenian hoplites were at a great disadvantage in the broken country that they were trying to conquer. It was fortunate for the Athenians that this lesson about untried allies and broken terrain was taught to them so thoroughly on a small scale that they did not have to learn on a large scale. Thucydides does not spare the Athenians in telling of their mistakes and shortcomings. After suffering considerable losses, Demosthenes finally withdrew.

In 425 Demosthenes blundered into a great success on the west coast of the Peloponnesus, at Pylos. As he lay encamped there with a small force, a superior force of Spartans pounced on him. After the Athenians had defended themselves heroically for two days, a detachment of their fleet came up in the rear of the Spartans and put their ships out of action, leaving 420 Spartan hoplites and their attendant Helots on the island of Sphacteria, just off shore, where they had based themselves for further attack on the Athenians of Demosthenes.

Nothing could show better than this incident what a formidable figure the well trained and heavy-armed soldier, especially the Spartan, was in ancient warfare and what weight each of these soldiers had in the political thinking of the Spartans. The thought of losing these 420 first-line soldiers struck terror into them. Each man was important not only for this war, but also for the continuing life of Sparta. They immediately proposed an armistice; they handed over their whole fleet on condition that the men on Sphacteria be supplied with food. They then sent an embassy to Athens to propose that the two states end the war and make an alliance. Cleon urged the Assembly to demand the surrender of the men on Sphacteria and the cession of a number of key points as a preliminary to serious discussion of peace. The Spartan embassy went home.

On second thought the Assembly wished that it had been more reasonable. It was proposed that Cleon and someone else be sent to inspect the situation, for the Athenians were maintaining a force of 14,000 to watch the handful of Spartans, so great was their respect for them as fighting men. But Cleon, with his usual violence of tone, insisted that action was needed. When he drew the obvious answer that if he thought the Spartans could be defeated, he ought to go and command the operation, he hesitated, then responded to the jeers of the Assembly by accepting the command, setting sail, fighting a battle on Sphacteria, and coming back almost at once with 192 Spartan hoplites as prisoners, the remnant of the force.

The Athenians now freed themselves from invasion by proclaiming this handful of precious Spartan lives to be hostages who would be lost to Sparta if she invaded Attica. Sparta made repeated offers of peace, which were refused. By the year 424 Athens seemed to have prospects of being able to end the war on highly favorable terms.

In that year the Spartans were ingenious enough to send a force to northern Greece under Brasidas, a commander of quite un-Spartan dash and charm, to raise difficulties for Athens among disaffected allies. After a number of preliminary successes he captured the city of Amphipolis and gained control of the revenues and ship timber of the region, two welcome additions to Spartan resources. His fair and frank manner also won many friends for Sparta.

The historian Thucydides, who commanded a small fleet based at Thasos, was summoned, but arrived too late to reinforce Amphipolis. The Athenian people in their anger at the loss of the city exiled the admiral, thus allowing him the leisure to gather more material for his history and at the same time giving posterity a priceless account of these events.

At last, in 423, both sides were willing to sign a year's truce. Each still had a war party, however, with an active man as its leader—Brasidas in Sparta and Cleon in Athens. Under their influence the truce was somewhat less than completely observed. When it ended in 422, Cleon organized a great expedition to go to the North and undo all that Brasidas had done there. The Athenian and Spartan forces met at Amphipolis, and it was the good fortune of both sides that both Brasidas and Cleon fell in the engagement.

Peace negotiations began in earnest, for both sides wished to return as closely as possible to the state of affairs when the war started. But Argos, which had been neutral, seized the opportunity to make demands on Sparta as the price of renewing the treaty of neutrality. Her attitude was in the end to have much to do with the failure of the peace agreement. The Boeotians were also unwilling to make peace on the terms that satisfied Sparta. The result was that Sparta and Athens drew nearer to each other and made a treaty of mutual support and aid. The peace, concluded in 421, is called the Peace of Nicias, from the name of the chief Athenian negotiator, of whom we shall soon hear much more.

An Uneasy Peace (421–415 B.C.)

Sparta's chief problem was to bring back into line her disaffected allies. The difficulties of the Spartans were caused by the ambitions of Argos, which as a neutral had escaped the damage of the war, as well as by the disgruntlement of the Corinthians and others. For two or three years a number of ingenious statesmen among these malcontents tried to spin webs of diplomacy that would bind together new combinations to the advantage of their several states and to the disadvantage of Sparta. The air was cleared by Sparta's putting a splendid army in the field in 418;

the army defeated the Argives and their allies easily and restored all the prestige of Spartan arms.

Athens also had difficulty with her allies. In this connection one incident deserves mention. In 416 the Athenians decided that the island of Melos must be forced into their alliance. An expedition went there with an invitation to join; the Melians politely declined, saying that they preferred neutrality. Thucydides reports a discussion of the matter that he represents as having taken place between the Athenian and Melian leaders. It is generally known as the Melian Dialogue.

This dialogue is of interest because it is an independent work of art, because it shows "the first scientific historian" following the bidding of his strong artistic nature, and because it informs us on an interesting incident of the war. The factors of power politics involved in the situation were clearly set forth to the Melians by the Athenians, who were influenced solely by considerations of power. The dialogue is sometimes taken to illustrate the coarsening and hardening of the Athenian character under the stresses of war; this is perhaps an example of the sentimental attitude that often slightly distorts discussions of the Greeks. The Melians, after all their arguments for asserting their freedom were beaten down by the enemy towering over them, decided that in defiance of logic and common sense they would fight for their independence because it seemed right to them to do so. The Athenians took Melos, killed all the men, and enslaved the women and children.

The Sicilian Expedition (415–413 B.C.)

At this point Athens embarked on an adventure purely to satisfy ambitions of empire; it is known as the Sicilian expedition. The debate leading to the expedition and the expedition itself brought forward two Athenians of very different types, Nicias and Alcibiades. Nicias, who gave his name to the peace of 421, was an elderly and wealthy conservative who represented a goodly number of men who were not so blindly conservative as to wish for Spartan success and an oligarchic government at Athens, but who were cautious and a little old-fashioned. He was a religious man in the old style, believing in omens, a belief that cost the Athenians dearly during the campaign in Sicily.

Alcibiades took over something of Pericles' role as leader of the popular party and opponent of Sparta. Nature had lavished upon him every gift except that of a healthy personality. He was of noble birth and wealthy. He was vigorous and handsome. All accomplishments came readily to him. He was a man of great charm. He was intelligent and had at his disposal a great fund of resolution and energy which allowed him to do well whatever he wished to do or to play effectively any role that pleased him.

His personality, however, was of a type sometimes found in our own time in connection with a profusion of gifts. Alcibiades seemed almost unaware that other people had rights. To satisfy his own convenience or merely his whim he was capable of treating anyone with disregard or insolence. He was thoroughly unscrupulous; he could not be trusted to do the kind, the honest, or the pledged thing. Yet he could direct the overpowering charm of his personality at an individual or at the whole Athenian people and make people forget the injuries he had inflicted and that he obviously would inflict again whenever it suited him.

The debate on the Sicilian expedition began after Segesta, an ally of Athens in Sicily, asked to have envoys sent to her and convinced the men who were sent that she was able to finance an Athenian attack on Selinus, a city that moved in the Syracusan orbit, and even on Syracuse herself. The idea of attacking Syracuse at this time had no real connection with the rivalry between Athens and Sparta, even though Syracuse had been founded by Corinth, Sparta's ally, and kept up a connection with Corinth. To attack Syracuse was essentially a piece of exuberant Athenian imperialism. As the expansive genius of Alcibiades saw it, Athens would be able in the end to dominate all Sicily, Carthage, and the Greeks of South Italy. These and the Etruscans were regarded as the civilized peoples of the West, for no one then had any idea of what Rome would become.

Alcibiades threw all his influence behind the proposal, while Nicias opposed it with his usual cautious conservatism. The people should be considered an active partner in the decision, for they were never a mere passive mass dictated to by their leaders. In this case they were so enthusiastic that when Nicias named a prohibitive (as he thought) number of ships and men as necessary, they promptly voted that number. Athens had recovered very well during the years that had combined nominal peace and actual maneuvering with hostile intent. Her trade and tribute brought her a good income. The energy of the Athenian character was still there. The idea of conquering the great powers of the West did not seem fantastic to the people. If successful, they would have an empire that could guarantee employment and pay to the people and put them beyond fear of the Spartans or even in victorious control of them. If the price was likely to be high, they felt ready and able to pay it.

In June, 415 B.C., the great Athenian armada was ready to set out for Sicily. Almost the night before the fleet was to sail someone went about the city systematically mutilating the stone statues of the god Hermes that stood in every part of the city. Such a deed of sacrilege shocked and frightened people, and there were those who said that it was the prelude to an oligarchic revolution. An accuser came forward to point to Alcibiades as the leader of a group who had defaced the Hermae during a drunken frolic. To this was added a new charge, that he and his friends had enacted a parody of the mysteries on another drunken occasion, again a sacrilege, this time against the goddesses Demeter and Persephone, the holy persons of the Mysteries of Eleusis. Alcibiades hotly denied the charges and demanded an immediate trial. But he, with Nicias and another man, was to command the expedition, and this was declared no time for such a trial. So at the June solstice the armada sailed.

But superstitious fears did not disappear. New accusations were made as a result of which some men fled the country, while others were imprisoned. Finally a respectable citizen, Andocides, finding all the men of his family in prison with him, turned informer and told a story of the affair that led to the execution of four men and the temporary exile of a few others, while the state galley *Salaminia* was sent to bring Alcibiades home for trial. Perhaps Alcibiades was not unwilling to dissociate himself from the expedition, which instead of immediately assaulting the Syracusans with all its great force had bogged down in preparations and trivial operations. On the way home he escaped to Sparta.

The Athenians in Sicily soon learned that for the third time in this war they had put too much trust in their allies, whom they expected to carry out a major operation in concert with them. The western Greeks were now cool and not very helpful. In the autumn of 415 a belated attack was made on Syracuse with little success. The Syracusans appealed to Sparta for help, and Alcibiades, who was at Sparta, urged that the help be given. In 414 the Athenians moved on Syracuse again and by summer could feel confident that they had reduced the defenders to near starvation. The arrival of the Spartan Gylippus in command of relief forces from Sparta and Corinth was the turning point. Gylippus succeeded in breaking up the blockade of the city and winning some minor engagements. Nicias sent home a gloomy letter admitting the sorry state of the affair and asking for reinforcements.

With great effort the government sent out reinforcements under Demosthenes, an able commander. He tried to make a decisive attack at once. It failed. He urged Nicias to give up and go home, but Nicias resisted. A far tougher man than he might well have hesitated to return and report to the sovereign people that their great dream of empire in the West had turned into a nightmare. When at last Nicias was convinced, there was an eclipse of the moon (August 27, 413 B.C.), and both he and the majority of the troops accepted the soothsayers' assertion that they ought not to move for twenty-seven days.

This piece of superstitious behavior cost the Athenians dearly. Gylippus and the Syracusans managed to construct a barrier to contain the Athenian fleet in the great harbor of Syracuse. Nicias and Demosthenes attempted to escape overland with their confused group of soldiers, marines, sailors, rowers from the galleys, and slaves. The gloomy genius of Thucydides is at its best as he tells of the flight, the many swift deaths, the one-sided battle, the imprisonment of the captives in the quarries of Syracuse, the lingering and painful death of many there, and the sale of the survivors into slavery. This was the worst disaster ever suffered by a Greek armed force or by a Greek state.

The Last Stage of the War (413–404 B.C.)

The terribly costly defeat of the Sicilian expedition was a turning point in the Peloponnesian War and in the fortunes of Athens. Certainly it strengthened the sentiment of both conservatives and moderates that the democratic policy had been too ambitious and not cautious enough. It should be noted, however, that the great energy that was characteristic of the Athenians remained unimpaired and that the effort they still put forth was the wonder of outsiders.

At this juncture the Persians decided to take a hand in the war. The Peace of Callias (448 B.C.) had been reaffirmed some ten years before, but in 414 the Athenians had unwisely given aid to a revolt of the Carians against Persia. Perhaps for this reason, perhaps because of the disaster in Sicily, the Persians decided to regard the treaty as abrogated. They reasserted their claim to tribute from the Greeks of Asia Minor and began to pay naval subsidies to Sparta so that she could oppose an effective fleet to that of the Athenians in the waters off Asia Minor. The Spartans in return disclaimed the role of protectors of the Asiatic Greeks against the Persians.

Athens' difficulties in carrying on the war were also increased by the revolt of some of their allies. Thucydides would have us believe that they were ready to revolt at all times out of resentment of Athenian high-handedness and insistence on democratic institutions. A careful reading of his own details shows that they do not support his general remarks. The common people everywhere favored Athens, which supported the cause of the many. A large number of the revolts were plainly inspired by the few, as in the case of Mitylene. The few generally hoped for or could count on the support of either the Spartans or the Persians, both of whom were ready in this last phase of the war to support the few anywhere as opponents of Athens.

The Sicilian expedition had essentially resulted from a plan of the common people, who had looked forward to benefits for themselves from its success. After its failure the more conservative elements demanded to be heard, and the populace at large may well have been disposed to listen to more sober views. In 413 a newly created board of ten commissioners was elected; it was intended to be the highest ranking board and was to have an important voice in policy.

The conservative, or oligarchic, element must be separated into extremists and moderates. The extremists would take away all political rights from the mass of the people, while the moderates would only have strengthened the prerogative of the few to lead and direct. All along the extremists had banded together in clubs that did not call attention to themselves, but actively assisted their members in any situation where union seemed useful, as in campaigns for election. Not only did the conservatives take heart at the spectacular failure of the democratic policy in Sicily, but they also suddenly received an unexpected offer of assistance from Alcibiades.

In Sparta Alcibiades, after having given the Spartans such an idea of Athenian long-range plans in Sicily and south Italy that they decided to renew open warfare against Athens, won their admiration by playing the Spartan to perfection, living in strenuous simplicity. He added his own touch by seducing the wife of one of the kings and is reported to have said that the bloodline of the royal family would be improved thereby. He then found it advisable to change his residence and slipped away from the Spartan fleet, with which he was serving, to the Persian satrap Tissaphernes. The Persian grandee was also charmed as the recent Spartan ascetic slipped easily into the role, as Tissaphernes' guest, of the devotee of elegance and luxury. Soon a plan suggested itself to Alcibiades' fertile imagination.

He sent a message to the officers of the Athenian fleet at Samos: if an oligarchy were established at Athens, he would get the aid of Tissaphernes for Athens rather than for Sparta, which would give Athens a new advantage in naval power. The condition that Athens must change to oligarchic government seemed natural, since the Persians preferred to deal with the more stable governments dominated by the few.

Even to the moderates the establishment of an oligarchy of some kind seemed preferable to defeat by Sparta. Word of Alcibiades' proposal was sent back from the fleet to Athens, and there the efforts of the conservatives increased. The moderate faction debated the matter and prepared to propose a change to oligarchy. The extremists, on the other hand, began with the murder of several democratic leaders, which spread dismay among the people.

A group of conservatives serving in the fleet had gone to meet Alcibiades and Tissaphernes. But Alcibiades had sensed in the meantime that Tissaphernes was not going to fall in with his plan, and in order to keep the blame for the failure of the scheme from falling on him he managed to make the Persian price for cooperation seem so high as to be prohibitive. The disappointed envoys prepared to act on their own. Returning to Athens, they obscured their failure with Tissaphernes and proposed to the Assembly that a group be appointed to draw up a new constitution. By implication it was to be a moderately conservative arrangement.

In June, 411, a meeting was called to hear the report on the new constitution. The meeting was set for Colonus, a part of Athens that was outside the walls and was dangerous for a man without armor, so that the assembly that met there would be small and well-to-do. The assembly abolished all existing offices, decreed that there should be no payment for any public service, and set up a group of four hundred, who were in turn to choose five thousand, all of them men of enough property to furnish themselves with full armor. These five thousand were to be the voting public for the rest of the war.

The Four Hundred did not proceed to the nomination of the Five Thousand, as they had been directed to do, but surprised and drove out the regularly elected *Boule* and then murdered or deported whichever democratic leaders remained. They then offered to talk about peace with the Spartans, who received them very cautiously, having some doubts about their powers. The new leaders also sent envoys to the fleet at Samos. But, in the meantime, the men of the fleet had made up their minds that they must represent the democracy of Athens for now. In addition, perhaps because they thought that he still had access to Persian money, they had invited Alcibiades to join them and had elected him general.

Thus two governments claimed to be in charge of the Athenian state. Alcibiades made a suggestion that prevented conflict between them, however: the Four Hundred should proceed at once to appoint the Five Thousand and get on with the war. In the summer of 411 the Five Thousand were appointed—perhaps only half the men who had property enough to arm themselves fully. Apparently it was intended that others should serve in turn. Although it is not entirely clear how the new system worked, it seems that there was no pay, that the propertied class monopolized the offices and the places on the *Boule,* thus guiding policy, and that the rights of voting in the Assembly and serving on juries (without pay) were open to all. The people could still exercise a final check on policy, but all the initiative lay with the propertied class.

The Five Thousand prosecuted the war energetically. In May of the next year the Athenians won a naval battle at Cyzicus that caused the Spartans again to propose peace. Alcibiades, formally recalled from exile and put in command of the fleet, had won this engagement by his dash and vigor. Many were in favor of peace, but Cleophon, a businessman not unlike the late Cleon, persuaded the people not to settle for anything less than Spartan capitulation. The government of the Five Thousand was quietly put aside with no disturbance and full democracy was restored.

At this point the Athenian fleet, under the command of Alcibiades, dominated the eastern waters. In 407 he returned to Athens with the fleet and was received by the citizenry with great enthusiasm. The command of all the forces was given him, and in the autumn of that year he sailed back to the East with a strong force, planning to recover all the former subject cities there that had revolted from the league.

The rest of the war became a drama of futility and folly. Alcibiades fell into disgrace again, this time because a subordinate disobeyed direct orders and brought defeat to a part of the fleet. Knowing his fellow countrymen, Alcibiades retired to a fortress he had built for himself in the Chersonesus. The Spartans, having found a good admiral, won some naval engagements. Then the Athenians achieved an impressive victory at Arginusae. But in the rough weather the men of a dozen disabled ships and a good many men swimming and clinging to wreckage were not picked up. Embittered, the people tried the generals in charge as a group, condemned them, and executed them.

Again the Spartans asked for peace and again the people, urged on by Cleophon, decided to press on in the hope of victory. The active part of the war ended on a note of pure folly. An Athenian fleet of 180 ships, based at the long open beach of Aegospotami on the north side of the Dardanelles, was trying to open the strait by defeating a Spartan fleet, based in a harbor on the south shore. Each day the Athenians offered battle to the Spartans, who stayed in their harbor. Late each afternoon the Athenians went back, beached their ships, and scattered to prepare their supper. Alcibiades, whose fortress was in the neighborhood, came and advised the Athenian commanders to move to the protection of the naval base at Sestus, but his suggestion was scorned. Next day, when the Athenians came back and beached their ships, the Spartans swooped down and captured 171 of them. Sparta now ruled the Aegaean.

By late autumn (the year was 405) the Spartans were blockading Athens. After a few weeks starvation began. For a time Cleophon could inspire the people to defiance, but presently they sent another man, Theramenes, to Sparta to treat. The terms in the end were not unreasonable, and they were gladly accepted because many were dying of starvation. The Long Walls and the fortifications of Peiraeus were to be demolished, the fleet, except for a small police force, was to be given up, the empire was to be abandoned, exiles were to be recalled, and Athens was to follow Sparta's lead in foreign policy. In April, 404, the Spartans entered the city and the demolition of the Long Walls began.

THE CULTURE OF THE LATE FIFTH CENTURY

Much of the lively intellectual activity of the Periclean Age and of the time immediately after it took the form of conversation and debate, lost to us, of course, except for reports of it. Furthermore, only a few of the tragedies and comedies have been entirely preserved, although we have references to many others and sometimes quotations of a few lines from them. Also lost are many specialized essays and books, such as, for example, the books of architectural theory that discussed general principles and specific buildings. Other specialized books have survived (on military principles, the interpretation of physiognomy, and on dreams) that have not been influential since their own time and that offer almost nothing to the modern reader. We must remember that the surviving literary works of the Greeks (and of the Romans) were not the only books of their time or the only plays, but were a few of the many conceived and executed in an atmosphere of lively competition.

We shall here consider four great men of the late fifth century—Socrates, Thucydides, Euripides, and Aristophanes—all formed in the Periclean Age and all active until about the end of the century. It must be emphasized that Socrates wrote nothing. His enormous influence was exercised through conversations and the great charm of a completely developed and honest personality.

Thucydides wrote one book, his account of the Peloponnesian War, which he did not live to complete. His life was that of an Athenian aristocrat, active in government and in the intellectual life of the city and very much influenced by the attempts of the Sophists to analyze the methods by which governments are conducted.

Euripides wrote a great many tragedies; the twenty-one that we have are perhaps a quarter of his output. He, like Socrates and Thucydides, was a master of keen analysis of the ways of society and was to exert great influence after his death, as they did, both in the ancient and in the modern world.

Aristophanes was one of the masters of comedy and the only one whose works are at all preserved for us; we have eleven. His plays show a strongly conservative temper. He analyzed life in particular, rather than in general as the other three did, for we have many sharp criticisms of Athenian society and of political matters, like the war with the Spartans, but we seldom have the feeling that the plays lead to reflection on life in general. The structure and manner of Athenian comedy of this period did not lend itself at all to imitation, either by the Romans or by the early European dramatists, as so many Greek and Roman tragedies and comedies did.

Socrates

The conditions that started the Sophists on their characteristic activity also started Socrates on the long career that led at last to his condemnation for impiety and his death by drinking hemlock in the year 399 B.C.

He was an Athenian citizen, born in 469. He learned the trade of stone-cutter and worked at it for some years in his early life. At some point, perhaps by the time he was thirty, he stopped working at stonecutting and thereafter devoted himself to his life's real work. That work was to further as much as he could the development of a science of man. Socrates saw correctly, as did the Sophists, that the time had come for careful and systematic study of the conditions by which man really lives. The Sophists were more inclined to study the activities of man, especially oratory and politics; the aim of Socrates was to lay the foundation of a philosophy of human existence.

The rest of his life was spent in this quest. Unlike many men with a mission or a quest, he did not go to some other place or into retirement. He needed people who would discuss problems with him and whom he could observe. These men he could find in Athens and would have been able to find there even if Athens had not been the intellectual capital of the world.

In spite of the fact that so much was said about Socrates, it is diffi-cult to be precisely sure what he talked about and what his beliefs were, because we know him chiefly through a follower of towering greatness in philosophy—Plato. Socrates appears often as the chief character in Pla-to's philosophical dialogues. We simply cannot be sure of how much of what he says there is his own and how much is the later thought of Plato. We can be sure, however, that the interest of the young man in the inadequate natural science of the earlier philosophers yielded to an inter-est in man. His questioning of the Athenians and of visitors to Athens, according to Plato and others who heard him, was always on human values, either of the individual or of society as a whole. His chief idea seems to have been that virtue depends on knowledge and that to know the good is to desire it. The most important thing in life, then, is to con-sider carefully the nature of life and to attempt to learn what the good is.

Socrates may have been pursuing his quest for about forty years when he was brought to trial in 399 B.C. During that time he had never left Athens except on military service in the Peloponnesian War, when he distinguished himself by his calm bravery in battle. He must have had some property, since he fought as a hoplite, or heavy infantryman. We must not suppose that he spent all his time accosting people in the street and asking them to give definitions, or indeed that he spent any great proportion of his time with unselected companions.

In the year 423 Aristophanes caricatured Socrates in his *Clouds*. The two main points of the caricature were that Socrates was one of those who taught the younger generation to argue in an irresponsible and dis-honest way—"making the worse cause appear the better"—and that he was interested in "things in the heavens and below the earth," which was a way of referring to astronomical studies, which were forbidden by law as being atheistic. Socrates could not have been both the things that Aristophanes here suggested, a Sophist, on the one hand, instructing pupils in oratory, and an atheistic Ionian scientist on the other. No one combined these two careers. In fact Socrates did neither. He had long ago decided that natural science was not useful to him, and he insisted anyway that he taught no one, but only discussed and tried to learn. Probably many of his contemporaries did think of him as a Sophist, however, even though he may be distinguished from them in four ways. First, as was just said, he did not profess to teach. Second, he took no pay from anyone. Third, his interest was in the principles of the good life rather than in the rules for worldly success. Fourth, although many of the Sophists are known to have published their writings, Socrates wrote nothing.

Thucydides

The historian Thucydides, who lived from about 470 B.C. to about 400, was almost of an age with Socrates, Euripides, and Aristophanes and presumably knew them all. Like the other men he had grown up at a time when an exhilarating new freedom of thought was being asserted in Athens, but his mind had not been formed exactly as theirs had, for he belonged more to the class and the group that by tradition held the offices and managed the affairs of Athens, so that he saw political and social questions as one who knows what it is to form a policy and to take responsibility for it. He was much impressed with the Sophist idea that it was possible to construct a sound body of rules for the conduct of public affairs, thus adding to knowledge of the sort that is handed down within a governing class.

Thucydides tells the reader that when the war broke out between the Athenians and the Spartans in 431 he decided to write the history of what was likely to be the greatest war that had ever been fought. Because he had had the benefit of the Sophists' studies of government, he thought that he could write an account of the conflict that would throw new light on the behavior of groups of men and offer guidance for the future. It would be not merely the entertainment of an hour (an unfair remark aimed at Herodotus's book), but a permanent possession. This sober prediction of his own literary immortality has so far been justified. He was exiled, as we have said, for his failure to forestall the Spartan capture of Amphipolis, and it is to be presumed that he spent some of the time of his exile in Sparta and used the opportunity to work up his material from the point of view of the other side. It is not known when he returned to Athens. He was able to carry his story only as far as the deposition of the Four Hundred at Athens in favor of the Five Thousand in September, 411.

The traditional opposition between Herodotus, the amiable teller of stories, and Thucydides, the austere scientific historian, has been abandoned by serious scholars. Herodotus has come to seem far more than a quaint primitive in the writing of history and Thucydides has come to seem no mean artist as well as a fine historian. Although his admirers still sometimes refuse to admit them, Thucydides is also recognized as having some slight weaknesses, the chief of them being that his conservative sympathies sometimes influence his judgments unduly. His stature as artist is considerably greater than used to be allowed. In many parts of the book his narrative Greek prose style is awkward and difficult compared to that of some later authors, for the technique of the elegant and perspicuous complex sentence had not yet been fully worked out. Thucydides' prose is generally thought to represent the result of the earlier attempts of the Sophists to write effective and elegant Greek. Yet the story moves on straightforwardly and swiftly, and some of his narratives, such as the description of the later part of the Sicilian expedition, rise to greatness. His art is displayed, too, in the selection and reporting of speeches, many of which he could have heard himself. The fact that he gives what purport to be the speeches of important people in their own words aroused much unnecessary distress among the sober-minded historians of the nineteenth century, who fancied themselves as truly scientific historians and considered this procedure unscientific, although they generously thought of him as scientific in other respects.

For the historian to present the opposing points of view at certain crises is plainly necessary; to present them as formal speeches pretended to be in the words of the speakers is not necessary. It is highly effective, however, and the attentive reader of Thucydides may well come to feel that the author is wise to rebel at the self-imposed task of straightforward exposition and analysis and decide to allow himself the pleasure of following his creative imagination for a little while.

Euripides

Euripides, the last of the three great Athenian tragedians, is another of that company of Athenians who have been dear to the modern Western world because of their rationalistic and individualistic thought. The manner of Aeschylus and Sophocles in examining the ancient and traditional ways might be described as conservative and gentlemanly. Euripides dropped the restrictions and reservations of the conservative and the gentleman and worked in an uninhibited and realistic manner. His first plays were shown in 455, and he was still active when he died in 407. He wrote at least eighty-eight plays, but won only five first prizes. He was highly popular in the fourth century and thereafter. His great appeal to the Roman Seneca, who wrote adaptations of Greek plays, resulted in a strong Euripidean influence on the early tragic drama of France and England, both of which used Seneca's plays as models.

It was customary to say that Euripides was not a favorite of his own time, despite his later popularity, until recent re-examination of the evidence cast doubt on this assertion. We should remember that the officials who chose the plays must have been sensitive to public taste; if they repeatedly allowed Euripides to show his work, they must have felt that it would be well received. The plays, as has been said, were in accord with the temper of the times. The form in which they were cast, however, was somewhat unusual, so that it is possible that the audiences enjoyed the plays and that the judges, somewhat baffled by certain features of them, did not often wish to award them first prize.

War, women, and religion are the favorite subjects of Euripides. *The Trojan Women* is a vivid play that concerns war. It was produced in 415, just after the cruel Athenian capture of Melos and during the preparations for the great expedition against Syracuse. It was the third play of a trilogy, the first two parts of which we know to have been about earlier parts of the story of the Trojan War. In this, the third, the plight of the conquered Trojans and the hollowness of the Greek victory are vividly brought out.

The play has very little plot in the modern sense, and what unity it has comes from the presence through most of it of Hecuba, or Hekabe, the widowed queen of Troy. She learns that she is to be the slave of Odysseus, then that her daughter Polyxena has been sacrificed at the tomb of Achilles. Her prophetess daughter, Cassandra, is told that she will be the concubine of Agamemnon, although she was vowed to virgin priesthood. Andromache, the widow of Hector, is to be the slave of the son of Achilles; her little son is taken from her and cast from the wall, since Odysseus says that it is dangerous to leave a male of the royal blood alive.

After this pitiable series of events Menelaus appears to take Helen from the group of captive women, and a debate ensues of the sort that the Athenians enjoyed. Helen skillfully sets forth the argument that she was the plaything of the gods and is not really guilty of desertion and adultery, whereupon the aged Hecuba leaps into the debate with a passionate argument that Helen must take full responsibility for her own acts. Menelaus promises that Helen shall pay the penalty when she reaches home. At last it is time to go, and the Greeks, with their booty and their slaves, depart to the dreadful disasters that the audience knows are waiting for them on the sea.

Medea is a story of revenge. It raises again the question, constantly implied in Aeschylus's *Agamemnon,* whether it can be right to repay evil with evil. The audience, which almost inevitably sympathizes with Medea's first impulse of revenge, finally finds itself confronted with deeds of horror that follow naturally from the beginnings, but with which no one could sympathize. The play also raises questions about the position of women in society.

The story of Medea was an old one, the story of the oldest Greek penetration of the Black Sea, dramatized as the story of Jason and his quest for the golden fleece. He found the fleece in Colchis, at the far end of the Black Sea. The princess Medea, who possessed magic powers, was smitten with his manly charms and helped him to get the fleece from her father, than ran away to Thessaly with him. Jason could not marry a barbarian, of course, but they lived together and had two children. When Medea used her powers to repay a slighting remark from another young woman, she and Jason found it necessary to flee from his home in Thessaly and accept the protection of the king of Corinth. The king proposed that Jason marry his daughter, assuming that the barbarian mistress would retire into the background, where she would be adequately provided for. But Medea was not ready to be put aside, for to her this was the basest betrayal on Jason's part, not merely the way of the world.

Euripides was a master of the debate scene, and his debate between Jason and Medea is beautifully done. One amusing touch is Jason's assertion that he has done Medea a great and lasting benefit by giving her an opportunity to see the civilized society of Greece. The sympathy of the audience is with the rejected Medea, who now plans to send Jason's intended bride a poisoned robe. The poor little princess tries it on, and her flesh is consumed by the burning of the poison, as is her father's when he tries to help. Then, as a last revenge on Jason, Medea kills her own two children and carries away their bodies as she flees in the dragon-drawn chariot that she has summoned. Eight hundred years later Saint Augustine, telling in his *Confessions* of his days as a university student in Carthage, speaks of evenings spent in the theater, with a visit to the tavern afterward, and then down the street with his friends, all lustily singing "Medea Flying," by which he means Medea's farewell speech set to music as an aria. *Medea,* translated or adapted, has always been and still is good theater.

To portray so wicked a witch on the stage doubtless seemed unsuitable to the conservatives. Discussing a woman's station, especially that of a barbarian mistress, probably seemed a little ungentlemanly, too. Yet a woman's revenge in such a situation has a poignancy that an ordinary male revenge for an injury could never have.

Euripides' *Bacchae* was the third play of a trilogy that his son produced after his death, presumably the occasion on which one of his plays is said to have won a posthumous first prize. The subject is the power of Dionysus. This is not a criticism of the gods, nor yet the avowal of a return to religious orthodoxy, as some critics have interpreted it. The portrayal of the peculiar power of Dionysus and the nature of Dionysiac worship made excellent dramatic material. As Euripides viewed it, the god's power and his worship corresponded to basic elements in human nature that are no more open to criticism or approval than is the functioning of the liver, but that do make good theater.

Dionysus was the god of the vine and of fertility, but also of certain irrational urges in human beings that are difficult to formulate precisely and prosaically. Our irrational joy in beauty and the swelling of sex impulses in us are both Dionysiac, as are occasional acts of irrational cruelty. Sometimes the Dionysiac within outrages the soberness of our Apollonian side.

The story of the *Bacchae* is fairly simple. Dionysus came to Thebes to be with his worshipers. Pentheus, the king, opposed the rites and tried to arrest the god, who was in human form, but Dionysus brushed him aside with ease. Then Pentheus was tempted to go out to spy on the women's rites out on the mountains. He was detected by them, and in their religious frenzy they tore him to pieces as they customarily tore to pieces some captured animal as part of the ritual. His own mother carried his head in triumph, fancying in her frenzied condition that it was the head of a mountain lion. The play gives a very strong impression of the inexorable and irresistible power of Dionysus, or of the impulses that he symbolizes.

Aristophanes

Aristophanes lived from about 445 to about 380 B.C. His work has never been so popular in modern times as that of the other men whom we have discussed. His themes lack the universality of the tragedies, and his plays contain a great many local references that obstruct the enjoyment and comprehension of the modern reader. He wrote over forty comedies, of which eleven have survived. All except the last of these, *Plutus,* are of the type known as Old Comedy. *Plutus* is called Middle Comedy in the usual classification; this was a transitional stage which, by 300 B.C., led to New Comedy or what we nowadays would call comedy of manners.

The other ten plays of Aristophanes are the only surviving examples of Old Comedy. They are a curious blend of uproarious slapstick comedy, political and social commentary, personal abuse of individual Athenians, and lovely lyrics for the choruses. It must be remembered that comedy, like tragedy, grew out of the celebrations of the festival of Dionysus. The combination of actors and chorus in comedy is much like that of tragedy.

The abusive and indecent language that was tossed about at festivals for apotropaic purposes (that is, to avert the ill will of the unseen powers) appears in the comedies.

In the typical comedy of Aristophanes a character comes forward with a great idea, one full of comic possibilities, but often with overtones of sober sense. For instance, in *Acharnians* (produced in 425) one of the charcoal burners who made up most of the population of the deme Acharnae had the idea of making a separate personal peace with the Spartans, since there seemed no possibility of a formal ending of the Peloponnesian War. The ending of the war was a favorite subject with the conservative Aristophanes, and Athenian freedom of speech made it possible to bring up such a serio-comic proposal to change public policy. The charcoal burner, who exemplified "the little man," rose in his wrath, as the little man would always like to do, and proposed to conclude a peace between himself and the Spartan state, no matter what the rest of the Athenians did.

Then, in the comedy of Aristophanes, there is a debate about adopting the great idea. An opponent speaks against it and is heckled; the proponent speaks for it and is heckled. There is a vote, and of course the great idea is adopted. Sometimes the plot goes on to the end very logically and sometimes a succession of scenes follows that are loosely grouped around the great idea and come to no strictly logical conclusion.

Lysistrata (produced in 411) is named for the chief female character, whose great idea was that the women of Athens and the women of Sparta should refuse to have intercourse with their husbands as a means of blackmailing them into ending the war. The idea was adopted, and the ladies persevered until they had gained their end. The fun is increased by the fact that one or two of the weaker vessels among them have difficulty in standing by their own decision. One of the women teases her husband by pretending that she will yield to his importunities and have intercourse with him then and there. She keeps thinking of one thing and another that will be necessary—a blanket, a pillow, a drop of perfume behind the ears—and finally runs away, leaving him in the lurch. The scene is constructed with great skill to extract the last possible laugh from the audience. Yet, with all the fun, the serious idea that the war is a piece of tragic folly is never left aside for long, and at the end there is a rousing and effective lecture on the real bonds that do and should unite the two nations.

The simpler forms of humor have an ample field in which to disport themselves in a comedy with this plot. Aristophanes uses every device that might make people laugh. He has ludicrous situations and subtle plays on words, farcical ideas and slapstick. Through it all run the twin motifs of sex and elimination, the twin bases of the physiological joke.

There is no use in pretending that by some standard Aristophanes is pure-minded. He is indecent in the extreme. Probably not all his audiences enjoyed his kind of humor; probably most of them did. What is funny may be more funny for being indecent, and the festival was based on the spirit of lusty and energetic life, not out of keeping with his great play with the slang words for the sex organs. He calls attention to the embarrassing evidence of the condition the men were in, and at the end he leers at the thought of how the reconciliation will be celebrated.

12

THE FOURTH CENTURY:
POLITICAL HISTORY

Outside Greece the general situation was little changed by Sparta's triumph in the war with Athens. The Persian Empire was still the largest and richest entity. The Persians could believe for the moment that their longe-range diplomacy had weakened the threat of the Greeks of Greece proper to their western possessions and had allowed them to restore full sovereignty over the Greeks of Asia Minor.

The Greeks of Sicily must have been greatly relieved at the defeat of Athens, for it was plain that she could not rise to such a pitch of aggressiveness again for a very long time. In fact no threat ever came from Greece again, and in the following century the Greeks of the West, under the leadership of Syracuse, prospered greatly.

The defeat of Athens was probably a relief to the Carthaginians. Their empire, with its chief city near what is now Tunis, comprised a certain amount of rich farming land in Tunisia, but essentially was based on control of the western seas and on maritime trade. In the century that lay ahead they prospered greatly but continued their struggles with the Greeks in Western Sicily.

To the Spartans the victory over Athens and her allies brought no great profit, either immediately or in the long run. The Spartans attempted to exercise their influence in a wider sphere than before and in a sphere where they lacked the necessary experience. In spite of their sober virtues they did not know how to exercise the hegemony that they now found to be theirs, as we shall see in a moment when we turn to details. Their reputation suffered from the unwisdom and brutality of some of their acts, and their defeat at the hands of Thebes at Leuctra in 371 was to mean the end of their old primacy among the Greeks.

The defeat of Athens was a setback for democracy, since the Athenians had been the vigorous champions of the democratic form of government. Athens herself was far from being finished as a power among the Greeks, for the wartime losses in men and materials were capable of being restored, and the bright Athenian energy had not been extinguished. The true greatness of Athens, her greatness in the domain of the spirit, was not broken by the war. Naturally we cannot say what the result would have been had the war never been fought or had Athens been the winner. It is plain, however, as we shall see, that in the fourth century the cultural life of Athens went on as an orderly continuation of her life of the fifth century. But let us return to our narrative.

Spartan Management in Greece

The Spartans were as convinced of the superiority of rule by the few as the Athenians were of the superiority of the rule of the many. Naturally they wished to reshape local constitutions everywhere so as to place power in the hands of the few, the more wealthy and aristocratic elements who had long had to endure the predominance of the many under Athenian influence. Lysander, the most influential Spartan at the time, chose governing boards of ten local aristocrats in all the cities formerly allied to Athens. The boards, or decarchies, were charged with devising new aristocratic constitutions and supervising the installation of governments thoroughly sympathetic to Sparta. In the spirit of Greek factional strife the decarchies confiscated property and put many of the popular leaders to death, relying on the support of small Spartan garrisons under commanders known as harmosts.

As usual, our information is best for Athens, and there a stirring story played itself out. A group of thirty aristocrats, rather than ten, was chosen to manage the reorganization. They came to be known simply as "the Thirty." Backed by an unusually strong Spartan garrison, they instituted a reign of terror. The energy of one Critias and his uncompromising insistence on complete oligarchic control soon brought him to the head of the Thirty. He had once been one of the group that liked to talk to Socrates, although he is said soon to have given Socrates up, thinking that he had no more to learn from him that would be practically useful. He had been prominent in the oligarchic revolution of the year 411. The moderate element among the Thirty was led by Theramenes, who had also played the role of moderate during the revolution of 411.

Critias forthrightly accused many prominent democrats of treason and had them executed, then moved to a systematic assault on wealthy men, some of them citizens, some resident aliens, confiscating their wealth. The speech of Lysias, *Against Eratosthenes,* delivered in 399 B.C. and bitterly attacking the member of the Thirty who had arranged the murder of Lysias's brother, gives a vivid description of the cynical way in which the members of the Thirty enriched themselves personally by their misuse of power. It was later estimated that fifteen hundred persons were murdered, with or without a pretense of judicial process.

The Thirty then reduced the list of those with full citizen rights to three thousand, all "politically reliable," instead of allowing full citizen rights to all those whose property allowed them to equip themselves as hoplites, the usual formula for a conservative government. Systematically they eliminated the friends of Theramenes and at last forced Theramenes himself to end his life by drinking hemlock. Hundreds of citizens fled to such friendly nearby cities as Megara.

Thrasybulus, who had played an important part in opposing the oligarchic revolution of 411, escaped to Thebes, which had already begun to be estranged from Sparta. Gathering seventy other bold spirits, he launched a counter movement. The little group found its Sherwood Forest in the half-dismantled fortress of Phyle, in northeastern Attica near the Theban border. The troops sent against them were unable to take the difficult place by assault and were prevented by fierce wintry weather from blockading it and starving out the democrats.

By the spring of 403 Thrasybulus had some seven hundred men, and his forces were growing steadily. He also had a colleague, Anytus, who was to be prominent in the democratic party thereafter and who is best known as one of the accusers of Socrates. Presently the little army made its way down through Attica to Peiraeus and there defeated the government forces in a battle that cost the oligarchs the life of Critias. Faced with his death and with the growing power of Thrasybulus and Anytus, the more moderate among the oligarchs were able to force the appointment of a new board, this time a board of ten, to head the government, only two of whom had belonged to the Thirty. The rest of the Thirty withdrew to Eleusis, which they had seized before as a possible refuge.

Yet the Ten were unable to make any agreement with the steadily growing democratic forces at Peiraeus. Finally they appealed to Sparta, and Lysander answered their call. Presumably he would have been able to crush the democratic forces but for the fact that opposition to him at Sparta became so strong as to force his removal from command. King Pausanias, who took over command of the forces and the management of this affair, showed a conciliatory spirit, perhaps partly because the more sensible element at Sparta realized that she had already lost much of the general popularity and influence that she had enjoyed only a year or two before.

After it had heard emissaries from both Athenian factions, the Spartan government entrusted the settlement to Pausanias and a board of commissioners. The result was that the Athenians of both factions committed themselves to an amnesty, or act of oblivion, late in the year 403. This amnesty, which for Greeks showed surprising wisdom and restraint, provided that all that was past should be forgotten, if not forgiven. The surviving members of the Thirty were to stay in Eleusis as in a separate state. No acts of vengeance for wrongs done under the Thirty were to be allowed. The Spartans did not interfere in the formation of a new constitution, which naturally was a democratic one. The restored democracy took Eleusis in 401, executed the members of the tyrannical government who were captured there, and then again made Eleusis a part of the Athenian state.

The Trial of Socrates

It was probably the strain of recent events that caused the prosecution and condemnation of Socrates in 399 B.C. after the Athenians had allowed him to go his way for some forty years. Athens had lost a war, a long, bitter, costly war. She had been convulsed by the terrible rule of the Thirty and by the civil war that had led to the restoration of the democracy. The ordinary citizen of Athens must have felt that now was a time for Athens to apply all her forces to the task of reconstruction. Those men who represented disruptive forces or were too present reminders of recent events were likely to encounter strong enmity.

Socrates was not the only man against whom such feeling was directed in the years just after the restoration of the democracy. In the corpus of speeches ascribed to the orator Lysias we find an attack delivered in 399 against the orator Andocides for his impiety. Another speech contains a bitter attack against one Agoratus, who had acted as *agent provocateur* for the Thirty. Other speeches, some of this year and some of later years, show that the bitterness engendered by the Thirty lasted long, in spite of the amnesty. As late as 382 B.C. a man named Evandros, elected archon, was attacked at his *dokimasia,* or scrutiny, with the charge that he had been active under the Thirty. To the people of the time some of these trials may have seemed more important and interesting than that of Socrates.

Socrates was exposed to bitter feelings partly because the infamous Critias had once liked to talk to him. The equally infamous Alcibiades was thought to have been formed partly by his intimacy with Socrates. Socrates had long been regarded, although erroneously, as one interested in astronomy and other science and therefore to be presumed an atheist. The ordinary citizen might easily feel that he had had an unfortunate connection with the Thirty, that some slight odor of atheism clung to him, and that he was ready to make the worse cause appear the better. He might also feel that Socrates was hindering rather than helping the restoration of Athenian morale and strength. If he made the young men less ready to hear and follow their fathers, he loosened one bond in the state. If he refused to interest himself in the daily affairs of the polis in general and ridiculed the system of choosing officials by lot, he did some harm to unity of feeling.

Socrates' real accuser was Anytus, the prosperous tanner who had been one of the leading figures in the restoration of the democracy and was a leader of the democratic party afterward. He persuaded a young poet named Meletus to bring the formal accusation and he himself gave the principal speech. Anytus had done good service for Athens. He had played a man's part in some of the most stirring events of Athenian history— the end of the war, the terror of the Thirty, the adventures of the group that led the resistance and the restoration. We might expect him to plan now for the material and the spiritual restoration of Athens and see himself as naturally responsible. We might also expect him to attempt to silence an old man who had not fought in the resistance or the restoration, who attempted to depreciate the importance both of material prosperity and of the sense of unity, who lessened the respect of the young for their elders, and who plainly did not adhere to the simple old-fashioned faith, whatever he believed about the gods.

Anytus may be said to represent the man who identifies himself with the group and gives his interest and his enthusiasm to the promotion of common practical ends. Generally little love is lost between this type and the more individualistic, analytic type of which Socrates is so distinguished an example. Often, too, there is little mutual understanding when they differ; as in this case, they are hardly able to argue, but can only state their differing points of view.

The speeches of the accusers have not been preserved. Presumably they treated Socrates as a Sophist and emphasized his supposed taint of atheism. The need for public unity must have been mentioned. The charge— disbelieving in the gods of the city and holding other ideas of divinity, and demoralizing the youth—probably seemed to the accusers fairly well proven. Nor was Socrates' answer preserved. Plato, Xenophon, and several other men wrote their own versions of his defense, or *apologia*. Plato's *Apology* probably reproduces much of what Socrates said. It is not, in fact, a very good defense; it is the sort of thing that the detached and analytically minded man says when charged with not furthering the purposes of a society of men—more a statement of attitude than an answer to charges. The jury voted for conviction, 281 to 220.

Socrates might have saved his life by fleeing into exile before the trial. He might have saved it afterward by proposing a counter penalty of exile or fine, as the convicted defendant was allowed to do. Probably everyone expected him to make such a proposal and agree to cease his unacceptable activities. But his attitude now was even more intransigently individualistic and analytic than before, for he suggested that he should be rewarded for his service to the state in keeping the Athenians awake and up to the mark and that the reward should be free maintenance at the public expense. Then he added, without enthusiasm, that some of his friends were willing to contribute money for a nominal fine and that he was willing to let them pay such a fine for him.

Naturally enough the jury replied to this defiance by confirming the death sentence originally proposed by Meletus, voting it by an even larger majority. Socrates went to prison, where he would have been forced to drink the hemlock very soon had it not been that no execution could take place until the return of a religious embassy that had been sent to Delos.

During the month that he waited in prison he had a third opportunity to save his life. Plato's account of the affair in his *Crito* is probably trustworthy because he presumably had to keep close to the known facts. The wealthy Crito, Socrates' friend for many years, insisted that Socrates allow him to bribe the jailer, as could readily be done, so that Socrates could escape and flee to the protection of Crito's friends in Thessaly. Socrates' refusal, as given by Plato, is a strong affirmation of his loyalty to society, the loyalty that had been questioned at his trial. He refused to harm by disobedience that society whose terms he had accepted, and by implication he affirmed that his past conduct had not harmed society.

It is easy to accuse the Athenians of murdering Socrates because he tried to assert freedom of speech, but the matter is far from being that simple. The trial and condemnation of Socrates stand not as a foul blot on the good name of Athens, but as an example of the difficulty of conducting a human society with justice to all.

The March of the Ten Thousand

Two years before the trial of Socrates, Xenophon the Athenian accompanied some Greek mercenary troops hired for an attempt by a member of the Persian royal family on the Persian throne. His account of the expedition not only throws light on the condition of Persia at this time, but presents us as well with a true adventure story. Cyrus, the able and charming younger brother of King Artaxerxes, tried to supplant his brother on the death of their father, Darius II, in 404 B.C. The elder brother made good his claim to the throne and arrested Cyrus, but the queen mother managed to save her favorite son from punishment, and he was allowed to return to his satrapy of Lydia in Asia Minor. Cyrus made his preparations carefully by gathering a force of about 13,000 Greek mercenaries in addition to his regular troops on the pretext of crushing some unruly mountaineers within his satrapy and set out openly to conquer his brother the king.

The title of Xenophon's book, *Anabasis*, means "a journey upcountry from the sea." The expedition started inland toward the unruly mountain region. Xenophon names the Greek captains and brings their characters before us. We see the slow progress of the army and a number of such vivid incidents as the futile attempts of Greek cavalrymen to catch ostriches. Soon the soldiers realized that they were being led against the king, far from the sea, which to them was a friendly highway and the center of their world. They balked, but finally were induced to go on. The narrative leads us into the far country by the banks of the Euphrates where at last the battle took place.

The formidable Greek hoplites easily prevailed over the troops opposed to them, and the victory would have been theirs had not Cyrus dashed forward to attack his brother personally. He was killed, and his Persian troops at once submitted to the king. Tissaphernes, the satrap of Asia Minor whose guest Alcibiades had once been and an old enemy of Cyrus, advised the king to entice the Greek captains into a conference. They rashly agreed to come, and all were treacherously put to death.

The *Anabasis* records that the Greek soldiers, deprived of their officers, held a meeting in true Greek style, and that the proposals of a certain Xenophon, an Athenian (the author, of course), seemed good to them. They elected new officers, of whom Xenophon was one, although he had come on the expedition only as a gentleman adventurer, not as a soldier. Then the ten thousand Greeks marched and fought their way northward to the Black Sea. Xenophon's best picture is that of the long line of men coming over a ridge and of the great cry "The sea! the sea!" that went down the line.

It is easy to overestimate the weakness of the Persian Empire as it is suggested by this exploit. Although there were intrigues over the throne, although the satraps could make war on each other, and not all the nominally subject peoples could be held to strict obedience, the size and resources of the empire were such that it was not to be shaken by any existing power. As for the Greeks, the mercenaries of the *Anabasis* were a repulsive group of ruffians, although historians have not always chosen to call attention to the fact. The latter part of the narrative tells of their adventures as freebooters and mercenaries after their arrival at the coast of the Black Sea. During the rest of this century such bands of roving soldiers caused considerable trouble in Greece. The book ends with Xenophon's complacent account of his finally making a profit out of the expedition by organizing some of his comrades to kidnap a rich Persian of Asia Minor for ransom.

Further War with Persia (400–387 B.C.)

After the death of Cyrus the king promoted Tissaphernes to the management of western Asia Minor. Tissaphernes naturally planned reprisals against the Asiatic Greeks, who had helped Cyrus. They appealed to Sparta even while Tissaphernes was asking the Spartans, by virtue of the treaty between Persia and Sparta, to help him in asserting Persian authority over them. The Spartans, appealed to by both sides, repudiated the treaty with the Persians and the ignominious position in which it had placed them in the eyes of all Greeks.

For the next twelve or thirteen years the Spartans had a most unhappy time. For several years they warred against the Persians in Asia Minor. The Persians finally hired an Athenian exile to build a fleet and defeat them, thus ending Spartan control of the sea. Their army was forced to come home by a revolt of the Inferiors, those who were unable to be elected to the Equals or who had lost their position as Equals through selling their land for whatever reason. One Cinadon had organized a revolt of the Inferiors, bringing in the *perioeci* and the Helots. The revolution, apparently the only one of its kind, was nipped in the bud. However, hostilities with the Persians were still carried on in a desultory manner.

The heavy-handed and arbitrary Spartan manner toward the other Greeks had dissipated the advantages gained by her conduct in the Peloponnesian War. Corinth and Thebes felt that they had had no share in the gains of the war, and other states found the Spartans demanding and unhelpful. In 396 the Persians sent an agent to Greece with money to be spent in encouraging anti-Spartan movements in Argos, Corinth, Thebes, and Athens, and the resulting hostilities dragged drearily along for several years. It was not until 387 that the Persians were able to take the initiative in making a general peace on terms largely of their choosing.

In that year the Persian king offered a final formula for peace to Antalcidas, the Spartan representative.

King Artaxerxes regards it as just that the cities in Asia and the islands of Clazomenae and Cyprus should be his, and that the other Greek cities, large and small, be independent, except Lemnos, Imbros, and Scyros, which should belong to the Athenians as formerly. Whatever parties do not accept this peace, I shall fight against them, along with those who are of like mind with me, on land and sea, with ships and money.

In 386 Sparta and the other Greek states ratified "The King's Peace" or "The Peace of Antalcidas," as it was called. The Thebans claimed the right to sign for all Boeotia, but yielded to a direct threat of force from Sparta.

For the Spartans it was a great gain to be free from war with the Persians and to feel sure that Persia would support whatever they did in their role as guarantors that the others would abide by the terms of the peace. The cities of Asia Minor could at least hope for a period of peace in which they could pursue their commercial affairs undisturbed. Thebes had lost the hegemony over Boeotia which she had been building up, and Athens suffered financially from the precise limit set on any attempts to regain her old influence among the island states.

Spartan Control in Greece (387–371 B.C.)

Just as they had interpreted "the freedom of Greece" (said to have been won in the Peloponnesian War) as an opportunity to advance what they considered to be their own interests, so the Spartans now interpreted the autonomy of all the Greek states as guaranteed in the new peace to mean that they should attempt to weaken all the other states for their own advantage. This did not mean commercial or any other tangible advantage, but was an unconstructive policy of breaking up combinations between other states, presumably with the idea of forestalling the rise of any power that could challenge her.

The Thebans were ordered to give up their claims to preside over all Boeotia. The Corinthians and Argives were ordered to dissolve their alliance, and the Corinthians had to recall their oligarchic exiles. The city of Mantinea, in the Peloponnesus, was forced to dismantle its fortifications and dissolve itself into the five villages that had united a hundred years before to form a polis. The people of Phlius were forced to recall their oligarchic exiles and to accept an oligarchic constitution drafted by the Spartans.

Worse than this, the Spartans broke up a useful league centered at Olynthus, on the Chalcidic peninsula in the North. This league, which had existed for a long time, had ably defended the interests of the Greeks of the region against the kingdom of Macedonia. A quarrel over territory led Amyntas, king of Macedonia, to appeal to Sparta. The Spartans could see only that the Olynthian League seemed stronger than they wished any Greek political unit to be, for they lacked the elementary wisdom to see that Macedonia could be an even more formidable enemy to the Greeks and one much less easily negotiated with on the usual Greek terms. After four years of war the Spartans were able in 379 to break up the league and to force its members to enter into treaties with Sparta.

In 382 the Spartans treacherously seized control of Thebes. A Spartan officer passing through with troops being sent to the war with the Olynthian League was approached by a member of the oligarchic faction at Thebes, and a plot was formed to seize control of the citadel during a festival. With the help of the Spartan troops the oligarchic faction gained control. The "rules" of these struggles between oligarchs and democrats are well illustrated by the fact that at the very beginning of this affair some three hundred democrats fled to the protection of Athens. By gaining control at Thebes Sparta had apparently neutralized all possible opposition in Greece, yet within four years the Athenians were able to offer enough assistance to allow the Thebans to shake off Spartan control.

Next the Athenians resolved to organize a full-scale movement against the Spartans and invited all their old allies (except, of course, those given to Persia by the King's Peace) to join in a new naval league whose purpose was to force the Spartans to permit the Greeks to be free, autonomous, and in full possession of their own territories. The Athenians guaranteed that they would respect the rights of their allies and especially that they would not try to acquire property for Athenian settlers, a feature of the old confederacy that had been highly distasteful. The allies were to have a federal council that would be sovereign equally with Athens; Athens, however, was to be the executive. By the year 377 the Second Athenian Naval Confederacy was a going concern, and within three or four years the number of members apparently rose to about sixty.

The Thebans were fortunate at this time in finding two very able leaders, Epaminondas and Pelopidas. These men resolutely resisted further Spartan attempts to dominate Boeotia. Their most important move was to reform the army by the formation of "the Sacred Band" of three hundred hoplites of good family, a permanent and strong regiment that was reinforced by the usual militia when necessary. Little by little the Thebans persuaded the other cities of Boeotia to rejoin them and accept their leadership.

The rising power of Thebes so impressed the Spartans and the Athenians that they soon made moves toward a general peace, and in 371 the three powers had a meeting for that purpose. The meeting failed because Sparta and Athens, trying to check Thebes, insisted that the cities of Boeotia sign the new agreement separately, as Sparta had insisted they do at the ratification of the King's Peace. Epaminondas, strong in the feeling that Thebes had a new army and a new spirit, insisted that Thebes represent them. The Spartans, as usual, prepared to implement their demand by force.

Not only did the Thebans have a new army, they had a new ally in Jason, the tyrant of Pherae in Thessaly. This region of Greece, which lies north of Boeotia, appears so seldom in the full light of Greek history that we know regrettably little about it. Apparently the nobles there, who were organized in the old style of clans and families that had prevailed in the earlier days of aristocratic domination elsewhere, were able to hold the agricultural workers in subjection. Jason appears shortly after 380 B.C. as ruler of Pherae, and shortly thereafter he became *tagus,* or military chief, of all Thessaly. He joined the new Athenian naval league, but soon withdrew to cultivate the friendship of the Thebans and their league in Boeotia.

During his rise to power Jason had been able to find money to hire large numbers of mercenary soldiers. Presently, however, he instituted a new sort of army, a forerunner of that soon to be developed by Philip II of Macedonia. He organized and trained a national army of no less than 20,000 hoplites and eight thousand cavalry, supported by large numbers of peltasts, or light-armed and highly mobile soldiers. A country that could support an army of this size was indeed a formidable neighbor to the small and divided states of Greece, just as Macedonia was soon to prove formidable. The organization of the country as a whole, however, depended upon the personal abilities of Jason, and when he was assassinated soon after the great trial of strength between Sparta and Thebes in 371, Thessaly lapsed into its former division and ineffectiveness. The character of Macedonia was much like that of Thessaly; the great difference in the history of the two countries in the fourth century was that Macedonia was unified and made effective by a far greater man, Philip II, who was succeeded by his brilliant son, Alexander the Great.

The armies of Sparta and Thebes met at Leuctra, in Boeotia, in the year 371, and the decision went to the Thebans. Epaminondas drew up his army with a very strong concentration of hoplites, led by the Sacred Band on the left wing to meet the usual Spartan concentration on the right wing. The right wing, upon which the Spartans relied to break the line of their opponents, was crushed by the Theban left wing, and the Spartans were forced to withdraw to their entrenched camp. They lost a thousand men, of whom four hundred were full citizens, a terrible loss in view of the small number of full citizens. When it arrived, a Spartan relief force found that Jason of Pherae was on the scene with a strong force. The Thebans wished to push the matter to a conclusion, but Jason prevailed on them and the Spartans to make a truce.

The battle of Leuctra brought a minor era to its conclusion. It ended the supremacy of Sparta in Greece as well as the long established idea that the Spartan army was invincible, and henceforth she was only in the second rank of military powers. If Greece as a whole was benefited by the reduction of Spartan power, the fact that the Peloponnesian League no longer served as a solid federation of many Greek states was, in general, a loss.

Thebes in Power (371–362 B.C.)

The hegemony now briefly exercised by Thebes was unfortunately no better than that which had been exercised by Sparta. Every plan of the Theban leaders was based on the idea that Thebes must be strengthened and other states weakened. By the end of the year 370 they had organized a federation of central Greece that reached from the island of Euboea in the East to Aetolia in the West. They also had interfered successfully in the affairs of the Peloponnesus by supporting the new Arcadian League there, an organization of peoples formerly under the domination of Sparta. As might have been expected, the Athenians were disturbed by the rise of Theban power and drew closer to the Spartans.

A curious feature of the opposition of the Greek states to one another at this time is their attempt to gain the favor of the Persians. The shadow of the King's Peace still lay across all their moves. The Greeks as a whole felt a certain resentment at Persian dictation, but realistically accepted it when it was advantageous to do so.

The idea that the Greeks might someday unite in a great imperialistic war against the Persians had been proposed in a speech at the Olympic Games in the year 408 by the Sophist Gorgias, who called on the Greeks to drop their senseless struggles against one another and combine in a great effort against the Persians. About 380 B.C. Isocrates, the leading teacher of oratory at Athens, urged the same arguments in a pamphlet called *Panegyricus* and claimed the primacy in the enterprise for Athens. For the present, however, the Greeks engaged only in an undignified competition for Persian endorsement. In 367 the king gave his approval to the new Boeotian League.

In the year 362 the Thebans led an army into the Peloponnesus, where the Arcadian League was beginning to crumble, since about half its members were looking to Sparta rather than to Thebes, and the Thebans, like the Spartans, felt that force was the only answer to such opposition. A battle took place near Mantinea, the center of the Arcadian League. Epaminondas was mortally wounded while his forces were getting much the better of the fighting, and with his dying breath he urged his countrymen to make peace. The Boeotian League continued, but without Epaminondas it could exert no great influence on its neighbors. The brief period of Theban hegemony, like that of Sparta, had brought only further confusion to Greece.

THE GREEKS OF THE WEST IN THE
FOURTH CENTURY

There was no essential difference between the life of the Greeks in the West and those of Greece proper in the fourth century, although our information about the West is rather less detailed. Like their kinsmen in Greece they were harmed by struggles with one another that could, it would seem, have been prevented. The western Greeks also had the Sicilian natives, Carthage, the tribes of southern Italy, and the Romans to contend with. Like Greeks elsewhere the western Greeks found the fourth century a rather prosperous time in spite of their military and political difficulties. Many of their cities were rich and brilliant, and the drama in particular flourished among them.

If we shift for a moment to the long perspective in history, the western Greeks had a very important role to play, for it was through them that the Romans first became acquainted with the Greek style of civilization. Although the full flood of Hellenism did not burst on Rome until the second century B.C., when the Romans campaigned in Greece and Asia Minor and learned to know the achievements of classical Greece, during the fourth and third centuries they were constantly learning about contemporary Greek civilization from the Greeks of south Italy and—especially during the First Punic War, which was largely fought in Sicily—from the Greeks of Sicily. The Romans could have been disposed to reject the Hellenic style of civilization partly or entirely, as some peoples did reject it, but they embraced it, assimilated it, and transformed it into the Greco-Roman style that was the foundation of the civilization in the later West.

Dionysius I, Tyrant of Syracuse

In 408 B.C. the Carthaginians invaded the Greek part of Sicily for the first time since their disaster at Himera in 480. They captured some territory, took a rich booty, and retired, leaving garrisons in the new territory. In 406 they came again in even greater strength and attacked Acragas, the second city of Sicily. After months of struggle, betrayal, gallantry, and carelessness the combined Greek forces that had come to help Acragas withdrew, and the Carthaginians took the city and wintered there. In the spring of 405 they destroyed it.

Dionysius was a soldier who had distinguished himself at Acragas. In

405 he spread stories among the Syracusans about the incompetence of their generals and got himself elected as one of a new board of generals. He then gathered a group of mercenaries and went to Gela, where he posed as the supporter of the people, confiscated the property of the few, and kept the money to pay his mercenaries. On his return to Syracuse he had his colleagues on the new board of generals deposed on the ground that they had done nothing for the city while he had been active in her service. Late in 405 the people elected him sole general with full powers. He increased his personal armed force, put his family and close friends into magistracies and military posts, and took the government of Syracuse firmly under his control. He was tyrant from 405 to 367 B.C.

After he gained control of the city in 405, Dionysius still had the invading Carthaginian army to deal with. His first battle was a defeat, perhaps through his own fault. His Syracusan cavalry would have killed him had he not been protected by his mercenaries. At it was, the cavalry went ahead of him back to Syracuse and stirred up a revolt that he overcame by a lightning march and midnight attack at the head of his mercenaries. Then a stroke of pure good fortune saved him from the advancing Carthaginians, for a sudden onset of the plague so reduced their forces that they offered him a treaty that left Syracuse free, although a good part of Sicily was either to be in Carthaginian hands or to pay tribute to Carthage.

Almost at once Dionysius broke parts of his treaty with Carthage by extending his power over some of the cities of eastern Sicily that had been recognized as free in the agreement. He drove some of the peoples whom he conquered from their homes, sold some as slaves, and brought some to swell the number of the inhabitants of Syracuse, where labor was needed. The territories that he gained he gave to people whom he wished bound to him by obligations. In this way he created some new communities of Sicels, the original inhabitants of the island, and some of mercenaries imported from Campania, the part of Italy between Rome and Naples.

Dionysius was singularly indifferent to all claims of propriety or sentiment. The claims of Greek blood seemed to mean nothing to him. Old ties of sentiment, blood, or common citizenship were of no use to him in maintaining his position, but to pardon fellow citizens who had revolted and whom he could have destroyed was to create an obligation on their part. Early in his reign he brought back many men who had been exiled during the democratic regime, men whose continued prosperity rested as a result upon the existence, at least, of a conservative regime, if not of the regime of Dionysius. But when he made Syracusan citizens of captives or of mercenary soldiers and gave them land, he was beyond doubt creating supporters of his own regime who had everything to lose if he fell. The people whom he settled on the land of conquered cities must also be supporters of his regime, if they were to hold their lands.

His policy of lively trade and of wars undertaken for loot brought prosperity to the people of Syracuse in general, for the manufacture of weapons and ships went on constantly and trade in general was good. The magistrates were elected as usual and the assembly met and passed resolutions, but Dionysius was firmly in control, as Peisistratus had been in Athens. He had the good sense to refrain from direct personal injuries to the citizens. Enough people were eager to assassinate him without his provoking the revenge of an outraged husband or brother or the anger of the relatives of some murdered man. He made a fortress on the island of Ortygia in the harbor and lived there with his mercenaries.

In 398 he attacked the Carthaginians; the resulting war lasted until 392. He is said to have been a forerunner of Philip II of Macedonia and of Alexander in that he sometimes campaigned in the winter (a new practice in the ancient world), developed an artillery arm for sieges, and was expert in the coordination of all the branches of his forces. Twice more, in 383 and in about 368, he engaged in short wars with Carthage, the results of which were so equivocal that there is reason to believe that Dionysius stirred them up to justify his tyranny, but did not prosecute them so vigorously as to drive the Carthaginians away.

His policy also aimed at control of the harbors of Italy nearest to Sicily and of certain good harbors in other parts of Italy and in parts of Greece. After making peace with Carthage in 392 he embarked on the conquest of southern Italy, allying himself with the Lucanians, an Italian people, in order to get the better of the Greek cities in Italy. By about 385 he had gained control of most of *Magna Graecia*, or "Great Greece," the large region of southern Italy peopled by the descendants of Greek colonists. He also took control of the island of Elba from the Etruscans, iron being its attraction. He gained control of harbor sites on both sides of the upper Adriatic, on the west coast of Greece, and the east coast of Italy. He did good service by suppressing for a while the traditional piracy of the Illyrians on the west coast of Greece. He was so widely and respectfully known that the Gauls who moved into North Italy about 400 B.C. and sacked Rome in 387 sent an embassy to him offering to make an alliance. Whatever the outcome, we know that he hired some of them as mercenaries.

Dionysius died in 367 B.C., having ruled the polis and then the state or empire of Syracuse for about thirty-eight years. He had, at the very lowest estimate, shown himself a master of unscrupulous devices by which to gain and hold power over a free people. Often he showed great daring and personal courage. Accounts of him imply that he had considerable administrative ability and was able to surround himself with effective and loyal subordinates. He extended the power of Syracuse over most of Sicily and into Italy so that, except for Persia, she was the most powerful state in the world. He did endless damage in Sicily and Italy, however, both material and psychological. He aroused such hatred among parts of his own people that he lived in constant fear of assassination, and he provoked such hatred among the other Greeks that at the Olympic Games of 388 the great orator Lysias made a speech condemning him, stirring the assembled people to attack his ambassadors and prevent them from offering their sacrifices.

Although he cannot be said to have advanced Syracuse culturally as some of the great earlier tyrants had done both in Sicily and Greece, Dionysius showed a very human weakness in fancying himself as a writer of tragedies, which he tried long and unsuccessfully to get produced in Athens. Just before his death, when he had made a treaty with Athens, pressure was put on the officials of the festival of Dionysus to "give him a chorus." Dionysius's work at last had its day in the Theater of Dionysus and was then forgotten.

The poleis of Sicily continued to struggle with one another and with Carthage generation after generation until in the third century they came under the power of Rome. To put briefly a story that we shall tell in more detail later from the Roman point of view, a body of Italian mercenaries who called themselves "Mamertines," or sons of Mars, made themselves masters of Messana, on the shore of the narrow strait where Sicily is nearest to Italy, shortly after 290 B.C. and harried all eastern Sicily with their raids. The Syracusan Hiero finally had such success in campaigning against them that he gained the position of king of Syracuse in about 265. The Carthaginians, seeing the port of Messana, so usefully located on the strait between Italy and Sicily, possibly about to fall into the power of Syracuse, sent a garrison to help and kept the Syracusans from taking it. The Mamertines, made uneasy by the presence of the Carthaginians who had saved them from Syracuse, ingenuously called upon the Romans to save them from the Carthaginians.

The decision of the Romans to help the Mamertines is not easy to understand and is much discussed by modern historians of Rome, who find it hard to agree that any obvious Roman interest was served by helping the Mamertines. The action of the Romans brought on a long war with Carthage (264–241 B.C.) that is known by its Roman name, the First Punic War. Syracuse and some other cities joined the Romans. The long and costly war ended with victory for the Romans and their appropriation of Sicily as their first possession outside Italy. The Greek cities that had supported them were left free, while the rest of Sicily was made subject to Rome. In Rome's second war with Carthage (218–201 B.C.) the

Syracusans went over to the Carthaginians and forfeited their independence for so doing, since Rome was again the victor.

Other Western Greeks

The conquests of Dionysius I seem to have broken some of the strength of the Greek poleis in southern Italy, as had been the case with the poleis of Sicily. Two Italian peoples, the Bruttians and the Lucanians, were the most dangerous enemies of the Greeks. The people of the city of Tarentum tried to avoid domination by the threatening Italian peoples by calling for help from Greece. Sparta was her mother city, and Sparta's king came to her aid with a force of mercenaries, probably in 342 B.C. After three or four years of campaigning against the Italians he was defeated and killed. A few years later Tarentum again asked for help. This time they brought in Alexander, king of Epirus and uncle of Alexander the Great. The uncle, desirous of equaling the exploits of his nephew, started off well and in a short time had gained control of much of southern Italy, but the Tarentines somewhat illogically objected to the strength of the man who was strong enough to deal with their persistent Italian enemies and turned against him. He was finally defeated.

In the end all the Greeks of southern Italy, as well as the Italians who had caused them so much difficulty, were swept into the Roman net. Slowly the Roman federation had moved southward. The great Samnite wars of the late 300s and early 200s ended with a victory for Rome and the incorporation of these sturdy people into Rome's organization. Finally the Tarentines brought on a war with Rome by attacking a little Roman squadron cruising off their shore. Again they called in a Greek captain, the dashing, generous, able, but inconstant Pyrrhus. His erratic behavior, followed by his withdrawal from the struggle and his return to Greece in 275 B.C., left them helpless before the Romans. They and all the peoples of lower Italy ended as members of the Roman federation.

The Greeks of Massilia (modern Marseilles) dealt with interesting peoples in Gaul (modern France), many of whom belonged to the large group known as the Celts, who were found all over western Europe and in the British Isles. Occasionally they wandered. For example, the Gauls who moved into the Po Valley of northern Italy and later (387 B.C.) sacked Rome were Celts. In the third century many of them wandered farther toward the East, and some were absorbed by the peoples of the Balkans. One group wandered into Greece, was driven back northward, and finally settled in central Asia Minor. We hear of them there as the Galatians, a name that comes from the Greek word for Gauls.

The Greeks of Massilia exported Greek wares to the Celts. The Celtic workmen had a flair for the arts and transformed the decoration of the Greek objects into exuberant and attractive decorations in which the Greek motif could be recognized, but which were clearly Celtic. The Celts did not develop an urbanized civilization, but they did develop effective agriculture and a woolen industry. Furthermore, they lived an orderly enough life in large parts of Spain, France, the Low Countries, and the British Isles for their own people, the Massilians, or the Etruscans to be able to travel regular trade routes with some degree of safety.

The merchants of Massilia traded in eastern Spain, reached the Celts of the Alps and of northern Italy, and went up through Gaul and as far as northwest Germany. The city had earlier been a rival of the Etruscans both on the sea and in northern Italy and thus had a community of interest with Rome in her opposition to the Etruscans. The friendship of Massilia and Rome endured and was useful to both until the time of Julius Caesar.

THE RISE OF MACEDONIA

The rise of the kingdom of Macedonia from about 360 to about 330 B.C. brought the end of what the Greeks thought of as freedom—that is, freedom to manage their own affairs and to dominate their neighbors if they could. One could say that the system of city states, or poleis, proved its inadequacy. At least it had proved inadequate to keep the peace and allow all men to pursue their own affairs without interference from others. In this respect the Greek system seems to have been no more and no less successful than the Sumerian system of city states or the Egyptian system of small principalities during the periods when national unity could not be maintained. The nations of Europe in modern times, although much larger than the Greek polities, have likewise been unable to prevent wars among themselves.

If we are to strike a balance of achievements for this typically Greek political form, however, we must be sure not to set its real virtues to one side. Our study of the Greeks up to this point has made it plain that many real and permanent advances in civilization were made in the polis largely because of the city-state form of organization, which intensified the life of the citizen. We must also remember that although the era of such entirely independent political entities and of endless struggle between them was now to pass away, the culture of cities remained the chief characteristic of the civilized world. The lively and intense life of cities was the most important part of the life of the combined Greco-Roman world and was the thing that most clearly distinguished it from its less civilized neighbors.

Earlier Macedonia

Macedonia's rise under its great king, Philip II, to a position of dominance is the chief feature of the period before us. The social, economic, and cultural condition of the kingdom at the beginning of his reign was much like that of Thessaly. The people were recognized as akin to the Greeks and therefore eligible to compete in the Olympic Games. City life was little developed, and the effective organization of society was by tribes and clans. There was no conception of an impersonal government that ruled on a basis of fixed laws. There was no indigenous artistic or intellectual life. It was natural that in general the Greeks should regard the Macedonians as not quite belonging to the distinctive Greek way of life.

The first of the strong kings of Macedonia seems to have been Archelaus I, who ruled from about 413 to about 400 B.C. He made a great effort to create something like a truly national government, tried to develop a national army, fortified strong points here and there, and began a road system to facilitate military movements. He was an admirer of Greek culture and he invited Greeks—the tragic writers Agathon and Euripides, the painter Zeuxis, the musician and poet Timotheus—to his court.

In one way or another the Macedonian kings were frequently involved in the affairs of the Greek states. Amyntas II, who ruled from 393 to 370, invoked the aid of Sparta against the Olynthian League, as we have seen, and later and at different times was the ally of Athens, of Jason of Pherae, and of Thebes. The Thebans concerned themselves somewhat with the affairs of both Thessaly and Macedonia during the period of their hegemony, and from 367 to 365 the young Philip was kept as a hostage at Thebes in the house of Epaminondas, tutored in Greek philosophy, and apparently allowed the privilege of serious discussions of statecraft with Epaminondas himself.

Philip II Assumes Power

In the year 359 the Macedonian king Perdiccas suffered a crushing defeat at the hands of his western neighbors the Illyrians and lost his life. The twenty-three-year-old Philip, who had already been granted some governmental responsibility, was chosen regent for his nephew, the infant son of the dead king. He managed to dispose of five other members of the family whose ambitions might have been inconsistent with his. A year later he led the Macedonian armies against the western neighbors and defeated them decisively. After these victories the people made him king instead of merely regent for his small nephew.

Finding himself at the head of a kingdom with a recent history of weakness and disunion, frequent defeat in war by the neighboring tribes, and inadequacy in dealing with the Greek poleis, Philip wished to organize Macedonia into a strong and well functioning national state. He wished to gain the respect of the Greeks, for he had learned to know and to admire their ways. There is no evidence that he ever had any imperialistic designs for subduing the states of Greece and compelling them to pay tribute. If the latent strength of his kingdom was such that his efforts brought Macedonia to a position where it was more powerful than all the states of Greece, we need not therefore accuse him as a sinister enemy of Greek freedom, rather, he used his sudden authority as a friend of the Greeks.

In 357 Philip captured Amphipolis, a city in Thrace that Athens regarded as rightfully hers. It had indeed been founded by her, but the sentiment of its citizens was as much pro-Macedonian as pro-Athenian. This conquest gave him a good port on the Aegaean and accesss to the gold mines of Pangaeus, from which he is said soon to have taken a thousand talents a year. This he used in a splendidly devised new coinage, the first gold coinage in Europe. These fine coins were a means of representing Macedonia as a civilized state, over and above their use as money.

Athens and the Greeks of the northern regions were alarmed. Philip reassured the Olynthians by offering them a treaty. He then captured two coastal towns, Pydna and Potidaea, both dependencies of Athens and both founded on coastal sites that logically belonged to his kingdom. The forthrightness of these conquests was somewhat obscured by the fact that he returned without ransom all Athenians captured and that he presented Potidaea to Olynthus.

The Athenians, who had known Macedonia as a rather weak kingdom exposed to raids by its neighbors, began to realize that under this king it could be rather troublesome, so they made treaties with the Paeonians, Illyrians, and Thracians, the people who in the past had caused Macedonia most trouble, and encouraged them to invade. But Philip retained the initiative. His general Parmenio, a most valuable right-hand man, defeated the armies of all three peoples. Philip was now technically at war with Athens, since she had made alliance with his enemies, but for the moment he preferred to make nothing of the fact.

Since the difficulties that Athens was then having with some members of her naval league left her no energy to oppose Philip, he was able to consolidate his conquest of Amphipolis and the region of Mount Pangaeus, just beyond, and then turn his attention to the more general situation. In 356, the year in which Potidaea was captured, Philip's four-horse chariot won at Olympia; he evidently was losing no opportunity to assert the membership of Macedonia in the Greek community. In that year, too, his son Alexander was born. Philip is said to have received the

news of the birth of his son, the victory of his horses, and the capture of
Potidaea all on the same day. As the story goes, he raised his hands and
prayed, "O gods, send me some minor misfortune!"

The so-called Sacred War offered Philip a chance to present himself
and his nation as useful members of the community of Greeks. This was
perhaps the most trifling of all the wars of this unhappy period. The
Amphictyonic League was an ancient organization around Delphi and in
Boeotia, which counted its members by tribes and could be pretty well
controlled by Thebes. The league was in charge of the shrine at Delphi.
In about 357 the Thebans decided to use it to chastise the people of
Phocis for withdrawing from the Boeotian League of Thebes immediately
after the Theban defeat at Mantinea in 362. The Amphictyonic League
voted to impose heavy fines, nominally for sacrilege, on some leading citizens of Phocis. The Phocians saw no hope but in seizing Delphi and the
temple, hiring mercenaries, and preparing to fight.

The league formally proclaimed a "Sacred War" against the violators
of Delphi. The Phocians at first acquitted themselves well. When presently they suffered a serious reverse, they began openly to "borrow" the
treasures of the temple at Delphi. The irreplaceable gifts of many generations were melted down into their original gold, silver, bronze, or iron
to make coins or to be fashioned into weapons. Now that there was
money, new troops of mercenaries could readily be found, for all over
Greece there were men who had lost full citizen rights in their own cities
or were merely restless and glad to make a little money by warfare.

The Phocians made one serious long-range mistake by using some of
the money as a gift to Lycophron, the tyrant of Pherae. The other Thessalians, taking fright at the thought of such an alliance, appealed to
Philip. The possibility of interfering in the Sacred War was much to his
liking and in the year 353 he marched into Thessaly. The Phocian mercenary army went north to meet him and defeated him twice, but in the
next year he brought a larger army and defeated them decisively.

The Athenians, who had nominally been at war with Philip since 356,
were following these events carefully. They were in alliance with the
Phocians as a way of checking Thebes. As Philip prepared to march into
central Greece and end the Sacred War by defeating Phocis at home,
the Athenians sent a force to the pass of Thermopylae sufficient to block
his passage. Philip, who did not believe in doing things the hard way,
withdrew for the present. He had been invited to be commander-in-chief
of the Thessalians and had taken a most correct step in assisting the
Greeks to chastise the Phocian robbers of the treasures of Delphi. These
were real practical and psychological advantages, and he was willing to
let the final defeat of the Phocians wait rather than fight with the Athenian force. When, in 347, he did settle the affair of the Phocians, it was

done with comparative ease. For the present, however, he withdrew from Greece proper, turned around, and marched instead across Thrace to the Hellespont, making alliances with the Thracian chiefs and with such Greek cities as Byzantium, which lay along the shores of the waters on which Athens' wheat supply was conveyed.

Demosthenes Against Philip

Many of the Athenians remained indifferent to Philip's activities, or Demosthenes says that they did. In three speeches known as *Philippics,* from the name of the king, and in three others known as *Olynthiac Orations,* because they deal with Philip's advance against Olynthus (by the time these speeches were delivered Philip had become hostile to Olynthus), Demosthenes scolded, warned, advised, and encouraged the Athenians to wake up and take measures against Philip before it was too late.

Demosthenes, born in 384, was a year or two older than Philip. As an orphan he was badly treated by his guardians and prosecuted them successfully when he came of age, recovering some of his inheritance from them. Having learned something of oratory, he found that he could gain some income by writing speeches for others to use in court. Then, at the unusually young age of thirty, he began to offer himself as a speaker before the Assembly on public affairs. Now, with Philip's march to the Hellespont in 352, the Athenian lawyer, speaker, and self-recommended adviser of the Assembly recognized that his contemporary, the king of Macedonia, was a man to be reckoned with. Both had been exercising their powers as vigorously as they could for many years, Philip in war and in the other duties of ruling a somewhat wild people, Demosthenes in the arts by which the courts or the sovereign Assembly of the most civilized people of the time could be moved. Philip was soon to recognize that Demosthenes, too, was a man to be reckoned with, and the careers of the two men were thenceforward involved with each other until the murder of Philip in 336.

Both men, politically, were the products of their time. Philip's aims reflect his political background. He wished his kingdom to be strong and to be accepted among the Greeks. He knew that the order of the day was power politics, each state trying to make sure that its own position was secure and trying to weaken its most threatening rivals. His moves seem to have been consistently directed to creating a position of strength and safety for his people in such a world. Probably he himself was somewhat surprised at the power that Macedonia could generate and at the success of his own measures. Unlike some others, he sensibly aimed at building good will whenever he could do so. To ascribe to him plans for

building a superstate to dominate the obsolescent city states would only
be to read later history and our own ideas into his purpose.

Demosthenes, too, grew up in a world of power politics. His aims for
Athens were much the same as those of Philip for Macedonia: safety lay
only in pre-eminence. We must be equally wary about reading modern
ideas into the mind of Demosthenes. His purpose was not to strike a blow
against the evils of autocratic government. He spoke with ungrudging
admiration of Philip's energy and of the desire for glory and achievement
that drove him on. There is drama enough, without making the conflict
one of ideologies, between the king who wished his people to be strong
and secure and to gain recognition in the family of Greek states, and the
greatest orator of the Greeks who tried to spur his fellow citizens to
strive as their forefathers had for the same pre-eminence and security at
which Philip was aiming.

Demosthenes' first *Philippic,* probably delivered before the Athenian
Assembly in 351, was a call to the people to rouse themselves. The tone
was simply that of power politics: Philip is a danger to us and he is not
too strong for us to do something about him. Demosthenes urged the Athenians not to allow Philip the complete exercise of the initiative and to
have two modest armies always in readiness to check whatever move he
might make.

In 351 B.C. Philip began to move against the Olynthian League, which
had asked the Athenians for an alliance and was entertaining two of the
old pretenders to the throne of Macedonia. He began by diplomatic representations. In 349, having completed operations to make his western
marches more secure, he gave the Olynthians his full attention. They im-
plored the assistance of Athens, and Demosthenes, in his three *Olynthiacs,* urged his countrymen to oppose Philip. The Athenians were having
financial troubles at this time, since they no longer had tribute from
subjects, and their new naval league had lost some members. Philip
showed his understanding of their problems by persuading some of the
cities of Euboea to withdraw from the league. At last they agreed to send
help to Olynthus, but too little and too late. Philip captured the city in
348, destroyed it, and made slaves of its people. Such cruelty was unusual
with him, in spite of his custom of doing whatever furthered his aims.
Sometimes his actions were cruel and deceitful, for (like Julius Caesar
later) he carefully studied his problems and solved them variously by
clemency, personal charm, or barbarous cruelty, according to his estimate
of which would achieve his immediate and long-range purposes.

A new figure, some of whose speeches we still possess, now joined
Demosthenes in the limelight at Athens. This was Aeschines, who had had
experience as a teacher and as an actor. Both as a speaker and as a
counselor on public affairs he could rival Demosthenes in every way but

one: he remains in the second rank in both fields for lack of the deep conviction and fiery energy that animated the public policy and the speeches of Demosthenes.

The Peace of Philocrates

The Athenians decided that it was time to end the state of war that had existed since 356, when they allied themselves with the native chiefs on Macedonia's borders. Aeschines and Demosthenes were both members of the embassy that waited upon Philip at his city of Pella. The discussions, in which Philip treated the envoys with truly royal courtesy, resulted in an agreement to make peace on the sensible basis of the existing situation, with one exception, on which Philip insisted, that no mention be made of Phocis. After some movement of embassies back and forth the Athenians accepted Philip's assurance that he had no designs on Phocis and concluded the treaty. The peace, which was concluded in 346, was known as the Peace of Philocrates from the name of the man who proposed in the Assembly that negotiations be instituted.

Philip's next act was highly distressing to the Athenians. He suddenly moved his troops to Thermopylae and accepted the surrender that under the circumstances was the only course open to the Phocian commander. The mercenary soldiers were discharged and allowed to depart. The Phocian government surrendered, having no means of resistance. Philip called the Amphictyonic Council to decide the fate of Phocis, and it was decided that their cities must be dissolved into villages. A yearly tribute was imposed on them as restitution to the shrine at Delphi for what they had taken from it, and Philip acquired their votes in the council. His pretensions to complete Hellenism were also recognized, at least in these circles, by his being chosen president of the Pythian Games, whose regular celebration at Delphi was about to begin. The Assembly at Athens, unable to do anything but offer useless insults, was ready to boycott the Games and refuse Philip's formal request that every member of the Amphictyonic League accept him as a member, but Demosthenes, still trying to preserve a long-range view, persuaded the Athenians not to make insulting and ineffectual gestures.

Another Athenian whose words we can still read chose to make his views public at this point. Isocrates, the aged teacher of oratory and political essayist, published an address to Philip that he entitled *Philippus*. He argued that Philip ought to exert himself to create a military alliance of all the Greek states and then lead a combined expedition against Persia. Philip was not in any sense to be in control of Greece, but merely to preside over the alliance and lead its joint army. It has been argued, and reasonably, that the chief purpose of Isocrates, as a man of property, was to induce Philip to enlist the many mercenary soldiers who seemed to menace peace and the security of property throughout Greece, draw them away in a war of imperialistic conquest against the Persians, and then settle them on conquered territory. It was a practical plan, and it is interesting that Isocrates was willing to have Philip in charge, but nothing came of it at the time.

One of the less pleasant sides of Greek life is displayed in the records of Athens in the next few years. Demosthenes decided to prosecute Aeschines for treason and the acceptance of bribes during the proceedings that led to the Peace of Philocrates, his motive presumably being to hamper Aeschines' activities, which were in opposition to his own. As men who instituted a prosecution often did, Demosthenes had an associate in the prosecution, one Timarchus. Aeschines countered with a slashing suit to disqualify Timarchus from public life on the ground of his immoral ways and specifically on the ground that he had prostituted himself. His able speech, *Against Timarchus,* makes peculiarly disagreeable reading, but he was successful and inflicted a check on Demosthenes. The next move was for another associate of Demosthenes to prosecute Philocrates for treason on the ground that he had instituted the negotiations leading to the peace of 346. Public resentment at the unfortunate results of the peace was so strong that Philocrates saw that he could not possibly defend himself, reasonable as his proposal had been when he made it and when the Assembly accepted it. His only course was to flee into exile. Demosthenes now reactivated his prosecution of Aeschines. Although he himself had been a member of the embassy and although, to judge by his speech and that of Aeschines, both of which we have, he did not have a good case, he almost succeeded in getting a conviction.

It was because of the distastefulness and danger of such proceedings as these that a few decades later the philosopher Epicurus urged his followers to avoid public life, a piece of advice that was less pusillanimous than it has seemed to many critics of Epicurus. The extreme case was that of a man who, like Philocrates, proposed a reasonable plan that the Assembly accepted but that went wrong because of the guile of someone else, or the able general who lost a battle to a genius or because of some unavoidable contingency; either one might meet death or exile for his unsuccessful attempt to serve his country.

Philip Triumphs

Meanwhile Philip was rounding out and securing his gains. He gained friends in the Peloponnesus by diplomacy and the use of money, but was obliged to make a show of force from time to time to counter the restlessness of his rude western neighbors. His main effort was directed toward securing control of Thrace and moving into the Chersonesus. Here he came into conflict with the interests of Athens, which felt that she must maintain her prestige in this region and safeguard the wheat route from the Black Sea region.

In 341 Demosthenes delivered his third *Philippic*, in which he called for vigorous action in the Chersonesus and the formation of an alliance against Philip. Although the other Greeks did not respond, the Athenians at last decided to put forth a real effort against Macedonia. Their power on the sea still made it possible to check him here and there, although his land forces were far greater than theirs. In the year 340 his attempts to capture the cities of Perinthus and Byzantium on the grain route were foiled by Athenian assistance, and in 339 he abandoned his efforts in that region.

But the Athenians now became involved in a dispute with the Amphictyonic League, a dispute that may have been fostered by Philip's subterranean diplomacy. The league called upon Philip, who promptly marched south. Instead of taking the action that was expected, he suddenly occupied the strong point of Elatea in Boeotia, whence he sent a message to the Thebans, announcing that he intended to invade Attica and asking for their cooperation. A messenger arrived at Athens one evening to announce that Philip was at Elatea. Early next morning the Assembly was convened and the herald asked who wished to address the people. After the invitation was repeated, Demosthenes arose to propose an alliance with Thebes and active resistance. An embassy to Thebes managed to secure the desired alliance in the face of Philip's envoys.

Surprisingly, the decision by force was delayed until the next summer. Philip called for reinforcements from home and considered his moves carefully. In the summer of 338 the large Macedonian force, some 30,000 men, met an almost equal force of Athenians, Thebans, and mercenaries at Chaeronea in Boeotia. The decisive Macedonian victory made Philip master of the situation.

As usual, he carefully considered what conduct would best advance his interests. Thebes was treated severely; the captives were sold into slavery, and other Boeotian cities were declared free of her. The Athenians, who made preparations for a last-ditch resistance, were surprised to learn that their captives were to be returned without ransom and that Philip had no further warlike intentions toward them. It is to be supposed that he recognized the difficulty of reducing a naval power with a strongly fortified city and realized the advantages of having such a power as an ally. He must also have recognized that Athens was what Isocrates and Demosthenes had proclaimed her to be, the spiritual leader and center of Greece, and that his purposes would be best served by clemency. He did, however, force her to give up control over her naval allies.

He now circulated the word that he would soon embark on the great war against Persia that had long been discussed in Greece. He also, late in 338, called for the formation of a new Greek league, which came to be known as the League of Corinth, because the convention that formed it met there. Again the league was in form what the Greeks called a *symmachia*, or military alliance. Philip was commander of any military operation, the war against Persia being planned as the first one. Every member was to supply troops. A congress was to meet at stated times. Although Philip was not to be a member of the congress, his office as commander of the armed forces, added to his prestige and power, obviously gave him sufficient control over the activities of the league.

This league, the formation of which was the culmination of Philip's long years of military and political action in Greece, was essentially the sort of organization that other influential states had tried to form. It did not represent a mere act of conquest designed to make sure that the economic surplus of the vanquished would be regularly transferred to the victor. To form such a league was rather the one method of ensuring the security of the dominant state that had presented itself to the political thought of the Greeks and was very like the attempts of Athens, Sparta, and Thebes to consolidate their power. It was superior in that Philip did not interfere in the internal organization of the members as others had done. Athens had tried to promote the democratic form and Sparta the oligarchic form. Philip probably had no strong feeling for either.

The invasion of Persia began in 336, but with the assassination of Philip shortly afterward in that year, the forces that had already crossed the Hellespont were withdrawn to await developments. The army was soon to be sent into Asia Minor again by Philip's son, Alexander the Great.

CHAPTER

13

THE CULTURAL LIFE OF THE
FOURTH CENTURY

I t is reasonable to regard the fourth century among the Greeks as a historical period. As a historical entity it may be said to have begun in 404 B.C. when the fall of the Athenian Empire necessitated new arrangements in Greece and to have ended at the death of Alexander the Great after his brilliant conquest of the Persian Empire. Modern historians feel that another new period, the Hellenistic Age, began after Alexander, and they date it arbitrarily from his death in 323 B.C.

Fourth-century political and military affairs were conducted along much the same lines as those of the fifth century, as we have just seen, but from other points of view we do seem to have a rather different period. The historians of art generally will not allow the happiest years of Greek art to extend beyond the fifth century; new tendencies inconsistent with perfect classicism become prominent, they say, in the fourth century. The great period of Attic tragedy was the fifth century; in the fourth no great writers worked in this field. During the fourth century Attic comedy changed from the public-minded Old Comedy of Aristophanes and others to the New Comedy, a polished drawing-room comedy concerned with the complications of individual private lives. There is significance in the fact that the young Plato of the late fifth century wrote tragedies and the mature Plato of the first half of the fourth discussed great problems, not in tragedies, but in the new form of philosophical essays. The progress of individualism in the fourth century is shown by the construction in that century of four great systems of philosophy, rational and complete systems, by which an individual, practically without support from God, clan, or polis could undertake to understand the scheme of things and his place in it, order his life, and find the courage to live it.

It is customary to find a real break in Greek history at the time of Alexander the Great; thus we say that his death marks the end of the fourth century as a period. After Alexander the Greek world of independent small or middle-sized poleis was largely gone and the eastern Mediterranean world was largely dominated by the kingdoms of the successors of Alexander; life was different in many ways, most of them caused by the existence of the kingdoms and the increase in individualism. Furthermore, the history of the Greeks before Alexander has a certain unity, interest, and glamor that are not found in their later history.

Greece and the Greeks elsewhere were not unimportant after Alexander's time, for some of their greatest achievements came then. Many Greeks played important parts in the history of Rome, and the achievements of the Byzantine Empire are Greek. There is a temptation to look on the fifth century before Christ as a high point in history that has some biological foundation, as if it were a man's prime of life, and to see all later Greek history as a slow decadence from that height. More than this, there is a temptation to seek and find in all Greek history after the fifth century signs of decadence to support the notion that some grand design was slowly working itself out. We shall discuss the history of Greece after Alexander and up to the sixth century of our era in connection with the history of Rome, making every effort to avoid unjustified schematization.

Economic Life

Athens remained an important commercial city in spite of her reverse in the Peloponnesian War and the loss of her empire. Peiraeus was still centrally located for the trade of the Mediterranean and still had its magnificent facilities. Ships could dock in a well sheltered place. There were warehouses although it was more customary to dispose of cargoes at once, either for use in Athens or for shipment to and sale in other places. At this busy port buyers were readily found. The bankers of Athens, mostly metics, were experienced in financing business ventures.

During the first third of the century the ascendancy of Dionysius I in Syracuse was helpful to trade. In spite of the frequent wars between Dionysius and Carthage, the Carthaginian ships called at Syracuse in times of peace, thus connecting the Greek trading complex with that of Carthage. The Carthaginians remained in control of all the ports of North Africa and southern Spain and continued their policy of policing the western Mediterranean to exclude the ships of other peoples.

Athenian wares were also popular in Etruria, north of Rome. The

Etruscan fleet had been destroyed in 474 and Etruscan sea power ended, but the export of Athenian vases that has made the present-day museums of north central Italy treasure houses of Attic ware continued, presumably balanced by the export of Etruscan iron and bronze and objects made of those two metals. By the fourth century the Romans were at the head of a little league around Rome and had begun to encroach on the territory of Etruria. They still had only rare contact with Greece, however, for they had no port of their own for seagoing ships and were regarded as only one of the groups of less civilized peoples on the periphery of the Greek world.

It is important to realize how prosperous the Persian Empire was in the fourth century. It controlled Asia Minor, Egypt, and the Near and Middle East, the territory in which civilization first developed and in which, materially at least, it was farthest advanced in the fourth century. Probably many of its subjects had under Persian protection the best opportunity ever offered in these territories for economic development.

In the far eastern part of the Persian realm were rich territories— Bactria, Sogdiana, Margiane—of which we hear little until the great campaign of Alexander. A little to the west of them the Medes still lived a feudal and tribal life, pasturing cattle in the highlands east of Mesopotamia. Mesopotamia retained all the traditional skill of its old and highly civilized past and prospered in both agriculture and manufacturing. Egypt, too, retained its old organization and skills, as did Palestine and Phoenicia. There was a lively interchange of goods with the Greeks, chiefly through the ports of Phoenicia and Palestine.

Commerce by sea followed a few main routes. The Carthaginians had long ago worked out an ingenious roundabout route for their navigation of the western sea, following prevailing winds and currents. If a ship from Carthage went north in the early summer to Sicily, Sardinia, and Corsica, she could easily go west to the Punic depots around the lower tip of Spain, calling at the Balearic Islands on the way, and come home in the autumn with favoring winds and currents along the coasts of what are now Algeria and Tunisia in North Africa. Only one trip a year was possible on the important grain route from the Black Sea to Athens. The ships that went out in the early summer would have a difficult time making their way against the prevailing northerly winds up past the Chalcidic promontory, along the coast of Thrace, and up through the Dardanelles, the Propontis (Sea of Marmora), and the Bosporus to the Black Sea. On the return trip, however, they would have favoring winds all the way.

The entrance to the port of Peiraeus could be closed. On one side was the navy yard, with shops and long sheds to house the warships. On the other side was a long stone quay where the merchant ships tied up.

Behind it were five large colonnades where business could be done, whether it was the expediting of goods for Athens or the exchange of goods to be shipped along to other ports. Officials examined and inventoried every incoming cargo and collected a tax of two percent, even on goods that were in transit. This tax was a revenue-producing device rather than a protective tariff, something that was unknown in antiquity.

The bankers of Athens had facilities for storing money left on deposit by their patrons. They could also, through their connections, arrange for payments in other places without the actual transport of coins. They changed money, an activity that could be as useful and even more profitable than it is now, because there was not yet a stable and active international money market in which standard relations of currencies could be established.

Athens was more dependent on imports of food than any other state of the time, and we know something of the measures taken by the Athenians of the fourth century to make sure that their grain supply did not fail. Only a third of any cargo of grain that entered Peiraeus could be forwarded to another port; two thirds had to remain. No grain could be handled by a citizen or a metic unless it was destined for Athens. Out of each cargo of grain arriving a wholesaler could buy no more than about seventy-five bushels, so that a corner in grain was impossible. At times Athens, like many other cities, found it necessary to appoint commissioners to buy grain wherever they could and bring it to Athens for distribution at normal prices.

It has been suggested that during the fourth century the peoples to whom the Greeks exported their wares began to be able to produce comparable things for themselves, or at least things with which they were satisfied. The idea rests on archaeological evidence from many places— the Persian Empire, Thrace, the Greek colonies, and the native cities around the Black Sea, Etruria, and the Greek communities of southern Italy. The comparison of the contents of innumerable excavations (and this sort of thing is the supreme achievement of the scientific archaeologist) and the classification of their contents by origin and periods seem to show that the flow of goods from Greece to these places was slowed down and that the market was partly taken over by goods that betray to the trained eye that they were locally made in imitation of the goods imported from Greece.

Society in the Fourth Century

Athens in the late fourth century had perhaps 20,000 adult male citizens, if we can trust the casual remarks of the orators. Assuming two or three other people in the average family, we have a total of about 70,000 free Athenians. There are only scanty data about the number of citizens in each of the financial classes. We hear of a man who left an estate of forty talents and of another who left twenty. Others in the small group of the richest men are known to have had only two or three talents. Men who had nearly one talent were thought to be well-to-do, but not in the top group.

In the year 322, we are told, there were nine thousand men who owned more than twenty minae, that is, a third of a talent. These men were liable to service as hoplites, and the top one thousand were required to serve as cavalry. The thetes, or fourth class, were those citizens, 12,000 in number, who owned fewer than twenty minae, a sum which would more or less correspond to the value of a subsistence farm, a place of five or six acres with an adobe house and the usual animals. Others owned no land, lived in the city rather than out in Attica, and had little enterprises of some sort, often shops that they handled by themselves or with the help of a single slave. In Athens there was no desperately poor and downtrodden group of citizens, as there was in some other places.

During the fourth century Sparta underwent the curious phenomenon of a rapid shrinkage in the numbers of those who held land that entitled them to be Equals, to fight as hoplites, and to take part in the government. This situation resulted from letting the system get out of hand, not from a sharp drop in the birth rate. In 480 B.C. there were eight thousand full citizens, in 371 only two thousand, and a few generations later only seven hundred. It has been suggested that in the fourth century many Spartans made money as mercenary soldiers and, eager to invest in land, breached the system that connected land and citizen rights, concentrating land in the hands of fewer people, some of them even women, and leaving many pure-blooded Spartans without land and thus without full citizenship.

Many Spartans may well have felt no regret at being excluded from the rigorous life of the first-class male Spartan, even though that life was subsidized. To engage in a trade or to take the gold darics of the Persian king and live a companionable, perhaps luxurious life as a soldier in Babylon or Susa, with no one to insist on black soup or visiting one's woman only by stealth, may have seemed far better.

We get the impression that in the fourth century men in many places were reluctant to marry, as they had not been before. With the growing sense of individualism the sense of responsibility to the commonwealth lessened, and one result was less feeling of duty to produce children. On the other hand, there must have been hundreds of Greek communities where life was not so confined as in the larger poleis, where there was enough territory to support the people well, and where life remained more natural, vigorous, and prolific.

The Mercenary Soldier

The Assyrians hired Greeks as mercenaries as early as the eighth century, and in the seventh and sixth centuries there is evidence that mercenaries fought for the kings of Egypt and for others. During the fifth century there was some employment of them among the Greeks themselves. It is somewhat surprising, however, that the Spartans hired Arcadian hoplites in the Peloponnesian War and that both the oligarchs and the democrats sought to bolster their forces with mercenaries in the struggle that finally ended the reign of the Thirty at Athens. The Persian satraps learned that the Greek hoplite was superior to the ordinary soldier of the Persian Empire and used him as a bodyguard and in their provincial troops. At any time after the Peloponnesian War a force of Greek mercenaries could be recruited without any difficulty other than that of paying them, whether it was a Greek polis, a tyrant, a Persian satrap, or the Great King himself who wished to have an offensive or defensive force.

Consideration of such men and of the *condottieri,* or mercenary captains who led them, throws light on the condition of Greece in the fourth century. That so many men from so many poleis wished to run the risks of mercenary service for the pay and the possibility of booty shows that life in the poleis was more difficult and less satisfactory than it had been. Probably money was becoming more important and the possession of cash more desirable. It is plain that we cannot speak of the polis as a tightly integrated political and social unit when so many of the citizens were ready to leave and risk their lives for money in the service of anyone who would hire them.

The Growth of Individualism

The growth of individualism, which must be so often mentioned in a history of Greece, deserves a little systematic discussion. Like many other things, individualism can be explained in part by saying what it is not. Those who live in an age of extreme individualism may find it hard to imagine any other kind of existence. The life of the Greeks as we saw them first emerging from the Dark Age, however, allowed very little room for individualism and is an excellent example of a way of life different from ours.

The clans of that early age entirely controlled the lives of their members, but if oppressiveness represents one side of such comprehensive authority, the other side is complete support. The members of such a group could expect it to support them with all its power whenever need arose. As it grew, the polis arrogated to itself functions that had formerly been discharged by the clan: the maintenance of internal order, the management of affairs with outsiders, and public dealing with the gods. The supervision exercised by the elders of the clan was replaced by that of a council of elders in the polis—for example, the Council of the Areopagus at Athens. The supplanting of the clan by the necessarily looser authority of the polis did not mean that social life became like ours, for the family was far more tightly organized than it is in the twentieth century. Parents still retained real authority, and women had not asserted their individualism. Marriages were arranged for them, and they had no other career. The head of a family was obligated to find husbands for the females as they grew to maturity or when they were widowed, for a woman had to have a male protector. Of course the world of the fourth century was a livelier place than that of the ninth century, and it was easier for a young man who wished to go away from home and make a new start far from his family. There were more ways of making a living than merely farming or piracy, of which the most obvious was mercenary soldiering.

ART AND LITERATURE IN THE FOURTH CENTURY

Architecture and Fine Art

During the fourth century some fine Ionic structures were built in Asia Minor, the home of this order. The architect Pythius built the temple of Athena in the little town of Priene on the coast and also wrote a book about it. He also was one of the two architects of the Mausoleum, the tomb of King Mausolus of Caria (one of the "seven wonders of the world"), and the two architects together wrote a book about this building. Of the building itself nothing remains except some fragments that were reused in later buildings but some of the book, we think, is preserved in the shape of remarks by later writers. We know that the Mausoleum had a high base about a hundred feet square, on which was an arrangement of thirty-six Ionic columns, which suggested a temple, and above the columns was a pyramid of twenty-four steps. On a platform at the top of the steps, 136 feet above the ground, was a sculptured four-horse chariot. The building had three separate friezes and a number of other sculptures, the remains of which show the tendency of the sculptors of the fourth century to represent figures in vigorous action and with every suggestion of emotion. The best-preserved of these figures are from the frieze depicting the struggle of the Greeks with the Amazons.

An interesting and distinctive form of Greek architecture that has rarely appeared elsewhere was the circular building, a type that also provoked a book, this one written by the architect of such a building at Delphi. *Tholos* is the Greek word for these structures, which had a conical upper part as did the tombs of the Mycenaean Age that are known as tholos tombs. A few such tombs were constructed after Mycenaean times and into the Classical Age of Greece. There was a tholos in the sanctuary at Olympia, too; its use in such places has never been understood in modern times.

In spite of the glorious success of some kinds of Greek buildings, notably the Doric temple, the Greeks did not in general distinguish themselves as architects and builders. Their intense theorizing was exerted in narrow areas, and they were not bold or enterprising. They ignored such useful devices as the arch and did not show much ingenuity in transporting and lifting their materials.

Although art historians distinguish subperiods within the sculpture of the fourth century, it will suffice for our purpose to characterize the whole century as a time when sculptors were increasingly realistic and increasingly fond of portraying highly animated subjects. Their work represents almost the opposite of the restraint that we customarily call characteristic of fifth-century art; it may be said that the extreme realism and the somewhat wild action and emotion of the fourth and the following centuries were just what the sculptors of the fifth century avoided by their restraint.

The Athenian sculptor Praxiteles was active in the middle of the century. His Hermes, the work by which he is best known, was one of the many famous statues erected at Olympia. It shows the god, young, graceful, and relaxed, offering a bunch of grapes to the baby Dionysus. His figure is too realistically constructed to please all critics. The Greeks painted their statues, however, and a scheme suggested for this one would stain Hermes' skin a sunburnt red, leave the child Dionysus white, give Hermes red and gold hair, accentuate his eyes, lips, and eyebrows as skillfully applied make-up now accents a woman's face, make his sandals golden, and the draperies yellow and gold. Such a statue, seen in the bright outdoor sunlight, would be a fine piece of artificiality to portray a god rather than mere realism.

The Hermes was one of a group of pieces of Greek art preserved for us by accident. Unfortunately work in gold or silver was likely to be sold or melted down by those for whom the beautiful had no appeal at all— soldiers, perhaps, who took fine small pieces as loot. Bronze, too, was much in demand as mere metal, mostly during the several simpler ages between the classical Greek and the modern. Although marble statues could not be used to build other structures, as the dressed stone blocks of other buildings were, they could be burned down into lime with which to counteract acidity of the soil. Many works of art were carried from their original places by the Romans. Later others were taken to Constantinople. In the eighteenth and nineteenth centuries a new wave of such polite vandalism enriched the museums of England, France, and Germany.

The Hermes appeared during the great excavations at Olympia carried out during the 1870s by the Germans. Pausanias described the statue in his guidebook and gave its exact location. The site of Olympia was shaken by an earthquake soon after the closing of the games at the end of the fourth century, then flooded several times. The excavators had to clear away a deep deposit of soil. They looked for the Hermes where Pausanias said that it was and found it there.

The bronze charioteer of Delphi, now a chief exhibit of the museum there, was part of a complete charioteer, four-horse team, and chariot of bronze dedicated at Delphi in the early fifth century to celebrate a victory in the games. Soon afterward a landslide buried the whole combination. Excavators late in the nineteenth century dug up the charioteer and found a few fragments of the chariot and the horses. Presumably somebody dug up the rest and melted it down for the metal; at least the long ages of burial saved the charioteer for us.

But to return to Praxiteles, who produced a great deal according to the remarks of Greek and Roman authors about him and his works, he was a successful businessman, turning out statues of both bronze and marble. It may well be that many were made by him, reproduced a number of times by his assistants, and sold in different places, just as nowadays a shop in a small town will guarantee that it has sold no other copy of a certain dress in that locality.

The sculptors of the fifth century had already developed several techniques for representing clothing in marble. Sometimes they draped it closely over the figure to reveal the limbs; sometimes they made it fly free; sometimes they simply clothed the figure with it. In the battle frieze of the Mausoleum the draperies are part of the vivid motion of the figures.

Scopas, of the island of Paros, was active at the same time as Praxiteles, in the middle of the century. A sculptor and designer of great skill, Scopas tended to specialize in animated figures showing great emotion. Ancient tradition made him one of the four noted sculptors to whom the queen of Caria entrusted the sculpture of the four sides of the great bottom structure of the Mausoleum. Unfortunately we do not know to which of the four men the few surviving pieces belong. We may suppose, however, that for some time Scopas and most of his establishment moved to Halicarnassus, the Carian capital, and worked together on this large commission.

Lysippus of Sicyon is another fourth-century Greek said to have organized a shop that turned out many statues; one estimate is fifteen hundred, which is probably high. We do not have a single statue that is surely an original of his. If any judgment can be made from what are said to be copies of his work, his tendency was to produce quiet, realistic statues suggesting scenes from life. One often ascribed to him is *Apoxyomenos,* a representation of an athlete scraping himself with a *strigil,* a metal object used to scrape off the oil with which he anointed himself and with the oil the dirt.

During the fourth century some unidentified shops in Athens produced beautiful tombstones. In the early years they were simple low reliefs of rather formal style, but as the century went on, the reliefs became higher. The figures became less formal, more active, and the note of emotion became stronger. Instead of one figure or perhaps two in stiff and formal poses, there are little groups that suggest the poignancy of the eternal parting.

Our lack of knowledge about Greek painting is tantalizing. It seems, however, that there was a movement toward realism in the fourth century analogous to that in sculpture. We gather from our literary references that late in the fifth century the range of colors was widened and that the use of perspective and chiaroscuro, or strong contrasts of light and shadow, was developed. The painters, like the sculptors, had long ago developed the ability to do what they wished in literal representation, as is shown by the story of the contest between Zeuxis and Parrhasius. Zeuxis painted grapes so lifelike that birds flew down to peck them, but Parrhasius painted a curtain so realistic that Zeuxis asked him to draw it back and let his picture be seen.

Athens and Sicyon were the centers of painting. The subjects are said to have been individual figures and groups of gods and men. Some were narrative scenes and some were pictorial. There were also portraits. Interest in still life as a subject in itself seems hardly to have begun, and the same is true of landscapes. The Greeks were more interested in people than in nature.

Oratory

In fifth-century Greece the Sophists had begun the formal study of oratory as part of their program of what we now should call higher studies. The influential Gorgias had sought to create an artistic prose by introducing principles borrowed from the practice of verse, especially those of balance, antithesis, and ornament of all kinds. Others, especially Corax of Syracuse, studied the most effective arrangement of an argumentative discourse and laid down the basic structure that is still used: introduction with an attempt to gain the favor of the hearers, narrative of the facts, argument, refutation of the opponent's case, and a conclusion that attempts to clinch one's own case. Athens was the home of the greatest Greek oratory, and later critics made a selection of the "ten best orators," which they called the canon of Attic orators, beginning with Antiphon, who died in 411 B.C., and ending with Deinarchus, who was born in 369.

Antiphon employed his skill in the oratorical art in the service of the oligarchic party by assisting other oligarchs in court or by assisting members of the party of the few from the cities of the Delian League with their court business in Athens. When the opportunity for an oligarchic revolution came in 411, he was a leader. He was convicted of treason at the end of the revolution in spite of a speech in his own defense that Thucydides praises highly.

Lysias, another of the early orators, was a metic. His father was a wealthy manufacturer who had been persuaded by Pericles to come to Athens from Sicily. The Thirty, in their lust for money, murdered the brother of Lysias, and he was fortunate to escape. The loss of the family property to the Thirty forced him to take up the profession of speech writer for others when the terror was over and he returned to Athens. Lysias had great ability in the intimation of character, and the speeches seem to reflect the men who ordered them—a frank and generous young man, a careful and sober middle-aged man, or whatever was needed. Their language is pure and elegant Attic. Beyond this, they have a charm that is universally recognized and has never been satisfactorily analyzed.

Isocrates (436–338 B.C.) was more a teacher and essayist than an orator. He frankly admitted that his voice and nerve were not adequate for addressing the Assembly and the courts. The financial misfortune of his family during the Peloponnesian War forced him, too, to become a writer of speeches for other men to use in court. In 392 he opened his school in Athens, which soon became very successful, and in later years he liked to forget his speech-writing period. He was a highly successful teacher of what he preferred to call philosophy but we should call forensic and political oratory. He believed that a real oratorical education produced a man of broad views who could express himself forcefully in speech or in writing. This was to be the view of the Roman Cicero. The style of Isocrates, both of itself and through its influence on the style of Cicero, was the foundation of western European prose style, for he developed all the possibilities of the periodic sentence, a complex sentence in which a number of subordinate ideas are grouped around the main idea.

The school of Isocrates in Athens was a strong influence on the life of the Greek world in the fourth century. Rich young men from Athens itself, from other cities of Greece proper, from the Greek cities of Asia, the Black Sea region, Sicily, and southern Italy attended. Many of the minor kings of the regions around the Greek world liked to send their sons to Athens to be educated, as in modern times Oxford has educated many young members of royal families of Asia and Africa, and the natural place in Athens was the school of Isocrates. This was the first school to attract so wide a clientele.

Isocrates expressed himself frequently on literature and government, generally casting his essays in the form of orations. In *Areopagiticus* he argued (as we have said) that the broad supervisory powers once possessed by the Council of the Areopagus should be restored to it—not a surprising suggestion from a conservative in an age when individualism was rising. As a trainer of princes, he took a sympathetic view of monarchy. He wrote one essay on the duties and behavior of a king, and from his other essays remarks could be collected to make a typical manual of the "Mirror of the Prince" type, a type that we find often among the Romans and later peoples.

He was more interested in foreign than in domestic affairs, and his chief theme was a common one: the desirability of a combined Greek offensive against the Persians. His *Panegyricus,* which dates from about 380, is in the form of a speech given at the Olympic Games; the Greek word means a speech given at a great assembly rather than a speech of laudation. Here he argued that the Greeks should unite under the leadership of Athens to make war on Persia. We have mentioned his *Philippus,* an open letter to the Macedonian king published in 346, which called instead on Philip to take the lead. Greece was in fact ready for a new movement of population overseas, and an imperialistic campaign against Persia, which would use the restless part of the population and then leave it overseas in colonies, was a practical measure, especially from the conservative and propertied point of view.

Demosthenes (384–322 B.C.) stands first among the orators of Greece and of all time. His political orations show a firm grasp of Greek affairs and great powers of expression and persuasion. He also enjoyed a high reputation as a writer of speeches for others to deliver in court. He was not first in every aspect of oratory, but if others could surpass him in elegance or charm or resourcefulness in argument, he was admittedly first in the indispensable quality of the orator, the combination of earnestness, energy, and power of expression that leads to the persuasion of the hearer.

His *Philippics* and *Olynthiacs,* two groups of speeches on the rise of Philip II, were powerful efforts, but his last pronouncement in this field was the greatest of his orations. In 336 a certain Ctesiphon proposed that Demosthenes be presented by the polis with a golden crown for his public services. Aeschines, the old opponent of Demosthenes, thereupon prosecuted Ctesiphon for proposing an illegal decree (*graphe paranomon*) because the crown was to be presented at a different time and in a different place from those set by law and because, as Aeschines claimed, Demosthenes had not in fact benefited the state by his long activity in opposition to Philip. For some reason the trial did not take place until six years later.

Aeschines in his speech (which we have) made an excellent case for the irregularity of Ctesiphon's proposal. He would have done better to rest his whole case on this aspect of the matter without adding the assertion that Demosthenes had not benefited the state. Demosthenes' reply to him is known either by a Latin title, *De corona,* or an English title, *On the Crown.* It can also properly be called *In Defense of Ctesiphon,* for it was Ctesiphon who nominally was on trial.

Demosthenes had no good answer to make to the charge that Ctesiphon had proposed to present the crown under the wrong circumstances, and his political activity had indeed failed to stop Philip. Yet, by his characteristic combination of oratorical skill with earnestness and depth of feeling, and by his appeal to the pride of the Athenians in their history and their past glories, he won a crushing victory over Aeschines. Aeschines received only a small part of the votes, so few that he suffered the penalty of exile provided for those who prosecuted and could not carry a fifth part of the jury for conviction.

Other Thought and Writing

In literature the full development of Attic oratory was the great achievement of the fourth century. The Hellenistic Age (the age that followed the death of Alexander the Great in 323 B.C.) produced no orators considered great now or in their own time. The study of oratory did go on, however, especially in the Greek communities of Asia Minor, where the florid and artificial style called Asianic was developed. The Attic style was more practical, more designed for persuasion, and less suited for display. Romans later studied with the great Hellenistic teachers of oratory, and even at Rome, as we shall find, there could be theoretical disputes about the merits of the Attic and Asianic styles as applied to Latin oratory.

Tragedy hardly survived the fifth century. In the fourth century the most able men preferred to work in other fields. It was found advisable to allow revivals of the work of the important men of the fifth century, a good sign that tragedy was now only an entertainment rather than a vehicle for lively and debatable ideas. Comedy, as has been said, developed into the comedy of manners known as New Comedy, which we shall consider in connection with the Roman comedies derived from it, for New Comedy itself survives only in fragments.

Earlier we described the great adventure of Xenophon the Athenian, his participation in the attempt of Cyrus the Persian to overthrow his brother the king with the help of Greek mercenaries. Xenophon became a great admirer of Agesilaus, the king who commanded the Spartan troops in Asia at that time. He stayed for some time with Agesilaus, then returned to Sparta with him when Agesilaus was called home, and took the field with him in 394 in a battle against his native Athens. Many an Athenian must have sympathized with the conservatism of Sparta and had friends there. Such feelings could be understood, but it is hard to see how an Athenian could fight for Sparta against Athens. The Athenians banished him, and he lived in Sparta for many years as a country gentleman.

The writings of Xenophon are those of a man of the second rank in thought and in ability to write, yet a man of amiable nature. A surprising number of his books have survived. The *Anabasis,* his story of the great adventure, is a clear and vivid narrative. In the days before he went on the expedition he was a friend of Socrates and wrote a book about him, *Memorabilia,* that tells us much of what people said in criticism of him and in defense of him, a useful collection of information that we otherwise should not have. He also attempted an *Apology,* or defense speech of Socrates, and a *Symposium,* or account of a drinking party at which Socrates had much to say.

He wrote an encomium of the Spartan Agesilaus and another on Cyrus. His essay on the Spartan constitution gives some valuable information on that subject. He was a great lover of horses and dogs and wrote essays on hunting and outdoor life. His most serious work was his *Hellenica,* in which he attempted to continue the history of Greece from the point at which Thucydides left off, 411 B.C., to the defeat of the Thebans at Mantinea in 362. Although Xenophon did not have the penetration and intensity of Thucydides and was hopelessly biased in favor of Sparta, he may be called a respectable historian, and here again he left an account of something that otherwise we should know very little about.

Natural Science

During the fourth century mathematics and astronomy progressed in a straightforward and regular manner that led to brilliant work in the Hellenistic Age. Although that age will more properly be discussed later, the early developments made in the fourth century cannot be overlooked.

Until the middle of the fifth century mathematics was only one of the interests of any man who was advancing knowledge. At about that time, however, there was a strong movement toward differentiation and specialization. Although a few men still tried to work in many fields, within the next few generations most became specialists, so that when we come to the time of Plato we may speak of mathematicians.

Mathematics was an important part of the work of Plato's Academy, although we do not have much idea of how it was approached in detail. The figures of mathematics have a certain relation to Plato's Forms, or ideal essences, which we shall discuss presently. The sphere or the triangle of mathematics is perfect, as are the Forms. Although no instrument could ever be devised to draw those figures with the perfection that belongs to the Forms, the mind may see the figures in perfection as it may hope to reach the perfection of the Forms. It is possible that the little company in the Academy found that their attempts to conduct rigorous mathematical discussions helped them to make their philosophical discussions more rigorous.

The mathematics of the fourth century consisted in the main of arithmetic and geometry. Algebra was yet to come. The very first steps were taken in conics, however, and work done on the method of exhaustion in considering volumes was an ancestor of the calculus. Trigonometry was to come in a few centuries. Much of our information is brief and tantalizingly incomplete, but it is sometimes possible to see in detail what the mathematicians of the fourth century were doing. At the end of this century and the beginning of the third the great geometrician Euclid was active, from whose work we can learn all that had been accomplished in his field up to this time.

We saw that the Pythagoreans at some earlier time had grasped the idea of irrationals. In the fourth century arithmetic and geometry were so extended that it was possible to discuss any proposition with irrational numbers or with irrational lines without any awkwardness arising from the fact that the matter could not be expressed in terms of integers. This was a step into real mathematics.

The discovery that there are only five regular solids was another characteristic piece of work from this century; the author is not known, but the proof is found in Euclid. The five are the pyramid, with four faces, the cube with six, and the polyhedra of eight, twelve, and twenty faces. To discover this fact and construct a proof of it is a nice piece of mathematical work. The other side of the mathematical thought of the age may be illustrated by Plato's reaction to this discovery. He decided that some great principle must have been at work to limit the number of the regular polyhedra. Seaching for five of something with which to make an analogy, he finally hit upon the four elements proposed by earlier philosophers, plus one to represent the totality of matter. This kind of thinking, which we are tempted to call silly, is likely to occur fairly often in the early stages of a system of thought.

Although specialization had begun, not every mathematician of the fourth century was a specialist. The same man could work out new refinements of the theory of proportions, devise an ingenious solution of the old problem of the duplication of the cube, begin the science of theoretical mechanics, and be highly regarded as a practical statesman. The combination of mathematics and astronomy was a natural one for scholars, even though it was forbidden to teach astronomy. By the early fourth century the Greeks had made some observations of the heavenly bodies and some men probably had access to the results of Egyptian observations. Possibly some had also learned the results of Babylonian observations, but there is no proof. The great Babylonian astronomer Kidinnu is believed to have discovered in the fourth century the precession of the equinoxes or the fact that the spring and the autumn come a few seconds earlier each year because of the tilting of the earth's axis that makes the fixed stars seem to shift. This theory rests on the fact that over periods of hundreds of years it can readily be observed that the fixed stars seem to have changed their positions a little. The Babylonians made a long series of systematic observations from which this fact could be seen. The Greek Hipparchus discussed this matter in the second century.

To return to the fourth century, the universe was thought to be spherical and finite. The earth was believed to be a planet like the other planets and to rotate eastward on its axis. The great addition of the fourth century was an attempt to explain all the movements of the heavenly bodies by a theory of spheres. The theory postulated twenty-seven spheres, all having the same center as the earth. Each heavenly body was fastened to one of these spheres, described as having no other function than to carry the heavenly body around, and each could have its movement influenced also by the action of one or more other concentric spheres. The theory attempted thus to explain all the movements of the planets, which are very complex if observed from the earth. Although the astronomical observations on which the theory was based were incomplete and often inaccurate, the theory was genuinely scientific, for it attempted to take account of all the known facts and ignore metaphysical considerations. This was the beginning of scientific astronomy, which flourished greatly in the next three or four centuries.

PHILOSOPHY

Although the term "pre-Socratic philosophy" is commonly used and understood, we do not say "post-Socratic philosophy," since it is well understood that the greatest achievements of Greek systematic philosophy come not only after Socrates, but also in large measure because of Socrates. It was Socrates who saw that philosophy, in the sense of a system for living, had become very necessary. The questionings of the earlier philosophers, of the Sophists, and of the dramatists, combined with the fact that men no longer lived in the tight traditional organization dominated by clan and family, made it impossible for men in the poleis of

Greece to live in the old fashion and by the simple old beliefs. Like Adam and Eve, they had lost their innocence and must now go out to find a set of reasoned beliefs that would serve as a basis for living in a world more complex and not to be taken for granted.

It often is difficult for the modern to understand the place of philosophy in the lives of many people of the ancient world. For the intelligent man a philosophy was a necessity, because he was not content to live without some coherent view of the world and man. Perhaps this need is less felt nowadays because people vaguely assume that natural science explains everything about the universe and because the shocks of life are cushioned in a number of practical ways. The ancient philosophies must be understood as serious guides to living. They performed a real function that nowadays is often not performed (with unhappy results) or for which people turn to self-help books and other stopgap substitutes for a genuine philosophy.

The Cynics and Cyrenaics

Surprisingly diverse philosophical views were offered as offspring of Socrates' thought. It is perhaps natural that different people should claim to have been inspired to different views by him. Antisthenes, the founder of the Cynic school, was a mature man when he first met Socrates. He was a minor Sophist, a boorish man who in spite of his abilities was rough in speech and dress. His abilities did not include depth and subtlety of thought, so that he was inclined to reject those parts of philosophy that he found difficult.

Antisthenes seized on the fact that Socrates had let go all worldly ambition and led the simple life in order to devote himself to philosophy. This relinquishment of interest in fame, wealth, and family seemed to him the best road to happiness and successful living. When, after the death of Socrates, he returned to his career as Sophist, the essence of his message was that a man must strip himself of all those things that are subject to the whims and sudden reverses of fortune. If it has been stripped down to essentials, life is no longer at the mercy of other people or of mischances.

Antisthenes not only renounced wealth and fame, but also argued against ordinary comforts and such institutions as the state, marriage, and conventional courtesy, which are not found in a state of nature and have been devised by men for the ordering of human relations. If it is possible to construct a serious argument for discarding all such institutions and replacing them by the supposedly good impulses of a state of nature, there is no record that Antisthenes offered one. Apparently it was possible for him to make a modest living by promulgating his message, for people were interested in this question of how to live. Any seeker after truth or happiness who insisted on serious handling of the deeper philosophical questions would presumably have left Antisthenes; those to whom his main teachings were acceptable, and who, like him, cared little for a complete philosophy, would be satisfied to have such questions cavalierly dismissed.

The Cynic philosophy persisted as a recognizable discipline until the rise of Christianity. Its first hundred years, those of the fourth century, were its best, for the rise of the Stoic philosophy about 300 B.C. incorporated all the best of the Cynic ideas into a better system, and with the best ideas took from the Cynics the best people.

Aristippus of Cyrene, another follower of Socrates, elaborated another philosophy that purported to represent the essence of Socratic thought. As the somewhat boorish Antisthenes had seized on the simplicity of Socrates' personal life as the essence of Socrates' way, so the elegant aristocrat of the rich and pleasure-loving Greek city of Cyrene seized on Socrates' frank enjoyment of worldly pleasures as the key to the happiness of Socrates and the gospel to be proclaimed for the happiness of others. Naturally the two men had had little sympathy with each other when they were together in the company around the living Socrates.

The arguments of Aristippus about pleasure, which appeared again nearly a hundred years later in the system of Epicurus, started with the naturalness of pleasure. All human experience tells us that good functioning is pleasurable and that bad functioning is either painful or unpleasant. If, then, one is looking for a standard, the rightness of things that are pleasurable has a strong claim, especially since it is supported in so many cases by the painfulness of things that are harmful. Aristippus drew his conclusions straightforwardly and declared that the pleasure of the present moment is the surest guide to conduct, because both past and future pleasures are unreliable as guides. He felt, as did Antisthenes, that more abstruse philosophical reflections were not useful.

Plato (427–347 B.C.)

A great deal of difficult work had been done before Plato to raise and debate all the basic questions of philosophy. The time was ripe for a great attempt to construct a complete philosophy that would absorb all that was worth while in earlier attempts. It is not surprising that all subsequent philosophy echoes some part of Plato's work or seems indebted to it in some way. Plato is said to have regarded the viva-voce discussions of the Academy, which he founded in 387, as the most important part of his work. From time to time he did publish, and it is inconceivable that a literary artist of his ability should have been content not to do so. He cast his works in the dialogue form, except for a few, to which he gave the form of letters, and made Socrates the chief speaker in all but his *Laws*.

One of the first necessities was to establish some firm ground, because he had been exposed both to the Heraclitean notion of universal flux and to Socrates' attempts to make correct definitions and to win sure knowledge of basic matters. For this purpose he developed the concept of the Forms. The Greek word is *idea;* Form (with the capital letter) is a better English word for it than the English "idea." The Forms represent the perfect version of qualities, virtues, human relations, and things. There is a Form of justice and a Form of horse. The relation between the Form of tree and the individual tree, for example, is not clearly explained by Plato, yet one can see that if individual trees come and go, there is plainly something preserving the Form of tree, for this does not change from generation to generation. Unlike ideas in our sense, the Forms are not in the minds of men nor are they engendered by the minds of men. They exist from everlasting to everlasting and may be apprehended by men's minds, but only with effort and difficulty. The Forms are the only reality; all else is a somewhat dim version of the Forms. This conception allows the philosopher to recognize the changes of matter that we see while it preserves something that is above and beyond change and can serve as a basis for the rest of the philosophy.

A theory of the origin and nature of the world is an important part of any philosophy, although in modern times this part of the subject belongs to the offshoot of philosophy known as natural science. *Timaeus,* the dialogue in which Plato dealt with the origin of the world, contains the famous story of the lost continent of Atlantis. The essence of the dialogue is that God (for Plato regularly speaks in such terms) decided to impose order on the chaotic mass of matter in the universe and for that purpose constructed a world-soul by using the Forms, which had always existed. When the world-soul had been properly constructed on the best principles, God fashioned the chaotically brawling elements of matter into that most perfect of all figures, the sphere, and endowed his new creation with the soul that he had already created. Then he proceeded to the furnishing of this fair habitation with minor divinities, with man, and with the backdrop of the heavens.

An ancient philosophy also had to have an epistemology, a theory of how we know what we know. It followed from Plato's theory of the nature of the Forms and of matter that the objects apprehended by our senses are not real, but are rather representative of the ceaseless flux and are illusion. The Forms, which are real, are to be perceived by the soul, which has an innate knowledge of them persisting from one incarnation to another. Great effort by the individual is nevertheless necessary; the

philosophically trained person may hope for some success in the arduous
task of knowing the Forms.

In the beautiful dialogue *Symposium* (*The Drinking Party*) Plato explains the nature of what has come to be called Platonic love. Starting
from the ordinary love aroused by a beautiful person, one rises step by
step to a wider and higher love, and at the end one arrives at the loving
contemplation of Beauty in her essence, the Form of Beauty. In Plato's
scheme this love is practically synonymous with knowledge.

In this system the soul must be immortal so that it can carry its knowledge of the Forms from one incarnation to another. Souls, then, do not
perish with bodies, but undergo a thousand-year period of purification.
Once in a while some soul has been so defiled with baseness during an
incarnation that it cannot be cleansed and is not allowed to return to
another incarnation. On the other hand, sometimes a soul has been so
uplifted toward virtue that it is allowed release from the cycle of incarna-
tions and is freed for an eternity of contemplation of the Forms, the highest bliss to which the soul can aspire.

The ancient philosophy also had to have a theory of government. In
Politeia, generally known as *The Republic,* Plato presented a picture of
a well-ordered state as a means of writing justice large, so that anyone
could read its features and understand what it is. He would put the
populace under the direction of a worthy few—the philosophers—who
would be rigorously trained and tested. Philosophy-and-ruling is a career
open only to talent. Women are eligible equally with men. The ruling
group is not weakened by considerations of money or family. Its wants
will be supplied and its status assured without any need for wealth. The
children will not inherit the position of the parents, for people will be
bred like animals and the children raised by the state. There are careful
prescriptions for the moral and physical and intellectual education of the
guardian, or philosopher, class, all conservative and static in nature. The
education of the less able citizens will teach them to work and to obey.

The warrior class is to be composed of those who make some progress
in the training for the philosopher class, but are not able to pass the
tests for the final stage. The artisan and farmer class will be chosen early
from those who show no aptitude for any but practical training. As the
guardian class especially uses the intellect, so the warrior class uses its
courageous spirit, and the artisan class uses its practical talents. The
three classes may be compared to the brain, the heart, and the stomach in
man. In the state as in the body a division of functions is best, with each
part performing its own function without wishing or striving to be another part.

The Republic has had enormous influence. Modern states planning to
reorganize their societies and integrate them more closely have studied

the book and used it, and its literary influence is visible in a great many books, of which Orwell's *1984* will serve as an example. *The Republic* did not have any practical effect in its own time.

A philosophy must also, of course, have a system of ethics. In minor dialogues Plato offers discussions of some of the traditional virtues like courage or self-control. In others he deals with the question of whether virtue can be taught. The figure of Socrates is little by little built up in the dialogues into a most appealing picture of the virtuous man. Socrates defending himself before the Athenian jury for his attempts to inform himself about right living, Socrates in *Crito* refusing to harm the state by defying its judgment on him by escaping from prison, Socrates in prison among his friends at his final hour—these immortal pictures are pictures of the virtuous man. The honesty and elevation of Plato's writing are such that many a man, like Cicero, has felt that in philosophical questions he preferred to be wrong with Plato than right with others.

Plato's thought remained influential in Greece throughout antiquity. The Academy was active until all the universities, or philosophical schools, of Athens were closed by order of the Christian emperor Justinian in A.D. 529. The Aristotelian, Epicurean, and Stoic schools of philosophy, which maintained the other three schools, were all largely indebted to the thought of Plato. The Roman appropriation of Greek thought included the appropriation of philosophy; if more Romans professed themselves Stoics than followers of Plato, they nevertheless were much influenced by Plato and helped to transmit his influence to the modern world.

Platonic influence on Christianity was enormous. The idealistic system of Plato was naturally congenial to Christianity, and the able Christian scholars of the third and fourth centuries of our era, laboring to complete the philosophical structure of Christianity, used Plato and Aristotle constantly. The Neoplatonic philosophy, a somewhat mysticized version of Platonism developed by Plotinus in Rome late in the third century, served for many as a preparation for Christian thought. In the thirteenth century Aristotle was exalted to the first place in Western thought, but with the Renaissance Plato again became the favorite Greek philosopher of the West and has remained so.

Aristotle (384–322 B.C.)

Aristotle was the son of a physician of Stagira, an Ionian colony in Chalcidice. His father was court physician to the kings of Macedonia. Aristotle went to Athens when he was about eighteen and was enrolled in Plato's Academy, where he stayed for nineteen years. When Plato died in 347 B.C., Aristotle was invited by a former student of the Academy, Hermeias, to come to the little principality in Asia Minor of which he was tyrant, and there he spent three happy years. Then he accepted the invitation of King Philip of Macedonia (who may well have been a companion of his boyhood at the Macedonian court when his father was physician there) to come to Pella to tutor the thirteen-year-old Alexander. After some years with Alexander, Aristotle returned to Athens in 335 and founded the school that he called the Lyceum, from the name of a gymnasium, or outdoor sports ground. His group is sometimes known as the Peripatetic school of philosophy from the fact that much of his work was done with a small number of people who often strolled about rather than sat. For twelve years he lectured, at the same time turning out a great number of writings. But in 323 Alexander died, and there were threats against Aristotle for his pro-Macedonian views. He withdrew to Chalcis, saying that he would not allow the Athenians to sin again against philosophy, and died in the next year, 322 B.C.

Aristotle's first task was to work out his independence of Plato in metaphysics. He could not follow Plato's belief that reality is only in the Forms and not in the world with which we are surrounded, for he believed that reality is both in the world of individual objects and in the other world of Forms or universals, that the Many have as much reality as the One, and that the Good is attached to life in this world as well as existing remotely in that other world. He did have a large area of agreement with Plato's beliefs, for he believed in universals and abstractions, in the Good, and in a living God, the supernatural cause of the movements of the physical world.

In the *Physics* and the *Metaphysics* Aristotle dealt with major problems of cosmology; in spite of modern connotations, the title of the second treatise originally meant only "what comes after *Physics*." He attempts to explain how primeval matter was shaped into the world, the nature of being and becoming, movement, and causes. There is an elaborate discussion of causes as formal, material, efficient, and final. The work of the pre-Socratic philosophers is discussed in detail, and at the end he devotes two of the eleven books to a discussion of Plato's theory of Forms.

It was typical of Aristotle's attitude and interest that he investigated the processes by which judgments and statements are made. His *Categories* classifies the objects of thought. We may regard things under such headings as substance, quality, quantity, relation, place, time, position, state, and so on. He examines the propositions that we can make, trying to determine how we can set them up so that they will not be ambiguous or contain traps or pitfalls. In the *Analytics* he makes his greatest contribution to the subject of logic by developing the theory of the syllogism.

Aristotle is said to have collected the constitutions of one hundred and fifty-eight Greek states in preparation for writing his *Politica*. Presumably not one of these constitutions was written. They must have been

The Palace at Knossus. South Propylon (restored)   *Photograph by the author*

View from the Citadel of Mycenae   *Photograph by the author*

Athenian geometric vase, 9–8th
century B.C.
*The Metropolitan Museum of
Art, Fletcher Fund, 1941*

Athenian black-figured amphora,
c. 525 B.C.
*The Metropolitan Museum of Art,
Gift of Mrs. Leonard A. Cohn, 1941*

Athenian red-figured amphora,
5–4th century B.C.
*The Metropolitan Museum of Art,
Fletcher Fund, 1944*

Cretan seal ring of jaspar, 15–1100 B.C.;
women approaching seated divinity. Enlarged
sixty-five percent.
*Courtesy of The Metropolitan Museum of Art,
Bequest of Richard B. Seager, 1926*

Archaic marble head of a youth.
Second quarter of 6th century B.C.
The Metropolitan Museum of Art,
Rogers Fund, 1921

Archaic gravestone from Attica.
Third quarter 6th century B.C.
The Metropolitan Museum of Art,
Hewitt Fund, 1911 and Anonymous
Gift, 1951

Marble statute of Aphrodite. Copy,
probably Hellenistic, of 4th century
Greek work.
The Metropolitan Museum of Art,
Fletcher Fund, 1952

Bronze figure of Eros sleeping
(250–150 B.C.)
The Metropolitan Museum of Art,
Rogers Fund, 1943

Delphi, temple of Apollo

Photograph by the author

Epidaurus (Peloponnesus), the theater

Photograph by the author

Olympia, temple of Hera   *Photograph by the author*

Paestum, 5th century temple (Doric Order)   *Photograph by the author*

The temple of Nike (Victory), on the Acropolis of Athens (Ionic Order)

Photograph by the author

Taormina (Tauromenium), Sicily, the theater

Courtesy of Trans World Airlines, Inc.

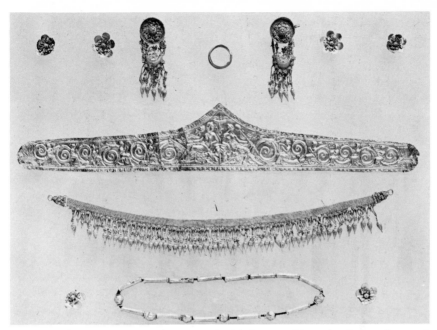

Greek gold jewelry, soon after 350 B.C. Diadem, necklace, beads, earrings and rosettes in the form of flowers.

The Metropolitan Museum of Art, Rogers Fund, 1906

The Acropolis of Lindus, Rhodes   *Courtesy of Pan American Airways*

The Porch of the Maidens (Caryatid Porch) of the Erechtheum, on the Acropolis
of Athens   *Photograph by the author*

described by him or by his students and collaborators after observation and questioning. We have a large part of a preparatory study, *The Constitution of Athens*, thanks to its preservation on a papyrus in Egypt. It gives an account of the constitutional development of Athens and of the form of her constitution.

Politica has generally been translated *Politics*, a slightly misleading title, for the book might better be called *Life in a Polis*. Likewise it has been suggested that Aristotle's famous remark, "Man is a political animal," should rather be rendered, "Man is a creature who lives in a polis." Aristotle and Plato have both been criticized for basing their political theory on life in the polis instead of realizing that the polis was doomed by the advance of such kingdoms as that of Philip. Such criticism is inaccurate, for the city continued to the end of the ancient world, whether or not it was an independent state, and a large part of what the two men said continues to apply.

Aristotle has an elaborate discussion of the theoretical schemes of government known in his day and of famous existing commonwealths. Plato's plan for a commonwealth comes in for some very sharp criticism. Being of a middle-class rather than an aristocratic temper, he presumably had little sympathy with Plato's idea of reversing recent tendencies by forming an aristocratic, conservative, static society. He discusses the virtues and defects of various kinds of states. Complete democracy and complete oligarchy rank very low, and the best kind of state is a mixture of democracy and oligarchy, inclining to the democratic.

The possibility of revolution was always present to the mind of the Greek political thinker, since the history of almost every Greek state was full of revolutions of the many against the few or of the few against the many. Aristotle realistically discusses the relations of the different elements in the several possible kinds of states and points out the probable form that revolution would take in one or another set of circumstances and how to guard against it. Another aspect of his theory is the consideration of the possibility that a political form will degenerate into a worse version of itself, as monarchy can degenerate into tyranny or democracy into mob rule.

In *Ethics* Aristotle discusses the classical virtues of the Greek—courage, wisdom, justice, temperance—and other virtues useful to the member of a polis. He gives successful life in the polis (in society, we should say) as the Good to which all these virtues are directed and which makes them worthwhile. In his eyes every virtue is a mean between two extremes: liberality is between prodigality and meanness, and pride is between vanity and undue humility.

His interest in all forms of human life and in the world did not cease when he had considered the usual parts of systematic philosophy. His

Rhetoric is a masterly examination of what rhetoric really is, the art of persuasive speech. He examines the mechanics of effective speech and the psychology that must be used in addition if one is to persuade. In *Poetics* he examines poetry; the construction of tragedy is the topic that has aroused most interest among modern readers of it. In the Renaissance and just afterward *Poetics* served as a set of rules for the construction of plays. *Oedipus the King* was Aristotle's favorite play, and he tends to find in it all the virtues possible in a tragedy.

But far more earthy subjects than these could claim his attention. He described many animals and Mediterranean fishes, sometimes so minutely that it seems that he must have dissected specimens, perhaps even with the aid of some sort of magnifier. Here, as elsewhere, his mind worked systematically, and his observations on animals and fishes and on their classification were the beginning of this branch of natural science.

Aristotle's work was not highly influential in antiquity; perhaps it was too factual and precise to correspond to the temper of the ancient world. Sometimes the Christian fathers used him in their task of building the philosophical structure of Christianity. In the fourth and fifth centuries of our era there were a number of learned commentators on his work who helped to make it better known. In the thirteenth century St. Thomas Aquinas made a fruitful union of the Aristotelian and Christian systems which for a short time ruled the world of serious thought.

The Epicurean and Stoic Philosophies

The son of an Athenian citizen who had gone to Samos, Epicurus seems to have developed his system thoroughly before settling in Athens in 306 B.C. He did not undertake to teach in Athens, but lived in a large house with a garden suitable for walks and discussion, from which his system is sometimes called "the philosophy of the Garden," and gathered a company of disciples about him. His was the first dogmatic philosophy. He laid down an elementary version of its most important principles to be memorized, then an intermediate version. In the third stage the learner might consult treatises rather than memorize rules or outlines. Epicurus and his associates and disciples busied themselves with treatises on every aspect of philosophy, with attempts to refute the assertions of the other schools, and with letters to the communities of Epicureans which were soon to be found in many places in the Greek world. The Epicurean was expected to attempt to make converts. The dogmatic clarity of the philosophy and the warmth of the Epicurean groups combined to win a fair number of people in every generation.

This was a materialistic philosophy. Its cosmology, requiring a world free from the intervention of gods, whether to help man or to punish contribution made by the political part of their philosophy, to preach that all men are brothers, rich or poor, Greek or barbarian, slave or free. It was a new idea in the world and one that helped to prepare the way for Christianity.

These four schools—the Platonic, the Aristotelian, the Epicurean, and the Stoic—especially represent the Greek effort to cope with life by reason, which at the same time is the high point of Greek individualism. Adherence to such philosophies meant that a man was not relying much on traditional values and supports. After a few generations a time came when men began to feel uncomfortably exposed in this rational individualism and began to start edging back toward the comfort of more emotional and more communal attitudes and ways of living.

14

ALEXANDER THE GREAT

The death by assassination of King Philip II in 336 B.C. left his son Alexander the king of Macedonia. Alexander, who was twenty years old, had been carefully educated to succeed his father. He had been trained in government and in the Macedonian art of war by his father and his father's helpers. At the age of sixteen he commanded one of the armies and crushed a rebellion in Thrace while his father was busy with the siege of Byzantium. At eighteen he commanded the left wing of his father's army at the meeting with the combined Greek forces at Chaeronea. His polite studies were watched over by tutors of whom the most notable was Aristotle.

Even as a youth Alexander was very serious minded and determined to fill his royal position with credit. He was ambitious for glory. He is said to have exclaimed when he visited Troy at the beginning of his campaign against the Persians: "O fortunate Achilles, to have found Homer as the herald of your glory!" Notwithstanding the loftiness of his ideas, he was practical and very careful about every detail. Both his courageous spirit and his practicality are illustrated by his mastering of the horse Bucephalus. He wished to have the wonderful animal, which his father's grooms were unable to manage at all, and by a combination of force of personality, observation of the horse's nature, and skillful riding he made a conquest of Bucephalus and kept him as his favorite mount for years.

His contemporaries were impressed with the fact that a man of so strong and commanding a disposition was not intemperate with wine or women, for his father was a roisterer, and his mother Olympias apparently was unconventional and of a fiercely hot temper. Perhaps Alexander's self-control in these two areas was partly a reaction against the occasional wild behavior of his parents.

At his father's death Alexander had two sets of difficulties to contend with. First, he had to gain the throne. Second, he had to handle the problems that other peoples would naturally create for Macedonia when they saw the redoubtable Philip replaced by a young man of twenty. Alexander's first moves to gain the throne were to make sure that the army would accept him, to put to death the very few conspirators against his father's life who had not already fled the country, and to rid himself of three competitors for the throne—a pair from another royal house who had some claim and his cousin Amyntas, the one whom his father had pushed aside as an infant. Alexander's excellent qualities were probably so well known that all the people recognized, as the generals did, that he was the best man for the throne, in addition to his claims as Philip's son.

The second set of difficulties occupied him for two years. First he went to Thessaly, where the anti-Macedonian party had gained control. A swift show of force without fighting gained him election as *tagus* of Thessaly, a position Philip had held. Then he moved southward into Greece, which was grumbling and disaffected, but not ready to unite and fight against him. The members of the League of Corinth sent representatives to Corinth at his call and elected him to his father's position of commander of the league's forces for a war against Persia.

In the spring of 335 he moved north against the Thracian tribes subject to Macedonia, who needed to be assured of the firmness of the new king, and defeated them. The Illyrians on his western border had to have a similar lesson. Then he had to go down into Greece once more, for the democratic exiles from Thebes had regained control of the city from the oligarchy that Philip had installed there and had driven the Macedonian garrison into the citadel. Other Greek states, including Athens, were preparing to help the democrats. Alexander made a lightning march, appeared before Thebes, and called upon the Thebans to honor their oath of allegiance to the League of Corinth. On their refusal he attacked the city, took it, and destroyed it except for the temples and the house of the poet Pindar. He sold the citizens into slavery and divided the territory of the city among the neighboring cities.

The War Against Persia: Asia Minor

In the spring of 334 Alexander set out for his great adventure in Persia, from which he was not to return. He left Antipater, an elderly and reliable general, in charge of Macedonia with troops enough to overawe the Greeks. Alexander also had hostages from the peoples of Greece in

the form of soldiers and sailors whom they had contributed to the expedition. Philip had sent the reliable general Parmenio into Asia Minor in
336, and even after Philip's death Parmenio had continued to hold a
bridgehead there that enabled Alexander to cross the Hellespont without
difficulty.

In his army there were over 30,000 infantry and over five thousand
cavalry. The flower of the army was the heavy cavalry, the first cavalry
force in history to be used as a striking arm rather than for scouting,
skirmishing, and pursuit, as cavalry generally had been used. A special
section of the cavalry, two thousand strong and drawn from the best families of Macedonia, was known as the Companions.

The famous Macedonian phalanx consisted of nine thousand men who
were known as the Foot Companions, hoplites of a specialized kind,
equipped with helmet, breastplate, greaves, and shield, and for offense
short swords and very long spears. The long spears seem to have been
specially fearsome to opposing soldiers. The nine thousand were divided
into tactical units of 256, or 16 square, which were drilled intensively, so
that even in the midst of battle they could change their shape, reverse
themselves, or divide to face and fight in two directions. This formidable
array of men was sometimes used to "fix" the enemy hoplites, or hold
them by its presence so that they did not dare to maneuver or change formation while they were attacked on the wings by the formidable Macedonian cavalry. Macedonia also provided a special body of three thousand
heavy infantry, drawn from the upper classes and known as the hypaspists.

In addition to a fleet of 160 ships, the League of Corinth contributed
seven thousand hoplites. Five thousand Greek mercenaries had been enrolled. Six thousand light-armed soldiers, of whom one thousand were
Cretan archers, completed the army proper. Alexander's force also included a siege corps that could build towers on rollers or on wheels tall
enough to top the ordinary city wall, and catapults that could fire large
arrows accurately for two hundred yards or throw stones of fifty or sixty
pounds for the same distance. This corps could also build pontoon bridges.

Alexander's whole force was engaged on only a few occasions; most of
his battles were small ones. Even in the small battles, however, all
branches of the army were represented and used in combination. Alexander's dashing manner and glamor have sometimes obscured the fact that
he was so practical and a master of detail. Not only did he combine his
different kinds of soldiers as no one before him had done, except perhaps
Dionysius I of Syracuse, but he also insisted on and received excellent
performance from his quartermaster's corps and from those at home who
enrolled and forwarded his reinforcements.

Alexander's intellectual interests are reflected by his remarkable entourage of noncombatants. A surveying corps recorded the distance of

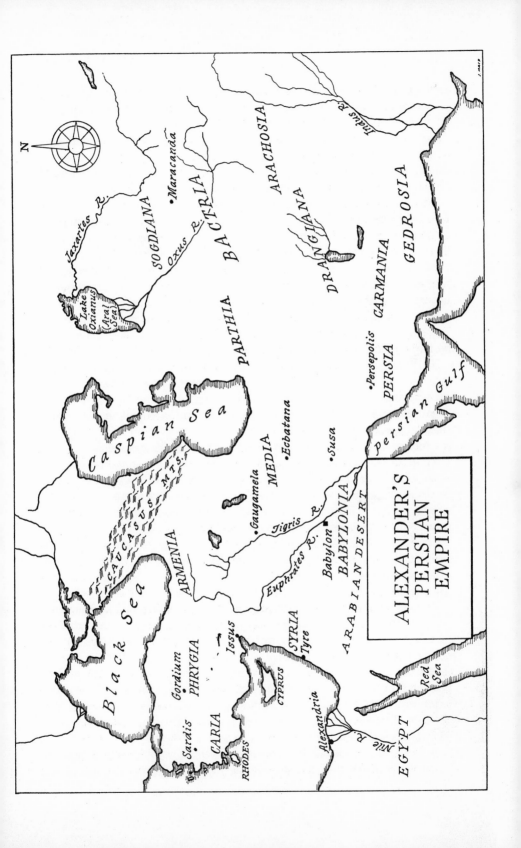

ALEXANDER'S
PERSIAN
EMPIRE

each march and collected data on the geography of each region. The
secretarial division kept a running record of the events of each day. Two
or three historians apparently were expected to produce at some future
time an artistic account of the campaign; no one could know that most
future accounts would actually be based on the private journal of Ptolemy,
one of the generals. There was a small group of biologists and botanists,
one of whose functions was to send specimens back to Aristotle.

The Persians had no heavy infantry of their own that could match the
Greek hoplite or the phalanx of Alexander, although there were perhaps
20,000 Greek hoplites employed by them in various parts of the empire.
Their heavy cavalry was plentiful and useful. The Persian archers were
good. The chief Persian mistake was that in spite of the arrival of the
first detachment in 336 they did not take the Macedonian threat seriously
enough to gather a major army to oppose it. Another mistake was to
reject the recommendation of a high officer that they retreat before the
Macedonians, removing all supplies as they went, and wear them down
by harrying them informally. Such tactics seemed beneath Persian dignity.

The Persians of Asia Minor opposed Alexander at the Granicus River
in 334, soon after his landing. The Macedonians won the battle, killing
many of the Greeks on the Persian side and capturing two thousand of
them, whom Alexander sent as slaves to labor in Macedonia on the ground
that they were traitors to the league. He reported the victory as won by
the forces of the league under himself as the league's general.

To take the Greek cities subject to the Persians along the coast of
Asia Minor was not difficult, for they were governed by Greek tyrants
or Greek oligarchies who were overthrown by the democrats of each city
as soon as the word got around that Alexander would favor democracies,
so that he had almost no fighting to do there.

His strategy at this point has other interesting elements beside his
support of democracy. He showed signs of moving away from the policy
of acting as head of the league. For instance, he now began to take into
his own service, not that of the league, the Greek mercenaries whom he
was able to capture. More striking is the disbanding of his fleet, even
while the Persians had an active fleet on the sea and were trying by means
of subsidies to raise Greece against him. His judgment that Greece could
not be so raised proved correct. He did not need to fear that the Persian
fleet could stop the transportation of his reinforcements across the Hellespont, for so tight a blockade was not possible. He knew that he could
count on the defection of many units of the Persian fleet that were supplied by the Greek cities of the coast, for when the news got around that
their cities had gone over to Alexander and had democratic governments,
the rowers of the ships, who were of the people, would simply slip away
from the fleet and take the ships home. He looked forward to capturing

the remaining bases on the Phoenician coast, which he was in fact able to do in the following year, 332 B.C., thus ending the activity of the hostile fleet entirely. His judgment that he could himself get along without a fleet was correct. Further, he was very short of money and could hardly pay for the upkeep of one.

The interior of Asia Minor seemed likely to yield him money. He could hardly demand from the Greek cities of the coast the tribute that they had been used to paying to the Persians, but inland in Asia Minor the natives paid rent to the king for their lands. He moved through the interior, and as he conquered it, sometimes by rather sharp fighting, he put Macedonian officers in as governors and trustworthy men in charge of collecting rents.

His long swing through Asia Minor brought him to Gordium, the old capital of the Phrygian kings and still an important center of communications. Here, as the story goes, he was shown the chariot of the original king of the Phrygians. On the pole of the chariot was tied a knot that showed no end, and, according to the local story, the man who could untie it was promised rule over all Asia. In spite of its being proverbial that Alexander slashed through the knot with his sword, the other story is rather more in character, that he simply took out the pin that held the pole and slipped the knot off the end of the pole, for his disposition was serious and he did not care for puzzles and games.

Presently he felt that he had done what he could afford to do in the interior of Asia Minor and came down through the Cilician Gates, a pass at the angle where the southern coast of Asia Minor joins the north-south coast of Syria. His purpose was to find the army of the king and fight a decisive battle. Darius's army was near, but somehow Alexander passed it and left it in his rear. Then, learning at last where it was, he turned back and met it at Issus in October, 333 B.C.

The inadequate infantry of the Persians could not stand up to the Macedonians, nor could even their archers, but their Greek mercenaries gave the Macedonians a good fight. Darius himself fled ingloriously as soon as he saw part of his line yield to a charge headed by Alexander. Although he captured the money that the king had brought for the campaign, thereby solving his immediate financial problem, Alexander was not able to capture the person of the king. The Macedonians won the battle and inflicted fairly heavy losses on the Persians. Some of the Greek mercenaries in the Persian service were able to rejoin Darius a little later; a group of eight thousand others decided to leave his service and went off to fight for other masters in Egypt and then in Greece.

After the victory Alexander decided to eat the dinner ready to be served in the luxurious tent of Darius. "So this is being a king," he remarked reflectively; he may well have been genuinely impressed. Presently he heard the weeping of women and was told that the mother, wife, and two daughters of Darius had been captured and were wailing for their lost lord. He sent to tell the royal ladies that Darius was alive and uncaptured, and thereafter he treated them with courtesy and consideration.

The Campaigns in Phoenicia and Egypt

Alexander had now fulfilled the original purpose of the war, to capture and hold the rich territory of Asia Minor, and had in addition defeated a Persian army just outside Asia Minor at Issus. His successes naturally changed his point of view somewhat. In addition, he presently received a letter from Darius asking for the release of the ladies of his family as a piece of royal courtesy and offering Alexander his friendship and alliance. Alexander sent him in return a statement of the grievances and the aims of the League. This, he told Darius, was a war of revenge for Xerxes' invasion of Macedonia and Greece. Both Macedonia and the league had more recent grievances, too, for the Persians had committed many warlike acts against them and had given aid and comfort to their enemies. He also accused the Persians of having caused the murder of his father. He said in conclusion that he regarded himself as the king of all Asia (although he did not publicly make this claim and act on it until after the final defeat and subsequent death of Darius) and that Darius must ask him as a vassal for what he might desire.

He went on with the conquest of Phoenicia, which he had begun before receiving the letter. Although most of the cities submitted to him readily, the siege and capture of Tyre took seven months. This was the last base for the Persian fleet, and before the siege was over that fleet had disbanded. Tyre was on an island two miles in circumference and half a mile from the mainland, and the chief part of the siege was the building of a causeway out to it so that it could be assaulted as if on land. It was captured in July, 332 B.C.

Ambassadors from Darius came to Alexander while he was busy at Tyre. The King sought again to make peace and secure a treaty of alliance by offering ten thousand talents, the cession of all territory west of the Euphrates, and a daughter to marry Alexander. Alexander is said to have called a conference of his generals and laid the proposal before them. Parmenio, the most distinguished of them, said that if he were Alexander, he would accept the proposal, to which Alexander replied that if he were Parmenio, he would accept it. The story will serve to represent the caution and limited horizon of the older Macedonians and their lack of interest in the further possibilities of adventure, gain, and accompanying danger. Alexander replied to Darius that he would not consider any proposal.

After the capture of Tyre Alexander turned toward Egypt and reached it late in the year 332. The Persian satrap of Egypt yielded at once, for his troops were few and poor compared to the invading army, and the people would plainly be glad to be in Alexander's hands rather than those of the Persians. He went through all the ceremonies necessary to symbolize his taking of the position of Pharaoh. He founded Alexandria, the city that has borne his name ever since. He was to found more than a dozen other Alexandrias when he got to Asia, none of them so successful as this one was.

It was highly politic for him to make the long trip to the desert oasis where the famous shrine of the Egyptian god Amun gave oracles that ranked with those of Delphi. Some scholars have conjectured that this was the beginning of a belief on Alexander's part that he had a certain divinity, especially because he is reported to have said that the priest addressed him as the son of Amun. The priest was only being correct; he would naturally use that name in speaking to the Pharaoh, who was officially regarded as the son of Amun-Re. Alexander found it politic later, after his complete victory over Darius, to receive the honors, some of them semidivine, traditionally offered to a Persian king. He even sent requests to the Greek states to give honors to him as to a god. He himself conceived of the idea as nothing other than a useful piece of political management.

Victory

After leaving Egypt Alexander went in pursuit of the main armed forces of the Persians. The battle that finally broke the power of Darius began on the first of October, 331 B.C., at Gaugamela, past the Tigris and in the home territory of Persia. Although the Persians could not form a seasoned army fit to meet Alexander's, they did the best they could by forming a corps of the scythed chariots that they had not used for a long time, hoping that they might thus be able to break the phalanx. Although the battle was in the end a great victory for Alexander, it was not a rout of cowardly Orientals, but a long and bitterly fought affair from which many of the Persians withdrew at last in good order and unpursued.

The Persians had chosen a flat place where they thought that the scythed chariots could be used to good advantage, and Alexander was willing to meet them on their own ground. The battle was begun by the cavalry, each side sending in more and more for a determined struggle. Then the chariots charged, but Alexander's light-armed men brought down many of the horses with arrows and javelins as they came, and the heavy infantry, or hypaspists, whom the chariots attacked first, skill-fully opened lanes for them and destroyed them as they drove through. The cavalry of the Persian left wing tended a little more to the left as they struggled with the Greeks, and the other Persians drifted over to give their left more support. Alexander charged the thinner place thus created in their line, and so broke through, and again Darius fled, as he had at Issus.

The battle was far from won, however, for the Persian right had pressed the Macedonian left so hard that Parmenio called for help, and Alexander turned back from the pursuit to help him. A large group of the Persian cavalry had also broken through the Macedonian line as part of it moved forward to charge the Persian line. Finally they were driven off and the left under Parmenio drove off the Persians who had pressed it so hard. Alexander was off again in pursuit of Darius and those with him. After it became dark, he and his men rested until midnight, then went on until in the morning they reached Arbela, more than sixty miles away, where they gave up the pursuit. Darius' two thousand Greek mercenaries had retired from the field in good order, as had the bulk of the Persian forces. The victory was nevertheless decisive, for the Persians did not attempt to put another major army in the field against Alexander.

Alexander marched southward for over two hundred miles, then crossed the Tigris westward into Mesopotamia and went over to Babylon, on the Euphrates. Here the commander of the Persian right wing at Gaugamela came out to surrender to him. Alexander made him governor of this dis-trict, the first Persian to be appointed to an administrative position, al-though Egyptians had been left at the head of the administrative system of their country. The Persian was to have two Macedonian associates in charge of the army and finance, however. The people of Babylon wel-comed Alexander, who gave the inhabitants the right to follow all their native customs.

The army then moved southward into Persis, the original territory of the Persians, where the troops of the local satraps put up the resistance that duty required. Alexander took the royal cities of Susa, Pasargadae, and Persepolis. Again he chose Persians as civil administrators of districts based on the former satrapies, giving them Macedonian colleagues to watch over the military and financial tasks. He deliberately burned the palace at Persepolis, the original royal city of the Persians, not as a crude act of vandalism, but as a symbol of the end of Persian power.

In the royal treasuries of the three cities he found gold and silver coin and bullion worth about 180,000 talents, as well as gold and silver plate and purple dye. He put a large part of the coin and bullion into circula-tion, largely by the making of lavish gifts to his officers and soldiers. It is impossible today to assign a purchasing power to the royal treasure or to compare it in amount to the money already circulating, although we do know that subsistence farming and home manufacture were so common that the number of wants supplied by the payment of money was so much smaller than it is now that the effect of putting much new precious metal into circulation must have been very great. Our evidence, scanty as it is, suggests that there was a general rise in the level of prices.

Darius was still at liberty in Ecbatana, the old capital of the Medes. In March, 330 B.C., Alexander started north from Persepolis. At his approach Darius fled eastward to Bactria, allowing Alexander to occupy Ecbatana without a struggle. Here Alexander dismissed the troops that the League of Corinth had sent for the expedition. They could re-enlist if they wished, but in the forces of the king of Macedonia, Egypt, and Persia, not in the expeditionary force of the League of Corinth. This gesture made it plain that Alexander felt that the panhellenic war of revenge on the Persians was over and that he was monarch of all the territory that had been taken.

At this time, too, he began to wear Persian dress on some occasions. Presumably he was revolving in his mind methods of bringing the Greeks and the Persians together and thought it advisable sometimes to adopt the behavior of a Persian. The Macedonians were not pleased, for they could not see beyond the simple idea of conquering the Persians and lording it over their rich country.

In the middle of the summer Alexander, hearing that Darius was collecting a new army in Bactria, decided to forestall him. He moved swiftly eastward and presently heard that the satraps of the East had foresworn their allegiance to Darius and made him a captive. Alexander took a small force and raced after them. At his approach they stabbed Darius and fled, so that Alexander captured only his body. He was saved embarrassment by not having to deal with Darius living. Now the only hindrance to his claiming to hold the throne of Persia in the fullest sense was that he had not marched through the eastern territories.

Alexander in the East

Most of Alexander's high officers were men of noble blood and some could even claim royal blood. Naturally they liked the old Macedonian idea that the king was chief among peers and resented the clear signs that Alexander proposed to stand alone above all other men. They might have admitted that this attitude was best for a Persian king, but they found difficulty in understanding Alexander's growing intention of ruling Persia as one responsible for the welfare of all his subjects, not merely the conquering Macedonians. A tangible point of difference of opinion was his attempt to introduce among them the Persian custom of *proskynesis*, or prostrating one's self before the king. Among the Persians it was only a sign of deep respect, but among the Greeks a man prostrated himself only before a god. Some Macedonians merely laughed at the idea, while others resisted and argued. Although he agreed to confine this practice to Asiatics, Alexander was deeply annoyed that he could not gain the cooperation of his high officers in the matter.

He was to have worse troubles with his officers. Philotas, son of Parmenio, commanded the Companion cavalry. In the autumn of 330 a conspiracy against the life of Alexander was reported to him, but he said nothing and took no action. The news of the conspiracy reached Alexander by another route, and he crushed it. Philotas and two others were tried for treason in the old-fashioned way, before the army. Philotas was found guilty and executed, and the other two were acquitted. Alexander then bowed to the hard necessity of government and sent messengers to kill Parmenio, the father of Philotas, who had been left in charge of the troops in Persia proper, for by the code of the time the death of his son left Parmenio no alternative to rebellion.

Eastward in Samarcand came another incident in 328 that was less dangerous but dramatically illustrative of the tensions. Probably all the company had drunk too much. Cleitus, a dear friend of Alexander, who had saved his life in the thick of the battle at the Granicus River, fell to taunting him during the evening, comparing his present attitudes to those of his father Philip and reminding him that the Macedonians from whom he was now withdrawing himself had by their strength and valor brought him to his exalted position. In spite of Alexander's attempts at self-control and the attempts of others to quiet Cleitus, the matter proceeded to the point where Alexander killed his friend with a javelin. For three days he was beside himself with remorse and raged up and down his tent without eating.

Meanwhile his expedition fought its way slowly through a part of the Persian Empire that refused to accept the decision of Gaugamela. Bactria and Sogdiana were rich territories, fertile and mostly well watered. Alexander saw the northern part of modern Iran, northern Afghanistan, and the southern part of the Soviet republics of Turkmen, Uzbek, and Tadzhik. Much of the years 329 and 328 was spent in fighting in this region.

By now he was regularly using Asiatics in his army. This policy was in accord with his political strategy of cooperation between the Greeks and the local peoples, although he also needed more men than his steady reinforcements from home could supply, for many were lost in the fighting and many were needed for garrisons, new cities, and military colonies. For political reasons, too, he married a beautiful Bactrian girl named Roxane. He founded military colonies in this region rather than the poleis of the Greek type that he had founded in the more pacific parts of the

Persian realm. These colonies were composed of men still capable of active fighting. Although they had fortified centers and land enough to support the men, the military colonies did not have the complete civil and religious organization of the poleis.

India

Alexander apparently believed that India, just beyond the Indus River, was on the edge of the eastern ocean as well as being the farthest province of the Persian Empire. In 326 he reached the Indus. There he was greeted by Taxiles, king of a large realm, with whom he made a treaty of peace and alliance. Then he marched eastward to the Hydaspes River, on the other side of which was the rich kingdom ruled by Porus, against whom he fought the most difficult of all his battles, especially because of Porus' use of elephants. He left both these kings in charge of their respective kingdoms, demanding only a nominal acknowledgment of his suzerainty.

When the troops had marched another hundred miles to another river, their patience came to an end. They had willingly followed Alexander through incredible difficulties and over incredible distances, not troubling themselves overmuch about those considerations that had made their officers uneasy. Now they were shaken by their battle with Porus and by the thought that there might be more elephants to meet. Beside, the land of Asia seemed to stretch out indefinitely. They refused to go farther.

Alexander was bitterly disappointed, for he had counted on reaching the eastern ocean and establishing the eastern end of an empire that could be served by water. He had brought shipwrights to build a fleet in which the army was to sail back. He shut himself up in his tent and sulked a monumental sulk like that of Achilles, but the men had already walked 11,000 miles and they did not care whether the ocean was to be seen from the next hill. Alexander gave in.

Back to Babylon

Back at the Hydaspes River, on the edge of Porus' kingdom, Alexander had a fleet of ships built. Late in the year 326 the army started down along the banks of the river, while many men and the supplies traveled in the ships on the river. In the summer of 325 they reached its mouth, where Alexander founded a city as part of his prospective system of trade. Then the fleet set out to go up the Persian Gulf, while the army marched along the shore. In the spring of 324 he was at Susa.

On his return Alexander found that a number of his friends had betrayed his confidence by flagrant misbehavior in the posts where he had put them. They were put to death. He abolished the Persian coinage and decreed that all his empire should use the Attic system of coinage. He married one of the daughters of Darius (the Macedonians were polygamous) and persuaded eighty of his officers to marry noble Median and Persian women. Many of the common soldiers had already contracted marriages with native women. Furthermore, Alexander had earlier ordered that a group of 30,000 native youths should learn Greek and be trained in the Macedonian fashion for military service; they were now enrolled in the army.

When he proposed to send home ten thousand veterans, all his old soldiers mutinied. He discharged them all, saying that he would use a Persian army if he was to be abandoned far from home by his Macedonians. A great reconciliation scene followed. He then organized a huge banquet both for his officers and for leading men of every sort from the new empire. Nine thousand persons took part in a libation, or ceremony of pouring out a little wine for the gods before drinking. All had drawn their wine from a huge mixing bowl, and he prayed that he might unite them all as if he had mixed their lives like the wine. This prayer of Alexander's is generally taken to be the first expression of the idea of the brotherhood of man, an idea that has made only modest and irregular progress in the years since.

In 323 he went to Babylon and settled down to hard work on the many plans for his empire, but he was not to be able to watch over the empire and try to govern it in accordance with his own ideas or even try to work for their acceptance. He died of a fever in June, 323 B.C.

THE HELLENISTIC AGE

The period from the death of Alexander in 323 B.C. to the death in 30 B.C. of Cleopatra, queen of Egypt, and the appropriation of her kingdom by the Romans is generally known as the Hellenistic Age. The death of Alexander does mark the beginning of a new time in the Mediterranean world, for he was no longer present to apply his great powers to organizing the realm that he had conquered. However, the movement toward the hellenization of the former Persian Empire was widened and systematized and became the chief feature of the three following centuries. The death of Cleopatra and the inclusion of Egypt in the Roman Empire was the passing of the last of the monarchs of the Hellenistic kingdoms into which Alexander's realm was divided and the end of the last of the kingdoms. Henceforth Rome was to rule the whole Mediterranean world, and another period had arrived, that of the Roman Empire.

The Romans are now waiting in the wings, and as soon as a brief description has been given of the formation of the Hellenistic kingdoms after Alexander's death, they shall have the center of the stage and we shall see them develop to the point where, in 200 B.C., they dominated the whole West and presently turned to conquest in Greece and the East. From that point on we shall consider the Mediterranean world as a whole, describing first the gradual Roman conquest of the eastern part during the last two centuries of the Roman Republic (which nearly coincide with the last two centuries B.C.), then the management and culture of this large and varied area for more than five centuries under the Roman Empire.

After Alexander's Death: Attempts to Preserve the Empire

The Macedonian generals and soldiers were in firm control of Macedonia and of the newly conquered empire; the wishes of others were not taken into account. At first some of the powerful men attempted to preserve the unity of the empire for which they all fought under Alexander. One way of doing so was to join in loyalty to a king. Alexander had a half brother, Philip Arrhidaeus, a young man of no qualifications except that of descent from the Macedonian kings. Alexander's wife, the beautiful Roxane, whom he had married as part of his plans to unite the peoples of his new realm, was expected to be delivered of a baby soon.

Such attempts as were made to maintain the unity of the empire by the principle of succession came to nothing, for Philip and Roxane and her baby son all perished in the struggle among men who either aimed at power or conceived themselves to be protecting their persons and the territories in their charge. By ten years after the death of Alexander it was plain that the empire could be held together only by a combination of his former generals or the supremacy of one of them. One of them, Antigonus, attempted to impose his will on the others.

Antigonus, one of Alexander's father's generals, had been left by Alexander in control of Macedonia and of Phrygia, in Asia Minor, to control the supply lines. Despite his age, he attempted to enlarge his power and territory, provoking opposition from the other leading men—Lysimachus, who controlled Thrace and part of Asia Minor, Seleucus in the East, and Ptolemy in Egypt. All had by now proclaimed themselves kings as part of their measures for governing firmly in what they thought of as their permanent spheres. The attempts of Antigonus to dominate, which may be said to characterize a second stage after Alexander's death, were ended by a definitive battle at Ipsus, in Phrygia, in 301 B.C.

The next twenty years or so may be said to constitute a third period. Lysimachus ruled a strong kingdom in Thrace and Asia Minor until he was defeated by Seleucus, who thus had control of practically all the original Persian possessions. During this period a series of contests for the control of Macedonia and Greece was sharply punctuated by a succession of raids by groups of the Celtic people whom the Greeks called *Galatoi* and the Romans knew as *Galli,* or Gauls. In 279 B.C. a large body of them raided Macedonia and plundered without trying to settle down. A horde of many thousands came as far into Greece as Delphi before being driven back by the Aetolians. Still others crossed into Asia Minor, where they did some damage, but were finally settled in a part of Phrygia which took its name of Galatia from them.

The Balance of Power: Egypt

After 275 B.C. the three leading kings, Antigonus in Macedonia, Ptolemy II in Egypt, and Antiochus the son of Seleucus in what is generally called the Seleucid kingdom in default of any other name for the large territory, seem not to have had any further idea that one of them might conquer the others, but to have based their policy on a balance of power among their three kingdoms. A fourth period, that of this balance of power, lasted until the beginning of Roman interference just after 200 B.C.

The Ptolemies had the wealthiest and most powerful kingdom of the three. They controlled the rich valley of the Nile, profitable trade routes into central Africa, and others down the Red Sea. For the sake of their safety in international competition as well as for trade, they tried to be strong on the Aegaean Sea. Earlier, at a time when Seleucus was very weak, the first Ptolemy had helped him against Antigonus and had at that time taken possession of Palestine and Syria for the sake of their important old Phoenician seaports. Egypt was safer if she could control these ports, their immediate hinterland, their pool of trained seamen, and their timber for shipbuilding.

Naturally the Seleucids claimed Palestine and Syria as properly part of their territory; they also felt the need to keep doors open to the Aegaean by either possessing these ports or by having free access to them. They fought Egypt more than once for these reasons. The Macedonians likewise felt that complete Egyptian control of the Aegaean would be contrary to their interests, both because they needed to import food from the Black Sea region and because other parts of their vital communications were by sea, but they impressed Egypt and the Seleucids more by the threat of force than by the actual use of it.

The reigns of Ptolemy I, which lasted until his death in 283 B.C., and that of his son Ptolemy II Philadelphus, which lasted until 246, were the best period of the three centuries of Ptolemaic control of Egypt. No small part of the success of Ptolemy II was due to his putting away his wife and marrying his sister Arsinoë, a woman of force and ability. Her most spectacular feat was the management of Egypt's war in Syria against the

Seleucids; her energy and sound measures brought the languishing conflict to a successful end. She may have furnished the broad plan that led Egypt in 273 to make an arrangement with Rome, of which we are poorly informed, but that resulted in parallel series of silver coins in Egypt and Rome and may well mean that Egypt was furnishing silver to the Romans and had an agreement with Rome for Egyptian trade privileges in Rome's sphere, especially to get iron from Etruria, which had just come under Roman control. Arsinoë's marriage to her brother may well have been the means of endowing her with formal powers adequate to allow her to act in matters of state.

Alexandria served as headquarters of the royal administration, as the chief commercial center of the kingdom, and as a show place to glorify the kings. The city was laid out on a regular plan with wide streets forming a grid. The palace and administrative buildings and the chief storehouses formed a group of large and handsome buildings that helped to make the city very different from such older places as Athens. The temples, the spacious gardens, the quarters of the great scholarly institute founded by the first two Ptolemies, and the tomb built to receive the body of Alexander added to the beauty and impressiveness of the city. There were a gymnasium, a stadium, and a hippodrome for horse races. The city had a double harbor; there was also a river harbor on Lake Mareotis, connected with the Nile. On the island of Pharos, which the kings connected to the mainland by a mole, stood the lighthouse, nearly four hundred feet high, with a place at its top for a fire of resinous wood.

Macedonia

The Macedonian kings of this period had as the center of their power the old Macedonia, which had fertile soil, gold mines, and a strong peasant population with some sense of unity. The story of their relations with Greece is very different in tone from the story of the relations in the sixth, fifth, and fourth centuries. The political and military power of Athens was ended permanently as a result of her joining Ptolemy II in an unsuccessful war of several years against the Macedonian king. Sparta was now only one of the several minor powers found in the Peloponnesus.

New powers and constellations of power appeared on the scene. The kingdom of Epirus, in northwest Greece, came to seem more a recognizable entity and less a mass of barbarians always ready to trouble the west flank of Macedonia. The Aetolians gradually gained control of most of Greece just north of the Gulf of Corinth, including Delphi. They had a large part in defending central Greece from the invading Celts. They were recognized by the other peoples of Greece and could even gain diplomatic recognition from Egypt and Rome as a power in world affairs.

They had no great achievement in the cultural sphere; like the majority of Greeks, they consumed the material and spiritual products of the few great producing Greeks. Their cooperation with the Achaean League made a combination of forces in Greece almost equal to the power of the Macedonians, whom they opposed successfully in active war just after the middle of the third century.

The Achaean League, formed in the fourth century, was powerful in the later third century. It gained control of Corinth, which the Macedonians had long held as a strong point for the control of the Peloponnesus, and persuaded many cities to join. The league might have controlled all the Peloponnesus but for the old traditions of the Spartans, which made them unwilling to join a league that they could not control, and the energy of the king of Sparta, Cleomenes.

In 235 B.C. Cleomenes seized and nationalized all the land of Sparta. As we have seen, many of the full citizens of Sparta alienated their land and thus lost their full citizen rights. Cleomenes presumably thought that he was restoring the constitution of Lycurgus and rebuilding the power of Sparta by assigning much land to the support of men who would live the military life, as in the old days. His move may have seemed to many people in Greece, as it might to us, a redistribution of the land on equitable principles and for the benefit of all. As he took the next step in his program, which was to eliminate Macedonian power and establish Spartan hegemony in the Peloponnesus, the poorer people in many of the cities of the Achaean League and elsewhere were ready to go over to him. The result was that an Achaean leader, fearing the rise of the poor, gave the Macedonians control of Corinth again, and they defeated Cleomenes at Sellasia in 222 B.C.

In 221 B.C. Philip V came to the throne of Macedonia. In the same year Ptolemy IV became king of Egypt. In 223 Antiochus III had become king of the Seleucid kingdom. The Greek Polybius, whom we shall discuss later, took the accession of these three kings as the starting point of the history that he wrote to explain to his fellow Greeks the rapid rise of the Romans in the Mediterranean world. We shall see that Philip V and Antiochus, both able men, were to engage in great struggles with the Romans. Ptolemy IV and his successors did not fight with the Romans, with the result that Egypt was the last of the three kingdoms to come under direct Roman domination.

The Seleucid Kingdom

We know only the broad outlines of the political history of the Seleucid kingdom during the third and second centuries. It was a large kingdom, claiming, if it could not entirely control, Syria and Mesopotamia and regions beyond the Tigris as far as India that the Persians had once controlled in a loose way. The kings were kept very busy by contests with their neighbors, in trying to hold some of the sections that attempted to assert their independence, and in struggles for the throne within the royal family. In the territory at the southern end of the Caspian Sea and just to the East a new power, the Parthians, began to arise around 250 B.C. and became an independent power that will appear later in our account of the dealings of the Romans with the peoples of the East. The Seleucid kings were generally named Seleucus or Antiochus. Antiochus III, who came to power in 223 B.C., was a strong monarch, but had the misfortune to come into conflict with the Romans. We shall tell his history and the further history of his kingdom in connection with Roman dealings with the Greek world.

CHAPTER

15

EARLY ITALY;

ROME'S NEIGHBORS AND RIVALS

The Romans often seem closer to us than do the Greeks and the earlier peoples of the Near East. Their nearness in time has helped to preserve more records of them and has allowed more of their buildings and roads and walls and aqueducts to survive in the inhabited places of the West. Italy, the home of republican Rome and the center of the Empire, is geographically closer to us, and much of the more Western and therefore nearer world as well—North Africa, the upper Danube, western Germany, Switzerland, France, Spain, the Low Countries, and England— was the scene of the history of imperial Rome. People living and working in these areas a few dozen generations ago can seem much less remote than people in the Near East.

The language, the way of thinking, and the set of values of the Romans, too, are much closer to ours. The Latin language is far more commonly known among us and seems less mysterious than the earlier languages even to those who have not studied Latin. Roman institutions are readily comprehensible to us. The careers of many of their great men are familiar to us and can serve as recognizable types for the study of human affairs.

Yet all these similarities must not make us forget how important the early peoples of the Near East and of Greece are in the background. Those peoples literally invented civilization as we know it. To them are due most of the great basic discoveries and inventions, as well as in- numerable minor techniques in every field from government to weaving. The Greeks reshaped many of the ideas and methods of the Eastern peo-

328

ples to produce a general style of thought and living that appealed strongly to the Romans and so passed into Western life and that still appeals when we go back to study it in its pre-Roman form.

The Romans grew from a small community occupying Rome and the small surrounding region of Latium to the ruling power of the Mediterranean world in an atmosphere created largely by these other peoples. As the administrators of a powerful republic and then of an empire they automatically drew on all the knowledge and techniques that the nations of the Near East and the Greeks still possessed. If Asia Minor, for example, ordinarily receives little mention when the framework of events and trends in Roman history is described, it was still a most important place in Roman times, for it was filled with old and cultivated cities and with people who played a useful part in manufacturing, trade, and the transmission of both abstract and practical ideas, and in the service of the Roman imperial government.

The Geography of Italy

The remoteness of the Italian peninsula from the older seats of civilization left the early peoples of Italy mostly untouched by the new ways until fairly late. Awareness of copper was slow in developing before 2000 B.C. It was well after 1000 B.C. that any considerable number of people resident in the peninsula could be said to be abreast of the times by the standards of the older civilizations of the Near East—in this case, enjoying the benefits of the Iron Age.

In the earliest times Italy was connected (we think) with Africa by land, but the land bridge sank many thousands of years before Christ, leaving Sicily as a remainder. When the Romans had finally brought all Italy under their control and had prevailed in their series of struggles with Carthage, it became plain that Italy was well placed for domination of the lands of the western Mediterranean, for the projection of the peninsula into the Mediterranean, augmented by Sicily, makes the great sea so narrow that it can be patrolled here fairly readily by ships.

The continental part of Italy, the most northern part, was a rich possession, for its soil was richer than that of most Mediterranean lands and was well watered. The Alps, which bound this territory on the North, formidable as they may seem, were not enough a barrier to prevent the arrival of new peoples in early times.

The Apennines seem to form the backbone of Italy. They are nearer the east coast than the western one and make the eastern side of Italy too steep and broken to be highly prosperous or to develop large cities. They slope more gently toward the west. Grapes and olives can prosper on such hills, and where the slopes are too steep or the soil is too thin, sheep can be given their summer pasture to spare them the heat and the dryness of the lowlands.

The long coastline has almost no good deep-water harbors. The ancient ship, however, could operate in fairly shallow water, and the goods carried were often such—pig iron, jars of oil, small luxury objects—that they could be loaded or unloaded in convenient units with the aid of small boats.

Italy as a whole seemed a rich country to the Romans when they came to compare it systematically with other countries. Crops of all sorts grow well there. In ancient times there were magnificent forests that were treated with the usual recklessness and with no systematic replacement, so that the topsoil was not held on the hills and was washed away.

Italy has fairly good supplies of ordinary building stone. The quarries of Carrara, in the North, supplied much fine marble for the buildings of the Empire. The structures of the late Republic or of the Empire are now well weathered, but still solid. Many a more modern structure in Rome was largely built of materials from ancient structures, as the Palazzo Farnese is built of stone from the Colosseum. The presence of clay suitable for bricks was an excellent asset, too, as was the presence of the cement with which the Romans made their wonderful concrete. Everywhere in Italy one can see the bricks of ancient times, which usually have lasted as well as the quarried stones.

Italy was not rich in metals. The region that was known as Etruria and now is Tuscany had a fair amount of iron and copper, with some lead and tin, and the island of Ilva, modern Elba, supplied a considerable amount of iron, much of which was worked in the city of Populonia, nearby on the mainland, down to the beginning of the Christian era.

The Early Peoples of Italy

Between about 2500 and 2000 B.C. the Neolithic dwellers in Italy were introduced to copper. The presence of a limited number of copper implements probably did little to modify the simple life of these people, who were general farmers keeping a few animals and grouped in small villages. Presumably their life was like that of average people of the time even in the Near East. Around 2000 B.C. and later, villages of lake dwellings appeared in North Italy; the new people probably came down from central Europe. They made very good stone implements, imported copper ones from Hungary and Bohemia, and eventually began to have the superior bronze tools of the type that was developed in Bohemia.

Somewhere around 1600 B.C. a new group of people appeared, known

CENTRAL ITALY
500-400 B.C.

to archaeologists as the Terramara (black earth) people from the name given locally to the mounds from which the evidence of their way of living was excavated. They used bronze. They burned their dead and buried them in urns of an interesting shape in formal cemeteries outside their towns. Such a cultural trait is welcome to the archaeologist, for it offers a way of distinguishing a people from those who simply bury their dead. This trait seems to coincide with others, like language, to indicate that during the Bronze Age and after 1000 in the early Iron Age there was a certain division between the peoples resident in Italy.

If a line be drawn on the map straight northward from Rome, it will touch the *eastern* coast of Italy near the mouth of the Po River. On the west side of the line were people who burned their dead and spoke languages not of the Indo-European group, and on the east side were people who buried their dead and spoke languages that were of the Indo-European group, so that the classification of societies by the criterion of incineration or inhumation of the dead coincides roughly with their classification by the criterion of language.

The Bronze Age culture on the west side of the line—the incinerating and non-Indo-European-speaking side—seems to have lasted to just beyond 1000 B.C. The arrival of the Iron Age seems to have been caused by the slow importation of iron articles and technical knowledge from central Europe rather than by the mass arrival of new people. Unfortunately archaeological finds cannot furnish us with information for even a fairly exact reconstruction of this considerable stretch of history, in which this group of peoples, not joined by any large new group, but probably with some infiltration of individuals and small groups, moved from the age of copper through the age of bronze to the age of iron.

If we now return to the Bronze Age to consider the inhabitants on the eastern side of our imaginary line on the map, we find that we are dealing with several peoples who seem to have entered Italy from the East sometime before 1000 B.C., perhaps as early as 1500 B.C. They may have come from Illyria, in the western part of the Balkan Peninsula, or from farther east. A certain kinship among them is attested by the similarity of their languages, which belong to the Indo-European group. One language, Latin, became so important politically with the rise of the Romans that the others went out of use for writing or for commemorative inscriptions and even ceased to be spoken.

The Latins—the division to which the Romans belonged—were a fairly small group that may have appeared on the Italian scene as late as 1000 B.C. and gradually moved or was pushed into the coastal region of the lower course of the Tiber, where the city of Rome was to be. Another important group was the Umbro-Sabellians, who occupied the mountainous regions of Central Italy. In later times the Romans had a long struggle with the southern group of them, known as the Samnites.

ROME'S RIVALS

Although the early history of Rome is one of continual struggle, most of the peoples of Italy whom she finally overcame and incorporated into her federation can hardly be called rivals in the sense that they, like the Romans, might have been capable of leadership among the nations. There were four peoples of early times, however, who can properly be called rivals of the Romans: the Celts, the Carthaginians, the Etruscans, and the western Greeks.

The Celts

Herodotus could speak of the Celts as a people well known to the Greeks, and in the fourth century the historian Ephorus called them one of the four great barbarian peoples of the world—the Celts, the Scythians, the Persians, and the Libyans. Archaeology suggests, however that it was around 1000 or 900 B.C. that they began to be a recognizable group, for their artisans were skillful and original, so that their work early began to have a style of its own that serves as a cultural trait that can be used to identify Celtic materials. There is plenty of later testimony that they were thought to have a characteristic appearance—tall, blond, fierce— that marked them off as a group. They began, too, to have a distinctive language of their own, the ancient form of which does not exist in any piece of connected writing, but is displayed in the names of many people and places and the names of many objects of common use in Gaul that are mentioned by the Romans.

By the seventh and sixth centuries the Celts were enjoying an iron-using culture called Hallstatt from the place in Austria where the first notable excavation disclosed its nature. All the evidence of it comes from the burials of princes and leading men. They were using horses by that time as well as iron, and they buried their dead, unburnt, in an underground chamber, accompanied by some food and pottery, an iron sword, a spear, a wagon (sometimes dismantled), and gear for a riding horse. These rich burials, the oldest of which are in upper Austria, Bohemia, and Bavaria, moved across to the West, as if during the sixth century the princes and lords had migrated to Switzerland and the upper course of the Rhine and during the fifth century had gone a little farther, to the middle course of the Rhine and to the Moselle. By the fifth century, too, the tombs contained gold and two-wheeled chariots, both of which came in direct trade from the Etruscans of northern Italy.

In about 500 B.C. a new culture known as La Tène, again from an archaeological site, arose among the Celts and persisted until the late first century, when the political activities of the Celts finally failed and a cloud was cast on their artistic activities. Both Etruscan and Greek influences can be seen in their work, but they transformed what they took into their own idiom in an attractive way.

The Celts moved into the light of written history when, around 400 B.C., several tribes of them moved down to settle in northern Italy, the fertility of which they probably knew from traders who had gone to the Etruscans there. They took territory from the Etruscans and settled down to farming. Some decided to wander down into Italy, not once but several times, and we shall hear of their encounters with the Romans. Some entered the service of Dionysius of Syracuse as mercenaries. Some went farther east and settled just below the Danube. We have seen that a group went down into Greece in the early third century and was repulsed by the Aetolians and that another group settled in Asia Minor, becoming known there as the Galatians. Members of this group served widely as mercenaries in the Hellenistic armies.

The separated units of the Celts were conquered in detail by the Romans, who, in the late third century, fought a fierce war with the Celts, or Gauls, in Italy and later gave a thorough chastisement to the Galatians of Asia Minor. In the late Republic and early Empire they subdued all the peoples of the Alps and those below the Danube, many of whom were Celts. They conquered Spain, then Gaul, then Britain, in all of which a considerable number of Celts joined the Romans of necessity, generally turning out to be contented and useful Roman citizens.

Carthage

The Carthaginians came from Phoenicia to found Carthage a little before 700 B.C. Other Phoenicians had come earlier to settle Utica, Hadrumetum, and other places, but Carthage soon took the lead and made its power felt all over the western Mediterranean. The Romans spoke of them as *Poeni,* from which they derived the adjective "Punic," and as *Carthaginienses.*

The city was called Qart-Hadasht, or the "New City"; in Latin its name was *Carthago.* Its site, very near to that of modern Tunis, gave it a good agricultural hinterland and put it in position to patrol the narrowest part of the Mediterranean, that between Africa and Sicily, to enforce its demand that ships of other nations stay out of the western Mediterranean.

Ships entered its merchant harbor through a narrow passage that could be closed and found there facilities for hauling 220 ships out of the water for loading or unloading. There was a separate naval harbor with a great arsenal.

Aristotle and other writers on government classified Carthage as an aristocratic republic, comparing it with Sparta and Rome. It never had a tyrant. The two annually elected executive officers were called *shofet* (plural *shofetim,* in Latin *sufetes*). As in Athens, the people elected generals. The over-all guidance of the state was in the hands of a senate, and a council called the Hundred and Four had power to review and correct all acts, somewhat as did the Ephors at Sparta.

The empire skillfully built up by Carthage (outside her home territory, which roughly coincided with the modern Tunisia) was not large contiguous areas of land, but colonies and trading stations on the shores of the Mediterranean, usually with very little territory under their control. They ran all the way along the coast from east of Tripoli to the Atlantic. There were even some on the Atlantic coast; there is record that in about 500 B.C. an expedition went some distance down the coast, far enough to report seeing gorillas and hearing tom-toms.

The colonies and trading stations tended to be about a day's sail apart (most of the sites are known to us), for the ship of those days was hardly more at home in the water than the airplane is in the air and needed to be drawn up on land as much as possible so as not to become waterlogged (later techniques of pitching and calking improved this). The stations were often on islands near the shore or on capes, at the mouths of rivers, or at some other place where a route from the interior could easily reach the shore. Lepcis, for example, near Tripoli, was the sea terminus of a great caravan route from the interior that brought slaves and gold dust, ostrich feathers and ostrich eggs.

The Carthaginians had colonies and stations on the southern shores of Spain and made some slight progress toward conquering the interior, which was rich in metals. The northeastern coast of Spain, however, was dominated by the Greek colony of Massilia (Marseilles), as were the whole southern coast of France and part of the coast of Italy where it adjoins France. The Carthaginians dominated the Balearic Islands, Malta, and some of the smaller islands around Sicily and early established themselves in the western part of Sicily, probably in the late eighth and seventh centuries when the great age of Greek colonization was bringing many Greeks to the eastern end of Sicily and to southern Italy. Their relations with the Greeks have already been mentioned (see Chapter 12).

The hinterland of Carthage in Tunisia was fertile and was worked by slaves or sharecroppers on large capitalist estates. Their industry seems to have specialized on rather cheap, plain things that could be offered to the simple people who came to barter with the trade stations in the western Mediterranean, where Carthage had a monopoly of trade. Such goods—combs and mirrors, for example—were generally copied from those made in Phoenicia, Egypt, and Greece. They also manufactured amulets (for some protection of a magic sort was a necessity), jewelry, plain metal utensils, and glassware. The one luxury product was the gorgeous crimson dye generally known as Tyrian purple, made from a shellfish, the murex.

Commerce was the chosen field of the Carthaginians; theirs may be called a commercial state, since considerations of trade had great influence on public policy. Trade was the motive for their colonies, trading stations, and exploring expeditions. It was necessary to keep a strong navy in order to keep the western Mediterranean as a *mare clausum,* or closed sea; they also tried to repress piracy. There are surprisingly few clues about the merchandise they traded. They doubtless carried plain pottery for sale or barter. It is said that they carried wine, women, and cloth to the Balearic Islands to be exchanged for slaves. Ivory from the elephants of Africa was a luxury product that they could offer in the richer world of the eastern Mediterranean.

There is a pleasant story that the traders would sail to a certain point on the west coast of Africa, go ashore and set out an array of their goods, and withdraw to the ships. The local people would then come out of the woods, consider the wares set out for their inspection, and put beside them a quantity of gold. The Carthaginians then came ashore again, and if they found the gold enough, they would take it and leave, but if it were not enough, they would go back to the ship and wait, whereupon the customers would bring forth more gold.

Their ships went up to Cornwall for tin, which they knew how to use to make copper (presumably from Cyprus) into bronze. They probably also carried the tin around for sale. In Spain they could get silver and lead and esparto for ropes. At many of their stops they could pick up wild animal skins, hides of cattle, and wool.

We are not well informed about their culture. Their language, one of the Semitic group, is known from a considerable number of funerary inscriptions and from names, single words, and technical terms found in the Greek and Latin authors. There is no trace of art or literature, nor any sign of fine taste or originality in their manufactures. Their chief divinities were Baal, a common divinity among the Semites, and the lady Tanit, the queen of Heaven, and religion seems to have been a gloomy business of formal observances that were thought to placate the Unseen.

The Etruscans: Their Predecessors, the Villanovans

A new stage in life in Italy was initiated by the arrival, or perhaps the emergence, shortly after 1000 B.C. of an iron-using people whom archaeologists call the Villanovans from their interesting settlement at Villanova, near Bologna in northern Italy. Whether they came from more eastern regions or merely learned the new techniques of the Iron Age, their material remains give the impression that their life was very different from that of the Bronze Age peoples who preceded them in Italy. Besides using iron, they made larger and more complex settlements that verged on being true cities; their agriculture was carried on in a more expert way, as is shown by the remains of large farms and irrigation works still to be seen; they cremated their dead and buried the ashes in urns in cemeteries that the archaeologists call urnfields. Such urnfields are found in several parts of Europe. From Bologna they moved down the west side of the imaginary line of the last chapter so that the southernmost group was just north of Rome in the region that was soon to be known as Etruria and is now called Tuscany. They thus occupied the region formerly occupied by the Terramara people, and even more. The Villanovans may have been the Terramarans emerging into a new phase, although it seems rather more likely that they were new arrivals. It may also be that there never was a Villanovan community, but only the sharing of a few cultural traits, like the use of iron and burial in urnfields, among a fairly large number of people.

The three or four centuries—part of the tenth, the ninth, the eighth, and part of the seventh—in which the Villanovan civilization flourished were the centuries thought of as a Dark Age in Greece, and consequently little was exported from there to the Villanovans. Italy apparently also received a mere trickle of goods from the Near East until about 800. The graves now and then yield a scarab from Egypt, a bit of glass that suggests Phoenicia, or a sword of a type that hints a connection with the workshops of Greece. There are also traces of trade between Italy and Central Europe, like swords of a European type.

The evidence of objects deposited with the Villanovan dead suggests that trade from the Near East and Egypt to Italy increased after about 800, as it did to Greece and the islands. We do not know why. In the early part of the seventh century—about 675 B.C.—the eastern note became much more prominent among the articles placed in tombs, partly in articles that seem to have been imported, like faïence from Egypt, and partly in representations of things that seem to owe their shape or style to eastern patterns, like the hairdo of the women, the pose of standing or seated figures, the shape of objects. In a rough way this movement coincided with the surge of eastern influence in Greece. In Villanovan Italy both eastern articles and those produced in the reawakened Greece were in use. Some of the large tombs contain interesting combinations of the traditional local articles and motifs with those that were brought from the Near East (perhaps by Phoenician traders), with some from Greece in the new style affected by the Near East, and even with some made at home under the new foreign influence.

The Etruscans

By about 700 B.C. the traditional style in Italy and the styles of objects imported from Egypt and the Near East had merged into a new artistic mode that we know as the Etruscan. During the century that followed, from 700 to 600, we get some knowledge from other sources than art of the emergence of the Etruscans as a large group with rather more traits in common than the Villanovans had had—enough traits in common to justify us in calling them a people.

The obscurity of the early history of the Etruscans has caused a great deal of scholarly debate that has led to an increasingly clear statement of differing viewpoints rather than to agreement. The most widely held view has been that the Etruscans were an eastern people who came to Italy by sea; this is the opinion of most of the ancient authors who mention them. Their tombs are different from anything found in Italy before this time and resemble some tombs of Asia Minor. Their gay and by ancient standards elegant life, as shown in the striking frescoes found in the tombs, suggests the life of the Near East at that time rather than that of Italy as we conjecture it to have been. Their mysterious language, which is not Indo-European, has affinities with the language of an inscription found on the island of Lemnos. The sudden increase of Near Eastern imports and influence in Italy has been taken by some scholars to mean that a new people must have arrived, bringing new objects and the new style with them.

The opposite view, that the Etruscans were a fusion of peoples and practices in Italy, was held by one ancient authority and has found supporters among modern scholars. These scholars point to a development of Villanovan art toward the new style, which was therefore not necessarily borrowed from abroad. They also believe that Etruscan tomb styles were foreshadowed in Italy and were not a real break with tradition. If the new objects and style appear somewhat suddenly, this is only parallel to the history of their adoption in some of the Greek communities of Asia Minor, which were slow to get into the stream of intercourse with the Near East, then suddenly did so with vigor and enthusiasm. Emphasis is put on the undisputed fact that the Etruscans learned to write their still-mysterious language after their appearance in Italy; their writing, therefore, cannot be used to show that they were ever in Asia Minor.

It is quite possible that both views are right. There is no improbability in the idea that the peoples of Villanovan Italy—those on the western or non-Indo-European side of the imaginary line northward from Rome—gradually grew together in culture to some extent and were joined by one or even two fair-sized groups of immigrants from Asia Minor or the islands who had useful cultural traits to contribute to the life of the region. Such a large number of people could progressively take on a certain style and self-consciousness of its own, as the Etruscans appear to do when they come into full view. We always assume that the Greeks, who were a widely scattered people with many variations in character, formed themselves gradually into a group sharing enough cultural traits—especially liveliness, self-confidence, toughness, a common language, and a common religious outlook—to be called a people. The Etruscans, who were also highly gifted, may have done the same. Fortunately there is no need for the historian to settle the question of the origin of the Etruscans, for in spite of our inability to read those remains of their language that we have, we are fairly well informed on what they did and about their influence on the Romans, for there are many remarks about them in the Greek and Roman authors, with a goodly amount of archaeological evidence to help.

The Etruscans resembled the Greeks in being organized into city-states. It was not inevitable that the Etruscans should be so organized, for the form was novel in the newer part of the Mediterranean world, that is, the middle and western part. A tribal organization with no center that could be called a city was much more common in Italy, as it had been at one time in Greece, where it still existed. The Etruscan cities, like the Greek, were generally built on hilltops so as to be easy to defend. Each had a well defined territory of its own. Although some of the cities had kings, the kings were gradually reduced by the nobility to being simply members of the nobility or were driven away, as had been the case in Greece. Twelve Etruscan cities had a league that seems to have been formed largely for purposes of religion. Like the Greeks, the Etruscans could readily organize for worship and sometimes for practical ends, but did not unite either for aggression or defense at times when it would have been advantageous to do so. In the seventh century they gained control of a good deal of Campania, or Italy between Rome and Naples, apparently settling somewhat inland from the Greek cities on the coast of the Bay of Naples and just above; Capua was the most important of their cities.

Although the Etruscans were competent navigators and pirates, the Greeks of southern Italy were aggressive enough on the sea to make a land route of communication with Campania desirable, which the Etruscans gained by getting control of Rome about 600 b.c. and of the Latins in the neighborhood of Rome. The century of Etruscan domination that followed was of great importance in the history of Rome, although Etruscan customs appear to have had less effect on the Latins than on the Romans, whom they thoroughly schooled in the attitudes of a conquering people.

Late in the sixth century the Etruscans suffered serious reverses in southern Italy. In 524 b.c. they lost a battle under the walls of the Greek city of Cumae, near Naples, and in 504 they were defeated farther north. At about the same time the nobles of Rome ousted their Etruscan king, Tarquin, in the unostentatious way in which the nobles of the Greek city-states persuaded their kings to retire to private life; the traditional date was 509 b.c. At more or less the same time the Latins and other peoples, especially the Aequi and the Volsci, moved across the route from Etruria to Campania, completely blocking it to the Etruscans. The Etruscans did not try very hard to regain Campania, probably because they were engaged in a great effort farther north in the rich valley of the Po River, where they took possession of a large area and founded twelve cities to match those of Etruria. One of these, now known as Marzabotto, with its grid of streets and plans of temples and markets, is clearly the result of unified city planning. Bologna, which they called Felsina, was perhaps the chief city; Greek vases found there can be dated as early as 530 b.c. Spina, at the mouth of the Po on the Adriatic coast, also seems to have been built according to a master plan. Both Spina and Adria, another important settlement a little farther up the coast, had a number of Greek residents. There are traces in the remains of both of a trade with places farther north. This rich and lovely land was taken from the Etruscans by a great invasion of Celts around 400 b.c.

The Etruscans were a power on the sea to the west of Italy, which became known to the Greeks as the Tyrrhenian Sea from the name, Tyrrheni, that they used for the Etruscans. Their power and aggressiveness were such that the Greeks regarded them as pirates. In the year 535 the Etruscans and the Carthaginians combined to fight a great naval battle with the Phocaeans of Corsica, of whose mass departure from Asia Minor we have heard. Although they won the battle, the Phocaeans were so battered that they decided to give up in Corsica and went to the south Italian coast. In 474 b.c. the Etruscans and the Carthaginians fought a great naval battle off Cumae with the Cumaeans, who had the help of

Syracuse. This battle seems to have broken the naval power of the Etruscans, although their merchant ships continued to sail the seas.

The original group of Etruscan cities in Etruria maintained themselves longer than those of Campania or those of the Po Valley, but in the end they all fell before the power of the Romans. The first serious incursion of the Romans was their capture in 396 of Veii, the Etruscan city nearest to them. The other Etruscan cities did not rally to the defense of Veii, although the ten-year struggle might have given them time and cause to reflect that it was very much to their interest to unite against so determined a power. But when the Romans became involved, toward the end of the fourth century, in a great struggle with the Samnites of Campania that lasted into the third century, the Etruscans, along with other peoples of north central Italy, allowed themselves to be drawn into the struggle against the Romans and were defeated and forced to join the Roman federation.

Etruscan Life

The original territory in which the Etruscan people came into being—that north of Rome—was rich in metals: there was iron on the island of Elba, and on the mainland were iron, tin, and zinc. All three Etruscan regions were more than adequate for agriculture. Wood was another product that was very useful at home and could be exported, especially to Greece.

A large part of the evidence known to us comes from tombs. Some tombs are like houses cut from the soft volcanic rock a little below the level of the ground, having a central room with other rooms at the sides as a house would. The cemetery at Cerveteri, the ancient Caere, not far north of Rome, has interesting tombs cut from the solid rock and with conical tops; it has been made an official show place. Many of these tombs were robbed at some time before the beginning of modern archaeology. Every kind of object of daily use was found in those tombs that had not been plundered, things put there to serve the dead in the other world. Beside tools, furniture, and eating utensils we even find representations of the things used in the kitchen, such as a long thin rolling pin like that which the Italian housewife uses nowadays to make the pasta. The paintings on the walls tell us of Etruscan painting techniques and give an idea of their typical figure, features, hair styling, clothes, shoes, dances and musical instruments, games and festivals, and beliefs about the afterlife.

The new techniques of aerial photography have shown that in Etruria there are hitherto unsuspected fields of tombs with mounds on top. The modern archaeologist, instead of opening them to look for new materials, bores a hole and lets down an apparatus with a light and a wide-angle lens that can be rotated to allow him to look all around the tomb to see whether there is anything of interest there.

The Etruscans fabricated some things of iron and shipped some iron abroad as pigs. Beside iron they manufactured weapons and tools of bronze, innumerable little religious images of bronze, often about two inches high, and many fine large bronze statues. They made beautiful little bronze boxes and chests of the sort that a woman might use for her jewels and cosmetics. They apparently used much wood in their temples and houses, but not stone. They were expert makers of terra cotta statues and architectural ornaments. The tomb paintings show us that they made graceful clothes of wool and linen and fine leatherwork; they could also make fine jewelry.

They imported some tin and lead from Spain or central Europe. They were in touch with the lands of the Near East and imported their characteristic luxury wares, like ivory, tapestries, and perfumes. Their greatest enthusiasm, however, was for Greek work, and some of our finest Greek vases are those that were imported by Etruscans. Although the influence of Greek processes of manufacture and Greek decorations may be seen everywhere in Etruscan wares, they were not mere copyists of other people, as the Carthaginians so often were, but impressed what they did with a style of their own.

The Etruscan Language and Literature; Religion

The Etruscan language presents a tantalizing problem. Our knowledge of it comes chiefly from about ten thousand inscriptions, practically all of which are epitaphs or are connected somehow with burials. They are written in an alphabet practically like the Roman one and probably borrowed from the Greeks of South Italy. The words can therefore be read, even when they cannot be translated. We can translate only a little, for we can recognize some of the words of relationship—father, son, and so on—in the epitaphs, some of the numbers, and some of the names of the magistracies that the deceased had held.

One very interesting document was found in 1964 in excavations at Pyrgi, north of Rome. The important city of Caere was built back a little from the sea, as ancient cities so often were, but was so flourishing a place that it had a port town, Pyrgi, as Athens had Peiraeus and Rome was to have Ostia. Two pretty little gold plates, about 15 by 3 centimeters in size, were inscribed in Etruscan letters, and a matching third one was inscribed in Punic, the first Punic inscription found in continental Italy.

Although all three inscriptions seem to refer to a dedication made at the shrine of Astarte at Pyrgi by Tiberius, a priest or high official at Caere, and although the longer Etruscan inscription, about forty words long, is matched in size by the Punic one, it has not been established that the two say exactly the same thing.

Although they did not have a literature in the sense that Greece and Rome did, the Etruscans produced some books of a sort, which was rare among most of the ancient peoples. We have brief references to writings called *Tuscae historiae,* or *Etruscan Studies,* and to a man who wrote tragedies in Etruscan. We are better informed about the religious books that made up what the Romans called the *Etrusca Disciplina.* These books were translated into Latin, since the Roman priests were very respectful of Etruscan rules of religion. One part dealt with the art of the haruspex; the haruspices were religious experts who could divine the will of the gods by examination of the livers of animals sacrificed to the gods, a kind of divination long known among the older peoples of the Near East. Another part dealt with the interpretation of lightning; its location, its sound, and its color all gave clues as to which god had sent it and what he meant by it. The third part gave rituals for many occasions, like the setting up of a new temple or the founding of a city. All these attempts to import some certainty into dealing with the unseen powers were congenial to the temper of the Romans.

Etruscan religion seems early to have borrowed from Greece the idea of twelve primary anthropomorphic deities. Their attributes seem to have corresponded pretty well to those of the major Greek deities. The Etruscans, however, had a strong feeling for organizing them into threes and for building temples to such triads of gods. The great temple on the Capitoline Hill in Rome, which was built in 509 B.C. under the influence of an Etruscan king, was dedicated to Jupiter Optimus Maximus, and in it were also housed Juno and Minerva. The Etruscans also believed in infernal gods, or those of the underworld, as did the Greeks. The practice of putting all sorts of equipment into the tomb implies a belief in an afterlife.

The Greeks

The Greeks of the West were far less important to the Romans as political and military rivals than they were as a cultural inspiration. The story of Greek colonization in the West was told in Chapters 6 and 12. From the point of view of the Romans, who did not have independent political views until they got rid of their Etruscan overlords just before 500 B.C., the Greeks of South Italy and Sicily were established people, not newcomers. A less vigorous people than the Romans might not have expanded into southern Italy, but the course of events did bring the Romans into conflict, as we shall see, with their Greek neighbors, and Rome absorbed them in a fairly short time. From here on they will appear only as a part of Roman history.

16

EARLY ROME:

THE CONQUEST OF ITALY

The Latins and Earliest Rome

The Latins were a people who made their appearance rather late in the history of Italy—perhaps 1000 B.C.—coming to settle in Latium, a district of Italy near the lower course of the river Tiber. Their language, Latin, was closely akin to many of the other languages of Italy. The whole group of languages is known as the Italic group and forms one of the main divisions of the Indo-European languages. The growing political importance of the Romans caused the Latin language to be more and more widely spoken and brought about the decline of the other Italic languages.

Historians have often been tempted to conclude that the character of the Latins, and then of that segment of them that became the Romans, was such as to lead them inevitably to the conquest of Italy and then of the whole Mediterranean world. Whether national characteristics exist is a nice question for the historian. The Romans were indeed remarkable in their willingness to absorb other peoples. They did not do so indiscriminately; at times they refused to permit people who seemed incapable of being absorbed to enter their territories, as when on several occasions groups of Germans asked for grants of land and offered to serve as soldiers. Nevertheless their willingness to admit new elements is characteristic of them, on the one hand, and played a part in changing the nature of the group slightly as time went on, on the other hand. The unusual persistence of the ruling class of the Romans at almost any period in pursuing the government's aims is also noteworthy. In many crises the Romans succeeded purely because of their pertinacity. We shall not attempt, however, to describe the Roman character as a consistent and permanent set of traits. Again and again there will be occasion to tell how the Romans acted in a definite set of circumstances and to give an account of what they had to say about themselves. The sum of what is told about their acts and their thoughts will be a basis for a judgment of their character.

Latium was at first most inhospitable, for its many volcanoes remained active until around 1000 B.C. After their eruptions became infrequent, the volcanic ash, rich in potash and phosphates, slowly gathered organic matter and became soil, and it is supposed that presently the Latins wandered in and settled. The Latins seem to have been in a more primitive state than many of the peoples who lived farther north in Italy. They were a pastoral and agricultural people, who pastured the usual sheep, cows, pigs, and goats, and raised the usual wheat, vegetables, and fruits. The culture of the olive and the vine, for which Latium is so well suited, was not introduced until later. The crude simplicity of life was not relieved by the practice of the mechanic arts or the fine arts.

There is archaeological evidence that the site of Rome was inhabited for some time during the second millennium B.C. These early people, Neolithic in their culture, probably stayed for some hundreds of years, perhaps until 1500 or 1400 B.C. The evidence suggests that after them there was a time when the site was not occupied, making a clean break between them and the Latins of Iron Age culture who came there later.

The Forum, back in the days of the ninth, eighth, seventh, and early sixth centuries, before anyone had faced the task of giving it thorough drainage and making it fit to use for everyday life, was a necropolis, or cemetery, about which little was known until the twentieth century. Although the Forum became the heart of Rome in its great days, in early modern times it was again a quiet place where goats grazed and where, as one can see in the pictures and prints of Italian artists like Piranesi, the remains of the ancient monuments were half buried and picturesquely covered with grass and flowers. But the steady progress of scientific archaeology late in the last century and early in this century led to the clearing away of many of the glamorous deposits surrounding the larger monuments. The area of the cemetery had to be cleared of several feet of soil that was ancient Roman and of some that was modern. Far below the modern surface lay the evidence that the forum had been used for burials from the ninth to the sixth centuries B.C.

There are traces of small early settlements on the Quirinal, Esquiline, and Caelian Hills. On the Palatine the excavations have disclosed the bases and traces of the walls of Iron Age huts, which can be seen by the present-day visitor. The few simple things, mostly fragments of pottery, found on the lowest, and therefore oldest, level of these excavations belong to the Iron Age and seem to come from the eighth century B.C. These oldest articles resemble the oldest ones found in the graves of the Forum and are earlier than the materials found on the other hills. We may say, then, that the Palatine settlement, which was only a small village, was the beginning of Rome and that it began in the 700s. The tradition of the Romans themselves, as we shall see, also put the beginning of the city in the middle of the eighth century.

Another stage of the city began when it came under Etruscan influence. We cannot be sure that the city fell under Etruscan domination of any sort other than cultural, but it does seem reasonable to suppose that it was political pressure of some sort that led to the introduction of Etruscan workmen and their products and to the presentation of all sorts of Etruscan ideas to the Romans. The Roman tradition held that there were Etruscan kings.

Most important in the new stage was the draining of the Forum by the great sewer, the Cloaca Maxima, that led down to the Tiber River and the beginning of the long use of the Forum as a center of political, commercial, and social life. The change can be dated to about 575 B.C. The archaeological finds, after about 600 B.C., begin to show more things that suggest the Etruscans; we cannot be sure, however, that Etruscan ideas began to be imported this early. Rome now became a city in the proper sense of the word, not merely a group of people who happened to live together and made their livings separately as agriculturists or herders. The last stage of early or prerepublican Rome came late in the sixth century with the inclusion of the Capitoline Hill in the official boundaries of the city. Upon the Capitoline was built the great temple to Jupiter, Juno, and Minerva, which Roman tradition ascribed to Tarquin the Haughty, the last of the Etruscan kings thought to have ruled in Rome. The traditional date of the expulsion of the Tarquins by the Roman nobles is 509 B.C. This period, no less than the twentieth century, was a low point in the curve of the utility and the prestige of kings. Etruscan people and Etruscan influence did not disappear from Rome, for there was no need to purge the supporters of the Tarquins after a quiet revolution of this sort.

The Roman Tradition

The foregoing is a very simple version of the views generally held by scholars about the early centuries of Rome. The Romans themselves did not know the history of the city in its early period in satisfactory detail, since systematic written history was not developed early enough among them to serve for this period. There was a strong oral tradition, however, that was supplemented by study of the antiquities of the early period. The records of the priests and of the great families preserved a few facts that could be used.

The Greeks were fully conscious of the existence of Rome by the end of the fourth century. Since they knew nothing reliable about Rome's origin, their writers ascribed it either to the mythical founder whom they called Rhomus or spun a pleasant story of the flight of the Trojan prince Aeneas from the ruins of Troy and his voyage to Italy with the other survivors, with whom he founded a city from which came Rome. He was said to be the son of a Trojan prince and of the goddess Venus. Rome was not the only city of Italy, of course, that was proud of its heroic past and claimed that some god was its especial protector. We catch echoes in Latin literature of the legends of other cities and learn that many of them, despite the eventual dominance of Rome, maintained a stiff-necked pride that looked down a little on the Romans as late comers in the circle of the cities of Italy. It was Rome, however, that found writers to embellish its founding, sing its glories, and draw the portrait of the old Roman. Only Athens had ever been able so to advertise its beauty, its role as the center of everything, and the fine qualities of its ideal citizen.

Vergil's version of the founding in his *Aeneid* is based on the story of Aeneas. Earlier Romans had already met the chief difficulty of this story of Rome's founding, namely that they all believed that Rome was founded in the eighth century (as indeed the archaeological evidence indicates), whereas the traditional date of the fall of Troy was 1183 B.C. Vergil followed a version already worked out at Rome that had the Trojans under Aeneas settle on the coast not far from the mouth of the Tiber, then move to the city of Alba Longa in the Alban Hills south of Rome (now Castel Gandolfo, summer seat of the Pope), then rule there until the eighth century, when Romulus would found the Palatine settlement at Rome. Vergil endowed the Trojans with the power and the splendor of his Rome, the Rome of the beginning of Augustus' reign. The Trojans, however, could contribute to the Roman pedigree the prestige of old Troy, which was not less real for being derived from Homer's poems, and Aeneas' descent from a goddess. Vergil also seemed to foresee what would be the best traits of the Roman Empire and foreshadowed its achievements in his story of the establishment of its Trojan ancestors in Italy. Even Athens in the accounts of its great writers did not come to birth trailing such clouds of glory.

The historian Livy (Titus Livius of Padua) also worked under Augustus and also consciously glorified Rome. He dealt briefly with Aeneas, then dealt at length with the whole later story of the twins Romulus and

Remus and the founding of Rome. Like Moses and others, the twins were said to have been exposed to die by a wicked usurper and to have been saved by fate and the kindness of humble people; they were reared in obscure circumstances until finally they were grown and were strong enough to depose the usurper.

The later Romans, who held the tradition that the modest early city had been ruled by Etruscan kings, put their number at seven. Although it is plain that many of the stories told about them are inventions, there surely is something in the tradition. Perhaps the most interesting of them is Servius Tullius, the sixth, whom the Romans thought of as a great innovator. Before his reign the basis of citizenship was membership in a *curia*, of which there were thirty; membership in a *curia* came from membership in a clan. Servius divided the city into four regions that he called *tribus*, plainly what we call wards; the word "tribe" is customarily used for them, and they replaced the *curiae* (which were simply allowed to wither on the vine) as the basis of citizenship. He replaced, as Cleisthenes had done in Athens, a system that depended on traditional groups and bonds of kinship with one that realistically grouped people by their place of residence. The members of the four tribes lived in four divisions of the city, and sixteen rural tribes were formed in the territory outside the city. Others were formed later, the thirty-fifth and last being formed in 241 B.C.

The chief purpose of the new system was presumably to fit new people readily into the citizen body. We may assume that people were attracted to Rome by its being larger than some other cities and economically livelier under the Etruscan influence. Although newcomers could not readily be accommodated in the old kinship system so as to become full members of society and especially to be available for military service, the new system could find places for them, since one needed only to be a free man and to reside within the Roman territory. The tribes were used as the basis for the census, the institution of which was attributed to Servius in later times.

The declaration of a man's property before the censors made him liable to a certain tax and determined his military responsibility. The richest men, who were synonymous with the nobility at this time, were expected to provide horses and fight in the cavalry, as the leading people generally did in the ancient world. Probably the men who could provide body armor and fight as heavy infantry—those who were known as hoplites in Greece—formed another group, and the poor would be skirmishers or noncombatant helpers in the army.

After the reorganization of the people by Servius Tullius, a new assembly, the *Comitia centuriata*, or assembly by centuries, may have come into being beside the *Comitia curiata*, the old assembly by *curiae*. The word "century" seems to have been applied both to a grouping within the tribe from which a number of soldiers could be drawn each year and to the men actually serving in a given year as a unit in the army. Our evidence does not show unequivocally that this assembly existed before the end of the monarchy or that it ever met then; some scholars maintain that the assembly was devised in the middle of the fifth century.

Perhaps the institution of the tribes by the king allowed the new people to be fitted into the citizen body by the king, rather than by the leaders of the great families, and thus gained their loyalty for the king. The men who formed the heavy infantry and were a middle class that had formerly had no recognition and were partly of the new people may have felt themselves to be supporters of the king rather than of the well-to-do who formed the cavalry.

Nevertheless the monarchy fell, and in so quiet a manner that we know almost nothing about the event. Tarquin the Haughty, who was the successor of Servius, was deposed and driven into exile, probably as the result of a quiet comparison of strength that convinced the king that he had no hope of matching the force in the hands of the nobles. The occasion of the confrontation may well have been some attempt on his part to make a new arrangement to improve his position.

THE UNIFICATION OF ITALY: 509 TO 265 B.C.

Rome and Her Neighbors

The Latins, the larger group of whom the Romans were ethnically a part, were overshadowed or directly controlled by the Etruscans during the sixth century, as Rome was. The Etruscans had not crushed them nor broken up their organization, the Latin League, nor imposed an entirely new culture on them, any more than they had on the Romans. They had, nevertheless, given them many elements of advanced culture, as they had the Romans. The Etruscan remains at Palestrina, for example, the ancient Latin town of Praeneste, make a brilliant showing in the local museum along with the things made by Praenestines under Etruscan influence.

The fifth century was a dangerous time for the Romans and the league, for the peoples of the Apennines were a restless lot who bred well, like the Greeks, and periodically sent out swarms of surplus population to find places for themselves as best they could. The Samnites, farther south than Rome, thus overflowed into the good land of Campania, capturing both Etruscan Capua and Greek Cumae late in the fifth century. The peoples nearer Rome, the Aequi and the Volsci especially, had pushed their way down until the Aequi threatened Latium from the east and the Volsci had cut across below Latium to reach the Mediterranean coast, in position to move into the lands of the Latins if they could. The struggle went on all through the fifth century; fortunately the Etruscans to the North were too busy with their new adventure of conquering the rich lands of the Po Valley to bother the Romans at this time. By the year 400 Latium was cleared again, and the relative power of the two sides had become such that the Aequi and the Volsci never were again a threat.

The Latin League founded a number of military colonies in places taken from the Aequi and the Volsci or in locations where a watch on them would be useful. Volunteers from members of the league were sent out, and Romans were eligible. The new cities, although colonies in origin, were full members of the Latin League and were autonomous, owing no deference or allegiance to any other city, but regarding the Latin League as a parent body. The fact that the Aequi and the Volsci ceased to give any real trouble may have been due to the presence of these colonies. A number of cities of this sort could keep watch over a fair-sized territory, constantly testing sentiment and watching for signs of coming trouble and providing a well trained body of citizen troops to deal instantly with any disorder or concerted movement. Any such movement would consist of the gathering of irregulars for a raid or of a citizen army that would be almost entirely infantry and could act only by walking across country, either of which operations could usually be detected by the watching Latin city before it was fully organized or at worst could be contained or stopped before it did much damage. We have, of course, seen both the Greeks and some of the earlier peoples using such military colonies.

During the fifth century Rome made no long strides toward her future greatness, although she maintained her independence of the Etruscans and played her part in resisting the encroachments of the Aequi and the Volsci. Although she was stronger than many members of the Latin League, she was no match for them all. Some of them, like Tibur (modern Tivoli) and Praeneste, were as strong individually as Rome and had as much of a tradition of culture with an Etruscan tinge as did the Romans.

The Conquest of Veii

In 405 B.C. the Romans began an attack against Veii, the nearest of the Etruscan cities, only about fifteen miles away, up the Tiber and on the right, or opposite, side, and took it in 396. The captured territory was appropriated and formed into four new voting districts, or tribes, of Romans. The new landholders and voters were Roman citizens, most of whom probably had had no land and thus had been unable to serve in the army and vote effectively in the *Comitia centuriata*. Such a sudden increase in territory, in real wealth and in men competent and liable for military service must have given Rome a sudden and considerable advantage in power over her allies of the Latin League. Rome's system was more effective than that of the other Latins, for she made the men who held the new territory members of the original Roman organization, merely increasing the number of the voting districts as a means of administering it, while the usual Latin system was to found colonies that were independent members of the league and could not be controlled as the new parts of the Roman territory and population could. The accession of the territory of Veii may have made Rome nearly equal in power to the whole Latin League.

The Gallic Invasion

It was natural that some of the large group of Celts who swirled into North Italy around the year 400 and overran the Etruscan possessions there should decide to investigate Italy further. The Romans, incidentally, always spoke of these people as *Galli,* or Gauls. In 390 B.C. by the Roman reckoning and 387 by the more exact Greek reckoning, one group of these Gauls wandered down into Italy, presently decided to attack Rome, and left aside other hopes of plunder to descend on her. A Roman force met the advancing horde at the river Allia, a little above Rome, and was routed. Some cool-headed Roman officer saw that the best hope was to rally what men he could and take them to the shelter of the walls of Veii, thereafter to fight some other day. In Rome the priests and the Vestal Virgins gathered the sacred objects and fled to Caere. The few fighting men left in the city and those who had gathered there after the rout went up to the citadel on the Capitoline Hill. Three days later the Gauls arrived. They looted and burned the city, which had no wall or other means of holding them off, and then settled down to besiege the Capitoline. They were not persistent people, however, and they suffered from fever. When news came that their home territory in the North of Italy was under pressure by new arrivals, they allowed the Romans to ransom themselves and went away. This simple story of a disaster that did not become utter ruin was embroidered by the later Roman historians both to show off the character of the old Roman and to save the credit of the Roman people.

This disaster raises an interesting question as to the source materials of Roman history. Some scholars believe that all written records must have perished at this time and that we therefore cannot believe that any account of Rome's history before the descent of the Gauls had any written records as its substructure. Probably more scholars believe that some records must have survived in the temple of Jupiter on the Capitoline, that some records kept in the temples down in the Forum may also have been saved because the Gauls were too superstitious to destroy temples, and that the collective memory of the senators could easily have restored the text of all the treaties in existence and a large part of the other records.

After the departure of the Gauls the Romans built the wall around the city mistakenly known as the Servian Wall. The stone came from quarries near Veii; the quarry marks show that Greek workmen were brought in. The wall was five and a half miles long, twenty-four feet high, and twelve feet thick. It has been calculated that the area enclosed was 425 hectares, or 1053 acres, or 1.63 square miles. Probably not all this ground was densely inhabited. Nevertheless, it is useful to know that Rome's walls at this time enclosed more space than those of any city in central and northern Italy except Veii. Four of the old Greek cities in the West had more enclosed space: Croton and Tarentum in Italy, and Syracuse and Acragas in Sicily.

In the year after the Gallic raid the Etruscans attacked Sutrium and Nepete at the northern edge of the territory taken from Veii. The Romans were able to beat them back and then invited the Latins to join in the founding of military colonies there to look northward, just as those at the southern edge of the Latin territory looked southward toward the Aequi and Volsci. In the year 381 the Romans took the people of Tusculum into the Roman state completely, thus acquiring a substantial piece of territory that stretched eastward from Rome and that divided the Latins into a northern and a southern group. Again a large piece of territory and a goodly source of soldiers had been added to the unitary state of the Romans. It is worth noticing that they gave the aristocracy of Tusculum a welcome to the ranks of the upper class at Rome and that before the end of the century more than one man from Tusculum had attained the Roman consulship.

Rome's Final Struggle with the Latins

Although the conflicts that terminated with Rome's gaining control over all Italy south of the Po River were on a larger and larger scale, their causes remained the same as before. The straightforward expansion of the Etruscans in the sixth century, of the Aequi and Volsci in the late sixth and the fourth centuries, and the equally straightforward expansion in the fifth century of their neighbors to the South whom we know as the Samnites created strong pressures. Naturally a people in the situation of the Romans, or of the Latins, content as it might be with its own situation, was forced to continual consideration of its power in relation to that of others and to an attitude at least as much offensive as defensive.

Even if they did not intend, as the Aequi and Samnites did, to take land from someone else every few years to provide room for their own expanding population, they could easily come to feel in the course of the struggle that a purely defensive attitude was bound to defeat itself if not combined with an occasional offensive move of prevention.

We may still ask ourselves why Rome rather than some other power rose to be mistress of Italy, but we cannot really answer. Other cities got as good political training from the Etruscans and had as good soldiers, man for man. We do know that the Romans were very persistent, yet others were as much so, and the optimistic view that perseverance conquers all is not supported by experience.

By the year 350 or a little later it was plain that the Latins did not intend to follow Rome's lead in their foreign affairs without having a voice in determining policy. They made the realistic demand of the Romans that one consul and half the Senate should always be Latins, which would have welded Rome and the Latin League together. The proposal was on the border line between the practical and the impractical. It was a highly practical way of combining the two powers without any need of an elaborate treaty or a new constitution, but it was impractical to suppose that it could be done, no matter how shrewd the Romans were about making use of any good thing that they could draw to themselves, for it meant the sharing of the consular office and the senatorial status. Further, the proposal would have introduced into the Roman government that very division and lack of unity that hampered the Latins when opposed to the decisiveness of the Romans.

The Romans refused to consider the proposal and prepared to prevent the Latins from terminating their relation to Rome. In 340 B.C. one of the Roman consuls led an army to the South, where it joined a Samnite force and won a difficult and bloody victory over the Latins. In 339 the Romans won two more victories, each over a part of the Latin forces. The fact that the Latins could not match the unity and discipline of Rome counted heavily against them, and in the year 338 the Romans disposed of the last scattered resistance and ended the war.

Having insisted that the Latins must stay with them and having fought a war to force them to stay, the Romans were now faced with the problem of how to treat them so as to be able to direct them, yet as allies rather than as subjects. A great deal of the later history of Rome was to consist of her gaining control of other people and fitting them into her system with some success, first in Italy, then overseas. Her first principle was always to assure her own control, but in such a way, if possible, as to serve the interests of the other people as well and insure their loyalty. To make certain that she could control the military forces of the alien groups was an important element in consolidating the whole Empire.

The Romans dealt with the situation of 338 B.C. in several differing ways. The Latin League was dissolved as a political entity, although there was no interference with the traditional annual religious ceremony of the Latins. The members of the League were regrouped in four ways. (1) Full Roman citizenship was given to a group of the Latins whose territories were close to Rome: Lanuvium, Aricia, and others. (2) A group of Latin communities that had been sent out earlier as colonies of the Latin League, thus becoming autonomous members of the league, were kept in their former status of Latins in alliance with Rome. Their old Latin privileges of *conubium* and *commercium,* or marriage and trade, however, were henceforth to be valid only in relation to Rome, and not, as before, in relation to all the other Latin cities. Thus Rome intended to divide and rule them. These communities were to be the nucleus of what the Romans henceforth called *nomen Latinum,* "the Latin name," and what the modern historian, when speaking of the following centuries, calls "the Latins." (3) Tibur and Praeneste, as well as Laurentum on the coast near Rome, became federated states (*civitates foederatae*), which meant that they were allied to Rome, as were the Latin communities of the second group, and were obliged to furnish soldiers to Rome, but were not to enjoy in relation to Rome the rights of *conubium* and *commercium* and the further right enjoyed by the second group of becoming Roman citizens by moving to Rome—one of the old rights that every member of the Latin League possessed in relation to every other. (4) A small colony of Roman citizens was sent to Antium to keep a watch on this seaport, which had in the past repeatedly made trouble for the Romans. This was a Roman colony, composed of Roman citizens sent out from Rome, who were to retain their Roman citizenship, the inducement being the goodly grant of land offered to each colonist.

The Latins had thus lost the right and ability to form foreign policy independently of Rome, that is, they had lost what they saw the Romans gradually taking from them and what they had fought to keep. Their closer association with Rome was to be profitable to them, however, and they in turn were to contribute much to Rome's successes by the service of their men in the Roman legions. The Romans had now formed a larger state than they might have dreamed of a century before. They controlled the military forces of their allies, but the arrangements as to citizenship were reasonable, if not palatable, and no attempt was made to make the others give up their economic surplus. It was rather the Romans who paid, for they would even compensate the allied troops in time of war.

The Samnite Wars

The attempts of the Samnites to expand caused their wars with the Romans. The first conflict began in 326 B.C. and ended in 321, and we know very little about it except that a gifted Samnite general seems to have led a Roman army into a trap where it had to surrender. We are told that the loyalty of some of the allied communities was shaken by this misfortune and that measures were taken to hold them steady. Some land near the Samnites that was at the disposal of the Romans was distributed to Roman citizens and organized into new tribes, thus carrying the organization of the full Roman citizens with all the rights of those resident in or near the city to a point nearly a hundred miles from Rome.

The second phase of the war began in 316 and ended in 304 and was marked at first by a Samnite victory and the revolt from the Romans of some of the people in their federation. If the list of the disaffected peoples is divided on the basis of time and place, the fact comes out that the number disaffected at any one time was never enough to break the Romans and that the revolting people were not a geographical entity; we know, too, that there was no harmony of sentiment or command among them. The offensive against the Samnites consisted of expeditions into their country that conquered limited areas and led to the setting up of Roman outposts, since there were no major cities whose capture would have forced the Samnites to submit. In 304 the Samnites were willing to cease hostilities and renew their treaty of 354 B.C. with the Romans.

The Romans had thus met the threat of Samnite expansion into Campania. They had held their alliance together and made new treaties, some of which were with the Apulians who were beyond the Samnites. They had taken territory from some of the allies who had revolted and from strategic places on the borders of the Samnites; part was used for Latin colonies, and part was distributed to Roman citizens, who were organized into two more tribes, or voting districts. The acquisition of this land should be regarded merely as one phase in foreign affairs; it surely was not an end in itself.

The Samnites still were not ready to settle down and allow the control that they could see the Romans preparing to exercise over them. They invited the Gauls to join them against Rome; the high point of this effort was a desperate battle at Sentinum in Umbria in 295 B.C., one of the most northerly points where Romans had been. The victory of the Romans meant that they were to extend their dominion a little northward into central Italy, where they already had some alliances. By 290 the Samnites were willing to give up, and apparently the old treaty was renewed.

The Celtic peoples of Europe were still restless, however, as they had been for more than a hundred years. Now a large group of them began that journey eastward that we have already mentioned; it took some of them down into Greece and others to inner Asia Minor. In the year 285 a group of them invaded Italy; this was the sixth time. After the usual reverses the Romans, now far more powerful than they had been a century before, boldly took the offensive and drove the Gauls out of their excellent territory just below the Po. The land they took from them was known as the *ager Gallicus,* "the Gallic territory," and later in the third century there was to be a notable political struggle over its distribution to poorer Roman citizens.

The War with Pyrrhus

Tarentum, which was located on the southern shore of Italy, retained its early prosperity in spite of the brutal career of Dionysius I of Syracuse and the incursions of the Italic peoples. The Tarentines, not great soldiers themselves, had been in the habit of hiring *condottieri,* or captains of mercenaries, from Greece. As we have seen, mercenaries were plentiful and were something of a problem in Greece in the fourth century. Even Spartan kings could be hired. Archidamus of Sparta was the first great *condottiere* hired by Tarentum; he died in a battle with some neighboring Italic people in the year 338. In 334 the Tarentines brought in Alexander of Epirus, an uncle of Alexander the Great. He was able at first to defeat the Lucanians and Bruttians and tried to set up an empire of his own in Italy; he even had friendly diplomatic intercourse with the Romans. His enterprise failed, however, when he died in a defeat of his army. Although two more such adventurers both disappointed the hopes of the Tarentines and aroused the hostility of everyone else in southern Italy, we still must concede that the Tarentines played this difficult game with some success for about sixty years until in 281 B.C. they requested King Pyrrhus of Epirus to help them against the Romans. The quarrel was brought on by an attack of the Tarentines on a Roman fleet of ten ships cruising the southern shore and an attack on a garrison that the Romans had sent at the request of Thurii, a southern city that was hard pressed by the Lucanians, one of the difficult Italic peoples. Apparently Tarentum meant to claim that all of southernmost Italy was under her protection.

In the spring of 280 Pyrrhus arrived. He was a famous professional soldier and brought with him a seasoned professional army of 25,000, with three thousand cavalry and two thousand archers among them. He was a dashing and brilliant man, a tactician of such quality that Hannibal later spoke admiringly of his battles, but no strategist by temperament, for he lacked persistence and was so subject to fits of optimism and pessimism that he could not follow out any consistent plan.

Pyrrhus won the first battle, in 280 B.C., and moved quickly northward toward Rome, prepared to see the alliance of the "barbarians" fall apart. But the Romans made ready to defend the city; Rome's allies shut their gates and manned their walls, and the Samnites did not revolt and join him as he had been led to expect. He stopped and sent a legate to negotiate, making what seemed reasonable demands, but the Romans refused. The two armies met again in 279 in a battle much like the first one in that Pyrrhus won, but at a cost in casualties that he could not afford. His brief statement that another such victory would ruin him gave rise to the phrase "Pyrrhic victory."

At this point he was asked by the Greeks of Sicily to come to help them against strong Carthaginian attacks and was tempted by the idea of creating a kingdom there. He went in 278, showed his usual brilliance, but tired of the plan and was back in Italy in 275, disappointed and with his army much depleted. After almost defeating the Romans at Maleventum (afterward renamed Beneventum) he withdrew to Greece, never to return.

In 272 the Romans captured the citadel of Tarentum, granting the city the status of naval ally, which left it free, but obliged to furnish warships or transports. Other Greeks of southern Italy were glad to enter into alliance with Rome. All Italy, from the Po River in the North to the very toe in the South, was under Roman control.

CHAPTER

17

EARLY ROMAN INSTITUTIONS
AND CULTURE: 509–265 B.C.

THE DEVELOPMENT OF
EARLY REPUBLICAN INSTITUTIONS

The nobles of Rome were doing the current thing when they sent King Tarquin into unwilling retirement in 509 B.C., for both Greeks and Phoenicians had got rid of their kings in many polities and were managing well with a government of the powerful few. At Rome the Senate, or council of elders, had long been used to watching the course of events and convening at the king's request to hear and advise him, and it was now ready to serve as a continuing organ of government. The idea of the nobility's choosing one of its number to serve as executive officer for a year was common enough among the Greeks of Greece and of South Italy, although it had been first thought of less than two hundred years before. The Romans decided to have a pair of annual chief executives, known at first as *praetores*, or praetors, and then as *consules*, or consuls. The word "praetor" reappeared presently as the title of two officers created to take some of the duties of the consuls.[1]

In certain emergencies the consuls could appoint a dictator who could hold absolute power for six months, although he customarily resigned when his task was done. Sometimes the task was the spectacular one of taking command of the army in a difficult situation that called for a gifted general. To assume the religious functions of the king the *rex sacrorum*, or "king of the rites," was probably added at the fall of the

[1] See pp. 365–366.

monarchy. In Greece, too, as we have seen, an official was given the religious function of the kings who were deposed.

Two methods of assembly seem to have been inherited from the monarchy. The *Comitia curiata,* or assembly by *curiae,* was retained throughout the Republic to perform such tasks as ratifying the adoption of patricians into other clans and the formal confirmation of the power of the elected magistrates. The *Comitia centuriata,* the assembly by centuries that reflected the organization of the army and that probably originated in the late years of the monarchy as part of the reforms of Servius Tullius, had as its its chief duties under the fully developed republic the election of magistrates and the declaring of war.

Some of the people—probably fewer than a twentieth—were considered patricians; the rest of the citizens were regarded as plebeians. The patricians were able to claim for themselves the right to hold all the offices, including the priesthoods, of the new republican government. People in general were willing to accept the idea of the inheritable superiority of a small group of prominent citizens. Some patricians were not rich. Not all plebeians, on the other hand, were poor and downtrodden; some of them were energetic, well-to-do, and assertive.

We must remember that Rome of the Republic, in spite of what it was destined to become, was only a rather small city surrounded by a modest amount of farming land. To the west the Tyrrhenian Sea was only a few miles away; one could look eastward across the plain and see the hills where the neighboring commonwealths of Tibur and Praeneste were. The great Romans of those days were only the owners of farms that nowadays would seem diminutive. The domestic and foreign problems of this little state were simple, and the working of its new government was equally so. Yet Rome was beyond the primitive stage of clan government and had arrived at the stage that in Greece would have entitled it to be called a polis. There was a defensible center of population and government instead of a number of scattered independent villages through the territory. The government had taken control of the army, the administration of justice, and the relation of the group to the gods, all of which functions must have once been under the control of the clans.

The Struggle of the Patricians and the Plebeians

The creation of an organization belonging to the plebeians and of the office of tribune of the people was the first step in the plebeian advance. We are told by the ancient authors that the plebeians of the early days suffered considerably from the lack of sufficient land and the demands of the wars on their time. The man who was called off to war might find on his return that his little crop had failed for lack of attention, or hostile raids might have ruined his farms—at least the trees, vines, animals, and house. Many holdings were too small to feed a family anyway, and some men had no land at all. There is evidence of more than one severe famine in early Rome; such famines, caused by persistently adverse weather conditions in most cases, always hit the small farmer harder than the larger. The poor man who found himself in difficulties would be tempted to pledge his person as security for a loan, and the result might be the loss of his freedom.

In 494 B.C., according to Roman tradition, the plebeians, returning from a campaign, refused in utter disgust and discouragement to enter the city, and their secession led to the recognition by the patricians of the *Concilium plebis,* or plebeian council, and of two tribunes, leaders of the plebeians. No matter how credible we find this secession, it seems likely that in 471 the patricians formally recognized the existence and competence of the *Concilium plebis,* an assembly for plebeians only, and of a college now of five tribunes, annually elected by the *Concilium,* that could also pass *plebiscita,* or resolutions, that were binding only on the plebeians unless confirmed by the *Comitia centuriata,* which made them *leges,* or statutes. The powers of the tribunes included convoking the plebeian assembly and making proposals to it and perhaps from the beginning, as later, proposing to it that fines be imposed on the patrician magistrates for acting against the interest of the people. The tribunes also had the power of coercion, which enabled them to veto the acts of magistrates or even veto the summoning of an assembly, so that they could prevent the *Comitia centuriata* from meeting. They could protect individual citizens from arbitrary action by the magistrates, and the fact that the tribune could not leave the city during his year of office and that his house door had to stand open day and night suggests that the race for sanctuary sometimes was a spirited one right to the last stride.

By the middle of the fifth century there was another assembly, the *Comita tributa,* an assembly of *all* the people, both patricians and plebeians organized on the basis of the tribes, presided over by a consul rather than a tribune and needing a declaration that the auspices were favorable before it could legally meet. A cardinal aim of the liberal leaders of the plebeians was that this assembly should become able to legislate without need of the concurrence of either the Senate (an advisory council of leading men inherited from royal times) or the *Comitia centuriata,* a right acknowledged only by the Hortensian Law of 287 B.C.

All these arrangements look like the work of men who believed that the whole people should be represented in government, as did Pericles and other leaders in fifth-century Athens. To them *plebes* probably meant the whole people rather than merely the poor and underprivileged. They seem to have been trying to find ways to limit the broad supervisory and punitive powers exercised by the consuls as heirs of the kings. At Athens similar powers were sharply limited in this same century, and at Sparta the Ephors were established (somewhat earlier) as annual officers to represent the people and to supervise and correct magistrates and commoners alike. We may assume, although there is no direct proof, that the Romans studied the Athenian, Spartan, and other systems of government. At Rome, as elsewhere, there was no inconsistency in believing that the power of the magistrates must be limited in the interest of the whole population, but that those magistrates ought to be chosen from a limited and privileged group rather than from all classes.

The Laws of the Twelve Tables

The next incident known to us in the development of the constitution was the adoption of the so-called Laws of the Twelve Tables, Rome's first written laws. Probably the pressure for the preparation and publication of the code came from the liberal-minded men, patrician as well as plebeian, who felt that it would be well to replace an indefinite authority with a definite and impersonal one. Regulation by a well considered code that took advantage of Greek experience and limitation of the indefinite authority of magistrates and priestly experts in legal matters were in accord with the temper of the times. This was a step toward the establishment of the impersonal governments based on law that were characteristic of the Greco-Roman way of life.

A tribune is said (some doubt it) to have proposed in 462 that the people assert their power as the source of law by drawing up a set of laws to limit the imperium of the consuls—a logical way of beginning. A commission of three is said (some doubt it) to have been sent to Greece in 454 B.C. to study constitutions. Then a commission of ten patricians, or decemvirate, was appointed (most scholars accept this) to govern for a year in the place of the ordinary magistrates and to produce a code of laws. They produced ten tables of law, which in 451 B.C. were accepted by the *Comitia centuriata,* thus becoming one long *lex,* or statute, and were posted in public view with general approval. The rest of the story is again open to some doubt. A second commission of ten is said to have been appointed, to have produced two more tables, and to have acted so tyrannically that popular resentment forced their resignation. For the year 449 there were two consuls again, but ten tribunes instead of five.

Although the Romans of later times must have known what was in the tables, since Cicero tells us that schoolboys were made to learn the whole code by heart in his day (first century B.C.), the code is not preserved in any of the collections of Roman legal materials that have come down to us, and what we know comes only from scattered quotations of rather small parts or from references to the principles embodied in the code. Cicero and other authors often quoted bits of it while discussing political and legal matters. Some of what we know comes from the writings of the jurists.

The Rome reflected in the laws of the Twelve Tables was a simple and conservative agricultural community. The fact that the Etruscans had brought it somewhat into world trade is not reflected, at least in the parts of the code that we have. We do find that there was free testamentary disposition. In practical terms this means that the property of a family was not a whole upon which all members of the family lived and worked and from which they were supported, like the simple manor of Homeric days, but was in the more advanced stage of being parceled out among the smaller units that we call families today, a stage in which it would be practical for the head of each small family unit to have full control of a property and be able to alienate parts of it.

The law regarding land had become somewhat sophisticated, for the rules on boundaries included the case of a branch that overhung a neighbor's land and that he could remove as a nuisance, as well as the right to gather the fruit of one's tree if it fell on the neighbor's side of the boundary. Wood was scarce enough for the case to be envisaged of a man's recognizing a beam that had been stolen from him and proposing to remove it from the structure into which it had been built. The use of magic charms against either people or crops was dealt with; the belief in the possibility of such actions persisted through the most rational period of Roman civilization.

Further Development of the Constitution

To continue with our scanty information on the development of the Roman constitution, in the year 447 B.C. a pair of quaestors was elected (by the *Comitia tributa*) for the first time, to serve in 446. Quaestors were patricians, and their function at this time was probably to relieve the consuls of financial administration, as it surely was in later times. They did not have the imperium, which may be loosely defined as the full power of the State and belonged only to major offices. This office was opened to plebeians in the year 421.

One of the two tables of laws published by the second set of decemvirs had forbidden marriage between patricians and plebeians. This rule, so impractical for a privileged class that numbered perhaps only five percent of the population and was confronted by wealthy and vigorous outsiders whom it might absorb by marriage, was repealed by the Canuleian Law of 445. Many of the rather small list of Roman statutes known to us are identified by the names of their sponsors—Canuleius, in this case.

The censors, another pair of patrician officials without the imperium, first took office in 443 B.C.; the office was not opened to plebeians until 351 B.C. It has been suggested that taking the census suddenly became much more difficult than it had been, for the Romans had just adopted a new system for their army based on heavy infantry of the kind that the Greeks called hoplites. According to this explanation the census now needed, for the first time, to show the amount of each man's property so that men of the higher financial classes could be required to equip themselves with the better and heavier armor of the hoplite. Another body of opinion holds, however, that men had been classified by property since the days of Servius Tullius.

A pair of censors was elected every five years. Their first duty was to take the census, which meant to make a list of all the free citizens according to their tribes and also according to the amount of their property. The most affluent men were liable to service as cavalry and were known as the *equites,* "cavalrymen." This group supplied the senators and the magistrates from the beginning of the Republic, and a noted scholar has called the distinction between those who fought on horses and those who fought on foot a fundamental feature of the Roman social order. Every free man was liable to military service. In the fourth century the censors acquired the right to fill vacancies in the Senate and to remove undesirable members. They were also given charge of the building and road making done by the state. The office became important and desirable.

After the Gallic invasion of 387 B.C. there was a period of sharp struggle in both economic and political matters. There were two kinds of opposition, that between rich and poor and that between patricians and plebeians. The poorer plebeians wanted relief from economic distress, and the richer plebeians wanted to become eligible for the consulship. Licinius and Sextius, tribunes of the people in 376 B.C., were elected every year for ten years to continue their struggle to get a bill passed, that would satisfy some plebeian demands. In 367 B.C., with the approval of the Senate at last, they got the so-called Licinian-Sextian Laws through the *Comitia tributa,* although some of the plebeians, as well as the patricians, had opposed them.

The new laws provided that plebeians be eligible for the consulship; presently it became the rule that one consul must be plebeian. Relief was also given from the harshness of the law of debt, for many men had lost their freedom by falling into debt, as in the Athens of Solon's time. The new laws provided that interest that had been paid be regarded as payment on the principal, a measure that could do no more than give temporary relief. It was not until 326 that the *lex Poetelia-Papiria* forbade the practice by which the debtor was delivered (or delivered himself) into the power of his creditor and was forced to work for him; it is surprising that such a custom persisted so long.

Although the state had regularly taken land from other peoples to give to landless men, starting with the conquest of Veii in 396 and continuing with the appropriation of some land from almost everyone with whom the Romans struggled, there continued to be all too many free citizens with too small farms or with no farms. Some of the conquered land was declared *ager publicus,* or public land, and was rented out by the censors on five-year leases for farming or pasturage. Naturally the rich were most able to rent this land, and it is also natural that some of them rented more than the probable legal limit of five hundred *iugera,* or 310 of our acres, and renewed their leases again and again so that the land was practically in their permanent possession. Licinius and Sextius tried to enforce the legal limit on the renting of this land so as to make some of it available to landless men.

Just after the passage of the Licinian-Sextian Laws two new offices were created, that of praetor and that of curule aedile. A praetor was given as one duty the administration of the city itself when the consuls were away, and like the consuls, he was clothed with the imperium, so that in their absence he was qualified to perform any of their functions. After a generation plebeians could hold the praetorship. Two curule, or patrician, aediles were added to two aediles who long had been the assistants of the tribunes; the function of the group was to take care of the details of the management of the city of Rome.

The most important duty of the praetor was the administration of the courts of private or civil law. Roman law was not in general created by *leges,* or statutes, although some *leges,* like the Twelve Tables, were important. The changing of the law or the creation of new law was done through the discussions that surrounded the cases in the praetor's court, and new principles of law made their appearance in the praetor's edict— the list of actions-at-law that would be entertained, a list that was published by every praetor at the beginning of his year of office. Naturally the list was composed almost entirely of principles and remedies established in other years. The praetor would sometimes add one or drop one; his decision would rest on careful discussion by the responsible men who were used to the study and practice of the law.

In 242 B.C. another praetorship was created, that known as *inter peregrinos.* The man was called the *praetor peregrinus,* and the original praetor came to be called the *praetor urbanus.* The *peregrini* were non-Romans whose states were in some friendly relationship to Rome. Some of them were merchants from overseas; most of them were subjects of Rome who had not attained the full Roman citizenship. The legal arrangements that these people made with one another and with Roman citizens were dealt with in the court of the new praetor, and the dealings in this court with cases based on systems of law that were slightly different from that of the Romans lent detachment and perspective to Roman legal thinking. Useful features of other law could be imported into Roman law by being incorporated in the praetor's edict.

Between the years 367 and 287 B.C. the plebeians had slowly and without any one resounding contest gained access to those posts that formerly had been reserved for patricians, and they were at last eligible for the three magistracies that, in ascending order, came to be the chief prizes of a career in public life: the quaestorship, the praetorship, and the consulship. *Honos,* or "honor," was the word usually applied to those magistracies, and the three were often called the *cursus honorum.* Plebeians also became eligible for the censorship, and members of both orders were eligible for the aedileship. This post, homely as it was in one way, came to be an important element in a political career because its holders could please the voters by their generosity in managing the festivals. The tribunate was by its nature reserved for plebeians. In the year 300 the colleges of pontiffs and augurs were opened to plebeians, which left as the exclusive preserve of the patricians only the positions of *rex sacrorum,* the *interrex* (or interim king of the old days on the death of a king), who now was appointed if there was any delay in the election and installation of the new consuls, and the chief three of the fifteen flamens, who were priests, each appointed to serve a specific deity.

When the Hortensian Law of 287 B.C. provided that the resolutions of the *Comitia tributa* and *Concilium plebis* should have the force of law, theoretical sovereignty was at last vested in the whole group of free citizens rather than in a limited group determined by birth or by the ability to arm themselves. Rome nevertheless remained an aristocratic republic rather than a democracy, for it continued to be directed by the aristocracy rather than by popular leaders and the popular assembly, as we shall see repeatedly.

The reorganization of the *Comitia centuriata,* which probably took place in 241 B.C., was the last major event in the formation of the republican constitutional system. Before the reform the army and the *Comitia centuriata* had 193 centuries. There were in the army eighteen centuries of cavalry, the richest men, followed by eighty centuries of the first class, the heavy infantry. The second, third, and fourth classes furnished twenty centuries each, and the fifth class thirty. There were four centuries of smiths and musicians, and the poorest people were grouped in one. This arrangement provided Rome with an army and also with the centuriate assembly. Since each century had one vote in the assembly —a vote that was determined by a ballot within the century—and since the eighteen centuries of cavalry and the eighty of heavy infantry voted first, and since their 98 votes were a majority of the 193, the well-to-do could control the decisions.

We do not know why the *Comitia centuriata* was reorganized on a tribal basis. We do know that after 241, in addition to the cavalry, seventy centuries (instead of eighty) were men of the first class and that each of the thirty-five tribes provided in this class a century of *seniores,* or men over forty-five, and a century of *iuniores,* or men from seventeen to forty-five. Later mentions of elections by the Roman historians often refer to the tribal basis of the electing assembly.

A Summary of the Constitution

The tribunes strictly speaking were not magistrates, since they stood apart from all other officials. They still had the duty of being available at all times to their fellow plebeians to protect them from the arbitrary exercise of the powers vested in the magistrates. After the rise of the new nobility some of the tribunes came from families that were regarded as noble. More than once thereafter they showed more sympathy with the economic interests of the few than with those of the many.

The quaestors soon were four in number, then eight. Some served at home in the treasury, while others took the field to manage the military pay chest. This was the office with which young men ambitious for a career began.

The aedileship was not required as part of the *cursus honorum,* although ambitious young men usually aimed at this office after their quaestorships. The aediles watched over buildings and streets, markets, the water supply, policing, and festivals.

The praetors and the consuls were elected by the *Comitia centuriata.* The number of praetors slowly increased, for Rome began in the middle of the third century to acquire provinces overseas and needed praetors to govern them beside those two praetors who were in charge of the courts at home. Sometimes an official was prorogued, that is, continued in his office. A consul might be left in charge of an army for another year; his title was then proconsul. Sometimes after he had served a year as praetor or consul a man continued in office and was sent to govern a province for a year or more as proconsul or propraetor. During the Samnite Wars, when this practice started, there often were one or two minor rebellions to be dealt with beside the main operations, and in the Second Punic War, a century later, there were several major armies to be commanded for years at a time. The greatest importance of prorogation, however, was that when Rome began to acquire overseas provinces in the third century, they could be governed by men of at least praetorian experience, that is, the supply of men of sufficient dignity to be entrusted with the government of a province could be expanded at will by giving the praetors and consuls additional terms of office, even for several years at a time.

Until the end of the Roman Empire the consulship was the chief prize of political life. Since they were in a sense the successors to the kings, the two consuls presided over the Senate, commanded the armies, and had the right to inflict death sentences at home as well as on campaigns. Their power had been somewhat curtailed since the beginning of the Republic by the right of appeal to the people from death sentences, by the giving of control over the treasury to the Senate and the quaestors, and by the power of the tribunes of preventing arbitrary action on their part. They still had absolute power when heading the army.

The Senate came to be composed in practice of all the men who had held consulships or praetorships, plus others less successful politically who had to be added to fill its three hundred places. Men to fill vacancies were chosen by the censors. More plebeians were included after 367 B.C., since they could hold office. The Senate could not meet formally unless called by the consuls or praetors; its function when called was to advise them. Its continuity and experience as a group gave it a practical authority for which there was no theoretical or legal basis. Although it did not elect the magistrates, it acquired the power of determining their spheres of activity during their year of office. It also acquired the power to prorogue praetors and consuls. Although it did not make the laws, it could often by its prestige prevent or hasten the passage of laws by the assemblies and could also influence a law's form by preliminary discussions. It gained control of the treasury, and it alone could authorize the quaestors to disburse monies. Although it could not declare war, which was the privilege of the *Comitia centuriata,* it often planned the general course of the wars; even in peace it directed the general course of affairs, for governmental experience and knowledge were concentrated in the Senate. No magistrate could hope to initiate a policy and put it into action during his one year of office. A man who had a policy could advance it best by gathering support for it among the senators, unless it was a radical one dear to the people, in which case he would try to get it enacted into law by the *Comitia tributa.* Yet, in spite of the fact that the weight of the whole Senate was generally too much for the consuls in a dispute over large issues, the consuls often confidently defied the Senate on the details of civil or military administration.

There were finally four assemblies: the *Comitia curiata,* which met in the form of a representative for each of the thirty *curiae* only to ratify adoptions or to confer the imperium on the new consuls and praetors; the *Comitia centuriata,* which elected consuls and praetors, declared war, and heard appeals; the *Concilium plebis,* which enacted legislation; and the

Comitia tributa, which elected tribunes, aediles, and quaestors and could enact legislation.

It is sometimes said that the plebeians created a state within a state and forced the patricians to recognize it. It would probably be more accurate to say that the plebeian leaders thought of themselves as fighting for the conception that all free men constituted the plebes and that no segment of the people, in this case the patricians, should be allowed to arrogate power and privilege to itself.

ROMAN CIVILIZATION: 509 TO 265 B.C.

At the beginning of the period that we are discussing, Rome was only a fair-sized Italian city whose nobles had just shaken off the power of a king; at the end of the period, although she was only moderately larger, she had acquired political dominion over an area about a hundred times as great as her own five hundred or so square miles. In spite of some advances in culture, the Romans of 265 B.C. were plainly a far less cultivated people than the Greeks of Greece or than the Greeks and other people who lived and worked in the other countries of the old world eastward from Greece. A time was to come, however, and soon, when these barbarians, as they seemed to the Greeks of the time, were to conquer the old world and embrace the Greek accomplishments eagerly and create a new Greco-Roman culture.

The Economic Basis

Agriculture was, of course, the chief occupation of all Italy, as it was everywhere else in the ancient world. As we have seen, Italy had good soil, a climate suitable for the vine and the olive tree as well as cereals and vegetables, and suitable places for the pasturage of horses, cattle, sheep, and pigs. We can see from the property qualifications for the army how small the ordinary farm of the early days was. The man of the first class had about twenty *iugera* of workable land, or about thirteen acres, with some animals and some simple tools, and about 160 bushels of wheat each year when the reaping and the threshing were done. It is surprising that the property of the second class was three-quarters as much, of the third half as much, and of the fourth a quarter as much, although nowadays to distinguish between so small a farm and one three-quarters as large would seem useless.

From the beginning to the end of the Republic the question of land for small farms, or subsistence farms, was important in politics and was closely connected, of course, with the fact that the poor were often in distress. Some census figures are mentioned by Roman authors for the very early Republic, and we may suppose that they represent all the free people, whose number was generally a little more than 100,000. We also have figures for the later years of our period, and in 275 B.C. the number was over 250,000. There is reason to suppose that this figure means only adult males, so that we should probably put the number of free Romans at about 750,000. Although the government had done well in finding land for the increased Roman population, there still was pressure from landless men through the rest of the history of the Republic.

As the city of Rome grew in size, there must have been some development of industry, although the evidence eludes us. The supplying of the army with weapons kept many men busy, wherever their workshops were. In spite of the prevalence of home manufacture and the probability that many people living in the city had farms on which their clothes could be made, as well as their dishes, chairs, tables, and so on, there must have been many artisans in a city of well over 200,000 people, but we do not have precise evidence.

The treaty made by the Romans with Carthage in 348 B.C., presumably at the request of Carthage, who had extended her sway and now wished all the powers who had had former treaties with her to recognize her claims, shows that the Romans could not have had any real official interest in trade, since they made no objection to the Carthaginian policy of keeping other ships out of the parts of the sea that she regarded as hers. The Romans were more interested in securing the agreement of the Carthaginians not to try to establish themselves anywhere on the coast of Latium. Although some of the Etruscan cities and those of the western Greeks were plainly founded near the sea so as to be in position for sea trading while a little removed from the shore to be safer from the attacks of pirates, the founding of Rome, as our account has shown, was done with no thought at all of the sea, and the future greatness of Rome owed nothing to her being only twelve miles from the coast and connected to it by a navigable river.

The Romans, like the Greeks, did not have a group of people who could be called "labor," since the artisans of the period were not numerous enough and did not have enough of a distinct common interest to form such a class. Often the work in shops was done by the owner and one or two slaves working together, and the owner of a small farm, if he had a slave, naturally worked with him. Neither the farm hand nor the worker in the shop need have felt his slavery unbearable, for both had honest work to do and company in doing it, a living and a recognized place of their own. The slave lived with the master and his family on terms of some equality, since both were essentially the same kind of people, although one had the misfortune to be born a slave or to fall into slavery, most often in warfare.

The Family

For the modern observer the most striking feature of Roman family life is the *patria potestas,* the comprehensive power of the head of the family to manage and control the family property and the lives of the other members. We must realize, of course, that the low state of the family in the twentieth-century West is the exception rather than the rule and that a strongly organized family has been the rule rather than the exception. The *patria potestas* was a genuine legal form of control, correction, and punishment. Such powers of punishment now are generally vested only in impersonal governments. In spite of the growth of government in Rome, this family organization remained with little modification except the mitigation of some of its harsher features, such as the power of inflicting the death penalty.

The oldest male was *paterfamilias,* or head of the family, even if he had grown sons and grandsons. The members of the family were the agnates, or those who were related in the male line. A man would therefore not count his mother's or wife's relatives, the cognates, as members of the family. There were forms of marriage, however, by which a man could bring his bride under his *manus,* or power (the word means literally "hand"), with the intention of making her a member of his family. The family was a genuine social unit and was governed by its head, whose authority was such that his wishes guided the members of the family in all their activities. The idea of the family as a unit more important than individual desires is illustrated by the rule that the consent of the *paterfamilias* must be given to a marriage that a grown son had sought and arranged because the issue of the marriage might someday be the head of the family. If such a family seems impossibly harsh and confining to us today, we must remember that its full power could be mobilized to support any one of its members and that it could give the security that is often so deeply missed in modern times.

Marriages ordinarily were arranged by parents. The bride's father expected to furnish her a dowry. The day of the wedding was more difficult to set than it is with us, since there were so many beliefs about the ill-omened or well-omened quality of days. Neither state nor church had asserted control over marriage; there was no license to be procured, no notice to be given beforehand, no registration of the marriage in any public archive. The blessing of the gods or their forbearance could be solicited by the parties to the marriage without the aid of a priest, except that in the patrician ceremony of *confarreatio,* the most formal kind of marriage ceremony, the Pontifex Maximus presided.

When the union was blessed with offspring, the baby was laid before his father, who accepted him into the family by taking him up in his arms; he could legally be rejected. The baby had the name of his *gens,* or clan, to begin with, which took second place among the three names, or *tria nomina,* and was called the nomen. Claudius, Valerius, Cornelius are famous names of *gentes.* The personal name, or praenomen, which stood first, tended to run in the family, as names do in conservative families in our own time. Marcus, Lucius, Publius, Gaius are familiar praenomina. The third name, the cognomen, which plain people often did not have, showed what branch of the family its owner belonged to and often came from a peculiarity or an exploit, as Torquatus came from the slaughter of a Gallic chief by a Roman general named Manlius, who took the *torques,* or gold collar, from his foe's neck.

The first great ceremony for a girl was marriage, and for a boy it was the assumption of the *toga virilis,* or plain white toga of manhood, at about the age of seventeen. At that time the father added his son's name to the list of citizens, and the boy was felt to have become a man.

The funerals of the great families of Rome, who early learned, as oligarchies do, to prize and emphasize the honors gained by their members, were marked especially by processions in which were carried death masks, or *imagines,* of those members of the family who had gained high office or performed great military exploits. The masks were kept from generation to generation, as were records of the offices and exploits.

Religion

Clear traces of the practice of magic survived from the early stages of Roman religion, and indeed the practice never disappeared, even in the time when the Empire had become officially Christian. The Twelve Tables forbade the use of *mala carmina,* or charms, against people or against crops. We also find survivals of taboo, or the feeling that certain things, persons, or places can do harm if approached or touched. For example, the flamen Dialis, or priest of Jove, might not touch iron nor ride a horse, wear a ring, have any knots about his clothing, see an army ready for battle, go near a dead body, nor eat numerous things nor even mention certain things.

Animism, or the belief that everything has its own numen, or spirit, is also well attested. Often the numina were so undifferentiated that they were taken as groups, and they never became anthropomorphic. There was a spirit of the doorway called Janus, founded on a symbolism that we can readily imagine. Vesta, the spirit of the hearth, never was ascribed a human form, important as she was. The lares and penates as spirits of the household are familiar to us as an expression, at least. All household worship was conducted under the presidency of the *paterfamilias;* this, of course, included the ceremonies around the farm to purify and protect the ground and the animals and to bring increase of everything.

Jupiter, Juno, and Mars seem to have been fairly definitely thought of as gods rather than as spirits from very early times, and to have been commonly worshiped among other Italic peoples as well as at Rome. The Etruscan and Greek influence had brought the conception of anthropomorphic gods to Rome by the beginning of the Republic. The first monument of such ideas was the great temple of Jupiter Optimus Maximus, Juno, and Minerva on the Capitoline Hill, dedicated in 509 B.C. Such gods needed houses in which to live and statues of themselves to symbolize their presence.

From regal times the state had a body of officials in charge of religious matters. The Pontifex Maximus, or chief priest, headed a college of *pontifices* whose function was to regulate and watch over all the official observances of religion and to lay down rules for all religious matters. One of their duties was to manage the calendar; they determined which days were fit or unfit for legal and other business and which were the festival days.

The college of augurs was charged with the supervision of all the processes by which information was sought as to whether the gods approved of an action going on or about to go on; augury was not an attempt to foretell the future in general. The augurs ordinarily attempted to obtain and interpret signs of some sort at the request of magistrates engaged in some action, whether the holding of a meeting of the people or the sending of an army into battle.

A third group of priests was the college of fifteen flamens, three of whom belonged to major gods, Jupiter, Mars, and Quirinus (or the deified Romulus), while the other twelve belonged to less important deities. Their chief task was to sacrifice to the god whom each served. The Vestal Virgins were a society of six maidens whose chief duty was to tend the sacred fire of Vesta, goddess of the hearth.

The Army

The earliest army had a thousand men from each of the three pre-Servian tribes and a century of cavalry from each. The whole was known as the legion. Before long the army was doubled, and by the time of the Samnite Wars it had been doubled again, to four legions. The cavalry was raised to eighteen centuries. Although they first used a phalanx, or mass of men, as did the Macedonians, the Romans changed presently to a legion divided into thirty maniples, or companies, of 120 men each; it has often been suggested that the rough-country work of the Samnite Wars necessitated this more flexible formation. The men were drilled to maneuver and fight in the smaller units. Each legion was now composed of three divisions, known as the *principes, hastati,* and *triarii.* If one were hovering above and looking down on the army just before the fighting, it would seem to be three rows of neat blocks of men, 120 men in each block, or maniple. Between the maniples of the first row were large spaces; the maniples of the second row were placed behind those spaces. The third line was thinner and more continuous. On either wing were squadrons of cavalry, near whom were light-armed skirmishers.

As the two armies neared each other, the light-armed troops and cavalry inflicted such annoyance on the enemy as they could. When the main bodies of infantry came into contact, the Roman custom was to advance close enough to throw the javelin that each infantryman carried and follow them with a sharp charge. The next stage of the fighting was done with the sword. If some of the enemy moved into the gaps between the maniples of the front line, the men on the sides of the maniples could easily turn to meet them. If the enemy relied mostly on spears and a close formation, they were less likely to try to move into the gaps, for they themselves could not turn readily to fight men at their sides. Practice in swordplay and in keeping formation was very important in keeping down casualties. As the men of the front rank in each maniple tired, those of the second or third rank could step forward to relieve them. The maniples of the second row could move up to the gaps to give relief to the maniples of the first row, who could slowly pull back, leaving gaps where they had been. Thus the Romans could keep up a steady pressure of skilled sword work on the enemy for a considerable time. Sometimes suddenly sending a small force that the general had held in reserve into battle would be enough to rout a foe whom the pressure of the main line had worn down and tired. When this happened, the cavalry gave chase, and the slaughter of men who broke and ran was often fearful, for pursuers could easily strike them down and leave them to be dispatched later.

The fact that the Romans had given the other peoples of Italy a place in their imperium instead of merely subjecting them was a source of immense strength for the armies that fought the battles of the Roman organization. Drawing from this great pool of manpower, the Romans could have nearly 100,000 men in the field and on the sea year after year in the great wars with the Carthaginians, known as the First and Second Punic Wars, which they fought in the middle and at the end of the third century B.C. They ordinarily requested contingents of infantry from their allies in the federation that would equal the number of the Roman infantry, plus a larger number of cavalry. The allied infantry were armed and trained as were the Romans and formed the wings in battle while the Romans took the center. The commander of the whole army was a

Roman consul, although in such massive wars as the Punic Wars some armies had to be commanded by proconsuls, praetors, and propraetors.

The thorough and systematic way in which the Romans made their camps is typical of their deliberate and farsighted methods of warfare. The usual careful progress of a Roman army across a countryside was made even more deliberate by its stopping at a fairly early hour to make camp for the night. Morale and discipline were both helped by the fact that at night the men had a safe and orderly lodging. Further, if it were worsted in the field, the army had a prepared fortress to which it could often retreat before its losses became too heavy.

The ceremony called the triumph was the culmination of a successful campaign. The Senate early arrogated to itself the right to decide whether or not the general might have the triumph, or perhaps the lesser reward known as the ovation. Gradually informal rules and then specific ones grew up as to how many of the enemy must have been killed. Only the major magistrates—dictator, consul, or praetor—might win a triumph. The commander and the army might not cross the pomerium, the religious boundary of the city of Rome, until the Senate had awarded the triumph. Then they marched through the streets to the Capitoline Hill, the general in a special chariot adorned with gold and ivory, clad in a special toga and wearing a golden crown on his head. The Senate, the priests, and the white oxen for sacrifice came before him; he was followed by the soldiers and by wagons laden with booty and often by floats with symbolic representations of forts or hill strongholds or cities that had been captured. On the Capitoline the general laid a laurel wreath on the lap of the statue of Capitoline Jove and presented the oxen for sacrifice. His name was recorded in the *fasti triumphales,* the official record of triumphs.

18

ROME'S CONQUEST OF THE WEST

THE FIRST PUNIC WAR

The First Punic War was momentous in that it led to Rome's acquisition of her first territory outside Italy. The causes of the war are obscure, although the circumstances that led to its outbreak are plain. To assert that the Romans, now that they dominated all Italy, were bound to come into conflict with the Carthaginians, who in 265 B.C. were pressing toward their old goal of controlling all Sicily, is not to give a cause.

About 288 B.C. a group of Italians who had been serving as mercenaries for Syracuse seized the city of Messana, on the Sicilian shore of the narrowest part of the strait between Sicily and Italy, and proceeded to make continual raids for plunder in eastern Sicily. Finally the Syracusan Hiero succeeded in containing them and besieged them (his success made him king of Syracuse in 265 B.C.). The Carthaginians, fearing that he would take Messana, answered a call for help from the mercenaries, who liked to call themselves Mamertines from an Italian name, Mamers, for the god of war. The simple-minded Mamertines, fearing the Carthaginians now in their citadel, also sent out a call for help to the Romans.

The Senate refused the request. It may well have been mindful of the treaties with the Carthaginians and probably saw no danger that Carthage would try to close the strait to traffic with the foot of Italy. There seemed no reason why Rome should receive the Mamertines as allies or clients and thereafter protect them, since she had just chastised such a group who seized another city in the same region.

Presently, however, prominent people who liked the prospect of a war

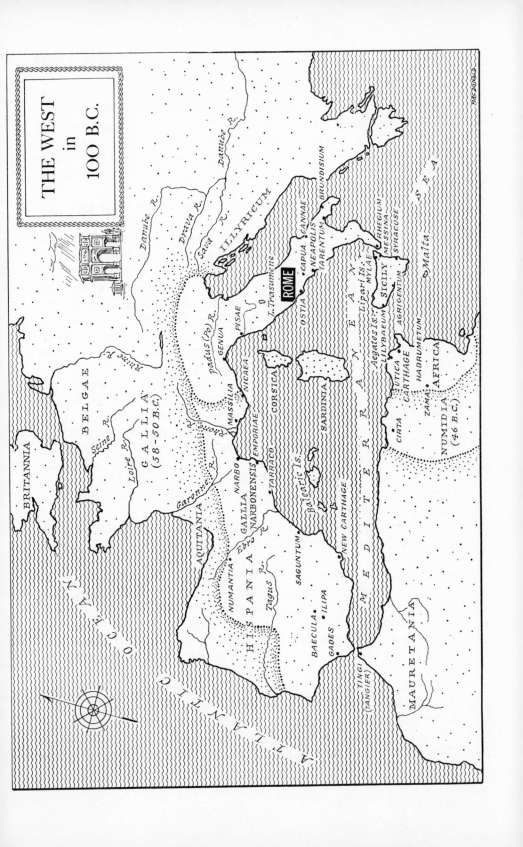

THE WEST
in
100 B.C.

BRITANNIA

BELGAE

GALLIA
(58-50 B.C.)

Seine R.

Loire R.

Garonne R.

Rhine R.

Danube R.

Drava R.

Sava R.

Danube R.

ILLYRICUM

AQUITANIA

Padus (Po) R.

GENUA

NICAEA

MASSILIA

PISAE

L. Trasumene

ROME

OSTIA

CAPUA

NEAPOLIS

CANNAE

TARENTUM

BRUNDISIUM

RHEGIUM

MESSINA

MYLAE

Lipari Is.

Agates Is.

LILYBAEUM

SICILY

AGRIGENTUM

SYRACUSE

Malta

GALLIA
NARBONENSIS

NARBO

Ebro R.

TARRACO

EMPORIAE

Balearic Is.

CORSICA

SARDINIA

NEW CARTHAGE

SAGUNTUM

Tagus R.

HISPANIA

NUMANTIA

BAECULA

ILIPA

GADES

TINGI
(TANGIER)

MAURETANIA

MEDITERRANEAN SEA

UTICA

CARTHAGE

CIRTA

ZAMA

HADRUMETUM

NUMIDIA
(46 B.C.)

AFRICA

ATLANTIC OCEAN

N

Rhone R.

in Sicily, chief of whom was one of the consuls of the year, carried the matter to the *Comitia tributa,* which voted to accept the Mamertines as allies, perhaps in response to the suggestion that there might be booty in a country long known as wealthy. This was not a declaration of war, which could only be made by the *Comitia centuriata,* and it should be understood that this account of the reasoning involved rests partly on conjecture.

The Mamertines somehow persuaded the commander of the Punic garrison to evacuate the citadel; his government crucified him soon afterward for doing so. The consul, Appius Claudius, to whom the Roman people had voted the command in this adventure, got his troops across the strait in ships of the south Italian allies and occupied the citadel of Messana from the water side. King Hiero of Syracuse had now joined his old enemies, the Carthaginians, in the face of the threat from the Romans, and their men were before the walls of Messana. Claudius ordered them to retire from the territory of an ally of Rome, and when they refused, war was declared on them. This was the formal beginning, in 264 B.C., of the First Punic War, as it is generally called.

The Romans attacked their enemies in turn. Hiero soon withdrew, and after some time an alliance was made between him and the Romans under which he supplied them with food during their later campaigns and to which he remained faithful, to his own profit, until his death in 215 B.C. Although they could have regarded the subsequent withdrawal of the Carthaginians from the neighborhood of Messana as sufficient recognition that the city was under their protection, the Romans chose to act as though there could be no stopping until they had driven the Carthaginians entirely out of Sicily.

They therefore put strong armies into Sicily and drove the Carthaginians back slowly toward the western end of the island. They captured the great Punic stronghold called Acragas by the Greeks, Agrigentum by the Romans, and Girgenti by the modern Italians and sold the people into slavery. Since the Carthaginians could be as stubborn as the Romans and had two very strong points at Panormus and Lilybaeum that could be provisioned and reinforced through their harbors, they, too, were ready to continue the struggle. They were also able to land troops or pick them up and ferry them to other points as they pleased, even for raids on the coast of Italy, since they controlled the sea.

The Romans therefore decided that for the campaigning of the year 260 they must have a fleet. They built twenty triremes and a hundred larger ships. Finding oarsmen was difficult, as we learn from the history of the naval empire of Athens. The Romans gathered young men from their allies, trained them in rowing on stages set up on land, gave them a few days of practice in the ships when they were built, and sent them against the enemy. Thirty thousand men were needed to row the hundred larger ships.

In the early summer the new fleet went down to Syracuse, where the ships were fitted with a simple but brilliant invention, a raised gangway near the bow that could be swung around and its outer end dropped on the deck of any ship that tried to ram or lay alongside. A spike would sink into the deck of the other ship and hold the gangway there, and the eighty legionary soldiers assigned to each ship would board the enemy vessel, where there would be no comparable force of fighting men. In August, 260 B.C., the consul Duilius met the enemy fleet off the northeast corner of Sicily (the battle takes its name from the coastal town of Mylae) and defeated them thoroughly by using the new device.

Striking as this victory was, however, and useful as it was in lessening Punic raids from the sea, it was not conclusive, for the Romans did not find any way to reduce the Punic fortresses in western Sicily. Three years dragged by in minor operations. In 256 the Romans sent a force to Africa that raided successfully, but was defeated in a major battle. The fleet that was taking the remains of the expedition back to Sicily was destroyed in a great storm with dreadful loss of life. For fourteen years the war continued, often with long intermissions. Again a Roman fleet was lost with great loss of life. The great Carthaginian Hanno is known to have opposed continuing the war and to have urged that the Carthaginians do the sensible thing by consolidating their hold on the fertile territory near them in North Africa and cultivating their profitable trade in the western Mediterranean.

The last stage of the war began with the revival of the Carthaginian efforts by Hamilcar Barca, representing the aggressive policy of his family, who as a group are referred to as the Barcids. His aggressive measures in Sicily caused the Romans to build still another fleet, with which in 241 B.C. they so defeated the Punic fleet that the forces of Hamilcar Barca in Sicily could no longer be supplied or reinforced. The peace terms were fairly lenient: the Carthaginians must withdraw completely from Sicily, restore to the Romans all the prisoners they had taken, and pay an indemnity of 110 talents a year for twenty years. The *Comitia centuriata*, by whom peace had to be declared as well as war, rejected the terms set by the general on the scene and had ten commissioners sent to Sicily to investigate the situation. In the end the indemnity was increased to 3200 talents to be paid in ten years, Rome took some small islands near Sicily, and the Carthaginians were forbidden to sail in Italian waters (perhaps for the benefit of the Greek commercial cities of South Italy) or to recruit mercenaries in Italy.

The Results of the War

The system that the Romans had followed in building up their power in Italy, that of giving the conquered a share of the labors and the rewards of either alliance or the Roman citizenship, did not seem desirable or practical for Sicily. It was understood that the Carthaginians were all to go and that Rome was to control the island, but without a precise theory of government or a formal installation of Roman officials. Hiero's Syracusan kingdom, which occupied about a quarter of the island, continued to be an ally of the Romans. Messana also was an ally. Five cities that had rendered service to the Romans in the difficult early days of the war were made *liberae et immunes*, or free and not subject to obligations, as the Roman commanders had promised them at the time. Syracuse and these others together held nearly half of Sicily. All other cities of Sicily were allowed to govern their own territories in their own way, but were subject to the payment of a tithe, or tenth, of their harvested crops, a fair system that did not grind them down in lean years as would a fixed tax.

Carthaginian troubles were far from ended. From late in 241 to early in 238 they fought a bitter war with some of their former mercenaries, who were joined by the North African neighbors of Carthage. At the end of this war some mercenaries in Sardinia appealed to Rome; the upshot was that Rome brutally took Sardinia and Corsica. In 227 B.C. the two islands were declared a province and put under one of the two new praetors. The tithe of Sardinia became an important source of supply of grain for Rome.

At first the only major Roman official in Sicily was a quaestor. In 227 B.C., however, it was decided that such a post required an official who had the imperium, and from that year on two extra praetors were elected (making four in all), one of whom was sent to govern Sicily and the other to Sardinia and Corsica. The praetor presided in general over "the province"; this word now began for the first time to have the meaning of an overseas possession instead of merely the sphere of duty assigned to a magistrate. He also presided over an equitable legal system, partly of suits as before in the local courts and partly of contests between citizens of different Sicilian cities and between Sicilians and Romans.

Hamilcar Barca, having brought the war with the mercenaries to an end, was sent by his government to Spain in 237 B.C. The Carthaginians had had some trading posts on the coast, but no control over territory in the interior. Basing himself at Gades (modern Cadiz), Hamilcar made substantial conquests in the interior of Spain before his death in 228, being followed by his son-in-law for seven years, then by his son Hannibal, now come to full manhood, thoroughly trained as soldier and administrator, and ripe for his great deeds against the Romans. The work of these three men brought Carthage considerable wealth, especially in silver from the rich mines, and a goodly number of soldiers from the able fighting men of Spain.

AFFAIRS IN ITALY

Between her wars with the Carthaginians Rome carried on three sets of operations to assure her security in the North. First, the Ligurians, who inhabited the coastal part of Italy that lies toward France, had lately expanded down the west coast of Italy, pressing the Etruscan allies of Rome back in that region. They also gave aid and comfort to the Corsicans, whom Rome was having difficulty in subduing, and preyed on the ships of Massilia, which was friendly to Rome. Between 238 and 230 the Romans drove them back up the coast and finally subdued them after the second war with Carthage.

Second, the Gauls were far more dangerous than the Ligurians. The Romans learned that the Gauls of northern Italy, who had been quiet for some time, were summoning to join them other tribes from farther north, even from beyond the Alps. A complete review of the Roman military forces at that moment showed that they could put 250,000 citizen infantry and 20,000 cavalry into the field and that the allies could furnish 350,000 men. If reserves and the forces of the Greek allies in the South were counted, the total was well over 700,000 men, a huge number for the time. In 225 B.C. a Celtic army of 70,000 did cross the Apennines and descend into Etruria and score a success against the Romans and take a great deal of booty, but as this army made its way back northward along the western coast of Italy, two Roman armies met it at Telamon, near the coast, and practically annihilated it, killing 40,000 and taking 10,000 prisoners. The Romans decided that they must have a better boundary to the North and in four more campaigns conquered Cisalpine Gaul, or "Gaul this side of the Alps," or what we are used to seeing on the map as continental Italy spreading out above the top of the peninsula. This was a major war, both difficult and important, but it has been overshadowed by the more spectacular war with Hannibal and the Carthaginians that followed it. The Romans also campaigned against the tribes around the head of the Adriatic and carried their frontier there to the Alps.

The third of Rome's operations between the Punic Wars was against the Illyrians of the Adriatic coast across from the eastern coast of Italy, who not only had made themselves a nuisance as pirates, but had allied themselves with Philip V of Macedonia in his contest with the Aetolians to the south of them and had proved so formidable that they caused a chill of apprehension among the Greeks in general. In 230 B.C. the Romans sent so strong a force against them that it would seem that the Illyrians had been represented as most dangerous. We notice, too, that the Romans gave formal notice to the Aetolian and Achaean Leagues and to the cities of Corinth and Athens that they had chastised the piratical Illyrians and had taken measures to contain them. We need not see here the beginning of a policy of aggression eastward. We may, however, suspect that the Romans were receiving information from the Greeks of their federation about the sinister intentions of the Illyrians against commerce and perhaps against the coast of Italy, and we may also suspect that the Roman Senate was as yet a little innocent about the affairs and the diplomatic assumptions and methods of the Hellenistic world and was capable of making brusque and awkward moves in response to the urging of those who professed to know all about the capabilities and intentions of the Illyrians or Philip V.

An interesting popular measure was passed in 232 B.C. by the *Comitia tributa* against the strong opposition of leading nobles and without any request for the approval of the Senate. A tribune, C. Flaminius, was the author of the bill, which provided that the *ager Gallicus,* the territory below the Po River taken over five decades before from the Gauls and in the meantime rented out by the censors as public land on five-year terms, should be given as allotments to individual Roman citizens. Senators might have objected that the allies were to receive no share in this, that Latin colonies would be fairer and more useful; they might also have resented losing profits gained from leasing the land cheaply and farming it or ranching on it. In view of the perpetual question of managing the voters, it should be noted here that Flaminius, who sorely offended the nobles as a class and was soon to do so again, was able to be elected to the highest offices. Although they could be influenced by the aristocracy to a surprising extent, this and other cases show that the voters would sometimes vote for measures and elect people most unpalatable to the governing class.

Some time later in the century Flaminius was the only senator to support an interesting but slightly puzzling measure enacted by the *Comitia tributa* that prohibited senators and their sons from owning any real seagoing vessel—any vessel, that is, of more than about 225 bushels capacity. A prohibition against senators' taking state contracts probably was part of the same law. Julius Caesar re-enacted these rules in his consulship (59 B.C.). An obvious, but far from satisfactory, explanation is that senatorial dignity was thought to be inconsistent with commercial interests.

THE SECOND PUNIC WAR: 218 TO 201 B.C.

The Second Punic War, or Hannibalic War, ranks with the Trojan War and the American Civil War as one of the great literary wars of history. As the Trojan War and Achilles found Homer to tell the story, so Rome's war with Hannibal and the Carthaginians found Livy, one of the great literary historians. We need not suppose that the Carthaginians planned a war of revenge against Rome, for they were used to making careful calculations based on their own interest rather than on emotion. If he acted in Spain in a way likely to bring on war with Rome, Hannibal is not likely to have done so for a revenge that would surely engender further war, but with the idea that the Romans were such incorrigible international bullies that it was necessary to reduce their power far enough to prevent them from interfering with other peoples. To destroy them might well have seemed to a Carthaginian merely an invitation to the almost equally aggressive Philip V of Macedonia to move into Italy and from there further west. Hannibal's conduct after his crushing defeats of the Romans early in the war seemed more an attempt to break up the Roman federation in Italy than to destroy Rome.

The Romans had been worried enough by Hamilcar Barca's successes in Spain to send an embassy to him in 231 B.C. to ask his intentions; he replied that he was only trying to help pay off the indemnity. In 226 B.C. the Romans made a treaty with his son-in-law and successor that bound the Carthaginians not to go in arms north of the Ebro River, which flows into the Mediterranean a little north of Tarraco, the modern Tarragona. They presumably agreed to recognize Punic power south of the river, for they needed to be free to deal with the Ligurians and with the Gauls. The Greek city of Massilia (Marseilles), which presumably urged the Romans to oppose Carthaginian expansion in their direction, had to let go three of its colonies south of the Ebro.

When Hannibal took charge in 221 B.C., he decided, after having scored some successes against the Spanish tribes, that he must reduce the town of Saguntum, south of the Ebro, which was an ally of Rome. We do not know when the alliance was made; it may well have been done hastily in 222 or 221 B.C. to give the Romans an excuse to interfere with the Carthaginians in Spain once the end of the great struggle with the Gauls was in sight, and it did serve that purpose, for the Romans made demands, such as that for the surrender of Hannibal and his staff, that left the Carthaginians no choice but war.

Hannibal Invades Italy

Hannibal marched to Italy by necessity rather than by choice, for Rome controlled the sea. Although crossing the Alps had not proved too difficult for whole migrating Celtic peoples, the local resistance that Hannibal encountered and the rigorous weather of the high places in early autumn made his crossing most arduous. Having lost several thousand men and some of his elephants, he came down late in 218 into the plains of North Italy with some 26,000 well seasoned troops and with hopes that the Gauls would rise to join him out of hostility to the Romans. He also had hopes that a determined invasion would cause Rome's allies to fall away from her. If in retrospect he seems not to have understood what bonds held Rome's allies, we may remember how much unattractive Roman behavior the Carthaginians had seen.

In the very first engagement, a cavalry skirmish, the consul Publius Cornelius Scipio was wounded and would have lost his life had he not been rescued by his son, who was also named Publius Cornelius Scipio and was to gain the added name of Africanus nearly twenty years later when he defeated Hannibal in Africa to end the war. Scipio's Gallic auxiliaries then deserted him, and he drew back. The other consul soon joined him and insisted on engaging Hannibal. The engagement was typical. Hannibal, having prepared and breakfasted his troops, took the field early and tempted the Roman into leading his men out with no breakfast and fording the Trebia River, which gave its name to the battle. After the wet, cold, and hungry Romans had worked on his center, which held well, he used his cavalry and wings to envelop their line, then called for a charge by a force hidden in ambush in their rear. Although two-thirds of the Roman force perished in this battle, ten thousand legionaries broke out and made their way to the fortified city of Placentia. Both sides then settled down for the winter. The later career of the young Scipio shows that he, at least, was attentive to the lessons in generalship that Hannibal was presenting to his adversaries.

Hannibal's Great Victories

In May, 217, when the passes were almost clear, Hannibal moved from his base at Bononia (Bologna) and marched with great difficulty through one of the Apennine passes to the western side of central Italy. The consul Flaminius followed him, but refused to let Hannibal entice him into battle by seeming to leave himself exposed. As Hannibal marched southward toward Rome, with Flaminius following him at a respectful distance because of his inferiority in cavalry, he turned off to the left, or eastward, toward Perusia and set a trap on the shore of Lake Trasimeno, where it was possible for him to catch Flaminius' army between the water and the hills around. When the Romans had marched along the lake in the early morning mist and had emerged onto a little plain, the Punic troops, who had been quietly waiting on the hills above the level of the mist until they could hear the Romans gathered below them, charged from three sides. Although the Romans fought bravely, they were almost wiped out, and Flaminius lost his life.

Hannibal freed those of the allied troops whom he had captured. In spite of this gesture and his great victory, not a single city opened its gates to him. He could have marched unopposed to Rome, however. That he did not, now and on a later occasion, has been attributed to a weakness in siegecraft. It seems likely that so brilliant a student of Hellenistic warfare would have been able to conduct a siege effectively, had that been his purpose; therefore the destruction of the city of Rome and of all Roman power must not have been his strategic aim. He turned and spent the summer going down the east side of Italy and ravaging widely, expecting to detach the hill people from Rome, again without success.

The Romans decided to have a dictator for this emergency, something that they had not done for a long time. The choice fell on an experienced and careful man, Quintus Fabius Maximus, whose policy of moving cautiously when in Hannibal's vicinity was to earn him the added name of Cunctator, which should be translated "the slow-goer" rather than "the delayer." The Fabian policy was to follow Hannibal and weaken him by attrition while refusing to meet him in the open field. Hannibal countered this strategy by moving over to the fertile fields of Campania and laying them waste, but Fabius did not let loud complaints and criticisms tempt him to offer battle. When the term of the dictatorship expired, it was not renewed, but Hannibal had not won another victory and had almost no success in detaching Rome's allies. Fabius had done well.

The year 216 brought the supreme disaster of the Battle of Cannae, fought near the east coast of southern Italy. Cannae was a classic battle of encirclement. The Punic center allowed itself to be pushed back slowly by the weight of the legions, which tended more and more toward the center in the process, until the Punic wings could come around, enclosing the Romans, and dispatch them without their being able to fight effectively. Over 60,000 were lost.

Hannibal's officers urged him to move quickly to take the city of Rome. Most historians believe that this time, too, he refused because Rome was strongly fortified and he recognized his own lack of skill in siegecraft. The fact is that his numbers and the numbers of potential defenders were such that he could probably have taken even so fortified a city by assault, if he had wished to, and could have had additional men soon to make the task easier, for in fact the Carthaginian Senate did not begrudge him support. It seems more likely that he did not intend to take the city of Rome.

Rome's Darkest Days

After Cannae several important cities of central Italy went over to Hannibal, as did most of the tribes of the Samnites. In southern Italy all the Italic tribes deserted, while the Greek cities in general remained true to Rome. Badly as the Roman confederation was shaken, there were still strongly fortified places all through central and southern Italy that could not be taken without considerable effort and that remained undisturbed. Farther north, the Etruscans and Umbrians remained solidly with the Romans. Capua was in a class by itself; it was an old and proud city and very rich because of its industries, built on Greek and Etruscan traditions. Hannibal met its demand for complete autonomy and freedom from conscription of its men for his war; the demands reflect its grievance against Rome. Early in 215 B.C. Hiero of Syracuse died, and soon the Romans found their Sicilian province ablaze with resentment and acts of resistance. Five years of effort were needed to regain control of Sicily.

In Spain Gnaeus Scipio, who had been sent there in 218, began by winning Tarraco as a base. In 217 his brother Publius, who had commanded in the first engagement of the war in northern Italy in 218, arrived as proconsul with twenty ships and eight thousand men, and in 216 the brothers won a major victory. In 212, however, the Carthaginians sent substantial reinforcements to Spain, and in 211 they crushed the two armies with which the brothers were attempting to campaign separately. Both the Scipios were killed. The small remaining Roman force, under a minor officer who had survived, was barely able to maintain itself north of the Ebro River.

Philip V of Macedonia, whose sphere of influence had been brusquely invaded by the Roman operations in Illyria, watched the descent of Hannibal on Italy with interest. On receiving the news of the battle at Lake Trasimeno he moved to ally himself with the Aetolians, some of whom had already spoken of the rise of Rome as a danger for Greece, so as to be ready to drive the Romans from Illyria in case of their defeat by Carthage. In the summer of 215 he made a treaty with Carthage. They were to deal with Italy, and Philip, in spite of his having dreamed at one time of invading Italy by land around the head of the Adriatic, was to stay away. Carthage could call on him for troops for their war with Rome. On defeating Rome they were to make it part of their terms that Rome must abandon any hold on Illyria and the islands near it and must agree not to attack Philip.

For the Romans the alliance offered hardly more than inconvenience, for they easily countered Philip's few moves against them in Illyria and on the Adriatic. It did bring them more into contact with the Greeks, for they detached the Aetolians from him and raised some of the other Greeks, who feared him, against him. A shrewd king of Asia Minor, Attalus of Pergamum, also joined the Romans. In 206 the Aetolians made peace with Philip, and the Romans did so in 205.

The few years after Cannae required the supreme effort. The only possible strategy was to avoid meeting Hannibal in the field and wage a war of attrition. Roman losses had been heavy, and to gather, pay, and equip the large forces now needed was very difficult. Continued command of the sea was essential, for which purpose two hundred ships and some 50,000 men were needed. At one point the commanders of the fleet wrote to complain that money and supplies had not reached them, only to be told that there was no money nor supplies and that they must feed and pay their men as best they could.

The year 212 saw a notable triumph, however, the capture by the Romans of the great city of Syracuse, which had been delayed for almost two years by those marvelous devices of the scientist Archimedes that will be described later. In 211 Capua fell to the Romans. Hannibal was unable to prevent the Romans from investing it closely with a double line of works that faced outward as well as toward the city and so could defy his attempts to raise the Roman siege. When taken, Capua was not sacked nor destroyed. Some of the nobles committed suicide, others were executed, and all the territory of the city was confiscated, after which it was allowed to continue as a commercial center without any political organization under the supervision of a prefect sent from Rome.

In 210 B.C. Publius Cornelius Scipio, the future Africanus, was irregularly given the imperium as proconsul by a vote of the assembly. He had been aedile, but not quaestor or praetor. He had, however, been tested in eight years of warfare and had probably shown clearly his remarkable ability to lead and inspire troops. There was a definite shortage of trained and able generals. Late in the year 210 he went to Spain with reinforcements. During the winter he drilled his army and made plans, and in the early spring he made a sudden attack of army and fleet together on New Carthage, the great Carthaginian base in Spain, taking it the day after he reached it. Thus he gained a most useful base, farther south than Tarraco, well fortified, possessing a good harbor, with shops and trained men for ship repairs and for making armor and weapons, filled with useful stores and money, and commanding the access to some of the silver mines. Another success was reported in the same year: the recapture of the strong city of Tarentum, which had been betrayed to Hannibal a few years before.

Rome Moves to the Offensive

Scipio began the offensive against the main Carthaginian forces with the Battle of Baecula in the following year, 208 B.C. He met one of the three Punic armies that were in Spain, commanded by Hannibal's brother, Hasdrubal, and inflicted heavy losses on it. Hasdrubal withdrew northward, crossed into Gaul, recruited new troops there, and descended into Italy in 207 to help Hannibal, as we shall see. Scipio has been criticized for letting Hasdrubal leave Spain; to pursue him, however, would have meant getting out of the proper range from his base and exposing himself to the joint attack of the other two Punic armies, thus inviting another disaster to Roman power in Spain.

During the rest of the year 208 and in 207 Scipio held his ground and nurtured his relations with the Spanish tribes, which was as useful as winning battles. Early in 206, however, the two Punic armies together moved out to seek a major engagement. The opposing forces made contact at Ilipa, near Seville, and encamped on low hills opposite each other. Several days in succession the Carthaginian commander led out his men; Scipio led his army out each day when the Carthaginians were in position, but refused battle.

When he was ready to fight, he passed the word one night for the men to be ready at dawn. He came forth with his Spanish auxiliaries in the center and his legionaries on the wings, the reverse of the usual arrangement. A brisk cavalry attack on the Punic outposts brought the enemy out before breakfast—a device that Scipio had learned from Hannibal at the Battle of the Trebia River in 218—and under constant pressure so that on seeing his changed order of battle they could not shift their own. His less formidable and less reliable Spanish allies were able to threaten the better Punic troops in the center and keep them in their position, while the heavy block of Roman legionaries on either wing unfolded as it approached the enemy and by orderly marching spread outward to enflank the Punic wings—what might be called a flying encirclement. Using his stronger troops against the enemy's weaker ones, Scipio crushed their wings and surrounded their center, inflicting such heavy losses that they no longer had any body of troops that could hope to oppose him. This was the end of significant Punic power in Spain.

In the Italian theater the chief event of these years was the utter defeat of Hasdrubal and his army in the Battle of the Metaurus River in 207 B.C.

As Hasdrubal moved down into Italy with a strong army, a Roman force of four legions under one of the consuls barred his way at the Metaurus River in Umbria, some thirty miles south of Ariminum. C. Claudius Nero, commanding the other consular army, was farther south trying to block a slow movement northward by Hannibal to meet his brother, when messengers from Hasdrubal were captured. It was learned from them that the plan was for the two Punic armies to meet in Umbria.

Taking six thousand infantry and one thousand cavalry, Claudius stole away, completely deceiving Hannibal by leaving some men in his camp to obscure the fact that he had gone. He is said to have marched 240 miles in six days, the country people along the way coming out to offer the soldiers food and to cheer them as they trudged past. He slipped into his colleague's camp by night, but the double bugle call in the morning betrayed to Hasdrubal that both consuls were there. He attempted a bold dash to get past them and join Hannibal, but the Romans overtook him at once, forced him to fight, and crushed his army. Claudius marched back and slipped into his camp without Hannibal's knowing that he had been gone. He freed two prisoners and sent them to tell Hannibal what had happened, while a cavalryman rode up to Hannibal's pickets and rolled Hasdrubal's head along the ground at them.

The aftermath of the battle also provides us with a note on the management of Roman elections. Two of the three men chosen to carry the news to Rome were known to be candidates for the consulship of the next year; their being the bearers of good news commended them so strongly to the people that they were elected. It is probable, although it cannot be proved, that the two messengers who were candidates for the consulship were political allies of the consul in charge in northern Italy and that he chose them with the intention of helping their candidacies. Naturally such opportunities as this were eagerly seized by candidates and by their supporters. Military achievement was highly acceptable to the voters, even in circumstances far less tense than these. To give another example, Scipio's great popularity with the people when he came home victorious from Spain surpassed, as we shall see, anything of the sort yet seen. He was triumphantly elected to the consulship, was able to secure the election of a group of his friends to the other consulship and to the other offices, and then was able to put great pressure on the Senate to adopt his plan to take the war to Africa.

The sponsorship of measures helpful to the people was also highly acceptable to the voters, as is shown by the career of Flaminius, the consul of 217 who was defeated and killed by Hannibal at Lake Trasimeno. As tribune in 232 B.C. Flaminius carried a bill for the distribution of the *ager Gallicus* to citizens for farms. In 227 he won the praetorship and served with distinction in Sicily, and the people made him consul for 223. It is believed that the prejudice of the senatorial order gave rise to the stories of his recklessness as general against the Gauls of North Italy in that year. Distasteful as the renewed candidacy of Flaminius must have been, the magistrate presiding over the consular election late in 218 would hardly dare to reject the name of so important and popular a candidate, although he had the power to do so. Flaminius' sponsorship of the agrarian law of 232 doubtless still counted in his favor with the people in 218, and there was also a feeling that the war had been mismanaged and that a man somewhat close to the people would manage it better.

The members of the nobility wooed the voters year after year, however, in pursuit of offices and influence, which are both means and ends in an oligarchy of this kind, and generally they found few special circumstances like those we have just mentioned that they could use in trying to commend themselves to the voters. Their constant method was to make alliances with the great and to offer patronage to the small. We can apprehend, sometimes clearly, the alliances of the great families, often cemented by matrimony and sometimes riven by personal quarrels—alliances that aimed at the acquisition of magistracies, priesthoods, governorships, and military posts for their members. There are times when it seems that a whole clan may be identified with a policy of some sort, just as Hanno and his group in Carthage were opposed to the aggressive policies of the Barcids for more than a generation. We cannot always be sure; perhaps the Cornelii as a group favored an aggressive policy toward Carthage and Hannibal, but this aggressive policy may have belonged only to the two Scipios, father and son. The lack of men holding magistracies is not always a sure sign that a clan was temporarily neither powerful nor influential, for it might have no men of the right age to hold office and still be strongly represented in the debates of the Senate by elderly members of failing health or good men defeated in close races for the consulship, to say nothing of the clan's influence through its alliances.

Patronage of the small man, like alliances with the great, was slightly uncertain when viewed as a means of achieving office. Probably the noble landlord could be consistently successful in controlling the votes of his tenants and could expect his political allies to be able to deliver votes for him, even after the introduction of the secret ballot in 139 B.C. The voters were conservative about preferring members of old families, so that any scion of the few greatest families who did not have some spectacular disqualification could expect to move steadily upward and hold the consulship. The influence of the great families was naturally exerted through a chain of lesser families as well as directly on the voters. The leading families of Rome made matrimonial alliances with families all over Italy.

They sometimes aided members of families who had never held office at Rome to establish themselves among the nobility at Rome. A striking example from the period of the Second Punic War is Marcus Porcius Cato of Tusculum, in the hills beyond the Latin plain, whom a Valerius Flaccus commended to the Roman voters, thinking that Cato would bring valuable votes from the region of Tusculum. Cato rose to be censor as well as consul, discharging his offices so as to outshine his sponsor.

The members of the nobility, even while they competed fiercely for offices and influence, were generally united in support of the interests of their own group. The man who espoused the theory of full popular sovereignty, like Flaminius, or who as consul tried to strike out with a policy of his own not approved by the majority, was subject to great pressure from relatives, friends, political allies, and the influential older men. The consul always had to remember that after one year of that office he must return to the bosom of his own social group.

The Offensive in Africa

Late in the year 206 Scipio returned from Spain and was elected to the consulship for 205 by an overwhelming vote. His political ally M. Licinius Crassus, who was Pontifex Maximus, was elected to the other consulship.

Scipio now urged an invasion of Africa to draw Hannibal out of Italy. Fabius "the slow-goer" urged that they drive Hannibal away by attacking him in Italy, fearing the mischances that could befall an expedition to North Africa. Although Fabius and the other more conservative members of the Senate could perhaps have gathered a majority in favor of assigning Scipio some other task than the invasion of Africa (opposing Hannibal in Italy was the obvious one), Scipio could surely have persuaded the *Comitia tributa* to vote him any province he wished and thus could have had his way with complete legality. One of the conservative senators asked him if he would leave the matter to the Senate and abide by its decision or would appeal to the people. He replied that he would do what he thought was in the best interest of the state.

The tribunes of the people were asked what their attitude would be. They jointly answered that Scipio must either trust the Senate or withdraw his proposal there and take it to the people, for they would intercede with their veto if he received an unfavorable answer from the Senate and then asked the people to override it. Once this point was established, the conservatives apparently agreed to a formula, and Scipio entrusted the decision to the Senate, which assigned Sicily as the province of one consul with permission to cross to Africa if he thought it necessary. Since Scipio's colleague, the Pontifex Maximus, could not leave Italy (and of course he was elected for that reason), Sicily was Scipio's province.

Scipio delayed until the spring of 204, when he sailed as proconsul for Africa with a force that he had raised to about 30,000 men. His very careful preparations had done much to win over some of the conservatives. The Numidian prince Masinissa joined him with a strong cavalry force. A rival Numidian, Syphax, whom Scipio had also made great efforts to win, had been brought back to the Carthaginian side by the offer in marriage of the beautiful daughter of one of the great Punic nobles.

Although Scipio accomplished little beside one minor victory in the first campaign, in 203 he won a major battle. He captured the port of Tunis, near Carthage, and his lieutenants defeated and captured Syphax. At last Hannibal was recalled from Italy, his great plan a final failure.

The Battle of Zama (202 b.c.) ended the war. It has been called the only battle in history where two great commanders gave their best performances. The Romans skillfully parried the opening charge of Hannibal's elephants, partly by opening lanes to let them run through and be brought down by attacks from the side and the rear, partly by frightening them back with loud noises so that they recoiled on their own line. The Roman cavalry then drove off the Punic cavalry. Scipio, now ready to operate his flying encirclement as at Ilipa, could see that Hannibal's third line, composed of veterans, was in position to withstand such a move. After some conventional fighting Scipio called off his army, and Hannibal was willing to let him do so. Scipio now lengthened his line, and Hannibal followed; Scipio let him do so, hoping for the return of the Roman cavalry. The two armies closed again, and soon the cavalry, which had thoroughly dispersed the Punic cavalry with its pursuit, rode in and decided the contest. Hannibal escaped.

Under the terms offered by Scipio, Carthage was to retain her autonomy, but must restore lands claimed by Masinissa as well as recognize his sovereignty in Numidia. She must give up all her elephants and almost all her ships. The indemnity was raised to ten thousand talents, to be paid in fifty installments. Early in 201 all was arranged; Scipio returned to Rome with his army and received his added name, Africanus, by popular acclaim.

The Romans took Spain as their great prize of this war. Although they did not completely subdue it until the time of Augustus, they gained agricultural and mineral wealth from it, sent it colonists, recruited soldiers there, and drew it into the mainstream of the Greco-Roman culture. It is customary to say that the Senate strengthened its position by its wise and tenacious direction of the war, and it surely must have gained greatly in skill and collective experience by having to deal with so many and so urgent problems through almost two decades. Many of the common people visited Sicily in the armed forces during the war or fought among the Greeks of southern Italy. In both these places many men must have spent time among Greeks who had never done so before, so that Greek words, ideas, amusements, and vices became familiar to them. As for the Romans as a whole, the winning of the war made them supreme in the western Mediterranean, and both they themselves and peoples and governments elsewhere were keenly aware of the fact.

CHAPTER

19

THE HELLENISTIC EAST

We shall turn aside here from our narrative to describe the culture of the East in the Hellenistic Age, not only for itself, but also because this was the point at which the Romans suddenly became far better acquainted with the East and felt its influence far more intensely as a result of their military operations and conquests. They brought the whole East under their domination during the time from the Second Macedonian War (200–196 B.C.) to the appropriation of Egypt as a Roman possession in 30 B.C. Their merciless looting brought to Italy fine objects of every sort, from clothing to statues. The money that they took as loot, or required as payments from vanquished opponents, or thereafter exacted as tribute did much to change the character of Roman life. The slaves whom they brought to Rome to render skilled domestic and personal service taught their new masters to accept comforts formerly unknown and vices formerly repugnant. Other skilled slaves now made in Italy products that had formerly been imported. Unskilled slaves were so cheap that men with capital began to develop large slave-manned plantations or ranches, with an unfortunate effect on the position of free men in agriculture. The Romans gained formal instruction, too, for many of the slaves were capable of giving instruction in the Greek language and literature and were able both to practice and to teach medicine, architecture, and other arts. Before long free men began to come west to Rome and Italy to engage in trade or the professions. There must have been few areas of life in much of the Italian peninsula that did not in some way feel the influence of Greece and the Old World.

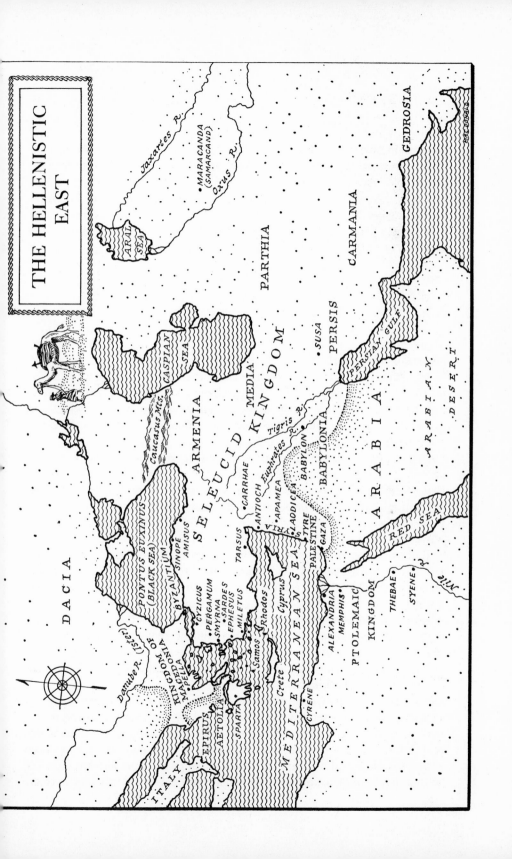

THE HELLENISTIC
EAST

JAXARTES R.

MARACANDA
(SAMARCAND)

Oxus R.

ARAL
SEA

GEDROSIA

PARTHIA

CARMANIA

CASPIAN SEA

SUSA

PERSIS

PERSIAN GULF

Caucasus Mts.

ARMENIA

MEDIA

SELEUCID KINGDOM

Tigris R.

Euphrates R.

CARRHAE

ANTIOCH

APAMEA

BABYLON

BABYLONIA

ARABIA

ARABIAN DESERT

DACIA

PONTUS EUXINUS
(BLACK SEA)

BYZANTIUM

SINOPE

AMISUS

TARSUS

LAODICEA

TYRE

PALESTINE

GAZA

RED SEA

Danube R. (Ister)

CYZICUS

PERGAMUM

SMYRNA

SARDES

EPHESUS

MILETUS

Samos

Rhodos

Cyprus

MEDITERRANEAN SEA

ALEXANDRIA

MEMPHIS

PTOLEMAIC
KINGDOM

THEBAE

SYENE

Nile

KINGDOM OF
MACEDONIA

PELLA

EPIRUS

AETOLIA

SPARTA

Crete

CYRENE

ITALY

As our story proceeds, we shall give more details of the impact of the older culture on the Romans. For the present we shall describe in this chapter first the economic and social life of the Hellenistic kingdoms and then their intellectual, religious, and artistic life. They felt a Roman influence in turn, to be sure, but it resulted largely from the fact of Roman power over them after the Hellenistic Age (that is, during the Empire) and was chiefly in the practical sphere. Greece and the other countries of the eastern Mediterranean and of the Near East were to form a very valuable, strong, and important part of the Roman realm in the late Republic and the Empire.

ECONOMIC AND SOCIAL LIFE

Greece

Ill-informed as we are in detail, we may believe that Greece prospered moderately in the Hellenistic Age. Living was better for those who had some advantage to begin with, like the ownership of land or capital for business, for such men could profit by changing conditions. If Alexander's putting into circulation of the huge Persian royal treasure did something to raise prices and if thereafter a greater volume of trade had the same effect, these propertied men could perhaps be gainers by the new price levels, whereas the workingman, who was unorganized, would find that the real value of his wages was less than it had been before. It is possible that more men fell into slavery because of warfare; piracy, too, was less restrained than it had been before, bringing more people into slavery. If there were more slaves and they were therefore cheaper, they may have offered more competition to free workmen than before.

The existence and competition of the great Hellenistic kingdoms affected life in Greece and the island cities in a number of ways. Greece and the islands did not escape the Wars of the Successors after Alexander's death. The attempts of the Macedonians to assure themselves of control over Greece caused a considerable amount of warfare. The attempts of the Ptolemies of Egypt to control the Aegaean waters and islands and the counter-measures of the Macedonian kings led to diplomatic pressure on the cities, occasional violence, and often gifts of grain or money from the kings.

The small size of Greece, the poor quality of its soil, and the fecundity of its people always tended to crowd it, and by the fourth century, as we saw, there was again need for a great migration, leading to frequent demands for an aggressive war against Persia for loot and land for colonies —the war that Philip II and then his son Alexander undertook. The resulting new opportunities in the Ptolemaic and Seleucid kingdoms were an extremely important new factor in the life of the cities of Greece, the islands, and the coast of Asia Minor, for in both kingdoms able Greeks were in great demand. Mercenaries were required for the armies, and men of high caliber were needed for administrative and military posts close to the kings and in every part of the kingdoms.

The Seleucid kings thought it desirable to establish cities of the Greek type with citizens who represented Greek knowledge and customs to serve as centers for the defense, administration, and improvement of the realm. Even though the people already there were the heirs of an older civilization than the Greek and often possessed both knowledge and skills superior to those of the Greeks, the kings thought it good to have nuclei of people in many places who knew more of the tradition of self-government than did the old inhabitants and who were bound to the new government by ties of self-interest. The man who joined such a colony could get a sizable piece of good land, which would be worked by slaves, and could count on making a good living in a place that, far as it might be from Greece, was made Greek in character by every article of its charter and every activity of his fellow colonists.

There were many openings, too, for people who went to the new kingdoms to engage in the professions or in trade. In Egypt there were many posts for Greeks in the elaborate system of government ownership and management of agriculture and trade that Ptolemy I inherited from the older Egypt and that he refined and extended.

Egypt

Ptolemy I Soter was that one of Alexander's generals who became satrap of Egypt after Alexander's death, then continued his control of the country during the Wars of the Successors, and in 306 proclaimed himself king of the territory he was holding, as did his rivals in the other territories. After his death in 283 his son Ptolemy II Philadelphus, associated with him since 285, ruled until 246. A rather small number of Macedonians were available to help Ptolemy I in his new kingdom. He invited Greeks from other places in considerable numbers. There is no evidence that he objected on principle to using Egyptians in his administration, but the fact is that the Egyptian officials of higher ranks were soon replaced by Greeks. The army probably had to be composed of Greeks trained in the methods of Greek warfare; native Egyptians would have had too much to learn, and their loyalty would not have been certain.

The many Greeks in Egypt lived mostly as a race apart. Many of them worked for the central government in Alexandria. Naturally this great port also attracted many other foreigners, among whom the Jewish element was prominent. Many Greek merchants lived in Naucratis, which had been an extraterritorial city ever since King Amasis made it so in the sixth century. Far to the south Ptolemy I founded a new city, Ptolemais, to be the administrative center of the southern part of the kingdom, to which naturally many Greeks were drawn.

Although they were not organized into poleis, the Greeks in Egypt did group themselves into associations in the three cities just mentioned and in the many other places in Egypt where there were considerable numbers of them. The government made a clear legal distinction between Greeks and Egyptians and expected a man's Greek status to be noted in formal transactions to which he was a party. They brought with them to Egypt the worship of their own gods. They formed social clubs, trade associations, and clubs for mutual help. In every place where there was at least a modest number of Greeks, a gymnasium was founded that served as a center for social life as well as for exercise and athletic contests. There are records of primary and secondary schools that taught Greek literature, rhetoric, practical mathematics, and doubtless Greek mores and values.

The first Ptolemy applied himself to continuing and even extending the detailed and authoritarian system that had been worked out in Egypt more than a thousand years before his time. The native Egyptian people, high and low, were regarded as being under his control, bound to abide in the places fixed for them and to exert themselves to make the king's land productive. A considerable part of the land was farmed by the king himself through his agents; whole villages were composed of peasants who were under the control of the king's agents. The other kind of land was that granted to individuals to manage. Soldiers were often given land to enjoy if they would undertake to be available at any time for military service.

The government kept careful registers of all the land, as is done nowadays. The probable yield of each man's parcel was calculated, and the government gave him enough seed to sow it and told him how many measures of the product—most often grains—he should produce and how many of those measures he must give to the government. Not only did the king's officials thus leave the peasant only about enough to live on until the next harvest, but they also forced him to give a certain number of days of labor on the maintenance of the elaborate irrigation system that brought the rich muddy water of the Nile to the fields. They could also compel him to allow the use of his draft animals for government projects. We get the impression that the peasant was incredibly patient, but he could be roused to strike by the exaction of extra work on the dikes or the requisition of his animals at busy times and especially by being beaten by the officials. Although the peasants could be punished, the officials naturally did not like it to be known that the peasants under their management had been driven to desperation.

There is very little trace of slavery among the Egyptians. Since the huge labor force was so well used to working for little return, there was nothing to be gained by anyone's investing money in slaves to do the work or even trying to capture them in raids.

The upper officials of this complex system were Greek, but the class of scribes among the Egyptians seems to have been encouraged to convert itself to working in Greek and thus to take the clerical posts in the new regime. Thus the Ptolemies acquired a reliable group of men, not on the decision-making level, who could handle both the Egyptian and the Greek languages and be useful in keeping up communication between the government and the people.

The workings of a typical government monopoly, that of oil, are made clear to us by a papyrus that is generally known as the Revenue Laws of Ptolemy Philadelphus. Before the coming of the Greeks olives were generally used only as fruit in Egypt, and cooking oil came from seeds: linseed, sesame, safflower, and gourd. The Ptolemies took measures as part of their control of oils to encourage the production in Egypt of olive oil, the only kind the Greeks would use, so that it need not be imported. Every step in the production of the oils was regulated. The government decreed that certain lands should be planted with the oil-bearing plants. The seed was given to the farmer, as it was with wheat. No such plants might be grown on private initiative. The gathering of the crop was strictly supervised. All mills were registered and were sealed except at the time when the seeds were pressed under supervision. The product was distributed to the consumer at fixed prices through retail outlets licensed and supervised by the government. The competition of the excellent oil produced in Greece and elsewhere was effectively counteracted by a fifty percent tariff and by the government's buying it at a fixed price and selling it at a price that would make it impossible for anyone to make a profit by sending oil to Egypt for sale. High officials who liked Greek oil could import it in their own ships, paying the high tariff, plus another tax for importing it for their own use. An attempt to sell it was subject to stiff fines.

The chief export of the Ptolemies was wheat, a basic product. Sometimes we find them giving large gifts of wheat for political purposes, for example to Greek cities. Such gifts could be even more welcome than those of money in the game of international politics, for famine or the threat of famine was not infrequent in an area of modest rainfall, which could fail entirely sometimes, and of uncertain transport; a gift of wheat could save lives where money would be of little use. The Ptolemies always needed money, in spite of the natural wealth of their country, since they could not operate their economy on a subsistence basis, having soldiers and a great number of officials who must be paid in cash. They also had to import certain necessities: timber and pitch for ships; iron for ship fittings, tools, and weapons; copper from Cyprus; and tin from other places with which to make the copper into bronze; and silver. Horses for the army were also a necessity; they were bought largely in Cyrenaica. Since the supply of Indian elephants was controlled by the Seleucid kings, the Ptolemies organized an elaborate service for the acquisition of African elephants, their shipment from harbors in Somaliland up to Egypt, and their training there.

There was a considerable trade in luxuries. Ivory, myrrh, frankincense, and cinnamon could be found in Africa. Much more of the incense, ointments, and spices, however, came from India and Arabia. India's rice, dyes, and spices came by sea to southern Arabia in the ships of Arab traders and then could be brought up the Red Sea, along with the spices, pearls, and coral of Arabia, or could be taken in caravans up through Arabia to the ports of Phoenicia (controlled by the Seleucid kings) and even to coastal cities farther north, like Ephesus. Naturally the people of the Seleucid realm took much of the supply, but enough was shipped across the Aegaean to make a profitable trade for the cities where it was transferred to ships.

The Ptolemies wished some of this trade to come to Egypt, both to supply their people and to give Alexandria some of the profit from shipping across the Aegaean. There was also money to be made in giving some of the goods further preparation for the market, for example, in final preparation of perfumes for the consumer and putting them into attractive containers. They tried to activate the Red Sea route by exploring and policing it, and even restored an old canal connecting the Red Sea with the Nile. The caravan route seems, however, to have been more attractive to the merchants. We can see indications that the Ptolemies strove to bring some of this trade out at the ports they held in Palestine, and they did get some of it to come up the Red Sea and to Alexandria. A time was soon to come when Greek traders learned the secret of the seasonal winds betweeen Egypt and India; then Alexandria did a large business, much of it in government factories, in working over the goods that were brought in, then shipping them to the Mediterranean world.

The island republic of Rhodes was a very important commercial ally of the Ptolemies, for it did a great deal of the carrying and distributing of grain and other products of Egypt: grain to the cities of Greece proper, the islands, Asia Minor, Rome, and other places in the West, and luxury products that were acceptable in all those areas and also in the rich cities of the Black Sea region, which had no need to import grain.

Rhodes had a good location, not only in that it lay between Egypt and its chief markets, but also in that the prevailing winds and currents favored its ships as they came up from Egypt to Asia Minor and beyond.

Even before the conquests of Alexander, Rhodes had a lively commerce and cohesive corps of merchants and bankers. The Rhodians were willing to assume the responsibilities of a mercantile state, especially that of trying to keep the sea clear of pirates. They also pressed steadily for the adoption of a uniform code of commercial law among the trading peoples of the Mediterranean.

Wine was Rhodes' chief product. She shipped it in amphoras, or large jars, with distinctive handles, and the Rhodian amphora handle is found by the thousands in excavations all over the Mediterranean, bearing witness to the course of Rhodian trade. Her ships carried grain from Egypt, olive oil, pottery and honey from Athens, lumber and pitch from Macedonia, wine from Samos and Chios, and marble from Paros.

The Seleucid Kingdom

Ionia, the region of the Greek cities on the western coast of Asia Minor, had a long history behind it, and its cities were well organized for both manufacture and trade. The Greek cities were important and useful to the Seleucid kings, for they were of strategic importance; they gave the kings a cultural and commercial connection with the Greek world; they could supply or find useful trained men for the army, the government, the colonies, and the other projects of the kings; and their continuing prosperity allowed them to contribute a large amount of money in taxes to the royal treasury. The kings naturally were unwilling to grant them the complete political independence that their tradition led them to demand, but they did allow them to have their own constitutions and local self-government, which involved no loss of royal prerogative or profit and saved the royal government some effort. We know the names of some two dozen new cities that the kings founded somewhat more inland in the more southern part of Asia Minor to serve as centers of administration.

Northern Syria was a second section especially important for the kings. There they founded Antiocheia, or Antioch, as a capital, giving it a dynastic name from Antiochus, a frequent name in the royal family. Antioch, which was a few miles from the Mediterranean on the Orontes River, was to be an important and brilliant city for centuries. On the coast were two great ports, Seleucia and Laodicea, and on the Orontes above Antioch was Apamea, the center of military preparations, where the horses, elephants, and stores of arms were kept. The Euphrates River and one edge of Mesopotamia were not far from northern Syria, and the flock of old and newly founded cities ran right up into Mesopotamia.

Mesopotamia was the third highly important part of the Seleucid Kingdom. The kings were very respectful of the ancient customs and learning of this region, which was highly civilized and full of expert craftsmen and businessmen. They encouraged the rebuilding of some of the great temples of Mesopotamia that had apparently lost some of their administrative functions under the Persians and were in a state of decay. From the earliest times the temples of this region had been centers of administration, manufacture, and finance, since the land was thought of as belonging to the gods, and the priests were the managers of the possessions of the gods as well as the stage managers, as it were, of the rites of worship.

Probably a great many people in these three most important parts of the Seleucid realm, and even more in the odd corners of the kingdom, were little affected by Greek ways. We do not find that the kings (and the same is true of the Ptolemies) made a systematic effort to hellenize their people, although the presence of so many Greeks in important positions and the fact that Greek was the language of government must have had some effect. The priest of a great temple in Babylonia might well learn Greek to watch out for the interests of his organization, but he probably would feel no need of borrowing anything from Greek religion, thought, economic practices, or customs of daily life.

The Seleucids may be said to have had four kinds of organization in their vast realm: that of cities, old and new; that of peoples such as the hill folk of Asia Minor or some of the larger Iranian peoples far to the East; that of small potentates or dynasts; and that of more formidable kings on their borders, such as the kings of Pontus, Bithynia, and India. The cities were useful and easy to deal with; the more loosely organized peoples did not give much trouble unless they were large, like the Iranians. The dynasts, or petty rulers, could be useful as agents of the kings administering a small region along its traditional lines. After the Seleucid kings decided that they could not hold the part of India taken by Alexander, they had a cordial relation with its king. The chief problem in the international field was their struggle with the Ptolemies over the possession of Palestine and Phoenicia. In this matter of administration, as in all others, the great diversity of the Seleucid Kingdom contrasts strongly with the simplicity of Egypt, where the Ptolemies had no independent cities or peoples to deal with and had deserts rather than kingdoms for neighbors.

The Peoples on the Periphery

In approximately 200 B.C., then, when the Romans were about to begin their conquest of the East, there was a circle of peoples who were economically and socially rather sophisticated. These peoples were surrounded, however, by others of less sophistication who from time to time made raids to try to relieve them of their surplus. Beyond the Seleucid Kingdom were many Iranians, who preferred to be apart from it, and beyond them were India and China, whose civilization had developed much as had that of the people whom we have considered in the early part of our study.

The more northern peoples of Asia appear only from time to time clearly to Western eyes. The Scythians and the Sarmatians were in southern and middle Russia for hundreds of years. Like the Iranians, they preferred an organization much simpler than that of the Greeks and without the three great characteristics of the Indo-European civilization: the high intellectual tradition with reading and writing, city life, governments based on laws rather than on loyalty to kings. Farther to the west the movements of late Neolithic peoples had resulted in the formation of the recognizable group of Celts. Some of them were now settled in Asia Minor as the Galatians, but some had found a place along the Danube, and many were in Gaul (modern France) and were presently to be brought into the Roman orbit by Julius Caesar. With them in Europe were Germanic and Slavic peoples who were to make their strong mark on Mediterranean peoples during the time of the Roman Empire.

On the southern side, the Arabians were to make themselves felt later in the great movement of Islam. Below Egypt were African peoples who never were much heard from in the life of the Mediterranean world. In North Africa the Carthaginians were soon to be destroyed by the Romans, and the Berbers of North Africa were to accept the Greco-Roman civilization in great numbers at the urging of the Romans. The intentional propagation of the Greco-Roman way by the Romans was an important part of the life of the Roman Empire, as was the frequent conflict with the more belligerent of the surrounding peoples. On the other hand, it was not always war to the knife, and the traders of the Mediterranean lands were generally welcome to take goods and some few ideas to the peoples on the fringe.

HELLENISTIC LITERATURE, SCIENCE, AND ART

Literature: The Alexandrians

The competitive efforts of the Hellenistic kings to glorify their kingdoms and regimes produced effects in all the three fields that we are about to discuss. Although the patronage of literature by the Ptolemies is best known, the Seleucids and the kings of Pergamum also supported libraries.

Ptolemy I founded the great Library in the Brucheion, the royal quarter of Alexandria; he also founded the Museum. The word meant "place of the Muses" rather than what it means to us, and the organization was like a great modern research foundation, offering to scholars of literature and science a living and a place for dwelling and working with like-minded men. The kings energetically sought copies of every important Greek book and play.

The activities of the librarians and of the literary men who worked with them evolved into what we know as literary scholarship. Authoritative texts of all the authors were established. The archaic words of the older authors—words, that is, no longer in use—were studied and arranged in lists, which was the beginning of lexicography. A catalogue was prepared comprising titles of books and information about their authors.

Ptolemy II Philadelphus supported the Library and the Museum as generously as his father had done and presided personally over the brilliant circle of literary men and scientists to whom his bounty was offered. Callimachus, a native of Cyrene, was perhaps the leading literary man in the history of the Museum; he was born a little before 300 B.C. Some of his work has been preserved. He believed ardently in brief and polished writing and produced a number of short, elegant, learned, and not very exciting pieces of verse, generally in the elegiac meter, composed of alternate hexameters and pentameters. One set of poems, called *Causes,* gave in four books of verses the stories from Greek legends explaining the causes of certain customs and rites among the Greeks, information that was a natural by-product of researches in literary history. His *Hekale* was an epyllion, or little epic, written in hexameters; the short epic was a characteristic product of his literary beliefs and standards, and such small, learned, polished epics (perhaps one twenty-fifth the size of *Iliad* or *Odyssey,* or as little as four hundred lines long) were written by other Greeks of the period and were imitated, along with other Alexandrian productions, by the Romans of the late Republic.

Callimachus also wrote epigrams, another form that was very popular through the Hellenistic period. The epigram, a very short poem—perhaps four to twelve lines—in the elegiac meter, often expressed a point or a sentiment with grace and charm. One of Callimachus's epigrams is well known from the translation that begins, "They told me, Heraclitus, they told me you were dead." He wished to predict the immortality of his friend's book of poems, *Nightingales,* and did it in three elegiac couplets. "Heraclitus," he says, "a man spoke of your death and moved me to tears, for I remembered how many times we two sent the sun down in conversation. But while you, my friend from Halicarnassus, were ashes, oh so long ago, your *Nightingales* live on. On them Hades, the snatcher of all things, shall not lay a hand."

Theocritus of Syracuse, the originator of pastoral poetry, was also of the generation of Philadelphus and Callimachus. He wrote charmingly of the singing matches of shepherds, an entertainment for long, quiet days that is still practiced by Greeks guarding their flocks. His poems are the country poems of a city man in spite of their wealth of realistic detail and the simplicity of the ideas ascribed to the shepherds. The references to hills and streams and busy bees, to raucous cicadas in the hot summer noontime, and to the grateful coolness where a rock hangs over a spring are most agreeable. As we shall see, the pastoral poems of Theocritus were to inspire Vergil's pastorals two centuries later and through him many pastorals in the modern languages of Europe.

Apollonius of Rhodes wrote an epic of medium size, *Argonautica,* which told the old and well-known story of Jason's quest for the Golden Fleece with much learned and often abstruse detail. The princess Medea, for all her dread powers, appears as an appealing young girl in love.

These men and many others whom we know only by a reference in some later author and perhaps by a few lines quoted by someone are known as the Alexandrians. Beside belonging to the third and second centuries before Christ and having lived for some time in Alexandria, they had in common an attitude to literature that can be described briefly as a belief in brevity, learning, and polish. The polish consisted chiefly of a careful choice of diction and the observance of strict metrical rules. Although they did not succeed in imposing their standards on all the Hellenistic writers, they did have considerable influence on the Roman writers of the late Republic, and their literary attitude is still known as Alexandrianism when it reappears in modern times.

Much of the other writing of the Hellenistic Age, however, was long-winded, popular, and carelessly written. To say that much writing was popular does not mean that it had the public character of previous Greek writing, which was more often heard than read and was intended for groups of people. In the older Greece, epic, lyric, and elegiac poetry were sung to groups, and the plays were performed before thousands. The writing of the Hellenistic Age, however, was meant more to be read in private; it was turning into belles lettres and ceasing to be aimed at a general public.

The many didactic poems of the Hellenistic Age are typical of this trend. Their subjects were often purely prosaic, and the poems seem to have been written only to show off the ingenuity of their authors. Aratus's *Phaenomena* was about the heavens and the weather. Nicander, who lived in the second century, wrote *On Snakes* and a book on countermeasures in case of food poisoning; apparently he simply took serious scholarly books and turned them into verse.

Although tragedies continued to be written, no one was able to make enough of a reputation in this field to ensure the preservation of his works. At Athens it became the custom to have revivals of the tragedies of the great writers of the fifth century. Plays, old and new, were presented at festivals of Dionysus all over the Greek world by members of the guild of Dionysiac artists, a body that was recognized by many governments and was given privileges to encourage it.

The comedy of the Hellenistic Age, the so-called New Comedy, was one of the few products of the age that remained Athenian rather than universal; Menander, whose first play was shown at Athens in 321 B.C., was its foremost writer. New Comedy was very like the modern comedy of manners. The topical allusions of the Old Comedy of Aristophanes disappeared, as did the frequent lusty references to sex and elimination. Bourgeois life in Athens was the general subject. Business trips often form a part of the plot, and we hear frequently of the prosperous mercenary soldiers in the service of the kings of the time. The love life of the young and their marriages are the most popular form of complicated plot; the twenty-one Roman versions by Plautus and the six by Terence are a great help to our knowledge of the plots, since little of the large body of the original Greek plays is preserved.

The writing of history increased greatly during this period, as did that of related forms like memoirs and accounts of travel. Although the official journal of Alexander's expedition perished, the lost private journal of Ptolemy as one of his generals and the lost account of Alexander's admiral Nearchus of the voyage down the Indus River and back along the coast to join the army were preserved in a way by being taken up into the *Anabasis of Alexander* written by Arrian in the second century of our era.

An interesting book on a far-away country was the lost *Indica* of one Megasthenes, whom the first Seleucus sent as envoy to the great Indian king, Chandragupta. We know of a book on Lydia and of one on Lycia.

The people of lands now under Greek control could also wish to explain their ways to the Greeks. We have already heard of Manetho; he was a priest of Serapis under the first Ptolemy and knew Greek well enough to write *Aegyptiaca*, a history of Egypt for the Greek-reading public. Berossus, a priest of Babylon, wrote a similar book called *Babyloniaca*.

In this atmosphere imaginative tales of far-off societies or commonwealths arose naturally, perhaps the most famous being that of Euhemerus, a Sicilian who was sent by one of the kings to Arabia. As reported by a later historian, he told a plain story of life in southern Arabia, from which myrrh and frankincense came, then gave a tall tale of an island commonwealth somewhat reminiscent of the society that Plato imagined. Physical conditions on the island were ideal; society was organized into classes, some highly privileged, but living was good for all. Hellenistic skepticism in religious matters comes out in the report of the traveler that the records in the temples showed that the gods were originally only men of great abilities.

Many historians wrote popular history; their works are now known only by quotations of passages or by references to them in other authors. One historian, Polybius, wrote to be useful rather than to be popular. He was born around 200 B.C. in Megalopolis in Arcadia; his family were rich landowners, and his father was a leading politician in the Achaean League. Polybius was in command of the cavalry of the league just as Rome's relations with King Perseus of Macedonia were coming to the stage of war.[1] When the Romans, after their victory of 168 B.C., decided to take a thousand Achaean hostages to Italy, Polybius was one. He was fortunate enough to become the friend of a young Roman, Scipio Aemilianus, and to remain his friend for decades as Scipio grew to a brilliant manhood of political and military achievement. The result was that he resolved to write a history that would explain to the Greek reader what we shall tell when we return to the Romans, that is, how Rome suddenly rose to be mistress of the civilized world in the fifty-three years between the end of the second war with Carthage and her destruction of that city and her subordination of Greece in 146 B.C. It was a large book, and what is left of it fills 1500 pages of translation in the Loeb Classical Library edition. The first five books, which get the story well into the Second Punic War, are almost complete, and there are several hundred pages of long excerpts from the rest of the work.

Hellenistic Science

In the Hellenistic Age philosophy and pure mathematics were regarded as the highest of interests. The geometry of Euclid, who flourished about 300 B.C., brings together and systematizes the work done in that subject up to his time. The work was the basis of the geometry textbooks of the Western world until the twentieth century.

Archimedes of Syracuse, the greatest mathematician of the ancient world, who was born about 287 B.C. and died in 212 B.C., may well have lived for some time in Alexandria, but spent most of his productive years in his native city. His outstanding work was done on the areas and volumes of certain curved figures and solids. We know of works entitled, for example, *On the Measurement of a Circle, On Conoids and Spheroids, On the Regular Heptagon,* and *On the Quadrature of the Parabola.* The modern mathematician regards the proofs offered by Archimedes as elegant and economical.

Archimedes developed the sciences of statics, or levers, and of hydro-

[1] See pp. 420–421.

statics, or floating bodies, working out principles far beyond the obvious ones and devising proper proofs for them. King Hiero II, his kinsman and patron, asked him to determine whether some silver had been put into a gold wreath ordered for dedication to a god. As Archimedes was considering this problem, he got into a too-full bath and caused it to run over. "Eureka!" ("I've got it!") he cried as he realized that he could measure the volume of such an irregular object as the wreath (or a human body) by putting it into a full vessel of water and measuring the amount of water that overflowed. Knowing the volume of the wreath, he could compare its weight with the weight of that volume of pure gold.

The story of the king's asking him to improve the fortifications of Syracuse is rather like a modern science fiction story of the development of a secret weapon and its eventual use against a brutal aggressor. Archimedes' improvements were made while Hiero was still alive and Syracuse was friendly to Rome. After the death of Hiero in 215 B.C., Syracuse went over to the Carthaginian side in the Second Punic War. In 213 B.C. a Roman fleet under Marcus Claudius Marcellus, the fine soldier who did well a little later against Hannibal in Italy, assaulted the city from the harbor side. Both Polybius and Plutarch (in his life of Marcellus) tell of the engagement. The naval attack was repulsed by Archimedes' superior catapults, by devices that could be run out from the walls to drop heavy rocks through the planking of the Roman galleys that came in close, and by a contrivance that caught them by the bow, lifted them, and dropped them stern first into the water. The Romans then settled down to a siege and took the city in 212 B.C. Marcellus ordered that Archimedes be found and brought to him, and he is said to have been killed by a soldier who found him working on a geometrical problem and who could not persuade him to break off and come to the Roman general.

Aristarchus of Samos, who flourished in the early third century, comes earliest among the Hellenistic astronomers known to us. He concerned himself with explaining the movements of the heavenly bodies, a matter to which a great deal of attention was given, for if one assumes the geocentric point of view, the observed movements are very hard to fit into a system, since the movement of the earth makes some of the bodies seem to stop and move backward at certain points.

Aristarchus said that the earth revolves around a stationary sun in the center of the universe, meanwhile revolving daily on its own axis (this movement had been suggested earlier). This heliocentric theory, which quite naturally seems a great advance in Greek astronomy to us, was not greeted with enthusiasm and before long was implicitly rejected by other men, partly because their conception was of circular rather than of elliptical orbits, and partly because so fine a telescope is needed to detect the different angle to the fixed stars at the opposite ends of the earth's orbit that this confirmatory observation was not successfully made until the nineteenth century.

Hipparchus, who lived in the second century and compiled a catalogue of stars, was perhaps more typically Alexandrian than Aristarchus. Refinements had been made in the dioptra, or sighting instrument, so that Hipparchus was able to establish the precession of the equinoxes by comparing his own observations of the positions of the stars with earlier observations. A gradual tilting of the earth's axis makes spring and autumn arrive a few seconds earlier every year; it also makes the fixed stars change their apparent positions very slowly. He also offered better figures for the lengths of the solar year and the mean lunar month.

Eratosthenes was the all-round man of Alexandrian studies. A description by a later man gives us one sample of his work, his attempt to measure the circumference of the earth. Starting with the idea that the earth is a sphere and with the fact that at Syene in Egypt the sun at its height on the day of the summer solstice casts no shadow on the sundial and therefore is vertically overhead, while at the same moment it cast a shadow of one-fiftieth of a circumference on the sundial at Alexandria, and considering that the two places were five thousand stades apart (the distance was measured by Ptolemy's royal surveyors, who were trained to pace it off like a football referee giving a penalty), he drew a figure to show that the distance from Syene to Alexandria was a fiftieth of the circumference of the earth. In spite of the fact that the two places are not on the same meridian and that we are not sure of the length of the stade that he used, the method is correct and the result achieved is at least comparable to the true figure.

Eratosthenes believed all the oceans to be joined and the world of Asia, Africa, and Europe to be an island. He asserted that one could sail down the west coast of Africa and around the southern tip to reach India and that one could sail westward from Spain around the world to India, even conjecturing the existence of the New World that lay between. He was learned in history and chronology, enough of a mathematician to have solved the old problem of duplicating the cube, wrote a history of comedy that was well thought of, and produced some poetry.

There was some medical study of the sort that we should regard as scientific. Herophilus, who worked in Alexandria, is said to have been given condemned criminals by the king for vivisection. He discovered the nerves and understood that they branched from the brain and the spinal cord. He perceived that the cerebrum should be distinguished from the cerebellum. He almost discovered the circulation of the blood, at least seeing that the heart is a pump and that the arteries carry blood rather than air.

Mechanical knowledge was increased by the study of the forces of compressed air and steam and the invention of devices to use those forces. Ctesibius, who lived in the second century, is said to have invented the cylinder and plunger, the force pump, the water organ, a catapult worked by compressed air, and other mechanical and pneumatic devices. It used to be said that in Greek and Roman times cheap labor discouraged the making of useful inventions, but in fact slave labor was not cheap, the slaves taken by the Romans in their eastern wars being one exception. The inventions had rather to wait on other factors: steam engines, for example, could not be made until iron pipes that could be fastened tightly together were available.

Although astrology hardly seems a science to us, the Hellenistic version of it was at least partly scientific in intent. Surely the conception that all parts of the universe are so related that the movements and conjunctions of the heavenly bodies have an influence on the lives of men, could we but gather facts enough to allow the connections to be deduced, is not entirely unscientific, degraded as the everyday practice of the astrologer's art might become. The personal astrology that we know now, with the practice of casting personal horoscopes, began in the Hellenistic Age and increased greatly in the early Roman Empire. The Hellenistic horoscopes that we have are for specific persons and are based on the computed position of the seven heavenly bodies (sun, moon, and the five planets then known) and the signs of the zodiac at the moment when that person was born; they give only the computations for that moment. We know, however, that a great system of doctrine on the evaluation of the data grew up, and it was in this part of astrology that there was so much room for charlatanry and superstition.

The rise of astrology gave new life to magic, which always asserted that it had means to force the powers of the universe to provide what the magician's client wanted, from worldly preferment to the death of an enemy. The methods are to be seen on papyri that give charms and describe ceremonies to be enacted, promising to achieve almost anything, usually by commanding the services of a demon or even of a major divinity. Calling his name was a potent device, so that prudent and ease-loving demons naturally kept their true names secret if they could. The secret names of gods and demons and even of cities formed an interesting minor department of knowledge. The crucial moment in any use of a demon is that when the powerful demon, inexorably summoned to do the will of someone else, is no longer needed and is dismissed firmly, unthanked and unpaid; spells were provided for managing this.

Religion and Philosophy

Naturally the cults of the gods in the poleis of the Greek world lost some of their strength during the Hellenistic Age as the formerly tight social organization of the typical polis was loosened still further by the greater mobility of its members, who could now go to Egypt, the Seleucid kingdom, and many other places on commercial trips, for service in the army, administration, or as colonists. A number of indications point to a decline in the worship of the Olympians who were thought to be the patrons of the poleis: the building of temples and the making of dedications especially slackened in this age, and the great oracles were consulted less than previously.

The impression that we get of an increased liveliness in the cults of Egyptian and Near Eastern divinities may be due partly to the more frequent mention of the divinities and the cults by Greeks who traveled on business or went to work in those regions and perhaps even began to worship.The Egyptian Isis was perhaps the most striking of the divinities of whom we now hear. Isis was woman and mother and as such was a divine source of warmth, love, comfort, protection, and help. Her worship was very different from the worship of an Olympian shared with all one's fellow citizens, for one had to be initiated to be a full participant in the worship of Isis. Not everyone could be initiated, for the goddess had to summon those who were to undergo a symbolic death that led to a full life, no longer at the mercy of Fate, no longer subject to death.

Others elevated that same Fate, or Tyche (the Greek word), or Fortuna (the Latin word), to the status of goddess, believing that pure chance, or contingency, continually showed itself the most important force in private and public affairs. Polybius and other writers discuss the role of Tyche in history in the same serious way in which the role of contingency in history is discussed in modern times.

Art: Architecture

The founding of cities of the Greek type by Hellenistic kings, most of all by the Seleucids, naturally meant that a great deal of building in the Greek style was done to let the inhabitants feel that a unit of Greek life had been set up. This implied a market place, which could be very elaborate with porticoes, a theater, a municipal hall, a gymnasium, and temples to one or more gods. The result was that a great deal of competent and commonplace work was done and that the same styles and methods became commonly known all over the Hellenistic world. The rise of colonnades along the streets, so that the citizens could be protected from the sun and the rain, was one new feature. The planned city, with streets in a regular checkerboard pattern, was an idea of the fifth century that now was often applied, since so many cities were built all at once by governments, and we hear more of regulations affecting the width of streets and public health.

The Ptolemies built an elaborate and beautiful royal quarter in Alexandria; indeed the whole city was a symbol of the brilliance of their reign. The Seleucids, too, gave especial care to their royal cities, like Antioch. Pergamum, which had a striking natural site, was beautified by its kings. Although the lower city of Pergamum remained a crowded Asiatic city of poor people and foreigners, the kings built magnificent structures on the long ridge above—a propylaea, or entrance gate, three gymnasiums, one rising above another, and a theater. In the citadel at the top were the palace, the library building, and the temple of Athena. Just outside the citadel was the huge altar of Zeus Soter, "Zeus who Saves."

Sculpture

The growing individualism of the classical Greek world had led by the fourth century to marked individualism in statuary. Statues were much less often idealized portraits of gods or types of mankind and were more often frank representations of individuals. This tendency was carried much farther in the Hellenistic Age, for actual people were often portrayed in rags or performing intimate acts. The well known statue of the boy sitting with one foot up on his other knee while he tries to get a thorn out of the foot is typical. The bronze prize fighter of the Museo delle Terme in Rome is a man of mature years and somewhat forbidding aspect who sits in a relaxed posture as if resting after a bout.

The Victory of Samothrace, now in the Louvre, reminds us that the artists of the period were also capable of elevated and idealized sculptures. The winged female figure is doing something to be sure, but only what is necessary to characterize a Nike or Victory; she is alighting on the prow of a ship. The prow is there beneath her, and in its original setting it stood in a pool, or basin, on a hillside in Samothrace above the complex of buildings devoted to the Mysteries of Samothrace. Water from a spring above filled the basin, so that the ship seemed to be floating in the water. The great wings of the figure are in the position that will finally stop the downward progress of the Nike and allow her to alight gently. Wings and draperies beautifully suggest the rush of the wind, which will cease in a moment.

The wealth of Rhodes and the strong spirit of its people made it a center of the manufacture of statuary. We naturally think first of the Colossus, a hundred-foot statue of the sun god cast in bronze that was made to commemorate the repulse in 305 B.C. of the great siege of the city in the Wars of the Successors of Alexander.

The sculptors of Pergamum had their greatest period (240–225 B.C.) when they were making the statues that commemorated the victory of King Attalus over the Seleucid king and over the Galatians of central Asia Minor. The bronze statues may be judged by such familiar marble copies as "The Dying Gaul" and the other Gaul who has just killed his wife and is about to kill himself. Among the other officially commissioned products of the sculptors of Pergamum is the frieze of the altar of Zeus, which shows the battles of gods and primeval creatures. This is in a way a marvelous production, for the altar was four hundred feet long and the work was done with great skill, but it lacks the fire and life of the more immediate and deeply felt victory over the wild Celtic robbers so near at hand in space and time.

Popular as they were among the Greeks, statues of bronze and marble were even more so among the Romans. Since we shall soon be discussing the impact of Greek civilization on the Romans after Rome turned eastward in 200 B.C., we may as well think for a moment now of the Greek side of this process. Many of the things and people that so affected the Romans were brought to Italy as booty; the Romans plundered Greek cities unmercifully and carried off many people into slavery. The works of art of the great masters that were stolen by the Romans could not be replaced. The people, too, whether humble or of the more educated classes, were sorely missed, but they could in a sense be replaced, and some of them found very comfortable positions for themselves in Rome and either stayed there as freedmen or returned to Greece after some time.

The Roman liking and respect for statuary and other works of art gave the Greeks opportunity to realize at least a little gain from the relation to the Romans. The making of several marble copies of a statue designed by the head of a large shop had long been a regular practice, so that it was now very simple to turn out wholesale for the Roman market replicas of the good, old, safe masterpieces or of other works that might successfully be represented as something new for the man who had confidence in his own taste. Divers have investigated the wrecks of a number of ships bound for Rome with such cargo, and we hear of a Roman firm in the business of finding originals in the East for such buyers and of great houses in Italy crammed with the loot of such expeditions. Naturally copiers of statues also set up in business in Italy.

Painting

Our slight knowledge of the painting of the period is based almost entirely on the paintings found on the walls of the houses of Pompeii and

Herculaneum (in the Greek part of Italy), which were buried by the great eruption of Vesuvius in A.D. 79 and excavated in modern times. Some of the paintings form an integral part of the house, like the ones that represent a garden, so that one seems to stand in the middle of a garden rather than in a room. Some, too, are formal decorations rather than representations of scenes and thus are really a part of the house.

A few of the finest examples show a talent for choosing the great moment from a well known myth or legend. In one picture we have the instant when Achilles, hidden among the girls by his mother so that he would not go to Troy and die there, betrays himself to Odysseus by leaping to arms at the sound of the trumpet. The great Alexander mosaic that is now on a wall in the museum in Naples is a copy of a picture of Alexander nearing Darius in the thick of the battle; even in the mosaic we can sense the technical competence and vibrant liveliness of the picture.

CHAPTER

20

ROME CONQUERS THE EAST: 201 TO 133 B.C.

The Second Macedonian War (200–196 B.C.)

In spite of the fact that Philip V of Macedonia joined Hannibal during the Second Punic War (these few hostilities are called the First Macedonian War), it is difficult to decide why the Roman Senate forced another war on him. Philip finished his first war with the Romans in 205 B.C. Late in that year the king of Egypt died. Soon afterward Philip and Antiochus III of the Seleucid Kingdom made a secret treaty, which later came to light. Antiochus would have liked much better to have Philip still engaged with the Romans, but that war had ended, so he made an agreement with him that they should respect each other's right to prey on the dominions of the little boy who had inherited the throne of Egypt. Antiochus began by taking southern Syria. Philip built a fleet and began a series of attacks on independent cities that lay along the approaches to the Black Sea, the Hellespont, and the Propontis, or Sea of Marmara. Rhodes and Byzantium, two great commercial states, and the kingdom of Pergamum, some of whose territory lay on the shore of Asia Minor near the Hellespont, naturally all were much interested in keeping open the waterways that Philip was trying to dominate by his conquests. They made representations to him that had no effect and fought him with their navies with inconclusive results. If their embassies to the Roman Senate represented him as a violent and ambitious man now embarked on a course of crude imperialism, there was some truth in it, and it may have been possible to convince the Romans that Philip was a danger to them.

The Senate's first request for a declaration of war to the *Comitia cen-turiata,* which was probably in the spring of 200 B.C., was flatly refused. Although the chronology of events is very puzzling, it seems that Athens, too, made an appeal shortly afterward and that the consuls explained to the people that Philip was trying to dominate the world and would soon be in Italy if he were not checked now. During the summer of 200 Roman ambassadors in Athens told one of Philip's generals, who had carried a raid right into the suburbs of Athens, that Rome demanded that Philip cease to attack Greeks and submit his dispute with Attalus of Pergamum to arbitration. The immediate effect was to make the general withdraw, presumably to await instructions from his royal master. Had Philip ac-cepted the demand of the Romans, for which there was no basis in inter-national law, since they had no relation with the other parties that would justify their position, he would in effect have confessed himself to be a client state of Rome and without an independent foreign policy. This would have been convenient for the Romans, who presumably intended their action this way. Of course Philip refused. Later in the summer the *Comitia centuriata* voted for war.

The war with Philip was not a very difficult one. In 200 B.C. the Ro-mans began with an expedition that devastated some of Philip's terri-tories. In the next year a little more was attempted; two minor victories were won over his army, and the Aetolians decided to join the Romans. The Greeks in general stood apart, wishing to see Philip's constant inter-ference in Greece stopped, but believing that Rome could probably ac-complish that result without their becoming involved. The Battle of Cy-noscephalae in 197 B.C. ended the hostilities. Philip was forced to evacuate all Greece and the places he had just taken on the Hellespont and the Propontis, to give up his fleet (another sore blow to his standing with relation to Egypt and Antiochus), and to pay one thousand talents.

The Aetolians, who were very helpful in the earlier stages of the final battle, urged the Romans to invade Macedonia and break its power com-pletely, which would have enabled the Aetolians to extend their own power. Not only would it have been an irresponsible and foolish act for the Romans to allow the destruction of Macedonia, which was so useful both to them and to the Greeks as a barrier against the rude peoples of the Balkans and farther northward, but Titus Quinctius Flamininus, the Roman commander in Greece (not to be confused, of course, with the earlier Flaminius), was also concerned with what seemed to be a danger from Antiochus. To be free to maneuver against him it would be better to have a reasonable peace in Greece. The recent weakness of Egypt be-cause of the youth of her king had helped Antiochus to recover territory from her in Palestine as well as in Syria. He judged the time ripe to com-plete the process by capturing areas in Asia Minor and across the straits in Europe that once his ancestors had held or claimed, and he began cautious advances into Asia Minor while Philip and the Romans were engaged with each other. Rhodes was immediately aroused, but he managed to pacify her. Then Eumenes, king of Pergamum, whose father Attalus had joined Rome in the two Macedonian wars, took fright at the growing nearness of Antiochus' power in spite of assurances that his boundaries would be respected and appealed to the Romans.

At the Isthmian Games of 196 B.C. (Corinth's great games) the announcement was made that the Romans wished all the Greeks whom Philip had seized, those of Asia as well as those of Greece, to be free, and it was received with tremendous enthusiasm by those present and by the Greeks in general. This great gesture may be taken as a token of Roman admiration for the Greeks, or as a fair pretext for repressing Philip's future ambitions, as the opening of a diplomatic campaign to put Antiochus in the wrong if he molested Greek cities of Asia Minor, or as all these things together. It also shut out Aetolian ambitions to take some cities as a reward for helping the Romans. Antiochus nevertheless continued with his plans, crossing in 196 to the European side of the Hellespont, where his ancestor Seleucus Nicator had had a foothold and which he regarded as the last piece of territory needed for the complete restoration of his ancestral kingdom. He began the rebuilding of the city of Lysimacheia, which the Romans had forced Philip to abandon after he had conquered it, and announced his intention of making it one of the capitals of his realm and the residence of his son Seleucus.

The War with Antiochus (192–188 B.C.)

The Romans sent an embassy to tell Antiochus that he must withdraw from Europe, must respect the cities belonging to Ptolemy and Philip, and must not attack those that were free. The king was ready to play at this game, reminding them that Asia was his sphere, as Italy was theirs, but that he had a historical claim to Lysimacheia. He also offered to submit any disputed question to the undoubtedly suitable arbitration of Rhodes. The Roman ambassadors went away with this reasonable answer and did not return. Their troops were withdrawn from Greece in 194, and Antiochus, thinking that they had left the field to him, sent ambassadors to Rome to make a final treaty.

The ambassadors were astounded at being told that the king must either evacuate the European side of the strait, in which case the Romans would pay no attention to Asia, or expect the Romans to continue to interest themselves in the Asian Greeks if he stayed in Thrace. The Aetolians now did their best to stir up unrest in Greece and to convince Antiochus that a war with Rome was inevitable. He finally yielded to their urging and to his own feeling that the Romans were so unreasonable that a limited war in Greece might best bring them to a definite and workable agreement. He was not properly prepared, since he did not want a war and had supposed until recently that ordinary diplomacy would bring a settlement with the Romans; the resources of his empire were vast, but took time to mobilize. He went to Greece in 192 with the limited force that he could put in the field on short notice.

Greece had already been "liberated" too often and was cool to him. The Romans sent an army the next year and drove him from Greece, then prepared to make war on him and drive him back from the part of Asia nearest to them so as to have a buffer. We must remember that to the people of the time his kingdom must have seemed the greatest of the Mediterranean powers and that the Romans at this time were rather likely to allow their ideas to be influenced by those of the smaller powers who hoped to use Rome for their own protection and advantage. Scipio Africanus seems to have urged this war when he was consul for the second time in 194 B.C. He was probably swayed by the fact that Hannibal was known to be urging Antiochus on. After the Second Punic War, Hannibal was elected to office at Carthage and employed his administrative ability without fear or favor in the cause of honest and efficient government, thus stirring up powerful enemies, who finally accused him of planning a new attempt against the Romans. The Romans demanded that he be surrendered to them, and he barely escaped. He fled to the court of Antiochus, which seemed to be one of the few safe places for a person whom the Romans were trying to hunt down.

Since Africanus had been consul so recently, he could not be elected again to take charge of the war against Antiochus. His brother, Lucius Cornelius Scipio, was elected consul and assigned the war with the king as his province; of course he asked the great Publius to go along as a member of his staff and as the real commander. The one real battle of this war was fought early in 189 B.C. near Magnesia, about forty miles eastward from Sardis. Antiochus had about 75,000 men, while the Romans had only about 30,000, but the Asiatic army, as usual, was composed of men with different languages, equipment, and methods of fighting, so that its elements could not be efficiently coordinated on the field. The individual elements fought well; the Romans won partly because they were able to stampede Antiochus' elephants, partly because King Eumenes of Pergamum, who was actively helping the Romans, led a fine cavalry charge on the flank of the enemy's phalanx once the elephants were gone, and partly because the legions were superior to the opposing infantry in the final phase of the battle.

The Roman general offered reasonable terms of peace that would have left the king the most important and defensible part of his realm. Unfortunately the Senate took a more timid view and sent out ten commissioners with the consul of 189 B.C., Gnaeus Manlius Vulso, who arrived and succeeded Lucius Scipio after the battle at Magnesia; they were armed with a new set of conditions for peace. Antiochus' freedom to make war in his own part of the world was denied, and he could not make alliances in the normal way; he had to surrender his elephants and all his fleet except ten ships.

Manlius and the ten commissioners settled the terms of peace in 188 B.C. by the Treaty of Apamea, named for a city in Syria. The king's western boundary was to run down through Asia Minor very roughly along the thirty-second parallel, excluding him from about the western two-thirds of Asia Minor. Eumenes received much of this territory for Pergamum, and the Rhodians obtained the territory lying farther south and nearer to them. There was a lively dispute over the Greek cities on the coast, the "freedom" of which the Romans had pretended to champion against Antiochus. Eumenes tried to get control of them, and the Rhodians, to combat his aggrandizement, urged the Romans to keep them out of his power. The resulting compromise had little to do with the pretensions of the Romans before the war.

During 189 B.C. Manlius Vulso also campaigned against the Galatians, the Celtic people who settled in central Asia Minor about 275 B.C. and constantly annoyed and attacked their neighbors from that time on. He reduced many of their strongholds with considerable loss of life on their side and sold many of them into slavery. The campaign was probably necessary and surely was a great relief to those who had been harassed by the Galatians, but the cruel methods of Manlius Vulso and the extortion that he practiced were most discreditable. He took a huge booty back to Rome, and there were those who said that the new standard of ostentatious luxury at Rome was due to this operation.

There was a tendency among the Romans and among some historians of the nineteenth and early twentieth centuries to regard the peoples of the Near East as of a stamp inferior to that of the peoples of Italy and of the other western parts of the Roman realm. The eastern peoples are said to have been poor soldiers and to have been unstable, excitable, devoted to orgiastic religions, and in general undesirable as immigrants to the western countries, and most of all to the city of Rome. The fact that the Romans could defeat Antiochus more easily than they did some peoples in the West contributed to this notion. As we go on, we shall see that the Near East, in addition to its glorious history of developing the early civilizations, was to continue to contribute many good soldiers and administrators, many shrewd merchants, and a large number of intellectuals of every sort, some of whom were exponents of lofty and closely reasoned religious ideas.

The Third Macedonian War (171–167 B.C.)

The Achaean League wished to unite the whole Peloponnesus under its leadership, but had much difficulty with Sparta's resistance to the project. The two sides conducted their quarrel with considerable bloodshed and bad feeling and sent several embassies to the Senate, which appeared inclined to let them settle things for themselves, even in an unruly manner. At one time four rival embassies from Sparta were in Rome, and the affairs of Greece must have seemed almost past understanding. Yet we find the Romans doing things unforgivable in the world of diplomacy: dealing separately with members of leagues that they recognized as leagues, not bothering to inform themselves about matters that they undertook to arbitrate, and being almost unfailingly haughty and overbearing.

The Romans were looking with a jealous and fearful eye on Philip V of Macedonia, who by good management was again increasing the prosperity and strength of his kingdom. Philip died in 179 B.C. and was succeeded by his able son Perseus. Possibly Philip had meant to fight the Romans, as many people of the time believed, and the idea that Perseus might do so caused a certain unrest in Greece.

Perseus' attitude toward Rome was most correct. Nevertheless the Romans, urged on by many Greeks and by Eumenes of Pergamum, declared war on him in 171 on the pretext that he was preparing to make war on them. Perseus had a good army of 40,000 men who acquitted themselves well in the short contest that followed, the Third Macedonian War. He could not hope to match the Romans in manpower, however, and he lacked an adequate navy. The geography of his country is admirably suited for defense, and his final downfall did not come until after the Battle of Pydna (168 B.C.), where he was defeated by the superior tactics of a new Roman general, Lucius Aemilius Paulus, and by the flexibility and efficiency of the Roman formations against the strong but rather inflexible Macedonian phalanx.

The Settlement of the East

Rome did not annex any territory after the war with Perseus. Macedonia was broken up into four republics that were barred from trading and from political dealings with one another. They had senates and chief magistrates. There were to be no armies except those allowed against the barbarians on the frontiers. In other places the Romans, apparently from sheer irritation at the Greeks, were less reasonable.

In many cities there was a systematic purge (as we have learned to call it when it occurs in our own times) of those who opposed Roman policy. Among the Aetolians there was a pretense of a trial before the execution of five hundred men not sympathetic to Rome. A thousand men from the cities of the Achaean League were taken off to Rome under the fiction that they were to stand trial; it was the year 150 before the survivors were allowed to go home. This was the group among whom the historian Polybius went to Italy. For some reason that we do not know the Senate was bitter against Epirus, in northwestern Greece, for Paulus is said to have destroyed seventy cities there and to have sold the whole population, 150,000 people, into slavery. In 167 B.C. Romans in Italy were relieved of all direct taxation—a dramatic illustration of the profit Rome made from her eastern wars.

Eumenes, who gave the Romans good help against Antiochus and Perseus, did not get what he hoped for in return, for the Senate was cool to him and interfered in his relations with the Galatians, who still were potentially troublesome. The Rhodians, who had offered to mediate between Perseus and the Romans, were punished for their presumption by having Delos made a free port, which cost them dearly because a good deal of trade that had formerly been handled at Rhodes was diverted to Delos.

Perhaps the most highhanded treatment of all was that given to Antiochus IV of the Seleucid Kingdom. At the time of the war with Perseus he and the Egyptian kingdom, now ruled by Ptolemy VI Philometor, an able monarch, were engaged in hostilities over the possession of Coele-Syria, the upper part of Syria. Antiochus had gained an advantage and was besieging Alexandria at the time when the victory of Pydna made it plain that no one in this part of the world could withstand Roman force. A Roman envoy, Popillius, was sent to order Antiochus to evacuate the territories of Egypt, whose old treaty of alliance with Rome, first made in 273 B.C., had recently been renewed. The incident is notorious: the king received the written demands from the envoy and said that he would like to take time to consider them, but Popillius drew a circle around him with his stick and told him to answer before he stepped out of the circle. Antiochus agreed at once to comply with the Senate's demands.

Neither Egypt nor the Seleucid Kingdom was ever strong again. Ptolemy VI Philometor lived until 145 B.C. and ruled ably, but with full recognition of the fact that the Romans had saved his kingdom from Antiochus and that they were equally ready to give brusque orders to him. The Senate more than once moved to weaken the Seleucid Kingdom; for example, it lent support to elements there who were eager for attempts on the throne and for civil war.

Pergamum remained the most important kingdom of Asia Minor. Eumenes, although checked by the Romans, still had a large realm; he was succeeded in 159 B.C. by his brother Attalus II, who ruled until 138 and was then succeeded by Attalus III, who, as we shall see, bequeathed the kingdom to Rome at his death in 133 B.C.

From this time on we shall find the Romans surrounded by a throng of client kings whom they could sometimes help and sometimes use, just as in modern times powerful nations have client nations, whom we now prefer to call satellites. Masinissa of Numidia had assumed this role at the end of the Second Punic War. From now on these kings regularly sent their sons to Rome to be educated. The young men could learn at Rome how the world was governed and could make useful friends. They were also safer from murder by rivals than they would be at home.

It became the custom, too, for the kings to ask for public recognition by the Romans. A new king naturally made it plain that he intended to honor all the treaties and relations of his predecessor, if he did so intend, so that his policy would be known. Kings became eager, however, to receive the message that returned from Rome when they sent to announce their adherence to the old friendship with the Romans, preferably a statement that the Romans regarded the king as a friend and an ally, but at least an assurance that they regarded him as king.

The Final Settlement in Greece

The new republics of Macedonia were reasonably successful until a pretender to the throne arose who gained such support by claiming that he was the son of Perseus that two Roman legions had to be used to put him down in 148 B.C. Macedonia was made a province, with Illyricum and Epirus also under its governor. The position of Macedonia on the map is worth studying, for although in Greek history the country almost always appears as a somewhat wild place far to the North and out of the mainstream, in the larger context of Roman history it is a zone that connects Italy and the East. This fact is emphasized by the completion during the second century of the *via Egnatia,* a great road primarily built, of course, for military purposes and running over five hundred miles from Dyrrachium (modern Durazzo) on the western coast of Greece all the way across Macedonia and the northern coast of the Aegaean to connect with the territories of the East. We shall see, too, that Macedonia and the regions between it and the Danube were to be very important during the late Republic and the Empire as sources of natural wealth and men, beside continuing to be an important link between the eastern and western parts of the large area controlled by Rome.

Some years after the Third Macedonian War Greece itself lost its nominal freedom. The Achaeans, seeing that the Roman armies were busy in various places, supposed that they could flout Roman orders. The Romans decreed, among other things, that Corinth should be allowed to leave the league. The senators who brought the Senate's word of freedom to Corinth were surprised at being attacked by a riotous mob, whose leaders the city refused to punish. The Achaeans were most bitter against the Romans, but the mass of citizens in every part of the country warmly resented the Roman support of oligarchy; to the Romans it seemed only natural to support the few rather than the many so that there would be a small group in each place to deal with and hold responsible. In 146 the Roman forces of Macedonia easily scattered those of the Achaeans, the only army available to the Greeks. Greece was not made a province until generations later. For now she was declared a part of the province of Macedonia.

Corinth was destroyed, nominally because of the attack on the ambassadors, but really as a warning to others. Another of the great international thefts took place as the treasures of this rich old city were carried off to Rome. A century later Julius Caesar, with his usual common sense, dismissed the notion of letting this fine commercial site be unused and refounded the city; he also refounded Carthage, another great commercial city destroyed in 146 B.C.

The days of Spartan greatness lay 250 years in the past, but Sparta as a symbol of disciplined valor, of the stern raising of the young, and of simple patriotism had established itself among both Greeks and Romans. The Romans probably thought it useful to leave Sparta to its aristocratic government in its fertile territory and to the pursuit of its old ways, which were occasionally mentioned in later times by writers. Plutarch, for example, at the end of the first century of our era, says in his biography of the Spartan lawgiver Lycurgus that he himself had seen how the Spartans performed some of their traditional rituals and acts.

Athens, like Sparta, was thenceforth to live its old life in the shadow of the Romans. At least the Athenian democracy could still wrangle, if it could not rule. The literary men no longer developed new fields, but there were fine teachers of literature. The four schools of philosophy, those of Plato, Aristotle, the Epicureans, and the Stoics, were from now until their closing in A.D. 529 the attraction for many students from all over the Mediterranean world, and Athens, like Sparta, could still inspire men.

Many another handsome and vivacious Greek city, especially those of the coast of Asia Minor, served as an intellectual and artistic center for centuries under the Romans. In both Greece and the other parts of the Greek world, however, there was henceforth a lively fear and dislike of the Romans. Not only did men resent their highhandedness, brutality, and greed; they also despised their crudeness and their indifference to the niceties of behavior and of art and the intellect as known among cultivated Greeks.

The Further Organization of the West: Africa

The Second Punic War had been terminated by a treaty that left Carthage no freedom in foreign policy and that set up Masinissa as ruler of Numidia. His kingdom was large, for it covered a little of modern Tunisia and most of modern Algeria and extended a little way toward Egypt south of the Carthaginian territory. Carthage still had a fertile territory of some size, by ancient standards, and many of her old trade connections as well. Masinissa ruled Numidia for more than fifty years before he died, probably in 148 B.C., at about ninety. He was the ideal client king from the Roman point of view, for he was always ready to obey the commands of the Senate and would anticipate them when he could. In one way he was unusual: he regarded Scipio Africanus, rather than the Senate in general, as his patron. In this respect Scipio was at the beginning of a long succession of great Romans who regarded kings or whole peoples or provinces as their clients. M. Claudius Marcellus, who had some successes against Hannibal in Italy and who took Syracuse, became the patron of Sicily, and the relation descended for several generations in his family.

Toward the Carthaginians Masinissa followed the predatory policy that suited him and that seemed to be indicated by the attitude of the Romans to his aggressions. Several times commissions were sent in answer to their complaints at his taking pieces of their territory by force, but the commissions either decided in his favor or left the matter unsettled, which meant that he could keep the land he had stolen. Presently, however, one of the commissions was instructed to make a complete settlement and fix a boundary, and the Carthaginians objected to their doing so.

Marcus Porcius Cato, of whom we shall hear more in connection with affairs at home, was a member of this commission and apparently became convinced that the Carthaginians were both strong and determined, for from now on he ended every speech he made in the Senate with the words, "Carthage must be destroyed." The other point of view was represented by Publius Cornelius Scipio Nasica, a former consul and censor, now Pontifex Maximus and soon to be *princeps senatus,* or first senator, the one who was first asked his opinion on each question before the Senate. We may assume that he objected to the immorality of Cato's view; the scanty evidence makes it plain that he believed that the *metus Punicus,* or fear of Carthage, was a salutary element in life as it had been lived in Rome and that the disappearance of Carthage would cause the Roman character to deteriorate. For fifty years, however, Roman policy had been to strike down peoples at a distance who appeared capable of sometime endangering Rome, and this emotional attitude was not to be changed by any kind of argument. The Senate was persuaded by Cato and others that Carthage must be destroyed as soon as a pretext could be found.

The Carthaginians supplied the pretext by resisting the final settlement of their boundary with Masinissa, by expelling some of their own people who were said to have favored Numidia, and finally by engaging in a formal battle with Masinissa, in which they were badly beaten. The Romans immediately began to prepare an army. The Carthaginians offered to give satisfaction, but the Romans declared war just before the arrival at Rome of an embassy which came to agree to do whatever the Romans wished.

The Senate demanded three hundred hostages and said that the Carthaginians must obey the commands of the consuls whom they were sending to Africa. When the consuls arrived in Africa with their army and fleet and had ordered the Carthaginians to surrender all the munitions they had—20,000 sets of arms and two thousand catapults—they disclosed the final condition: the Carthaginians must destroy their city and retire to a site ten miles from the sea. Technically they had broken the treaty made at the end of the Second Punic War by taking up arms against Masinissa, and technically they had left themselves helpless by their act of entrusting themselves to the will of the Romans (*deditio*). Nevertheless the action of the Romans cannot be excused; it was a shameful one dictated by an unworthy fear.

The outraged Carthaginians closed the gates, freed the slaves, and fell to making weapons. One of their generals had withdrawn from the city, so there was a force outside; the fortifications on the sea side were such that supplies could sometimes be brought in that way. Surprising as it may seem, the Romans achieved very little at first by their attacks on the city.

The hero who finally took the city was another Scipio. He was one of the sons of Paulus, the conqueror of Perseus of Macedonia, and had been given for adoption to the son of Scipio Africanus, an unwarlike man. He then took the name of his adoptive father, Publius Cornelius Scipio, and added to it his old name, Aemilius, with an adjective ending that made it Aemilianus. He is known sometimes as Scipio Aemilianus and sometimes as Africanus, like his adoptive father's father, because of his success in Africa.

Scipio went to Africa as one of the military tribunes at the beginning of the war and distinguished himself in the operations of the years 149 and 148. He was allowed to return to Rome to stand for the aedileship for the year 147, but his reputation and the glamor of the Scipionic name were such that the people elected him consul and voted that his province should be to conduct the war against Carthage. His friend Polybius the historian went with him when he returned to Africa. Little by little the Romans gained the advantage, and in 146 the city fell. Scipio Nasica remarked that now the Romans had no one to fear and no one to blush before.

What remained of the city was destroyed, and the site remained unused for a hundred years, until Julius Caesar refounded the city. The Romans made a province of Carthage's territory, calling it Africa (they did not use the word for the whole continent, as we do). Masinissa had died during the war, and Scipio, whom he had named to settle the succession in his hereditary role as patron of the Numidian kingdom, made a reasonable arrangement among the sons of the deceased king. Some land in the new province was given to cities there, like Utica, that had taken the Roman side in the war. A large amount of good land was vacant. So that prospective buyers could have some idea what to expect, the Senate had a translation made of a Punic handbook on farming, written by one Mago and presumably applying the rules of Hellenistic farming manuals to local conditions.

Affairs in Spain to 133 B.C.

While all this was going on in Africa, the Romans were also busy subduing Spain. At the end of the Second Punic War the Romans held a rather small territory on the eastern coast of Spain, as the Carthaginians had done. A fixed tribute, or *stipendium,* was demanded rather than a proportion of natural products such as was collected in Sicily. There may well have been rapacious exactions by the first governors, for they brought home extraordinary amounts of the precious metals. The historian Livy remarks that the Spaniards soon discovered that they had merely changed masters; the Romans, however, did not have the shrewdness that the Carthaginians had long since acquired in nursing along a lucrative source of income.

In 197 there was a great uprising of the Spanish tribesmen against harsh Roman treatment, and it became necessary to send M. Porcius Cato, the consul of 195, with a full army. He had little success in pacifying the country, although he seems to have done something to regularize the exaction of the tribute and to have instituted the regular working of some of the iron and silver mines.

The warfare in Spain dragged on until the year 179, when a treaty was made with the Spaniards by the praetor of 180 and proconsul of 179, Tiberius Sempronius Gracchus, the father of the famous tribune of 133 B.C., who bore the same name. Gracchus, who was highly respected for his upright character, persuaded the Spaniards to accept a fair treaty that granted them better land, but bound them to pay tribute and provide auxiliaries. The Spaniards were responsive to honest treatment and evidently regarded this treaty as fair, for they referred to it later as a model.

The character of Gracchus, too, evidently stood out as a paragon among those of the Romans whom the Spaniards had met, for some years later, learning that his son was in Spain, they insisted on his being present at a negotiation then going on to guarantee the Roman agreement by his personal integrity.

Twenty-five years later the peace was disturbed again; the Romans attacked a tribe that, though allied with them, had insisted on building a great tribal stronghold for itself. From 153 to 133 the Romans warred on the Spaniards with senseless cruelty and culpable inefficiency. At Rome there was great discontent about the war in Spain after its renewal in 154 B.C. The men found the fighting arduous, the booty scanty, and the terms of service long. The complaints of the men subject to be called for military service, who were also the voters, were communicated to the tribunes. In 151 B.C. the tribunes took the violent step of arresting and imprisoning the consuls in a fierce struggle over the levy of that year that evidently ended in a compromise, the choice of men for Spain by lot. At about this time, too, the tribunes had a law passed limiting service to six years, and we hear of an army being largely replaced because all the men had served their legal limit. In 138 B.C. there was another quarrel so bitter that the tribunes again took the consuls to jail. At last the wishes of the people caused Scipio Africanus to be sent to command in Spain with the tribunes helping to set aside the law of 151 forbidding a second consulship so that he could be elected consul again. In 133 he finished the war by ending the long siege of the little town of Numantia, where a small and heroic army was holding out against the Romans. We shall see that the Iberian Peninsula was not entirely pacified, however, until Augustus campaigned there. It should be noted that the resentment of the people at long service in the army in unrewarding wars and the struggles of the tribunes and the Senate are a prelude to the proposals of Tiberius Gracchus in his tribunate, which we shall discuss presently.

Spain in the second century may be called the Wild West of the Romans. There were periods of peace and periods of war, and the treatment of the natives was essentially conscienceless exploitation for the sake of the agricultural and mineral wealth. The natives were not set apart on reservations, but were sometimes enslaved to work in the mines and on the farms or enrolled as auxiliary troops. After 133 B.C., however, they were allowed to become a fairly prosperous provincial population.

Northern Italy

After the Second Punic War the Gauls and the other peoples of northern Italy had to be dealt with all over again. Rome was fortunate in that the Gauls did not assist Hannibal as they might have; it was not until the war was as good as over that they really rose against the Romans. From 210 to 191 B.C. the Romans were fairly steadily engaged with them, defeating their tribes separately until in 191 they conquered the Boii, the most bellicose of all. Many of the Boii left the country in the following years and went to the region farther north that took from them the name of Boiohaemum and is now called Bohemia.

The Romans made every effort to secure the country, sending colonists to Placentia (Piacenza) and Cremona, then to Bononia (Bologna), and a little later to Parma and Mutina (Modena). Major roads were built to allow the swift passage of troops along the more important routes. Ariminum, on the eastern coast, was the anchor point of Roman force in the North.

A separate effort was made against the Ligurians, who controlled another piece of territory that to us seems an obvious and normal part of Italy—the territory of the Italian Riviera, east, west, and north of Genoa. These were tough and stubborn people; they were not subdued until about 150 B.C. A similar effort was made in the northeast corner of Italy against the Istri, a little way down the east coast of the Adriatic. In 181 a Latin colony was founded at Aquileia, at the head of the Adriatic, between the modern Venice and Trieste. It was composed of veterans who were given large allotments of land and was plainly meant as a military colony. The site was excellent for commerce, however, and the time was soon to come when the city prospered on the lively trade with the new centers developing to the north of it.

It is hard to see in the wars of the fifty years or so after the Second Punic War the acts of a nation that had a great master plan for the domination of the Mediterranean or even a very strong urge toward that end. Perhaps it is fair to say that they were the acts of people who fumbled their way through situations as they arose and showed remarkably little aptitude for reflection about the general state of affairs and their own long-range interests, and especially so when they allowed themselves to descend to a policy of brutal terrorism.

THE ROMAN CULTURE: 265 TO 133 B.C.

New Ways of Life: The Nobles

As a group the senatorial order gained experience and increased its authority by conducting this long series of wars; it may be said that the time from the arrival of Hannibal in Italy to the tribunate of Tiberius Gracchus in 133 B.C. was the high point of the authority and prestige of the Senate. For the individual Roman of the senatorial order it was a stirring time. It was financially profitable, too, for the Romans took immense amounts of booty. Some was brought home to the public treasury, but some of it was sold and the profits divided, with a good share going to the commander and the officers and a small share to each soldier. It has been estimated that during the Second Punic War about 170,000,000 denarii were brought to the treasury and that the ten thousand talents, or 60,000,000 denarii, of the indemnity paid by Carthage would bring this to 230,000,000 denarii, or $46,000,000 in values of 1932.[1] Although all this booty did not pay for the cost of the war, we may suppose that there was a goodly amount of other loot that found its way into the possession of individuals.

At the end of our period there were six overseas provinces: Sicily, acquired at the end of the First Punic War; the double province of Sardinia and Corsica, taken just after Sicily; the two provinces of Hither and Farther Spain, which were organized in 197 B.C.; and Macedonia and Africa, both organized in 146. For each province a charter was drawn by a senatorial commission. This *lex provinciae,* as it was called, established the political organization of the province, often giving to cities that had been helpful to the Romans special status and privileges, then arranged the system of administering justice and that of collecting taxes.

The provinces were normally governed by magistrates whose power had been prorogued. The governor was in charge of both civil and military affairs. In a sense, it has been said, he did not govern, but kept the peace and administered justice while the local governments did the real governing. The Romans had no ambitious plans for the minute exploitation of resources in the style of the Ptolemies or for changing the attitudes of the people; their viewpoint was more like that of the Persians, who tried to protect their subjects and leave them alone, requiring only a modest tribute and contingents of troops for the common defense. The governor had to report at intervals to the Senate, render account to it when he came home, and submit to it any arrangements looking to permanence.

It is difficult to form a judgment on the quality of provincial government, since we know little of routine and unspectacular performances. If he was in the province only for one or two years, the governor was still of the governing class and knew the process of routine administration, and in his group of helpers, which was called his *cohors,* he would normally have one or two mature men of special abilities as well as youngsters undergoing the same kind of seasoning that he himself had had when he was young. Nevertheless a rapacious man could find many ways to make

---

[1] Tenney Frank, *An Economic Survey of Ancient Rome* I, 80–81. Other summaries of income and expense may be found in this interesting and useful volume, published in 1933. The denarius was reckoned there as worth 20 cents in 1932 on the basis of its silver content, and we may as well leave the reader to adjust that calculation to current values.

money, from the acceptance of improper presents to the outright selling of justice. Probably the majority of governors were not unendurably rapacious; some undoubtedly were.

The new opportunities for making money from warfare in rich countries and from the governing of the provinces had an unfortunate effect on Roman political life. Naturally more and more money was used in the competition for office, which had been keen enough before this new element was added. Not only could votes be bought outright, but also the voters could be offered games and spectacles and dinners, so that the cost of election became exorbitant, and the man who at last became governor of a province was likely to be in the mood to regain some of the money he had spent on being elected. Laws against electoral bribery began to appear, but plainly failed to check the evil. The *lex Calpurnia de repetundis* (recovery law) of 149 B.C. established a court in which the people of the provinces could attempt to recover money alleged to have been illegally taken by a governor; in exacerbated cases there could be a criminal prosecution besides.

The Businessmen (Equestrians)

From early times the army had eighteen centuries, or 1800 men, in the cavalry arm; there were normally more than one hundred men in the infantry century. Although originally the wealthier men had supplied their own horses, early in the Republic the state began to furnish the horses and the censors began to decide who should have the "public horse." Naturally the senators of military age came first, followed by their sons who had reached military age but were not yet members of the Senate, and then by relatives. It has been calculated, however, that no more than half the 1800 places are likely to have been filled in this way, and we assume that the other half of the corps was chosen by the censors from men who had the property qualification of the first class of infantry and seemed desirable members of what was clearly an elite group. Clearly those who served in the cavalry (and plebeians were eligible) were set apart from others. They received more pay than the legionaries, for example, and larger grants of land when colonies were founded. They were exempt from menial military tasks and took precedence over the centurions or noncommissioned officers, being classed with the higher officers.

There remained a group of men who had the property of the first class, but had not been given the public horse. These men gradually interested themselves in farming the contracts of the state, that is, in bidding as groups to collect the taxes in the provinces or to build buildings in Rome or build roads or whatever other work was done, thus becoming a loosely defined class of businessmen. Until the time of the Gracchi they were not thought of as constituting an order, yet it was understood that there was a loose grouping of those, not in the senatorial order, who fought in the cavalry with the public horse or had done so when of military age and of those who had the requisite amount of property, but had never been given the public horse; all might be loosely referred to as "equestrians," or "knights," so that the curious connection was established between large business and the cavalry.

There were also many businessmen, both large and small, who were not Roman citizens, but belonged to the peoples of South Italy whom we call the Italians, those who were allied to Rome less closely than the group whom we call the Latins. The casual references in the Latin authors and the evidence of inscriptions found in Greece, the islands, and the Near East show that great numbers of these people, many of Greek ancestry, were engaged in trade between Italy and regions to the East.

The Common People

The common man, if he were the holder of a little land, had to go to the wars. Perhaps his relatives kept the farm going while he was away; if fortunate, he returned with a share of booty that enabled him to buy more land and establish himself solidly. If he died in some far country in the service of the Republic, his widow might abandon the farm and go back to her family. It is certain that some farms were given up and either taken by the neighbors or made public land.

Another cause of the decrease in small farms was that the upper classes, who had profited far more from the wars than had the poor, naturally sought to invest at least part of their new wealth in land in Italy. Small holders could be tempted by good cash offers or could be bullied or driven away. Rome and many smaller centers began to have crowds of landless men who had drifted to the towns to find some way of keeping body and soul together.

The new masses of slaves made more difficulty for the free poor, since the huge numbers taken in the eastern wars could be bought very cheaply. The rougher ones were suitable for farm labor, and the large properties of the rich could be staffed with slaves at low cost, leaving no work for the poor on such farms.

Another handicap for the small farmer was the importation of cheap grain from Egypt and from the provinces of Sicily, Sardinia, and Africa. This factor could easily be given too much weight, since many small holdings were genuine subsistence farms that did not depend on a cash crop and since, too, many farms must have sold a modest cash crop in towns to which none of the imported grain ever came. It would be a mistake to suppose that small farmers disappeared; it would probably be proper to say that enough small holders had lost their land to cause some uneasiness about the recruitment of men for the army and to create a problem through the numbers of unemployed in some centers.

When he went to the city, the little man found the slave competing with him there, too. Many of the slaves from the East were cultivated people who made excellent workers. Some became house servants, some prostitutes. The many trained artisans could be put to work in shops. Slaves served as accountants, actors, teachers, musicians, architects, and physicians. Although to us it is surprising to find so much skilled work done by slaves in this and later periods of Roman history, it was a logical system, granted that the idea of slavery is accepted; talent could be sought out and enhanced by education (which was systematically given to promising slaves), and the person thus trained could be kept at work, being unable to strike or quit.

Coinage

The first Roman coinage appeared in 269 B.C. Before that time the Romans were content to use the coins of other governments or to use bronze bars for simple transactions. The denarius, which was mentioned earlier, was not the first coin used by the Romans, but is now believed to have been established as the basic coin shortly after the Second Punic War, perhaps in 187 B.C. It was a standard coin like the shilling, the franc, the mark of modern times, and the Athenian drachma of its own time, with which it was generally equated. The smaller coins were the as, ten of which made a denarius, and the sestertius, or two and a half asses, four of which made a denarius. We often speak of the talent, a measure of weight developed early in the Near East, which in Greece was divided into sixty minas or six thousand drachmas; the Romans used it and divided it into six thousand denarii.

Art

From the sixth century, when the Etruscans gained a style of their own and began to send the products of their shops to neighbors, Italy, or at least central Italy, can be said to have had a common style in art. The Greek influence, exerted directly on the Etruscans, the Romans, and others by Greek products and sometimes by émigré Greek workmen, was important in this style, to be sure, but there was also a native element, part of which we may call Etruscan and part of which was manifested in small local variations in the work done in various places: the cities of Etruria; Rome, Praeneste, and other cities of Latium; and the cities of Campania.

The Etruscan and Roman preference for statues of bronze or terra cotta is a salient point in the history of the things that were made with artistic intent. The general excellence of the bronze work of the Etruscans, from full-sized statues down to little boxes or mirrors, is another point. Still another is that the Romans early had a taste for pictures and reliefs that told the story of a historical event or were otherwise informative.

Temples, which were the most elaborate structures of this earlier period of Italian style, were ordinarily built on a podium, or raised platform, of stone. Unlike Greek temples, they could be approached only from the front, by stairs leading up to the podium. The walls and columns were of wood, and there were antefixes of terra cotta—large round pieces, decorated with pictures of heads and borders of formal ornament, all brightly painted—and *acroteria,* or pieces for the corners of the roof, and statues along the ridgepole of the pitched roof, all these, too, of brightly painted terra cotta. The largest of these early temples was that of Jupiter Optimus Maximus (perhaps 509 B.C.) at Rome.

At about the time of the First Punic War a complex set of changes in the art of Rome and central Italy began. The unification of Italy under the Romans may well have made communication of all kinds between the Greeks of southern Italy and the people of Rome and Central Italy even easier than it had been before. The sojourn in Sicily of many soldiers during the First Punic War probably caused many of them to have a new interest in Greek architecture and art; then many of them saw Greece and the East in the wars after 200 B.C., so that the Hellenistic styles in art became known in Italy and Rome. To these general causative factors may be added local ones in Rome: the increasing sense of power and importance that came to the Romans with their conquests; the larger amounts of money available for buildings or for smaller objects of art, the presence in Rome of many fine objects of art stolen as booty and of competent Greek artists taken as slaves or coming to Rome voluntarily to find work, and the realization of the Roman nobles that art could be used as part of their continual competition for honor and pre-eminence.

The results naturally were as complex as the causations. A new common style of central Italy began to form itself in the late third and the second centuries and matured fully in the time of Augustus. Although Augustus could boast that he found Rome a city of buildings of sun-dried brick and left it a city of marble (or at least faced with thin marble slabs), Rome did become in the third and second centuries a large city whose buildings could stand comparison with those of other cities of the Mediterranean world. It is characteristic of the competition of the Roman nobles that new buildings of any distinction were generally presented by a leading man or that he caused his name to be associated with the building if (as censor, for example) he had it built at public expense.

The Rise of Latin Literature

Although, as we have seen, the Romans were always ready to learn from the Greeks and did learn from them in many fields, the appropriation of Greek literary ideas and techniques for a written Latin literature did not begin until the middle of the third century. Not every people that came into contact with the Greeks wished to adopt their literary techniques. In fact, many peoples were indifferent or hostile to reading and writing and to the high intellectual tradition based on those skills, which makes it the more remarkable that the Romans eagerly studied Greek work in all branches of literature and then made their own significant contributions, thus building up in literature, as in other fields, a Greco-Roman tradition of great importance in forming the culture of the more modern West. No other literature influenced the Romans directly. Moreover, they did not develop forms of their own that might have been expected to produce a literature. Roman authors speak of early Roman ballads and of dramatic performances that seem to have been largely unrehearsed, but none of these was brought to a consciously literary form and put into writing.

Instead the Romans began with forthright adaptations of Greek work, beginning with an author known as Livius Andronicus. A senator, Livius, bought a Greek-speaking slave, Andronicus, who had been trained in Tarentum to teach, and made him tutor to his children. When the slave eventually was given his freedom, he called himself Livius Andronicus. He either knew Latin or learned it in Rome, and he organized a school in which he taught in both languages. Since there was no Latin literature for him to use in teaching, he translated Homer's *Odyssey* into Latin. We now have only fragments of the translation, that is, we have very short passages or single lines or parts of lines that were quoted by later authors, most frequently by grammarians of the third and fourth centuries of our era who wished to give examples of old-fashioned words and usages. Even from these fragments, however, we can tell that this, the first attempt ever made at an artistic translation, had a tone and spirit of its own and was lively.

In 240 B.C. Livius was asked to prepare a play for the *ludi Romani,* or Roman Games, in September, presumably by the aedile responsible for the festival, who may well have thought that he could woo the electorate for his next candidacy for office by adding plays such as there were at the Festival of Dionysus in Athens and such as he may have seen in southern Italy or on service in Sicily during the recent war with Carthage.

How Livius got copies of the Greek plays that he rendered into Latin we do not know, although we can suppose that copies of the fifth-century tragedies could be bought from bookstores in southern Italy or Sicily and that the copies of the comedies were either bought in southern Italy or sent directly from Athens, the one great center of New Comedy. Livius, like the early Greek writers of tragedy, was probably producer and chief actor, for the aedile who commissioned the play for a festival naturally wanted a complete production with no further effort or worry on his part. The plays were given in the open air, perhaps on a temporary wooden platform; Rome did not have a permanent stone theater for nearly two hundred years.

Naevius, who may well have been a Latin and who fought in the First Punic War, produced his first adaptation of a Greek play for the Roman stage in 235 B.C. and lived until 201 B.C. In him the purely Roman note begins to come out strongly, for he wrote an epic poem on the recent war with Carthage which was presumably the first original work in Latin literature. The fragments of the *Bellum Punicum* betray a strong consciousness of Roman achievement and show that in the story of early Rome that led up to the war Naevius emphasized the exploits of Aeneas, which brought the Trojans to Italy and led at last to the founding of Rome.

Ennius (239–169 B.C.) came from outside the city of Rome or even Latium, for he was born and brought up in Calabria, in southern Italy. A man did not need to be a Roman of Rome, however, to have a proud sense of being a member of a great commonwealth, and Ennius, in his *Annales,* a historical epic, did much to develop what might be called "the portrait of the old Roman," the picture of an idealized national type that was comparable in its social usefulness to the picture of the Athenian all-round man developed in the days of Pericles. Pride in Roman men shines through such lines as *"moribus antiquis res stat Romana virisque"* (Rome stands firm in her old ways and her men). Ennius knew the effectiveness of a liberal use of the word "Roman," as Cicero did after him and as Shakespeare did in *Julius Caesar.*

Ennius presented adaptations of Greek plays for the Roman stage as his predecessors had done. He also translated the adventure story of the Sicilian Euhemerus, which we have described, and invented a literary type, that known as *satura.* As he wrote it, *satura* was a mixture of prose and verse observations on life, anecdotes, and so on, not unlike a column in a newspaper conducted by a good writer. The acid note that we think of as characteristic of satire was added by later Romans who worked in this field.

Since no work of Livius Andronicus, Naevius, or Ennius exists as more than quotations ranging in length from one word to perhaps a dozen lines, it is a great pleasure to the student of Latin literature to come upon the twenty-one comedies of Plautus and the six of Terentius, or Terence. Their works are refreshingly different from one another, for the work of Plautus, the earlier of the two, is racy, full of local allusions and off-color jokes, with some of the dialogue made into arias, while that of Terence is lively without being either racy or coarse and is couched in language of almost untranslatable ease and elegance. Neither man wrote original plays; these are all adaptations from the Greek New Comedy.

With Plautus we come to an important aspect of Latin literature, its transmission of the Greek influence to modern times. The playwrights of early modern times read Plautus and Terence carefully and used them. Plautus' *Aulularia,* or *Pot of Gold,* is the story of a miser and of the circumstances that forced him to give up his antisocial ways; Molière's *L'Avare* is much indebted to it. *Menaechmi,* or *The Two Menaechmuses,* is an ingenious and funny play about twins who were separated when very young and met again with a great many mistakes at first as to their identities. This served as model for Shakespeare's *Comedy of Errors* and for the modern *Boys from Syracuse.* An excellent example of this Plautine influence is the Broadway hit of the early sixties, *A Funny Thing Happened on the Way to the Forum,* in which it is easy to recognize elements from several plays of Plautus blended with great skill to form a comedy that sounds thoroughly Plautine.

Publius Terentius Afer was brought to Rome as a boy slave and fell into the hands of the senator Terentius Lucanus, who gave him a good education and later freed him. He wrote only six comedies before his untimely death, four modeled on those of Menander and the other two on those of a close follower of Menander. His comedies surpass those of Plautus in elegance and are far behind them in vigor. There are no arias in the meters of song, but only quiet conversation. We do not find the Greek words that Plautus throws in for fun or to give the pleasure of recognition to an audience that had served in the army in Greek-speaking areas, nor do we find the same picturesque vocabulary of abuse. Terence has his own elegancies: his exposition at the beginning is skillfully managed and his narrative passages move with exemplary swiftness; the plots are tight and the characters are finely portrayed. His Latin is pure and elegant, easy in its movement, clear and exact.

During the second and first centuries playwrights continued to present Latin versions, sometimes rather independent ones, of the tragedies of the great Greek authors; we hear of their being presented at the public festivals in Cicero's time. After that we do not hear of new authors, although the performance of the old plays continued. The writing of tragedies on the old Greek themes came to be only an exercise for literary-minded young men.

The consciousness of the Romans that the civilized world was largely

Greek was displayed by the fact that Greek was the language used by the senator Fabius Pictor when at the time of the Second Punic War he wrote a history of Rome. This work may be compared to the nationalistic accounts offered in Greek to the Greek world by Berossus of Babylon and Manetho the Egyptian at about the same time. Fabius, who was sent by the Senate to consult the Delphic Oracle during the war and probably was instructed to sound out sentiment in Greece during his trip, could easily have come to feel the need for a book to interpret Rome and its history to the Greeks in the proper light and with the authority that his being a senator would lend it. His work, like that of some of the other early authors, has been preserved only in fragments.

Marcus Porcius Cato, whom we have seen as politician and soldier and who is often known as Cato the Censor because of his severity in that office, made shrewd use of the gifts that the Greeks came bearing, even while he carefully watched for concomitant dangers. He was known as an effective orator; the fragments of his speeches show that he had learned a good deal of the Greek techniques of effective speech. His lost *Origines* was the first history by a Roman written in Latin. It was characteristic of Cato to emphasize the origins and the importance of many other cities in Italy and to describe the wars as common efforts without naming generals rather than give credit for sound strategy or fine leadership to some noble Roman (we know this from what other authors say).

Cato's *De agricultura,* which has come down to us complete, is the first Latin technical work, a straightforward description of choosing and managing a moderate-sized farm as an investment. Cato's choice of farms for profit would be first a good vineyard, then a truck farm, a willow grove (for baskets and the like), an olive orchard, a meadow for hay, a cereal farm (wheat, barley, spelt), a piece of woodland, an orchard, and an oak forest where pigs could be pastured on the acorns. He gives detailed instructions for equipping it with slaves, some of them specialists, with animals, and with buildings and equipment, sometimes mentioning the prices of olive crushers and metal tools and the best places to buy them, as well as the proper rations for the slaves. For the extra work at harvest time outside help is to be called in; such seasonal work was normally done by free men. Factual writing was congenial to the Romans, and hereafter they did a considerable amount of it, sometimes on very practical subjects, like Frontinus' essay on the water supply of Rome, and often on literary or historical subjects that required scholarly investigation.

The Late Second Century

The younger Scipio Africanus, the conqueror and destroyer of Carthage in 146 B.C. and of Numantia in 133, was given Greek instructors of every

kind by his father Aemilius Paulus and was able to use the library of
King Perseus of Macedonia, which his father brought home after the
Battle of Pydna. As a very young man he formed a continuing friendship with the Greek historian Polybius and later became friendly with
the Greek philosopher Panaetius. We know that there were other Greeks
in Rome of some literary and intellectual pretensions (Polybius speaks of
them as what we should call "the Greek colony in Rome"), if not the
equals of Polybius and Panaetius, and naturally the patronage of great
Romans was most welcome to them, since their own country was in so
troubled a state. Scipio and other members of the Roman upper class thus
had excellent opportunities to learn the Greek language and its literature
and philosophy from men of some distinction.

Scipio did not write, although he has been regarded as the leading figure
in the Scipionic Circle of cultured Roman noblemen, so called perhaps because of Cicero's imaginative reconstructions of such a circle in his dialogues a hundred years later. Even if we do not subscribe to the idea that
there was a circle of which he was the leading figure and through which
he encouraged literary studies, we may still accept the idea that he knew
Greek well, was widely read in Greek literature, and was aware of the
main ideas of Greek philosophy, even while remaining a grim and bullying
Roman typical of his time. There was plainly a ferment of thought and
writing, too, in the middle and later second century, even if Scipio was
not the central figure.

One important effect of Greek studies was the rise of interest in effective
oratory in the Greek style, for oratory was a most important weapon of the
Roman aristocrat in his endless task of cherishing and protecting his clients and competing with his peers. Greek teachers taught him in Greek
the techniques of persuasive speech; such instruction was not available to
the ordinary man, who knew little or no Greek. When an attempt was
made in 92 B.C. to open a school of oratory with instruction in Latin, the
censors forthrightly ordered its closing as a *ludus impudentiae,* or school
of impudence, which would teach oratory to those not of the proper social
class to wield it. Another trait of life that we can trace to this time was
the acceptability of an interest in writing and literature among the upper
classes, as well as a feeling that the patronage of competent literary men
counted for something in the endless competition for glory and prestige.

It is worth remarking that Greek influence was not always welcomed
without reservations. Cato the Censor more than once made biting remarks about the sillier excesses of those who were delighted with Greek
learning and ways, and in 161 B.C. the Senate expelled all teachers of
rhetoric and philosophers from Rome. In 155, however, the Athenians
sent three major philosophers as an embassy to Rome, and when one of
them broke his leg, they all stayed until he was able to go home, passing

the time by giving lectures on philosophy to the Romans, the sophistication of which was both fascinating and repellent to them.

The first Roman philologist, Aelius Stilo, grew up in the atmosphere of the time of Scipio and lived on into the next age. Learned in the law, he offered legal instruction, then extended his interest to antiquarian questions of Roman history, the meanings of archaic words, and the establishment of a genuine corpus of Plautine plays selected from the many that bore Plautus' name. He was the forerunner of a number of fine scholars in language and literature, some of whose work we still have.

CHAPTER

21

POLITICAL LIFE: 133 TO 79 B.C.

The period from 133 to 30 B.C., the period of the fall of the Roman Republic, may for the purpose of description be divided into three parts. This chapter will recount the events of 133 to 79 B.C. Chapter 22 covers the years from 79 to 49 B.C., a period of the rivalries of strong men that led to the civil war between Pompey and Caesar. Chapter 23 tells the story from Caesar's crossing of the Rubicon to the establishment in power in 30 B.C. of his great-nephew Octavian, who was soon to be called Caesar Augustus.

Tiberius Gracchus

In 133 B.C. a tribune of the people, Tiberius Sempronius Gracchus, a man of a distinguished family, attacked the double problem of the diminution in the number of small landholders eligible and liable for service in the army and that of the presence in the cities and the towns of men who no longer had any land, making a proposal, with the support of some leaders of the senatorial order, to provide land for men who had none. His plan was a renewal of one part of the Licinian-Sextian Laws of 367 B.C., for it envisaged a strict interpretation of the limit of five hundred *iugera* (310 acres) for the renting of the public land.

Any lease or holding of the public land that amounted to more than five hundred *iugera* was to be reduced to that size; the lessor or holder might then have full ownership of the five hundred *iugera*. The land re-

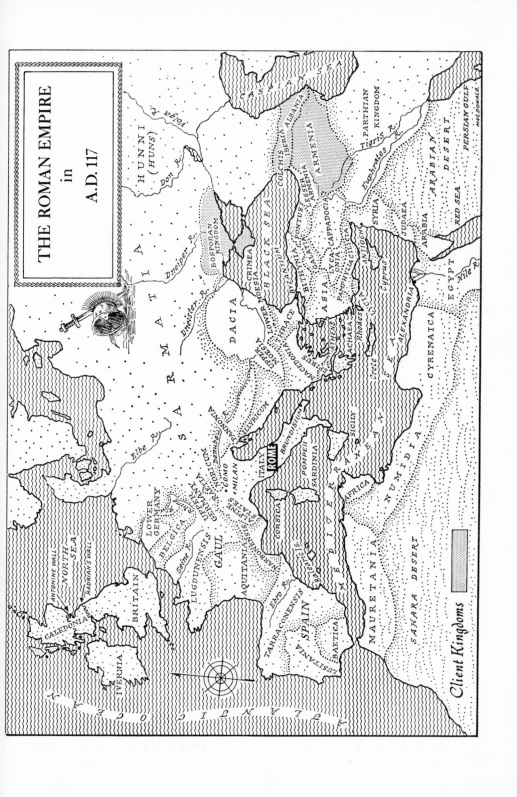

THE ROMAN EMPIRE
in
A.D. 117

HUNNI
(HUNS)

Volga R.

Don R.

Dnieper R.

SARMATIA

Dniester R.

CASPIAN SEA

CAUCASUS

COLCHIS
IBERIA
ALBANIA
ARMENIA

PARTHIAN
KINGDOM

Tigris R.

Euphrates R.

BOSPORAN
KINGDOM

CRIMEA

BLACK SEA

DACIA

MOESIA

LOWER MOESIA

UPPER MOESIA

BYZANTIUM
BITHYNIA
PONTUS
GALATIA
MESSENIA
ARMENIA
ASIA
CAPPADOCIA
LYCA
PONTA
PAMPHYLIA
PISIDIA
CILICIA
ANTIOCH

SYRIA

JUDAEA
ARABIA

ARABIAN
DESERT

RED SEA

PERSIAN GULF

MACDONALD

THRACE
MACEDONIA
EPIRUS
ATHENS
ACHAEA
Rhodes
Crete
Cyprus

ALEXANDRIA

EGYPT

Nile R.

CYRENAICA

MEDITERRANEAN SEA

Elbe R.

NORTH SEA

ANTONINE WALL
HADRIAN'S WALL

CALEDONIA

IVERNIA

BRITAIN

LOWER
GERMANY

BELGICA

UPPER
GERMANY

NORICUM

RHAETIA

ALPINE
STATES

LUGDUNENSIS

Seine R.

GAUL

AQUITANIA

NARBONENSIS

COMO

MILAN

ITALY

ROME

POMPEII
BRUNDISIUM

SARDINIA

CORSICA

SICILY

AFRICA

NUMIDIA

MAURETANIA

SAHARA DESERT

ANTONA R.

PANNONIA

Danube R.

ILLYRICUM

SPAIN
TARRACONENSIS
LUSITANIA
BAETICA

Ebro R.

Tagus R.

Balearic Is.

ATLANTIC OCEAN

Client Kingdoms

covered by reducing the size of large leaseholds would be used to establish landless men on subsistence farms.

Although Tiberius' proposal was legal and to modest renters of public land might have seemed desirable, since it gave them title to land that they were now holding on lease, to the large leaseholders it seemed intolerable. The leading men of the Latin and Italian towns, as well as Romans, were large holders, and some of them (or their ancestors) may simply have stayed on their land when it was declared public land of the Roman people and now felt that the land belonged to them by continued possession. To have to give up what seemed to them to be their own land for a dubious attempt to reinstate men who were failures was to all these large holders an unjust and foolish thing.

Tiberius offered his proposal to the *Concilium plebis* without first laying it before the Senate, which was legal, but tactless. Another tribune of the people, Marcus Octavius, forbade the *Concilium plebis* to consider the measure. Tiberius refused to be balked. After some maneuvering he submitted his proposal to the Senate, which received it coldly. After he had vainly appealed several times to Octavius to withdraw his veto, he called a meeting of the people and proposed his recall. The people voted to deprive Octavius of his office, elected another man in his place, and passed Gracchus' agrarian law. Octavius might have vetoed these proceedings, but chose not to.

Another vote of the people established a commission of three, with power to reclaim and assign lands and to settle disputes. Tiberius, his younger brother Gaius, and his father-in-law were the three members. But the commission needed some funds, which the Senate refused to give. At this point chance presented a strange source of money. Attalus III, King of Pergamum, died in 133 B.C. and bequeathed his kingdom to Rome, apparently with the idea of preserving the interests of the upper classes against the threat of revolution. Tiberius prepared a measure to earmark some of the revenue from Pergamum for the work of his commission; apparently this was enough to make the Senate grant him money.

By now he had surely alienated even the group in the Senate who had at first encouraged him. As the time for the elections drew near, he resolved to run for a second term as tribune, presumably to safeguard his program. A second term was not illegal, but long custom was against it. Somehow the discussion of the election between the tribunes and the *Concilium plebis* burst into a riot, and the other tribunes rushed to a meeting of the Senate and called for help in putting down a tyrant. The sensible caution of the presiding consul did not prevent the Pontifex Maximus from leading a party of senators, doubtless reinforced by clients and slaves who were in readiness, to kill Tiberius and three hundred of his supporters. This was the first time that the Romans shed blood over an internal question.

Although these murders cannot be condoned, Tiberius must bear the blame for having acted irresponsibly—a grievous fault in public life. The theoretical and legal sovereignty of the Roman people did not impart the needed experience, vision, and skill in handling affairs to the crowd of voters whom Tiberius might gather as the *Concilium plebis* on a given day. The Senate's traditional right to discuss and shape legislation and to handle finance and foreign affairs was in general practical in spite of some abuses.

To attempt to establish the re-election of tribunes and the right of the people to depose them may also be called irresponsible. There was no sound basis for the founding in Rome of a democracy of the Periclean type under a leader re-elected many times. As for the recall of the tribune whose acts were unpopular, this procedure should have been possible only for an informed electorate and by a somewhat protracted process.

The Senate set up a court that tried and executed a number of the partisans of Gracchus, but it did not attempt to have the agrarian law repealed or to stop the activity of the commission, which worked for ten years. The census of 125 B.C. showed an increase in the number of property holders since the year 131, some of which may well have been due to the work of the commission.

The work of the commission aroused resentment among the Latins and the Italians, since the allotments were to be given only to full Roman citizens, while public land could be reclaimed from well-to-do Latins and Italians. Marcus Fulvius Flaccus, a candidate for the consulship of 125 B.C., said that he would propose full citizenship for all the allies, or, if they preferred their present status, he offered them guarantees against arbitrary treatment by Roman magistrates, which was a very sore point with them. Flaccus was elected and proposed his bill, but a military emergency arose in Gaul and the Senate sent him to deal with it, so that the matter was never effectively pushed. Disappointment on the part of the allies was so intense that the town of Fregellae took the extreme step of seceding from the Roman alliance. The Romans besieged and took Fregellae, destroyed it, and settled its inhabitants elsewhere.

Gaius Gracchus

Gaius Sempronius Gracchus, the younger brother of Tiberius, served as tribune of the people in the years 123 and 122 B.C. His election to a second term as tribune caused no disturbance and gave him time and assurance for the development of his policy. He was a member of the land commission from its beginning in 133. Although our sources do not give the items of Gaius' program in strict chronological order, we can still get a good idea of what he was trying to do. He first induced the people to pass a law declaring that no court should exist with powers of capital punishment except by the order of the people. With dubious legality the law was made retroactive, so that the president of the court that had condemned the followers of his brother could be exiled for his part in the matter.

He then attacked the problems of landlessness and unemployment by founding two large colonies in the extreme southern part of Italy, both on sites suited to trade and both to contain a certain proportion of men of means to help in getting industry and trade started. Also, in his second tribunate, he carried legislation for a similar colony on some of the land taken from Carthage in the province of Africa. A figure of two hundred *iugera* is given for the allotments in this colony, showing that it, too, was meant to attract men of means. This suggests some concern for the businessman, the farmer of medium property, and for the grain supply of the city of Rome.

His care for the grain supply was also shown by a measure providing, as was not unusual in the Greek city-states, that the government should regularly buy and store a supply of grain and offer it for sale to all citizens at a price slightly below the normal market price. Although this has been called a move to buy votes, it was a statesmanlike measure to assure the basic food supply of a city that had outgrown the productive capacity of the neighborhood. It did at the same time, of course, make him more popular.

He also carried a bill providing that the tithes in the new province of Asia (Asia, like Africa, was a province rather than a continent to the Romans), the former kingdom of Pergamum bequeathed by Attalus III, should be farmed at Rome by the censors, which meant that the large companies of Roman businessmen would bid lump sums and that the winner would be empowered to collect for the government from the provincials. He also carried a bill that turned over seats on the juries of the extortion court set up by the *lex Calpurnia* of 149 to the business class, which was to be known from then on as the equestrian order. It is probable that an "equestrian census," or amount of property qualifying a man to belong to this group, was established by Gracchus, although the amount is not known.

It was probably at about this time that full citizenship began to be conferred *ex officio* on the magistrates of the Latin municipalities. We also know that Gracchus made an unsuccessful attempt to have the Latins moved up to full citizenship and the Italians to the Latin status. Had he succeeded, all the Latins would have become full citizens, and there would have been a steady flow of the leading men of the allied Italian (now become Latin) communities into the full citizenship as they became magistrates of their towns. Since almost all of them would be wealthy, they would also come into the new equestrian order, which would be composed, then, of men from all Italy, representative of every part of the peninsula.

Although the equestrians were essentially the same sort of people as the members of the senatorial order, the senators could hardly be expected to welcome the establishment of the new group and the fact that it had already been offered two kinds of leverage in the form of the farming of the tithes of Asia and the control of the juries in the extortion court. Whatever they may have thought of the merits of the idea in the abstract, it was natural that they should work together to defeat it in the concrete, and they succeeded at least in convincing the people that they would be giving away rights and privileges of their own if they raised the status of the Latins and the Italians. The Senate also induced another tribune, Marcus Livius Drusus, to attempt to alienate some of Gaius' popular support by outbidding him in the matter of land for the landless. Gaius had founded two colonies; Drusus now proposed a dozen colonies of five thousand men each, with no property qualifications required. He also had an interesting proposal to please the Latins: no Latin was to be beaten either by order of a magistrate or when on military service. This measure presumably went into effect, but there is no evidence that the commission for founding the dozen colonies ever really attempted to do so.

Gaius ran for a third term as tribune and was not elected, for the senatorial group had succeeded in detaching much of his support in spite of his good qualities. He remained a land commissioner, but after the end of the year 122 he held no other office. Early in 121 a tribune proposed the repeal of the legislation for Gracchus' colony in Africa, and in a minor row over the matter one of the servants of the consul was killed. The consul, a determined conservative and a harsh and cruel man, persuaded the Senate to pass a resolution asking the consuls to see that the commonwealth suffer no harm. This formula, which was used several times in later years, came to be known as the *senatusconsultum ultimum,* or ultimate decree of the Senate, and was nearly equivalent to our declaration of martial law. The consul gathered an armed force of senators and knights and attacked the company, presumably of clients, with which Gaius had occupied the Aventine Hill on hearing that force was to be used against him.

Gaius was slain in the rout of his supporters, and the consul then executed without trial some three thousand men who were on the Aventine or were thought to be connected with Gaius. Although no new reformer arose in the place of the Gracchi and the Senate had, for the moment at least, regained control of the commonwealth, it did not attempt to stop the work of the land commission, to cancel the measure to stabilize the grain supply of Rome, or to take from the knights the farming of the tithes of Asia or the seats on the juries of the extortion court.

Two provinces were added during this period. The Romans had had some difficulty in accepting the bequest of the kingdom of Attalus, for one Aristonicus, an illegitimate son of the king before Attalus, raised the common people and resisted, so that it was 129 B.C. before the Senate was able to set up a plan for the government of the province, which was called Asia and comprised roughly the western half of what we call Asia Minor. The Romans did not reach out for more territory here; instead they bestowed on native kings some of the more difficult interior regions.

In the West a new province was established in southern Gaul and was called Gallia Transalpina by contrast with Gallia Cisalpina, or Gaul on the *near* side of the Alps, which lay in what is now called continental Italy. The Romans, responding to the city of Massilia's calls for help against the persistent raids of its Gallic neighbors, had by their presence in Gaul aroused other Gallic tribes, whom they defeated in large formal engagements. By 121 B.C. they found themselves in control of a large strip of southern Gaul that reached all the way from north Italy to the Pyrenees, and they organized it into a province that surrounded the territory of Massilia. This province, beside its military value, was expected to yield grain to help in stabilizing the supply for Rome. The city of Narbo, the later Narbonne, was founded in 118 B.C. and so prospered that the province soon came to be called Gallia Narbonensis as well as Gallia Transalpina.

The Jugurthine War: The Cimbri and the Teutons

A very able Numidian named Jugurtha was determined to oust his cousin, who had a claim to the throne equal to his, and killed him in defiance of the Senate's arrangement that they should settle their dispute by sharing the kingdom. The Senate was forced by the general indignation to declare war and send one of the consuls of 111 B.C. against Jugurtha; he presently accepted the king's surrender and sketched terms of peace that left him the kingdom. One view is that this tough fellow was a desirable client king and that this was the best way to handle him, especially at a time when there was danger on two of the northern frontiers. Two northern Germanic peoples, the Cimbri and the Teutons, had started a mass migration to find land. In 113 B.c. they inflicted a severe defeat on a Roman army that went up and met them in southeast Austria. Fortunately the two peoples decided to turn westward through Switzerland into Gaul instead of invading Italy. At the same time the Romans had carried on heavy fighting for several years against the people north of Macedonia. The Senate had good reason to avoid military commitments in North Africa.

Another view rests chiefly on the *Bellum Iugurthinum* of the Roman historian Sallust (C. Sallustius Crispus), written between 50 and 40 B.C., which depicts the Senate at the end of the second century as corrupt and incompetent. The tribunes of that time surely thought so, for they prosecuted several senatorial generals for the terrible defeats that Roman armies suffered at the hands of the Cimbri and the Teutons in Gaul. A tribune summoned Jugurtha to Rome to tell what senators he had bribed to act in his interest, but Jugurtha suborned another tribune to forbid him to speak.

The war was renewed, and a new commander, Quintus Caecilius Metellus, slowly invested Jugurtha's large open country with forts and in two years had made significant progress. The powerful family of the Caecilii Metelli was known for persuading men of wealth to make the attempt to join the governing class and for bringing them along by its assistance, thus adding to its own great political strength. Such a protégé was with Metellus in Africa: Gaius Marius of Arpinum, a town some sixty miles below Rome, who owed to the Caecilii Metelli his election to the offices of quaestor, tribune, and praetor. He asked his patron and commander for leave to go home to campaign for the consulship and was told that it would be soon enough when Metellus' son was of an age to campaign with him for that office. After harsh words he was given permission and campaigned by accusing Metellus of prolonging the war, promising a quick decision if he were elected—a prospect acceptable both to the people and to the businessmen, who saw a good field of operations in the grain trade blocked by the hostilities. He was elected consul for 107 B.C. The Senate prolonged Metellus' command, but Marius persuaded the people to use their power as they had with Scipio Africanus in the Third Punic War to declare that Africa should be Marius' province instead.

Marius also enrolled more men, accepting volunteers who did not belong to any of the five classes of property, but were *capite censi* or *proletarii*—men without property. This measure has been regarded as harmful to the commonwealth. There is evidence, however, that the same thing had already been done in a very small way. It was no remedy for the shortage of men to create new small landholders and then take them away from their land for several years at a time for military service. It seemed rather more practical to take young men with no land, keep them in the army for perhaps sixteen years, and discharge them while still vigorous with a piece of land and a little money as a bonus in the hope that they would settle down.

Marius spent the years 107, 106, and 105 by conquering Numidia slowly along Metellus' lines, that is by reducing and garrisoning Jugurtha's strong points. Jugurtha drew in Bocchus, king of the more western territory called Mauretania, as his ally, but with no great subsequent success, and was finally reduced to flight and refuge with Bocchus. Here a new Roman, later to be very important, enters the story: Lucius Cornelius Sulla, a subordinate of Marius, persuaded Bocchus to win the gratitude of the Romans by giving up Jugurtha. The Romans did not take any land from Numidia to add to their province of Africa. Eastern Numidia, adjacent to Africa, was given to a half brother of Jugurtha who appeared tractable as a client king, and western Numidia was added to Bocchus' kingdom.

The Cimbri and Teutons had meanwhile made the proposal that they settle on the border of the Roman province in southern Gaul as friends and allies of the Romans; the Senate, fearing their fickle nature, warned them off. In a battle that followed the Romans were defeated; they were defeated again two years later. Then in 105, at Arausio, the modern Orange, they suffered their worst defeat since Cannae, losing 80,000 men.

Marius was about to return from North Africa. The people elected him consul for 104, although there was a law (already disregarded when Scipio Africanus was sent to Numantia) against repeating the consulship, and voted him the command against the Cimbri and the Teutons. He had more than two years in which to prepare before the barbarians decided to attack Italy. The people elected him consul for the third, fourth, fifth, and sixth times for the years 103, 102, 101, and 100, with the Senate wisely making no objection. He had all the men armed alike, dropping the distinction in weapons based on the man's property classification. Henceforth the legion consisted of ten cohorts, each of six hundred men and divided into six centuries. Each legion had its own number and name and a silver standard.

In 102 the barbarians moved, and Marius met the Teutons as they came across southern Gaul, defeating them at Aquae Sextiae, the modern Aix, so thoroughly that their remnants were not dangerous. The other consul had difficulty with the Cimbri, who came over the Brenner Pass, but at least managed to keep his army intact. In 101 he and Marius met and crushed the Cimbri at Vercellae, north of the Po. The credit for this victory, too, apparently belonged to Marius.

Marius in Politics: Saturninus and Glaucia

Marius informally joined forces with one Saturninus, who had prosecuted the commanders of the army that was crushed at Arausio in 105, and got a law passed that provided bonuses of land in Africa for some veterans of Marius' African campaigns, including some of the allied soldiers. In 100 B.C. Marius was consul for the sixth time and celebrated a triumph for his great victory over the barbarians. Saturninus was tribune for the second time, apparently having procured the murder of one of his competitors and having joined himself with another reckless character, Glaucia, who was elected praetor. Saturninus proposed another law to provide land for veterans. This time, since the land was in different provinces, there is room for a conjecture that Marius, through Saturninus, was trying to arrange and get credit for the grant of land to the veterans of other armies beside his, which had fought against the Cimbri and Teutons—those veterans for example, who fought on the north Macedonian front.

The Senate may well have felt that the situation was like those that the two Gracchi created, with demagogues promising gifts to the people (Saturninus had the price of the state grain reduced), courting the allies, and now gaining support among the veterans that would enable them to meet any force against them with force. It proved possible to persuade the people that their interests were not being well served, as had been done in the later days of Gaius Gracchus. Saturninus was vulnerable because of his record of violent measures. Marius was probably ready to desert him and Glaucia because they were embarrassing allies and because they probably were beginning to feel that they could act independently of Marius.

In the elections for 99, which were held in the late summer of 100, Saturninus was able to get himself elected tribune again. Glaucia kept up his reputation by having a rival for the consulship murdered. The Senate passed the *senatusconsultum ultimum,* which neatly separated Marius from Saturninus and Glaucia. They and their followers tried to use the Capitoline Hill as a fortress, but Marius forced them to surrender by cutting off their water supply and imprisoned them in the senate house. A mob of young men of the upper class, with some of the people apparently joining in, tore off the roof and pelted them to death with its heavy tiles.

The Social War (90–88 B.C.)

By the decade of the nineties the Italians seem to have become very eager for Roman citizenship, although we cannot be sure why. It would be natural for them to become impatient about their inferior standing in the alliance, especially since the Romans had been more imperious toward them since the Second Punic War. The fact that the equestrian order was better organized than before may have been prejudicial to the interests of the Italian businessmen abroad. If the Italians could get the full citizenship, they could make themselves heard in the political struggles of the Romans when they affected economic interests, and a number of the Italians would automatically become members of the equestrian order. The feelings of the Italians became strong enough to cause the Romans to enact in 95 B.C. the *lex Licinia et Mucia* to expel all noncitizens from Rome. Apparently a definite movement of revolt began to be organized during the burst of indignation at this action.

Marcus Livius Drusus, son of that Drusus who had outbid Gaius Gracchus for popular favor, was one of the tribunes for the year 91. He tried to gain popular favor by bills for cheaper grain and the foundation of colonies. His proposal to give the Latins and the Italians full Roman citizenship, however, aroused a storm of opposition in spite of the fact that the idea was not new. It soon became evident that he could not carry through such a proposal, and the Italians were furious with disappointment. The Senate declared all his earlier bills invalid on the ground that they had been illegally combined into "omnibus bills." Then Drusus, amid the ruin of his plans, was murdered by an unknown person for an unknown reason.

The murder seems, nevertheless, to have caused the Italians to put into action a scheme for revolt that must already have been prepared. The Latins did not join the movement; their status was apparently much more satisfactory to them. Two groups of the Italian allies, the Samnites in southern Italy and the Marsi in the east central part, took the lead. Northern Campania, Latium, Etruria, and Umbria preferred not to join. There was a little fighting in 91 B.C., and early in 90 the war was in full swing.

The Italians began the war on the offensive, with high hopes and an army of 100,000 men, but the Romans managed to deny them any decisive success during the first year. Toward the end of that year the *lex Iulia de civitate* made citizenship available to the Latins and to those of the other allies who had not revolted, offering it to them as communities and requiring them as communities to accept it. The *lex Plautia-Papiria* proffered citizenship to any individual who would present himself within sixty days before the urban praetor to be enrolled, apparently with the idea that some of the rebels could be lured away as individuals. The Romans tried at first to give their new citizens a second-class citizenship by proposing to enroll them in some new tribes, which in the *Comitia tributa* would vote last and thus would have no influence, but abandoned the idea when the new citizens scornfully rejected it. The fighting with the rebels continued through the year 88. Lucius Cornelius Sulla, who as Marius' lieutenant in Africa had persuaded Bocchus to hand over Jugurtha to the Romans, distinguished himself as commander in the southern theater of the war and was elected consul for 88. By that year only the Samnites were still fighting. The defeated Italians were given the citizenship and were put into eight of the thirty-five tribes. They had suffered grave losses in the war.

The Mithridatic War

The war with King Mithridates of Pontus resembled the war with Jugurtha in that it came from Rome's attempts to repress and manage an energetic king on her borders. Pontus, in Asia Minor on the southern shore of the Black Sea, was a kingdom of rich resources, fertile and well watered, and with a good supply of metals. It was a country of villages rather than of cities and was Asiatic in character, although the rulers and nobles were often susceptible to the attractions of Greek culture. The king's father, Mithridates V, maintained a friendly and compliant attitude toward Rome. Mithridates VI, a very forceful man and less ready to be dominated by the Romans, made his way to the throne by violence that included the murder of his brother.

Since a little before 100 B.C. he had been moving cautiously to extend his kingdom and had been hampered by arbitrary commands from Rome that he did not feel ready to defy. When the Social War broke out, he felt free at last to act decisively. He doubtless hoped that the peoples of Asia Minor and Greece would all join him against the Romans if he furnished impressive leadership. He seized Cappadocia and the kingdom of Bithynia. Probably to his surprise, the Romans sent out a commission and ordered him to withdraw from Bithynia, which he did. They then provoked the Bithynian king to attack him and threw their own one legion in the vicinity into the fray. Mithridates swept aside the attack. His call to the people of the surrounding territory to join him was answered, and he ordered a general massacre of all the Romans or Italians in the region—some 80,000 men, women, and children. Now, in the year 88, he decided to send a fair-sized force to Greece to secure that country and to meet the inevitable Roman attack.

Meanwhile, back in Rome, Sulla had been put in command of the troops that were ready to go out against Mithridates. But Marius decided that he ought to have the command in this campaign, and unfortunately there was a way for him to get it. He made a deal with a tribune, Servius Sulpicius Rufus, who was trying to get the new Italian citizens distributed through all the tribes, rather than only eight, so that they would have a genuine influence in the total voting. He gave his support to Sulpicius, getting in return a vote of the people that he should replace Sulla in the command against Mithridates, just as they had put him in Metellus' place against Jugurtha. Envoys were sent to Sulla, who was in South Italy and was ready to embark for Greece, to order him to give up the command. Some of his officers ordered him to yield, as Metellus had yielded or as the commander at Carthage had yielded to Scipio, but he ordered the troops to march back to Rome, and they obeyed. He easily captured the city, for his opponents had not thought that he might defy the state. Sulpicius was hunted down and killed; Marius managed to escape.

Sulla could not remain in Rome to adjust the situation because of the war with Mithridates. The steps that he did take were aimed at assuring the predominance of the Senate. It was provided that only measures approved by the Senate could go before the people and that they must go to the *Comitia centuriata* rather than to the *Comitia tributa,* since the tribunes could not preside over this assembly nor introduce bills in it. Then he started off for Greece, although he must have known that the situation was not entirely stable. Now Marius, aided by the consul Cinna, inflicted injury on Rome in his turn. Returning from exile, he gathered troops from among his veterans, captured the city, and then massacred all he could reach of his political opponents. The arrangements of Sulla were canceled, and he was declared an exile. The slaughter was ended by Marius' death early in 86 B.C.

Cinna managed the home government for three years by contriving to get himself elected consul for each year. During this time orderly government was maintained, the Italians were distributed through the tribes as had been planned, and a fair number of leading men took part in the operations of the government, although it was nominally antisenatorial. But no one could ever forget that the day was coming when Sulla and his army would return. Cinna's measure exiling him made it necessary for him to plan to return in arms.

When he finally got his five legions to Greece in the year 87, Sulla defeated Mithridates near Athens, then at another famous place, Chaeronea. The king was able to send another army, and Sulla defeated that, too, ending the campaign in Greece. The war then moved to Asia, where it went on somewhat sporadically until in 85 B.C. the king and Sulla met to discuss terms. Sulla, who wanted to return to settle affairs in Italy, was willing to promise that the king should be recognized as king of Pontus and an ally of the Romans, requiring only that he should surrender most of his fleet, withdraw from territories he had overrun, and pay an indemity. The real punishment for the war fell on the cities of the province of Asia, practically all of which had been on the king's side. They were fined 20,000 talents, ten times what the king had to pay, and for years afterward they were the prey of the Roman businessmen from whom they had to borrow much of the money.

Sulla's Return

In 83 B.C. Sulla and his army returned to Italy, ready to fight it out with the government, which still regarded him as an outlaw. Beside those who so thought of him there was a group that tried to stay neutral and a group of conservatives who believed in the supremacy of the senatorial class and thought that Sulla would represent it, much as they disapproved of his marching on Rome before he left. Now, of course, the opponents of Sulla had been guilty of illegality and sickening violence. Gnaeus Pompeius, a future great man who now was just past the age of twenty, raised an army of three legions, largely from his own estates in Picenum, and cleverly maneuvered them past the two consular armies to join Sulla in southern Italy. By a combination of force and promises Sulla made himself master of all Italy. Young Pompey served as commander in Sicily and then in Africa to end the resistance of the remnants of the government's forces.

Sulla's belief was that Rome should have a thoroughly conservative government, under the Senate, of the type that had prevailed (without specific legislation to help it) just after the Second Punic War, hampered neither by the pretensions of the equestrians nor the opposition of the tribunes. His first business was to murder all the opponents that he could catch and to confiscate their property. After a little of this he decided to post a list of those on whom there was open season. The Latin word *proscribere* means to post such a list, and the noun is *proscriptio,* giving "proscribe" and "proscription" in English. Forty senators were on the list, probably the officers of the government's forces, but there were 1600 equestrians. Rewards were given to their murderers, their property was confiscated, and their children and grandchildren were declared ineligible to hold office or sit in the Senate.

A law was now passed by which the people made Sulla dictator "to make laws and set the state in order." He began by filling up the Senate, which because of the civil war was down to 150 members. Although he naturally put in some of his own supporters and some younger men of noble families who would be expected to arrive in the Senate in a few years anyway, he also chose three hundred members of the equestrian order. Possibly he had spared a group out of that order that to him seemed most conservative and in agreement with the senatorial point of view even while he was butchering the 1600 others; he might well think that this would be the end of the equestrians as a political force. Henceforth there were to be twenty quaestors elected every year instead of twelve, and all of them were to become members of the Senate at the end of their year of office, so that there would be no need to have censors fill vacancies in the Senate every five years. A rule was made that the tribune would not be eligible for any further office, which naturally kept ambitious young men from wishing to hold the tribuneship. The tribunes were also to be unable to propose legislation to the people, and a limitation of some sort was placed on their veto.

Sulla's best measure, and one that lasted well into the Empire, was his establishment of seven standing criminal courts. We have seen that such a permanent court was set up in 149 B.C. to deal with extortion in the provinces. Sulla kept this one and added courts for major crimes: murder, assault, forgery, electoral bribery, embezzlement, and treason. Naturally the juries were to be chosen from members of the senatorial order.

Knowing political ambition as he he did, he thought it wise to insist on a law that thirty was the minimum age for the quaestorship, thirty-nine for the praetorship, and forty-two for the consulship, and that no office could be repeated within ten years. A man had to follow the *cursus honorum,* or regular succession of the three main offices. Since there were now ten provinces—Sicily, Sardinia-Corsica, two provinces of Spain, Macedonia, Africa, Asia, Cilicia,[1] Gallia Narbonensis, and Gallia Cisalpina—the eight praetors that were now to be elected every year and the two consuls would serve to govern them all as promagistrates, with the Senate assigning them so as to keep a watch somewhat on too ambitious men.

Although Sulla's dictatorship seems rather unlike the earlier ones in that violence brought him to the point where the people voted for it and its stated purpose was new in Roman history, he did fulfill that stated purpose and then resign, as earlier dictators did. He could safely live as a private citizen for the few months left to him, since his supporters and beneficiaries were everywhere. Those who disapproved of him could only assert that his life in retirement was more roistering and less virtuous

---

[1] A territory in southern Asia Minor, taken after a large campaign against pirates who had based themselves there.

than that of a simple country gentleman and that the disease that took him off was uniquely loathsome.

Cicero's Defense of Roscius of Ameria

A spectacular case, the defense of Roscius of Ameria (79 B.C.), was the first great opportunity of a tough and ambitious young man, Marcus Tullius Cicero, who was determined to make a career as an orator. He later published his speech both to do credit to himself and because of its political importance. Sextus Roscius of Ameria, fifty-odd miles upriver from Rome, was on trial for murdering his father, and the case had come to court in a strange way. The older Roscius owned thirteen good farms, most of them bordering on the river; he also had two cousins with whom he was not on good terms. One night, during a visit to Rome, he was murdered as he returned from dining out. The news was sent that same night to the cousin who was in Ameria, and he drove the victim's son, a quiet and timid man of perhaps thirty, from the properties by force.

Then, as in a modern mystery story, the criminals became too ingenious. They bribed Chrysogonus, a powerful freedman of Sulla, to put the name of the murdered Roscius on the proscription list, although the list had been officially closed; thus the elder Roscius became posthumously an outlaw. The younger Roscius fled to the protection of the powerful family of the Caecilii Metelli at Rome, the noble patrons of his family, and Cicero hints that they defended him from attempts on his life. The two cousins of his father then suborned a citizen to bring a charge of patricide against him in the standing court for murder.

The patrons induced Cicero to speak in defense of Roscius; they appeared in court, but no one knew who would make the defense until the prosecution completed its case. Then Cicero arose and explained that he had been asked to speak because he was not so prominent a figure that his defending Roscius would seem to represent an attack on Sulla. Then he suddenly loosed a savage attack on the two cousins of the dead man that in a few minutes blew the prosecution's case to bits and exposed the whole train of criminal acts that had led to the trial.

Dangerous as this could be under the conditions, his larger purpose was more dangerous still. Naturally Sulla did not wish to have the senatorial system upset by the actions of freedmen whom he could not constantly supervise. The jury, which was composed of senators, according to Sulla's new rule, must have known that it would be hard enough for the nobles to reassert their old relationships after the disturbances of the civil war and the influx of new citizens as a result of the Social War, but it would be harder still if the great Caecilii Metelli could not defend their client, the younger Roscius, from such an outrage at the hands of a freedman. With great skill and icy nerve the young Cicero lectured the jury and through them the irascible Sulla on this delicate subject. Roscius was acquitted, the wider principle had been resoundingly stated, and Cicero had put the whole nobility, not only the patrons of the Roscii, under great obligation to him.

22

POLITICAL LIFE: 79 TO 49 B.C.

The brief span of time between 79 and 49 B.C. is better illuminated by our sources than any other period of ancient history. Beside some histories we have Plutarch's lives of some of the chief actors, orations of Cicero, and, best of all, over eight hundred letters of Cicero's correspondence, some of them from his friends to him, but most of them written by him, which offer very detailed information. Many men can be known rather well—Gnaeus Pompeius, or Pompey, Marcus Licinius Crassus, Marcus Tullius Cicero, and Gaius Julius Caesar are the ones we know best—so that it is tempting to think of the period as being the acts of these important and fascinating individuals.

THE RISE OF POMPEY: 79 TO 70 B.C.

Challenges to the Senate's Control

One of the consuls of 78 B.C., Lepidus, tried to gather a following by appealing to those who wished the repeal of Sulla's arrangements. The matter went so far that during his proconsulship in Cisalpine Gaul his subordinates began to gather troops, and in 77 he found himself marching on Rome. Pompey, to whom the Senate had granted propraetorian powers, was able to gather troops hurriedly and defeat him. Unfortunately the command of troops and the role of savior of the state appealed to the young man, and he kept his troops under arms while he offered to go to Spain to deal with a knotty problem personified by one Sertorius.

Sertorius served against the Teutons and the Cimbri and in the Social War; then as praetor in 83 he fought against Sulla and in 82 went to Hither Spain as propraetor. Little by little, and with some reverses, he gained control of a large part of Spain, commanding the loyalty of the people there and claiming to represent the Roman government against the usurpation of Sulla. He repeatedly defeated the Roman generals sent against him. Pompey was on this mission from 76 to 71 B.C., finally defeating Sertorius by a combination of superior numbers and treachery. He did much to remove old grievances in Spain by grants of land and of citizenship; he also gained himself a number of overseas clients. Young as he was, he understood the game of politics rather well.

Military Problems

The Third Mithridatic War (the Second was merely an episode) was caused by the action of the king of Bithynia in 75 (or 74) in bequeathing his kingdom to the Romans, who accepted the bequest and declared Bithynia a province, which to Mithridates seemed an intolerable change in the power situation. In 74 he invaded Bithynia. Although the chief Roman commander, Lucius Licinius Lucullus, is the symbol of luxurious living, he was a good commander and in about three years he had destroyed or dispersed the Pontic army and driven Mithridates into refuge with Tigranes, king of Armenia. In 69 Lucullus captured some of Armenia, but his troops refused to follow him further, resenting the fact that he had not allowed them to loot the cities they had captured. He also incurred the enmity of the knights by adjusting the affairs of the province of Asia to prevent its ruin, for the exactions of Sulla had by now put the provincials hopelessly in debt to the Roman men of business. Lucullus brusquely scaled the debts down to what was harsh, but possible, and in four years they were cleared. We shall return to the account of this war and tell how Pompey completed it at last.

There were other military problems. The governors of Macedonia had to fight off and chastise barbarians who attacked the province in force. Rome also had not fully accepted her responsibility for dealing with pirates; we shall return to this theme, again with Pompey.

The threat of Spartacus was nearer home and more spectacular. Spartacus was a Thracian who had once served in the Roman auxiliary forces, then turned to brigandage, was captured and enslaved and sent to a gladiatorial school at Capua. The growing popularity of gladiatorial contests at the games in Rome and in smaller places made the training and leasing of slave gladiators a profitable business. In 73 Spartacus led a small group of gladiators in an escape, and they soon gathered a following of slaves from farms and ranches large enough to be called an army. It defeated troops sent against it, including the armies under the consuls. Marcus Licinius Crassus, praetor probably in 73, saved the situation.

Crassus, who was of a prominent family, fought on Sulla's side in 83 and 82 and enriched himself by buying the property of the proscribed cheaply when the market was glutted. He set himself with all his energy to making money, perhaps largely as a help to a political career. He is said to have profited greatly by training slaves for every expert task. In this emergency he was expert enough to drill and discipline the demoralized troops in a short time, drive Spartacus into southern Italy, and surround him. The slave army broke through, however, and moved northward, where it was turned back by troops returning from Macedonia, divided, then crushed by Crassus in separate engagements. Spartacus died in action. Several thousand of the slaves, fleeing northward, met Pompey returning with his army from Spain and were destroyed.

We may not assume that Spartacus was a champion of social justice, for he would probably have been a slaveholder himself, had he been able. Neither may we assume that the men who joined him had been miserably mistreated, although all had suffered the injustice of slavery, for the farm workers probably labored no harder than free men on their own land, and it is difficult to overwork a shepherd or a cowboy. Few of the town slaves joined Spartacus; they were the more intelligent and the more able.

The Consulship of Pompey and Crassus

Pompey and Crassus obtained senatorial approval of their candidacies for the consulship of 70 B.C. Pompey especially needed this because he had not held the quaestorship and praetorship, which were preliminary to the consulship. Since he had held military commands, regular or irregular, most of the time since 83 and had had the high rank of proconsul in Spain against Sertorius, he naturally objected to going back and working his way up through the minor offices. Such exemptions from the normal rules had been granted on other occasions.

Both men probably sensed that the extreme conservatives, who by now were beginning to refer to themselves as the *optimates,* or "the best people," might wish to and be able to gather strength enough to resist their canvass. Both therefore favored the demand of the *populares* (the group in the nobility that tried to advance itself by posing as champions of the people) for the return of the legislative powers of the tribunes, which had been taken away by Sulla's laws. Both seconded the idea of renewed participation on the juries for the knights. They also stood for the election of censors—the last censorship had been in 86 B.C. Many men were eligible for the equestrian order and desired to be admitted by the censors, and many of the Italians who had not yet been added to the lists of Roman citizens wished the censors to enroll them. Both men were elected to the consulship and helped to put an end to Sulla's ultraconservative system by supporting these vital changes. Although there were no great crusading tribunes thereafter, the tribunes occasionally did play an important role in political struggles. The censors enrolled many new citizens and probably admitted many eligible men to the equestrian order. Toward the end of the year 70, after a great deal of discussion, it was decided that the juries should be composed of one-third senators, one-third knights, and one-third *tribuni aerarii,* men who had a census (property qualification) slightly lower than that of the knights; the list of prospective jurors for each year had three hundred men from each of these three groups.

Cicero's Prosecution of Verres

Cicero's career meanwhile was progressing. His daring and skill in defending Roscius of Ameria and the consequent support of the Caecilii Metelli and others must have helped him gain the quaestorship for 75 B.C., the duties of which took him to Sicily for the year. When, in the year 70, the Sicilians decided to try to get redress for the enormities of Verres, who as propraetor had just governed them for three years, they turned to Cicero. Both before and after this case Cicero preferred to defend rather than prosecute, for it was a better role for a rising young man who wished to make friends without making enemies, but the request of the Sicilians that he be their patron and prosecute Verres on their behalf opened up great possibilities for him. Verres had stolen and extorted money, and for money he had connived at murders and had committed judicial murders. His love of the beautiful had led him to outrage women and steal treasures of art. The chances of convicting him were excellent, and a successful prosecutor would acquire Verres' precedence in the Senate, which would mean that when the presiding officers called for opinions in turn in the Senate, Cicero would be called on much earlier, having gained the place of a slightly older man who had been praetor several years before, and thus would have more chance to make himself heard while the presiding officer still thought it worthwhile to ask for further opinions. He took the case and initiated the prosecution by going to the praetor.

Naturally Verres' friends and all those of the senatorial class who thought that dishonest governors should be protected in looting the provincials gathered to oppose Cicero, and especially to try to block him until the end of the year, when newly elected magistrates very favorable to Verres would assume office. But Cicero pursued the case relentlessly, organizing his sources of evidence brilliantly and moving through the chief cities of Sicily with amazing speed as he put his case together. He was able to open his case when just a few days were left before the court holidays of the autumn, which would really end the court year. Instead of leading off with a speech of several days, he began to call his witnesses and let the story of the conduct of Verres as told by them build up such a crushing weight of utterly damning evidence that Verres' counsel, the famous orator Hortensius, could find nothing to say, and Verres gave up and went into exile.

Cicero now had Verres' place in the Senate and was acknowledged as the leading orator of Rome. He gained the support of the conservative leading men of the municipalities all over Italy, many of whom had come to Rome for the elections, which were in the early autumn, and had stayed for the trial or for other reasons. They saw in him a supporter of conservative principles who still would oppose corruption in high places and was known to be highly sympathetic, coming, as he did, from an equestrian family, to the claims of the upper class that did not belong to the senatorial order—the equestrian order and well-to-do people in general.

Caesar's Political Beginnings

Gaius Julius Caesar was born in 100 B.C. of a family that had not been important or powerful for some generations. Apparently he was ambitious and was resolved from his earlier years to win political honors. His first crisis came when Sulla ordered him to divorce his wife, the daughter of Cinna, and he refused; only the intervention of friends saved him from death. Other incidents of his early life show that he was bold and energetic. He was also a person of great charm—presumably the charm of the man of what we call the executive type, whose own ego does not obtrude itself and whose intelligence leads him to treat other people with full attention and courtesy.

Although there is some disagreement on the point, he seems to have decided early in life to cultivate the voters of the city of Rome, perhaps because so many of them on coming in from the country had become detached from their former patrons and might be won by a charming man of old family who would court them and try to serve their interests. He early became known as one of the *populares*. He stressed the fact that his aunt had been the wife of Marius by giving a eulogy of her at her funeral, and in his aedileship in 65 B.C. he restored the trophies of Marius, which had formerly been set up around the city and later removed. In 70 B.C. he spoke earnestly for the restoration of the full dignity of the tribunes. But even while emphasizing his interest in the people's cause whenever he could, he lost no opportunity to remind them of the antiquity of the Julian gens to which he belonged and of pointing out that it went back through Aeneas, the founder of the Roman people, to the goddess Venus, the mother of Aeneas in Greek and Roman legend.

THE TIME OF POMPEY'S ASCENDANCY: 70 TO 62 B.C.

The Reduction of the Pirates

In 67 B.C. the tribune Gabinius proposed that the *Comitia tributa* choose for the reduction of the pirates a man of consular rank, giving him for the term of three years an unlimited imperium on the sea and power on the land equal to that of the governors where his operations should take place, with an adequate supply of men, ships, and money. Pompey was obviously meant to be the man, although he was not named. The Senate was opposed to the bill, being plainly unwilling to see any one of its members get such extraordinary powers, with such opportunities to enrich himself with booty and add to his influence. The equestrian order and the people, however, were not so much interested in the even distribution of influence and booty among the senators as they were in the state of the nation, for the arrival of tributary grain from overseas could not always be counted on, trade by sea had been disrupted, and merchants and travelers by sea were often killed or sold into slavery by the pirates. When the Senate persuaded a tribune to interpose his veto, Gabinius threatened to depose him, as Tiberius Gracchus had deposed Octavius by the vote of the people. The tribune desisted, the Gabinian Law was passed, Pompey was chosen, and the price of wheat dropped at once.

Pompey's performance was brilliant. He chose able legates, divided the Mediterranean into two by putting a strong force at the narrow point by Sicily, and in forty days swept the western end of the sea clear of pirates by using one squadron to drive them into the arms of the other. The process was helped by his letting the word get around that those who surrendered would be treated humanely.

By the end of three months he had also cleared the eastern end of the Mediterranean. He had to fight one real naval battle and reduce several mountain strongholds in Cilicia before this part of the task was ended. He captured ninety warships equipped with bronze rams as part of the pirates' equipment. As he had done in Spain, he tried to give his prisoners a new start by settling them on available farming land.

Pompey in the East

Early in 66 B.C. the tribune Manilius introduced a bill in the *Comitia tributa* that gave to Pompey, in addition to his powers against the pirates, the command against Mithridates, superseding Lucullus, who had lost the confidence of the people and alienated the soldiers. Pompey moved northward from Cilicia after ending his campaign against the pirates and defeated the last army that Mithridates was able to raise. The king fled and presently ended his own life.

Pompey moved southward to Syria, which he annexed as a new province of Rome. He found that one of his legates had recently come out in favor of one of the two brothers who were struggling for the rule of Judaea; Pompey decided that he would aid the other. The disappointed contestant submitted with bad grace, and his followers, refusing to give in, prepared to stand a siege in the holy precinct of Jerusalem. Pompey occupied the lower town without trouble, but it took three months to overcome the stubborn band. Pompey yielded to his curiosity so far as to enter the Holy of Holies in the Temple, but he respected the temple treasures.

Now he turned to a general settlement in Asia Minor. The Senate had already declared Bithynia a province; Pompey added some of Pontus to it. The province of Asia adjoined Bithynia; Cilicia was organized as a province south of Asia. Then came the newly acquired and rich province of Syria, completing a line of provinces that covered almost the whole coast of the Black Sea and the Mediterranean from Armenia (which was left in charge of its king, Tigranes) down to Egypt. Behind the line of provinces was a group of client kingdoms that stretched over to the Parthian border on the Euphrates River. For all these petty monarchs there were advantages in accepting the friendship of Rome as offered to them by Pompey, for if they were from now on to have no independent foreign policy, they lost nothing but the opportunity to be swallowed by a neighbor. The Romans did not demand tribute nor interfere in domestic affairs.

Pompey also restored or rebuilt or recolonized some of the cities founded by Alexander the Great or by the sovereigns who succeeded him, and he created some completely new ones. Probably many of these cities consisted of agricultural land with a small urban center and were meant to be administrative units.

FROM 66 TO 62 B.C. AT ROME

Crassus was very busy during these years with schemes to strengthen his position. He was censor in 65 B.C. with the leading conservative Quintus Lutatius Catulus. Crassus attempted to arrange that the full Roman citizenship be given to the Transpadanes, or people of Italy above the Padus (Po) River. Pompey's father had sponsored the grant of the Latin right to them. Pompey, Caesar, and Crassus all wished to gain the credit of procuring the grant of full citizenship for them and the electoral support that their gratitude would insure. It was Caesar who in the end did get them this right, since Crassus was prevented by his colleague in the censorship, whose insistence on not changing anything naturally set him against the creation of thousands of new citizens who would not be clients of the great families.

In the summer of 64 Cicero was elected consul. The year 63 was "his year," as the Romans said, that is, he had reached the minimum age of eligibility, and to be elected in the first year when one was eligible was an extra honor, one which he had already had for both quaestorship and praetorship. In spite of the fact that none of his family had held high office at Rome and that he was therefore a "new man," he had acquired much influence, as we have seen. The entrenched nobles must have perceived that he was likely to uphold their interests, too, out of respect for the glamor of old names and because he naturally would support the system through which he advanced to the supreme honor of the consulate.

The fact that Catiline (Lucius Sergius Catilina) was again a candidate helped Cicero's cause. Catiline had advanced to the praetorship and then to the propraetorship of Africa, where his extortions were so barefaced as to lead to a prosecution when he returned to Rome. He attempted to run for consul in 66 B.C., but when the day of the election arrived, the presiding consul refused to receive his name. Catiline combined great energy and charm with a violent and dissolute nature, and he had allowed his expenditures to outrun his resources even more than was common among upper class Romans, so that he faced ruin unless he could get the consulship and then a governorship that would allow him to rebuild his fortunes at the expense of his province. He had attached many people to him by creating hopes that as consul he would bring about a cancellation of debts. Some were in debt for attempted political careers; there were Sullan soldiers who had failed at farming the lands given them as their bonus on discharge; others were simply in difficulties. Obviously the conservatives would do anything to keep such a man from the consulate. Since there was no candidate of old family who had any strength, they threw their support to Cicero, who was elected with a colleague who, if undistinguished, was not dangerous.

In the year 63, the year of Cicero's consulship, all the main actors in the events and politics of recent years—Crassus, Pompey (who was completing his arrangements in the East), Cicero, Catiline, and Caesar—made their characteristic contributions. Also a new conservative came forward, the thirty-two-year-old Marcus Porcius Cato, great-grandson of Marcus Porcius Cato "the censor."

Late in 64 Crassus induced a tribune, Servilius Rullus, to propose a commission of ten to acquire all possible land in Italy and the provinces and distribute it to persons needing land. We know something of Rullus'

Etruscan painted terra cotta antefix, used as an exterior adornment for a temple.
Ny Carlsberg Glypotek, Copenhagen

A street corner in the Etruscan cemetery of Caere (Cerveteri)
Photograph by the author

Republican temple; Largo Argentina, Rome   *Photograph by the author*

Etruscan bronze cover for a sarcophagus
Courtesy of The State Hermitage, Leningrad

Rome: Ponto Rotto (Broken Bridge) on the Tiber   *Photograph by the author*

The so-called Regina Vasorum; a brilliant example of Greek work
from southern Italy

The Claudian Aqueduct near Rome

The Appian Way   *Courtesy of Trans World Airlines*

Carthage: Remains of imperial Roman baths   *Courtesy of Trans World Airlines*

Hellenistic Cameo   *Kunsthistoriches Museum, Vienna*

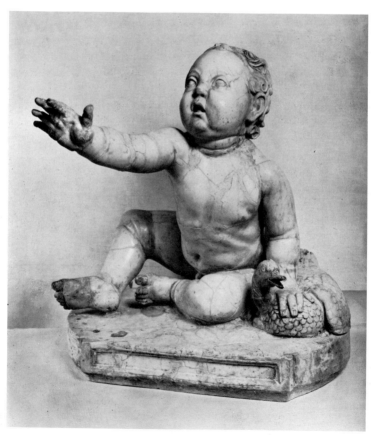

Hellenistic genre sculpture; Boy with goose   *Kunsthistorisches Museum, Vienna*

Bronze head of the early Augustan period, possibly the younger Cato
Courtesy of The State Hermitage, Leningrad

A panel of the Ara Pacis   *Photograph by the author*

A street in Pompeii　　　　　　　　　　　*Courtesy of Trans World Airlines*

A small-town theater; Tusculum　　　　　　　*Photograph by the author*

bill from Cicero's three speeches against it in January, 63, in which he doubtless magnified its undesirable features, such as the magnitude and vagueness of the powers of the ten commissioners. Apparently Crassus hoped that before Pompey's return he could get control of all available land through the commission and bargain with Pompey about land as bonuses for his soldiers or represent himself as the real giver of any grants of land. The bill was withdrawn, since Cicero's speeches seemed to have made the people cool toward it.

Caesar, as aedile in 65 B.C., had dazzled the people with the lavishness of his games. In 64, as presiding officer of the *quaestio de sicariis,* the permanent court for murder trials, he had pushed the prosecution of the men most active in the killing of the proscribed in the days of the Sullan proscription, but connived at the acquittal of Catiline, who had been one of the worst of them. In 63 B.C. he was elected Pontifex Maximus at the age of thirty-seven, although Catulus was the logical man for this desirable office. It was elective, however. Perhaps Caesar had added to his popularity by supporting a bill that restored to the people the right to elect the main body of priests, a right that Sulla had transferred to the priests themselves. Probably the deciding factor was Caesar's lavish bribery, presumably financed by Crassus.

The conspiracy of Catiline, which came late in 63, followed his unsuccessful attempts to be elected consul for 62 on a frank program of canceling all debts and giving all debtors a fresh start. For the first time he turned to organized violence, making a plan to seize Rome itself, with simultaneous risings in other parts of Italy. In spite of the reports of the agents who penetrated the conspiracy, there was a lack of evidence of the kind that would warrant arrests and prosecutions, but the Senate did pass the *senatusconsultum ultimum.* Catiline (who was a member of the Senate) had the effrontery to appear at a meeting of the Senate where Cicero planned to report on what he knew of the conspiracy, and Cicero seized the occasion to make a vigorous impromptu attack on him, now known as the First Catilinarian Oration, which stung him into leaving the city and openly placing himself at the head of troops waiting in Etruria. The other conspirators, still in Rome, foolishly tried to arouse some provincials to join them and allowed treasonable letters bearing their names and seals to be captured.

On the fifth of December the Senate debated their treatment. Opinion was unanimously for the death penalty until Caesar spoke, arguing for imprisonment and making veiled threats about the possible consequences of putting men to death without a trial. Then Cato spoke boldly to the wavering Senate in favor of the death penalty, and it voted as he urged. Cicero as consul acted boldly and promptly, taking the conspirators to the prison and having them strangled. Catiline's men began to desert when they heard that the government was resolute, and in a few weeks he died in a battle in which the regular forces crushed his band.

A formal prosecution would have been better and could have been done promptly. But Cicero had quelled a dangerous, if not a critically dangerous movement. This to him was naturally the high point of his career, and he spoke of it afterward repeatedly and with self-praise such that his contemporaries must have been repelled and the scholar who reads his writings finds this topic most tiresome. His words did not help his relation to Pompey, who fancied himself as the rescuer of the state in every emergency and had tried, through a tribune, to see if this crisis could be nursed along until he could get home to deal with it.

An incident that was both comic and serious occurred in the next year in December, 62. The festival of the Bona Dea, the women's goddess, was held in the house of Caesar, who was praetor this year. No man was allowed to be in the house during the ceremony. A young man who was called Clodius (the plebeian form of his real name, Claudius) made his way into the house disguised as a flute girl, whether because he was having an affair with Caesar's wife, as some thought, or as a prank, and was discovered when one of the maids asked him a question and he attempted to reply in a woman's voice. It was during the ensuing scandal that Caesar divorced his wife with the famous remark that Caesar's wife must be above suspicion. Clodius was tried for sacrilege and gained his acquittal by scandalous bribery. He claimed to have been in a town sixty miles away at the time of the incident; Cicero made an enemy of him by puncturing the alibi, testifying that he had seen him in Rome.

THE FIRST TRIUMVIRATE

Its Formation

There was some apprehension among the senators as to what Pompey would do when he and his soldiers returned from their victories in the East and landed at Brundisium in December, 62. Cato had made up his mind that Pompey would try to usurp the supreme power and in his characteristic way found it hard to revise that idea in the light of what Pompey really did. In spite of Cato's belief and perhaps that of Crassus, it is unreasonable to suppose that Pompey had any wish to make himself a tyrant, since tyranny offered him nothing in comparison with his role of the servant and frequent savior of the state. The two Romans who did so break through the constitution, Sulla and Caesar, both claimed to be driven to it and found safety rather than satisfaction in what they had done.

Pompey made two important and reasonable requests of the Senate, that it confirm his eastern arrangements *en bloc* and that it arrange the presentation of land to his veterans.

Cicero showed good sense in wooing Pompey at this point; he was much concerned with harmony between the equestrians and the senators and hoped that Pompey would support this worthy effort. Other men found their own standing of more consequence or feared that Pompey had become too important or thought him too insistent on his own glory. It was probably natural, but not good politics, for the Senate to insist on examining his arrangements in the East in detail. Pompey had had the advice of very able legates, and his arrangements were excellent, but the Senate had not been given the opportunity to send the usual senatorial commission. The Senate also delayed and obstructed every move that Pompey made to get the distribution of land to his soldiers started. It would seem that it should have welcomed the opportunity to manage the distribution itself, but the Senate as a whole had no *clientela* and probably feared that credit for any distribution of land would go to Pompey or to the commissioners in charge.

At this same time Crassus brought a request from one of the great equestrian companies to have lowered the amount with which it had won in the bidding for the farming of the taxes of Asia, alleging that the figure was unreasonably high. Cicero, practical again, supported the request, but Cato, virtuous and unbending, persuaded the Senate to refuse.

Pompey, feeling that he must do something for his veterans, asked a tribune to bring a bill before the people to provide them land, but here, too, the conservatives managed to obstruct. It is surprising that Pompey permitted himself to be so handled, but the fact is that he finally became discouraged and in the summer of 60 B.C. allowed the tribune to drop the bill. Meanwhile Caesar, who after his praetorship of 62 B.C. governed Farther Spain in 61, showed statesmanship in scaling down debts as Lucullus did in Asia, displayed military ability in dealing with the unpacified people on his farther border, and used some ingenuity in getting money to help with his debts.

In 60 B.C. Caesar, Pompey, and Crassus made a secret combination, apparently on Caesar's initiative, which only gradually became known and has been known ever since as the First Triumvirate. Caesar brought his influence with the city voters and the common people and wished to advance his own career. Pompey brought his prestige and the backing of his veterans and wanted the confirmation of his arrangements in the East and land for his veterans. Crassus brought his wealth and influence. What he wanted is less clear; perhaps it was a sense of power behind the scenes. One public step in the alliance was taken late in 60 when Caesar betrothed his daughter Julia to Pompey. She was a real bond between them for the five years that she had yet to live, for both men loved her dearly.

The conservatives could see that Caesar was likely to gain the consulship for 59; by a large campaign of bribery they at least brought about the election of a dull but tenacious conservative, Bibulus, as Caesar's colleague. After the election Caesar, as part of his plans for his consular year, made overtures to Cicero, probably asking him to be his adviser. The two men had been friends for years. Cicero admired Caesar and was susceptible to his great charm. Caesar may well have admired different qualities in Cicero and surely knew the value of his eloquence. Cicero, however, realizing that he might find himself involved in measures of which he deeply disapproved and that no possible operation of the new alliance could bring him anything he desired, sensibly refused to entangle himself.

The Acts of the Triumvirate in 59 B.C.

Caesar proposed in proper form to the Senate that a commission be set up to reward Pompey's veterans with land; some of the unemployed people in the city were also to be settled on the land. The senators refused this request and delayed by debating the matter. Caesar took the request to the people, disregarding Bibulus' attempt to stop him, and with the added strength afforded by the presence of many of Pompey's veterans got the bill passed. From now on Bibulus regularly reported that adverse omens had been seen when Caesar was legislating, a device that technically would invalidate all the legislation if the time should come when the Senate felt strong enough to maintain such an assertion. Bills to confirm Pompey's eastern arrangements *en bloc* and to allow a reduction of the bid for Asia of the great equestrian company satisfied the desires of Pompey and Crassus.

Next the Vatinian Law, carried by the friendly tribune Vatinius, provided that Caesar should have as his proconsular province Cisalpine Gaul and Illyricum for five years, with three legions, instead of the routine sphere of action that the Senate had provided for both proconsuls, knowing that Caesar would be one of them. Illyricum especially offered some opportunity for gaining military glory and booty, and troops in Cisalpine Gaul could control all Italy. The governor of Transalpine Gaul died at this time, and the Senate added this province to Caesar's command, perhaps thinking that thus it would be awarded to him for only one year instead of the five that the people might vote.

Caesar had now forced the Senate to allow him to carry bills through the *Comitia tributa* or the *Concilium plebis* in disregard of the tribunician veto and the claim that the auspices were wrong or that bad omens had manifested themselves. He had brought armed men to the meetings of the assembly and had forcibly prevented the other consul from addressing it.

Still he had by no means captured the Senate's power, which consisted partly of traditional respect, partly of the support of many persons who were humble clients of the senators, and partly of the continued support of many middle-class and upper-class people in Italy and the provinces who were not to be underrated. Caesar arranged all these acts. Crassus presumably was indifferent to the nature of the means if the ends could be achieved, but Pompey was made most uneasy by Caesar's violent and illegal deeds and made halfhearted attempts to dissociate himself without leaving the Triumvirate.

Fairly early in the year 59 it was commonly known that the three men were working together. Naturally the senatorial order was bitterly resentful of them and their acts. Not even all the city poor approved entirely, as is shown by incidents in the theater reported by Cicero in his letters, when the people greeted Caesar's entry with silence and cheered his opponents or applauded a line in a play that could be applied in criticism of Pompey. Those who came from all over Italy to vote in the *Comitia centuriata* in the late summer were less amenable to the influence of the triumvirs than was the assembly of the people, so that although the triumvirs were able to elect two men whom they could control as consuls for the year 58 B.C., they were forced to admit the election of some praetors and some tribunes who were hostile to them. Two of these praetors, after they took office, even attacked the legality of Caesar's acts as consul and had a sharp argument in the Senate with Caesar, who was preparing to go to his province. One of the conservative tribunes threatened to prosecute him for his acts, and Caesar finally made a sharp threat of force to gain a promise from the whole college of tribunes that it would not try to prosecute him in his absence.

THE YEARS OF CAESAR'S PROCONSULSHIP: 58 TO 50 B.C.

Caesar in Gaul

Caesar's motives in his subsequent invasion of Gaul are not clear. Most of his colleagues looked eastward to the countries of the Old World for fame and loot, but his conquest brought Rome a large country that easily took on Roman ways and was a great source of manpower and wealth for the Romans. It is the fashion to speak of Caesar as farseeing; yet it is questionable whether he could look farther ahead than anyone else. Apparently his first plan was to campaign in Illyricum; when the death of the incumbent governor opened up Transalpine Gaul to him early in 59, his plan to campaign there instead in 58 depended on a new and unforeseen set of circumstances. We can only be sure that he intended to develop an army on which he could rely, gather plunder to repair his finances, and keep his political fences in Italy mended.

He learned that the Helvetii, who lived in what is now Switzerland, planned to migrate in 58 B.C. to near Tolosa, modern Toulouse, in southern Gaul. He refused to allow them passage through the Roman province, turning them to the north and following them as they went westward, not without some damage to Rome's allies north of the province. When they turned and attacked him, he defeated them with great loss and ordered the survivors to return home so as not to leave their old lands invitingly open.

After defeating the Helvetii, Caesar moved, at the request of many of the chief men of Gaul, against the German Ariovistus, who had been invited to help one of the Gallic tribes and had stayed to oppress several of them. Caesar defeated him decisively and broke his power in Gaul. Caesar then left his army to winter in Gaul instead of withdrawing it to Roman territory, perhaps to show that he intended to protect Gaul from further German invasions, perhaps even to provoke the farther tribes of Gaul to attack him. In the spring of 57 the Belgae, a large tribe of northern Gaul, gathered their forces, whereupon Caesar moved toward them. He waited until, tired of waiting for an engagement, they went home, and so divided their forces; then he overcame them separately. By the end of the summer of 57 the Romans had won several battles and had marched successfully through a large part of Gaul.

Maneuvering in Rome

At Rome Pompey was leading a rather unhappy life, as was everyone else in politics except Clodius, the young man who had invaded the festival of Bona Dea. In 59 Caesar had helped this patrician to become a plebeian (by the means of adoption by a plebeian) and thus eligible for the tribunate; he was elected tribune for 58. Clodius persuaded the people to pass a set of laws, one of which provided that the censors could expel senators from the Senate only on formal charges heard by both censors, and another that magistrates could not stop business (as Bibulus had tried to do) by claiming to have observed ill omens. Two other laws provided that grain should be distributed free to the people rather than at a low price, as it had been since the days of Gaius Gracchus, and that the common people's *collegia*, or clubs, which had recently been suppressed, were again legal. Both these laws were aimed at intensifying the loyalty of the city poor to Caesar, who was helping Clodius and who wished to win them as his clients.

Clodius also proposed a bill, obviously aimed at Cicero, to exile anyone who had put Roman citizens to death without a trial. Since Cicero had refused to compromise his freedom of speech and action by any association with the triumvirs, Caesar thought it safer to have him removed from Rome, and Clodius had his own motive, that of hatred from the Bona Dea case. The final form of the measure named Cicero and stated that he must live not less than four hundred miles from Rome. Cicero went to Greece, where he was cared for by friends during his exile, which was very trying to his spirit.

The Triumvirate felt no need to exercise the all-pervasive control to which we have become accustomed in modern tyrannies, apparently assuming that the soldiers who were loyal to them would insure their continuance in power and their personal safety. No attempt was made, beyond hints of reprisals, at repressive measures for occasional displays of disapproval by the populace. The known active opposition consisted of practically the whole upper class, the *optimates*. During the years 58 and 57 the *optimates* tried hard, and with some success, to create dissension within the Triumvirate, especially by taking advantage of the fact that Pompey and Crassus had never liked each other and were held together only by Caesar and self-interest.

Cicero's friends worked unceasingly for his return, and at last Pompey, whose failure to protect Cicero from exile had been a sore blow to the orator, lent his authority to the project. In August, 57, after he had been in exile for more than a year, his recall was voted by the *Comitia centuriata*. His friends had managed to convene this assembly, in which the men of property were stronger, whereas his exile had been voted by the *Comitia tributa*. The elite of all Italy came to Rome to take part in the voting, and as Cicero traveled northward toward Rome he was given a great welcome all along the way. Nevertheless he was not free from now on to air all his views, for Pompey had exacted pledges from his brother Quintus Cicero for his good behavior as regarded the Triumvirate.

In the spring of 56 B.C. Caesar asked Pompey and Crassus to come to the little town of Luca in northern Italy, just inside his province of Cisalpine Gaul, to confer on their mutual interests. A hundred and twenty senators are said also to have gone there to pay their respects to Caesar and to hear what he might have to say. The triumvirs decided to continue to work together. Caesar was to have another five years of command in Gaul, until the end of the year 50 or early in 49; this is an oft discussed point, with the weight of scholarly opinion somewhat in favor of late 50 B.C. Pompey and Crassus were to be supported for the consulship for 55 B.C., and afterward Pompey was to have Spain as his proconsular province for five years, and Crassus was to have Syria. When, in the summer of 56, the Senate came to the usual task of assigning proconsular provinces and there were proposals that Caesar be replaced in Gaul, Cicero was required by Pompey to speak in favor of Caesar's retention there. The speech, "On the Consular Provinces," has been preserved; Cicero showed some skill in making the best of what he had to do.

Caesar's Further Work in Gaul

In the summer of 56 B.C. Caesar subdued areas of Gaul that he had not approached before or that were stubborn. The maritime people of the Veneti had imprisoned Roman ambassadors sent to them and had inspired other peoples of the coast to reconsider their submission to the Romans in the summer of 57. Caesar executed the magistrates and councilors as an example, giving their treatment of his ambassadors as a reason, and sold all the people to the slave dealers who followed the army. Although the wealth of Gaul could not be compared to that of the East, the people could be seized and sold if a suitable reason could be found, and Caesar found reasons fairly often. The campaigns in Gaul were highly profitable to him, and from being very much in debt from his attempts to build a career he became a successful middle-aged man having money with which to acquire and reward supporters. More than one of the conservatives at Rome was bought by Caesar in a polite way.

In 55 B.C. Caesar made his first visit to Britain, largely for exploration, since little was known of the island even by merchants, although it was believed that the Druids, or priestly class, of Britain were stirring the Druids of Gaul to unrest, and there was a story that Britain had pearls and gold. In 54 Caesar went again with a larger force and saw more of the country.

In 52 B.C. the central Gauls found in Vercingetorix a leader who could bring some unity to their fight for freedom. Caesar finally defeated him and made him retreat to the hill town of Alesia in east central Gaul. There the Romans blockaded him, defeated a relieving force, and starved him into submission. Some fighting was also necessary in 51; Caesar spent most of the summer of 50 organizing Gaul as a Roman possession.

Caesar's *Commentarii* (the usual word for an official's formal report on his term of office) were probably written in the winter of 52–51. The book is not easy Latin; it has been used in schools because the theme is simple and the vocabulary somewhat limited by the subject. It is beautifully pure and elegant Latin, however, for Caesar was gifted in language as well as a purist. It is also a masterly description of his campaigns as he wished people at home to see them.

The Roman acquisition of Gaul was of vital importance for the medieval and modern West. The character of the Gauls was so unsteady and their internal dissension so constant that in the centuries to come they would readily have fallen prey to the Germans, who became more and more eager to move and expand, had the Romans not organized and defended the country. As it was, it received all the Germans it could possibly absorb. Gaul became romanized enough so that when in the fifth century large numbers of Germans came in, they did not entirely submerge the Greco-Roman culture, which they admired but were not competent to maintain. Thus western Europe had a far earlier start in building modern life on the basis of the old Greco-Roman culture than it might otherwise have had.

The Struggles Leading to the Civil War

The unity of the Triumvirate became weaker after the year 55. In 54 Julia died, deeply mourned by her father and her husband; her passing weakened their alliance. In 53 Crassus died. Although his province of Syria was rich and he had plundered it well at the beginning of his term there, some impulse led him to seek an unnecessary war with the Parthians. The Parthian combination of heavy mailed cavalry and fine archers inflicted a crushing defeat on his forces at Carrhae, near the Euphrates, and Crassus died in the battle.

In Rome during the year 53 there was constant disorder. Pompey incited Annius Milo, an aristrocrat who needed little encouragement to violence, to organize a band of ruffians to counter the violence of Clodius' hoodlums, and from time to time the two factions clashed. There was no police force; the fact that the magistrates did not take the obvious course of bringing soldiers to stop such disorders was characteristic of the unsettled times. The elections of 54 were so often hindered by violence that there were no magistrates ready to take office for 53; it was July, 53, before the consuls of 53 were elected. The elections for 52, when Milo hoped to be consul and Clodius to be praetor, were broken up by disorders. In January, 52, Milo's toughs killed Clodius, and in the disorder that followed the senate house was burned. The Senate asked Pompey to be sole consul, the most irregular of all the offices he had held. Naturally he had no difficulty in restoring order in Rome when he really intended to do so.

Now a long series of maneuvers began, involving the nobles at Rome, Pompey, and Caesar. The ten tribunes jointly proposed and carried a law to exempt Caesar from the necessity of standing for a second consulship in person, so that he might be elected while he was still in Gaul and return to Rome as consul, thus avoiding a short period when he would be a private citizen and would not have a magistrate's exemption from prosecution. Then another law confirmed a decree of the Senate of the preceding year that there be an interval of five years between the holding of magistracies in the city and the holding of proconsulships. This was in a way a reform measure, since the interval between the magistracy and the promagistracy might have discouraged people from excessive campaign expenditures that could not at once be recouped in a province. It may also have been aimed at Caesar, since it would have made it possible to have a successor in Gaul ready to take over the day when his proconsulship ended, thus leaving him a private citizen for a short time before the beginning of his consulship, instead of his holding the proconsulship until someone could finish a consulship and get out to Gaul to relieve him.

By 51 B.C. it was plain that Caesar would soon have settled all the affairs of Gaul. The conservatives tried steadily to draw Pompey to their side against Caesar, knowing that on many occasions he had been glad to see an emergency, even to the point of creating one, so that he could gain glory by dealing with it. Outright attacks were made on Caesar by one of the consuls of 51, who also persuaded the Senate to reject a request from Caesar that his command be continued through 49 and had a discussion scheduled for March 1, 50 B.C. of the appointment of a successor to Caesar after trying to raise the question of having him relieved at once on the ground that the war was finished. He also attempted to assert that the law of the ten tribunes exempting Caesar from candidacy in person was not valid, but a tribunician veto stopped this attempt.

Caesar now brought over to his side, by a handsome payment, it was said, an able young tribune of the year 50 named Curio. The young man, one of the best propagandists Caesar had, stopped the discussion of March 1 by a veto and again during the year prevented proposals to relieve Caesar. In December, 50, the consul persuaded the Senate to vote that Caesar must lay down his command, while Pompey retained his proconsulship of Spain, which he had exercised through legates without going there. Curio managed to get a vote on the proposal that both should lay down their commands, and it passed by 370 to 22.

The consul answered by investing Pompey on his own authority with the command of the two legions that were available and ordering him to defend the commonwealth. The proponents of peace did their best, but the Senate became intransigent, perhaps because of threats from Pompey. Cicero said with deep discouragement in more than one of his letters that Pompey seemed not to want peace. He may indeed have planned to bring about a conflict and eliminate Caesar, the rising man, and then continue in the position of first man that he had so long enjoyed. Cicero's attitude was probably the shrewdest and most practical of all: that everyone had known for twenty years what Caesar was like and had lived with him as he was; that it was silly now to fight a civil war because he was that way; that it would be better to let him come home free of the threat of prosecution.

In early January, 49, the Senate voted that Caesar must lay down his command, and the tribune Marcus Antonius, whom we know as Mark Antony, vetoed the action. After a long discussion the final decree of the Senate, that declaring martial law, seemed imminent, and Antony fled to Caesar at Ravenna in Cisalpine Gaul. The *senatusconsultum ultimum* was passed soon afterward, commanding Pompey and other proconsuls to defend the state against Caesar.

Caesar's official view was that the other side had disregarded Antony's tribunician veto, had invoked martial law against him, and had taken away the immunity from prosecution given him by the law of the ten tribunes that provided that he could run for the consulate *in absentia* and come home already elected. He apparently saw the threats of prosecution as a real and great danger. Feeling that both his *dignitas,* or "face," and his personal safety were imperiled, he boldly crossed the little Rubicon River, leaving his province and entering Italy proper, an act of war, since he brought a small army with him.

23

THE FALL OF THE ROMAN REPUBLIC: 49 TO 30 B.C.

Caesar's crossing of the Rubicon, although it has come to symbolize the irreversible decision, the casting of the die, was not in fact necessarily final. Many prominent men attempted to compose the quarrel, and there were negotiations between the opposing groups on at least three occasions. Every attempt to avoid the war finally broke down.

THE CIVIL WAR

49 B.C.: *Italy and Spain*

Caesar moved with his usual speed down the Adriatic coast and gained control of Italy above Rome, capturing a good-sized force at Corfinium, toward the east coast and slightly north of Rome. He enrolled the men and dismissed the officers, for he had decided on a policy of clemency, and when some of those whom he had released returned to fight against him, he only said that they must be as they were and he would be as he was. Pompey found recruiting difficult and slow. The loss of the troops at Corfinium induced him to withdraw to Brundisium, the usual port of embarkation for Greece. Caesar rushed down with his forces to prevent him from getting away, but Pompey escaped to Greece with his army and the large group of senators who opposed Caesar.

The careers of many men on both sides of this struggle show that there was no clear division on the basis of principle or of past activities. There was a small group that was determined to uphold at all costs the privilege of the aristocracy. But in many cases personal ties outweighed other strong considerations. Cicero, who went to southern Italy with Pompey at first, refused to accompany him to Greece and was earnestly and repeatedly asked by Caesar to join him or at least stay neutral. Finally, after painful indecision, he chose Pompey out of gratitude for Pompey's past services to him and left Italy in June, 49, for Greece.

After his failure to stop Pompey from embarking for Greece and his failure to persuade Pompey to confer with him, Caesar went to Rome. There he opened the treasury and took what money he needed, pushing aside a tribune who tried to prevent him. Some feared confiscation of property or proscription, but Caesar was trying to leave the way open for resumption of peaceful life. One of Cicero's correspondents wrote that the usurers were well pleased with him, that is, he had not disturbed individual financial relations at all. He gathered all the senators whom he could persuade to make an appearance and tried through them to enter into new negotiations with Pompey.

Foreseeing that Pompey must try to gather strength from the provinces, he sent Curio to take control of Sicily, an important source of grain for the capital, and he himself led an army to Spain to try to win its resources from Pompey. Mark Antony was left in charge in Italy. Caesar maneuvered the able Pompeian legates in Spain to where they were cut off from their supplies. The word of his clemency had spread, and they surrendered. He sent the men home and pardoned the officers, having thus neutralized some good troops who might have helped Pompey.

On his return to Rome he held a dictatorship for a few limited purposes. He had an election (since the consuls were not in Italy) in which he was declared consul for 48, celebrated a festival that fell at this time, and had some minor laws passed by the people. Having done this in eleven days, he resigned, as the dictators traditionally did after finishing their special task.

48 and 47 B.C.: *Greece, Egypt, and Asia*

Caesar was not able, however, to neutralize Pompey's support in the East. With surprising speed Pompey built up in Greece a force of over 30,000 legionaries and three hundred ships, chiefly by calling on the armies posted in the eastern provinces and by requesting help from the client kings along the eastern borders, who owed their positions to him because of his settlement of the East in the late 60s. He also had some two hundred senators with him. Cicero was disgusted by the bloodthirsty talk and the plans for revenge and proscription that he heard almost daily among them. Caesar ferried seven legions over to Greece late in the year, and Mark Antony brought four more in the spring of 48. After long maneuvering and a minor victory for Pompey, the two armies met, early in August, in a decisive engagement near the town of Pharsalus, which gave its name to the battle.

Pompey had the larger army and more cavalry, on which he counted for a decisive stroke while the infantry were engaged, but Caesar anticipated the move and had a strong force ready to counter the attack of the cavalry. He followed with a general counterattack, which Pompey's practiced eye could see would win the day. He rode from the field and fled, and Caesar's career had come to a victory over Roman citizens and allies in civil war. "This is the way they wanted it," he said bitterly. "After such achievements I, Gaius Caesar, should have been condemned if I had not sought support in my army."

Pompey fled by ship with a few friends and finally came to Egypt, thinking to find asylum there, but was treacherously murdered. Caesar arrived three days later and was greeted with the news of the murder. The last three decades had been the Age of Pompey, although we, with a different perspective, think of them as the time of the rise of Caesar. Pompey's prestige was immense, and his services to the state were great, yet he had encouraged the growth of crises to enhance his own glory and had repeatedly tried to lessen the legitimate credit of others. No statesmanlike idea is associated with his name.

Caesar was not only pursuing Pompey; he had come to Egypt to collect six thousand talents that the late king, Ptolemy XI Auletes ("the flute player") had promised the Triumvirate for restoring him to the throne. He had died in 51, and the kingdom was in dispute between his daughter of twenty-one, Cleopatra, and her brother, who was thirteen. The second daughter also had a party among the palace officials and the soldiers. Cleopatra had been driven into exile. The murder of Pompey by "the palace gang" was intended to enlist the support of Caesar.

Although Cleopatra was perhaps not smuggled into Caesar's presence in a rug, as some said, she did return secretly and meet him. He probably assayed her at once for the intense, able, ruthless person she was and resolved to establish her in control of Egypt. With his support she could hold the country indefinitely, making Rome no trouble and sometimes supplying money. She would not be able to form any troublesome independent policy for years, if ever. As for their being lovers, it was the less important part of the relationship, except that for the lady there might be a political advantage in bearing a child to the most important man in the world.

Caesar had to spend several months in Egypt and had to run some very grave risks, as he was besieged by the royal troops and the Alexandrian mob through the winter of 48–47. When his reinforcements came, he defeated the Egyptians. Since young Ptolemy XII was killed, the throne was nominally given to a still younger brother, Ptolemy XIII, whom Cleopatra married in the usual fashion of the monarchs of Egypt.

Caesar now had to deal with a threat from Pharnaces, son of Mithridates of Pontus, who had overrun some territories in Asia Minor and had already defeated one of Caesar's legates. Leaving three legions in Egypt, Caesar met Pharnaces in a campaign of only five days. *"Veni, vidi, vici"* was his report to the Senate.

On his arrival at Brundisium in September, 47 B.C., Caesar found Cicero, who had been waiting there ever since the Battle of Pharsalus; he had refused to go to Africa with a large group of those who had escaped from the battle. Caesar treated him with friendly courtesy and pardoned him for following Pompey, as he did many others. Mark Antony, whom he had sent home from Pharsalus to supervise Italy in his absence, had on the whole done well, although Rome still echoed with his wild parties and Caesar had to make him disgorge some of what he had appropriated from the sale of Pompey's properties. He did not lose Caesar's favor, however, and we must continue to take him seriously as a soldier and administrator. Caesar also acted to relieve what seems to have been real misery among the poor by decreeing that low rents need not be paid for a year and that interest accrued since the beginning of the civil war be canceled.

Africa and Spain: 47 to 45 B.C.

Late in the year 47 Caesar began his campaign against the republican forces gathered in the province of Africa, boldly ferrying his troops across in the treacherous winter weather as he had to Greece. The republicans were helped by King Juba of Numidia, who brought infantry and a large force of cavalry. Again Caesar was hard pressed by the competent general and troops of the other side, but he overcame their early advantage and brought on the formal Battle of Thapsus early in 46 B.C., once more winning the day, as he had at Pharsalus, by shrewd generalship. He took for Rome the kingdom of Numidia (just west of the province of Africa), which was a good territory for the production of grain and which had been developed along Carthaginian lines by Masinissa.

The chief feature of the African campaign was the suicide of Cato, who was in command at Utica, up the coast from Thapsus. Realizing that the place could not be defended after the defeat of the main army, he made arrangements for its surrender and killed himself. The point of view of the *optimates* was that he was too great-souled to be willing to view the victory of Caesar and the tyranny that was bound to follow. Another view is that he was not great-souled enough to accept the pardon that Caesar would surely have offered him and join in the work of reconstruction under Caesar's leadership.

Again Caesar returned to Rome to stay for only a short time. He celebrated a huge fourfold triumph for his victories in Gaul, Egypt, Pontus (against Pharnaces in 47) and Africa (nominally over Juba). He gave presents of money to his troops and to every citizen and offered fabulous feasts and entertainment.

Before the end of the year 46 he was off for his last campaign, that against the sons of Pompey, who had collected in Spain an army that should be called a Pompeian faction rather than the last of the republicans. The campaign was brief, ending with the bitterly fought Battle of Munda, in southern Spain, in 45. Sextus Pompey escaped; we shall soon hear more of him.

CAESAR'S REFORMS AND RECONSTRUCTION

Although he began his legislative activity before he had disposed of all opposition, we may properly consider Caesar's whole attempt at reform and reconstruction here. He worked within the old constitutional forms as far as he could, although the occasional obstruction of tribunes caused his holding the dictatorship a second time, from late 48 to late 47, and taking a ten-year appointment to the office in 46 that was changed to a permanent dictatorship early in 44. He was consul in 48, 46, 45, and 44.

He made as much use of the Senate as possible. To the Romans the inequality of men seemed obvious, and a senatorial order was indispensable to give recognition and cohesion to the leading people in the commonwealth; a Senate that had power, held meetings, and reflected prestige on its members was necessary to allow these leading men to play their part in a well-ordered society. Caesar raised the number of senators to about nine hundred and was accused in his own time of admitting people unworthy either by birth or merit. From this distance the charges do not stand examination; he took in newcomers, but they were solid citizens, equestrians, bankers, local notables, or even executives who had been connected with manufacturing. Although he restored pardoned Pompeians to the Senate and enlarged its membership with new men, he cautiously held in his own hands for the present the control of finance and foreign policy and the bestowal of governorships and commands.

He had the number of quaestors increased from twenty to forty, of aediles from four to six, and of praetors from eight to sixteen, a move that brought more men into the system of responsible government. The number of consuls was left at two. The old-fashioned calendar, which required the addition of an intercalary month every now and then to make it come out right, had been manipulated by aristocratic politicians through the priests. In 46 B.C. it had been allowed to become wrong by two months. Caesar introduced a version of the Egyptian calendar that we have come to know as the Julian calendar. Although a great improvement, it still needed refinement and was replaced in 1582 by the Gregorian calendar sponsored by Pope Gregory, which was introduced into England and the colonies in 1752.

Caesar cut down the number of people receiving free grain from 320,000 to 150,000. The corollary of this was a huge program of founding colonies, many of them outside Italy. He refounded Corinth and Carthage; both sprang at once to vigorous new life. Veterans also were sent to colonies, some of them in Italy, others in Greece and the East, in Africa, Spain, and Gaul. To this new Roman element in the provinces were added new citizens, suitable provincials to whom the full citizenship was given, and the Latin right was extended to many whole communities. We cannot say that Caesar moved to put the provinces on a level with Italy, as was done later, for all his measures taken together show that he assumed the pre-eminence of Rome and Italy. Nevertheless, beside the grants of citizenship just mentioned and the bringing of some provincials into the Senate, he did try to help the provinces by setting fixed taxes, rather than tithes, so that the old taxgathering companies were not needed to collect them.

Surprising as the variety of his reforms seems, we must remember that he had been in public life for over thirty years, that he had advisers, and that he was willing to listen to elements that others had not cared to hear. It is also true that most of his reforms were straightforward improvements in the orderliness and efficiency of government. In the city he suppressed the *collegia*, or clubs, from which Clodius had drawn his hoodlums, leaving only genuine guilds of long standing and the associations of the Jews, which were recognized as nonpolitical. In the Forum Romanum, the original Forum, he built a great basilica for legal business, the base of which can still be seen there. He built the Julian Forum adjacent to the old Forum, and in it erected the temple of Venus Genetrix to assert the claim of the Julian family to descent from the goddess Venus. He commissioned the scholar Marcus Terentius Varro to gather books for a public library. He planned to drain the Pontine marshes, near the coast, to gain new land; it was also dimly guessed that the marshes had a connection with malaria. He required that at least a third of the workers on the great farms and ranches should be free men, perhaps partly for his discharged soldiers, but also in order to have some restraint on large slave staffs left unwatched by absentee owners.

Caesar undoubtedly grew more brusque and arbitrary as time went by. He made remarks that for a head of state were indiscreet, as when he said that the commonwealth was merely a name without substance. Many rather extravagant honors were voted to him by the Senate, but we have no reason to suppose that he demanded or invited them. As for the idea that Caesar had long had it in mind to become king, there is no clear evidence for so extraordinary and self-defeating a purpose on his part.

Something did move sixty senators to conspire to murder him. We can see that their act brought further woes and a monarchy to Rome. Caesar himself had said that only trouble could come from killing him. Yet they were all honorable men who knew Caesar well and banded together in complete secrecy to kill him; we can hardly dismiss them as dreamers who hardly knew what they were doing.

Caesar's greatness is beyond question. He was a man of high intelligence supported by the energy that is so essential a part of human achievement. From his early years his aim was to rise through the *cursus honorum* and to enjoy the position of a leading member of the nobility, and he worked carefully and ruthlessly toward this end. Not all his acts were legal; not all were decent. If he fell below the general standard of behavior of his time, however, it was not by much.

His was a less complex nature than some, as the nature of the strongly executive type is likely to be. His desires and interests seem to have been fairly few and straightforward. His fine intelligence ruled his planning and his making of judgments all the more because it was probably not obfuscated by a large number of interests, desires, and emotions. In civil and military life alike he made sound judgments and made them quickly, then acted with such speed and decision that he often forced his opponents into errors or seemed to be enjoying pure luck. His handling of people was extremely skillful and unhindered by intrusions of his own ego; the resultant charm was felt by everyone with whom he dealt.

Caesar's acquisition of control may be regarded as the end of the Roman Republic, even though after his death there were years of struggle before his great-nephew Octavian could also assert his predominance. We can easily see many things wrong with the late Republic, but to call it decadent or to say that its faults were so incurable that only monarchy could restore it to health is to resort to easy formulas. Strangely enough, what was wrong with the Republic did not bring about the end of the Republic; that was done by the presence of Caesar and Pompey. A shrewd governing class could have endured either one and could have kept itself in control, but two of them was one too many.

The Assassination of Caesar

Neither Brutus nor Cassius, the two leaders of the conspiracy to assassinate Caesar, had won real distinction; neither had shown extraordinary ability, as far as we know. Their fame, however, runs through literature from their time to ours. After their final defeat their names were officially symbolic of treason for their killing of Caesar. On the other hand, well into the first century of our era the opposition to the emperors used them as a republican symbol, for example, by celebrating their birthdays. At the end of the century the Greek Plutarch, in one of his biographies of noted Greeks and Romans, wrote the life of Brutus as of a tragic hero whose downfall was caused by a flaw in his character. Dante, early in the fourteenth century, put Brutus and Cassius in the lowest part of his Hell for their treachery to Caesar, whom he admired as the founder of the Roman Empire. Shakespeare, reading a translation of Plutarch, perceived that Brutus would make a tragic hero. With his fine feeling for Romans, he restored the Roman note, which is not to be found in Plutarch, and made of Brutus the chief example for the modern world of that symbolic old Roman on whose portrait Ennius, Cicero, and the historian Livy worked so effectively.

The conspirators apparently had no plans whatsoever for the effective seizure of power after their murder of Caesar on March 15, 44 B.C. The failure of the common people of the city to hail their deed with joy was a great surprise to them. Mark Antony held legitimate power as Caesar's colleague in the consulship, and Marcus Aemilius Lepidus was the master of the horse who assisted Caesar in his other role, that of dictator. Antony looked to his own safety as Caesar fell. The conspirators made their way to the Capitol as a symbolic act, planning to dedicate their bloody weapons there. They asked Antony to meet them, but he refused and busied himself with getting Caesar's papers and money from his widow. He also conferred with Lepidus, who had some troops outside the city. The troops were moved in to secure the city early the next morning, the sixteenth. Antony called a meeting of the Senate for the next day, March 17.

On the seventeenth in the Senate Antony made the conspirators a moderate proposal, although Lepidus would have taken vengeance at once. Antony pointed out the obvious fact that Caesar had so thoroughly reorganized the government that to cancel everything he had done would bring chaos and leave every man present with no valid appointment. Further, such a course would bring down the wrath of all the veterans settled on bonus land and of all the men now under arms. There really was nothing to do but acquiesce in the validity of all that Caesar had done. Cicero, who had been taken into the councils of the conspirators as soon as the deed was done, proposed that there be an amnesty for the killing, and this was agreed on.

On March 20 Caesar's funeral took place. Antony delivered a reasonable funeral oration to an audience that was ready to burst forth with an emotional display. The combination of the traditional reminder of the great deeds of the departed with the announcement that he had left his gardens to the people and three hundred sesterces to each citizen so stirred the crowd that they gathered wood and themselves cremated Caesar's body in a great bonfire in the Forum. The liberators hid themselves and before long left the city for villas far enough out to seem safe.

For some weeks all was peaceful. Antony was in control and speaking in conciliatory tones. A law was passed to confirm Caesar's acts, to abolish the dictatorship, and to continue the promised distribution of land to Caesar's veterans; all these provisions tended toward keeping the peace. Antony was said, however, to have taken bribes to issue forged decrees of Caesar that he pretended to have found among Caesar's papers.

In April Antony persuaded the Senate to vote him the proconsulship of Macedonia for five years and the six legions that Caesar had gathered there for a projected campaign against the Parthians. Lepidus had gone to take charge of the provinces of Gallia Narbonensis and Hither Spain, which had been assigned him by Caesar. Most of the other provinces were in the hands of men of Caesarian sympathies. Late in April Antony went to Campania to gather a force of Caesar's veterans to act as troops to insure order in Italy for the present. He persuaded some six thousand of them to serve and returned to Rome.

THE RISE OF OCTAVIAN: 44 TO 30 B.C.

His Struggle for Recognition

When he returned in May from Campania, Antony found on the scene that young man who was to upset the precarious equilibrium of forces that had been achieved and who was in the end to dominate Rome as Caesar Augustus. He was Caesar's grandnephew Gaius Octavius. He was eighteen years old at the time of Caesar's death and was at Apollonia, on the west coast of Greece, studying oratory and military matters and waiting to go with his great-uncle on the Parthian campaign.

The chief trait of his character, a resolve very reminiscent of Caesar to win his way to prominence by any methods and at any cost, showed itself at once. In spite of the opposition of his mother and his stepfather, the youngster went to Italy and landed near Brundisium. After sounding out the veterans there he showed himself to them and was warmly received, but was shrewd enough not to do more than let himself be seen. During the rest of April he was in Campania, living with his stepfather and conferring with men who had had some standing among the adherents of Caesar. He also called on Cicero and made a very favorable impression by his modest bearing and his deference to Cicero's opinions and advice.

Early in May he moved up to Rome, where he was well received because of his connection with Caesar. Caesar's will had provided for the adoption of Octavius; such posthumous adoption to keep up the families of men who had no sons was not uncommon among the Romans. Now Octavius was ready to announce that he accepted. By Roman custom he took the name of his adoptive father followed by his old name, with the adjective ending *–anus,* as a fourth name, as in the case of Scipio Aemilianus; thus his new name was Gaius Julius Caesar Octavianus. Historians know him by three successive names: Octavius, Octavianus, Augustus. He himself preferred to call himself Gaius Julius Caesar rather than Octavianus. By 38 B.C. he began to call himself Imperator Caesar, and we shall see that in the settlement of 27 B.C. he received the name of Imperator Caesar Augustus. For the stage of his career that began with his adoption we shall call him Octavian, as is customary.

When Octavian asked Antony to pay him his inheritance from Caesar (Antony had control of Caesar's money), Antony put him off. He apparently realized how dangerous a person Octavian was, for he moved to have Cisalpine Gaul rather than Macedonia as his province, although it already had a governor, Decimus Brutus, one of the assassins of Caesar, who had been assigned it by Caesar and was already installed there. Antony also persuaded the Senate to give Brutus and Cassius assignments that involved no troops.

Octavian's career at this point could have been ended easily, had the magic of Caesar's name not protected him. He built up his power by using the name of his great-uncle, bribing veterans, tampering with troops under arms, and suggesting future rewards. It was most unfortunate for the Republic that he imposed on Cicero as he did not on Antony, and Cicero persuaded the Senate to give him the rank of propraetor and a legal command over the troops he had illegally raised. Cicero apparently thought of Antony as intending himself to be dictator and as having thwarted the immediate return of the Republic at Caesar's death, and was foolish enough to think that Octavian could be encouraged in illegal courses until he had crushed Antony and could then be dismissed. Cicero made a series of speeches against Antony that he called *Philippics* to suggest that he was challenging a dangerous person as Demosthenes had challenged Philip II of Macedonia, and perhaps to invite comparison with the speeches of Demosthenes.

Antony tried to take Cisalpine Gaul by force from Decimus Brutus and was attacked by the forces of Octavian and those of the consuls of 43 B.C., Hirtius and Pansa. Several times serious proposals for peace were made, but somehow Cicero was able to keep alive the martial spirit of the Senate toward Antony and quell the talk of peace. A moderate defeat was inflicted on Antony, but he skillfully escaped toward the West. The consuls both fell in the battle; the troops of Decimus Brutus, whom Antony had besieged for some time, were in no condition for pursuit of Antony, and Octavian refused to pursue him. Octavian sent to the Senate to demand the consulship and rewards for his soldiers, which the Senate had to grant, having no power with which to resist.

Slowly the rest of the drama unfolded itself. The governors of the provinces of Spain and Gaul joined Antony, since their soldiers could see no reason to fight against him. Although they were theoretically bound to support the Senate against Antony, the governors were men of the world and may well have been unable to see what could be gained by the sacrifice of a single life more.

The Second Triumvirate

In November there was a meeting of the three leaders, Antony, Octavian, and Lepidus; the latter had been in Gaul and was the first of the governors to join Antony. Antony and Lepidus could easily have defeated the army of Octavian at this point, too, had it not been that again the veneration of their soldiers for the name of Caesar protected him. One result of their discussion was a law of November 27, 43 B.C., establishing them for five years as *tresviri reipublicae constituendae,* or a board of three to set the commonwealth in order. This is often called the Second Triumvirate. Antony, who might have been a sober proconsul and who could perhaps have guided the commonwealth back to a restoration of senatorial control, had now become one of the masters of the state, faced with a plainly ambitious and utterly unscrupulous colleague. Lepidus had almost accidentally gained a position for which he had neither taste nor talent and from which he soon was ousted.

Like Sulla, the triumvirs proscribed their enemies and rich men to get funds to pay the troops. They also planned to confiscate the land of eighteen of the wealthiest cities of Italy for the soldiers. Cicero was the most illustrious victim of the proscriptions. Mark Antony insisted on his death, and indeed Cicero had forced Antony into a role very different from that that he wished to play after Caesar's death and had used his great oratorical powers to belittle him.

Probably few men have ever been judged by such exacting standards as Cicero has been, with every moment of weakness, every flash of vanity, every mistake inexorably recorded and held against him. Cicero is the rare case of an intellectual, a fine writer, and a supreme orator who also somehow found the energy, the courage, and the ability to handle people that gave him a political career as well. To find the energy to do so much was unusual. To contribute more of permanent value to posterity by his thought and writing than any other Roman would have been enough for one man, even without a moderately successful career in active life in a rough age.

The Final Defeat of the Republican Forces

In the first division of territory and responsibility among the triumvirs Antony took Cisalpine and Transalpine Gaul, Lepidus was given the other part of Gaul and Spain, and Octavian had Africa with Sicily and Sardinia. The most important parts of the East—Greece and Asia Minor —were in the hands of Brutus and Cassius, who had gone there instead of to their assigned provinces. They found themselves able to gather a large army, and they thoroughly plundered the East for money to pay for it. In the early autumn of 42 they moved to Greece with nineteen legions and a large fleet.

Octavian and Antony went to Greece with a large army, leaving Lepidus as consul for 42 at Rome. They met Brutus and Cassius at Philippi, in eastern Macedonia at the edge of Thrace. In the first battle, on October 23, Cassius' wing was driven back in confusion, and this experienced soldier, mistakenly thinking that Brutus' wing also had failed, committed suicide. Three weeks later the army of Brutus was crushed, and he refused to survive defeat. Mark Antony rightly gained what little glory there was in this melancholy victory, for Octavian was no soldier, and for part of the campaign he was prostrated by some bodily frailty and illness that plagued him in his earlier years and more than once brought him near death, although he lived to the age of seventy-seven.

The hopes of the republicans were extinguished at Philippi, and many of their leaders were killed. Some of the survivors are said to have greeted Antony respectfully and to have spoken insultingly to Octavian, who to them was an unscrupulous and contemptible adventurer. Many who escaped fled to Sextus Pompey, the son of the great Pompey, who had escaped from the Battle of Munda in 45. Since then he had become the head of a large republican naval force, from one point of view, and from another point of view the formidable leader of a fleet of pirate ships.

Antony and Octavian, East and West

After Philippi there was a new division of territory and responsibility. Antony went to the East to restore Roman power there and raise money. Octavian was to stay in Italy, where his main task was to find land for 100,000 discharged veterans. Naturally the confiscation of land in Italy aroused resentment. Fulvia, the fierce wife of Antony, and his brother began a movement, apparently without his knowledge, to raise Italy against Octavian, but Octavian speedily crushed it. Antony meanwhile traveled through the East distributing rewards and punishments for people's behavior in the recent struggle. In the early mounths of 41 he summoned Cleopatra to appear before him at Tarsus in Cilicia to answer the charge that she had favored his adversaries. Plutarch, in his biography of Antony, gives a picture of the charming stateliness with which she presented herself before him, and Shakespeare, in *Antony and Cleopatra*, somehow improved on Plutarch's description. When winter came, it found Antony in Egypt, where for a few weeks he lived riotously with the queen. To Antony, as formerly to Caesar, it seemed a great advantage to have Egypt ruled by a monarch who would make the Romans no trouble and would willingly contribute money now and then. But early in the year 40 Antony went about his business and did not see Cleopatra again for four years.

Returning to his headquarters in Greece, Antony found his relations with Octavian worsening and went to Italy with his troops. Again war seemed imminent, but the soldiers refused to fight, and the rivalry between Octavian and Antony was calmed by the so-called Peace of Brundisium (September, 40 B.C.). There was a frank division of the Roman possessions into East and West by a vertical line on the map just east of the heel of Italy and going up through the northwest coast of the Balkan Peninsula, through the modern Albania. Lepidus was to have Africa.

Octavian was well assisted by trusty friends. Gaius Maecenas, whose name has come to symbolize the enlightened patron of the arts, was an Etruscan, a wealthy older man who attached himself early to Octavian. At first he often played an active role as man in charge at Rome in Octavian's absence, but after about 30 B.C. his poor health apparently allowed him to do nothing very active. Marcus Agrippa came from obscure people, was about Octavian's age, and was a man of action. In the early years he especially supplied the military ability that Octavian lacked. In 38 B.C. Octavian acquired a different and very valuable ally who was to be with him until his death. The beautiful Livia Drusilla was of the blood of the great Claudian family and had married Tiberius Claudius Nero, her distant relative. She had a little son, Tiberius, and was soon to give birth again. We shall meet her sons Tiberius and Drusus as men. Her husband now divorced her, and Octavian married her, both with a shameful swiftness.

For some years after the Peace of Brundisium, Sextus Pompey caused great difficulties in the West and the Parthians in the East. Antony and Octavian cooperated in dealing with these opponents, but with a great deal of friction. Sextus Pompey blockaded Italy with such success that the usual shipments of grain from abroad could not arrive, and there were riots in Rome over the food shortage. The plebeian population of the city, like the soldiers, saw no sense in the struggles of ambitious men and demanded that there be negotiations with Pompey. Although in 39 B.C. an agreement was made to take Pompey in as a fourth member of the governing group, Octavian soon tried again to overcome him by force, and the struggle went on until the year 35. Pompey was overcome, and Lepidus, too, was eliminated, for he was foolish enough to try to assert himself as of equal importance with Octavian and was abandoned by the soldiers, who knew that their rewards at the end of their service would not come from Lepidus. He was stripped of everything except his permanent office of Pontifex Maximus and lived most of the rest of his life, until 12 B.C., in compulsory retirement in a pleasant town of Italy.

The Parthians invaded Roman territory and did great damage while Antony was in Italy in 40 B.C., just before the Peace of Brundisium. One of his subordinates inflicted three sound defeats on them in 39 and 38, but he felt that a large punitive expedition was necessary. In 37 B.C. he set himself to dealing with the East in earnest, preparing for the expedition and carefully reviewing all the political arrangements there. He established a group of client kings—Polemo in Pontus and Bithynia, Archelaus in Cappadocia, and Herod, later known as "the Great," in Judaea. Cleopatra's kingdom was the southern bastion of this system of provinces and client kingdoms. Antony spent another winter, that of 37–36 B.C., in Cleopatra's company, and accepted as his children the twins born after his last visit, to whom she had given the resplendent names of Alexander Helios (the sun) and Cleopatra Selene (the moon). Another boy was born later. In 36 B.C. Antony marched out against the Parthians and was badly defeated, but held his troops together and brought them back by his skill and courage. Cleopatra gave him money and supplies for his army in this emergency. The Parthians, if not defeated, were at least impressed enough with Roman power to stay on their own side of the line for generations.

Antony's last great arrangement is known as the Donations of Alexandria. At a great ceremony in 34 B.C. he proclaimed that Caesarion, son of Caesar and Cleopatra, was recognized as such and should rule jointly with his mother as Ptolemy, King of Egypt. Kingdoms were assigned to the three children of Cleopatra fathered by Antony, somewhat as the heir of England is assigned Wales.

Octavian's sedulous propaganda against him must not deprive Antony of his due. His government of the East was competent; his choice of client kings was sound; he managed the people with tact and with understanding of their traditions and feelings. As for his relation to Cleopatra, we need not suppose that he was a weak man led by a sexually attractive woman, nor was her character so much stronger than his that she could lead him. His problem was that of managing a too-ambitious subordinate with a following of her own. We know that many men of good repute assisted him and were loyal to him.

The Final Contest (*33–30* B.C.)

Octavian complained of Antony's recognition of Caesarion and handling of Egypt, while Antony complained that Octavian had broken his promises to send soldiers and had taken under his control all the forces of Sextus Pompey and of Lepidus, of which Antony needed a share. He offered to lay down his powers as triumvir in 33, the end of their second five-year term, if Octavian would do the same. Octavian's propaganda spoke of loose women and orgies, while Antony's spoke slightingly of Octavian's descent on his father's side and of his lack of military ability, which it magnified into cowardice.

The consuls of 32, who were friends and supporters of Antony, planned to ask the Senate for a formal ratification of all his arrangements, but Octavian, fearing a fair discussion, came with soldiers to the meeting and made such threats that the consuls, and with them no less than three hundred senators, fled to Antony. Octavian forcibly took Antony's will, which was deposited with the Vestal Virgins, and published it. It declared that Caesarion was Caesar's son, left large legacies to his own children by Cleopatra, and directed that he be buried beside her in Alexandria.

The years 32 and 31 were spent in active preparations for the inevitable struggle. Antony's great problem was Cleopatra, whom he needed for her money and for the support of Egypt, but to have her along when he moved toward Italy was a great disadvantage, for he could not think of landing in Italy if she were with him. Many Romans detested her, and presently men started leaving him for that reason. Antony decided to start by going to Greece and met Octavian's forces in the Battle of Actium, on the west coast of Greece, on September 2, 31 B.C. Morale had so declined among Antony's forces that he could have little hope of prevailing. Cleopatra broke away with her fleet of ships and her treasure at the very beginning of the battle. Antony followed her, and they fled to Egypt. The army and navy that they had deserted were partly defeated and partly absorbed after some negotiation.

It was July of the year 30 before Octavian had finished his more pressing problems of asserting his own control in the East and could come to Egypt with an army to take it. Antony and Cleopatra were unable to make any real preparation against him, and after a brief battle Antony killed himself. Cleopatra, hoping to save the rule of Egypt for her children, tried to negotiate with Octavian, but found him impervious to her charms and disdainful of her claims. Realizing that he planned to take her to Rome and show her in his triumph, she had an asp, the Egyptian royal snake, smuggled in to her and died by its bite.

Octavian killed the young Caesarion because he was a competitor for the glamor of the Julian name. There was no wholesale slaughter of the Romans who took Antony's side. He appropriated Egypt, to be administered by himself through a personal agent of equestrian rank. With a part of Cleopatra's treasure he paid the overdue wages of his soldiers, some of whom were becoming restless and troublesome, and was able to buy land for them instead of confiscating it, as he had done when he first came to power and had to find land for veterans. He celebrated a series of triumphs for his victories, spending money lavishly for decorations, for gifts for the soldiers and the people, and for huge feasts. The injection of this money into the economy had a salutary effect, at least for his purposes, since the threatening discontent was thoroughly alleviated.

ROMAN LAW

The Types of Law

There were four chief divisions of Roman law. First was the sacral law, that connected with religion, which dealt with such matters as sacred days, the proper manner of holding ceremonies, and the choice of people for priesthoods. Apparently the Pontifex Maximus could impose fines in cases of sacrilege.

The second type was domestic law. As we have seen, the *paterfamilias* controlled the persons, property, and slaves of his family. The law governing such relations was carefully worked out except in the matter of grievances and injuries among the free members of the family; the comprehensive powers of the *paterfamilias* inhibited the growth of formal rules of law to cover such relations.

The third type is criminal law. We have seen that Sulla established a number of permanent criminal courts.

The fourth division may be called private law; in the United States it is known as civil law. Our expression would be somewhat misleading if applied to Roman law, for among the Romans the *ius civile* was the original Roman law, which applied to those having the full status of Roman citizen, and was contrasted with the *ius gentium,* or law of people in general, which the Romans saw in use among other people and of which they borrowed some features. Roman private law, the law of dealings between individuals, had as its main divisions the law of persons, the law of property, the law of obligations, and the law of procedure.

The Sources of Law

Only a small part of Roman law consisted of statutes, or *leges*. Some of the statutes of which we know were made law by the *Comitia cen-*

turiata; the Twelve Tables is the chief example. After the *lex Hortensia* of 287 B.C. had made the *plebiscita* of the *Comitia tributa* and of the *Concilium plebis* legally binding, these two assemblies of the people were the chief source of statutes; we cannot always be sure in which of them the people met when we are told that they voted something. *Senatus-consulta,* or decrees of the Senate, were another source of law, although they were more likely to be administrative rules, often of a temporary nature.

The Romans did not have great respect for statute law. They did not allow it overriding authority in the courts; they did not trouble to make accurate collections of it, so that we know almost nothing of the content of many statutes that the Roman authors mention in passing; they often allowed statutes to lapse into desuetude and even to be forgotten. The Roman writers sometimes complain that the great volume (as it seemed to them) of statute law on public matters was a hindrance to the proper conduct of society. Although historians tend to dismiss this remark as a commonplace thoughtlessly repeated, we should perhaps take it as evidence that to the upper-class Roman the best kind of government was the discretionary government that the *paterfamilias,* the magistrate of wide and loosely defined powers, and the Senate could conduct, the kind that the aristocratic Council of the Areopagus had conducted in Athens and that the democratic regime of the fifth century replaced by a government of definite legal rules.

The considerable body of Roman law not created by statute arose partly from custom and partly from proceedings in the courts of the praetors. Roman law, like the common law of England, which is the basis of much American law, recognized as obvious certain crimes (murder and theft, for example) and certain relations (for example, common-law marriage or marriage by cohabitation). Thus custom gave rise to a certain amount of law. Roman law did not, however, accept custom of all kinds as authoritative.

The proceedings in the courts of the urban praetor and the *praetor peregrinus* were a source of law and helped to keep the law flexible; we shall discuss these proceedings more in detail later. Here it may be said that the early Roman law, like most early law, had rather rigid forms, called *legis actiones,* in which a legal action could proceed; in early English law this was called forms of action. One has the suspicion that this system suited an aristocratic minority, for it required the plaintiff to choose exactly the right form and disqualified him entirely if he chose the wrong one; thus it would be easy to keep a troublesome and uninformed person from getting very far in a proceeding at law. The praetor of Cicero's day, however, presided over a discussion between the parties to the contest, which led to a careful definition of the issue between them and the choice of a formula, so-called, to be used at the trial. A very simple example of a formula is "If it appear that A owes B one thousand sesterces, let him pay it." The trial was, as with us, an attempt to establish the facts of the case.

The praetor of each year issued an edict at the beginning of his term of office in which he declared what legal remedies he would offer and what actions at law he would entertain during his year of presiding over the courts. Differently put, he gave a list of the formulas he would allow—each formula, like the simple one that allows an established debt to be collected, being a statement of a principle of law. Naturally almost all the content of the edict was the same from year to year, but the praetor could create new law simply by saying in his edict that he would give out certain new formulas or that he would create certain new legal remedies. This was not an arbitrary or capricious process. Although the praetor of any year was not likely to be highly learned in the law, he always, in the Roman fashion, surrounded himself with friends whose knowledge and good sense could assist him in his official duties. The cases that had come up in recent years would have been thoroughly discussed by all those members of the nobility who interested themselves in law. If it had become plain that some change in the law was very desirable, and if all Rome's legal experts were agreed that such was the case, they would offer the newly elected praetor a carefully drafted formula that he would publish in his edict. He could just as easily remove a formula that was now felt to be no longer useful or appropriate.

The Courts

The jurisdiction of the Pontifex Maximus in sacral law was exercised directly in what may be called his own court. The *paterfamilias* may be said to have had his own court when he sat in judgment on his family or slaves. Sometimes he would have friends in as advisers. An extreme example is the case of a senator of Cicero's time who accused his son of becoming the lover of the young man's stepmother and invited most of the Senate to sit as his advisers at his trial of his son, which ended in the disproof of the charge and probably was meant as a way to silence a malicious rumor.

Disputes of private law, or what we call civil cases, were taken care of in the courts of the urban and peregrine praetors. Matters of probate were handled in the court of the *centumviri*, or hundred men. The standing criminal courts made permanent by Sulla were much like our courts; these were the courts the composition of whose juries was a bone of contention between senators and equites. The aediles had a police court in which they could handle minor cases of disorder. Now and then the tribunes initiated criminal trials in the assemblies of the people, as when they prosecuted the generals who suffered the disgraceful defeats at the hands of the Teutons and the Cimbri. The courts of the municipalities of Roman citizens in Italy were presided over by prefects sent out from Rome by the praetors. Those cities that enjoyed the status of free allies of Rome —Tibur and Praeneste, for example—had their own legal systems and courts, as did the provincial cities that had the status of free allies.

In the provinces the Roman governor was the chief legal officer. He was bound by the terms of the province's charter, originally drawn up by a commission and approved by the Senate. He held court in a circuit of important cities. In the provinces, as at Rome, the Roman law was applied to Roman citizens, while the law of others was respected as binding on their citizens.

Legal advice, whether on the making of a contract, the drawing of a will, or on commencing litigation, was to be had from members of the upper classes who called themselves *iurisconsulti,* or jurisconsults, and whose chief interest was the law. They did not learn it in law schools, for there were none, but from their elders. Their advice and services were at the disposal of their friends, of other people who had some claim on them according to the complex system of mutual services among the nobility, and of still others who wished to enter into such a relation of mutual help and obligation. The jurisconsult did not expect to be paid in money for his services, since the obligations that he created were payable in a different and a valid currency. Many men not of the nobility undertook to give such advice and aid, expecting to be paid in money. Presumably the laws against taking money for legal assistance that were occasionally passed and then allowed to fall into desuetude were meant to curb the activities of these others, not that the nobles wanted fees for themselves, but because they wished to prevent men not of the nobility from practicing what they considered their profession and gaining influence thereby. Although the leading jurisconsults often held office, it is noteworthy that they rarely went beyond the praetorship.

The man who thought of going to law generally started by asking someone to assist him; the Latin word is *advocare,* and the person asked was an *advocatus,* from which comes "advocate" in English. If he were an ordinary man, he asked that noble who was his patron and whose client he was. If he were a member of the upper class and himself the patron of others, he was still likely to ask one or more friends to assist him. They approached the praetor and stated the case as it seemed to the man who felt himself injured. If the case seemed reasonable on the face of it (a prima facie case), the praetor gave permission to summon the other party, who also asked his patron or others to help him.

Each side needed an orator—one of the men who, like Cicero, made a profession of effective public speaking. If one of the parties was himself a good orator, he usually asked another to share the speaking in court with him. Perhaps one's patron was a fine orator, or a man might have rendered services in the past to a distinguished orator for which he would now expect payment in oratory.

Each side also needed a legal opinion. Nowadays the first man called on to help is a lawyer, who can attempt to form an idea of what the court will consider to be the law in the case by consulting his armory of books. The Roman orator had no volumes of statute law, few treatises on the law, and no authoritative decisions of a supreme court, for decisions were not appealed to a higher court. Decisions in earlier cases were not binding unless one orator could show that there was reason to be swayed by an earlier decision. The man who needed a legal opinion went to a jurisconsult and got an opinion as to whether he had a legal remedy according to the present state of the law as embodied in the praetor's edict. Obviously the two parties often came to the trial relying on conflicting opinions from their jurisconsults.

After getting their legal opinions the two contending groups came before the praetor for a discussion of the matter analogous to our pleadings, the formal moves leading up to the trial of a case. Questions could be asked by each side which the other side was bound to answer. The purpose of the discussion was to bring the matter to an issue, a clear-cut proposition that would serve as the basis for a trial. It had to be capable of being expressed in one of the formulas of the praetor's edict. A modern analogy would be that negligence can be culpable and that the formula, if we used such things, might be, "If it appear that the accident was caused by the negligence of the defendant, judgment shall be for the plaintiff."

Once the issue was joined, the praetor gave the formula to the *iudex,* or judge, whom he appointed to try the case, one of the upper-class Romans who constantly engaged in public business. Although he need not be a jurisconsult, he would, of course, not be unversed in legal and public affairs. His task was to hear the evidence and arguments and to find for one party or the other according to the terms of the formula that defined the legal question between them. When we use the plural of the word, *iudices,* for those trials that were heard by a large panel, we translate it as "jurymen." Sometimes there was a panel of three for civil trials; the probate court had a hundred and five.

LITERATURE

The New Poets and Lucretius

In the middle of the first century a movement for high standards of poetic craftsmanship took on a loose form. We have a slender corpus of the poetry of Gaius Valerius Catullus (84?–54? B.C.), who was probably the movement's most gifted member, the names of several other men, and a few fragments of their work. The Alexandrian ideals of brevity, learning, and polish appealed to the New Poets, as they liked to call themselves.

Catullus, the son of a prosperous landowner of Verona, came to Rome as a young man. He had a good education in the Greek and Latin authors and presumably had at least the beginnings of the usual instruction in oratory. Friends, love, and poetry were Catullus' real life. The informal group was pretty well agreed on its Alexandrian ideals, and some of his poems frankly herald the excellence of the learned little epics of his friends, contrasting them with the longer and less carefully written epics of others.

Catullus' great love affair was with the lady whom he calls Lesbia and who was probably Clodia, wife of a prominent senator and sister of Cicero's enemy Clodius. The affair brought forth some of his finest lyrics —tender, gay, vibrant, dainty—poems wrought with such skill that they seem as artless as the song of a bird, rather than the result of genius and hard work.

As the affair progressed, however, a note new to ancient poetry came into the poems—a note that foreshadowed, faintly and far away, the romanticism of the Provençal and Italian love poetry of the twelfth and thirteenth centuries. We can see the poet struggling to find words for a feeling unlike the plain passion or the rough-and-ready comradeship of a lusty love affair. He speaks of pacts, of sacred friendship, and of the pure sentiment a man generally feels for his sons and sons-in-law. He himself hardly understood this feeling, which probably arose from his unusual intelligence and sensitivity. Surely the lady did not understand, if indeed he ever tried to explain it to her. She added new conquests even while holding him and fascinating him by her physical charms. In the end Catullus plainly expressed the distress and sickness that he felt at finding himself still in the grip of a strong sexual attraction after love, liking and respect for the woman had gone. In so doing he expanded the short epigram into a new form, the elegy on one's own loves, which was to be effectively used by some of Catullus' successors.

Critics have sometimes asserted that there are, as it were, two Catulluses, the natural genius who wrote the love lyrics and the devoted craftsman who wrote the other poems of the collection. Nowadays it is thought that there was only one Catullus, a fine craftsman in all his poems, who wrote love lyrics, occasional poems of friendship, political lampoons on Caesar's henchmen, poems of coarse abuse and satire on his personal enemies and on the writers of long epics, and also some longer poems.

Among the latter are two wedding songs of considerable grace and charm, either of which could be read as a poem, offered as a poetic wedding gift, or actually sung at a wedding, and both have beautiful and tender passages. He wrote a little epic in the Alexandrian style, as apparently every one of the New Poets was expected to do. Catullus', which has just over four hundred lines, tells of the marriage of Peleus and Thetis and digresses for a little more than half its length to describe a tapestry on which was depicted the desertion of Ariadne by Theseus.

The influence of the Alexandrian ideas of the New Poets and of the work of Catullus can be seen for a generation or so after his early death. In Vergil we can see both the ideas and imitation of phrases and lines from Catullus. A group of elegists sprang up, as we shall see, to exploit the elegy of one's own loves. The lyric poet Horace was as insistent on high polish as any Alexandrian. These few men, the luminaries of the time of Caesar Augustus, were followers to some extent of Catullus and the New Poets and were men of great literary ability; after them most writing in Latin settled down again to much the same sort of thing that was written before the rise of the New Poets.

Titus Lucretius Carus (ca. 100–ca. 55 B.C.), a contemporary of Catullus, wrote a didactic poem, *De rerum natura,* or *On the Nature of the Universe,* following the older tradition in which didactic poetry was of high seriousness rather than mere versified information, as it so often was in the Hellenistic Age. The poem is an attempt to expound the Epicurean view of the universe as a great machine, the arguments for the mortality of the soul, the mechanisms whereby the senses give us knowledge of reality, the view that society and its laws are a natural and practical growth—all the things in the Epicurean philosophy that probably were hardest to commend to the attention of the Romans. Many important points of the Epicurean philosophy, like its ethics, which the Roman found perfectly intelligible, are not touched upon or are mentioned only briefly and without discussion.

Although many passages in Lucretius are prosaic, and all the genius of the poet could do no more than construct them in verse, the fervor of Lucretius and his great poetic ability make this a great poem. His Latin is pure and elegant. Many passages are elevated and stirring. Many keen observations of the world around us enliven the poem, and there is a conception, new in ancient literature, of Nature as something existing of itself, sometimes cruel, sometimes a great mother, full of mysterious ways, yet moving by majestic laws that occasionally reveal themselves to the philosophic eye.

Prose Writing

The *Gallic War* of Caesar was written swiftly toward the end of his time in Gaul and was offered to the public (the other Roman nobles, that is) as an account of what he had done there. It is a remarkable book, if one can read it as it was meant to be read instead of stumbling through its Latin before one is ready, for in it Caesar is the hero whose broad plans, lightning moves, and persuasive talks with Gallic leaders end all opposition, although the book seems candid and frank. Modern scholars have sometimes accused him of deliberate falsification, but this is not the right word. His choice of facts is naturally such as to put himself in a good light, his organization of the stirring and complex events is naturally such as to lead up to the favorable result that he achieved, and the deeds of his lieutenants naturally seem of secondary importance. There are descriptive passages of great interest—the general organization of Gaul, the Druids, the strange creatures found in the great Hercynian Forest.

Gaius Sallustius Crispus (86–34 B.C.), who is usually called Sallust, was one of Rome's best historians. After a disappointing attempt at a political career, he retired to devote himself to writing. His first effort was a monograph on the conspiracy of Catiline that gives us a picture of Cato and Caesar as the chief figures in the great debate on the fate of the conspirators, a fair-minded account of Cicero's part in the affair, and a vivid picture of Catiline as a nobleman who, in spite of his energy and intelligence, failed in the race for honors. His other monograph, the *Bellum Jugurthinum,* offers us many facts not to be found elsewhere concerning the preliminary events and the operations of the war with Jugurtha. He began his last work, called *Historiae,* a colorless title meaning merely "Studies" and used by many Greek and Roman authors, with the situation of 78 B.C., just after Sulla's retirement and death, and was able to complete the history of twelve years. We have only fragments of this work, which was intended as a full-scale account rather than as a monograph.

Marcus Terentius Varro (116–27 B.C.), who is usually called Varro, was the greatest Roman scholar. He was a friend of Pompey and served him as legate in more than one campaign; it was he who in 45 B.C. was commissioned by Caesar to collect books for a state library. Only his book on farming has survived. It is on practical agriculture and can be interestingly compared to Cato's book written 150 years earlier and to Vergil's *Georgics,* which took some of Varro's facts and ideas into its atmosphere of high symbolism. His greatest book was his *Antiquitates rerum humanarum et divinarum,* which is not entirely lost to us, since many of its facts of Roman life were used by later scholars and since the details of Roman religious observances that he gave helped Christian polemicists to make merry over the stupid practices of the pagans. His other researches covered almost every subject, for example, literary history, geography, and law.

Cicero's Intellectual Career

Cicero's father was an *eques* (knight) of the *municipium* of Arpinum. His connections were such that he could place his son under the care of Mucius Scaevola, one of the leading Roman jurisconsults. The young man was expected to be with his master during the conferences in which he expounded his view of the law to those who applied to him, during his attendance at the courts as an onlooker or as one called to lend his influence by being present when the case of a friend or ally or client was being tried, and during leisure hours at home, when the neophyte might be privileged to hear the conversations of his elders or to have private instruction in the law and the ways of the world of affairs. Everywhere in the Roman world—in Rome, in the headquarters of the armies, in the offices of the governors of provinces—young men of the upper class were being trained in this way by their elders.

Cicero soon turned to oratory as more likely than the law to serve his ambition, for his fierce and flaming ambition was manifest to himself and to others before he was twenty. He decided to make his way in public life in spite of the difficulties in the way of one whose family had had no consul in past generations.

Since the suspension of the courts during the Marian terror and afterward offered him no opportunity, Cicero was late in beginning his career at the bar. His first speech was in 81 B.C. After his successful defense of Roscius of Ameria in 79, he went abroad for three years, perhaps because he thought that he had offended Sulla by his defense of Roscius, perhaps because, as he said, he needed to develop a quieter and physically less demanding style of oratory. He heard the lectures of philosophers in Athens and elsewhere in the Greek East. Greek was the language used, of course, both by the philosophers and by the famous teachers of oratory to whom he went.

On his return to Rome his chief intellectual activity, along with his brisk practice at the bar, was the intense cultivation of the theory and practice of oratory. Until his praetorship in 66 B.C., he declaimed every day in both Latin and Greek, that is, he delivered a practice speech of some sort in both languages. This can be compared to the intense and faithful practice of modern musicians; presumably no orator does it today. His practice in Greek was partly because he studied the technique of the published speeches of the great Athenian orators like Demosthenes and partly because he wished criticism from the best teachers in Rome, many of whom knew only Greek.

His first major book, *De oratore,* was begun in the year 55, when his political influence had been reduced to practically nothing by the power of the Triumvirate. In this book, which plainly shows the influence of Isocrates and Plato, Cicero described his ideal orator not only as a man thoroughly trained in the techniques of the art, but also as a Roman strongly grounded in the *mos maiorum,* or the Roman way, and as an educated man, one who knew the philosophy and literature of the Greeks, the source of the quality that Cicero liked to call *humanitas.*

In 54 B.C. he began work on *De re publica,* or *On the Commonwealth.* Naturally we can trace an influence here of Plato and others who wrote on the form of the state, but the Greek influence is entirely assimilated, and Cicero's commonwealth is a thoroughly Roman commonwealth. After finishing this book he wrote no more until 46 B.C., when Caesar's government left no place for republican political activity. He produced two more books on oratory, both largely concerned with the question of whether the plain style called Attic should be preferred to the more luxurious style called Asiatic that had been developed by the Greeks of the East and that Cicero may be said to have represented among the orators who used Latin.

During his last two years he produced a series of books in which he attempted to represent to the Romans the main ideas of Greek philosophy. He himself had been interested in the subject ever since his father encouraged him to listen as a youngster to the lectures of Greek philosophers at Rome. He had even had a Stoic philosopher, Diodotus, as his house guest for several years, and it has been noted that his knowledge of Stoicism was especially detailed and exact.

In the first of the series, *Academici libri,* he treated the basic question of epistemology, or how we know what we know. In *De finibus bonorum et malorum (On the Outer Limits of Goods and Evils)* he attempted to compare the views of the Greek philosophical schools on values—what is important in life. Several other works treated other aspects of philosophy; of these *De officiis (On Duties)* stands out, for it is a careful and detailed discussion of what is right and right's frequent conflict with what is expedient, a discussion of morals as an art based on instruction and practice, and at the same time an essay on the obligations of a Roman gentleman.

Cicero's purpose was to represent to the Romans that quality of *humanitas* in Greek thought and writing (and, of course, he knew Homer, the lyric poets, the tragedians, and the historians), which to him seemed to combine so well with the *mos maiorum,* the solid basis of Roman life, to form a new kind of *humanitas.* This he succeeded in doing, creating a cultural idea of worth and vitality for his own time and for all the life of the western world up to now. His was the greatest individual contribution to the blending of Greek and Roman thought and writing.

Later Romans read and imitated his works and used them in the schools. St. Jerome, St. Ambrose, and St. Augustine, the three great churchmen of the fourth and early fifth centuries, were all deeply influenced by him. In the Renaissance he again exerted a great influence, for men who were ready to assert some modest degree of intellectual freedom found a guide in him. His influence became so great that many people cultivated a Ciceronian style and despised the Latin of their own day, with the unfortunate result that Latin became divorced from everyday life and the chance of a true international language was lost. Cicero's ideas have been so thoroughly worked into the fabric of Western thought that to the modern reader they inevitably seem commonplace, as indeed they now are. This is a lasting success beyond what this ambitious man could have hoped for.

CHAPTER

24

THE PRINCIPATE OF AUGUSTUS:
27 B.C. TO A.D. 14

Although Octavian and his party could feel that the long struggle for supremacy in the state was at last ended with the victory at Actium in 31 B.C. and with the death of Antony in the following year, they now had the problem of changing from the naked exercise of power to some way of assuring their position that would be both effective and acceptable to Roman sentiment. They also had the damage done by the civil war to repair and a large empire to govern.

The sixty legions that had been under arms were reduced slowly to twenty-eight, and the discharged soldiers were given bonuses and sent to colonies, twenty-eight of which were in Italy and the rest in Gaul, North Africa, Spain, and the East. The price of land rose somewhat, and interest rates fell sharply. Octavian also began a building program. This gave money in modest amounts to the poor for their labor, and from now on this was to be one of the purposes of the building program in the city of Rome.

Two considerations should be offered as a preface to the brief description of the events of 27 B.C. to A.D. 14, which follows. First, we must remember that the process of developing a new system was slow and often unsystematic, since a formal description of the events of almost half a century can easily give the impression that everything was done briskly and according to a complete plan. Second, we must remember that the changes were few if set against the totality of rules and practices at the time and that a great amount of the practice of the Republic continued into the Empire without any alteration.

The First Settlement (27 B.C.)

In 36 B.C. Octavian had had conferred on him by the Senate the sacrosanctity of a tribune, and in 30 B.C. he was granted the tribune's power of *auxilium*, by which he could protect men from unjust arrest. In 30 B.C. he was also granted the right to name new patricians to replenish the failing numbers of that class. In 28 B.C. as consul and with the help of his colleague Agrippa, he took the census of the people and revised the list of the Senate. He himself was named *princeps senatus*, the highest ranking member.

The first settlement, as the new arrangement of 27 B.C. is often called, began with Octavian's divesting himself of his extraconstitutional powers. This is the act of restoring constitutional government (*rem publicam restitui*) of which he spoke in his *Res Gestae,* or *Achievements,* a report on his work that he composed toward the end of his life and that has survived. The Senate, doubtless by prearrangement with a sufficient number of members, allowed him to lay down his unusual powers, then insisted that he take the garrisoned provinces—most of Spain, Gaul, and Syria—as a *provincia* and gave him the authority of a proconsul. He was to remain consul. This settlement put him in charge of twenty legions. He took the precaution of replacing the old commanders, although they were all of his party, with new men who owed their advancement to him and did not have the affection and loyalty of the troops as the old commanders did. It may well have been in this settlement, too, that the power to make war and peace and to make treaties was bestowed on him.

At the same time he was paying proper attention to the symbolism of his position, since the Senate voted that a golden shield be placed in the senate house in his honor to proclaim his old-fashioned civic virtues, and the doorposts of his house on the Palatine were decorated with oak leaves like those of the civic crown given for saving a citizen's life in battle "because he had saved the lives of citizens." This was very different from any symbolism used before for a head of state; the Assyrian kings, for example, had been portrayed on sculptured reliefs as mighty hunters of lions or at the head of their armies trampling their foes underfoot. Octavian's residence, too, remained a rather plain citizen's house rather than a large palace symbolic of the majesty of a king.

All the symbolism of January, 27 B.C. appeared immediately on new coins, for coinage was not the least of the devices for giving out propaganda. His new name, Augustus, was given, and *ex SC* for "by the decree of the Senate"; his head on the coins was bare, like a citizen, rather than crowned like a triumphing general; an eagle, however, symbolized his victories; the oak leaves were there, as well as the words *civibus servatis;* the golden shield was also represented.

His name now became Imperator Caesar Augustus. The first element had not been a name, but the word used by armies of the Republic to salute their commanders after great victories. The second element had been the cognomen, or third name, of his great-uncle's branch of the Julian family, so that using it now in the position where the name of the gens, or clan, usually appeared suggested that a new clan had been founded that ought to enjoy Caesar's prestige and popularity. The third element, too, had not been a name, but was an adjective meaning rather more than what "august" would convey now if applied to a great public man, for it suggested something more than human. So, having been Gaius Octavius, then Gaius Julius Caesar Octavianus, or Octavian, he became Caesar Augustus, or simply Augustus. The month Sextilis was now renamed Augustus and has been August ever since. He also liked to refer to himself as *princeps,* a word often used before to mean "leading man" and enjoyed by men other than Augustus in his time; as applied to him it had a good republican sound.

With the control of the armies in his *provincia,* Augustus combined a consulship every year until he resigned it in the summer of 23. He asserted in the *Res Gestae* that he had no more *potestas,* or power, than the other magistrates and that most of what he did was made possible by his *auctoritas,* or prestige. This was probably true; he had no need of more official power than the other magistrates because he could work through his great prestige and also, without mentioning it publicly, through his control of the army, of a great deal of money, and of access to honorific positions.

Late in 27 B.C. Augustus set out for the West and did not return until the year 24. Part of his purpose was to conquer the stubborn tribesmen of western Spain and what is now Portugal. There were also new arrangements to be made in the western provinces. Probably it also seemed desirable for him to leave Rome for a while so that the government could seem to function in republican fashion.

The Second Settlement (23 B.C.)

In 23 B.C., on July 1, Augustus resigned the consulship that he had held for so many years in succession. Probably it is significant that his place was given to a republican named Sestius, who had fought under Brutus and still boldly honored his memory. Augustus' making this consulship available to other men, instead of always filling one of the two himself, and beginning with Sestius was a good republican gesture. The office was still the great prize of the ambitious, and it was still felt that many tasks of government should be done only by men of consular rank.

Being determined to retain the substance of power, Augustus needed something to replace the formal control in Italy that the consulship had given him, and the legal fiction of the *tribunicia potestas,* or tribunician power, was devised. He was a patrician, to be sure, and could not hold the office of tribune, but the power without the office was more appropriate anyway. His taking the census without being censor was based on a similar fiction. The tribunician veto power was less important than the right to approach the assembly of the people and to propose legislation that up to now his consulship had given him. He was also granted two further powers that he had enjoyed as consul: that of convening the Senate at any time and that of laying any matter before the Senate at any time, even if it were done by a message rather than in person. Even though we must be always conscious of the hidden and indirect power that he wielded, it is interesting to observe that care was taken to insure legal correctness for his public moves. The tribunician power was conferred on him every year from 23 B.C. until the end of his life, and after him it was regularly conferred every year on every emperor until the late days of the Empire.

Shortly after this settlement he went to the East and stayed until late in 19 B.C. The fact that he made few changes in Mark Antony's administrative arrangements in the East is a further proof that Antony was an able and serious man. Naturally Augustus made as little trouble as possible for those kings, dynasts, and prominent citizens who had supported Antony in the recent struggle. The leading men of the East and of Rome had long since come to understand each other rather well, and Roman power in the East continued to be exercised largely by relations with the many important men who set the tone in the cities and were the owners of large estates in the country that they managed with authority, as did the owners of large estates everywhere.

The year 23 and the years immediately after it brought more than one difficulty to Augustus. In 23 there was an unsuccessful plot against his life of which we know little. In the same year came the premature death of his nephew Marcellus, son of his sister Octavia and her first husband, Marcellus, consul in 50 B.C. Augustus was moving the young man through the early public offices ahead of the usual age for holding them, presumably with the idea of grooming him to be his successor. Augustus' right-hand man, Agrippa, who doubtless could speak for strong elements in the party of Augustus, was opposed to the early preferment of Marcellus. His early death therefore removed a cause of friction, although it was a check to the plans of Augustus for finding and developing someone who could succeed him.

The Roman populace of free citizens showed plainly that it preferred to keep Augustus permanently in a dominant office by rioting when it was discovered that he was not to be consul for 22 B.C. In the winter of 23–22

the Tiber flooded, causing a pestilence, and the supply of food was dis-
organized. This, too, caused the populace to demand that Augustus protect them, and they called for him to become dictator. He says in the
Res Gestae that he accepted the *cura annonae,* or charge of the food supply, and speedily relieved the shortage; this was done through his agents,
of course, since he was away in the East. Later in the year 22 the people
refused to elect a second consul for 22, proclaiming that they were re-
serving the other consulship for Augustus, who refused to accept it.

Agrippa was induced in 21 B.C. to divorce his wife and marry Augustus'
daughter Julia. They had a son Gaius in 20 B.C. and a son Lucius in 17
B.C., both amiable, able, and destined not to live to full maturity. There
were two daughters, Julia and Agrippina. The last child, Agrippa Postumus, was said, perhaps falsely, to be of a brutal nature, and we shall hear
later of his end.

The Third Settlement (19–18 B.C.)

Augustus cut his work of organization in the East somewhat short to
return to Rome late in 19 B.C., for the people had again refused to elect
a second consul, and the man who served as sole consul for the year 19 had
great difficulty in maintaining order in spite of his ability and firmness.
Here a piece of symbolism was added: the day of Augustus' return was
made an annual holiday, as his birthday already was.

The powers voted to Augustus in January, 27 B.C., were for a term of
ten years, and in 18 B.C. they were renewed for another term of five years.
This time, however, Agrippa was granted the tribunician power and other
powers similar to those of Augustus (our sources do not use explicit language). This seems to have been the clearest indication yet given of who
was expected to succeed in case of Augustus' death. The tribunician power
was given to Agrippa every year as it was to Augustus and was numbered, as his were, so that we find "in his third tribunician power" as
part of the inscription Agrippa put on the famous temple at Nîmes,
France, known as the Maison Carrée.

In 18 B.C. Augustus also had a set of so-called Julian Laws drafted,
some dealing with morals, some with legal reforms, and used his tribunician power to introduce them in the assembly of the people. He says in
the *Res Gestae* that the people asked him to assume control over morals
but that he refused to take on any such task in his own person. To attempt to achieve the same result through the operation of the Julian Laws
was both more republican and less likely to lead to unpopularity.

In 17 B.C. a very special piece of governmental symbolism was offered
to the public in the form of the *Ludi Saeculares,* or the celebration of the
beginning of a new age. We still have the hymn, called *Carmen Saeculare,*

or *Hymn of the New Age,* written by the poet Horace to be sung by a choir of boys and girls. It calls on all the chief gods and mentions all the main Augustan themes—the antiquity and moral character of Rome and Roman assiduousness in worship of the gods and the signs that point to a new age.

The Succession

Not long after the birth in 17 B.C. of Lucius, son of Agrippa and Julia, Augustus adopted him and his other grandson Gaius, born in 20 B.C. At the same time the careers of a second pair of possible successors reached a fairly advanced point. Tiberius, the elder of the two stepsons whom Augustus acquired by his marriage to their mother Livia, was made praetor in 17 B.C. at the age of twenty-five, and his brother Drusus, who was four years younger, was made quaestor.

For a few years Augustus' plans for the government seemed to go along smoothly. He went to the West on another tour of reorganization and on his return in 13 B.C. was greeted with all the old enthusiasm and the offer of various honors, of which he accepted only one, the presentation of the *Ara Pacis Augustae,* or Altar of the Augustan Peace. The coinage had already spread the idea that peace could be Augustan, along with every other good thing, but to dedicate a great altar by this name was a fine stroke of symbolism.

Late in the year 13 Augustus was granted another five years of power over his large *provincia* outside Italy, since the term of five years granted him in 18 B.C. would expire in January of 12. The powers granted to Agrippa now put him nearly beside Augustus in power, but in 12 B.C. he died, although his health had in general been far more robust than that of Augustus.

The year 12 did bring a considerable satisfaction to Augustus, however, in that Lepidus, the former triumvir and still the Pontifex Maximus, died. An election was proclaimed, and Augustus was chosen by a huge crowd who came from all over Italy, as he says in the *Res Gestae.* Being Pontifex Maximus made it easier for him to control the state religion for governmental purposes. Later emperors, too, invariably held this office, at first going through the form of an election by the people, but before the end of the first century being elected in the Senate with an announcement to the people to represent popular participation in the election.

Tiberius and Drusus, the stepsons of Augustus, were mature and experienced men by now and able to assume the position that Agrippa had been filling, not only as reliable colleagues of Augustus but also as able and trustworthy generals. Tiberius distinguished himself in warfare in

Pannonia (modern Hungary), and Drusus advanced Roman arms into Germany as far as the river Elbe.

In 5 B.C. Augustus was consul himself and introduced his fifteen-year-old grandson Gaius to adult society by conferring the *toga virilis* on him in the traditional way; he held the consulship in this year in order to do more honor to Gaius. Gaius was designated as consul, to hold the office in A.D. 1, when he would be twenty, and was accorded by the Senate the right of attending its meetings. When these honors were given to Gaius, Tiberius was nearly forty and had commanded armies in wars as difficult and glorious, if not as glamorous and well described, as any that the Romans had ever fought. He was the leading member of a distinguished branch of the great Claudian gens, and probably felt that as to family Augustus and his grandsons were nobodies, whatever airy claims the Julian gens might make about its connection with the goddess Venus in one of her weaker moments. Tiberius went into retirement on the pleasant island of Rhodes shortly after Gaius' honors were conferred and remained there for seven years. Augustus' displeasure at Tiberius was such that when Tiberius' tribunician power expired in 1 B.C., he not only refused to have it renewed, but also forbade his stepson to return to Rome.

Augustus went ahead with the training of his grandsons in public affairs, but fate had another blow in store for him. Lucius died in A.D. 2 and Gaius in A.D. 4. Of necessity Augustus turned to Tiberius, who had been allowed to return from Rhodes in A.D. 2, and solemnly adopted him as his son. He also adopted his grandson Agrippa Postumus, the posthumous child of Agrippa and Julia, and forced Tiberius to adopt his nephew Germanicus, the son of his brother Drusus and Antonia. Antonia was the daughter of Mark Antony and of Augustus' sister Octavia and therefore possessor of some measure of Augustus' blood. Tiberius was given the tribunician power for ten years and was sent out for further work on the Rhine frontier.

When, in A.D. 13, Augustus received another of his periodic grants of power, Tiberius was given not only a renewal of his tribunician power, but also equal power with his stepfather in commanding the armies and administering the provinces. In addition he was the head of what may be called the Claudian faction, a large group of prominent people bound together by ties of blood, marriage, and interest. When Augustus died in A.D. 14, the great commands and the important magistracies were all held by reliable members of this group. The Senate, the magistrates, the soldiers in Rome, and the free people of the city at once swore allegiance to Tiberius personally, and the power passed smoothly to its new holder. There was a story that Agrippa Postumus was murdered as one fit for no serious work and therefore dangerous, since he was of the Julian blood. It is more likely that he died of illness at about this time and that the story of his murder was spread later by a faction interested in slandering Tiberius.

Augustus, the Senate, and the Senators

Augustus shrewdly used his great power and prestige after his success at Actium to gain control of the men of the senatorial order. In 28 B.C. he and Agrippa, beside taking the census, revised and reduced the list of senators. Some few men were induced to resign as unworthy; others were forthrightly removed. Again in 18 and in 13 B.C. he revised the list. One of the many ways in which Augustus used his wealth for political purposes was to enable men of good family and straitened circumstances to enter or re-enter the Senate by giving them enough money to make up the required property of 1,000,000 sesterces. Another way in which he could exert influence on the entry of men to the Senate, as distinct from his revising the membership of the Senate, was to further the early careers of promising and amenable men. Recruits were generally of families that had had earlier senatorial members, but Augustus early claimed the right to grant the privilege of wearing the *latus clavus,* the broad purple stripe on the tunic that distinguished the members of the senatorial order, to some young men of the equestrian order; they could then try to rise through the typical senatorial career, bringing in vigorous new blood for the highest class in the state.

The young man of the senatorial order had first to do a year of military service as a minor officer; many who had an interest in the art of war did more. The next step was to be elected to the vigintivirate, or Board of Twenty, whose members attended to such matters as the mint, care of the streets, special police work, and so on. Every year twenty of the young men who had reached the age of twenty-four could, as a third step, be elected quaestors and with the office gain a seat in the Senate. It is probable that the addition of these twenty members a year and a few older men kept the number of the Senate fairly steady. Augustus appointed the young men to their military posts and commended them to the people for election to the Board of Twenty and the quaestorship. The close watch kept over the rising crop of young men was meant to find energetic, able, and steady prospects for the service of the state who would recognize their debt to Augustus. In thus gaining so much influence over the careers of the senators, Augustus had skillfully used power to breed more power.

Legislation could be made by both *princeps* and Senate. The *princeps* could not only propose bills to the assembly through his tribunician power, but also could issue edicts with the force of law; he could, in addition, issue instructions to officials and replies to petitions that would in practice have the same force. The Senate continued to create a modest amount of formal law by its actions and decrees.

The courts continued to function as they had under the Republic, and under Augustus and his successors efforts were made to keep the business of the courts moving swiftly, efficiently, and fairly. It is worth noting that the prestige of Augustus and his successors and their insistence on honest provincial administration did not entirely prevent some misgovernment, for we have evidence of many justified prosecutions of dishonest governors.

In administration the Senate continued to be responsible for Italy. The cities and towns attended to most of the daily tasks of government, and the senators themselves (and other large landowners) handled the very simple management of great tracts of rural land. The management of the provinces controlled by the Senate remained much as it had been except for the presence of the financial agents of the *princeps* to manage his extensive properties.

The government of the city of Rome was improved by the creation of a formal fire and police department known as the *vigiles;* it had seven cohorts of one thousand men each, drawn from the class of freedmen; it was under a prefect of equestrian rank. Contact between the government and the people was made more easy by the division of the city into fourteen regions and 265 *vici,* or precincts, that elected their *vicomagistri* (precinct leaders). By the end of Augustus' reign there were three cohorts of the regular army known as the urban cohorts, stationed in the city under the command of a prefect of the city who was of senatorial rank.

Augustus also formed a separate corps known as the Praetorian Guard, composed of men of good family who came from old Latium, Etruria, Umbria, and the colonies of Roman citizens founded in Italy. They served as a force to guard the emperor and the city and were prepared to go out, as if from a military academy, to serve as lower officers in the legions of the active armies and keep up their quality. We shall see the Guard interfering in politics on more than one occasion. There were nine cohorts of one thousand, of which there were three in Rome and six scattered through Italy under Augustus; Tiberius concentrated them in Rome.

Although since the time of Gaius Gracchus occasional efforts had been made to insure a steady flow of grain toward Rome, no permanent government agency for that purpose was created until the shortages of 23 B.C. Resulting popular disturbances caused Augustus to set up a *cura annonae* (*annona* could mean both the yearly crop and the food supply) under a prefect of his own choice. The water supply of the city was likewise given new attention and care, for Agrippa saw to the building of two new aqueducts and developed a corps of his own slaves as specialists on the care of these and of all the minor parts of the system within the city, and after his death, Augustus asked the Senate to set up a permanent water board of three senators. Senators, too, were the members of the permanent boards of *curatores* to supervise the sacred and public buildings of the city and to take measures to protect the city against the floods of the Tiber.

The ordinary senator must have been a serious and busy man, although it is true that some hereditary members of the order chose to live a frivolous life—the sort of life that seems implied by the poetry of Ovid—rather than one of public service. After the beginner in this career had gained admission to the Senate by being elected quaestor, or, as often happened with mature men whose ability was called to the attention of the *princeps* was "adlected," or appointed to the Senate, he had many individual efforts to make. The younger men naturally wished to aim for the higher offices, or *honores,* but the years between offices were spent in work, not in idle waiting. A man could serve as the commander of a legion, as one of the staff of the governor of a province, or as governor of one of the less important provinces under Augustus' control. The emperor and his advisers kept a close watch on the careers of rising men, and imperial commendation for election to office was granted to those who did well.

Augustus recognized that his own repeated holding of the consulship was distasteful to ambitious men. Presently a statute fixed the term of the office at six months rather than a year so as to offer four consulships rather than two as prizes for ambition and to produce more ex-consuls, since certain tasks were traditionally imposed only on men of consular rank. An inscription discovered in Italy in the middle of this century and known as the *Tabula Hebana* gives us some detail of a process called *destinatio,* which was a preliminary to the elections after 5. B.C. (or possibly only after A.D. 5). Ten centuries of senators and equestrians chose their candidates, thus giving the assembly of the people a directive that it was rather likely to follow.

The ex-consuls went on to such tasks as the governorship of a more important imperial province, a place on one of the important and useful boards (like roads, buildings, food supply), the important post of prefect of the city, or the brilliant governorships of the senatorial provinces of Asia and Africa. Some of them served for long periods as commanders of armies. But there was much for the senator to do who had not even reached the consulship. All were wealthy and were responsible for their large estates and for the workers on them. All were patrons of many people, of towns and cities, or even of whole provinces. All these people needed help and representation in dealing with the government. Many men of senatorial rank were accomplished orators and worked hard on their technique, offering their oratorical assistance to their equals as well as to their clients, and other men put a great deal of effort into the study of the law. A man would frequently be called upon to sit with and assist a friend who was sitting as *iudex* on a legal question, had a difficult problem in some other official dealing, or needed advice on a private matter, for the Romans believed in asking for advice and discussion. We learn almost by accident that some men who seemed to lead very quiet lives were "friends of Caesar," that is, the advisers without office of Augustus and later emperors.

Augustus and the Equestrian Order

Augustus elicited hard work from the equestrian order, too, by opening to it new opportunities in the service of the state. He boldly used his implied censorial powers to reorganize the order with definite rules for membership, so necessary in any well ordered gradation of status. The property qualification was 400,000 sesterces; like the senatorial qualification, it was doubtless far less than the average estate of a member of the order. A man must have been freeborn and have done military service. He was formally entered on the list of the order and received the right to a public horse, the wearing of a gold ring, and the narrow purple stripe analogous to the broad stripe of the senator. Many experienced landowners and businessmen were drawn into the order, and it was open to the senior centurions of legions on their retirement from active service.

Augustus found many places for knights in the financial administration of the government at home and in the provinces that were under his control. The most brilliant opening for a knight was the prefecture of Egypt, a post that was forbidden to senators because the wealth, the grain production, and the geographical position of Egypt seemed to the Romans to make it a key to power in the eastern Mediterranean. Senators were not allowed even to visit Egypt without the express permission of the *princeps*. Other positions of real power open to knights were the *praefectura annonae,* or the office of prefect in charge of the city's food supply, and the commands of the Praetorian Guard and of the *vigiles*.

The common people of the city were the *clientela* of Augustus, although it must be understood that practically all of them were also clients of one or another of the leading men. Augustus could count on them to support his power if there were a test, and they could rely on him for the distribution of free grain, for a series of public entertainments and small gifts of money, and for a program of building that would supply a considerable amount of work.

Rebuilding and Reform

Augustus claimed in the *Res Gestae* to have restored eighty-two temples in Rome. He built the great new temple of Apollo on the Palatine in honor of his own adopted protecting divinity and the temple of Mars Ultor, or Mars the Avenger, which celebrated his punishing the murderers of his adoptive father by his defeating Brutus and Cassius at Philippi. This temple was given importance by being made the seat of many ceremonies, like the depositing of captured battle standards, the formal departure of magistrates for their provinces, and the enrollment of young men of the upper classes in the group of military age. Augustus added a forum of his own to the one that had been built by Julius Caesar; the temple of Mars Ultor was a part of it, and sculptured likenesses of a series of republican heroes contributed also to the republican symbolism that Augustus liked to use.

Augustus' remark that he found Rome a city of brick and left it a city of marble is often quoted; we should probably say that he left it a city of brick faced with thin slabs of marble. He built the Theater of Marcellus, which may still be seen, in honor of the dead Marcellus, his nephew, and Agrippa saw to the building of the Pantheon, dedicated to Mars and Venus, divinities claimed as patrons by Augustus. The present Pantheon is a new one, erected in the time of Hadrian. Augustus built himself a tomb in the Etruscan style, a round structure with a conical top that may still be seen near the Tiber in what was the Campus Martius. In all this building we do not find anything that we could call urban renewal except perhaps that the height of tenements was now limited to sixty feet.

The attempts at reform were directed at the social and religious life of the citizens rather than at buildings and streets. The Julian Laws of 18 B.C. attempted to push people toward marriage by rewards and penalties, for many people of the upper class had been discouraged from marrying by the protracted disturbances of the civil wars. Women as well as men were penalized for not marrying by limitations on their rights of inheritance. For men the rewards and penalties of marrying and procreating or not doing so could easily be linked to political life, the bachelor or the childless man being put at a disadvantage in seeking office or preferment.

Augustus also set limits on the manumission, or freeing, of slaves. One law limited the number of slaves that a man could set free by his will at his death, which suggests that many a man wished a great concourse of grateful freedmen at his funeral. Another limited the number that a person could manumit during his lifetime by providing that the owner must be at least twenty years old and the slave at least thirty. Freedmen were allowed to become Roman citizens, but were not permitted to hold

office nor to serve in the army; full citizen status was reserved for their
children who were born after they became free.

Augustus and Religion

Augustus knew that there was a strong feeling among most people that
Roman successes were largely due to divine support and that it was necessary to obtain the *pax deorum,* or kindly feeling of the unseen powers, by
religious observances. He became Pontifex Maximus when the death of
Lepidus gave him the opportunity, and before that time he had lent his
great prestige to various priestly boards by becoming a member of them.
He increased the dignity of the Vestal Virgins and appointed a *flamen
Dialis* or priest of Jupiter, a post that had been allowed to be vacant
for several decades.

The people of the East had long been accustomed to recognizing something of the divine in great men who served their fellows, and some Romans had been so honored in the two centuries in which the Romans had
been active in the East. After Augustus' rise to sole power it seemed
natural to institute a cult to honor Augustus and *Roma* jointly; it is
difficult to define in modern terms what *Roma* meant to the eastern
provincials. Cities even competed for the honor of having temples of
these two curious powers, and the priesthoods were esteemed as marks of
political honor. Whereas the Roman government needed only to give recognition to such spontaneous local observances in the East and to make
sure that the honors connected with it fell to politically reliable men, in
the West it had to take the initiative and have similar useful cults introduced. There is evidence of the priests and councils and altars of such a
cult in several places in the western provinces. Another kind of observance that seems to have been inspired by the government rather than
spontaneous was a cult of Augustus that the government encouraged
in Italy outside Rome, the officers of which were freedmen rather than
the leading citizens of the cult just mentioned.

Affairs Outside Rome and Italy: Army and Navy

The general conduct of foreign affairs presents every government with
one of its major never-ending problems, since there is no end to the particular problems that arise, whether in the area where force is used or
the area where diplomacy is used. The existence of the army as an instrument of foreign policy adds a separate persistent problem of governments:
that of managing a large body of men trained to the use of force and provided with weapons.

The government of the late Republic never brought itself to face the need for a permanent professional army, largely because, as we have seen, it saw no way to deal with the corollary problem, that of managing armies so as to keep them from being used by their commanders to influence or coerce the government. Augustus solved the problem by obtaining a grant of power that covered the places where there was most need to use armies, by causing the soldiers to look to him more than to anyone else for their rewards at the end of their term of service, and by gradually retiring some of the more ambitious generals.

The twenty-eight legions kept in service after 30 B.C. must soon have learned to think of themselves as a permanent professional army posted in certain strategic locations. In 13 B.C. Augustus made a rule that the term of enlistment for the men of the legions was to be sixteen years and that of the praetorians twelve years, and in A.D. 5 the term of the legionaries was raised to twenty years and that of the praetorians to sixteen, at the end of which time they could expect an honorable discharge and a gift, for the praetorians 20,000 sesterces and for the legionaries 12,000.

The legion now had 5500 infantrymen in ten cohorts and 120 cavalrymen. The legionary soldier was generally a citizen, as he had been in republican times, although a very modest number of noncitizens was enrolled in the legions and was given citizenship on being mustered out. Although the government assumed the right, as all governments must, to conscript men for the armed forces, there were ordinarily plenty of volunteers, for the service was reasonably well paid (at the rate of 225 denarii a year), would bring an occasional bonus or some loot and on retirement a gift of land or money, and for the average soldier was not really a dangerous occupation.

The armies were stationed in a number of great camps that were furnished with many of the amenities like baths and amphitheaters and that attracted settlements around them of traders and others who could cater to the needs and the pleasures of the soldiers, including often the common-law wives of soldiers, who were forbidden to marry. Often the settlements around the camps developed into regularly organized towns, and it was natural that many a retired soldier should decide to live in a familiar place of this sort where he had personal ties and had perhaps acquired a little property. The camps of the army must have done much to romanize the regions around them—a romanization consisting of some knowledge of the Latin language and of what the plain soldiers and the example of Roman organization and discipline could teach.

The shaping up and management of the soldiers was done by the centurions, of whom there were six in each cohort and therefore sixty in the legion. As would be expected in a country that had a well defined aristocratic class, the ranks above that of centurion were reserved for members of the senatorial and equestrian orders, the legion being commanded by a *legatus,* an ex-quaestor and therefore a member of the Senate, or an ex-praetor, serving in a military post for two or three years as part of the succession of civil and military posts and magistracies that made up the senatorial career. On his staff were a number of younger men ranked as *tribuni militum,* who were beginning equestrian or senatorial careers under the tutelage of their elders and with the instruction that could be given them by the seasoned centurions and *praefecti castrorum* (supply officers) and *praefecti fabrum* (engineer officers). Some men aimed at chiefly military careers from the beginning; they served more than one term as tribunes of the soldiers, later as legates, and then were recognized as military specialists and moved up toward higher commands.

As the legions of citizens in the republican army had had help from Rome's allies in Italy, so the citizen legions of the Empire had auxiliary troops of noncitizens organized into cohorts of infantry and *alae,* or wings, of cavalry. Augustus enlisted this large force (perhaps equal to the approximately 150,000 citizen soldiers) among the noncitizens of the imperial provinces, those under his rather than under senatorial control, giving them the promise of citizenship at the end of twenty-five years of service and romanizing them further by their contact with the army.

The navy of the Empire was essentially a maritime police force and communications service and was therefore composed of light and fast ships rather than the old-fashioned larger warships needed for large naval battles. The navy had a base at Misenum, at the north end of the Bay of Naples, one at Ravenna for the Adriatic, one in Gallia Narbonensis, one at Alexandria, one in Syria, and squadrons of river police on the Danube and the Rhine.

The Romans had long since found that to work through friendly and amenable kings was an excellent help in managing their foreign affairs, and especially so in the East since the wars with Philip V and Antiochus III and the assistance of the kings of Pergamum. The practice of having the sons of foreign kings in Rome for long periods as guests of the government was useful for everyone, since their fathers had less reason to fear assassination at the hands of sons impatient to assume the royal power and in a sense could feel that Rome guaranteed their thrones against usurpers by recognizing their sons as heirs to the throne. The princes were likely to assume a Roman point of view from ten or twelve years' residence in Rome and perhaps to wait with more patience for their time to ascend the throne, since for them, too, Rome offered guaranties against usurpers.

Augustus' common sense in foreign affairs was shown by his refusal to attempt to annex Armenia or Parthia, both of which lay outside the Mediterranean region that Rome could govern effectively. He bided his time and was able in 20 B.C. by diplomatic representations and some show of force to bring about the return of the standards of Crassus' legions, which had been the most glorious trophy of the Parthian victory over him in 53 B.C.—a diplomatic feat that was widely celebrated on coins and in works of art.

In regions other than the East warfare seemed necessary to secure Roman interests and was undertaken in that spirit. The pacification of Spain was completed early in the reign of Augustus, since the economic potentialities of the peninsula were too great for violent interference with them to be allowed. The suppression of the interference of the Alpine tribes with peaceful commerce, something that the Romans might reasonably have undertaken long before, was attended to. Eastward from the Alps Rome now planned to take Raetia and Noricum, which was more or less the eastern part of modern Switzerland and Austria, and then move eastward to Pannonia, or Hungary, and Moesia, which would extend its realm to the Black Sea and include everything below the Danube through practically its whole course. This territory was to be of the greatest value and importance to the Romans, for it brought them a tremendous supply of good soldiers, a fertile region, and control of a river that was useful both as a line of communication and commerce and as a barrier of some value against the peoples north of it.

The future emperor Tiberius distinguished himself by finishing the pacification of Pannonia in 9 B.C. and then suppressing a great revolt there in A.D. 9. In 12 B.C. his brother Drusus led an advance across the Rhine that was meant to reach the Elbe and create a narrow Roman province in Germany extending southward to the Danube and eliminating the awkward angle of the frontier where the Rhine turns sharply at Basel. Although Drusus died after a fall from his horse in 9 B.C., the work went on under the command of Tiberius until he and many of his troops were called away by the great revolt of the Pannonians. Then in A.D. 9 the German leader Arminius, the first national hero of Germany, trapped the Roman general Varus in the Teutoberg Forest and destroyed his three legions. Henceforth the Romans were content to hold only a very narrow strip beyond the Rhine and to give up the idea of reaching the Elbe.

This warfare, so lacking in drama and glamor, was probably as difficult as any that the Romans had ever engaged in, and the results were probably as important as those of any earlier war. The securing of the Rhine frontier meant that Gaul could develop in peace and become thoroughly romanized, so that before the end of the Empire it was able to absorb and romanize in turn a great many Germans who entered it in one way or another. The advance to the Danube also enabled the Romans slowly to assimilate a large number of people.

Economic Recovery

The end of the Roman civil wars and the prospect that pirates and brigands would be restrained were enough to bring a recovery of prosperity and a new enthusiasm for work and for economic ventures that were not the least significant trait of what has come to be called the Augustan Age. In addition the government of Augustus and those of his successors did more to promote trade than had been done under the Republic. More roads were built, and old roads were repaired. Improvements were made to rivers and harbors.

Italy may well have been the most advanced of all the divisions of the Empire and was officially regarded as the most important one. Italian property had not been subject to tax since 167 B.C., although there was a five percent tax on the value of slaves who were manumitted, a tax levied when slaves were sold, and an inheritance tax; the provinces had to pay a direct tax on land and on other property, and duties were collected on goods carried across the frontiers of the provinces. The customs duties were for revenue only, not to protect one area against the products of another.

The agriculture and the industries of Italy had long been prosperous (except as they were upset by the civil wars), and to them was now added a blossoming of expertly managed capitalistic enterprises that produced fine foods and luxury goods for the large market of the city of Rome, for Italy, and for export. The manual of farming written by Marcus Terentius Varro, who died in 27 B.C., describes larger operations than those covered by Cato's handbook of the early second century and shows us that enough of a luxury market had developed to make it worthwhile to invest in the production of such specialized items as thrushes and oysters. The processing of fine wines and olive oil was, however, by far the most important part of the luxury food industry.

Beside Varro's book we have casual references in many Latin authors to the famous wines and the fine oil of Italy. Archaeology supplies us with further evidence on the production of wine and oil from the remains of a number of villas in the neighborhood of Pompeii. The farms of which the villas were the centers can often be roughly traced, and although many of them are of moderate size, perhaps 25 to 125 acres, with equipment that betrays that they were general and self-supporting—evidences of the presence of cows, cheese-making utensils, wine and oil equipment, a mill, and a bakery—many others were far larger and were highly specialized. The villa of Boscoreale, near Pompeii, yielded a famous find of beautiful silver plate, and the house had fine ornamental paintings done directly on the surfaces of the walls, as well as elaborate heating and bathing facilities. The wine jars found there are thought to have been sufficient for an annual production of 20,000 gallons. Even this estate, however, could not compare with the really large commercial vineyards and olive orchards spoken of by Latin authors, which often spread over hundreds of acres and were manned by hundreds of slaves.

Archaeologists have found in many places amphorae for wine and oil incised with identifying inscriptions that give us facts about the course of trade. The wines and oils of Campania went westward to North Africa, Spain, Gaul, and even to Britain; they took a long land journey to the strip of Roman territory beyond the Rhine, or went up the Adriatic to Aquileia, not far from modern Trieste, and then on to the provinces of the Danube line.

The manufacture and distribution of other articles was much like that of food, with a considerable production at home—wooden bowls and buckets, simple dishes made from the clay pit on the farm, homespun woolen clothes, handmade shoes and other items of leather—and a large number of small shops producing for local needs, but with many large establishments dealing in the world market. Aquileia, for example, became a center for the manufacture of ornaments and little bottles or boxes of amber. The amber came down the land route through Germany, and the finished wares moved along the trade highways back toward Germany or the Danube provinces or by sea down the Adriatic and into the trade routes by water that went all around the Mediterranean. The silver, bronze, and copper products, some of them very beautiful, that came from the manufactories in several parts of Italy have been found throughout the European provinces and beyond in Germany, Scandinavia, and even Russia, for such things were regularly carried by traders to the neighbors outside every part of the Empire.

The red-glazed pottery of Arretium, the modern Arezzo, was probably more widely known through the world than any other product. Arretium was in the middle of north central Italy, not on a navigable river, so that its products had a fairly long haul over the hills before they could be put on a ship. Yet they were carried everywhere, even as far as India, as surviving fragments tell us, and were used in considerable amounts. Remains have been found of a mixing vat that would hold ten thousand gallons. In a very large establishment there was at least a little of that specialization that is the mark of the true factory; there might be a specialist designer, mixers, furnace men, and packers. The workers in such plants, and the managers and department heads as well, ordinarily were slaves, as skilled workmen usually were.

Our brief survey of economic conditions in other parts of the Empire should properly start with the eastern regions where civilization had flourished for more than three thousand years. Egypt's rich harvest of grain was a great asset to the Romans; 20,000,000 modii (a modius was

0.96 pecks, U.S.) of this grain went every year to Rome and was capable of feeding the city for four months. Industry, too, was active, the three chief products being the paper made of the papyrus plant, the linen made of the flax that grew in the marshy land near the Nile, and glass made from an especially fine sand. No less important was Egypt's share in the transit trade from farther east, which brought expensive goods from India, Ceylon, and Arabia. Some of the ointments, essences, fine fabrics, and ivory was passed along immediately toward the rich markets of Rome and Italy, profiting the Egyptians by their handling charges, but many of the materials were combined in the establishments of Alexandria into the perfumes and cosmetics that would bring the highest prices.

Syria had a share of the transit trade, too, and some exotic products of her own, like the balsam of Jericho. Syria's wine, olives, plums, figs, and dates were all highly regarded by gourmets. But textiles were her chief product, and the choicest were dyed with the Tyrian dye, a beautiful crimson (not purple) dye made of the shell fish found near the coast of old Phoenicia. Syrian looms produced fine fabrics of wool, linen, and silk.

Asia Minor and the islands were especially thankful for the cessation of the civil struggles of the Romans, since they had suffered so greatly from the exactions of whatever faction was on hand to drain their wealth to pay its soldiers. The people of the coastal cities and the islands, like those of Syria, had a long tradition of merchandising and needed only to be free of interference to rebuild their trade. They had a great variety of foodstuffs, fine woods, copper, silver, lead, iron, jewels, a kind of mica that could be split into thin panes for windows, and marbles, but most of all they had their ancient skill in manufacturing textiles.

The Danube provinces played a useful but not at all spectacular part in the history of the Empire: they were an agricultural country in which industry was never much developed; they supplied large numbers of men for the armies; and in the troubled days of the third century they produced a flock of competent generals, some of whom became emperors. None of their cities could compare in brilliance with the old cities of the East or the leading newer ones of the West.

Greece was a poor country. It still had some industries, but mainly culture, for Athens was the great university town of the Mediterranean world and a tourist attraction, while the art factories of Greece could still turn out a steady supply of works of art for the rich of the West. We cannot be sure how many of the Greeks who went westward to do every kind of skilled work for the Romans (and in many cases to live by their wits without doing anything useful) originated in Greece itself rather than in the Greek communities elsewhere. Other products of Greece, like its beautiful marbles or the honey of Mount Hymettus, could still command respect.

Gaul was divided into four provinces, the old province of Narbonensis and the new ones of Aquitania, Lugdunensis (with its center at Lugdunum, or Lyons), and Belgica in the North. The fertility of this pleasant land had long been exploited, and under the Romans certain of the products of the soil, especially wine and oil, could compete successfully in the international market. Gallic textiles were good enough to be in demand elsewhere, as were Gallic metalwork and jewelry. Although at the beginning of the Empire they were fairly large importers of pottery and glass, the Gauls were to become large manufacturers themselves of these two commodities as time went on. This, indeed, was a common occurrence in this large area of improved communications and free trade; unless there were some unique and unexportable raw material or an irreplaceable local skill, industry itself tended to be exported along with its own products, and here and there throughout the Empire energetic and ingenious men learned to make wares that they had formerly imported.

The forests and the waterways were interesting features of the economic life of Gaul. Archaeologists have often found the remains of little manufactories in wooded areas, since fuel was so necessary for the making of products like metalwares, pottery, and glass. The major rivers—Seine, Rhone, Saône, Moselle, Loire, and Garonne—often come close enough to one another to make short road communications between them possible, and the Rhine could also be thus linked to the Gallic system. Good profits were made from the carrying trade, and we can see that many towns and cities, like Narbonne, Arles, Bordeaux, Lyons, Treves, and Paris, prospered from being at the junction of important roads and rivers.

The Germanic peoples east of the Rhine were very important in relation to Gaul and to the Empire as a whole. Germans had come into Gaul, settled down there, and been somewhat assimilated into the Celtic peoples before the beginning of the Empire. The maintenance of the Rhine line and of the modest part of Germany that the Romans had conquered was a very important task for which Gaul furnished men and supplies. The Germanic people outside the boundary (and let us remember that they were also outside the Danube boundary) were not forever beating wildly against the boundaries of the Empire like waves in a storm beating against a breakwater. The people outside often were glad to serve the Romans as auxiliaries and to learn from them. The things they seemed least inclined to learn were the three great distinguishing traits of the Greco-Roman civilization: the high intellectual tradition that depended on reading and writing, the habit of living in cities, and government based on impersonal systems of law rather than on personal loyalty to monarchs.

Every now and then, as we shall see, something would impel them to try to enter the Empire, especially in the third and fourth centuries. Meanwhile their presence was one of the great facts of life for the people of Gaul.

Both Gaul and Italy supplied goods to these people outside the imperial boundaries, Gaul by trade across the Rhine and Italy by routes leading northward to the Danube. The nature of the goods supplied to the Romans by the people outside, unless it was cattle and slaves, is difficult to conjecture; presumably the Romans sent some money across the border as pay for auxiliary troops and some as political gifts. The scholars who have studied the many coins found in Germanic regions, even up into Sweden, think that Roman coins were valued and used as pieces of metal rather than as cash. Many silver vessels have been found and a number of bronze ones, many of them from graves in Jutland, the mainland of Denmark which projects northward from Germany, and from the islands of the Baltic. A magnificent hoard of silver vessels, about seventy in all, dug up near Hildesheim in Germany, where it apparently had been buried to preserve it from some danger, included one or two pieces that can stand comparison with any silverware from antiquity. Perhaps the collection was a diplomatic gift to some Germanic prince.

The great mineral wealth of Spain was the most important feature of its economy and the one most significant in the Roman handling of the country; the placing of roads and of administrative boundaries, for example, was often related to the location of important mines. Every metal could be found there: gold both in river beds and mines, silver in large deposits with lead as its by-product, tin, copper, iron, and cinnabar, an ore of mercury that would produce a vermilion pigment. Fine steel was made in Toletum (Toledo) and in two or three other places; the composition of the river water in these places was an important part of this process.

During the early Empire most of the mines in Spain came into the possession of the emperors. The process of acquiring property to be controlled directly by the emperors was an important part in the development of the emperors' role during the first century of our era, since a head of state who can dispose of the revenue from large crown properties is freer to act than one whose purse strings are held by a parliament or some other body.

The strip of territory that the Romans governed across the top of Africa is one of the more interesting provincial areas, since the people— mainly a stock of Berber natives, people much like southern Europeans— were so ready to express their feelings in writing or in inscriptions of various kinds that we have a useful body of evidence on their attitudes and on their relations with the imperial government. Many of them prospered, especially on agriculture, and there came to be dozens of cities of five, ten, or fifteen thousand, many of which have left visible outlines and large numbers of buildings.

ARTISTIC AND INTELLECTUAL LIFE

Art in the Service of the Imperial Government

In most respects the art of the early Empire was a continuation of the art of the Hellenistic Age. Although the critics do not entirely agree as to who the workmen were, and although it seems rather likely that very many of them were Greeks, we may still say that in the early Empire the art of Rome and of Italy attained great excellence and acquired a distinctive national character.

We have already seen the early governments of the Sumerians, Egyptians, Babylonians, and Assyrians using art for their own purposes, followed by the Hellenistic kings. Augustus doubtless had the Hellenistic examples in mind when he thought of using art and literature to strengthen his own position. We have already mentioned some such efforts; the rebuilding and building of temples, his new forum, the Theater of Marcellus, the Pantheon, and the tomb of Augustus were all efforts to bring architecture and art into the service of the government. Augustus was also one of the first of the long line of archaeological looters, for he brought two Egyptian obelisks to Rome, where they may still be seen.

The reliefs of the Ara Pacis are examples of significant detailed work in this field. In them there is a shrewd grouping of motifs that suggests the legendary origins of Rome and the protection of the gods even from that early time, the connection of the Julian house with the gods, and the membership of Augustus in that house; all these motifs are joined in the movement of a religious ceremony. Terra Mater, or Italy, is shown, as well as Mars and Aeneas, combining the human and the divine and leading toward Augustus. But Augustus appears in the role of a priest in the ceremony, thus uniting himself with the body of citizens, even while it is suggested that he is also head of the state and is accompanied by the attendants who belong to him in that role.

These motifs were promoted as governmental symbolism by their repetition in other places, perhaps most interestingly in the altars of the Lares, or household spirits, and also of the Genius, or guardian spirit, of Augustus in the 265 *vici* of the city. The altars of this combined cult that have been found all bear the oak wreath and the laurel with which Augustus' house was decorated, as well as representations of the Lares, the Genius, and scenes of sacrifice. They are so consistent in their scenes that they must have been officially inspired.

Greek Thought and Literature

During the early Empire the philosophical schools of Athens and the distinguished philosophers of Rhodes and the cities of Asia Minor continued to teach and to bicker with one another as they had been doing. The scientists in Alexandria and a few other places went on with their work, and everywhere that Greek was spoken the young were still trained in the traditional patterns of Greek education, while their elders retained a surprising interest in the Greek classics, in critical discussions, and in epideictic orations, or showpieces of oratory, offered by notable rhetoricians. Ever since about the middle of the second century B.C. there had been a steady drift of Greek intellectuals and literary men to Rome, some of them invited and honorably treated, some brought as slaves (for slavery could befall people of the upper classes), and some making their way to Rome by hook or by crook in the hope of bettering themselves.

Perhaps the most distinguished Greek literary man at Rome in the time of Augustus was Dionysius of Halicarnassus, a rhetorician who decided soon after Actium to come to Rome and did well there as a teacher of Greek literature. He and a number of other successful teachers seem to have made careers purely in Greek literature, probably never bothering to learn Latin or to take any notice of Latin literature. From Dionysius we have some interesting studies of the great Greek authors and a history of Rome in Greek called *Roman Antiquities* (he doubtless was helped by slave secretaries who could read Latin sources), which was written, he says, for the instruction of leading Romans, favorable in tone to Rome, yet firmly conscious that all good things originated among the Greeks.

One of the most interesting works that we have from this circle of teachers is *Peri hypsous,* or *On the Sublime,* a still profitable discussion of how an author succeeds in writing in the grand style.

The Nature of Augustan Literature

The chief ornaments of Latin literature of the time of Augustus are the elegists Tibullus and Propertius; then Ovid, who was the last of the great elegists and also wrote in other fields; the lyric poet and satirist, Horace; Vergil, who excelled in the three fields of pastoral, didactic, and epic poetry; and the historian Titus Livius, or Livy. Naturally there was at the same time a crowd of minor men and hangers-on of literature. In their technical excellence, elegance, and restraint, the most important of the qualities that we think of as Augustan, the great authors of our present period owe much to the work done by many Latin authors from the second century onward and perhaps most to Lucretius, Catullus, and the other New Poets. Although it is difficult to imagine what the elegists can have owed to the temper of their day, unless it were a resolve to stay away from public life as much as possible, we may conjecture with due caution that the state of the times had something to do with Horace's great desire to produce in Latin a corpus of lyric poetry that could stand comparison with Greek work and be shown off to the Greek world that surrounded the Romans, with Livy's glorification of the great Roman past and the idealized old Roman; and with Vergil's highly prophetic picture of the mission of a Roman Empire that was coming into being as he wrote. The work of these men brought the Greco-Roman literary tradition fully into being.

Tibullus, Propertius, and Ovid

Tibullus (ca. 55–19 B.C.) wrote with grace, tenderness, and polish, if not with a great deal of force or imagination, about two young women, Delia and Nemesis. Delia was a sweet and gentle girl, but Nemesis was hard and rapacious. In his first book of elegies he wrote of Delia, of country joys, and of his patron Valerius Messalla, a leading aristocrat and the center of a literary circle. The second book was more of Nemesis and the unpleasanter side of love affairs. The poems were written in elegiac couplets each of which consisted of a hexameter line followed by a pentameter line.

Sextus Propertius, who was born about 50 B.C. and probably died in 16 B.C. or a little after, wrote at the same time as Tibullus, but with far more fire, variety, and wit. One can learn something of him from studying his metaphors—the warfare of love, the slavery of love, the seafaring and the shipwreck of love, the fire of love; these were the ways in which he loved his Cynthia, had he stopped to count. Cynthia was a freeborn woman of the upper class, but she had emancipated herself from respectability and lived in her own establishment according to her own ideas. She was tall, stately, and imperious. They quarreled and wrangled and on one occasion stayed apart for a year, but the affair continued over several years with many phases.

Propertius was a member of the circle of Maecenas and was subjected to gentle pressures of the sort exerted on Vergil and Horace. Apparently it was suggested to him that he ought to write elegies like those of the Alexandrians to show the world that a Roman could produce a body of work in this field. He finally wrote some rather good elegies on Roman legends.

Publius Ovidius Naso, or Ovid (43 B.C.–A.D. 17), was another poet who could not bring himself to enter the service of the government in an equestrian post. His first poetic work, a set of elegies called *Amores*, celebrated Corinna, who was probably a composite figure of the women he loved.

His *Ars amatoria,* or *The Handbook of Love,* was a gay parody of Hellenistic didactic poetry. Beginning with an amusing statement of his own credentials, he offered instruction for lovers: how to find them, how to get them, how to hold them, making it plain that "they" were simply the light women whom the standards of the time allowed a man to pursue, if only he did not make a fool of himself or dissipate his resources.

Heroides, or *Letters of Heroines,* purport to be letters written by famous ladies who had been deserted. Medea writes to Jason, Penelope to Odysseus, and a dozen others display with charm and subtlety the feelings of a female heart bruised by the perfidy of a man. In all these poems Ovid has the brevity and polish of the Alexandrians and has added the fine expression of feeling that the earlier Latin elegists had cultivated.

His *Metamorphoses,* however, was a poem of 15,000 hexameter lines, based on the collections made by Greek writers of myths and legends involving changes of form, as when people turn to trees. Ovid strung together 250 of them, starting from the primeval chaos and coming all the way up to the glories of Caesar Augustus. Somehow virtue is generally rewarded and wickedness punished in the stories, although much harm is done by human blindness to values, especially the tendency to mistake female beauty for something worthwhile and lasting. Ovid's debt to Greek work is plain, but the Roman, or perhaps the Italian, charm and subjectivity appear in his work as in that of Lucretius and Catullus, the elegists, and Vergil.

We have already seen in the case of Cicero that the later influence of a Latin author might be exercised strongly at some times and very little at others. Ovid found most acceptance in the late eleventh, twelfth, and thirteenth centuries. His works were regularly read in the schools and were sources especially for writers who catered to the taste of the age for gay and elegant stories. Boccaccio and Chaucer, for example, made good use of him. The best example for our time is Shaw's expansion of Ovid's brief story of Pygmalion and Galatea.

Vergil

Publius Vergilius Maro (70–19 B.C.) was born near Mantua, in northern Italy, the son of a farmer and perhaps manufacturer of pottery who was able to give him a good education in the schools of the region and send him on to Rome to study rhetoric and to try to enter public life. The shy young man got as far as pleading one case in court, then withdrew to Naples to join a circle of Epicureans gathered around the philosopher Siro. There he spent a large part of the rest of his life, although he sometimes came to Rome.

His first work was his book of ten *Eclogues,* or *Bucolics,* probably written between 40 and 38 B.C. The pastoral idylls of the Sicilian Greek Theocritus were plainly his inspiration, for some of the poems imitate Theocritus closely in their themes of shepherd songs and country life, although others turn to Roman themes like the eviction of Italian farmers to make way for the discharged soldiers of Octavian. One, the so-called Messianic Eclogue, speaks of the imminent birth of a baby in whose lifetime a new age is to come on earth.

The Eclogues found many imitators in the early days of European literature, perhaps more among minor than major poets. Eclogues were written in every one of the chief modern languages and on a variety of subjects—on shepherds, as Vergil had done, on fishermen, and even on the life of Christ. The idea of Arcadia (actually a region of the central Peloponnesus) as a land of idyllic peace became a part of common literary property, for Vergil made his shepherds Arcadians in some of the poems.

In the *Georgics,* written during the thirties, Vergil challenged another Greek type, the serious didactic poem. Although Vergil's poem may seem at first glance to be a verse handbook of agriculture in four books, treating of dirt farming, the vine and the olive, cattle, and bees, it also proclaims itself to be in the spirit of Hesiod, whose poem on farming was really a cry for an order of justice in heaven and on the earth, and it plainly is meant to treat of higher things than how to run a simple subsistence farm. With an echo of Lucretius' new idea of Nature as an order of things that can be spoken of as an entity, Vergil seems to be writing in a highly symbolic vein of the way in which man must approach the earth and the great order of the world so as to live rightly.

Vergil next undertook to write an epic, partly at the urging of Maecenas, who for some years now had been his patron and friend. He decided to use the legend, well known to the Greeks, of the escape of Aeneas from burning Troy, his wanderings, and his coming to Italy to found a new people. The founding of the united Trojan and Italian people under the name of Italians could serve to suggest the refounding of Rome and Italy by Augustus. The Romantic preconceptions of the German scholars of the nineteenth century led them to a grotesque misconception of the *Aeneid* as merely an infelicitous attempt to produce an imitation of Homer. Vergil was challenging Homer rather than imitating him, and there are clear and intended reminiscences of Homer all through the poem, while the whole spirit of the work is different and foreign to anything in Homer.

The gods are not the careless aristocrats of Homer, but serious-minded cosmic powers. We learn early in the story that Juno, who gloated over the fall of Troy, is still pursuing the Trojan remnant with her hatred, but that Venus, the goddess mother of Aeneas, is watching over him and that Jove has given her solemn assurance that he will reach Italy, where he will found the Roman people, who are to rule all nations with no limit of space or time. The note of disciplined power restraining violence is sounded clearly as Jove gives his prophecy of Rome's role in the world.

The hero, like the gods, is of a new type that Homer could not have imagined. Achilles was a rather amiable and unusually sensitive young ruffian who had no responsibility but to the heroic code of his time and whose struggles not to break that code are most appealing. Odysseus was the most fascinating of adventurers. Aeneas, although he was a contemporary of theirs in the story, bore the weight of the great nation that Rome had become and of political responsibilities utterly unknown to Homer's delightful primitives or to Homer himself. The qualities desirable in a literary hero had changed, as they were to change again and again in the centuries to come. If we find it hard to imagine how anyone could see a hero in the dogged, dutiful, unglamorous Aeneas, let us remember that there were to be centuries in which the heroes were such men as the gentle St. Francis and that the man about whom Americans want to hear most was an awkward, sad man who bore a lonely burden of state often under contemptuous criticism.

In the sixth book Aeneas, with the help of the gods, visits the underworld to see the spirit of his father. In a sense the whole episode is taken from Homer, since Odysseus went to the edge of the underworld and conversed with some of the shades. Vergil's account is incomparably superior to that of Homer, for instead of being a mere adventure it is closely woven into the story of the spiritual advance of Aeneas and is full of rich description. On this trip Aeneas puts away from him all the claims of the old life and fully accepts the duties of the new. He crosses the River Styx on Charon's boat and sees the realms below and bids goodbye in turn to the shades of people who symbolized Troy and his journey to Italy. Then he goes to the Elysian Fields, where he finds his father and is allowed to see a group of souls of the future great men of Rome as they stand on the bank of the River Lethe; these, his father explains to him, are the coming men of the race that he is to found.

In the last six books Aeneas lands near the mouth of the Tiber, is offered the hand of the Italian princess Lavinia, then has to fight a war stirred up by Juno and Lavinia's former fiancé, and finally prevails. Juno, at Jove's command, gives up her opposition, only asking Jove to agree that Troy be forgotten and the Trojans absorbed into the Italians. At last Aeneas has fulfilled his great destiny and the foundation for Roman greatness is laid.

Quintus Horatius Flaccus (65–8 B.C.)

During the thirties Horace, as he is called in English, published two books of *Satires,* not of the acid type, but rather tolerant and amiable comments on life and values. He and Vergil were great friends, and he had been received into the circle of Maecenas. The *Odes* (23 B.C.) were Horace's chief effort; in the opening poem he says that in these he wishes to show himself a lyric poet, by which he means that he wishes to be recognized as having conquered this Greek genre for Latin literature. The *Odes* are written in the meters used by the Greek lyric poets. Many of them deal with Greek subjects, for instance, hymns to the Olympian gods. The first one in the Alcaic meter begins with a plain imitation of a drinking song by Alcaeus, perhaps to give the Roman reader a key to what the meter was intended to be. A number celebrate Augustus, for the republican soldier Horace (he fought under Brutus at Philippi) accepted the principate in the end. Probably Horace's odes about women have given more pleasure to his readers than any others that he wrote. The tone is always cool and detached and the sentiment almost always agreeable.

Horace had his greatest successes, perhaps, among the literary men of the modern European languages in a far different field from those in which we have seen Cicero and Ovid and Vergil exerting influence, for his superb craftsmanship has tempted innumerable poets (and jinglers) to attempt translations of him. A curious sideline of his influence was that exerted for some time in early modern literature by his *Ars poetica*. This poem was regarded as giving an authoritative set of literary standards, although Horace wrote it as a complimentary poem for two well-born young men who had literary interests and in it advised them to follow with care all the rules of correct composition: to revise and polish and wait nine years for publication—probably good advice for young dilettantes.

Titus Livius (59 B.C.?–A.D. 14? 17?)

Livy, who came from Patavium (Padua) and was a schoolmaster and man of learning rather than a man of affairs, was another in the series of men from outside the city of Rome who in their writings made the composite picture of the old Roman. He set himself in the early days of Augustus to produce a history of the Roman people, of which there were several already, and was so successful that his drove most of the others out of circulation. To him we owe many of our best stories of the stern virtue and public-minded devotion of the old Roman. He is our best source, for example, for the stories of Romulus and Remus, of the rape of Lucretia, and of Horatius at the bridge. When he comes to the Second Punic War, the Senate and the Roman people become the heroes. The fact that the Second Punic War is one of the great literary wars is largely due to Livy's account of it.

Although he did use archives to some extent and also secondary works based on the archives or on other sound primary material, we know that he did not bother with certain good sources that were available to him. He was not above projecting struggles of the late Republic back into the early Republic. He did not have a sound military sense, although some of his battle scenes are fine reading, and he was perhaps not aware of some things that a man versed in government would have known. He has nevertheless given a picture of certain parts of Roman history (a goodly part of the work did not survive) that offers most of the materials for a judgment on military or political affairs at certain points. Without his book we should have far less knowledge of Roman history and of the character of the Romans.

25

THE SUCCESSORS OF AUGUSTUS:
A.D. 14 TO 96

The first group of emperors [1] are known as the Julio-Claudians; in this group were Augustus, Tiberius, Gaius, Claudius, and Nero. At the death of Nero came the first armed struggle over the succession, and in A.D. 68 and 69, Galba, Otho, and Vitellius ascended the throne in quick succession and were driven from it, with Flavius Vespasianus gaining the position of *princeps* in 69 and holding it until his death in A.D. 79. He was succeeded by his sons Titus and Domitian and the three, whose reigns lasted until A.D. 96, are known collectively as the Flavian emperors.

TIBERIUS: A.D. 14 TO 37

Tiberius was armed at the moment of Augustus' death with every power that could help him assume the position held by his predecessor. All the armies were in charge of reliable men of his faction, to whom he immediately sent word of the death of Augustus. He was left as commander-in-chief through the proconsular power, and the armies accepted his succession quietly, so that he did not need to fear their setting up as a rival candidate any ambitious noble or Germanicus, his nephew and adopted son, who was very popular.

[1] Although Augustus asserted that he was restoring the Republic, historians nowadays agree in speaking of the system that resulted from his acts as a monarchy and of the successive heads of state as emperors. Augustus called himself *princeps*, an informal term, on those rare occasions when he put a name to his position. The word was used of his successors, but more often the reigning emperor was referred to as Caesar, no matter what his name was.

Having assured the obedience of the army, Tiberius had to gain a position that in a sense did not exist, since there was no office that Augustus could be said to have held, like king or president, and Tiberius already possessed the important proconsular and tribunician powers. After he had attended to the funeral and the official deification of Augustus, he called a meeting of the Senate and asked it to consider what should be done. Although the details of the process are not clear, we know from the account of the historian Tacitus that a drama was played out in which Tiberius asked the Senate to appoint one or more successors to the tasks of Augustus and that a number of senators perversely refused to play their parts, instead asking him embarrassing questions about his own attitude in the matter. In the end he seems to have been voted Augustus' place as *princeps senatus*, or chief of the Senate (which was not the same thing as the general and unofficial word *princeps*, which would have described his whole position), and a life tenure of the proconsular and tribunician powers; this was equivalent to putting him at the head of the government. He accepted with a reluctance that was probably genuine. The precedent set in the reign of Augustus that the powers of the *princeps* were granted by the Senate was thus confirmed and prevailed, at least in theory, for centuries. Tiberius was thus secure in the legal right to his position and reasonably secure against being robbed of it by force.

Through long experience during the regime of Augustus he knew how to exercise his power in its positive aspect, that of causing the tasks of government to be performed, and his general policy was simply to follow the methods of Augustus, although the pride and haughtiness (apparently mixed with sensitivity and shyness) of his heritage as a Claudian made it impossible for him to match Augustus' tact and graciousness and sense of what people in general would feel. The Senate had had time under Augustus to become used to the new system and was now composed of serious and experienced men ready to share with Tiberius the tasks of government.

Tiberius' acts and attitudes in government were conservative. He was careful about the minutiae of religious observance and severe toward the foreign cults and their devotees. In A.D. 19 the scandalous conduct of the priests of Isis in taking bribes to help a man complete a seduction led to their crucifixion and the destruction of their temple, and a fraud practiced in the name of religion by some Jews on a Roman lady led to the expulsion of Jews from Italy and the sending of four thousand Jewish freedmen to Sardinia as a police force. He was as ready to be severe with the Roman populace as with these foreign elements, for he curtailed the government's expenditure on the games and shows, which the people loved and at which they often amused themselves by riotous conduct. At one time he expelled all the actors from Italy when complaints had been made of their conduct, and he put restrictions on the size and cost of shows given in places outside Rome.

Not only was his task made more difficult by the insolence of certain nobles, but he also had difficulties with members of his own family. His mother, Livia, was a woman of strong personality who had married Augustus back in the early days of Augustus' career and felt qualified now and then to take a hand in affairs of state. His nephew and adopted son Germanicus had an ambitious wife, Agrippina, and was popular with the army and the people, so that Tiberius had some ground for uneasiness about him. When the army in the Balkans mutinied early in the reign with complaints of poor pay, poor land as bonus on discharge, and lengthened terms of service, Tiberius' son Drusus restored discipline with a mixture of remedies and severity, but Germanicus, who commanded the army on the Rhine, allowed the mutiny there rather to take its course, asserting his authority only after the men had committed excesses against their ringleaders of which they themselves repented. Germanicus' campaigns were marked more by attempts to gain glory than by sound political planning and good strategy. When Tiberius recalled him from his command and sent him to the East on an important diplomatic mission, he and his wife and the many nobles who can be said to have formed their party at Rome accused the *princeps* of jealousy. In A.D. 19 Germanicus died in the East under suspicious circumstances that we cannot interpret with certainty, although a legate whom Tiberius had sent out to the East was formally accused of murdering him.

The republican law of *maiestas,* under which it had been possible to prosecute those who diminished the majesty of the Roman people—for example, by outrageous neglect of duty or by incompetence that led to the defeat of an army—was extended by Augustus through the *lex Iulia de maiestate* to acts tending to diminish the majesty of the *princeps* and to words as well, which had been permissible under the old laws. The new law of *maiestas* was made the basis of a number of prosecutions plainly intended to determine how far one could go with it, for among the Romans as among the Greeks the absence of a district attorney or public prosecutor gave rise to professional prosecutors seeking a quarter of the victim's goods given as a reward, so that many prosecutions were motivated by greed rather than by public spirit. The historian Tacitus, who lived through a period at the end of the century when this law was made an engine of tyranny, speaks with more emotion than accuracy of its use under Tiberius. Although he used his authority to repel with scorn and anger some attempts to misuse it, Tiberius yet felt that the laws must be enforced. Although the subject of trials for treason under this law is a controversial one, there is good evidence for the view that the men convicted of *maiestas* (generally by the Senate sitting as a court) were probably guilty of genuinely treasonous activities and were dealt with by proper legal procedures.

In contrast to the many people who tried the patience of Tiberius, either intentionally or by being difficult people, stood Aelius Sejanus, prefect of the Praetorian Guard, whose efficiency and energy commended him to the emperor. He persuaded Tiberius shortly after A.D. 20 that the nine cohorts of the Praetorian Guard should all be in Rome and had a barracks for them built on the edge of the city. In the year 26 Tiberius took the strange step of retiring from Rome to Campania and then to the island of Capri, never to return to the city, presumably because he found life there utterly distasteful. Sejanus, since he was in charge of the military force in Rome and enjoyed the emperor's confidence, began to seem even more powerful than he had been before Tiberius went away. There are hints in the Roman writers of his devising a complicated plot to seize the throne for himself, year by year eliminating one and another of the members of the imperial house, among them Tiberius' son Drusus, whose birth would commend them for the succession. In the year 31, however, Tiberius is said to have been warned by Antonia, the widow of his brother Drusus, of what was going on and to have arranged a coup which should suddenly remove Sejanus from the protection of the guardsmen, give the command to a trustworthy man, and bring Sejanus down. Another possibility, a much less fascinating but rather more likely one, is that Tiberius became worried about the power that naturally attached itself to Sejanus during his own absence from Rome and decided that he had allowed him to wax too powerful and that he must somehow remove him.

Probably the most important aspect of Tiberius' retirement, which lasted until his death in A.D. 37, is that it was possible for the government to continue as it had. Although our sources speak darkly of orgies on Capri, we must suppose that the *princeps* took with him a large entourage of secretaries and serious advisers and that the business of the head of state was assiduously attended to, while in Rome the Senate also carried on the many tasks of government that belonged to it, and in the provinces the governors and generals were also working efficiently and were conscious that the government had an active head who was overseeing them. Obviously Capri was even more accessible than Rome for most of the reports that flowed in steadily from all over the Mediterranean world. The picture offered by some modern writers of a solitary and morose tyrant governing by decrees sent from a remote solitude can hardly be correct.

The "Tiberian terror" offers more of a problem to the modern historian. Tacitus speaks of unending judicial slaughters after the deposition and death of Sejanus. Tacitus, like Thucydides, often offers generalizations that can be disproved from his own detailed account, and in this case his report of a few trials warrants us only in believing that a certain number of people were prosecuted by due process of law for genuine crimes, not merely for adherence to Sejanus. On the other hand, the fall of Sejanus must have caused terror among the large party that surrounded him until it was plain whether the government did intend to persecute his former supporters, and the sudden removal of such a nucleus of power must have caused many painful adjustments for people who had attached themselves to him.

If the stream of domestic affairs was occasionally roiled by jealousies within the imperial family, by the affair of Sejanus or by lesser ones of the sort, or shadowed by professional informers who wished to fish in troubled waters, its current generally ran deep and true in the old republican channel as it had been modified by Augustus, for Tiberius aimed to imitate Augustus in his management of affairs. The Senate did do somewhat more legislating and did act as a court for important cases. The prefect of the Praetorian Guard and the prefect of the city became rather important. In general there was prosperity except for the financial crisis of A.D. 33. The amount of money in circulation seems to have fallen, interest rates rose beyond the legal limit, there were prosecutions for usury, and debtors and creditors alike were caught in the turmoil that arose from the attempts of individuals to free money to pay off obligations that no one had expected to have to meet so quickly. The emperor urged the Senate to make a large amount of money available for loans for a three-year term on adequate security in land, and the crisis quickly passed. Tiberius was officially generous to cities that had suffered disasters from earthquake or fire, and he supplied the money necessary for certain men of good family, whose ancestors had not conserved the family property, to be able to re-enter the active senatorial life.

Although there were no major wars during the reign of Tiberius, there were many minor operations needed to keep the peace in so large a realm. On the German border there was often some minor activity. The pressure of Roman settlement and of orderly ways in North Africa provoked the resistance of the nomad Musulamii, who saw themselves threatened in their ranging back and forth with their animals across the southern borders of the Roman territory. After several campaigns against an elusive group of opponents, the Romans put down the resistance of these people and began a long process of converting them to a more settled way of life that suited the provincial governors and the taxgatherers better and in the end brought some of the nomads, now grandees of the towns they had created, into the wider service of the Empire. A local revolt in Gaul, which soon was put down, probably was caused by a combination of restlessness under Roman rule, the strain on the men and money of the country caused by the campaigns of Germanicus in Germany, and possibly the suppression of the old worship of the Druids.

The trial and the death of Jesus Christ throw a bright light on one little sector of provincial government, where the incompetence and tactlessness of the procurator Pontius Pilate had aroused bitter resentment among the Jews, whose customs he neither understood nor respected. He had been there since A.D. 26, and by the time of the trial of Jesus, which probably took place in A.D. 33, he was anxious to settle any such difficult matters as expeditiously as he could, caring nothing for the life of one of "the natives." Three years later he was removed from his post by his superior.

Tiberius, like Augustus, tried to maneuver members of his family into position to succeed him and was frustrated by their dying before him. In his last years he summoned his great-nephew, Gaius, to live with him at Capri. This son of Tiberius' deceased nephew Germanicus had the nickname Caligula, or "Little Boots," from the fact that his ambitious mother Agrippina, who went to the German frontier with Germanicus, used to dress him in a little soldier's outfit and show him off to the troops. He was born in A.D. 12. His mother Agrippina gave him his Julian blood, being the daughter of Agrippa and of Julia, the daughter of Augustus. His father Germanicus was the son of Drusus, the brother of Tiberius; hence his Claudian blood. Gaius' cousin Tiberius Gemellus, son of Tiberius' son Drusus, was born in A.D. 19. Tiberius named these two young men in his will as his joint heirs. Neither had been given any of the training that a future *princeps* needed, either in warfare or in government, and neither had been invested with the imperium or the tribunician power. Gaius acceded to the principate in a simple way: on Tiberius' death the Senate declared his will invalid and bestowed the usual powers of the principate on Gaius, who thereupon adopted Tiberius Gemellus as his son.

GAIUS: A.D. 37 TO 41

The general and apparently genuine rejoicing at the accession of Gaius was natural enough, since a handsome and engaging young man, the son of the popular Germanicus, was succeeding an admirable but gloomy *princeps* and was promising to follow the methods of Augustus and to cooperate with the Senate. It is unfortunate that the part of Tacitus' work that dealt with this reign is lost and that sources like Suetonius' biography are not serious studies of government, for Gaius' attitude and policy changed radically before the end of the year 37 in the direction of frivolity and tyranny. He had a serious illness in September, 37, and the theory was put forward by senatorial writers that he became mad. It seems more reasonable to suppose that he was not mad, but was a young man who had been too much with an embittered widowed mother and with irresponsible eastern princelings living as hostages at Rome and not enough among men who were doing responsible work and trying to train him.

As soon as he recovered from his illness, we are told, he began to display a tendency to arbitrary and tyrannical rule. He misused the judicial power of his position to order the death of a number of people, among them his cousin Tiberius Gemellus. He gave large gifts from the treasury, apparently for the pleasure of feeling able to do so. He encouraged informers and professional prosecutors and confiscated the estates of wealthy men.

In the autumn of 39 he went to Gaul for great expeditions against the Germans and Britain. The resentment of writers of the senatorial class appears especially in the accounts of his campaigns as ridiculous pretenses. The assaults against the Germans in fact amounted to little, and the invasion of Britain was not attempted; probably the most successful part of his trip was the confiscation of some of the great Gallic fortunes. When he returned, in 40, he announced himself the open enemy of the Senate. He now proclaimed his own divinity. His rapacity and cruelty increased. In January, A.D. 41, he and his wife and daughter were murdered, the plot being led by a tribune of the praetorians out of personal resentment.

All the excesses of Gaius cannot be said to have shaken or changed the framework of government. He had rather thrown into relief the fact that there were no controls on the *princeps*. Nothing in the careers of Augustus or Tiberius called for such restraints. Checks on the power of a monarch can come only from the demands of minor wielders of power, like those who extorted Magna Charta from King John; in imperial Rome the Senate, the only group that could logically make such demands and support them with power, had been put at such a disadvantage by Augustus and was so shrewdly controlled by his successors that it could never combine to make an effective demand or a threat. Yet it would be wrong to say that the government was now an autocracy tempered only by the fear of assassination, for it remained in spirit a government of law and one responsive to tradition and to public opinion, in spite of the fantasies and illegal acts of Gaius.

CLAUDIUS: A.D. 41 TO 54

Claudius, who was born in 10 B.C., was the son of Tiberius' brother Drusus and thus was the younger brother of Germanicus and the uncle of Gaius. He had some disease or nervous injury in his early years or from his birth that affected the control of his muscles and the clarity of his speech, making him so unattractive and so apparently incompetent that Augustus had not allowed him to go through the civil and military positions that trained the young men of the imperial family. He was even kept out of sight on many public occasions. There is evidence in a letter of Augustus, however, that he recognized a surprisingly lively intelligence in Claudius. His intelligence may well have been high enough to alienate him from the generality, and his awkwardness of limbs and speech must have had much the same effect, so that he found it impossible to have even the normal social life of a prince and to learn something from experience of all the little adjustments that one must constantly make to maintain easy intercourse with people in general.

Just as he was a completely new type in the growing gallery of imperial personalities, so his accession was novel. After Gaius had been struck down, a soldier who was looking through the rooms of the palace found Claudius hiding behind a tapestry and with others carried him off to the camp of the Guard on the edge of the city. While the Senate was debating a proposal to restore the Republic and at the same time some of its members were trying to gather support for their own aspirations to the vacant throne, the populace was calling for Claudius as the man clearly in line for the position, and the soldiers of the Guard, too, were ready to accept him. He finally promised the Guard 15,000 sesterces apiece (the first of many times that presents were offered to them by aspirants to the throne) and was saluted as *princeps* by them. The Senate, which could not agree on a policy and had no power at hand to oppose that of the soldiers and the populace, recognized him and gave him the imperium, the tribunician power, and the position of Pontifex Maximus.

His Government

It would be interesting to have a minutely detailed account of the early part of Claudius' reign of nearly fourteen years so that we could see how this inexperienced and unsocial man of forty-nine went about taking control of the ponderous machinery of government, which was being managed by a great many men of more experience and, as it doubtless seemed to them, of more ability. We do know that he sensibly declared that whatever had been said and done in the two days when the principate had no occupant should be forgotten; the murderers of Gaius were punished, however. He immediately made it known that he would take Augustus as his model in government and would cooperate with the Senate, thus creating expectations of a reign pleasanter than that of Tiberius and better than that of Gaius. The people whom Gaius had sent into exile were recalled, what he had stolen in the way of money or works of art was restored, if possible, and some of his worst creatures were put to death.

To take hold of the routine work of the *princeps* that must go on from year to year was more difficult, especially since Claudius had not been allowed to participate either in social life or in the tasks of government. He either was aware, however, or was made aware of the great value of causing the coinage to present his personality and his ideas to the public in as favorable a light as possible. Some of the money in the unusually varied coinage of his first year carried the legend *ob cives servatos,* "because of saving the lives of citizens," which had been used in granting honors to Augustus and had since then become a symbol of cooperation between the *princeps* and the Senate. The legend on other coins referred to his acceptance by the Praetorian Guard. The figures and legends on some combined to symbolize a subtle combination of ideas that had been used since Augustus: peace, safety, prosperity, old-fashioned modesty. The design and workmanship of the coins was improved, and in general they give the impression that we often get from the study of this reign that a highly competent administrator was directing a good many aspects of the work in his own way.

Presumably many senators who might have worked directly with Claudius were unwilling to do so because they did not believe him competent and found him repulsive; he may well have hesitated to invite men to close cooperation. The sources tell us only that he found four freedmen of great ability (we must remember that much highly expert work, even of an executive nature, was done by slaves) and that he and this team, who constituted what we should call a cabinet, worked very hard and supervised closely all the business of government. One, Narcissus, was chief secretary; his control of all the correspondence made him a very useful man and gave him proportionate power and influence. Pallas was in charge of all financial matters. Two other secretaries dealt with petitions presented to the emperor and with the details of the matters brought before him in his judicial capacity. Although both earlier and later emperors made some use of slave and freedmen secretaries, this group of four was spoken of with especial distaste by people of the time, perhaps because Claudius did not have the natural executive manner that would repress arrogance in them and prevent misuse of their power.

Claudius can be said to have increased the part played in government by the *princeps* and his appointees and lessened the role of the Senate. More new posts went to equestrians than to senators. The efficiency of the freedmen of the cabinet also tended to draw functions under their control, especially in finance. Although the Roman authors often say that Claudius was repeatedly deceived by his freedmen and had little idea of what was being done in the government, the modern historian, having access to many imperial decrees found on papyri or inscribed on stone, tends to feel that he had an administrative style of his own that shines through repeatedly in the decrees and that he probably had a remarkable command of the details of government.

His Wives

We hear most of his last two wives, Messalina and Agrippina, the first of whom was a dissolute female and the second a managing one. The gruesome antics of these two are probably the high spots in the careers of the women of the Caesars, some of whom, like Augustus' Livia or Germanicus' Agrippina, were people of formidable managerial competence, while others tended through their frailty to complicate the task of keeping the royal family respectable. Messalina was said to have an insatiable appetite for men and to have inspired a deadly fear in youths of the upper class, who dreaded to be singled out for favors that they could not refuse and that brought with them the peril of death. Messalina at last went to the length of going through a marriage ceremony with a young noble named Silius, alleging that an oracle had said that Messalina's husband must die and that she was dragging Silius into that role to save Claudius. Narcissus, the most devoted to Claudius of the freedmen, insisted on her execution, which took place in A.D. 48. A contest is said to have followed to choose a new wife for Claudius, with the freedmen advancing the claims of various spirited ladies. The winner (A.D. 49) was Claudius' niece Agrippina (sometimes called Agrippina the Younger), daughter of Claudius' brother Germanicus. She was twice a widow—she was believed to have poisoned her second husband, Lucius Domitius Ahenobarbus, to gain control of his wealth—and had a son, Lucius Domitius Ahenobarbus, born in A.D. 37. The Roman feeling for propriety and legality was satisfied by the Senate's declaring that an uncle and niece were not within the prohibited degrees of consanguinity.

And so they were married. The lady, although her charms were capable of stirring the pulse of an uncle no longer young, was the other kind of bad woman. She set herself to gain power, apparently to advance the cause of her young son. In 49 the philosopher and writer Lucius Annaeus Seneca was recalled from an exile visited on him by the jealousy of the emperor Gaius and made tutor of her son. In the year 52 she succeeded in gaining the post of prefect of the Praetorian Guard for her nominee, Afranius Burrus. In the year 50 she persuaded Claudius to adopt her son, whose name was now to be Nero Claudius Caesar, and to make him guardian for his own son by a former wife, Britannicus, who was five years younger. In 51 young Nero was presented with the *toga virilis,* and a consulship was designated for him when he should be twenty. In A.D. 53, at the age of fifteen, he was married to Claudius' young daughter Octavia.

Agrippina might suppose that all had now been so arranged that her son would probably succeed Claudius; as a great-great-grandson of Augustus and the adoptive son of the reigning emperor he ought to eclipse any claim of the young Britannicus. But the old rivalry between her and the still powerful Narcissus was so intensified by circumstances in the year 54 that she became afraid that Narcissus might persuade her husband to change the arrangements that had been made for Nero. To prevent such interference with her plans she poisoned Claudius. The succession of Nero to the throne went off smoothly, since the Praetorian Guard was offered a gift equal to that that Claudius had given them on his accession and since they, the provincial armies, and the people were pleased with Nero's descent from Augustus and his attractive manner. They had reason to hope for a good reign from an ingenuous boy who was watched over by the daughter of Germanicus and by Seneca and Burrus, two very able men who came from the provinces and would understand the desires of the whole Empire. For the supreme power to pass thus from one person to another by domestic treason, common as it was in the Near East, was uncommon in the Roman Empire.

An Assessment of Claudius' Reign

Claudius may be said to have managed with some success the negative side of the imperial power, that of getting the position and holding it, in spite of the way in which he lost it, and he was successful on the positive side, that of using the imperial power to get done the work of government. He was punctilious in his respect for the Senate and attempted to encourage its functioning as a part of the government, even though some of his measures of efficiency transferred certain Senate functions to his own bureaus or to his procurators.

He seems to have given great offense to the senators by his legislative activity and his interest in the functioning of the courts. All through this century the increased agenda of the courts with the growth of the population and of business activity plainly necessitated the construction of new buildings for courts and the freeing of more days formerly forbidden for the holding of courts. Claudius offended the senators, however, by brusquely interfering in the procedures of the courts so as to promote the disposal of their business.

Claudius could deal with the people, the army, and foreign nations without encountering such rudeness as he provoked in the senators. Like Augustus, he seems himself to have enjoyed the simple bloody pastimes that pleased the people and to have been generous in presenting animal hunts and gladiatorial contests. He was happy in his choice of generals, in spite of their coming from the senatorial order; his nominees proved their skill in winning their battles and in disciplining their men and continued to distinguish themselves by good work under Nero.

In Africa the nomad Musulamii, subdued under Tiberius, revolted against the steady pressure of the Romans to make them settle down to agriculture, and to the West in Mauretania a revolt stirred by Gaius' deposition and murder of King Ptolemy lasted into the reign of Claudius. Such arbitrary deposition of client kings was not uncommon and usually did not provoke armed resistance. Two new provinces were formed, Mauretania Caesariensis, covering part of modern western Algeria, and Mauretania Tingitana farther west, with its capital at Tingis (Tangier) and with territory extending down the Atlantic coast. The area had been brought along toward civilization by its king, Juba II, whom Augustus installed and to whom he gave as wife Cleopatra Selene, one of the daughters of Antony and Cleopatra; probably she encouraged him in his attempts to make his capital of Caesarea a brilliant city by the importation of Greek artists.

Claudius added Britain to the Empire by a brisk campaign in A.D. 43. This conquest was suggested not only by the wisdom of an emperor's having a military exploit to show, but also by the desirability, seen by Julius Caesar in 55 B.C. and never forgotten, of removing the constant irritation and incitement of the peoples of Gaul by the Belgic element who controlled much of southern Britain. Britain remained something of an outpost of empire, hardly paying its way materially and contributing almost no notable personnel. Its four centuries under the Romans may perhaps help to give us a longer and broader view of history as we reflect that to the Romans the inhabitants of England were a part of the burden of empire and had a very long way to go before becoming really civilized.

Along the line of the Rhine and the Danube the Roman government was active and vigilant. A powerful German tribe was willing to take the king whom the Romans named for them. Noricum (roughly modern Austria), annexed in 16 B.C., was made an imperial province under the governorship of an equestrian procurator. Roads were built in the region of Noricum and Raetia (Switzerland). The troublesome Thracian kings were retired in A.D. 44, and their kingdom received another equestrian procurator as governor; Moesia (roughly modern Bulgaria) also was given a governor to replace its king.

Claudius' measures for improving the shipment of grain from overseas to Rome are interesting as an early example of arrangements that the government made with businessmen to get essential work done. Claudius' arrangement took the form of bounties and of agreements to make good any loss from storms for those who had ships or would build them and contract to have them available in early summer when the grain was ready to be carried. The government also improved the unloading facilities at Ostia by building two moles that formed the arms of an artificial harbor that could be entered through an opening where the arms almost met. Although not safe in rough weather, this simple harbor was a great improvement on the open roadstead where the ships had formerly unloaded into lighters. Many ships still discharged their cargoes at Puteoli, on the Bay of Naples, the nearest really good harbor; goods for Rome had then to go up the coast in small vessels.

NERO: A.D. 54 TO 68

His Accession and Early Years

Nero's accession was solemnized on October 13, 54 by the Senate's conferring the usual powers on him, for recognition by the Senate continued to seem the final seal of legitimacy, even for those who came to the throne by murder or the support of the praetorians or the army. He made a good impression by delivering a speech composed for him by Seneca in which he promised in effect not to encroach upon the province of the Senate as Claudius had done. Apparently Seneca felt that the Senate objected very strongly to such encroachment.

Seneca, who held no post except the unofficial one of friend of Caesar, and Burrus, the praetorian prefect, were in a delicate position because of Agrippina's desire for power, for both were nominees of Agrippina and both had assisted Nero to the throne. Agrippina's power was due in some measure to her descent from Germanicus and Augustus, and she had worked carefully to gain influence over men in the government. Pallas, for instance, who continued in charge of finances under Nero, was a useful ally. Her having influence of some sort in the mint, perhaps by controlling the official in charge, is shown by the prominence given her, with Nero, on the coins of the last few years of Claudius' reign and those of the first few months of Nero's. She frankly attempted to become coregent with her son. Tacitus tells that Nero, having been coached by Seneca, was about to receive some ambassadors, when Agrippina slipped in the side door of the hall, evidently intending to sit beside him and join in the proceedings. Seneca had him go quickly to meet her and send her away.

Only a few facts betray the struggle for position that doubtless was concealed from most people at the time. In A.D. 55 Britannicus was poisoned, and a handful of men who had some relation to former emperors were killed or exiled; this may well have been done to eliminate eligibles whom Agrippina might try to put in Nero's place if driven to desperate moves. The coinage of the year 55 tells the story of her gradual decline in power as succeeding issues made her less prominent. In that year Pallas was dismissed—a sore blow to her. Tacitus gives a vivid picture of the fury and the blandishments with which she tried to regain her ascendancy over her son.

Meanwhile Seneca oversaw the workings of the government and assiduously promoted the idea of an austere but benevolent regime. The governors of provinces and the tax collectors were watched more strictly, the obstructive powers of the tribunes (which had not been used for many decades) were taken from them, and the insolent conduct of some freedmen was curbed. The great empire was well governed and prosperous. Meanwhile the young head of the organization had taken to roaming about the streets at night in the company of some of the gayer spirits among the nobility, as well as some of lower origins. In A.D. 58 he fell head over heels in love with a beautiful and dangerous married woman, Poppaea Sabina. The lady, the young aristocrats, and ambitious men from the lower classes all urged him to assert himself, all thinking of possible advantage to themselves.

In A.D. 59 Nero had his mother murdered. If his less desirable advisers became more influential thereafter, the Empire still continued in general to be well governed. In 62 Burrus died, and Seneca, feeling that there probably was not much use in his trying to go on without Burrus, requested leave to go into retirement. Nero now divorced Octavia, daughter of Claudius, who had been his wife since 53, and added her murder to that of his mother. He then married Poppaea.

The Fire

The great fire began the night of July 18, A.D. 64, and spread rapidly through a city built of inflammable materials and without an adequate fire department. Nero, who was vacationing at Antium a little way down the coast, hurried to the scene and showed himself capable of taking charge in a disaster. He directed measures for fighting the fire and repressing disorder, arranged for shelter for the homeless, and reorganized the food supply for the emergency. The accusation was made that he had deliberately caused the fire so as to be able to build in the devastated area, but it must be rejected along with the charge that he sang arias on the fall of Troy of his own composing while the fire raged (his contemporaries did not say that Nero fiddled while Rome burned).

The persecution of the Christians belongs to the complex of events connected with the fire, for it was probably instituted to give the lower classes an outlet for the wrath aroused by the fire and thus to recover some of the popularity that in general Nero enjoyed among them and that he prized. The suspicion that Nero himself had arranged for the fire was doubtless increased by the fact that he took a huge tract of land, two hundred acres, in the most populous part of the city, to build himself a country place in the city, the chief feature of which was the Golden House, a palace. It was to have the forests, the meadows, and the little lake of an idyllic site well out in the country. Later the practical-minded Vespasian restored the land to general use and built the Colosseum for the people's pleasure where the lake had been.

Other areas of the city were rebuilt so as to be more beautiful, spacious, and fire-resistant. The populace apparently took this as another reason for believing that Nero had started the fire. Tacitus, on the other hand, described the fire in terms of the old republican associations of what was destroyed and spoke slightingly of the new broad streets because they did not keep out the sun as the old narrow ones had done, although he granted that the use of stone facings and the requirement of space between buildings would help to prevent other large fires.

His Policies

Nero encouraged Greek influence in art and education, in the glorification of the capital city by rebuilding it, and in the exaltation of his position to that of a divinely inspired monarch. He made some effort to change the character of public amusements in Rome toward the more refined and less bloody Greek type. He built a new amphitheater, a gymnasium, and baths as part of this program.

Although he had been interested for some years now in composing poetry and in singing, he gave his first public performance in the year of the fire. The fact seems to be that he was a passable artist and sincerely interested. Strange as it may seem to the modern mind, he apparently believed that his music would bring him nearer to the god Apollo, for it was possible for a king (or a man) in those days to believe that he had a connection with one or more divinities.

The great conspiracy of the year 65 aimed to murder Nero and to replace him by a popular nobleman, C. Calpurnius Piso. The populace was disenchanted with Nero, but powerless. The upper classes resented the growth of the emperor's power and their inability to retain their own functions in government; they found his appearances as artist degrading and shameful; they were disgusted and enraged by his appointing men from the East of no social standing, even freedmen, to the great prefectures and procuratorships. The emperor's control of the instruments of power was such that the senatorial and equestrian orders could not force a change on him. The conspiracy was betrayed as the great moment drew near, many people were executed, and thereafter the *princeps*, thoroughly frightened, carried on a campaign of terror against the upper classes.

Late in the year 66 Nero began a tour of the East to give artistic performances and perhaps attend to the frontier question. A great revolt of the Jews broke out almost at this moment, however, and engaged the armed forces for some time. For a whole year Nero paraded through Greece giving concerts and naturally winning first prize in every competition. He also started construction of a canal through the Isthmus of Corinth, a project that was abandoned at his death and not carried through until modern times.

Nero lost the imperial power by raising up justified opposition to himself, by somewhat neglecting the cultivation of his sources of power (he did not trouble to commend himself to the army), and by being irresolute in the crisis. Early in 68, Vindex, a romanized Gaul who governed the province of Gallia Lugdunensis, with its center at Lyons, led a revolt that was proclaimed as both against Nero and for Gallic autonomy. The governor of Spain, Sulpicius Galba, joined Vindex in opposing Nero and declared himself the representative of the Senate and the Roman people as a way of suggesting himself for Nero's place. He was joined by Salvius Otho, governor of Lusitania, and by the quaestor in charge of the province of Baetica in Spain, but by no one else. Although Vindex and his supporters in Gaul were overcome without great difficulty by the Rhine army, which guarded Gaul as well as the German frontier, the senatorial order at Rome was ready to do anything that it could against Nero. No strong military action was imminent, but Nero was unable to assert himself and take control of the armed forces; he finally gave up his own cause for lost when he learned that the Praetorian Guard had been persuaded to take the side of the Senate, which had proclaimed Sulpicius Galba as emperor. His death lacked even such dignity as had attended those of Gaius and Claudius, for he fled, then attempted to kill himself, but lacked the nerve and had to ask a faithful freedman to dispatch him.

THE YEAR OF THE FOUR EMPERORS: A.D. 68–69

Galba, Otho, and Vitellius

Galba's reign of seven months, from June, 68, to mid-January, 69, was a failure. He was of an old family, seasoned in affairs if never distinguished, and seventy-three years old at his accession. Tacitus says, "He was agreed by all to be capable of ruling, if only he had not ruled." Galba's misplaced firmness, his meanness with money where at least moderate generosity was indicated, his failure to exert leadership over the soldiers, and his alienation of the Senate by choosing advisers not of their number combined to keep him from building a secure position. He attempted to gain strength by adopting a younger man as colleague, but did not have sense enough to choose a strong young man with good qualifications.

Salvius Otho, who had joined Galba at the beginning, hoping to succeed him, and who had been spinning plots and spending money to that end, saw that he must act at once. On January 15, 69, he had both Galba and Galba's newly adopted son murdered and was himself proclaimed emperor by the Praetorian Guard, to which he had distributed bribes and promises. His principate did not last until the summer, although he avoided the mistakes that Galba made. The legions of the Rhine had refused to swear allegiance to Galba in the usual ceremony held in January, had proclaimed their general Aulus Vitellius as emperor, and had begun a march to Italy even before they heard that Otho had taken Galba's place. Naturally this news did not stop them, once they were on the way, and the fact that Otho had been elevated by the Praetorian Guard only inflamed them, since the advantages and the easy life of the praetorians were a source of annoyance to the soldiers of the frontier armies. Although the armies of the Danube and the East swore allegiance to Otho, they were far away. After much delay Otho gathered an army, met the forces of Vitellius in northern Italy, suffered a defeat, and took his own life.

The reign of Vitellius was as much a failure as those of Galba and Otho, for he was lazy and gluttonous as well as lacking in the qualities of a good chief executive. Tacitus' remark has often been quoted that the armies discovered at this time the secret that emperors could be created elsewhere than at Rome. This is true, but we must add that the armies created three singularly incompetent emperors. The whole complex of events underlines the fact that the Romans of the period could sometimes have very great difficulty with a problem that confronts almost all governments, that of keeping the army from interfering with politics, a problem that can never be forgotten by those who govern. Although the armies have traditionally been given credit for creating Vespasian, there is evidence that although a vigorous party of officers in the East organized a movement to raise him, they gained the adherence of several governors of provinces and of many people at Rome, so that his support really came from a well organized faction—so well organized that it was somewhat embarrassing later to find posts and plums with which to reward all who were active in the early stage of the movement.

Vespasian's Rise

Vespasian was not connected by blood with the former emperors, nor was he of the nobility, for his father had been a quiet member of the equestrian order. Vespasian and his brother became members of the senatorial order, however, and Vespasian was a good servant of the government in the usual series of both civilian and military posts, while his brother attained the high position of prefect of the city. Vespasian had commanded a legion in Britain, was consul in 51, had governed Africa, and for two years had commanded the forces dealing with the Jewish revolt. The movement for Vespasian was openly proclaimed on the first of July, 69, and before the end of December Vitellius was dead and Vespasian was acknowledged as *princeps*. There is no need to summarize the disgusting and depressing account of the intervening civil war given by Tacitus in his *Histories*.

THE FLAVIAN DYNASTY: A.D. 69 TO 96

Vespasian's Reform

Titus Flavius Vespasianus, who ruled from 69 to 79, is generally known as Vespasian; his elder son, who ruled from 79 to 81, is referred to as Titus; his younger son, who ruled from 81 to 96, is called Domitian; together they are known as the Flavians. Vespasian, who became emperor through civil war, had neither descent from Augustus nor senatorial ancestry to lend him prestige. The fact that he had two sons, of whom the elder by several years was already mature and experienced, had appealed to his supporters and now commended him to everyone. He faced the task of bringing back the general sense of peace and prosperity and of restoring the confidence of the whole body of the people. "The man of good sense," as a modern historian has called him, was well fitted to inspire trust by his obvious competence and his calm, matter-of-fact manner.

In the East the army, commanded by Titus, finished the slow reduction of Jerusalem in September, 70. Although those Jews in Palestine and elsewhere who had not joined the revolt suffered no punishment, and although the survivors of the revolt were not in fact severely penalized, the Temple was not to be rebuilt, and the peculiar Jewish combination of a religious and political government was ended, so the Jews, wherever they were in the Empire, were organized in local congregations rather than being able to look to a government of their own with its spiritual center in the Temple. Titus was able to return to Rome and to celebrate his triumph in 71. In addition to the ordinary powers, the proconsular and the tribunician, which would be accorded to a son to associate him with his father, he was given the command of the Praetorian Guard, possibly with the double purpose of establishing him more clearly as the destined successor of his father and of securing the succession (and public confidence) better by firmer control of the Guard. Both sons were given the title of Caesar at once, and both were associated more than once in the consulship with their father.

To repair the ravages of the public finances by Nero's expenditures on his pleasures and his large projects was necessary both to restore public confidence and for proper management. Vespasian put the sum needed at forty billion sesterces, or something like two billion dollars. He did not claim as inheritance Nero's very extensive personal properties and those he had confiscated as emperor, but had them managed as the property of the crown. He annoyed and scandalized some people by selling whatever he could, like some of the old palaces in Egypt. He raised the taxes, which probably was not unfair, since prosperity had increased and values had risen during the preceding century. He devised new sources of income, like the small charge for the use of the public urinals, which is said to have disgusted the elegant Titus. He instituted a great review of the land registers in an attempt to hunt out *subseciva,* or scraps of land left unsurveyed and unassigned in both Italy and the provinces. As cries of pain and rage arose from people who had long occupied such land and felt that they had acquired possession by usage, he agreed to stop, but did not relinquish what he had taken. The government's interest in a precise survey of all land did not cease, and a second-century writer on surveying remarks that in the provinces much of the work of the courts was on litigation between the municipalities and Caesar to establish precisely the boundaries between municipal lands and the very numerous estates that belonged to the imperial government.

Yet Vespasian was not a miser nor shortsighted about expenditure. The rebuilding of the temple of Jove on the Capitoline, which was burned during the civil strife, was done in proper fashion. He used the site of Nero's lake for the great structure for the people's pleasure that is properly called the Flavian Amphitheater, but became known as the Colosseum. He built the beautiful Forum of Peace next to that of Augustus. He gave grants to impoverished men to enable them to remain in the senatorial order, as earlier emperors had done; he gave subventions to literary men, and he even established the rhetorician Quintilian as public professor of the art of effective speaking with a generous salary from the treasury.

Vespasian's measures for the development and use of manpower were very shrewd. He encouraged many men of the sober municipal class, who hitherto had thought only of belonging to the equestrian order, to accept membership in the Senate, thus finding a new source of good men and incidentally bringing a new note of frugality and sobriety to the society of the capital. He began a steady pressure on the leading people of the provinces to romanize themselves, especially urging them to send their children to schools that would teach them Roman ways and the familiar use of Latin spoken with a good accent, and encouraging the building of cities with such Roman features as forums, capitols, and baths. Probably the prospect of entering the imperial service and gaining official and social advancement in another and wider sphere than the one they had always known was tempting to many in the provinces. Vespasian added some provincials to the Senate. The men of the provinces were called up for the army more than they had been before.

Although his principate was acceptable to the army, which recognized his competence and was pleased that he was training two strong sons to succeed him, and to the common people, who perceived his concern for their welfare, and in general to the Senate, which saw that he would do his work well, and to the provincials, whom he was calling to new responsibilities and participation in the Empire, Vespasian did have to endure some attacks. Suetonius says that there were constant conspiracies; this simple statement may mean that several people plotted against his life —perhaps men of certain families in which such plots seemed hereditary. A group of senators from these die-hard families was led by Helvidius Priscus, who criticized and rudely insulted Vespasian. The emperor patiently endured his rudeness and obstructiveness for several years, but finally condemned him to death on a charge not known to us.

Titus (79–81)

When Vespasian died after ten years of rule, Titus' succession was well prepared, and when Titus died prematurely in A.D. 81, Domitian succeeded him in equally uneventful fashion. Titus' ambitions had seemed excessive to some, and people spoke of the cruelty of his nature, but his efforts at popularity when he became *princeps* were highly successful. His short reign is marked chiefly by tragedies: a great plague, of which we know little, and the spectacular eruption of Vesuvius in August, 79, of which we know much and are still learning more as excavation and study progress in Pompeii and Herculaneum, which were buried by the eruption.

Domitian (81–96)

Domitian worked toward absolutism, as had Gaius and Nero. Like them, he was fascinated by Greek culture and tried to introduce new elements of it in Rome, especially those of public displays and competitions of a bloodless kind; presumably all three men thought of such cultural elements as supporting somehow the position of an absolute ruler of the Hellenistic type. The Senate resisted his pretensions, and he encouraged informers to bring prosecutions against senators. In 88 the governor of Upper Germany revolted. Domitian, unlike Nero, acted promptly and decisively, but even so was anticipated by the man in charge in Lower Germany, who quickly crushed the uprising. Domitian's increased pressure on the upper classes gave rise to a large and unsuccessful conspiracy against his life in the year 93, after which he persecuted anyone who showed the least sign of independence or made a tactless remark. When he became suspicious of his own family and personal servants, he caused a plot that led to his murder; the successor had been made ready, for no one could endure the thought of a civil war over the succession. Thus Cocceius Nerva became emperor in 96.

It is natural that senatorial accounts of Domitian's reign pant with rage at his treatment of the upper classes; Tacitus and his friend Pliny, for example, give us a good deal of detail about persecution of senators. The picture presented by the pieces of evidence from nonsenatorial sources, however, is that of a very able ruler with a firm intent to establish absolute power.

Although he gave the soldiers a raise in pay from 225 to 300 denarii a year, which doubtless was justified by the general rise in prosperity and prices, Domitian did not pamper them in any way. In A.D. 83 he personally supervised operations against the Germanic tribe of the Chatti, consisting of careful penetration of their territory and building of military roads until they belatedly perceived that they had allowed the Romans to gain a great strategic advantage. The Roman frontier that cut across what is now southwestern Germany from the Rhine to the Danube was revised and strengthened.

The Dacians, who lived above the Danube and beside the Black Sea, showed new strength and aggressiveness at this time, perhaps because a forceful king, Decebalus, had put new spirit into them. Again and again during the next two centuries we shall see that peoples outside the Empire suddenly asserted themselves or combined into new federations that showed an aggressive spirit. The invasion of the Dacians was answered by a punitive expedition, and there were several years of inconclusive war. Military operations under Domitian were active and sensible, the government's management of its armed forces was firm and efficient, but there was a clear warning of dangers from the peoples outside that presently would be more acute.

Domitian's government in Rome was both careful and magnificent. He amused the people with liberal shows of the usual kind and tried to introduce the more refined Greek contests in both athletics and literature. The charming Piazza Navona in Rome retains the shape of a small stadium that he built, and near it was an Odeum for literary contests. His building program furnished employment for the poor, enhanced the impressiveness of Rome as a monumental city, and emphasized his own claims to absolute power and an element of divinity. He did needed restorations, finished the Colosseum, and finished the temple to the Deified Vespasian (for the man of good sense had been granted the honor of posthumous deification, which was withheld from some emperors) and dedicated it to him and to the Deified Titus; a portico also was dedicated to them both. He finished the baths that Titus had started to build. He built a Forum, a temple to the Flavian family, and a temple to Jupiter the Guardian for helping him to a narrow escape in the civil warfare of the year 69. Another structure that glorified him was the gorgeous new palace on the Palatine Hill. The temple of Jupiter on the Palatine had been burned again during the reign of Titus, and it was restored with incredible magnificence.

To choose the elderly Marcus Cocceius Nerva, who was of a suitable family, had fitting experience for the position of *princeps,* and was acceptable to the Senate, to succeed at Domitian's death and hold the place until a younger man could be found to succeed him was a sensible plan with a precedent at least as far back as 1352 b.c. At that time, when the Egyptian king Tut-ankh-amun died without an heir, the powerful general and administrator Horemheb married the widowed queen to her aged grandfather to hold the throne for a year or so until he could work up proper sentiment to support his taking it himself.[2] But Nerva was barely able to hold out. The Praetorian Guard, who had been taken by surprise at the time of the assassination, rose in 97, demanding the punishment of the assassins, and could hardly be brought back to obedience. There were also grave financial difficulties. Nerva's health was failing, and he wisely moved to adopt his successor without waiting until the last minute, as Galba had done, and chose an experienced man, Marcus Ulpius Traianus (known as Trajan in English), who commanded the army of Upper Germany. The well publicized adoption had the desired effect, and the three remaining months of Nerva's reign, until his death in January A.D. 98, were not marked by any signs of weakness in the government. With the death of Nerva and the accession of Trajan the period of experiment and consolidation of the principate as the successor of the republic ended, and the era of the "good emperors" of the second century began.

LATIN LITERATURE

Naturally Greek literature and thought, both classical and contemporary, exerted a strong influence on Latin literature and thought during the first and second centuries. The study of Greek was customary in

2 See p. 57.

Rome, Italy, and the western provinces. The young men of the leading Roman families often spent some time in Athens studying philosophy and oratory and absorbing atmosphere.

Oratory

There was more need of oratorical ability during the Empire than ever before. The demands on the courts had so increased that new space had to be made available and more days of the year had to be declared open for legal business. There is evidence that many men acquired fame, money, and position by their oratorical performances in the courts. The man of high position had need of oratorical ability when he represented his clients, whether in the courts, the Senate, or in conference with someone who could see that the just needs of the client were attended to. For a man to pretend to a position of any importance without being a competent speaker would have been unthinkable.

The older Roman method of learning to speak was to follow an able, experienced man, in conference and in court, just as in the United States one used to "read law" in a lawyer's office and accompany him to court. But not every father in the society of Rome in the first century, composed as it was of many newly rising men, could find a well placed older man who would take his son for coaching. Naturally new schools of rhetoric sprang up to train young men, just as schools of law sprang up in the United States in the nineteenth century with the expansion of legal business. Any plausible person could undertake to teach rhetoric, and poorly trained youngsters could find people to represent in court. If, for example, he were a new member of the equestrian order, the father would have clients who could use his son's services. Many a young man, schooled in figures of speech but with little idea of how one convinces a jury, must have made a sorry figure on his first appearance in court and seemed quite unready to play the advocate.

Vespasian's appointment of Quintilian (Marcus Fabius Quintilianus) to a state chair of rhetoric was meant to remedy this situation by making a fine teacher available to many, thus raising the standard of teaching. Quintilian's *Institutio Oratoria* (*On the Training of the Orator*) prescribes a course of study from the cradle up. Like Cicero, he believed in a good general education for the orator. The training in speech is described with technical detail. Quintilian remarks again and again that many teachers, while striving to impart a high polish to the oratory of their pupils, cannot or do not inculcate that quality that brings to others a sense of conviction and assent. To Quintilian oratory seemed meant for genuine and spirited contests, and we must assume that there were many of them, some in court, some in great trials in the Senate, some among members of the emperor's circle of *amici*.

Lucius Annaeus Seneca

Seneca, Nero's tutor and guide, wrote tragedies on the themes used by the great Greek writers, but intended them rather to illustrate the Stoic principles on disturbances of the mind than as plays for public performance. The plays are modeled on those of Euripides—*Mad Hercules, The Trojan Women, Hippolytus, Medea*—and of Sophocles—*Oedipus Rex, Hercules on Oeta*—with an *Agamemnon* that can hardly be said to be modeled on Aeschylus' play of that name and a *Thyestes* for which no model is known, although the subject was popular in Greece. All have themes of unbridled emotion and resounding disaster resulting therefrom so handled as to bring out the Stoic idea of the unhappy consequences of irrationality and lack of self-control. In one sense they are philosophical essays.

The plays do have genuine dramatic virtues, however. They show off character and emotions effectively, and there are many fine passages of dialogue. If the things that happen are mainly in the minds of the characters, the same is true of many good Greek plays. Seneca has a gift of vivid description, as in Oedipus' description of how it felt to stand in the road below the Sphinx's perch and think out the answer to her riddle while she sharpened her claws and made little noises in anticipation of eating him. In many of the choruses there are touches of fine lyric poetry.

These plays, like those of Plautus and Terence, served as models for the early European playwrights, who were but slightly acquainted with Greek. Many passages in Seneca, some of them lyric, have a tone like that of Shakespeare. Seneca's scene in which Medea gathers poisonous herbs, for example, may well have suggested the scene of the witches' brew in *Macbeth*. Apparently the representation of violent emotions in Seneca was congenial to the Elizabethan playwrights.

Seneca also produced a number of philosophical essays. They are the philosophy of moral exhortation and excellent of their kind, full, as Montaigne said, of things that are true and useful. There are those who are distressed that Seneca, even while preaching contempt of wealth and mastery of one's soul, could amass a great fortune by being close to Nero and even write the speech in which Nero asserted that his mother lost her life in attempting to kill him. To attempt to balance such criticism against the enormous good that Seneca did while managing the Roman Empire, Nero, and Nero's mother is an excellent exercise in values.

Satire

Satyricon, more than a hundred pages preserved from a much longer book composed in mixed prose and verse, is probably the work of the senator Petronius Arbiter, a companion of Nero's lighter hours, and is one of the earliest examples of the picaresque novel, or novel of the exploits of a rogue. Much of it is reminiscent of Huck Finn's journey down the river on the raft with the King and the Duke, for it is the adventures of a boy and two rascals of ready wit with a fine perception of when it was time to get out of town.

The book is of great interest stylistically, for the author, like most men of his time, had a thorough literary training and could vary his style to suit his content. His normal style was elegant and swift. He could parody Seneca's high moralistic manner amusingly. The most interesting part of the book is the account of a dinner given by a rich freedman, Trimalchio, in which the behavior of vulgar people is represented in shrewd and fascinating detail, and their low language is reproduced with its incoherence, slang, faulty grammar, and admixture of bad Greek. This is the only sizable passage of everyday talk of uneducated people in Latin literature.

Juvenal, the most famous of Roman, and possibly of all, satirists wrote sustained blasts of indignation, resentment, and criticism of society. He is said to have begun writing only after an unsuccessful effort to gain advancement in the equestrian career. His first satire explains that Roman life arouses such indignation in him that he must write, and he gives many vivid examples of what he objects to. The third satire, which served as model for Dr. Samuel Johnson's "London," is the beginning of a literary subtype that might be called "leaving the city." Juvenal's friend Umbricius explains why a plain Roman citizen can no longer endure Rome and gives a picture of the big, dirty, rich, wicked city.

Epic

Some of the respectable and dull epics of this period have survived, the product of men who thought writing a respectable way of spending their time. The *Argonautica* of Valerius Flaccus retells the tale of Jason's voyage to Colchis in search of the Golden Fleece. Silius Italicus' *Punica* treats the Second Punic War with laudable historical accuracy, a fair sense of movement in the story, and properly chosen epic language. Pliny the Younger speaks of him as a most agreeable elderly gentleman of literary tastes who collected busts of famous authors, celebrated Vergil's birthday every year, and wrote with more industry than talent. The

Thebais of Statius is only a fairly good rehearsal of the famous old stories of lust and bloodletting in Thebes. One epic, Lucan's *Pharsalia,* tries to do something new, for it has a modern theme, the civil war of Caesar and Pompey, rather than a legendary one, and it omits the gods altogether.

The Two Plinys

The elder Pliny was the uncle of the younger Pliny. Both are excellent examples of the feeling that literary pursuits were highly respectable for members of the upper classes. We learn a little of the personal history of the uncle from two letters of the nephew to his friend, the historian Tacitus. The first letter answers a question about the uncle's writings. He served in the army in Germany and while he was there wrote an essay on throwing the javelin from horseback; he also wrote a full account of Rome's wars in Germany. When Nero came to the throne, Pliny confined himself to an essay on usage in speech, which seemed a safer subject. Under Vespasian he accepted high responsibilities and served the emperor well, but continued to work with almost frantic energy on his *Natural History,* the only book of his that we have. His nephew tells us that another man, not otherwise known, offered him 400,000 sesterces, the amount of the equestrian census, for his notebooks, plainly intending thus to buy a ready-made set of materials which he would write and publish as his own so as to seem an author.

The nephew's account in his other letter to Tacitus about his uncle tells of the uncle's death in the disastrous eruption of Vesuvius in A.D. 79. With considerable art Pliny manages to give the impression that his uncle, who was then commander of the fleet based at Misenum, across the bay from Vesuvius, died while heroically directing rescue work, although he does not say so specifically. Still another letter is about his and his mother's experiences after his uncle went out and did not come back and the wind changed so as to blow the smoke and fumes and ash across to Misenum.

Pliny the Elder's *Natural History* is a rather uncritical compilation of facts of all kinds, a mine of information about aspects of ancient life of which we should otherwise know little. It discusses natural products, from wheat to gems, often naming many varieties and giving facts about methods of production. It is equally detailed about animals, domestic and wild, about fishes, birds, and insects, all subjects that the ancient authors ordinarily treated only in passing. This book is a much more useful result of the urge to write (for the historian, at least) than the epics are.

The nephew became a senator, although his uncle had remained in the equestrian order. We have the panegyric on Trajan that he delivered on assuming the consulship in A.D. 100. He was a good speaker and appeared often in the centumviral court, which we should call the probate court. His *Epistulae* show that the value of publication as a status symbol was much on his mind as well as his uncle's, for he either wrote the letters for publication in the first place or revised them very carefully preparatory to publishing them, and his remarks in the letters are often on some aspect of literature, his oratory, his verses, his literary friends, or his constant preoccupation with the subject. A letter to one of his friends tells of a marvelous incident of a dolphin coming to a swimming place and riding a boy on his back, something that we have come to regard as quite possible. The subject is offered to his friend, however, as something that he could write about effectively. The friend plainly wished to write and did not know what to write about. Cicero had similarly suggested subjects to his brother, who was spending a long winter in camp in Gaul under Caesar.

Tacitus and Suetonius

Cornelius Tacitus ranks as a great historian because his writing is a fascinating development of a good subject rather than because he possessed the virtues of a historian. He was a friend of the younger Pliny, had much the same background and education, held the usual offices, and was even more noted than Pliny as an orator. His first major work was the *Histories,* an account of Rome from Galba through Domitian; unfortunately the part from the middle of the year 70 to the end did not survive. Then he went farther back and wrote *Annals,* a history of Rome from the death of Augustus to the death of Nero, where the *Histories* began. Roughly the first third and the last third of the *Annals* survive.

His point of view was that of the Roman senator, to whom affairs at Rome were most important of all, with the doings of the emperors, especially the details of their coming to the throne and their exercise of power, in the center. The relations of the emperors to the Senate and the senators were of cardinal importance, and in this field, of course, he had a long and often grisly story to tell, with the emperors gaining steadily in power. Foreign affairs are told from the Roman point of view and often with the interest directed to the careers of the generals commanding the great armies. Tacitus, like Pliny, tells us a great deal both directly and by implication about the practices, assumptions, interests, and prejudices of upper-class Romans.

Our often tantalizingly slender knowledge of the emperors of the first century is much helped by the *Lives of the Caesars* (published in A.D. 120) of Suetonius Tranquillus, a quiet and scholarly man who wrote these biographies of the first twelve Caesars, from Julius Caesar through Domitian, and a number of lives of literary men. These were neither panegyrics nor attempts at rounded judgments and interpretations of his twelve subjects, but were collections of information on the lives, deeds, and characters of the men. His position in the civil service was such that he could draw material from the imperial archives that was not available to everyone.

26

THE SECOND CENTURY

Nerva, Trajan, Hadrian, Antoninus Pius, and Marcus Aurelius are often referred to as "the five good emperors" and are often discussed together, their reigns extending from A.D. 96 to 180. We shall treat the rule of Commodus as belonging to that sunny time, but leading into a recognizably different period. In this chapter, then, "the second century" will start with Trajan, who really inaugurated the new period, and end with the end of the reign of Commodus in 192.

TRAJAN: A.D. 98 TO 117

Since he was born in Spain, Trajan may be called a provincial, although he was of an Italian emigré family. Nerva's choice of him for adoption was made on the basis of Trajan's ability, personal force, and authority among the soldiers and officers of the armies, not on a theory that a provincial or a representative of the armies was needed at this point. The effectiveness of the choice in meeting the forces that seemed to threaten Nerva is shown by the fact that all was quiet from his death in January, 98 until Trajan's arrival in Rome in the summer of 99. Trajan already had the affection and loyalty of the armies; he soon won that of the Senate. Although he had held more military posts and fewer civil ones than was customary, he showed a good sense of how to handle the civil affairs of government. Trajan ruled as an autocrat to be sure, but a most enlightened one.

His Government

The facilities at Ostia were improved by the addition of a large octagonal ship basin surrounded by piers and warehouses; this made safer the unloading of the many ships that brought grain and other products to Rome and also was far better for the handling of the heavy blocks of marble and the huge timbers used for the imperial buildings.

The imperial city was of constant concern to the imperial government. Work was done on the bed and banks of the Tiber, and a drainage canal was built to carry off flood water. Trajan built another of the great bathing establishments which were one of the choice gifts of the emperors to the Roman people. For dwellers in cramped apartment houses without bathrooms it must have been most welcome to go to large and splendid buildings for bathing and for companionship, both in the pools and in the luxurious social halls, and in the winter for warmth, since apartments and houses were generally heated only by braziers. Apparently there were women's hours for the use of the baths. Many commercial bathing establishments must also have continued to serve the public.

A supply of good water was a convenience dear to the Romans. Trajan's choice for the head of the water department, Frontinus, wrote a book on the subject as well as one on the military art. The waterworks were maintained by public slaves, trained as specialists of several kinds as in a modern water department. Frontinus bluntly records that through influence it was possible for individuals to enjoy the assistance of these workmen on their private water systems, although they should have been engaged only in the service of the public, until he instituted a strict system of accounting for their time. He also records that the private systems that were allowed to draw from the public system had been using public water without paying the proper fees, in many cases, until he reformed this part of the department's work, too.

Trajan's Forum, the most splendid of all the forums built by the emperors, had as its chief feature a great basilica, of which the floor, with bases of columns, can still be seen. Beyond this were a Greek and a Latin library surrounding a courtyard in which stood the great one-hundred-foot column of marble with a spiral band winding upward on which were carved scenes from Trajan's Dacian campaigns. A gallery ran around the courtyard so that one could see the upper parts of the column better than from the ground, as the visitor now must do. Hundreds of shiploads of fine marble from the East were brought in for this project; the satirist Juvenal mentions the wagons hauling marble slabs up from the Tiber wharves, with their noise and crowding of the streets and occasional collapse, as one of the annoying features of life in Rome. Adjoining one end of the Forum was a complex of market structures, dignified and useful; in the largest building there was room for over 150 small shops.

Although the highly skilled work on this great project and others, like the baths, was presumably done by slaves, as was usual, there must have been years of employment for many of the poorer free citizens. Since the improvement of the port of Ostia probably made the grain supply a little more regular, this was another part of the emperors' care for the people of the city. We know that Trajan arranged that any Latin who ran a bakery in Rome for three years could gain full citizenship. The bakery, like the baths, was a great convenience to dwellers in rudimentary apartments, since one could take a fowl there to be roasted, or a pie of some sort, as well as buy things that had been prepared and baked there. Trajan was generous, too, with the bloodshed that gladdened the heart of the Roman. The games offered on his return in A.D. 107 from the Dacian War are said to have lasted 123 days and to have involved ten thousand gladiators and eleven thousand animals. He was generous with the *congiaria,* or systematic gifts of money. During his reign he may have given each citizen in the city something over three hundred dollars at present values, a total sum that over a period of nearly twenty years would represent a series of very welcome windfalls to a poor man.

The replacement of freedmen by knights in some important positions in the civil service, which had been begun by Vespasian, was carried further by Trajan. The composition of the Senate was changed somewhat by the introduction of men from the eastern provinces and North Africa in greater numbers than before. Nearly half the senators continued to be Italian during the second and third centuries. Those who were not were compelled to have Italian land as a third of their property, since there was a tendency for senators for some provinces to be indifferent to Italy and never even pay it a visit.

An institution begun by Nerva and known as the *alimenta* was extended. All over Italy the government gave loans to farmers at five percent, a low rate for the time, the interest being used for the support of poor children. More evidence would be welcome for both sides of this process: it would be interesting to know what kind of farmers (probably small) were to use this money and for what purposes the state was concerned with the upbringing of poor children.

His Wars

Trajan spent the winter of 98–99 on the Danube frontier surveying the situation and planning his war against the Thracian king Decebalus. The war, which was begun in 101 and ended by a decisive Roman victory in 107, yielded a rich booty of gold and gave the Romans possession of the

Dacian gold mines, which were worked henceforth under state management. A new province of Dacia was formed above the Danube adjoining the Black Sea, while below the river a great effort was made to establish colonies of veterans and to encourage settled life and the formation of towns and cities. Since the Rhine frontier had already been well secured, the strengthening of the Danube and of the region behind it was of great importance for the safety and the prosperity of the Empire.

Trajan's wars have been criticized for being unnecessary and for injuring peoples who might have acted as buffer states. The annexation of Nabatean Arabia, to be sure, was a very quiet affair, since it lay among territories now part of the Empire. Roman trade with India was now increasing, and with this annexation a great through road was built to carry goods from India from the port at the head of the Gulf of Aqabah, which branches off from the Red Sea, up to the commercial cities of Syria, thus making an old route more readily usable.

To fight the Parthians was a different matter. Trajan moved against them in A.D. 113 and by the end of 115 had overrun their territory, even to the bottom of Mesopotamia, and had captured the Parthian capital of Ctesiphon. The Parthians were still able to fight back, however, and when Trajan's health failed him and he died, in August of the year 117, the war with Parthia had still not been completed.

HADRIAN: A.D. 117 TO 138

Publius Aelius Hadrianus, Trajan's nephew, was protected by him as a young orphan and was taught by him in civil and military affairs. Hadrian asserted that Trajan adopted him in the last days of his life; there were doubts at the time that have never been resolved. Although Trajan trained him, he did not attempt to maneuver him into position for the succession. The army in the East acclaimed him, however, and Hadrian boldly used their support to put pressure on the Senate to accept him. But he must have been nearly the best man, if not the best.

He was born in A.D. 76 in Spain. He was well educated and had a passion for Greek culture, yet was virile and vigorous enough to be very fond of hunting, to climb Mount Etna to see the sunrise from its height, and to take part in his mature years in the exercises of the soldiers. He allowed himself to be elected an honorary archon of Athens to show his enthusiasm for the ancient greatness of Greece.

Hadrian's first great decision was to abandon Trajan's recent and insecure conquests in the East; the method was to give the territories to client kings. He would have abandoned Dacia had it not been argued that its consolidation into the Empire was already largely achieved. There were revolts of the Jews and other peoples, all of which were firmly repressed. Some of the barbarians from outside needed to be taught once again that they could not raid when the Romans seemed busy; the Pax Romana rested on such ready use of force. It is interesting that Hadrian, like Vespasian and Trajan, did not arrive in Rome until a year or so after his accession. This suggests that the new man might be securing some outlying regions, but also that he might be allowing some of the harsh measures needed to confirm his power to be taken by lieutenants in his absence, as Vespasian's agents had finished the distressing civil war. While Hadrian was settling the affairs of the East, his chief lieutenant saw to it that four of Trajan's leading military men who might be expected to object vigorously to Hadrian's more pacific policy were accused of treason and put out of the way. There was great resentment, but the deed was done before Hadrian came. On his arrival so great a parade was made of remission of taxes, of games for the people, and of fair promises to the Senate that it all seems like an attempt to buy final approval for his position.

His Imperial Policies

Hadrian's policy was to secure and develop the Empire as it was. Its boundaries were now as logical as they could be. In Africa the Sahara Desert was a boundary; the nomads who might spring from the desert sands toward the Roman territory were only a minor threat. The Atlantic Ocean was an effective western boundary for Spain and Gaul. In Britain it was decided to make no further effort to subdue the Scots, and the great work now known as Hadrian's Wall was erected as a barrier strong enough to control peaceful traffic and check any attempt at invasion. The Rhine and Danube lines, on which so much effort had already been expended, were effective as formal barriers to control traffic and slow down invasions; in the terrible times of the third century the attacks on the Rhine and Danube were almost always encouraged by the absence of the defending forces in some civil war. Since there was no logical boundary in the East, it was probably more economical and safer to deal with the great power of Parthia by diplomacy than to try to conquer and rule it. Egypt, which completes the circle, was protected on the south by geography and the absence of any powerful neighbor. To the advantages of so many natural frontiers was added that of the great internal communication and transport routes offered by the Mediterranean Sea, supplemented by many navigable rivers.

Hadrian spent almost twelve of the twenty-one years of his reign traveling through the Empire. His inspections of units of the army were rigorous and detailed. Everywhere he encouraged the municipalities to strengthen and beautify themselves, even to the extent of having a retinue of architects and artists with him who could suggest appropriate public buildings for the towns and cities and could leave plans from which to build them, sometimes as the emperor's gift, sometimes at the expense of a public-spirited citizen. He also encouraged attempts of communities to gain higher status. The simplest organization recognized by the government was called a *civitas ;* it would correspond roughly to an American township or simple government of a fairly large and thinly settled area. As economic activity and population increased, the place could gain recognition as a *municipium,* which would correspond to an American town. Then a few could hope to be raised to the grade of *colonia,* or city, the title of colony implying a fiction that citizens had come from Italy to settle it.

Hadrian's belief that the provinces should be encouraged to play as strong a role as they could in the Empire led him to bring many of their leading men into the equestrian order and into the civil service. The service was given a more formal table of organization, as it would be called nowadays, with carefully graded ranks and titles. Knights were now heads of the four great departments that Claudius had instituted and put under freedmen and of new departments as well. It was unfortunate that Hadrian's idea of efficiency led him to separate the civil and military careers; the old republican idea of forming a career from a mixture of civil and military posts perhaps seemed out of date, but the time came when the civil and military officials had little idea of one another's duties and knowledge and little sympathy with one another.

Hadrian's enthusiasm for every side of Greek culture showed itself in the furthering of Greek literature and art at Rome. He also presented buildings to Athens and attempted to revive its past glory. In Rome and nearby are fine examples of the imperial architecture of his reign. Across the street from the Colosseum one can see the remains of his temple of Venus and Rome, a cult that he took pains to promote, especially in the East, and for which he thought it worthwhile to build a large and costly temple in Rome. The Pantheon, too, is imperial architecture of Hadrian's reign. The porch is all that remains of Agrippa's original building; it leads to a circular hall with a huge hemispherical vault above it, and at the top, over 140 feet above the pavement, there is a large hole to let in light. It is a feat of engineering and a notable example of the growing tendency to use space and light as architectural components in large interiors.

Hadrian's tomb, now known as Castel Sant'Angelo, lies across the river and near enough to the Vatican and St. Peter's for the popes to have made it a fortress in the days when their power could be rudely threatened. It is essentially another imitation of an Etruscan tomb like the Mausoleum of Augustus. Out on the Latin plain, where the ground slopes up to the hills of Tivoli, Frascati, and Palestrina, Hadrian built his Versailles, a great complex of buildings, lawns, porticoes, and pools where a hard-working monarch could go with his entourage of secretaries and advisers and officials to work in comfort in hot weather.

In Hadrian's later years a vein of moodiness and cruelty came out, for his was an intense and complex nature. He devised an elaborate and not very wise scheme of adoption to provide himself a successor, which failed partly because of the early death of the chief person. Afterward, early in 138, he adopted the man who did succeed him and who is known as Antoninus Pius, requiring him in turn to adopt at once two boys whom Hadrian had chosen. The elder, who did succeed Pius and was known as Marcus Aurelius, was in his sixteenth year, and the younger, Verus, who was the colleague of Marcus Aurelius for a few years and died in 169, was about eight.

THE ANTONINES: ANTONINUS PIUS: A.D. 138 TO 161
MARCUS AURELIUS ANTONINUS: A.D. 161 TO 180

Antoninus began his reign in 138 as a man of mature years. His family was of Nîmes, in southern Gaul; he was extremely rich and went through the offices of quaestor, praetor, consul, and proconsul governing Asia with credit to himself. He was practically unacquainted with military life and with the frontier areas of the Empire. He showed little or no enthusiasm for Greek culture beyond what every educated Roman felt.

As emperor he stayed at home in Italy, working hard on the routine business of government. Although there is no great and striking event from his reign, we can learn much of its minor happenings from inscriptions. It became more and more the custom for men to inscribe dedications to the emperor on a building or some other gift that they made to their municipalities; the milestones of the roads often indicate that repairs were made or new roads built under a certain emperor, and the epitaphs of the men who made their mark became increasingly specific and detailed. Minor wars broke out and were repressed; earthquakes now and then rocked cities, whose wounds were healed partly by the application of imperial money; in general the twenty-three years of Pius' reign were as peaceful a time as a great empire has seen. The historian is tempted to make portentous but unjustifiable remarks about Indian summer.

It is true that there were severe troubles in the next reign—troubles that the emperor and his people met with magnificent courage, skill, and resolution—and in the third century there was a terrible storm of troubles, but they were not the troubles of an autumn of the Roman Empire, nor were they the troubles of the advancing old age of that Empire, for the analogy with the seasons of the year or with the stages of life of a biological organism is false. For a people or an empire there is no such thing as April showers or dreary November, nor is there youth or old age; there is only excellent organization that brings out the best efforts of the members of the group or some less effective organization that exposes them to difficulties and does not inspire them to do, dare, sacrifice, and achieve. Nor are there troubles and problems of old age, as there are diseases of old age in men; the troubles and problems that the Roman Empire had to face in the third, fourth, and fifth centuries were those that had exercised the Romans of the Republic, who knew all the difficulties that later men experienced—Hannibal in Italy for fifteen years, fearful invasions of the Germans, civil war.

When he succeeded Antoninus Pius in A.D. 161, Marcus Aurelius took the surprising step of asking the Senate to grant complete equality with himself to Verus, even to the title of Augustus, so that for the first time there were two equal rulers. Verus had only eight years to live, since he died suddenly in 169, but in those years he gave no evidence of being comparable to Marcus in character or ability. In 162 the Parthian king declared war on Rome and invaded Syria. Marcus planned the grand strategy of the war that followed, the generals were competent, and Verus was largely an onlooker. The strategy and successes of Marcus surpassed even those of Trajan, and victory was in sight when, in 165, the plague struck the Roman army in the East, then spread to the provinces of the East, to Rome, and even to Gaul. Peace with honor was granted to the Parthians, and the Romans withdrew to their own territories.

In A.D. 167 a great war began with the Germans that was to last until the death of Marcus Aurelius in 180, so that the philosopher king, the product of a most intense Greco-Roman education, who would have preferred to live merely as a quiet member of the upper class with strong philosophical tastes, was compelled to preside over another great war, to spend most of the rest of his life in the field, and to show himself perhaps as good a military man as Rome ever had. He wrote (in Greek) his *Meditations* as a solace for his spirit during the long and weary years that he spent in directing this war.

By the year 175 the operations against the Germanic peoples seemed to be complete. Suddenly the governor of Syria, Avidius Cassius, put himself at the head of a revolt of the whole East, proclaiming himself emperor. The old sentiment of superiority and of differentness that the East felt for the West, even if it could subside while the Empire protected the borders and made great prosperity possible, could not disappear in so short a time as two and a half centuries, and it may well have been strengthened by Pius' strong Italian feeling and failure to visit the East, by the inferior quality of Verus as he had been seen during the recent war with the Parthians, and by the obvious difficulty that Marcus was now having with the barbarian neighbors of the middle and western Empire.

Fortunately Cassius was murdered by a centurion, and the revolt collapsed with his death, but the seriousness with which the government viewed the disaffection of the East is shown by the fact that the emperor judged it best to visit every important part in person, removing officials who had joined the movement, offering clemency where possible to those who had to be prosecuted for their part, showing himself as the product of a thorough Hellenic education, but reminding men everywhere of the majesty of the head of the Empire.

The work of driving back the Germanic peoples from the neighborhood of the Danube had not been completed, after all, for there were new restlessness and trouble there, which took the emperor once more to that frontier, where he died in the year 180. He was succeeded by his son Commodus, who made a compromise treaty with the troublesome peoples, although his father had hoped that he would finish the task of reducing them.

COMMODUS: A.D. 180 TO 192

Commodus was in his nineteenth year and had all the formal powers of coregency, including the title Augustus, for his father had made great efforts to assure him the throne. His reign, once peace was made with the Germans, was a time of unbroken peace. The combination of great enthusiasm for the culture of Greece and the East combined with pretensions to some connection with the divine came out again in Commodus. Whereas Nero had presented himself to the populace as a musician like the god Apollo, Commodus appeared in the arena and slew lions from horseback, perhaps to suggest Hercules or possibly emulating as a mighty hunter the old kings of Assyria and Egypt.

The excellent men whom his father had chosen continued to do their work outside Rome, but at the seat of government corruption and inefficiency soon set in as unscrupulous men played on the young emperor to win positions of power and then exploited their opportunities for gain or for revenge on rivals. A conspiracy against his life failed and was falsely attributed to the Senate, leading to a steady campaign of terror against the senatorial order like those of Nero and Domitian after the unsuccessful conspiracies against them. Occasionally Commodus roused himself and left his athletic exploits or the company of his many concubines to replace one favorite with another. His assassination was due to a small group in the palace that thought itself threatened.

THE GOVERNMENT OF THE FIRST TWO CENTURIES

The Emperor

The set of formal powers regarded as necessary for the emperor remained as it was after Augustus had finished his careful experimenting. The emperor held the consulship only occasionally as a means of dramatizing his position, not as an office that he really used. The proconsular imperium gave him control of the armies in the provinces where there might be warfare, and with it went the power to determine conditions of recruitment and service, to choose the officers, and to decide on war or peace.

The tribunician power made his person inviolable, gave him the right of intercession, and allowed him to convene the Senate to receive motions that he wished to make. The censorial power allowed him to exert an influence on the composition of the Senate, especially by adlecting men of mature years who had not been through the normal preliminary career but whose unusual ability came to his attention. His right to commend men for offices, a right unconnected with any magistracy, enabled him to exert further control over the careers and honors that were so precious to the upper classes. The position of Pontifex Maximus allowed him to use religion both in the service of the government and to enhance his own power.

In spite of the great differences in personality of such men as Augustus, Tiberius, Vespasian, and Hadrian, the role of emperor changed very little, remaining that of the hard-working servant of mankind. Efforts to change the role to that of the monarch endowed with a share of the divine nature, as had long been customary in the East, were made by Gaius, Nero, Domitian, Hadrian, and Commodus, but with the different trappings suggested by their different natures. All of them, however, attempted to glorify Greek culture even more than was customary. It is interesting that the emperors who had such ideas were generally followed by men who asserted the ideals of Italy and the West effectively, but without saying much about it.

The Senate

The Senate governed Rome, Italy, and certain provinces. It had become the legislative organ of the government and acted as a court for outstanding cases with political implications and as a court of appeal.

The members of the senatorial order had important activities and duties. They had to have fortunes of a million sesterces; their status was hereditary. Roman conservatism was such that certain primary offices and duties were reserved for members of the senatorial order and often for those who had risen to the praetorship or the consulship. There was work to be done in the armed forces; the many men who held commands were also likely to take with them friends as advisers (or younger men to give them experience), as did the many men holding civil posts all over the Empire. Beside the civil magistracies there were embassies and many kinds of commissions, although the pressure of this kind of work had to be eased by putting some of the minor tasks in the hands of equestrians. The priesthoods were both an honor and an occasional duty. The senator also spent a great deal of time in doing what an American senator would call "taking care of my constituents." The clients, however, or the people whose patron a Roman senator was, did not belong to a definite district, and of course they did not elect him. Rather they were partly the inhabitants of the several places where he had estates; partly the towns, as entities, of these regions; perhaps other towns in provinces where he had seen civil or military service; or even whole provinces as entities. He must represent these individual or corporate clients when they made requests of the Senate or of the emperor and must appear for them in the courts or find some skillful orator to do so. If all the six hundred senators did this sort of work and had in addition the responsibility of managing and controlling their own large estates, their services to society and their influence must have been very great, even if they could not make a stand against a tyrant or as a group insist on initiating policies of government.

The Equestrian Order; The People

The members of the equestrian order, whose rank, unlike that of the senators, was not hereditary, gained entry to the order by being able to declare property worth 400,000 sesterces, and by being appointed by the emperor. Membership in the order, which historians sometimes refer to as "knighthood," was a very satisfactory kind of nobility, and the equestrian was not overawed by the senator's rank. The knights who served the government were organized in a carefully graded hierarchy of dignity and salary. In the lower grades were those, for example, who functioned as lawyers representing the interests of the imperial treasury, and the heads of the departments of water and coinage. Above them were the heads of the departments that dealt with affairs of the whole Empire and the governors of some minor provinces. The summit of an equestrian career was the prefecture of Egypt, of the food supply of Rome, or of the Praetorian Guard.

The citizens who lived in the city of Rome were maintained by the emperors as a privileged class whose presence was desirable, presumably to represent the Roman people of earlier days and to furnish a body of free citizens in the city to keep it from being peopled only by slaves and freedmen, to act as clients of the great men, and in the case of the poorest, to be available as a seasonal labor force. About 150,000 persons were eligible for the distributions of grain by the government, thus getting their basic food free.

All the territory of Italy and the provinces was carefully surveyed, and every part had some kind of organization, as is the case with us, whether it was the rudimentary *civitas*, which we have likened to our townships, the *municipium*, or *colonia*. The leading men of the municipalities and colonies were organized into a group known as the *curiales*, or those who were of the proper class (which later became hereditary) to serve in the Senate, or *curia*, of their town. Two or four magistrates were elected every year from this group. The man who was elected to an office was expected to donate a stated sum to the town in recognition of the honor. Rich citizens often presented buildings or statues or improved the forum.

The towns gained a modest revenue from their small taxes, from the rent of the land owned by the town, or from the investment of its funds. The expenses also were small, since the towns offered almost no public services except the maintenance of roads and bridges. Other services, called *munera*, were performed by the leading citizens under the direction of the *curia* and according to rules set up by the imperial government. To go on an embassy to Rome was such a *munus ;* also to oversee the collection of taxes and charges, to supervise the supplying of horses, mules, and oxen for the imperial post, or to manage the collection in a provincial town of the tribute grain or oil. The visiting or passing Roman magistrate must be entertained. The *munus* of the poor man was to work on the roads.

In communities that did not have the Roman citizenship, but were legally *socii*, or allies of Rome, there was great variety of local government. In the East there were such curious forms as temple estates. In many places there were old tribal organizations. On the other hand, there were already cities in many places, especially the old and famous cities of the East. These were recognized as entities and moved up to the formal grades of *municipium*, in which the magistrates got Roman citizenship, and *colonia*, in which everyone got it. The Romans required as much self-government from the provincials as they could and imposed as little uniformity on them as possible. Although the people of the provinces had no voice in imperial policies, and although there was nowhere anything that could be called democracy, the people of the provinces, like those of Italy and Rome, could feel that their opinion would be respected and their just demands heard. The presence in the two higher orders of men from the provinces meant better communication between the provinces and the government, as did the activity in the provinces of many responsible officials. There were official provincial councils that could send requests or make complaints to the government, even to asking for the prosecution of imperial officials. There is ample evidence, especially in inscriptions, that the provinces and towns requested favors or complained of abuses and were answered by the emperor.

Finance

We have already seen something of the ups and downs of imperial finance. Augustus spent great sums on the state out of his own ample resources and died comparatively poor; Tiberius pursued a cautious policy that left a good balance in the treasury at his death, which Gaius then did his best to dissipate. After Claudius had restored economic wisdom, Nero's great plans again brought the treasury into difficulties from which it was rescued by the good sense and ability of Vespasian and afterward of Domitian. Trajan seems to have prospered on the booty of Dacia and on its mines, but to have spent far more on his eastern wars than was wise. Hadrian and Antoninus Pius built up a surplus that was consumed by the wars that Marcus Aurelius had to fight. Even so bare a recital reminds us that the government lived from hand to mouth, with no way of floating loans, no proper method for acquiring and keeping a surplus, and on a slim basis of taxation for so ponderous an organization.

Although our evidence will not allow us to form even a rather tentative idea of a yearly budget for the Empire, we can say something of its expenditures and income. It was free of many of the normal costs of a modern government, like those for social services, at least outside the city of Rome. Its soldiers were paid rather modest wages. Although the officials of senatorial rank were expected to be wealthy enough to support themselves while serving the government (senatorial governors of provinces did receive a salary), regular and generous stipends were paid to the equestrian officials, and a fair number of permanent lower personnel had to be paid. Obviously the payroll comes to little when compared with that even of an average government of a century ago. The expense of supporting an adequate capital seemed necessary to most kings of the ancient world and was not shirked by the Roman emperors. The emperors maintained a suitable populace, brought in free grain for it and a great supply of pure water, entertained it with costly shows, handed out recurrent modest presents of cash, and furnished employment by public works which also gave the city a suitably monumental character.

The sources of income also differed from those of a modern or semi-modern state. Industry could not be taxed as it is now. The provinces were still frankly taxed as subject, the chief levy being that on land. Some of the provinces, notably Africa and Egypt, paid taxes in kind by sending

large amounts of grain for the provisioning of the city. Although they
had not paid a property tax since 167 B.C., the people of Italy continued
to be burdened with a five percent tax on inheritances and a tax of five
percent on the manumission of slaves. The goods of condemned people
were claimed by the state.

The property of the emperors or of the government was a source of
income. The revenues of Egypt were at the disposal of the emperors. The
emperors received many legacies, although it must be understood that
their policy in this respect, with very few exceptions, was to accept bequests only from people they knew well and who did not have relatives
who would more properly inherit. Some of the heavy-handed earlier men,
like Nero, forthrightly executed rich men and took their property. Nero
is said to have done this to six men and seized half the province of Africa,
which belonged to them; here we may wonder if just once an emperor
thought that a group of great landowners could command power enough
to make a stand against the central government. The word *fiscus,* literally
"basket," as well as "patrimony" and other words was used to describe
the property of the emperors.

Large areas of land acquired by the government were partly let out on
long leases and were partly farmed through agents. The State also acquired mines and quarries—generally by confiscation—and exploited them
through its managers. Much land was declared public that had been
royal land of monarchs whose realms the Romans took. The conjecture
has been made that from all these sources the government might have
had an income under Augustus of half a billion sesterces and under Vespasian of a billion.

The Army

The army, which had been reduced to twenty-eight legions under Augustus, had thirty under Hadrian. Vespasian began to reach out more
widely for recruits for the army as he did for men to be equestrians and
senators, and our evidence indicates that by the time of Hadrian the recruits for the legions came from the less romanized regions of the Empire
and nearest to the places where there was fighting to be done. Auxiliary
troops, especially of cavalry, were still enlisted along the borders; they
received the citizenship after their term of service. The pay of the legionary soldier was 225 denarii a year until Domitian raised it to 300 and
Commodus to 375. This was modest, indeed; but maintenance, occasional
opportunities for booty, and a bonus on retirement were additional in-
ducements, as was the steady employment in a world that was difficult
for the free workman.

The army had significant weight as a formal group of 150,000 to 200,-

000 trained and organized freemen, beside being the instrument of force in foreign policy. To manage such a large army would have been far beyond the capabilities of any earlier power, a fact that Americans can scarcely appreciate, since we take for granted feats of organization that most other people find extraordinary. The equestrian procurator in charge of the Gallic province of Belgica was responsible for the provisioning of some 80,000 persons in the army of the Rhine, and the production of all Gaul looked toward the supplying of that army with animals, food, arms, tools, and other supplies. Another aspect of the military was its great effect in romanizing many of the men who joined it and in romanizing the people of the region where the army of the province was stationed.

THE CIVILIZATION OF THE FIRST TWO CENTURIES

Now that we have told of the development of the imperial government and of the chief events of the first two centuries of our era, we shall attempt to give some idea of the social and economic life of that time and of the relations of the Empire with the world outside it, then describe educational, intellectual, and artistic affairs, and finally review religious beliefs and movements.

The Eastern Empire: Greece and the Lower Danube Provinces

Greece could export culture by receiving students, mostly at Athens, and tourists who came to see all her illustrious cities and to attend the famous festivals of Olympia and the other centers, which were still regularly celebrated. Both Athens and Sparta enjoyed a nominal independence and freedom to preserve their old institutions. Athens received practical benefits to bear witness to the philhellenism of Hadrian: he gave the city a subsidy and presented her with new buildings. He also founded a league of all the Hellenes that was meant to foster among all the Greeks a sense of their common descent and their duty to be worthy of their past glories. Marcus Aurelius endowed four chairs of philosophy, one for each of the four systems that had long held their place as the chief philosophies of Greece. Sparta lived in moderate prosperity on its good agricultural land and preserved those old customs that so fascinated the other Greeks. The once great kingdom of Macedonia prospered on the products of its farms and forests and once again supported a hardy peasantry.

The Thracians were given cities of the Greco-Roman type to serve as centers among them, since the great line of communication from Italy and from the Danube toward Byzantium and Asia Minor passed through Thrace. Roman control of the Danube region also meant new life for the Greek cities on the west end of the Black Sea, since they were protected from barbarian pressures and could trade in the agricultural output of their hinterland and the products of Asia Minor that were sent up the Danube to supply the armies and the prosperous agricultural communities there, and also the barbarians above the Danube, who had a well developed taste for the amenities and the luxuries enjoyed in the Roman Empire.

Asia Minor

Asia Minor in general had its greatest flowering in the first two centuries of our era. Its great cities continued to be the old ones on the coast, but many newer cities had some wealth and importance, and far back in the hills there were smaller places that in this more prosperous age could afford for the first time to bedeck themselves with the stone public buildings and other paraphernalia that served as symbols of civic status. The Greeks had founded the great cities of Asia Minor back in the Dark Age and they had prospered; the Seleucid Kingdom had offered them good conditions as a matter of policy. Many Italians settled there after the Romans gained control, and there were many other strains of population of less privilege. It may perhaps be said that the second century was a second great age of the flowering of the Greek city. This occurred under the aegis of the Romans, to be sure, and was accompanied only by a rather high level of artistic and literary accomplishment instead of the extraordinary brilliance of the first great flowering of the Greeks in the sixth, fifth, and fourth centuries before Christ. The wars of the older age were missing, too, the eternal contentiousness of the Greeks being represented only by the competition of the cities in decorating themselves with buildings and comforts and standing high in the regard of the imperial government.

The propertied classes in the East had been favored by the Romans from the very beginning, and in the early Empire they gained even more an advantage over the masses than before, with the result that there was as sharp a conflict between the rich and the poor, the few and the many, as there had been in the great old days of Greece, but the rich were supported by all the power of the Romans. Not only were there economic differences, but there was also a clear division between those who could claim to be Greeks and those who could not, as there had been in Hellenistic times all through the Seleucid Kingdom and in Egypt. The Romans, like the Seleucid kings and the Ptolemies, gave special advantages to the Greeks in general and to the more affluent Greeks in particular— those who would have been called the supporters of oligarchy in the older days of Greece.

The constant ill-feeling and friction between rich and poor and between Greeks and non-Greeks produced a milieu in which Christianity could make its most important early advances, for the alienation of the poor and underprivileged in the cities, cut off as they were both from the social organization and the means of making a living that the man on the soil would have, was greater than the alienation of country people, so that even to the end of the ancient world the dwellers in cities were more receptive to the message of comfort and status spread by the Christians than were the country people.

Syria and Palestine

Syria and Palestine were a little different from Asia Minor in that many of their people were of a Semitic strain and were more in touch with the world to the east of them, since there were no barriers like the mountains at the eastern edge of Asia Minor where it joins the continent. Northern Syria, near the great bend of the Euphrates, was always in close touch with the upper part of Mesopotamia, and from middle Syria or Palestine the caravans had always traveled across the desert to southern Mesopotamia. The route to northern Mesopotamia continued to the Iranian plateau and went eastward just below the Caspian Sea to meet the silk route from China. The caravans to southern Mesopotamia could go on to the harbor at the mouth of the Tigris River, at the north tip of the Persian Gulf, where the ships from India put in with their cargoes of pepper or rare woods like teak and ebony.

We have seen that when he annexed Nabataean Arabia Trajan improved the highway that led down from Palestine to the north end of the Gulf of Aqabah, an inlet of the Red Sea. The incense of Arabia and the ivory of Ethiopia had come up the Red Sea since the days of the old Egyptians. In the first century one Hippalus discovered that a bold shipmaster could make use of the monsoon, or etesian wind, which from the end of June until September regularly blows from the southwest. It brings the rainy season to India and can also blow ships from the southern ports of the Red Sea straight across the course of more than a thousand miles to India. In the winter the wind blows steadily in the other direction. This discovery made regular trade with India far more practicable than it had been, since the route that hugged the shore was long, difficult, and infested by pirates.

The three great staples of the trade between Rome and the East were pepper, incense, and silk. Naturally other articles of luxury and utility also played a part in the trade of the Empire with the peoples outside it. The ivory of Africa and the amber of the Baltic were especially prized as imports.

Syria had manufactures of its own to sell as well as the goods that its merchants imported from China, India, and Mesopotamia, blown glass and the deep crimson dye being the most distinctive ones. There was a lively textile industry, and all the other manufactures in metal or stone or wood, as well as the making of parchment, were practiced as they had been for a long time. The Syrians were the great middlemen between the East and the West, since the coast of Syria and Palestine has many usable harbors. Their own goods and those they imported flowed out to go to Rome, up the Danube, to Carthage and other ports of North Africa, to Marseilles or Cadiz or Britain; with the goods went many keen businessmen. The evidence of the presence of these businessmen in far places often comes from small stone statues or reliefs of their gods with inscriptions dedicating the statue to the god and naming the worshiper or the group of worshipers.

We know the political history of China during Roman times rather well (at least much better than we know that of India) because the Chinese developed a tradition of historical writing. From about 200 B.C. to A.D. 200, the time of the greatest success of the Romans, there was a large unified area in China controlled by a strong central government through an imperial bureaucracy. The emperors who headed the state were far-sighted and hardworking men who successfully controlled large armies and could find labor for such projects as the Great Wall, which defended the boundary for 1500 miles, and for large works of flood control and irrigation. They, like the Romans, found the neighboring barbarians often inclined to raid the civilized and rich empire that stirred their imagination. They also, like the Romans, found the barbarians more and more competent at warfare as they learned the methods of the empire. Sometimes the barbarians achieved cooperation like that of more civilized people or sometimes they would produce a gifted leader who for a generation would make them more formidable. The long successful period of the Chinese proved, like that of the Romans, to be an interlude between long periods of restless movements of peoples, and alternations within China of good government and poor government.

Egypt

The Romans managed Egypt as a vast estate, as the Ptolemies had done. The native Egyptians were regarded as *dediticii*, or conquered persons with no rights. The Greeks were favored in Egypt as they were elsewhere, although city life, as under the Ptolemies, was largely in Alexandria. As in Hellenistic times, a share of the wares that were brought up the Red Sea from Arabia and India came to Alexandria.

The Culture of the East

The general culture of the eastern part of the Roman Empire, like its economic life, was a continuation of the culture of the Hellenistic Age. There was probably a rather higher level of education than there had ever been before among the Greeks, since an education in the Greek classics had now become the mark of membership in a superior and privileged class, as was the practice of manly sports in the gymnasium, which was a central part of the life of every Greek city. The quality of this literary education is probably reflected by some of the display speeches preserved for us which were meant as entertainment for educated people and which assume a very high level of literary knowledge and interest on the part of the audience.

The tradition of the speech for display and entertainment went back to the Sophists of the fifth century in Greece. In the first and second centuries after Christ this literary type flourished as never before, and the Sophists were important men, much as the great performing musicians are among us, going on tours from city to city with elaborate retinues. Not all the Sophists published their speeches, of course, nor have many of those published come down to us. A notable speech among those we have is the *To Rome* of the second-century Sophist Aelius Aristides, a speech that belongs to the type given in praise of the city where the man was performing. The important trait of this speech is its commendation of Rome for having created a civilized community that covered the whole Mediterranean world and that enabled men to live well—not, of course, that a Greek of Asia Minor would recognize a Roman or Latin civilization, for he would laud Rome only as having made it possible for a Greek civilization to flourish widely. Still this was far different from the note of haughty superiority toward the Romans that the Greeks had maintained since they first learned of Rome's existence.

We know the names of scores of men who had the impulse to put pen to paper and the energy to finish what they started; we have dozens of fragments of their writings that have appeared on papyrus or were quoted by other writers, and we have the complete works of a few.

Lucian, who began his career as a Sophist, developed a new literary type, the satiric comic dialogue in prose. He is very funny, but is so much the cynic and the mocker that he ranks only as a minor author who is useful to us for the information he gives by the way. Yet his irreverent dialogues, his vivid imaginary civilizations in imaginary places, and his satire on men, manners, and literature are fun. Arrian set himself to rival the Athenian Xenophon and wrote an *Anabasis of Alexander,* the best surviving biography of the great conqueror, as well as books on hunting dogs and cavalry techniques. This man was a soldier who reached the consulship in A.D. 146 and as governor of a province drove off an invading force of Alani from beyond the Caucasus. Appian of Alexandria went to Rome and probably served as a treasury lawyer, near the bottom of the equestrian hierarchy. He wrote an interesting series of books on the wars of the Roman Republic, a separate work for each country with which Rome fought—*The Mithridatic Wars, The Punic Wars, The Spanish Wars,* and so on—the best of them being *The Civil Wars,* an account of the Roman civil wars from the Gracchi down to about 35 B.C. Lucian, Arrian, and Appian all wrote in Greek, of course.

Plutarch of Chaeronaea is unusual in that he came from Greece itself. He, too, went to Rome, in the time of the Flavians, won the friendship of important Romans, and learned a fair amount of Latin, which not every Greek would bother to do. He is best known for his *Parallel Lives,* in which a series of Romans who made their mark in government and warfare are compared with a series of Greeks distinguished in those same fields (not the fields in which the Greeks were admitted to be strongest), probably as a reminder to the Greeks of the greatness of their people even in the area where the conquering Romans claimed to be masters.

The leading philosophers were active more in teaching and argument than in writing, for the great philosophical schools had so probed, assaulted, outflanked, and bespattered one another's systems that there was not a great deal left to be said or to be written except for each school to explain its system anew to whoever seemed interested.

The religious beliefs of the East were indeed complex and constituted one of the great exports from the East to the West. The Syrian and Palestinian corner of the East produced many thinkers in this field. Judaism was an old religion of this area by now, Christianity was born there in the time that we are discussing, the Gnostic beliefs that led to the great system of Manicheism were partly developed there, and Islam was to arise nearby in the seventh century. For us the chief religious significance of the period lies in the development in this part of the eastern world of the two great religions that we still know: the Jews in this difficult time were busy with the beginnings of the Talmud, while the Christians were about to become a recognizable group and gain enough organization to enable them to continue as a group. The details of early Christianity may be left until we discuss the western Empire and can discuss the early history of the Christians there, too.

The science of the Greeks continued to progress slowly, partly at Alexandria, where the emperors continued the subsidies formerly provided by the Ptolemies, and elsewhere as well. We know fewer names in this field than in the more popular ones of literature and philosophy and can form less idea of the large number of lesser lights who must always be present in the background if there are to be a few stars whose works and fame outlast their own time.

Dioscorides, a Cilician of the first century who served as an army doctor, wrote a book, which was accepted as authoritative well into the beginnings of modern times, on plants as sources of drugs to be used by the physician. His book can perhaps not be called scientific in the modern sense, since he treated symptoms rather than diseases or people. Soranus, another man of the first century, wrote competently, for his time, on gynecology. The greatest of the physicians was Galen of Pergamum, who lived in the second century. He acted for a time as surgeon to gladiators in Pergamum, and one would think that he might have had numerous opportunities to see bodies that had been laid open and were still alive. He did indeed have a great interest in anatomy, but made mistakes precisely because he did not know enough of the human interior. Galen was full of theories, like that of the teleology, or purposive forming, of the body. His work was also full of exact and useful observations.

Alexandria remained the chief center of astronomical studies and the companion study of mathematics. Ptolemy, who lived in the second century, was the chief writer on astronomy in our period. His book, *Mathematical Collection,* remained a standard work until in early modern times the work of Copernicus made it obsolete. It is often known as *Almagest,* the Arabic name for its translation. In it he developed a system explaining the movements of all the heavenly bodies. He also made an attempt at scientific geography, attempting to work out the positions of places on the earth's surface by the use of astronomical observations, a method that was excellent in conception but beyond the techniques of the ancient world.

The Western Empire: The North African Provinces

If we leave the East and continue our trip around the ancient world in the clockwise direction, we come first to the provinces of North Africa, the easternmost of which was called Tripolitania from its three chief cities of Lepcis, Oea (modern Tripoli), and Sabrata. They had modest harbors and a small hinterland that could be cultivated and were termini for caravans coming up from central Africa with slaves and gold dust and ostrich eggs and feathers. The remains of Lepcis are very imposing, for Septimius Severus, who was emperor from 193 to 211, was born here and presented his *patria,* or native city, with a great set of public buildings as a gesture of patriotism.

Farther west are Africa, the original province taken from Carthage after the Third Punic War, and beyond it the larger province of Numidia. Next was Mauretania Caesariensis, with its capital at Caesarea on the coast, which became a glamorous city of the Greek type under Juba II, whom Augustus set up as king there. This province covered much of modern Algeria. Mauretania Tingitana, with its capital at Tingis, the modern Tangier, occupied the northern part of modern Morocco. The Roman management of the provinces of North Africa was a masterpiece of economy of effort, since from the beginning client kings were used as much as possible and the Roman influence spread slowly westward by its appeal to the natives almost as much as by forcible conquest.

In the northern part of the North African provinces there is enough rainfall to make wheat and other cereals a regular and plentiful crop, so much so that the Romans relied on the cereals of North Africa for the provisioning of the capital, drawing two-thirds of what was needed from the African provinces and one-third from Egypt. Farther south, where there is less rainfall, cereals are more difficult to grow, and the olive is better, for the trees are spaced, they strike their roots deep in search of nourishment, and they can be grown on hilly ground more easily than cereals can. In the area of reduced rainfall remains of stone olive presses have been found, as well as stone reservoirs and little cisterns from which stone conduits lead to distribute water to the olive trees. This scanty evidence makes it seem likely that the cultivation of the olive was begun in this region on a large scale in the early second century by the managers of the great imperial estates, who were in a position to know that in Syria methods had been developed for growing olives in regions as dry as this by careful conservation and use of what water there was. They also knew that it is useful to rake the ground lightly at nightfall to break the baked surface and open the soil to capillary action that will absorb the heavy dew. One of the Arab conquerors of North Africa in the seventh century remarked that one could ride all the way from Tripoli to Tangier in the shade of olive trees, which may have been almost literally true, since the route would lead through the olive zone.

The inhabitants of these provinces were apparently much like southern Europeans, although among themselves they distinguished a number of groups by such local names as Libyans or Gaetulians. The Carthaginians may have left some Punic blood when they disappeared as a political entity, for we know that Punic religion did not die out and that in the early 400s St. Augustine, Bishop of Hippo, had to find a Punic-speaking priest for one of his backwoods parishes. Italians were traders here before 100 B.C. and some remained permanently. The veteran colonies of Caesar and Augustus added more men from Italy. A modest number of Jews was settled in small groups. Although all these people seemed to have lived harmoniously and the whole area became enthusiastically Roman over a space of several centuries, less Roman influence by far persisted here than was the case in Italy, Spain, and France. The Semitic influence of the Carthaginians and of the Arabs, who came in the seventh century, apparently was more congenial and is the dominant note in our time.

Spain

It has been remarked that the provinces of the West were brought up by the Romans from what was essentially the culture of the early Iron Age to a state of civilization somewhat comparable to that of the older peoples of the East. In spite of the attention paid to Spain by Phoenicians and Greeks and Carthaginians, its culture, like that of the African provinces, was different from and simpler than that of the provinces of the East.

The mineral wealth of Spain was important to Rome from the time when she took Spain from Carthage. By the end of the second century of our era the emperors had gained possession of most of the best mining properties. The elder Pliny gives a vivid description of the method of mining the gold ore, which was also rich in silver; the great efforts made to bring water down from high places so that it would flow with force for hydraulic operations impressed him. We have some inscriptions that throw light on the rules of exploitation of these mines. The inscription giving the rules laid down by the imperial procurator in charge of the whole operation shows that he ran what used to be called a "company town" in the United States, in which every service—for example, barbering, shoe repairing, the fulling of clothes for cleaning, and bath establishments—was provided only by the appointees of the procurator's office.

The soil of Spain was rich for agriculture, too. Pliny speaks of the plentiful yield of wheat and of its high quality. In the first and second centuries the export of Spanish oil and wine to the markets of Gaul, Britain, and the Rhine increased greatly. Much of it came from large estates owned by the emperors. We have an unusual kind of evidence of the imports to Rome, for behind the docks on the river where goods were unloaded there is a hill now called Monte Testaccio, "The Hill of Broken Pots," which consists still of the remains of millions of jars, many of which, it seems from the study of a number of the fragments, bore marks showing that they came from Spain. The large jars were cheap enough to make it better to break them up than to send them back to be refilled with wine or oil.

Gaul

The province of Gallia Narbonensis, founded in 121 B.C., was well used to Roman ways by the second century. The elder Pliny speaks of this region as an extension of Italy, and certainly the modern traveler there could readily imagine himself in Italy. There are still impressive remains of the amenities provided for the cities. At Arelate (Arles) are a theater and an amphitheater. At Nemausus (Nîmes) are a fairly well preserved amphitheater, now fitted up for bullfighting, and the temple known as the Maison Carrée. Arausio (Orange) has an impressive theater and an arch. The most beautiful monument of all is out in the country, the Pont du Gard, the arched bridge that carried the aqueduct of Nemausus across a little river that flows down a fairly deep valley.

The rest of Gaul, the part that Caesar conquered, was divided into three provinces under the control of the emperor (Narbonensis was a senatorial province): Gallia Lugdunensis, with its center at Lugdunum (Lyons); Aquitania, whose chief cities were Bordeaux and Toulouse; and Belgica in the North. The predominantly Celtic population of Gaul found little difficulty in making the changes that the Romans required, for Celtic emotions and reactions were much like the Roman. The Latin language could readily be learned by speakers of Celtic and was much used, although Celtic remained a genuine spoken tongue. The Romans saw to it, of course, that Latin was required for advancement in their system, and schools were founded everywhere, many of them becoming famous for their thorough instruction.

Gaul was one place where the Romans believed it necessary to interfere with religion, since Druidism was so strong a political influence and so nationalist in character. Augustus forbade Roman citizens to take part in its rites, a ruling that had its real effect on the many Gauls who won the Roman citizenship and aspired to be leaders in their communities. Claudius thought it better simply to forbid Druidism. The cult of Rome and Augustus was cheerfully accepted. The old local deities lived on, occasionally allowing themselves to be equated with Greco-Roman gods, as Teutates was with Mercury.

The industry of Gaul developed naturally from old Celtic manufacturing processes that had long been practiced there. The craftsmen were expert in the handling of metals, and their fine work in gold, silver, bronze, and enamel was known beyond Gaul. Their textiles and their products in wood, like casks and coachwork, were also famous. Two industries, those of pottery and glass, were developed after Gaul came into world trade. The pottery at first imitated that of Italy and most of all the famous Arretine ware, then in several great centers the Gallic potters learned to make attractive types that could undersell the Arretine and became able to send their products over all the western provinces, as the archaeological finds testify. The manufacture of glass was begun in imitation of the Alexandrian and Syrian work and also became a very prosperous industry.

Britain

Britain was one of the less important provinces, although its position made it very useful, in Roman hands, for controlling the whole Atlantic coast of Europe. Roman activity and influence were pretty well confined to the lowlands of Great Britain. Among the chief urban centers were London, Lincoln, Gloucester, York, Verulam (St. Albans), Winchester, and Leicester.

The roads and two great walls are plainly visible features of Roman engineering in Britain. Some of the roads ran considerable distances over thinly populated areas to connect centers of population. Like many other examples, they do not support the generalization that Roman roads drove straight as an arrow to their destination with magnificent disregard for the difficulties of the terrain. In fact Roman roads were generally planned to avoid the necessity of real feats of engineering; those in Britain tend to run along ridges and to cross rivers at the easier places.

Hadrian's Wall and that of Antoninus Pius are fortified *limites,* or borders. Hadrian's is seventy-three miles long, running from a little above Carlisle on the west to near Newcastle-on-Tyne on the east. Those who approached it from outside first met a deep ditch, beyond which was a wall, mostly earth, about twenty feet high. The garrisons lived in forts that were part of the wall. Apparently mass attacks on this wall were not expected and did not occur, but the physical obstacle of the wall was a great deterrent to smugglers and raiders, and the small legitimate traffic could be channeled through a few gates. The Wall of Antoninus Pius, only thirty-three miles long, crossed the island at the very narrow point farther north and was of the same design.

Germany and Raetia

Although the large armies along the Rhine had a powerful romanizing effect in the narrow strip of Germany held by the Romans, and although the Germans outside the empire had something of a taste for Roman goods, the Germans in general put up a strong resistance to the Greco-Roman civilization. Many people in the Near East resisted it because they already had a well developed system of a rather different kind, but the Germans and the nomadic peoples who roamed in southern Russia and on the Iranian Plateau and in parts of central Asia resisted it, not because they had some mystic objection, but simply because they did not want what the Greco-Roman culture had to offer. Individuals, sometimes in considerable numbers, would come over, but the masses kept their old ways, the very simplicity of which may have been the secret of their lasting appeal and their strength.

The province of Raetia, which included modern Switzerland and the rather narrow projection of western Austria, was conquered in the time of Augustus. Its population, which was largely Celtic or had been subjected to Celtic influence, was able to settle down readily to being a part of the Empire. If the province was not important either economically or culturally, its strategic importance was great.

The Upper Danube Provinces

Our starting point in this clockwise tour of the provinces was Greece and north of it the provinces of the lower Danube, which may be said to have been a part of the East. When under Diocletian in the late third century a formal division was made between the eastern and the western parts of the Empire for administrative purposes, the provinces that we first discussed belonged to the East, and those of the upper Danube, which we are about to discuss, belonged to the West. A glance at the map will show that a nearly vertical line so drawn as to leave Italy in the West and Greece in the East would, when it reached the Danube, divide the provinces in this way. It is also true that the culture of the upper Danube was more Celtic, Latin, and Western, while that of the lower Danube was more Greek and Eastern. Many of the people in the provinces of the upper Danube came there in the movements of the Celts in the fifth, fourth, and third centuries before Christ.

Raetia was a Danube province as well as a Rhine province. Next to it on the Danube was Noricum, which was more or less the modern Austria, below which was Pannonia, which was virtually the modern Hungary. Immediately south of Pannonia lay Dalmatia across the Adriatic Sea from Italy. The usual Roman methods were employed in Noricum, Pannonia, and Dalmatia. The Roman citizenship spread, and cities were built. Archaeological finds show that the products of Gaul, apparently shipped through Cologne (Colonia Agrippina) on the Rhine, were distributed in this countryside, and that goods in considerable volume came up the Danube, originating largely in Asia Minor, and other goods came on the roads that radiated to these provinces from the port of Aquileia, at the head of the Adriatic.

In the first and second centuries the center of the population and economic activity in the Empire shifted somewhat northward, since the vigorous people in its northern part became more and more prosperous and the barbarians outside became more interested in goods from the Empire. Northern Italy gained in prosperity for this reason, since it helped to supply the Danube provinces, and a time was to come in the late third and the fourth centuries when Milan was more important than Rome as a seat of government.

THE RISE OF CHRISTIANITY

During the first two centuries Christianity was born and became an organization of some strength, with members spread widely in the Empire, in spite of the fact that it was illegal. This was a startling achievement, even if we remind ourselves that it took more than 150 years, and it is explained partly by the nature of the message of Christianity and partly by its organization.

The message of Christianity, if we try to explain its appeal rather than undertake the almost impossible task of describing it accurately, was one of fellowship and hope for the downtrodden, not that it did not have an attraction also for many intelligent and educated people. The idea of a single god who was concerned with his faithful worshipers had been promulgated by the Jews. The mystery religions of Greece, the Near East, and Egypt had long since made familiar the idea that the initiate might hope for something beyond this life. The idea that God sometimes reveals his purposes to man was familiar all over the ancient world. The Gnostics had tried to promote the idea of a redeemer who should restore perfection to the universe and then rule over all. Added to all these factors favorable to the Christian message was the personality of Jesus and his role as the Christ.

The poor and the lowly, especially those in the great cities of Asia and Syria, found great comfort in the idea of a heavenly father, in the promises of immortality, and in the belief that Christ was their defender against the powers of evil, which to them were not merely an expression sometimes used, but a terrifying reality. They found a new social standing and a satisfying warmth in the little Christian communities where there was a brother's welcome for everyone, even the slave. The members of the group were not exclusive, but evangelistic, and in the end the success of Christianity was a triumph of hard work more than anything else. It did not take the ancient world by storm, but was spread by long and patient effort.

The first great organizer was St. Paul, who was born at about the same time as Jesus. *The Acts of the Apostles* gives us some idea of his travel and preaching at about the time of Nero. Paul also had a new conception of the relation of Christianity to Judaism, for he believed that the Jewish law and the code of observance based on it had been superseded by the coming of Christ and that the basic thing in religion was now a proper inner relation to the divine Christ. Such a view could hardly be acceptable to most other Jews, nor was it reasonable to them that the chosen people should welcome a large number of newcomers who had not been brought up in the consciousness of the history of the Jews, their hopes, their tribulations, and the high morale that held them together. As Christianity spread more and more widely and began to have something like the beginnings of a world movement, largely because of Paul's organizing ability, it was only natural that it should no longer regard Jerusalem as its center and that its ties with Judaism should grow weaker as its likeness to Judaism grew less. Rome was a more natural center for Christianity, and by the end of our period the primacy of the Bishop of Rome was widely recognized.

It can be said in a general way that during the first century Christianity was exuberant and growing, with new ideas and new assertions of prophetic inspiration, while the second century was a time of conservation and consolidation in which the freely flowing fountains of inspiration and enthusiasm were channeled so as to run strong and deep. The New Testament was written during the first century, and we have much evidence that many persons who were far less important in the movement than the authors of these writings undertook to speak with prophetic voices. In the second century there were several good organizers who attempted to strengthen the authority of the bishops so that they could look after the daily welfare of their flocks better and could insist on the received essentials of Christian doctrine while opposing their authority to attempts to introduce new varieties of doctrine that might well have harmed the church by their diversity.

Against the Heresies, written late in the second century by Bishop Irenaeus of Lyons, was important in refuting many of the unacceptable beliefs of this time and thus in defending the main body of doctrine. For us it is a glimpse of some of the varieties of doctrine that were not found acceptable. The beliefs that Irenaeus describes are so inane, as someone said about little children's favorite games, that it is hard to see how any adult could possibly think them up. But intelligent adults did think them up, for it was an age in which thought was not conditioned by natural science, as it is with us, and the intelligent could readily people the world with swarms of invisible powers in choirs and in hierarchies and could invent all sorts of abstract spirits that could operate for good or for evil. Perhaps the most surprising thing about the heretical beliefs that Irenaeus describes is that nothing is said about what would seem to be the most important beliefs about Christ—his birth, life, teaching, death, and resurrection—nor about many of the questions that come up in Paul's epistles. We may suppose that early Christianity brought forth a good deal of belief, mostly under the influence of the Gnostics, that we should not recognize as Christian at all if it were described without reference to Christianity.

Christianity was illegal in the eyes of the government and highly unpopular among people in general. The younger Pliny wrote to Trajan from his post in Bithynia to ask for instructions about dealing with them.

He expressed surprise that they did not seem guilty of cannibalism, incest, and other crimes of which they were accused, but made it plain that they refused to sacrifice before the statue of the emperor as a symbolic act of loyalty. Trajan ruled that they were not to be sought out, but when found must demonstrate their loyalty to the Empire in the usual way. There is ample evidence that the common people hated them for their atheism, as the Christians' insistence on their own one god seemed, and because they seemed to refuse to join with others in loyalty and enthusiasm for the emperor. Many a time the governors of the provinces, before whom they would be brought for trial, wrestled mightily with them to persuade them to perform the simple ritual of sacrifice that would save them from prosecution and death. The Christians insisted that their prayers for the emperor would do more for the Empire than their sacrifices before the emperor's statue. To aver that their own magic was more potent than the magic of the others, as we might put it, was, of course, to destroy the last possibility of any meeting of the minds. The governor, hearing the mob outside shout "The Christians to the lions!" would at last have to send the Christians to the lions. The base passions and the inhuman cruelty directed against the Christians have been paralleled in other times by the resentment and the cruelty of people who found that someone else was unwilling to support the values that to them seemed most important in life.

CHAPTER

27

THE THIRD CENTURY:
A.D. 192 TO 284

We shall take the liberty of giving our own definition of the third century, as we did of the second, and shall choose a date for its beginning which marks the opening of a "time of troubles" and a date for its closing which found Diocletian on the throne and ready to begin an effective recovery. Perhaps the listing of the many things that went wrong during these ninety years or so will make it seem that there never was a moment free from disaster, so that the reader will have to stop to remind himself that ninety years is a long time and that there was room in it for a good deal of quiet and peace.

Pertinax

Since there was no logical successor to Commodus, the Praetorian Guard found no difficulty in securing the throne for Pertinax, a senator who had the usual mixture of civilian and military posts and who promised them a donative of 12,000 sesterces apiece. Unfortunately Pertinax was so stern in the economies with which he sought to restore financial soundness and so insistent on strict discipline that the praetorians murdered him. They then opened a negotiation with another candidate and were very pleased with the arrival at their camp on the edge of the city of a very rich (and foolish) senator named Didius Julianus, who wanted to buy their support. After spirited bidding Julianus finally offered them a donative of 25,000 sesterces apiece, and they proclaimed him emperor, forcing the Senate by threats to accept him. They could not protect him, however, against the forces that now arose.

Septimius Severus (A.D. 193–211)

The situation was like that of A.D. 68–69 in that the great frontier armies sought to decide who should be emperor, but this time Septimius Severus, commander of the Danube army, was able to move into Italy swiftly and without opposition to take the throne, then deal successfully with his rivals afterward. There was a great deal of useless fighting, and many supporters of the losing contestants were executed and their property confiscated. Septimius Severus was not a crudely harsh and cruel man, but was like Julius Caesar in his careful calculation of the relative advantages of harshness and clemency.

Indeed Severus has been accused of being only a rough soldier and of basing much of his policy on the fact that his wife's family were Syrians and that his family came from North Africa. He was not a rough soldier, but a product of the usual senatorial career of civil and military offices, a man who knew a great deal about the resources and problems of the Empire as well as how to handle armies and direct the processes of civil government. He did not favor Syria or the African provinces (except for Lepcis in Africa, the city of his birth), but continued the policy of his predecessors of developing both areas and bringing more and more of their people into the government.

A number of his measures worked against the privilege of Italy and of the upper classes. He stationed a legion in Italy and began to recruit the Praetorian Guard from legionaries in general rather than from Italians. He granted other privileges to the provinces that had formerly been enjoyed only by Italy, especially by grants of the full Roman citizenship to whole cities. He used more and more equestrians from all over the empire in the service of the government (this continued the policies of his predecessors) and even put some of them in positions, like the command of legions, that had formerly been reserved for senators. He also made it possible for enlisted men to work their way up through the post of leading centurion of a legion to the equestrian order and the imperial civil service. A new name, *res privata,* "the private property of the crown," was now given to the vast possessions of the crown. More procurators were needed in the imperial service to take care of all this farm land, mines, quarries, and other properties.

It was plainly becoming more difficult to find the men and the money to make the government run. The government began to impose on the *curiales* of cities all over the Empire a number of duties for the imperial government, like collecting the imperial taxes, in addition to the already burdensome tasks that they were required to perform in the local sphere. The government also tightened its control over the merchants and shippers who served it in the matter of the *annona*, the food for the city of Rome. These did not have to give their services free, as did the *curiales* when they collected taxes, but the regulations that insured that they would perform regularly and efficiently became very strict.

Severus was determined that his two sons should succeed him by natural inheritance, since he, like Vespasian, came to power as the result of a civil war over the succession and was very conscious of the value of securing a peaceful succession. For this purpose he claimed that he had been adopted by Marcus Aurelius and advertised his supposed Antonine ancestry on coins and in long inscriptions. He also named his older son Marcus Aurelius Antoninus, although he became known as Caracalla from the name of a military garment that he liked to wear.

The Severan Dynasty

Septimius Severus died in A.D. 211. In spite of his attempts to train his sons and to have them rule jointly and well, the two young men detested and feared each other so intensely that their desire was to rule a divided empire and never see each other again. Their ambitious mother, Julia Domna, persuaded them to give up this wish, believing that she could preserve harmony between them and avoid the splitting of the Empire. Caracalla soon found a simple solution to their quarrels by having his brother Geta murdered, accusing Geta of having plotted to kill him.

The short reign of Caracalla (A.D. 211–217) saw many acts of cruelty caused by his fears and suspicions. Perhaps the most interesting event was the promulgation in 212 of the *Constitutio Antoniniana*, an imperial enactment that made Roman citizens of all freemen in the Empire except for the group called *dediticii*, who were conquered people without rights. This was not a great humanitarian measure, but was intended to subject the whole population to the inheritance tax.

Caracalla was not without military ability, beside which he was obsessed with a desire for military glory. He directed a successful campaign against a threatening coalition of Germans and then embarked on an eastern campaign, apparently planning to conquer Parthia to gain glory for himself. He lost his life in 217 because one of the praetorian prefects, Macrinus, learned that a local astrologer had predicted that he would become emperor and knew that he could not live long when such a story reached the ears of Caracalla. He was able somehow to persuade some of the soldiers to murder the emperor, after which the troops proclaimed Macrinus himself emperor, although he had gained his position as prefect by great legal ability, not by military prowess. The Senate was willing to accept him, although he was a Mauretanian and of the equestrian order—the first emperor not of the senatorial order.

The ladies of the house of the Severi, however, were unwilling to see power pass out of their family. Severus' wife, Julia Domna, died soon after the death of Caracalla, but her sister Julia Maesa had two daughters, Soaemias and Mamaea. Soaemias now modestly let it be known that her fourteen-year-old son was the offspring of her cousin, the deceased Caracalla. The ladies managed to present the boy to the troops, who welcomed him because of his supposed parentage. The plan succeeded, for in June, 218, the soldiers deposed and killed Macrinus after he had ruled rather unsuccessfully.

The boy held the priesthood, hereditary in his family, of the local *baal* of the town of Emesa in Syria, and he now began to call himself by the god's name, Elagabalus (or Heliogabalus), "the lord of the high place." He ruled Rome from 218 to 222, since he was acceptable to the army. He brought his god to Rome and made a shrine for it on the Palatine, outraging even a public opinion now used to oriental customs by his performances of rites as high priest. His offenses to feeling in Rome were such that his grandmother, Julia Maesa, realizing that he was courting assassination, persuaded him to adopt as colleague his cousin, the son of her other daughter, Mamaea, arguing that he needed to free himself for his religious duties. Soon afterward he and his mother were murdered by the Praetorian Guard, and it is not unreasonable to suppose that his grandmother and his aunt Mammaea may have given the process at least a tiny push.

His cousin succeeded him as Severus Alexander and ruled from A.D. 222 to 235. In its way this reign was even more improbable than that of Elagabalus, since for thirteen years the Roman Empire was rather well headed by a nice Syrian boy, his mother, and his grandmother. There was no striking new policy to characterize the period. The Senate was treated with somewhat more honor than during the last three regimes, and in the traditions of the senatorial order this reign was later regarded as a golden time, so much so that we must accept with caution the accounts written with a senatorial bias that would make Alexander something of a restorer of the governmental methods of the early Empire.

The establishment of the New Persian Kingdom in A.D. 227 repeated in a way the events of 549 B.C. when Cyrus the Persian freed his country from the domination of the Medes and began a career of conquest. The great Persian family of the Sassanids led a movement that overthrew the Arsacids, the ruling family of the Parthians, and aimed at restoring the territory and the glory of the old Persian kingdom, which involved taking some territory back from Rome. Beginning with a great raid on Cappadocia and the siege of Nisibis, in northern Mesopotamia near the Armenian border, the Sassanids were able at first to take advantage of the unreadiness of the Romans for so strong an attack.

Severus Alexander and the ladies of his house had no taste nor talent for war. We shall see again and again in the following decades, as we do here, that it was unfortunate that the Roman system of this time required the head of state to be the leader of the armed forces. The Roman army was moved tardily and timidly against the Persians, and although it was possible to break off hostilities after three years of warfare in which the Persians were fairly well balked in their invasion, the troops were resentful that they had not been led to a full-scale counterattack. When, in the year 235, the young emperor tried to buy off some troublesome Germans by giving them subsidies (by now a regular device) instead of expelling them by force, the cumulative dislike of the troops was so great that they murdered him.

A Period of Succession Troubles

Severus Alexander's successor, Maximinus, was a Thracian peasant whose valor and vigor had raised him from plain soldier to the command of a legion, equestrian rank, and a governorship. He vigorously attacked the Germans whom his predecessor had tried to buy off and decisively defeated them. His short reign (A.D. 235 to 238) was satisfactory from the military point of view, but he had little idea of civil government. His persecution of the upper classes and his exactions of money led to a movement against him in the year 238 in which two men named Gordian, father and son, were made emperors and were unable to maintain themselves in that position. The Senate then chose two of its members as joint emperors, but they were murdered by the Praetorian Guard, which set up the thirteen-year-old Gordian III, grandson and son of the other two.

The reign of the young Gordian III lasted until early in the year 244. As with Severus Alexander, he was supported by the professional personnel of the Empire, which was perfectly capable of keeping the great organization running smoothly if it were not violently prevented from doing so. For the last three years of his reign the Empire was virtually headed by the very able praetorian prefect Timesitheus. In 244 Timesitheus died suddenly of natural causes. His assistant was an Arab, M. Julius Philippus, another able man of considerable experience. Not being content to be praetorian prefect and second man in the Empire, he incited the soldiers to have Gordian murdered and himself proclaimed emperor. The elevation to the throne of Philip, son of an Arab tribal chief, is sometimes said to be symbolic of Roman degradation at this time, but it was Roman tradition to make good Romans of aliens. In A.D. 247 Philip presided over the celebration of Rome's thousandth birthday. If at the end of Rome's first thousand years the emperor was an Arab by birth, an able, conscientious, hardworking chief executive, the fact is consistent with the course of Roman history up to that time.

In the last years of Philip's reign three pretenders to the throne were set up by different armies. In the next few decades there were many such pretenders. Sometimes we can see why they arose, sometimes not. At least one of those under Philip was expected to do something about excessive taxation. One was put forward by the Danube army, which began at this time to regard itself and the area that it guarded as the true defenders of the Empire. Fortunately no real warfare followed these attempts to raise generals to the throne. These three pretenders, as was to be the case with several others later, lost their following before making a decisive move and quietly disappeared.

There was more danger in a new invasion of the Goths, who had not been paid their annual subsidy. Although Philip was in such despair that he proposed to abdicate, his general Decius drove out the invaders. Apparently the troops felt that a general who could restore discipline among them and lead them to victory should be emperor and they probably felt, too, that they might succeed if they attempted to raise him to the throne, for in 249 they proclaimed Decius emperor. He is said to have wished to remain subordinate to Philip, but such reasonable conduct was not possible, and during the conflict that followed Philip fled, leaving the throne to Decius.

The Germanic and Persian Invasions (ca. A.D. *250–ca. 270)*

There now was a storm of incursions by Germanic peoples which lasted for more than twenty years and which, in conjunction with the new aggressiveness of the Persians, almost brought the Romans to ruin. For the civilization of the West it was a good thing that the Germanic people of this period raided rather than seriously invaded, since the civilization of the Germans seems to have advanced markedly through its contact with the people of the Empire in the 150 years before the Germans came in large groups to stay and finally gained control of the West. Even at that later time they were not really ready to manage the complex Roman system, so that they had to simplify it, but they were at least much nearer to being ready to handle it than they were in the third century.

Decius was the first of a distinguished line of emperors from the Balkans. His short reign is noted for a more serious persecution of the Christians than they had had to endure for several decades, probably caused by his feeling that he must do everything possible to gain the favor of the gods. Every man, woman, and child was required to obtain a certificate of having made the pagan offering that was required. The excavations of Egypt have yielded a fair number of such certificates on papyrus, issued by magistrates. Had Decius been spared to continue the persecution in its original rigor, the Christian church might have been brought to an end.

In the year 251 Decius went to meet another invasion of the Goths, but through the treachery of one of his high officers he was defeated and killed, the first of the emperors to lose his life on the battlefield. For a year or two the succession to the throne was uncertain, although one pretender came near to establishing himself. Meanwhile the Goths invaded again, even going into Asia Minor and pillaging the famous old city of Ephesus. In 253, Valerian, an elderly senator of considerable prestige, was able to establish himself as emperor.

Valerian associated his son Gallienus with him as ruler of the West, taking the East as his own sphere, and together they faced steadily rising storms on the frontiers. The Goths occupied Dacia; this was for now the one instance of Germanic people attempting to settle and stay within the boundaries of the Empire, and this province was the only one that was not brought back under the control of the central government when it presently re-established its authority. In the West a number of the fortified posts of the *limes* of Germany fell, and it seemed best to retire the boundary westward to the Rhine. A raiding band of Alemanni penetrated well into southern France, and the Franks went all the way to Spain on a great raid. The forays of this short period of intensive pressure were probably the most destructive that Gaul ever suffered, and from this time on many Gallic cities enclosed themselves in smaller and stronger fortifications than before, and the villas, or country houses, of Gaul never flourished again as they had up to this time.

In the same period changes took place among the Germans, too. The old confederations lost some prestige, and new confederations grew up, as was easily possible, since the basic unifying principle of German social life was loyalty to a personal leader, not to a tribe or nation. Both Alemanni and Franks were new confederations. At about this time, too, the Germanic peoples of the northern seacoasts began to take to the sea; A.D. 285 is a well attested date for their operating as pirates. Some of them also drifted southeastward to where, above the lower Danube, they made contact with the Scythians, Sarmatians, and Roxolani, steppe peoples of Iranian origin who taught them about the life that had been appropriate to the Iranian steppes and to southern Russia.

In spite of the efforts of Gallienus the situation in the West became worse. Often the raids from the outside were encouraged by the appearance of frequent pretenders to the throne, for the people beyond the frontier could easily learn when the army inside was engaged in putting down a pretender instead of being available for its proper work. The pretenders were always commanders of armies, impelled sometimes by their own ambitions and sometimes by the desire of the soldiers to get a large donative in return for making their commander emperor. The pretenders were always of senatorial rank, for even after such leveling of society as had taken place, a nonsenator would ordinarily not entertain such aspirations. Gallienus found it necessary to remove practically all the important commands in the army from the reach of senators and give them to equestrians, who would feel that they could not find any support for attempts at usurpation.

The greatest of the pretenders or usurpers in the West was Postumus, a general in the Rhine army who appears to have been moved by a combination of ambition and a quarrel with Gallienus' young son, who was nominally in charge there. He was able to control Gaul, Britain, and Spain until A.D. 269, and for a short time parts of North Italy. He seems to have intended to bring the whole Empire under his control. His government of the territory that he did hold was efficient; one notable feature of it is the fine gold coinage of his two mints.

The condition of the Empire during this period of usurpations and invasions just after the middle of the third century is often called an anarchy. It is true that the imperial government often could not regulate the succession to the throne, control the army, or defend the frontiers and was in great financial difficulties. Nevertheless there always was a regime that had a claim to legitimacy and was attempting to discharge the functions of a government with a definite policy. Whenever the armies set up pretenders, there was an attempt at the exercise of government. The use of the word "anarchy" does much to obscure the nature of the situation.

The greatest success of the Persians against the Romans was their capture of the emperor Valerian during the campaign of the year 260. The accounts of it differ as to whether the Persian king Shapur I, son of the founder of the New Persian dynasty, used base treachery or made a bold capture. The brisk propaganda methods of the king are shown by the fact that five representations of the capture still exist in rock reliefs. Shapur I made a serious mistake, however, in rebuffing the overtures made to him by Odenathus, prince of the caravan city of Palmyra, about 125 miles northeast of Damascus and the same distance southeast of Apamea. Odenathus, who commanded a strong force of mailed cavalry and archers, fell on Shapur as he was returning from his campaign of A.D. 260 with Valerian as captive and with a huge booty, inflicting heavy losses on him.

Gallienus made the best of the situation by bestowing titles on Odenathus and by encouraging him to fight some of the government's battles and to stand guard for now against the return of the Persians. For several years Odenathus watched over the eastern extremity of the Roman realm as Postumus took care of the western extremity, and when he died in 267, his queen, the famous Zenobia, took control of the government in the name of her young son and was able even to extend her power to Egypt while the Romans struggled with the Goths in 267 and another Germanic people in 268.

The nonmilitary arrangements of Gallienus are striking. He brusquely changed the relation between emperor and Senate, among other things by giving over many of the high commands held by senators to members of the equestrian order and by suspending the bronze coinage long managed by the Senate and regarded as a symbol of senatorial authority. He also ended the persecution of the Christians, probably because he doubted the value to the Empire of the device of combining against a minority. He seems, on the other hand, to have felt that morale could be somewhat improved by a restoration of the old pagan values, and he supported a new philosophy now called Neoplatonism, which was a reaffirmation of Plato's philosophy of permanent values and of the worth of the intellect and asserted the value of the old ways of pagan culture. Plotinus, the founder of Neoplatonism, and many Greek literary men were encouraged by the emperor, who also allowed himself to be elected archon at Athens and was initiated into the Eleusinian Mysteries. He appeared to see himself as champion of a revived common culture capable of being widely accepted.

Gallienus was murdered in A.D. 268 by his chief officers, who had conspired because of his interest in cultural values which lay beyond their horizon and because they felt that he had neglected the defense of the Danube lands, from which practically all of them came. The officers chose one of their number, Claudius, as emperor and were able to commend him to the Senate with little or no resistance, but to the army, which had admired Gallienus as a fine general, only with great difficulty and the payment of a liberal donative. Claudius went at his military duties with determination and scored an important success against one group of invaders, but died of the plague early in the year 270.

Recovery Begins

Aurelian, his successor, began by pursuing a large body of raiders as they retired across the Danube with their booty and by treating them in the following negotiations with a sternness that had not been seen for a long time. They had apparently assumed that even after being defeated they could demand the payment of an annual subsidy from the Romans. In the next year, A.D. 271, Aurelian began the wall around the city of Rome much of which remains and is still known by his name. The wall was twelve miles long and in most places twenty feet high, with towers for catapults. Many of the eighteen gates still stand. Another defensive move was formal withdrawal from the province of Dacia, beyond the Danube, which was too exposed to the first shock of invaders to be practically defensible.

The next move was against Zenobia. Aurelian easily made his way to her home territory and defeated the formidable army of 70,000 that she was able to bring against him. In A.D. 274 he recovered the western provinces from Postumus by one battle and could now call himself the restorer of the world.

He attempted, too, to deal with the financial and social difficulties that beset the Empire as a result of the invasions and the civil wars with the pretenders. Analysis of the coins of the reign shows that an attempt was made, though not a very successful one, to improve the real value of the coinage and reverse the trend of inflation. Another way of attacking the problem was to set a price on bread to protect the poor, to distribute baked bread instead of the grain that had long been usual, and to offer pork, oil, and salt in occasional distributions.

The necessity of making the succession to the throne more orderly must have been on many men's minds, and Aurelian found time even among his many campaigns to inaugurate a new policy. He told the troops flatly that the power of the emperor was divinely bestowed and protected, in spite of the fact that he himself had been raised to the throne by the army. He instituted a cult of the sun god that was apparently based on the deity called Elagabalus, who had been brought to Rome by the emperor who took his name, but the form of the cult was Roman: there were no orgies, a temple was built in the Roman way, and a college of priests of senatorial rank was formed to supervise the cult. The religion was broad enough to allow comfortable room for every worshiper of the sun in any style, so that the Easterner, the Egyptian, and the Greek devotee of Apollo all might join. There are indications that this new attempt to find a basis for unity implied a persecution of the Christians as a group who openly refused to subscribe to the values that unified other people. The new cult was not a great success, however, and the persecution was never really begun.

Aurelian's death in A.D. 275 was caused by his displeasure at a secretary whom he found deceiving him, and who, to save himself, forged a list of important military men who were to be executed and showed it to the men. The times were such that they rose to this bait and murdered the emperor. Finally an elderly man was chosen who worked well for a few months, then collapsed and died. Thereupon a usurper arose, but he was thrust out of the way by an experienced soldier put forward by the armies, Probus (A.D. 276–282). In the end Probus was put aside by his own troops, excellent emperor that he was, apparently because he had burdened them heavily with campaigns and public works in the intervals between campaigns. Again there was a brief period when two men held the throne for a few months each and were deposed. In 284 Diocles, who was soon to call himself Diocletianus, or Diocletian in the anglicized form, came to the throne. In 285 he secured his power by eliminating a rival. He was now fully in power and free to attempt his sweeping plans for ending forever the disorders through which he had lived.

THE LIFE OF THE THIRD CENTURY

Economic Life

The damage and change caused by the troubles of the Empire were the salient factors in the economic life of the third century. A great plague in the middle of the century also upset economic life while it was raging and left a shortage after it of women and children as well as of men.

Property losses occurred with the destruction of buildings, olive trees, and vines in the raids and with the carrying off of people and tangible property. We must also reckon the money paid out to the peoples on the borders, which seems to have been much more during this period than previously. On the other side of the account we may put the purchases made by the barbarians of goods from within the Empire during the intervals of peace, which must have brought back a fair amount of the protection money.

The government—and we must remember how many emperors there were during this century and how distracted they were by purely military tasks—responded to the economic losses and dislocations by increasing the devices, which began as early as Trajan and Hadrian, for regulating the communities and individuals so as to make sure that they would perform the tasks they did for the central government. As we have seen, under Septimius Severus the liabilities of the *curiales* toward the government were increased. Again and again during the third century these men, the chief property owners in their cities, were confronted with extraordinary demands for supplies for the government and for extra taxes. Somewhere in the latter part of the third century the *curiales* were legally fixed ("frozen," in the modern terminology) in their position, and their heirs inherited their duties along with their property, so that the holder of the property, whoever he was, also had the duties.

A corollary of this was to fix the tenants (*coloni*) of the large landowners, so that the state could be sure that the land would be tilled and that the payments in kind to the state would be regularly made. The shipowners and the people who performed other services in connection with the food supply were also frozen in the performance of their duties.

They were paid for what they did, of course. The soldier, too, was fixed in his occupation, and his sons after him were to follow it.

The already large properties directly owned by the state were increased during this century, especially by the acquisition of industrial plants. The state had long been the owner of great brickyards that were originally the personal property of members of the imperial family. State-owned factories that supplied the army with clothing, weapons, and tools are mentioned more and more often. The workers were often free men, but subject to military discipline and not at liberty to change jobs.

Another feature of this age was the rise of large estates owned by the more able people who took advantage of the ruin of some of the less prudent and less fortunate. The requisitions and the strict rules of the state for the *curiales* bankrupted many, for the man who could not perform the duties demanded of him on the basis of his property would be sold out by the state, and his property would ordinarily be bought by someone in the neighborhood who was a successful manager of land.

There was no theory behind the measures that the successive governments in this century took to get the work of the government done. There was no objection to the rise of larger private properties; the government probably welcomed them as being more efficient and making it easier for it to get the supplies and services that it needed. In the next century, as we shall see, some of the great property owners were able to play the role of "the barons" and to defy the tax collectors and other agents of the central government—something that the government had not had to contend with since the very beginning of the Empire.

There is ample evidence of the dismay and disgust of many people on whom the system bore hard, so much so that many people tried to flee and lose themselves in the population or even outside the Empire among the barbarians. There is also evidence of attempts to find a way to escape from duties. Although many people lost their land because they could not meet the obligations of ownership, in the absence of detailed and statistical knowledge we may not assert that the new conditions brought misery to almost everyone, for in the intervals of the invasions and civil wars, which left large areas of the Empire untouched for considerable periods, it was possible to live along under this system without being in misery from day to day. It may well be that a man of this period would have recoiled in horror at a vivid description of life in a large American city in the latter part of the twentieth century, wondering how human beings could endure the incredible network of taxes, the noise, the dirt, the polluted air, the crime, the subway, the parkways, the job from nine to five, the loss of ties of family, church, and community. It is true, of course, that men were frozen into their jobs in the third century, but they perhaps did not mind very much, since they did not have to fear being frozen out of their jobs.

Pagan Literature and Learning

Among the works in Greek that stand out from a mass of mediocre writing and published oratory of this period were a group of romantic novels, the successors of earlier ones that have not been preserved. Most famous of them is *Daphnis and Chloe,* a tale of the love, adventures, dangers, and marriage of two simple and innocent young people, set against a stylized bucolic background. Slight as the story is, it is charming and has had influence in modern times of every kind—translation by the great Amyot, imitation in Bernardin de St. Pierre's *Paul et Virginie,* embodiment in a painting of Corot and the music of Ravel. The popularity of romances of this sort led the Christians to compose romances of the lives of the saints to serve as competitive offerings for the reading of the faithful.

A great influence was exerted by the doctrine that has come to be known as Neoplatonism offered by the philosopher Plotinus. For him all things in the universe are connected by bonds, not of sympathy so much as of intelligence, and he believed in the power of the various kinds of intelligence to cause changes in the universe. Contemplation, too, is a creative activity. The supreme human experience is to rise by intellectual activity and effort to the point where one can experience the one, the absolute, and, leaving one's self behind, simply *be* in its presence. Perhaps because of the purposes of Gallienus, this philosophy tended to be a rallying point for the more intelligent pagans against the rising claims and influence of Christianity, and a part of Neoplatonism was the support of all the old familiar and dear practices of paganism. On the other hand, Neoplatonism served in many cases as a preparation for Christianity, since it directed the mind to the idea of a single and absolute force in the universe. But the two were by no means the same thing, and if Neoplatonists were sometimes converted to Christianity, Christians were sometimes converted to Neoplatonism.

Although there is hardly a pagan Latin author of the third century worth mentioning, Latin education was widespread in the West. There were schools everywhere, and the standard liberal education, essentially a literary education with strong training in oratory, was a necessity for the young man who wished to make his way in polite circles or in the civil service. Chance has preserved works on correct usage from this later period of the Empire that were meant to help those to whom Latin was an acquired language or who spoke it with a provincial accent and with provincial solecisms.

Christian Thought and Writing

In the second century several memorials were addressed to the emperors by philosophically trained Christians, urging them to examine the facts of Christianity rather than merely listen to the slanders that were aimed at it. At the end of the second century or the beginning of the third came Minucius Felix's *Octavius,* a charming and sunny little dialogue written in good Latin with many echoes of Cicero's phrasing. Two friends go down the river to Ostia, where one of them attends to some affairs, after which they take a walk on the beach and fall into a discussion of Christianity. In this more artistic form the dialogue asks, as did the memorials to the emperors, that slanders on the Christians be disregarded and the facts considered.

In the third and fourth centuries the Christians became more confident in their written debates with other people. To the Jews they offered the argument that Christianity was a logical development of Judaism. For the pagans they adapted the old idea of *daemones,* found in Greek and Persian thought, to fit the major gods of the official religion of the time, asserting that the gods were only a part of the unseen crew of beings, partly divine, but also seeming rather human, that moved about between heaven and earth and caused a great deal of trouble in human affairs. Although the word meant only a spirit of some sort, good or bad, it now acquired the exclusive connotation of wickedness that "demon" has in English. The Christians had full confidence that they were in possession of revealed truth that superseded all other systems of belief, and they promulgated their ideas briskly, brashly, and often offensively.

Julius Africanus' large book on chronology was an excellent example of careful Christian scholarship. He made comparative tables of chronology according to the Jewish reckoning from the birth of Abraham, the Greek reckoning from the first Olympic Games in 776 B.C., the Roman reckoning from the founding of Rome in 753 B.C., the dynasties of Egypt as described by Manetho, and one or two less important systems, listing a great number of important events from all these spheres so that they could be dated by any one of the systems. Many important dates are known to us only because they found a place in Africanus' work, which was continued and expanded by later scholars. These Christian chronologers naturally regarded the time after the birth of Christ as different from the time before the birth of Christ and thus began the development of the idea that there are periods in history and that great events often cause the beginning of a new period.

Clement of Alexandria was one of the first of the great scholars and teachers who worked on the philosophical substructure of Christianity. He was a highly educated man who wished Christianity to accept the best in Greek and Roman thought, especially its long philosophical tradition, while insisting that the pagans must recognize the revelation through Christ of the realities of the governance of the universe.

Origen was born about A.D. 185 and died in 254–255?; tortures during the persecution under Decius in 250 are said to have broken his health. Most of his writing took the form of commentaries on the Scriptures rather than of separate treatises. He combined philosophy with Scripture by making allegorical, or symbolic, interpretations of Scripture to show that the two things had essentially the same meaning. The allegorical method, which some scholars regard as a sign of the intellectual weakness of Christianity, had already been extensively used in the best Greek circles, largely for the purpose of making the great authority of Homer seem consistent with matters of a later time of which Homer could have known nothing.

Origen may properly be called a Platonist philosopher as well as a Christian theologian. In both these roles he recognized a supreme and incorporeal Being, eternal and uncreated, and beside that Being he recognized also a principle, called the Logos even before Plato, and appearing briefly on earth as Christ. The Holy Spirit came from Christian thought rather than from Plato. The three formed a Trinity of three rather than one, and unequal rather than equal. Origen's theology, which can be worked out in detail from those large parts of his exegetical work that survive, is thus decidedly different from the theology of a simple Christian who knew nothing of philosophy or chose to keep separate what he did know.

An instructive example of Christian thought and procedure at this time is the condemnation of Paul, Bishop of Samosata, on the ground that his view of the nature of Christ and of Christ's relation to God was heretical and dangerous. The condemnation was the work of the Bishop of Rome, acting on complaints, for by now the authority of Rome was widely recognized in the Church. To depose Paul was another thing, for Samosata in A.D. 268 was in the territory of Zenobia, near Antioch; Paul naturally maintained that he was right and kept physical control of the church in Samosata. After he defeated Zenobia in 272, Aurelian ordered that the matter be settled to conform with the views of the Church in Rome.

A far greater heresy than that of Paul (and many other minor heresies) was that of Mani, who began in A.D. 246 to preach in the New Persian Empire a new form of Christianity that presented a serious challenge to its orthodox form during the fourth century. Plain as the oriental elements are in his new religion, Mani called himself the disciple of Jesus, and his followers thought of themselves as the best Christians. Like the Gnostics, he believed in an original state of perfection in which all was dominated by the principle of Light, which included everything good, and a falling off from that state because of the rise of the principle of Darkness, which included everything bad. There was an elaborate account of the advance of Darkness (one result of which was the creation of our world), of the place of Christ in the struggle of Light to restore the original perfection, and of the role of mankind in the process, which was to live in such a way as to help the restoration of the original state of things. Although all this may seem rather far from Christianity, Manicheism, as it was called, was an important form of Christianity in the fourth century.

CHAPTER

28

THE END OF THE ANCIENT WORLD

Diocletian's success in stabilizing the situation and the fact that he made important changes justify our calling his accession the beginning of a new period. That period, which we may as well call the fourth century, may be said to have ended with the death of the emperor Theodosius in A.D. 395. The fourth century was one of the great germinal periods, for in it the foundations of European life as it was to be for a long time afterward were laid. Those foundations remained in spite of the fact that after 395 there were new political and military difficulties that resulted, during the fifth and sixth centuries, in the passing of control in the West to Germanic kings and leaders.

RECOVERY AND A NEW AGE: A.D. 285 TO 395

Diocletian (A.D. 285–305)

Diocletian, who came of an undistinguished family in Dalmatia, joined the army and rose to governorships, a consulship, the command of the imperial bodyguard, and thence the throne. To keep himself alive, to keep himself on the throne, and to prevent the army from interfering with the government were his immediate problems. He made himself less accessible to the soldiers and the citizens than other emperors had done, partly to lend dignity to his office and partly to make assassination less easy. For these same purposes he borrowed from eastern kings elaborate court ceremony, the use of costly silk and purple clothes for the members of the court, and a system of resounding titles for officials and functionaries.

The best way to control the army was to lead it well in its proper work. Diocletian began by exercising command himself in successful operations in Moesia and Pannonia. When a peasant revolt in Gaul brought forward a pair of pretenders to the throne, he sent his lieutenant Maximianus, who quickly led the army in Gaul to a series of easy successes. In the next year Diocletian made him his colleague in charge of the West with the title of Augustus to show full equality of rank.

Diocletian now had to deal with enemy armies in Pannonia, Moesia, and Raetia. On two occasions he had to fight against the Sarmatians of southern Russia, and on another occasion against invaders of Syria from the South. By his exercise of diplomacy he persuaded the Persians to give up some of their claims on the eastern border and installed a Roman nominee as king of Armenia. Maximian fought all three of the great German tribal alliances of the Franks, the Alemanni, and the Burgundians. He made one of his subordinates, Carausius, an admiral to direct defense against the groups of Franks and Saxons who had recently taken to the sea and were harrying the coasts of France and Britain with their piratical raids.

It was probably in 292 that Diocletian took two younger associates who were given the title of Caesar in 293. Diocletian took Galerius as his Caesar and married his daughter to him. Maximian's Caesar was Constantius, a good soldier and the father of the emperor Constantine. Diocletian and Galerius ruled the East, dividing some parts between them, and Maximian and Constantius similarly ruled the West. It was understood that presently the two Augustuses would retire and allow the two Caesars to move up to the senior position, choosing two new Caesars as their juniors.

For five or six years after the formation of the tetrarchy, as this team of four rulers is generally called, the storms of war continued to rage, for the world had been too long unused to a heavy hand ready to enforce the Roman peace to settle down readily now. Carausius, the admiral of the Channel fleet, revolted and took all Britain with him when accused of conspiring with the pirates to enrich himself, and it was nearly ten years before the central power was again firmly in control in the island. Finally, however, the general military situation was stabilized.

The partition of the army among four efficient leaders who had a nearly unbroken record of successes brought almost automatically a reform of spirit and discipline among the troops. The organization of a mobile army, strong in heavy cavalry, ready to meet invasions at any point, thus supplementing the fixed forces on the frontiers and supplying a defense in depth behind them, meant that the great need of an additional force would not have to be met in haste each time it arose.

The provinces were divided so as to make about twice the number for efficiency's sake, although it has often been suggested that this was done to prevent any governor from having enough troops at his command to raise a revolt. Even the peaceful provinces were divided, and we can see that new officials were provided to administer justice promptly and to handle finances. There were over a hundred provinces, with a grand division into East and West and two large divisions called prefectures on each side. Some idea of the government of the provinces and the disposition of the troops at this time can be gained from the *Notitia Dignitatum* (roughly "list of offices" in English), a rather long list of officials and troops in the many administrative divisions of the Empire that was composed a little after A.D. 400, but goes back to a document of the time of Diocletian.

The Edict of Diocletian, published in A.D. 301, is an interesting administrative document that gives long lists of maximum prices set by the government in an attempt to combat the rise in prices. It begins with a list of thirty-five cereals and vegetables, after which are nineteen kinds of wine, twelve of oil, and fifty of meat. Later come wages of every kind, from those of a teacher of shorthand to those of a man with a mule, and prices of a great variety of manufactured goods, so that the student of economic history can learn much about the products available at that time. It was a good move against inflation to mint a good gold coin, the aureus, but unfortunately the government did not back it up with an equally sound coinage of silver and copper. There is even room for suspicion that the government tried to manipulate these other coinages in such a way as to outwit the public and extract a profit from the operation.

The government did well, however, in making the many requisitions in kind more regular and reasonable. Apparently a series of censuses of property was made in order to determine the taxable value of units of land, animals, and the labor of rural people, in some places distinguishing land by its degree of cultivation and in others only by its area, while there were also variations on what constituted a *caput*, or individual, with some fascinating combinations adding up to one. There was much to be said for the government's taking as taxes many of the things that it needed for soldiers and officials, then distributing them through its own agents without any use of money in the transaction. Cereals, oil, meat, and wine were obvious needs, while clothing seems a less natural thing to acquire by taxation. Riding and draft animals were also exacted from the taxpayers, as were men to work for the government, and recruits for the army were drafted in proportion to the units of population set up by the census. This system was fairer than anything known before, and it was the nearest to a governmental budget yet seen. The government's carefully calculated body of demands was called an indiction.

After Diocletian had for years allowed the Christians to cherish their beliefs, celebrate their rites, and build their churches, in A.D. 303 he issued a ruinous edict against them, probably at the instigation of his Caesar, the strong pagan Galerius. Their churches were to be destroyed, and they were forbidden to meet for worship; their sacred books had to be surrendered to the magistrates, and as a class they lost their legal rights. Such an edict, if strictly enforced, would have meant the end of Christianity, as indeed could have been the case in some of the earlier persecutions. It was never really enforced in the West, however, and in the East Galerius was apparently the only highly placed person who was at all enthusiastic about it.

Constantine (A.D. 306–337)

In A.D. 305 Diocletian retired and with him his fellow Augustus, Maximian, and the two Caesars, Galerius and Constantius, moved up to the senior positions. On the death of Constantius in 306 his army proclaimed his twenty-one-year-old son Constantine as Augustus, ignoring the Caesar of the West who had been appointed to help and succeed Constantius and raising a threat of the sort of civil war that had been so common in the third century. Constantine, who had an urge to dominate much like that of Octavian over three hundred years before, moved toward power slowly and carefully. In A.D. 311 Galerius' death not only ended the persecution of the Christians (actually he issued an edict legalizing their religion just before he died), but also encouraged Constantine to further advances, so that he took an army to Italy and in 312 won the famous battle near the Mulvian Bridge in the northern outskirts of Rome. This was the battle before which he claimed to have had a vision that inspired him to have his soldiers mark a symbol of Christianity in their shields—a combination of the first two letters of the Greek word *Christos*, a *chi* and a *rho*, which resemble an *X* and a *P*. The cross was not yet established as the Christian symbol. Constantine's action should probably be regarded as a direct test of what the god of the Christians could do for him.

Constantine was now in control of the whole West, and by the year 313 another ambitious man named Licinius emerged as master of the East. The two met early in 313 in Milan and agreed to give the Christians complete freedom of worship and restore confiscated property to them. Apparently no formal "Edict of Milan" to that effect was published, but the policy is made clear in letters from Licinius to the governors of provinces. The agreement of the two men on this policy did not make them real partners in administration, however, and with the passage of time their rivalry became more open, leading at last to a contest of arms in 323–324 that left Constantine as sole ruler of the Empire.

Constantine continued most of the tendencies in government begun by Diocletian, like the increase of court ceremony and insistence on the lofty position of the emperor, which made the center of government begin to seem more medieval than old Roman. He continued the good gold coinage, enlarged the mobile field army, and enrolled many barbarians, especially Germans, in the armies, while bringing in large groups of barbarians to settle in scantily populated areas under obligation to military service. The system of requisitions in kind was continued, and those who served the government, whether soldiers or civil servants, were largely paid in kind.

From the *Notitia Dignitatum* and other sources we learn of the existence of a very complicated bureaucracy. Constantine entrusted several important functions to men whom he called *comites* (from which come the French *comte* and English "count"), or "companions." The "count of the sacred largess" for example, had wide financial powers, controlling mints and mines and payments to government personnel, and the count of the crown properties managed the imperial estates.

Constantine undoubtedly knew a fair amount about the beliefs and practices of Christianity before his vision and thought of it as efficacious in supporting his regime when he came to sole power. Although he first granted tolerance to Christianity, then made it a favored religion, he realized the power of pagan sentiment and the numerical superiority of non-Christians and did not attempt to make Christianity the only recognized religion. He did, however, make some interesting attempts to promote church unity, presumably so that the church could be more useful to the government. The Council of Nicaea, which he convoked in A.D. 325, was the first of many church councils called by the emperors at the request of the churchmen to settle quarrels by establishing the official position of the Church on doctrinal points. The emperor attended the Council of Nicaea, took part in the debates, and tried hard to help in composing the doctrinal quarrel that the Council was to heal. In the end he put civil power behind the decision of the Council that what was called the Arian position was heretical and that the Arian bishops were to be deposed. The question was on the nature of the Trinity: whether the nature of Christ is the same (Greek *homos*) as that of the Father, the Catholic position, or like (Greek *homoios*) that of the Father, the Arian position, first stated and argued by a persuasive and stubborn bishop named Arius. The fact that the words differed chiefly because of an *iota*, the English letter *i*, gave rise to the saying that something does not make an iota, or jot, of difference. The Council's position was expressed by the words of the Nicene Creed, which it composed, "being of one substance with the Father."

The Arian heresy was far from being ended by the Council of Nicaea and the government's attempts to enforce the Council's decision. Not only did it stubbornly attempt to maintain itself within the Empire, but the

Arian party also produced the great apostle to the Goths, Ulfilas, who was consecrated bishop to the Christians held in captivity among the barbarians in A.D. 341. He taught the Goths Arian Christianity and translated the Bible into their language. The Arian faith of several Germanic tribes was thereafter a political fact to be reckoned with until well after A.D. 496, when Clovis the Frank moved from Arianism to Catholicism and thus gained the support of the Catholics of Gaul against the Arian Germans in Gaul.

The senatorial order opposed Christianity strongly because its members conceived their status to rest largely on a pagan structure of society. Even when they became Christians for reasons of policy they held to the pagan culture. Constantine adlected a large number of Christians into the Senate, but the new members, instead of attempting to support and spread his views, eagerly embraced all the old pagan symbols of superior status. Such opposition to his plans for a Christian Rome may have led him to hurry his plans to transform Byzantium into a new city, to be called Constantinopolis, which was founded in A.D. 330 and was from the beginning an officially Christian city, an "anti-Rome" in this respect.

The new city was naturally larger than the old Byzantium had been, since a capital city for the administration of the East was badly needed. Constantine took many senators with him, adlected others, and started his new city with a devout Christian Senate to balance that of Rome, with fourteen regions like Rome and a mob of plebeians to inhabit them and receive bread and circuses, with great public buildings, notably the Hippodrome, scene of horse races and riots like those of Rome, and with treasures of art taken from all over the ancient world, some of which are still to be seen in the modern city of Istanbul.

Naturally estimates of Constantine differ. From the exclusively Christian point of view he must seem the bringer of a great good in that he made possible a vast spread of Christianity. At the other extreme is the view that he betrayed the Empire by assisting Christianity to supersede the pagan system and by introducing far more Germans and other barbarians than the Empire could assimilate. Our estimate of him should probably be that he was a man of great energy and desire for power whose chief achievement was to put himself alone at the head of the government and who, when there, turned out to be only an ordinarily competent administrator.

The House of Constantine (A.D. 337–363)

Constantine died in A.D. 337. He had trained all his sons in government, and at his death he left the three youngest (he had brought accusations against the eldest and executed him) in positions of power. Constantine

II was in charge of the West; Constans in charge of Italy and Africa; and Constantius in charge of the East. Unfortunately they were unable to cooperate, and in the year 353 Constantius emerged as sole ruler, a position that he held until his death in 361. In 354 Constantius, having eliminated all the active members of the family, decided to call on his cousin Julian (who had spent his early years with tutors in a retirement that was carefully guarded, but recently had been allowed to study in Athens) and sent him to Gaul. Soon, in spite of his inexperience and limited authority, Julian began to display a talent for imperial tasks, and in 357 he was given command of the troops in Gaul. Within three years he led the army to considerable successes against the Alemanni and other troublesome Germanic peoples and re-established the defenses on the Rhine.

Constantius surrounded Julian with agents who were to watch him and report his every move. A war with the Persians was arising in the East, which gave him a reason (or an excuse) to demand that Julian send him some of his best Gallic troops. The soldiers, appalled by the thought of going so far from home, mutinied and proclaimed Julian as Augustus (A.D. 360), leaving him the choice of riding a whirlwind that he had not raised or being destroyed. He chose to attempt to reign and asked Constantius to recognize him. Constantius refused, and the two moved to meet each other in the Balkans in another senseless struggle, but the battle was averted by the natural death of Constantius late in A.D. 361. On his deathbed he named Julian as his successor.

Constantius was a man of more than average ability. The evidence for his reign, much of it consisting of rulings preserved in the law codes, is plentiful enough to give us a picture of the multiplication of officials and of the financial pressure that the government exerted on everyone. We hear of the growth of a sinister secret police who spied everywhere, something that had been done in a modest way as far back as Hadrian. An entirely new phenomenon was the rise to power of the eunuchs who made up the staff of the Sacred Bedchamber, as the emperor's household was called. Constantius was accustomed to say in jest that he had some influence with Eusebius, their chief.

Constantius' first visit to Rome was a pleasant and distinctive feature of his reign. He passed the first part of his life in the East, then spent five years of work and warfare in Italy. The court was at Milan, for the center of the Empire had long since shifted northward, as we have seen, and there was much military pressure to be resisted on the northern frontiers, so he had never been to Rome. In A.D. 357 he came to Rome, escorted by an army, riding into the old center of his realm on a high chariot, gorgeous in his imperial raiment, aloof and impassive as if he were another image of an eastern deity being brought into the city. The Roman crowd gave him a noisy welcome, and on the following days the senators escorted him around the sights of Rome. Constantius was enormously impressed. In the preceding year he had decreed, as a Christian monarch, that there should be no more celebration of pagan occasions; now he recalled that he himself was Pontifex Maximus and not the least part of all this mellow splendor, and he made appointments to vacancies in the pagan priesthoods of Rome and stayed the enforcement of his decree against pagan ceremonies. The old was yielding to the new, but was not yet entirely overcome.

Julian, during his brief term as emperor (A.D. 361–363), made that attempt to turn back the movement of affairs that earned him the title "the Apostate." His studies in the old university town of Athens had influenced him strongly, and he had put off the Christianity in which he had been raised. Able as he was, he had lived, like Claudius long before him, so much in retirement with tutors and servants in his earlier years that he had not acquired any sense of how to manage people in groups that could not be commanded or coerced, and he fancied that he could command a return to paganism. He innocently thought that the philosophical paganism of the Neoplatonists could serve as the faith of a pagan church organized in the manner of the Christian Church. His attempts at constructive measures and at penalties for noncompliance were distasteful to most people, and there probably was a sense of relief among pagans as well as among Christians when in A.D. 363 he died of a wound in a war against the Persians which better sense might have kept him from undertaking. The conduct of both Constantius and Julian toward the Christians shows that there was as yet no fixed governmental policy in regard to them.

The army chose as Julian's successor Jovian, commander of the bodyguard, who thought it best to disengage his army by yielding to the Persians the farthest Roman possessions. As soon as he was firmly seated on the throne, he put an end to the attempt to return to paganism. He died in A.D. 364, and after him came a new imperial house.

A New Dynasty: Valentinian and Theodosius (A.D. 364–395)

The army now selected Valentinian, a Pannonian officer of some experience, and he took as his colleague his brother Valens. Valentinian took the West for his sphere because he believed that the defense of the Rhine frontier, where the Germanic peoples had for some time been restless and troublesome, was the most pressing task of the government. He was able to chastise severely the peoples on the Rhine and the Saxons, and one of his generals drove out the inhabitants of northern Britain who had invaded the Roman part. In the East Valens was able to deal with the Persians and to repel an invasion of the Goths, who often gave trouble on the lower Danube frontier. The Roman armies of this time could fight and did fight.

A new and more fearsome enemy was added at this time, however. The Huns, responding to an impulse of their own or to some pressure not known either to written history or to archaeology (no sure connection can be made with what we know of Chinese history), came westward and in A.D. 373 overran the East Goths, or Ostrogoths, in the Ukraine (the southwestern part of the Soviet Union), then moved against the West Goths, or Visigoths, on the Dniester River, farther southwest. In all peoples of the West, even the pugnacious German tribes, the Huns inspired aversion and fear, for they seemed hardly human, having the gnarled forms of nomads who lived on horseback and features different from those of the Westerners.

The Visigoths, retiring before the Huns, presently asked permission to cross the Danube and settle down in Roman territory with a permanent obligation of military service. This proposal and other similar ones from outsiders were tempting to the emperors, since the newcomers would provide unpaid soldiers. The Visigoths were allowed to cross, but were scandalously mistreated and cheated by the Roman officials who were to supply them with food while they were getting settled. Thus they took to brigandage and presently, reinforced by some Ostrogoths, they had to be regarded as a hostile military force in Roman territory. In A.D. 378 Valens and his army met them near Adrianople, in Thrace, and were utterly defeated. Valens lost his life.

The Visigoths remained in the Empire, like a foreign body in an organism, it has been said, tearing tissues and causing hemorrhages. Such analogies are dangerous in their inexactness; the body politic need not suffer the damage that a human body might thus undergo. It must also be said that the Visigoths were often rather badly treated by the Roman government during the three decades and more before the government settled them permanently in southwest Europe. The continued presence of the Huns frightened them so that they did not want to go back to the territories outside the Empire where they had formerly lived.

Valentinian and Valens may serve as examples of the less cultivated class of men who often came to power at this time. They were Pannonians of little background or education, and they hastened to appoint many Pannonians of their own type to governorships and other high offices. Both seem to have been hostile to gentlefolk of education and high social standing, and both were desperately afraid of the powers that might be summoned by magic, so that in both East and West many accusations of magic practices were leveled at senators and other persons of the upper classes. We are told that many people in the East destroyed their private libraries because Valens was so ignorant that to him the possession of books seemed to make a man a practitioner of magic.

Even before the death of Valentinian in A.D. 375 his two sons, Gratian and Valentinian II, had received the title of Augustus, but they were young and neither possessed the toughness to hold and exercise the position, although both did last for some years. The important man of the next decades was Theodosius, whom Gratian put in charge of the East in 379 and who was more and more important until his death in 395. He began by negotiations with the Goths who were troubling the East. We know little of the negotiations, but the result was a grant of land for the Goths inside the Empire and a treaty allowing them to live there as an independent people under their own government. There are those who call this a shrewd and intelligent move, while others regard it as a shameful example of doing the easy thing that is harmful in the end. Theodosius enrolled many Goths in the Roman army as a simple way to avoid insisting on the conscription of Romans, a policy soon to seem very mistaken.

Theodosius was a very devout Christian of a rather unintelligent kind, and his Christianity gains in interest from the presence at Milan, the seat of the western court, of the belligerent and forceful bishop Ambrose, a former imperial administrator and a member of the senatorial order who became Bishop of Milan in A.D. 373 under spectacular circumstances. He was a popular administrator, and his conversion to Christianity aroused great interest. At that time there was a bitter contest over the vacant bishopric of Milan, and someone, said to have been a little boy, cried out that Ambrose should be bishop, and he was acclaimed by one and all and made bishop almost before he had joined the Church. Times were changing when a Roman of a great family could appear as bishop.

Ambrose had scored an outstanding success for the Christians during the reign of Gratian, in A.D. 383. The young Christian emperor had been persuaded to order the removal from the Senate house of the Altar of Victory, which had been there since the days of the Republic. The pagan senators sent him a memorial, written by the noted senator Symmachus and still extant, a dignified statement of the claims of tradition. Ambrose wrote an answer in which he rejected all the claims of antiquity in favor of the new truth of Christianity, and to make sure of the decision he threatened the young emperor with excommunication, thus preventing the return of the altar. In another contest he had prevented the mother of the young Valentinian II from getting the use of a church for an Arian congregation, and in his most famous contest he compelled Theodosius to do public penance for a massacre that he had ordered in reprisal for bloody civil disturbances.

Another notable statesman of the Church at this time was Damasus, Bishop of Rome, who began his episcopal career with violence, but then was able to settle down to the exercise of a velvety diplomacy. At the time of his election in A.D. 365 he and a rival fought several pitched battles fierce enough so that about two hundred dead were left each time. With his reign the primacy of the Bishop of Rome may be taken as established, and he also quietly developed the principle that the secular arm could regularly be called upon to enforce the decisions of the Church, for example, to expel from their sees bishops deposed for heresy or for other reasons. To him may also belong the credit for persuading Theodosius to take a sterner line against the pagans. The worldly setting of his bishopric was magnificent, and like a secular prince he was a patron of letters and the arts.

Theodosius was persuaded to issue an uncompromising edict forbidding pagan sacrifices or ceremonies of any kind. Even to worship the Lares in the privacy of the household was forbidden. Of course many of the pagan ceremonies, like rites of rejoicing at the coming of the spring, could be turned into Christian ceremonies like Easter. One which conspicuously could not was the Olympic Games, for a festival of horse racing and a track meet in honor of Zeus was a little too much to adapt. With the games ended, the site was deserted, was shaken by earthquakes, then covered with deep mud by floods of the nearby river. It was actually unidentifiable until the eighteenth century, then was triumphantly excavated by German scholars in the 1870s with the result that enough interest could be stirred up for the successful revival of the Games at Athens in 1896.

The civil administration of Theodosius was not an unqualified success in spite of his putting down usurpers. He did not properly face the arduous task of maintaining a citizen army, for he enrolled foreigners in too large numbers. He did not give the poor and the middle class the protection they needed against some of the rich, with the result that many little men were ruined and had to become protégés of the powerful, who thus became more able to assert themselves against the central government and shirk their duties of paying taxes and providing men for the army. He did take a firm stand in favor of Christianity, but we do not know whether the Empire gained or lost in strength and unity as a result.

THE FIFTH CENTURY

Troubles in the West

Theodosius, on his death in A.D. 395, left the *magister militum*, or head of the army, the German Stilicho, as guardian for his son Honorius, who had been proclaimed to the troops as his successor in 393 and was regarded as being in charge of the West, and probably also guardian of his son Arcadius, who had been proclaimed in 383 and was in charge of the East.

In fact Arcadius was much more under the control of a succession of high civil officials. During the fifteen years that followed the death of Theodosius there was frequent conflict between Stilicho and the men most influential in the East, a conflict that contributed to the troubles of the Empire.

Although historians have varied widely in their judgment of Stilicho, it is perhaps fair to say that he was the new type of German high in the service of Rome, well educated and cultivated, that he had the virtue of unswerving personal loyalty, in this case to his ward Honorius, and that he had very little policy other than to take proper care of the interests of Honorius and the government and to gain for the West the prefecture of Illyricum, which had belonged sometimes to the West and sometimes to the East and was prized by both as a recruiting ground. If he had had a more distinctive policy, there might be less difference of opinion as to his merits.

At the end of December, 406, a large group of Vandals, Alans, and Suebi, withdrawing before the pressure of the Huns, crossed the frozen Rhine and entered Gaul, where they are said to have spread destruction far and wide. The British army at the same time set up a claim to establish a strong emperor for the West, and finally its nominee, Constantine, crossed to Gaul in 407 to try to deal with the invaders. Stilicho had done nothing so far to help Gaul, but in the following year he made plans to send both Alaric, the Visigothic leader, and some Roman troops to Gaul to attempt to repress both the invaders and the usurper Constantine. He had enemies at the court of Honorius, however, who were able to use his failure in Gaul to bring about his deposition and execution.

In both East and West there were active anti-German parties who objected to the presence of so many Germans in high positions in the army and the civil service. Many of these Germans, like Stilicho, were three or four generations removed from the forests of Germany and were well educated persons who had a somewhat exaggerated respect for Rome and for what they thought of as old Roman traditions. The reaction against them in the East led to the removal of all of them from important positions for more than a generation. The East also made more effort than the West to enforce universal military service and consequently had a somewhat more reliable army. Stilicho, as the effective head of government in the West, naturally had been the chief object of the anti-German feeling.

Honorius attempted now to exert more control over affairs, but was kept too busy by Alaric and the Visigoths to be able to help Gaul. For a long time Alaric had been able to hold together a group that could be called the tribe of the Visigoths and had tried again and again to find a secure home for them. This time he marched on Rome and allowed the

Senate to buy him off with five thousand pounds of gold, ten thousand pounds of silver, and three thousand pounds of pepper. After more negotiations Alaric again marched on Rome, but desisted on learning that a force of Hunnic *foederati* (a term used for outsiders who fought for the Romans) was ready to move against him. Finally, after the failure of further negotiations, he marched on Rome in the year 410 and sacked it.

The sack of Rome by Alaric, if taken in its context, does not constitute a turning point of any sort. The symbolic importance of the city of Rome was such, however, in spite of the fact that the emperors had for a long time made Milan or Ravenna their seat, that the act sent a shudder of horror through the Roman world. The pagan party, which was still able to make itself heard, cried that this was the result of the abandonment of the pagan gods by a Christian government, and the Christians tried in turn to fit the event into their framework of world history, their deepest voice being that of St. Augustine in his *City of God*.

Alaric next made an unsuccessful attempt to take his people to Sicily, after which he died in southern Italy. His brother Athaulf was elected king in his place. To him is attributed the interesting remark that he had long thought that there ought to be a new and great kingdom of Gothia, but finally decided that the Goths were not ready for this and would do much better to attach themselves to the Romans and learn *romanitas*, as the Germanic peoples were wont to call the Roman way, which they so admired. In 412 he took his people to Gaul, where he hoped to find a place for them to settle. He married a Roman princess with Roman ceremonies and attempted to set up a sort of permanent government with Roman advisers in Bordeaux, but could not get the support of the Roman government and felt that it would be better to go to Spain. There he was murdered, possibly by a faction of his nobles who were unwilling to take on the Roman way of life.

In the year 411 the Roman general Constantius came to the fore in the struggle in Gaul against the usurper Constantine. The three peoples who had invaded and ravaged the country had all moved on to Spain, as had the Visigoths. Until 421 Constantius was in command in Gaul with the title of patrician, which came to be the regular title for a commander in chief, and succeeded in establishing the imperial authority there in a precarious way. An especially interesting part of his work is his settlement of the Visigoths (whom he recalled from Spain) in southern Gaul in A.D. 418. His measure probably had as its first cause a great rebellion of the common people, who called themselves the Bagaudae, which broke out in Gaul and especially in Aquitania after the disturbances caused by the invading Vandals, Alans, and Suebi during the year 407 and was not subdued until 417. Constantius summoned the Visigoths from Spain and settled them on the good farming lands of this region of France according to the system called *hospitalitas,* which was developed from the methods formerly used for billeting troops on local populations. The Visigoths were given two-thirds of the farm land and half of the pasture and wood-land of the Romans here and there who were their "hosts." They were so distributed as to mix them thoroughly with the Roman population and to make them available as troops anywhere through the countryside if there were any further attempt at an uprising. This arrangement may reasonably be regarded as an act of Roman policy, not forced on them by the Visigoths, and we have no record of complaints from the former own-ers of the land, who presumably were willing to pay this price to intro-duce a new and vigorous element of believers in the rights of landlords. It appears that the effect on the Visigoths themselves was to loosen their tribal organization somewhat and to turn their nobles into typical Ro-man landlords.

As the years went on, the Alans and the Suebi were either conquered by the Romans or broken up and settled, as were part of the Vandals. The Burgundi, who had come across the Rhine from Germany in the wake of the invasion of 406–407, were settled in what is now Burgundy and Savoy, the parts of eastern France nearest to Switzerland. In A.D. 443 they were offered the same *hospitalitas* as the Visigoths had been offered earlier, presumably because it was thought that they would be useful in preserving order.

After the death of the patrician Constantius in A.D. 421 another man, Aëtius, rose slowly to be patrician from about 433 to his death in 454. Although he was an excellent soldier, his chief claim to power was his cordial personal relation with the people of the court of the Huns, where he had spent several years as a hostage in his youth. It was an army of Huns, in fact, that helped him to establish himself, but his greatest achievement was to repulse the Huns in the great battle of Châlons, or the Battle of the Catalaunian Plains, in France in A.D. 451.

Attila, whose name is always associated with the Huns, had become their ruler in 433 and immediately made them much more formidable to both parts of the Empire. From his headquarters in Hungary he could bully the Ostrogoths and the Slavs of southern Russia and the Germanic peo-ples on the Danube and could make demands on the Romans.

In A.D. 450 the undistinguished new emperor of the East refused to pay further tribute to Attila, perhaps out of misjudgment of his own strength, and the West followed with a similar refusal. There is a story, too, of a willful daughter of an emperor who to gain her own way contrived to send a message to Attila asking him to marry her, so that he claimed the Ro-man West as the dowry that should go with her. Be that as it may, Attila moved westward and in 451 drove his way across the Rhine into Gaul, where Aëtius met him with the Roman forces and with the troops of the

Visigoths, who Attila had hoped would remain neutral. The men of the West stood firm, and after a bitter battle Attila was driven back to his camp, shorn of the aura of invincibility.

This has been called one of the decisive battles of the world. Probably the kingdom of the Huns would have become far less efficient after the death of Attila, even if the Huns had won this battle. It has been suggested, however, that if Europe had been the kind of steppe, like Hungary or their old Asian home, that suited the nomadic life of the Huns, they might have stayed and been able, barbarians that they were, even without the genius of Attila or another like him, to prevent the appropriation of the Greco-Roman civilization by the people of the West and the growth of modern Europe.

Attila returned to Hungary, gnashing his teeth, and in 452 marched into northern Italy, capturing some of its cities. His army was struck by famine and disease, however, and the Romans received reinforcements from the East. Pope Leo I is said to have represented the majesty of Rome and the Church most impressively at the head of the delegation that the Romans sent to urge Attila to go away and that succeeded, perhaps largely because of the adverse factors, which he had already considered. He went home and began to prepare for an attack on the eastern Empire, but died. All the neighboring peoples rose against the Huns at his death and in A.D. 454 inflicted a terrible defeat on them, driving the survivors eastward to Russia. The history of this region during the following century may be described as a comparatively harmless scramble among the peoples who lived there, with the Romans skillfully encouraging them to weaken one another.

The Vandals

The history of the Vandals before they crossed the frozen Rhine with other peoples the last night of the year 406 is of no interest to us, nor are their precise movements as they, with the Alans and the Suebi, went plundering through Gaul in 407 and on to Spain in search of further booty and food. In A.D. 428, Gaiseric, also known as Genseric, became the Vandal king. He was, for a German, a political genius, since he devised the prettiest arrangement that any of the Germanic peoples ever got at the expense of the more civilized world. In 429 he gathered enough shipping to ferry 80,000 of his tribe across the Strait of Gibraltar to North Africa, where the government was having difficulty with a revolt of the Moors and with the unrest of the popular element of the Donatists.[1] The Vandals seem to have proceeded eastward across North Africa in a leisurely and dignified manner, applying a little violence here and there,

[1] See p. 633.

but often overawing the inhabitants. The Roman possessions in the West, those in the two Mauretanias, had already been abandoned by the Romans, but were not the sort of place that Gaiseric was looking for. He planned to settle his people in the middle of the best area of the Roman provinces, where even with their limited numbers they could dominate the lands lying to either side of them.

He gained a treaty of *hospitalitas,* probably in 435, that gave his people possession of land more than adequate for their needs in return for the not burdensome duty of defending it, and in 442 he was formally recognized as an independent sovereign. The loss of this territory with so rich a yield in grain and tribute was a heavy blow to the Empire. Although the lands held by *hospitalitas* here and there still paid a revenue to the central government, the territory of the Vandals after 442 did not. On the other hand, the people who found themselves under the control of the Vandals in Africa do not seem to have been oppressed. They had been used to a life, under the joint control of the great landowners and the Church, that may well have resembled that of Europe during the Middle Ages. The Vandals, when not engaged in battle, seem to have been reasonable people bent on achieving ease and comfort. Much property in Vandal territory remained in Roman hands and was subject to Roman law.

The ill repute of the Vandals must have come most of all from their being the original Barbary pirates. From their position in North Africa they could readily raid all along the southern coast of Europe—their greatest venture was that at Rome in 455, when they plundered for three days—and they could make commerce and communication very difficult on the great interior waterway of the Mediterranean. Not only had they recognized the dream of all the Germans—a place of easy living—but they also found the excitement that they craved by going out as pirates and bringing in the cargoes of merchant ships or the loot of cities. The loss of Africa, however, was more important to the Romans than the loss of occasional loot and must be regarded as one of the sorest blows they suffered in this century. There are those who believe that the piracy of the Vandals permanently crippled communication by sea between the eastern and the western empires, although others feel that this did not happen until the Arabs took control of the Mediterranean at about the time of their conquest of Spain in A.D. 711.

In the century between the arrival of the Vandals in North Africa and their defeat (A.D. 533) and consequent dispersal by the forces of the eastern Empire, they did not impress themselves at all on the life of North Africa. Their language apparently gave way readily to Latin. They were Arians and spasmodically persecuted the Catholics, but not with conviction and persistence. There is no sign that they brought with them any cultural trait whatsoever that had the strength to survive. They left no trace of any custom or tradition: nothing in literature, religious peculiarities, monuments, or clues to unusual burial customs, clothing, or weapons. Like the Philistines, however, they had the misfortune to antagonize people who had the power to turn their name into a term of opprobrium forever.

Conditions in the West

The emperors of the fifth century in the West hardly seem worth mentioning separately, for they were not men who could take control of affairs. The Germanic *magistri militum* were more likely to make the important decisions of government. We must not assume for that reason, however, that there was no orderly government or that all governmental affairs were managed in a barbaric fashion. These Germans were no longer crude barbarians, but had had time and opportunity to become romanized, and even the coarser Germans were very respectful of Roman methods of management. One of the better known of these masters of the soldiers was Ricimer, who from 457 to 472 held the titles of patrician and *magister militum*, controlled Italy, and was able to make and unmake a series of emperors. The central government in Italy was functioning somewhat in the old way, but with a painful weakness. The Vandals had taken a large part of the provinces of Africa, their manpower, their grain, and their money tribute. The Visigoths, Franks, Burgundians, and others had been granted *hospitalitas* in many parts of Gaul, with some weakening of the central government, even though some tribute continued to be paid and no army needed to be supplied for the regions whose defense had been taken over as part of the treaty of *hospitalitas*. Toward the year 500 Clovis the Frank began to extend his power in Gaul, and with his victory over the Visigoths in A.D. 507 he became master of almost all Gaul. Here began the modern history of France. Clovis is known as the first of the Merovingian line of French kings, and after his death in 511 his kingdom held together, in contrast to the temporary kingdoms built by other forceful men of the time.

The western Empire is sometimes said to have fallen in A.D. 476 with the replacement in Italy of Romulus Augustulus (himself a usurper) by the German soldier and king Odoacer.[2] There is a modicum of truth in the idea, since now every major part of the West had come under the control of the Germans. Odoacer spread his people over the Italian countryside according to a treaty of *hospitalitas* as other Germanic leaders had done

[2] Recent work has indicated that the coins of Nepos, the eastern emperor's nominee for the West, show that he was recognized as titular ruler of the West, even by Odoacer, until the year 480, so that this year should probably have the mystical significance generally given to 476. See John Kent, "Julius Nepos and the Fall of the Western Empire," in *Corolla Memoriae Erich Swoboda Dedicata* (Graz, 1967), pp. 146–150.

elsewhere. On the other hand, he had the title of patrician and ruled those parts of the western Empire where he could make his writ run, chiefly Italy, through the Senate and other typically Roman agencies of government with great respect for the Roman tradition as he knew it.

In a way the fact that in the fifth century the western Empire slowly slipped away into the hands of Germanic kings can be taken as the result of a financial shortage, for there were probably enough people to man the frontiers against the steadily increasing pressure of the peoples outside, had it been possible to pay and supply them. Historians are fairly well agreed that to maintain so large an area of peaceful and settled life in so turbulent a world had been a task of great difficulty from the beginning and one that allowed little margin for mistakes of judgment, for inefficiency, or for adverse contingencies. The Pax Romana cannot be taken for granted; we must see it as something created with difficulty and maintained with difficulty and constituting an exception between the time before it and the time after it.

It is surprising that the Germans who took over the management of the West could be so admiring of the Romans and at the same time for themselves almost automatically reject the three cardinal features of the Greco-Roman civilization—the high intellectual tradition based on literacy, the intensity of life lived in cities, and impersonal governments based on the rule of law. We may be sure, however, that the Germans respected the practical abilities and the administrative efficiency of the Romans and that they made much use of Romans to tend the machinery of government and that they allowed the Romans to live under Roman law. The names of the officials tended to be the same; the financial structure, including the specific taxes, was very similar. The cities were sometimes lively, but in the areas given over to the Germanic guests they tended to be neglected and to shrink still further, and often they were put under the temporal dominion of a bishop.

This was the real decline of the Roman Empire in the West: its falling in the fifth century into the hands of men who were worthy and no doubt virtuous and who probably, had they cared at all for the things of the intellect, might have shown themselves intelligent, but did not belong to that continuing group, from the Sumerians and Egyptians to the Greeks and Romans, whose strenuous efforts had brought into being for men the bittersweet joys of high civilization. The strenuous class created civilization and the strenuous class maintains it. The West did not become a desert where a visitor from another planet might have seen a few half-naked savages skulking behind trees. It was dominated by a large group of people who did not care for the highest possessions of those whom they had conquered and felt no urge to prepare themselves or exert themselves to live as the Romans had lived. They farmed and fought (or more often brawled) and had the Romans among them handle the government and trade as best they could. The result, while surely not a disaster, was just as surely a decline.

The fact that Roman history begins in the West and contains a fairly easy conquest of the East by the forces of the West must not cause us to forget that the East was the home of civilization and that in the fifth and sixth centuries of our era the East was probably more densely populated, had better-developed industry, and was financially stronger than the West. It is also true that the armies of the East had no such assaults to cope with in the fourth, fifth, and sixth centuries as did those of the West. The eastern, or Byzantine, Empire, although new forces like those of Islam and the Turks and the predatory Crusaders arose to assault it, had nearly a thousand years of brilliant civilization yet before it.

29

THE CIVILIZATION OF THE LATE EMPIRE

The fourth century has been well called one of the great germinal centuries, for in it the Christian was combined with the Greco-Roman way of life. The fact that the Germans took control of the West and handled it far less efficiently than the Romans had done did not prevent the transmission in the West of a less intellectual and less intense version of the culture of the late Empire. The culture of the Byzantine Empire was a continuation of the combined Christian and Greco-Roman culture as it developed in the East in the fourth century.

THE GOVERNMENT

Emperor and Court

Although there was no legal system of hereditary succession to the throne, the soldiers liked to keep the succession in the imperial family, and Constantine was succeeded by his sons and then by his nephew Julian; Gratian and Valentinian II succeeded Valentinian, and the sons and grandsons of Theodosius succeeded him. Only twice after the third century did the throne seem to become really vacant, when at the death of Julian a council of leading men chose Jovian and presented him to the army, and when at the death of Jovian a few months later Valentinian was chosen in the same way. In the eastern Empire there were almost no attempts at usurpation of the throne, and the few attempts in the West either failed or succeeded only temporarily. The problem of regulating the succession to the throne was dealt with far better than in the turbulent third century and perhaps not much worse than in the first century.

Once a man became emperor, he had much the same powers that emperors had enjoyed since Augustus. To be sure, only traces were left among the pagans of the cult of the living emperor, but he was regarded by all as the viceregent of God. His person was to be adored, and the words "sacred" and "divine" were freely applied to everything that appertained to him. Although all the emperors were guilty of occasional unfortunate acts, they all protested that their being set above the law did not lessen their respect for the law. In the fourth and fifth centuries the great landowners were able for the first time during the Empire to gain such strength that they could at least resist the payment of their taxes to the central government and could shelter little men from the government, although they never got to the point of banding together to make major demands on the emperor.

The emperors lost their power in general by natural deaths. There is nothing to parallel the murders of Gaius and Nero for their excesses or of Claudius by Agrippina to gain the throne for Nero or of Domitian for his sternness—all of which occurred in what is regarded by most historians as an era of better management than that of the fourth century. The women of the imperial family exercised power more than once for those emperors who came to the throne as boys, and their hands were firm on the helm. On one or two occasions eunuchs high in the palace staff similarly directed the government. Perhaps the extreme case of management by someone not the nominal head is the German *magister militum* in the West, able German servants of the state who could not mount the throne because they were not of Roman descent, but who could hold power and command loyalty and keep the government going when the nominal emperor was a man inadequate to the demands of the position.

The Senate had less power and less involvement in affairs than in the first and second centuries. Its members did not hold as many offices and positions in the government as they did then, and did not hold high commands in the army at all. They occasionally functioned as a high court, but almost never legislated, although they frequently petitioned the emperor for legislation, which he thereupon enacted. The senators were rich men who owned a great deal of land and controlled a multitude of people and presumably exercised an influence that was taken for granted and is therefore seldom mentioned in our sources. The scanty evidence on their estates seems to show that, while there were some very large contiguous holdings, most of them were composed of units scattered through several provinces. This latter kind of estate might enable a man to speak for the interests of a great many tenants without being able to organize any group that could possibly act at his bidding. There is plentiful evidence

Hadrian's Villa; Tibur (Tivoli)

Photograph by the author

Part of the large building providing many small shops in Trajan's Market

Photograph by the author

Gold death mask of a Bosporan client king
Courtesy of The State Hermitage, Leningrad

Herculaneum; the edge of the excavation, showing the deep layer of volcanic mud
that covered the town in the eruption of 79 A.D.   *Photograph by the author*

Aquincum (now in the suburbs of Budapest): remains of the baths of the military camp, showing how the heating system under the floor was built.

Photograph by the author

The Roman amphitheater at Pula, on the Dalmatian coast

Courtesy of Isabel Montesinos

Spain: The Roman Aqueduct at Segovia   *Courtesy of Trans World Airlines*

Hadrian's Tomb (Castel Sant' Angelo)   *Courtesy of Trans World Airlines*

Petra, Jordan: The Treasury   *Courtesy of Pan American Airways, Inc.*

Roman North Africa; the Arch of Caracalla at Djemila
Courtesy of Trans World Airlines

The Arch of Constantine; Rome   *Photograph by the author*

Three-story house emerging in excavation at Ephesus   *Photograph by the author*

from this period that the imperial government continued to be aware of the importance of keeping information flowing steadily to it about the affairs of the realm and that it encouraged senators, bishops, officials, the *curiales,* the groups (shipowners, for example) that served the state, and private citizens to send petitions and make their views heard. It is naturally true that it often was not informed of passive resistance of various kinds to its ordinances, as when, for example, provincial governors did not persecute dissident groups with the rigor that was ordered.

Finance

Although the structure of the Empire had become too expensive for the resources of the Empire to support, the government managed to keep a system of finance going with reasonable success in the fourth and fifth centuries. Our sources are rich in taxpayers' complaints and evidence of strain here and there that raised an outcry. The solidus was kept at 1/72 of a pound of gold until well after our period. The silver coinage, on the other hand, fluctuated in purity and was finally abandoned, and the copper coinage became inflated. The system of collecting obligations to the government in kind which had been inaugurated by Diocletian continued and naturally obviated much of the effect of inflation for those persons, such as soldiers and civil servants, whose remuneration was largely paid to them in kind—clothing as well as food. When the scanty data available allow us to calculate in gold the price of some such staple as wheat, it appears that there was a slow rise in prices.

The tax structure, like that of earlier centuries, was much too simple and bore more heavily on agriculture than on trade. There is not enough evidence for us to attempt even a rough statement of the income and expenditures of the government during the fourth and fifth centuries. The occasional remarks about surpluses in the treasury, however, make it seem that in spite of the excessive expense of occasional wars, the standing army, and the civil servants, and in spite of the absence of the methods of financing governmental expenditures that are available nowadays, the imperial government was consistently in what seemed an endurable financial position until the losses of large amounts of territory in the West and the revenue from them in the early fifth century. It should be said, however, that there was one extremely serious financial mistake: the government of the late fourth and early fifth centuries regularly used foreigners in the army, allowing them land instead of money payment, and excused the native-born tenants of the great landowners from military service for a money payment, thus causing a shortage both of citizen soldiers and of citizen veterans who could be recalled in an emergency. Had there been ten thousand veterans in Gaul who could have been called to the colors in 407, the three invading peoples might have been driven out.

The Army

The army of the East was not subjected to the pressure that wore relentlessly on the army of the West during these two centuries, although the Persians and the Huns could be troublesome. The Black and Caspian Seas and the Caucasus Mountains between them, as well as the fortifications of Constantinople in its excellent defensive position, protected the East somewhat from the Germanic peoples and from the Huns when they moved over into southern Russian and Hungary. In the long run it was the pressure of great numbers of invaders that wore down the West.

As we have seen, Diocletian made a beginning of having a mobile field army in addition to the fixed forces that covered the boundaries of the Empire, and Constantine developed it further. The army was enlarged, and the cavalry force was increased sharply, which gave the army more mobility, added to its expense, and led toward the military style of the Middle Ages. This general disposition of the armed forces was strategically sound, since the pressure on the borders was such that there had to be fighting units fairly well spread along them to prevent small raids that could have been very damaging, and since there were also larger incursions that could be dealt with only by a greater force that ought to be capable of dealing with them without thereby leaving some part of the frontier unguarded.

It has been suggested that the fighting quality of the armies was not what it had been in earlier centuries (the reader will recognize that we are now in the realm of theories about the so-called decline and fall), but the fact is that the armies were well organized, as we have just said, and that the men were good fighters. There is no logic in theories as to why they should have been poor fighters, whether Christianity or socio-economic disgruntlement or Asiatic genes are offered as reasons.

The army was not a great political problem in the fourth and fifth centuries, as it had been sometimes in the first century and so often and so disastrously in the third century when the soldiers tried to raise their commanders to the throne. The management of the army to keep it out of politics is a perennial problem of government and one that the Romans knew well, but fortunately one that did not trouble them as much in this period as it had before.

The emperors have been blamed for using Germans in the army and relying on them too much, and there is justice in the charge in the sense that they could have and should have insisted on universal military service for citizens. It should be said in justice to the Germans that they had a remarkable sense of loyalty and that the emperors did not encounter treachery in German soldiers and German officials.

Industry and Trade

By the end of the second century of our era the Roman Empire had reached its greatest extent, and trade had had an opportunity to penetrate every part of it and push beyond its borders to the Germanic peoples, those of Africa below the Sahara, and to India, Ceylon, and China. The processes of manufacture were known, although the full use of the water wheel came in the third and fourth centuries, and a few pieces of industrial knowledge were yet to be imparted by the barbarians to the Romans. The chief differences between these activities in the second century and in the fourth and fifth were that a great deal of economic life was taken under state control in the third and early fourth centuries, that internal trade was sometimes disturbed by civil war in the third and early fourth centuries, that the course of trade with the peoples outside the Empire was more often disturbed then, and that probably more money was paid to peoples outside the Empire, much of which came back into the Empire for purchases that pleased the barbarians.

Another difference seemed important to historians of the nineteenth and early twentieth centuries who were nourished on what then seemed classical economics. They thought it a fatal weakness in the Empire that industries formerly concentrated in Italy, like those of fine pottery and glass, should have been exported to the provinces along with their products, so that these and other products were manufactured in several provinces instead of chiefly in Italy. Perhaps this line of thought depended on the assumption that the economy of an empire is healthy only if the manufacturing is monopolized by the power that controls the empire. For us it is hard to see why it was not just as good to have lively production in the provinces and save the cost of rather inefficient transportation. It is likewise difficult for us to see what was very harmful about the government's controlling large sections of the economy and exacting taxes in kind to be used in paying the soldiers and the civil servants, although such practices naturally were repugnant to the economic thinking of seventy-five or so years ago.

No serious attempt has been made to show that the economic system of the fourth and fifth centuries caused the loss of the West, and we may feel free to consider it for itself, regarding it as a trait of the culture of the late Roman Empire that led up to the medieval economy, but was still too much of a "world-wide" economic system, with too much freedom of movement within each province and about the whole Empire, to be considered medieval. Within the Empire there had always been a great market for everyone, with no barriers other than nominal customs duties to impede the free flow of trade. The solidus was a reliable medium of exchange, which even influenced the coinages attempted by some of the Germanic kings, serving as an example to keep them honest.

We must try to be very careful in marking off the limits of the structure of compulsion that began to be built during the struggles of the third century. Ideologies had nothing to do with it, and its only purpose was to allow the government to perform its functions more efficiently in a difficult time. The first item of supply for the government was food for the armies and for the officials, who were more and more organized along military lines. The *coloni,* or tenant farmers of the imperial estates and of the great private estates who were the most important persons in the production of food, were bound to their tenancies before the early fourth century, and the obligation was presently made hereditary. Service in the army was likewise made a permanent burden, up to a reasonable age of retirement, and a son of a soldier inherited the same duty. The manufacture of weapons was handled by the state from the time of Diocletian onward, and the *Notitia Dignitatum* gives the locations of shield factories, arrow factories, a bow factory, and others for swords, breastplates, and the *ballistae,* or large catapults, that served as artillery, and separate factories for producing the officers' armor of bronze adorned with gold and silver. The workers were organized with military ranks and titles and were bound to their work with a hereditary obligation. A repulsive feature was that recruits both for this service and for the army were branded to make desertion more difficult. The state also had its own facilities for producing some of the clothes of the soldiers and civil servants and the more elegant garments of those in higher position. There were dye works, linen mills, and woolen mills. Their workers, curiously enough, seem to have been slaves owned by the state, but their practical condition of life was that of persons hereditarily bound to labor in the factories. These plants produced only a rather small part of the clothes that the state needed for its personnel, and the rest were levied in kind in the indictions as part of the taxes or were bought. Every part of the Empire manufactured plain clothing, whether by home manufacture or in small commercial establishments.

Marble for public buildings came largely from the state's own quarries, with the addition of what came from a tax in kind of a tenth collected on the production of private quarries. The precious metals for coinage and for other purposes like the decoration of armor or of robes of state came from the state's own mines, while the less precious metals were exacted as taxes in kind from the owners of private mines. Even the charcoal needed for the mint and the arms factories was levied rather than bought. Labor was drafted to erect or repair public buildings.

The *cursus publicus,* or official post, was organized in the early Empire, but was not a Roman invention (we are all familiar with the words of Herodotus, paraphrased by our own Post Office, about the courier of the Persian royal post, who was not stopped by weather or any obstacle). The Roman post had fast riders for messages and wagons for the conveyance of goods or of officials traveling on public business. The many references to this service in the imperial enactments of this time show that the improper granting of permits to private persons to use it was of constant concern to the government. The *cursus publicus* was part of the structure of compulsion, for the government levied the personnel and the horses, mules, and oxen. It also had to feed them, of course, as it did all the other men and animals in the government service.

The *curiales,* or decurions, were not the least part of the structure of compulsion, since they had to attend to the government of all the cities and towns and the innumerable demands that the government made through the cities and the towns on the land and the people. Apparently all the emperors of the fourth and early fifth centuries still believed that urban life was a most important factor of civilization and characteristic of the Empire, so that they made every effort to support the organization of cities and towns. Even the later Germanic leaders felt that the structure of the cities should be maintained, little as the Germans themselves cared for living in them.

In their capacity as agents of the imperial government, a role that had first been thrust on them by Septimius Severus and had been intensified by later emperors, the *curiales* had to collect and be personally responsible for the taxes and the levies in kind demanded by the imperial government, which included finding men for the army and men and animals for the *cursus publicus;* they saw that the roads and bridges were kept in condition. In their original capacity as members of the city councils they governed the cities, which involved some use of their own funds for the routine tasks of management and to supply the baths and games that were regarded as part of city life.

The *curiales* varied greatly in their worldly station, for some were rich men in the large cities or on great country estates and some were humble men in tiny towns. They all seemed, however, to find their curial duties extremely irksome and to exercise much ingenuity in thinking of ways to escape from them. Not only the money but the frequent demands on their time must have been dreadful burdens, at least to the less affluent, who would not have well trained slaves or freedmen to act for them.

The rich decurions, who could perfectly well bear the expense of their duties, tried to escape by joining the imperial aristocracy of officeholders, which brought them higher status and was also desirable from the point of view of the government, which needed constantly to recruit its higher officials from the propertied class in the Empire. The law codes contain many enactments aimed at securing the government's interests: the decurion could not apply for a post in the imperial service until he had served as a member of the *curia* for a stated number of years, and he must be able to prove that he had done so, since a traffic sprang up in certificates issued by *curiales* for the benefit of other *curiales* purporting to show that they had discharged their duties to the *curia* of their own city. A man also had to have a son to inherit the property that entailed the eligibility and duty to be a *curialis* and must leave a son to perform the personal tasks that it entailed. One son must stay; if there were others, only one could become a senator.

The poorer men bore more than their share of the burden, since the richer ones were likely to find ways to avoid their obligation. The poorer men tried to escape appointment to the *curia*, often by attempting to join the more modest grades of the civil service. Periodically the imperial government conducted a search through all its personnel, including the army, to find men who had not yet been *curiales*, or perhaps had not fulfilled their years of duty, and sent back those who had not yet earned their freedom from these duties by performing them for the required number of years, usually fifteen.

Physicians and the municipal teachers of grammar and rhetoric constituted a small class that was excused from these duties for professional reasons. To Constantine it seemed natural to confer such immunity on the priesthood. Human nature being as it is, there was a rush for the priesthood by men seeking to evade their obligations as *curiales*, and soon the government provided that the man could go, if he wished, but that the property must stay behind. The last resort was flight. Some men abandoned the property that was overburdened with charges (most often because their richer neighbors had evaded their share of the obligations) and either put themselves under the protection of a richer man, tried to lose themselves in one of the larger cities, or fled outside the Empire. The grammarian Priscian tells of going on an embassy to the Huns from Byzantium and finding there a merchant who said that he had been driven out of the Empire by the exactions of the taxgatherers and much preferred life among the Huns.

The *navicularii,* or shippers, and the *pistores,* or bakers, will serve as examples of others whose services to the state became compulsory and hereditary. We hear of the organization of fleets to carry the tribute grain of Africa and Egypt to Rome in the reign of Claudius. Probably from the beginning the merchants who would guarantee that their ships would be available received immunity from their burdens as *curiales*. This was steady work, and the government made provisions to indemnify the merchants for the loss of ships, so that over the years the calling may have brought in a modest profit. Presumably the *navicularii* contracted to perform their duties only for limited terms until, during the disturbances of the third century, the state felt obliged to make the arrangement a permanent one and attach it to the real property of the *navicularii,* which made it hereditary. We cannot be at all sure that we should regard this guild, or that of the *pistores* or of other groups who supplied food, as especially downtrodden if the government gave them steady work with certain provisions against risks and with a very modest profit (or sometimes no profit) and exemptions from other charges that may well have taken the place of a profit. They were, like so many others at the time, frozen into their occupations.

There were people who lived outside this great structure of compulsion, either wholly or in part. The shippers who carried the tribute grain could do a little trading of their own at the same time. The *curiales* found an open market for the residue of their agricultural product that was not required as tribute or as tax in kind. That the market was open enough to fluctuate is shown by several remarks of authors of the time to the effect that the rich preferred the harvest not to be too bountiful so that it would not depress prices too much.

THE NEW PAGAN-CHRISTIAN CULTURE

The Church as Institution

The Church began its legal existence with its recognition by Constantine and during the fourth century was favored by all the emperors except Julian. Theodosius was the first of the emperors to attempt to make Christianity the official and only permissible religion, and this in general was the attitude of his successors. During the first three centuries the formal organization of the Church had been well worked out, even though it was not recognized as a legal entity. Every city of any importance had a bishop; the word comes from the Greek *episcopos,* one who oversees others. The bishops of the more important cities were known as metropolitans and those in charge of whole provinces as patriarchs. By the fourth century the primacy of the Bishop of Rome was recognized by most of the others, although it was a primacy that needed to be exercised with tact.

There were many minor members of the clergy, as is shown by occasional mentions of the members of the staff of a large church. Many people who felt drawn to the religious life but did not wish to join the clergy or could not (for women were not eligible, of course) became monks or nuns. The retired life of the religious communities seemed to many devout people a place where sin was less likely to raise its head, pure piety could quite simply direct itself to God, and the difficulties of the world could be avoided, while on the purely social side there was membership in a little community of like-minded people. The anchorites of Egypt withdrew even farther from the world. The Greek *anachorites* means literally one who goes upcountry, that is, out of the valley of the Nile to the comparatively desert region that lies on either side of the valley. There they lived solitary lives of meditation, of abstinence and prayer, self-accusation and self-flagellation, varied, as St. Jerome tells us of his own case, by highly colored fancies of worldly delights that would persist in presenting themselves unbidden. In the monasteries of the East it was the custom to work; they turned out fabrics or other products almost like factories, earning money that supported them and left a surplus for godly purposes. In the West it was more usual for the monks or nuns to live in idleness on the alms of the faithful.

The question inevitably comes up whether these devoted people were merely a burden on a society that had no great surplus with which to feed idle people. The clergy (the priests and their staffs) may well have been as numerous as the civil officials of the Empire, and it is possible that as a group they were paid as much as the officials were. It can be argued that in a culture in which Christianity was one of the strongest social forces, these people had a very considerable social utility. The monks and nuns, if they lived under a rule that required them to work, surely supplied themselves with the necessities of life, which was as much as most people did. A great deal of property was bestowed upon the Church, however, the income of which went for the support of some of the monks and nuns as well as the salaries of priests, the building and repair of churches, and the relief of the poor. Some resources did therefore go to support people in idleness, but not enough to represent a serious drain.

Even in the second century the Church had found it necessary to stigmatize certain doctrines as heretical for the sake of keeping the faithful together and marching forward as a unit. There had been those, for example, who believed that the God of the new religion could not be the God of the Old Testament. The Gnostics, another heretical group, had an elaborate system that promised the advent of a redeemer sent to heal the unfortunate breach between pure spirit and impure matter and restore the world to its pristine unity and cleanliness. They seized upon Christ as the redeemer promised by their teaching and claimed to be the most logical of Christians. Although the Church rejected them as heretics, their beliefs lived on into the early modern age. The disciples of Mani, to name another such group, whom we have already seen preaching in the middle of the third century, were regarded as technically Christians, but held beliefs that now seem more like Zoroastrianism, with a dualism of the powers of Good and Evil. They were called Manicheans, or Manichees, and St. Augustine was at one time a believer in their doctrines.

Some heresies appealed especially to national groups and combined theology with national feeling in such a way as to weaken the unity of the Empire. The Monophysites of Egypt, whose name derived from their belief in a single nature of Christ, were united partly by their theology and partly by their Egyptian nationality. The Priscillianists of Spain likewise combined theological deviation with local patriotism. The Donatists of Africa also belong in the context of the combination of theological difference with other differences, in this case socioeconomic rather than national differences. The claim that no bishop could be regarded as properly ordained who had yielded up the sacred books on demand during Diocletian's persecution became for some reason a rallying cry for the poor peasant and the laborer of Numidia and served to accent a sense of difference of interest between them and the well-to-do so strong that a recognizable Donatist group in North Africa stubbornly held itself apart for more than two hundred years.

The attitudes of Christianity, which may seem more suited to the poor and the downtrodden, were often adopted by the rich. Riches came to be regarded as a danger to morality, an attitude that lingered on into the twentieth century and is often illustrated in the literature of the nineteenth. From the desire for the salvation of one's soul and the hope thereof, presumably, came the exaltation of virginity and celibacy, since sex can be the great promoter of sin, if one wishes to look at the matter that way. This subject was developed with detail that can easily become preposterous and boring to the modern reader.

The triumph of the Church did not mean the utter end of paganism, for there is plentiful evidence that genuine pagans existed in the fifth, sixth, seventh, and eighth centuries in all parts of the Empire. Perhaps the Christian would have disdained to call their beliefs a religion. The evidence refers to the cities as well as to the country and to traces of rather sophisticated cults, like that of Isis, as well as to rather simple ones.

Christianity as a Culture

The combination of Christianity and the Greco-Roman culture was the final form of the culture of the ancient world, the form in which it was transmitted to the age that lay ahead. Christianity had indeed developed into a culture, or a complete and practical way of life. It had come to satisfactory terms with the temporal power in the shape of the Roman Empire and had then captured it, so that the ordinary physical requirements of a workable culture were taken care of. It had an ethical code and a system of values to prevent living from being mere confusion. Beyond this, it inculcated in the believer an attitude that relations between the members of the Church and the invisible powers were such that he could go about his daily life with confidence and hope and could even withstand severe shocks and disappointments through his faith that for eternity all would be well with him. It is such a set of values, ideals, and hopes that does most to engender in men courage and energy with which to meet their daily or their extraordinary tasks.

The formal education of this new culture remained mostly what it had been before, the study of the Greek and Latin classics and of effective speaking. The latter was still necessary for a man who wished to engage in public life to the slightest extent. The Christians opposed the study of those authors who, like Lucretius, had expressed doubts that the gods play any role in this world or even exist, but we need not grieve too much for the young man who could read anything in classical literature except the atheists.

Education is, of course, what society wants the young to learn, and it comprises far more than what can be taught in school. The Christians had ample means of inculcating both facts and attitudes. Devout parents taught children their own points of view and innumerable facts about worship and festivals and the sacred books. The sermon was a continuing instrument of Christian education. Participation in the church service was in itself education, especially insofar as the ceremony was enriched with beautiful objects or music or there were festivals of emotional appeal. The priests were naturally the most important agents in the educational process that secured the transmission of this culture.

Pagan and Christian Art and Literature

There is a difference of scholarly opinion about the characteristics of the art of the later Empire. Until a few decades ago it was regarded as merely decadent art, but scholars have come to regard it as a new kind of art. There is at least agreement that mosaic work, an art that did not reach its full popularity until this later age, achieved its highest point in the fifth century with the great mosaics of the churches of Ravenna, the imperial capital of the time.

Some of the art of the Christians was consciously used to further religious purposes. With the legalizing of the religion and the sudden growth of its resources, the building of churches of considerable size became possible, and the larger churches were the work of the best architects. They continued the tendency of the designers of the great imperial baths to use empty space and light as architectural components, or in a sense as raw material, a method of building that is familiar to us in our churches and our great railway stations.

There are many humbler examples of Christian art, springing from belief rather than officially used to inspire it. Many sarcophagi bear scenes of religious meaning. Some of them are crude, and naturally many would be executed by indifferent artists. Others show interestingly the features that were new in the pagan art of the time—the representation of the emotions of people, deep cutting of reliefs, and the grouping of crowded scenes with perspective, as if one were looking down on the group from a balcony. Incidents from the Bible were popular for sarcophagi or as decoration elsewhere, and the fact that there is a story often leads the artist to use a kind of narrative art that is very close to our comic strips, giving a succession of frames in which the characters are shown acting out three or more of the chief points in sequence.

In the fourth and fifth centuries there were almost no writers of belles-lettres whose works now seem of high quality. The poets Ausonius and Claudianus and the historian Ammianus Marcellinus are probably the only authors of any distinction in the literary sense. If we are to give a description of the literary scene, however, it must include works of inferior merit and technical works like those of the great grammarians of the period and the encyclopedists. It must also cover the great mass of Christian writing, almost none of which can be called belles-lettres, but which represents a huge intellectual effort and shows us one of the methods by which the Christians created a new culture. During the fourth and fifth centuries the pagans and the Christians felt themselves to be in lively competition, and literature was one of the several areas of rivalry. The Christians mastered all the learning of the ancient world and turned it to their own purpose with spirit and wit, while the pagans fought as best they could against opponents who seemed to them to be stealing a goodly heritage to transform it into something less worthwhile. Naturally the fact that many of the best minds and literary talents were busy with Christian subjects did something to lower the level of literary achievement among the pagans.

Although he was a Christian and wrote some few pieces of nominally Christian content, the poet Ausonius should be regarded as a writer of pagan poetry. He lived in the fourth century (his exact dates are unknown) and for thirty years taught grammar and rhetoric at Burdigala, or Bordeaux. His poetry did not show high inspiration, but for us it is more important that it displays a thorough acquaintance on the author's part with Greek and Latin literature and that it tells us much about life and manners at the time. The poet was plainly an agreeable man. His verses picture a happy life on an estate near Bordeaux on the river, with easy access to the city by water. His best piece is *Mosella,* an account of a journey on the Moselle, which shows us a beautiful river covered with cargo boats, with vineyards on the steep hillsides on the banks and beautiful villas above, and at the same time discloses a poet of good taste, some imagination, and a feeling for nature.

Claudius Claudianus, who is generally called Claudian, lived a generation or so after Ausonius and began his career in Latin poetry with a panegyric on the consuls of A.D. 395 after having already published poetry in his native Greek. His later work continued to attempt the grand style, recounting some of the wars of the time and praising the virtues of Stilicho. It is remarkable that he recaptured something of the loftiness and vigor of earlier Latin poetry, although it is possible to find his themes tedious at times. To the modern he seems at his best when with a deep and sonorous note he sounds the praises of eternal Rome, mistress and keeper of the world, gorgeous in her glory.

A lesser poet, Rutilius Namatianus, wrote in the same vein early in the fifth century, plainly echoing Vergil as he praised Rome for achieving the imperial tasks that Vergil had assigned her in Anchises' great speech in the sixth book of the *Aeneid*. These are utterances of the feeling that the greatness of Rome lies in her pagan achievement of ruling the world for its own good, attempting to counter the Christian assertion that a new and better dispensation had arisen for Rome and the world.

The historian Ammianus Marcellinus was a contemporary of Claudian and, like him, wrote in Latin rather than in his native Greek. He produced a history of Rome from the end of Tacitus' work (A.D. 96) to the death of Valens (378) in thirty-one books, of which the first thirteen are lost, leaving us the account of the years from A.D. 353 to 378. He set himself a high standard of accuracy and responsibility and often offered vivid and penetrating judgments on people, but was also able to see the Empire as a large enterprise and pay proper attention to the problems of the whole.

The scholarship of some of the pagans of the fourth century deserves our admiration. Aelius Donatus wrote a grammar that has been preserved in full and also in an abbreviated form. He is one of the late classical authors whose work was useful and popular during the Middle Ages and early modern times. He also wrote scholarly and useful commentaries on the comedies of Terence and on Vergil. He was very popular as a teacher of rhetoric in Rome. The commentary of one Servius on Vergil, written late in the fourth century, shows good sense and a wide range of learning. Apparently both he and Donatus had excellent libraries at their command.

It has been remarked that probably many of the books of the Greeks and Romans that have not come down to us perished because of the increased use at this time of the codex, or book in our style with a binding and leaves, which replaced the rolls on which books had formerly been written. In the gradual replacement of books on rolls by codices many of the older authors, or the less popular works of some authors, probably were not copied and therefore did not survive.

The literary product of the Christians, all of which was directed to Christian purposes, contains some imaginative, forceful, and charming writing. It may well seem that the more able authors of the time were Christians. The larger part of the Christian output, however, whether in Greek or in Latin, was theological and lacked literary grace, even though much of it was good expository writing.

The poet Prudentius wrote an epic arguing that the whole history of Rome led up to the adoption of Christianity just as it had led to the general improvement of Mediterranean life under the Roman Empire. He echoes Vergil, the prophet of the Empire, and implies as did Rutilius Namatianus that Rome had fulfilled the task that Anchises set for her in the *Aeneid,* but in a Christian rather than a pagan sense. He also wrote elaborate hymns, not at all suited to be sung as part of the church service and clearly modeled on the lyrics of great pagans like Pindar and Horace even while filled with Christian doctrine and Christian feeling— beautiful examples of the Greco-Roman-Christian culture that had now come into being.

St. Ambrose, the great administrator, really did write hymns for the church service, some of which, like the Palm Sunday hymn "All glory, laud, and honor" are still in use. His *De officiis ministrorum* (*On the Duties of Priests*), which plainly utilized the thought of Cicero's *De officiis,* is an interesting example of the adaptation of earlier thought for Christian purposes.

St. Augustine was a teacher of rhetoric in his earlier years and naturally was an untiring student of Cicero. His *Confessions* give us a charming picture of his life as a boy in the North African town of Thagaste and as a lively university student at Carthage. Early in life, he says, he was turned to the study of philosophy by Cicero's *Hortensius,* which was written just for that purpose, to turn people to philosophical studies. To Augustine this meant the beginning of his long progress toward Christianity, for Christianity to the men of this time was much like philosophy in being a reasoned coming to terms with the nature of the world. Finally, after teaching in Rome, he gained a desirable post as teacher of rhetoric in the imperial city of Milan and came into contact with Ambrose, who was able to answer some of his doubts about Christianity (doubts expressed in philosophical terms) and won him at last for Christ.

Augustine returned to his native Africa, where he soon became Bishop of Hippo, on the northern coast, and remained there until his death in A.D. 430, when the Vandals were overrunning the countryside. He says in the *Confessions* that he did not care for Greek in school, and the fact that he never really mastered the language caused him difficulty with his writing, since the Christian scholars of the East were so important in theological studies. From now on we hear more and more of men in the West who knew little or no Greek. Augustine nevertheless wrote a great deal on theology, and the proof of his success is that many later writers found in his thought the materials from which they could develop whole systems of their own. He wrote against the Manicheans, of whom he once was one, vindicating the unity of the universe and of the divine nature against their dualism. His writings against the Donatists were along a different line, since there he was arguing more on church administration and the question of how the succession of bishops was to be ordered. His other great controversy was on the nature of original sin, on which he held very firm views because of the great strength of his own passions (of which he tells us in *Confessions*), views that were rather well criticized by Pelagius, whom Augustine finally drove from the field and caused to be branded as a heretic. We have mentioned the fact that his *City of God* was an elaborate answer to the pagan charge that Christian government had caused such disasters as Alaric's sack of Rome.

St. Jerome, or Hieronymus, came from Dalmatia and received the best of educations in Rome under Donatus. In mid-career he left Rome and went to the East, where he improved his knowledge of Greek until he could use the language with ease and learned Hebrew. He was a hard worker and produced many scholarly commentaries on the Bible, as well as the famous translation of the Bible into Latin know as the Vulgate, or "received version."

The intellectual history of Jerome has been carefully studied, for his voluminous and frank writings show off the course of his thought plainly. Cicero remained a great influence on him, and he tried always to keep his Latin pure by referring to the norm of Ciceronian usage. One of the pleasantest passages is his account in a letter of the dream wherein he seemed to be haled before the Judgment Seat and accused of being a Ciceronian rather than a Christian. His Greek studies appear not to go back to the great writers of antiquity, except possibly Herodotus, and many things that he knows about the older Greeks seem to come from his intimate knowledge of Cicero. His real interest in Greek was in the writings of the theologians, and his knowledge of them goes back to Origen, almost the earliest of the great workers in that field.

Eusebius, who wrote (in Greek) a history of the Church from Christ to Constantine, is another of the Christians who changed the conceptions and the writing of history, for he was the first to give authorities in the modern manner with copious quotation of documents, some of them letters of bishops, others the published rescripts of the emperors. The Greek and Roman historians had often referred to their sources or spoken of the disagreement among earlier writers, but none of them had gone this far in bringing in source materials in their original form for the reader to see and judge. We have already seen that the Christians of the third century did useful work on chronology and introduced the idea of the division of history into periods as well as that of a grand purpose in history.

Although the works of the great Greek and Latin Fathers have been well translated into English, they sometimes make very difficult reading. One reason is that the reader often has to fight his way through thickets of pious expressions and protestations of sinfulness and unworthiness. The flood of allegorical interpretations of Scripture is also likely to repel the modern who tries to penetrate the argument of these books, for allegory had become a regular way of explaining away the crudities of the Old Testament and of showing that very many of its passages, if taken allegorically, show forth the coming of Christ and of the Christian dispensation. Although the Christian practice of allegorical interpretation can be defended, it is almost impossible for a modern reader to drive himself to read much of this kind of writing.

EPILOGUE

Complex and intense life styles are fragile, at least when compared to the simpler life style of the late Neolithic people whose numbers had steadily increased everywhere in the world while the Near Eastern and Greek civilizations were being developed. They also, since they develop wealth, arouse the cupidity of the simpler people, who tend to try to take wealth from the more highly developed people. So all these more complex and intense forms of society, being more fragile within and under attack from outside, tended in ancient times either to subside a little into something more sturdy and less complicated or to succumb to attack, and none of them could endure in its most developed form. Some disappeared completely.

If the Roman Empire perhaps lacked some of the refinements of Athens in its great age, as a whole it may be called the most strenuous of all the efforts of the ancient world, for it covered more territory and tried to govern it more carefully and efficiently than any other empire, and within this framework more people tried to take advantage personally of the complexities of life—the refinements of day-to-day living, the complex joys of literature, of art, of philosophy, of travel—and with all this there was a sentiment of the unity of man and of the duties of a great empire that had not existed before. Such a great organization could be kept up only by the unrelenting efforts of a strenuous class with high morale, and it automatically gave rise to pressures from the people outside it. Its quality was diluted by its efforts to take in and use the barbarians outside, and its difficulties were increased by the pressures of those who raided it. Meanwhile China, too, had developed a strenuous civilization, although not so complex as that of the Roman. Both found themselves unable to continue indefinitely to support a high civilization and to withstand the pressure of simpler people from the outside. Both, however, were able to hand on to later times a considerable amount of the content of their civilizations.

BIBLIOGRAPHY

This bibliography is not intended to be in any sense complete or even well balanced. The books have been chosen because they should be interesting and useful to the ordinary reader and because they are likely to be readily available in the library or in the bookshop. The less expensive editions, generally paperbacks, are marked with an asterisk. If the reader who wishes to go deeper will start with the books listed here, he will find that the bibliographies listed in them will lead him by stages and as far as he wishes to go in the direction of purely technical and scholarly presentations.

GENERAL WORKS

The Cambridge Ancient History. 12 vols. Cambridge: Cambridge University Press, 1923–39.
   The best ancient history. In 1961 separate fascicles began to appear of a new edition of the first two volumes, which depend largely upon archaeology and have partly become obsolete because of the advance of archaeological knowledge.

*Bailkey, Nels M. *Readings in Ancient History from Gilgamesh to Diocletian.* New York: D. C. Heath, 1969.

Kagan, Donald D. *Problems in Ancient History.* 2 vols. New York: Macmillan, 1966.

*Lewis, N., and Reinhold, M. *Roman Civilization.* 2 vols. New York: Harper & Row, 1966.
   Readings from the sources, clear summary notes, a good bibliography.

*McDermott, W. C., and Caldwell, W. E. *Readings in the History of the Ancient World.* 2nd ed. New York: Holt, Rinehart, & Winston, 1970.

The Oxford Classical Dictionary. 2d ed. Oxford: Oxford University Press, 1970.

Van der Heyden, A. A. M., and Scullard, H. H. *Atlas of the Classical World.* London: Nelson, 1960. Paperback, Dutton.
   An unusually interesting and informative text accompanies the many maps and charts.

The reader interested in archaeology will find many interesting articles in two popular journals of archaeology, *Antiquity* and *Archaeology*. Technical reports of recent discoveries appear in *The American Journal of Archaeology*.

THE NEAR EAST AND EGYPT

*Albright, William F. *The Archeology of Palestine*. Baltimore: Penguin, 1960.

*Albright, William F. *From the Stone Age to Christianity*. Garden City: Doubleday, 1957.

*Aldred, Cyril. *Egypt to the End of the Old Kingdom*. London: Thames & Hudson, 1965.

Bevan, E. R., and Singer, Charles. *The Legacy of Israel*. New York: Oxford University Press, 1929.
A collection of essays by different hands covering several aspects of the legacy of ancient Israel to the modern world.

*Bibby, Geoffrey. *Four Thousand Years Ago*. Baltimore: Penguin, 1965.
A reconstruction of the life of man in the second millennium before Christ. It is especially interesting and useful because it attempts to show what life may have been like in such places as China, Scandinavia, and southern Africa on the basis of the archaeological evidence.

Bibby, Geoffrey. *The Testament of the Spade*. New York: Knopf, 1956.
Great archaeologists and the rise of archaeology in the nineteenth century.

Ceram, C. W. *Gods, Graves, and Scholars*. New York: Knopf, 1951.

Ceram, C. W. *The March of Archaeology*. New York: Knopf, 1966.

*Chiera, Edward. *They Wrote on Clay*. Chicago: University of Chicago Press, 1938.
An interesting and authoritative account of the method of writing on clay tablets and the things that were written.

Childe, V. Gordon. *Man Makes Himself*. New York: Mentor, 1951.
An account of very early man.

*Edwards, I. E. S. *The Pyramids of Egypt*. Baltimore: Penguin, 1955.
An interesting description of less-known pyramids as well as the greater ones.

Finegan, Jack. *Light from the Ancient Past*. Princeton: Princeton University Press, 1959. Paperback, 2 vols., 1969.
Very informative about the archaeological basis of the history of the Near East and Egypt.

Forbes, Robert J. *Man, the Maker: A History of Technology and Engineering*. New York: Schuman, 1958.

Frankfort, Henri. *The Art and Architecture of the Ancient Orient*. Baltimore: Penguin, 1958.

*Frankfort, Henri. *Before Philosophy*. Baltimore: Penguin, 1966.
A stimulating discussion of early thought and belief (entitled in the original edition *The Intellectual Adventure of Ancient Man*).

*Frazer, James G. *The Golden Bough*, edited by Theodore Gaster. New York: Doubleday, 1959.
A classic of anthropology condensed and modernized.

Glanville, S. R. K., ed. *The Legacy of Egypt.* Oxford: Clarendon, 1942.
A collection of informative essays by different scholars.

Gordon, Cyrus. *Before the Bible.* Evanston: Harper & Row, 1963. Paperback, Norton, 1965.
Careful and detailed description of the early period in the Near East by a scholar working in the field.

*Gordon, Cyrus. *Hammurapi's Code.* New York: Holt, Rinehart, & Winston, 1960.
A brief and interesting description of an important document.

*Gurney, O. R. *The Hittites.* Baltimore: Penguin, 1952.

Hayes, William C. *The Scepter of Egypt.* 2 vols. New York: Harper and The New York Metropolitan Museum of Art, 1953, 1959.
The most useful single work on Egypt. The scholarly and interesting account of Egypt is connected with the great Egyptian collection in the Metropolitan Museum by many illustrations and references.

Kees, Hermann. *Ancient Egypt: A Cultural Topography,* edited by T. G. H. James. Chicago: University of Chicago Press, 1961.
A great deal of significant and interesting information about Egypt is given in connection with places in Egypt.

*Kramer, Samuel N. *History Begins at Sumer.* New York: Doubleday, 1959.
Popular in tone, giving a list of "firsts" to be credited to the Sumerians.

Kramer, Samuel N. *The Sumerians: Their History, Culture, and Character.* Chicago: University of Chicago Press, 1963.
A serious and thorough treatment of Sumerian civilization.

*Mallowan, M. E. L. *Early Mesopotamia and Iran.* London: Thames & Hudson, 1965.

*Mellaart, James. *Earliest Civilizations of the Near East.* London: Thames & Hudson, 1965.

*Moscati, Sabatino. *Ancient Semitic Civilizations.* New York: Putnam's (Capricorn) 1960.
An interesting discussion of the chief Semitic peoples of antiquity, including the Arabs and Ethiopians.

Oesterley, W. O. E., and Robinson, T. H. *A History of Israel.* 2 vols. Oxford: Clarendon, 1932.

Olmstead, Albert T. *History of Assyria.* New York: Scribner's, 1923.

*Olmstead, Albert T. *History of the Persian Empire.* Chicago: University of Chicago Press, 1948.

*Orlinsky, Harry. *Ancient Israel.* Ithaca: Cornell University Press, 1954.
A concise, interesting, and scholarly account of ancient Israel.

Pritchard, James B., ed. *The Ancient Near East.* Princeton: Princeton University Press, 1958.
A valuable collection of pictures and texts in translation.

Roux, Georges. *Ancient Iraq.* Baltimore: Pelican, 1966.

Singer, Charles J., ed. *A History of Technology.* 5 vols. Oxford: Clarendon, 1954–58.

Steindorff, G., and Seele, K. *When Egypt Ruled the East.* Chicago: University of Chicago Press, 1957.

*Wilson, John A. *The Burden of Egypt*. Chicago: University of Chicago Press, 1951.
Available in Phoenix paperback edition under the title *The Culture of Egypt*.

Woolley, Charles L. *Digging Up the Past*. London: Benn, 1954.

*Woolley, Charles L. *Excavations at Ur*. New York: Barnes & Noble, 1955.

Zeuner, F. E. *Dating the Past*. 4th ed. London: Methuen, 1958.
A scholarly book on all the methods of dating that do not depend on literary records.

GREECE

Barker, Ernest, ed. *The European Inheritance*. Vol. 1. Oxford: 1954.
Has summary articles on prehistory and Near Eastern, Greek, and Roman history.

Barker, Ernest. *Greek Political Theory*. London: Methuen, 1918. Paperback, Barnes & Noble, 1960.
A standard book by a specialist in political thought.

Bieber, Margarete. *The History of the Greek and Roman Theater*. 2d ed. Princeton: Princeton University Press, 1960.

Blegen, Carl W. *Troy*. 3 vols. Princeton: Princeton University Press, 1950–53.
The detailed report of a great modern excavation.

Blegen, Carl W. *Troy and the Trojans*. London: Thames & Hudson, 1963.
A report for the reading public.

Bonner, Robert J. *Aspects of Athenian Democracy*. Berkeley: University of California Press, 1933.

Bowra, Cecil M. *The Greek Experience*. Cleveland and New York: World, 1957. Paperback, Mentor, 1957.
The reflections on Greece of a distinguished British classicist.

*Bulfinch, Thomas. *Mythology of Greece and Rome*. New York: Collier, 1962.
This pleasant book has been a favorite for several generations under its original title, *The Age of Fable*.

*Burn, Andrew R. *The Lyric Age of Greece*. London: Edw. Arnold, 1960. Paperback, Minerva, 1967.
A description of Greece from 700 to 500 B.C. that treats the Greeks all over the Mediterranean world instead of concentrating on a few notable places.

Claster, Jill N., ed. *Athenian Democracy*. New York: Holt, Rinehart & Winston, 1967.

Dinsmoor, W. B. *Architecture of Ancient Greece*. London and New York: Batsford, 1950.

*Dodds, E. R. *The Greeks and the Irrational*. Boston: Beacon, 1957. Originally published by the University of California Press, 1951.
This book has done great service in explaining one side of the Greek character and in correcting sentimental ideas of the Greeks as disembodied intellects. It is not easy, but repays study.

Finley, Moses I. *The Ancient Greeks*. New York: Viking, 1964.

Finley, Moses I. *Slavery in Classical Antiquity*. Cambridge: Heffer, 1960.
A collection of reprints of useful scholarly articles.

Freeman, Kathleen. *Greek City States*. New York: Norton, 1963.
An account of some of the lesser poleis.

Fuller, B. A. G. *A History of Philosophy*. 3rd ed. New York: Holt, 1955.
The author takes great pains to make Greek philosophy intelligible in modern terms.

Glotz, G. *Ancient Greece at Work*. New York: Knopf, 1926. Paperback, Norton, 1967.

Graham, James Walter. *The Palaces of Crete*. Princeton: Princeton University Press, 1962. Paperback, 1969.
An analysis of minor as well as major palaces, with many interesting sidelights on ancient Crete.

Guthrie, W. K. C. *The Greek Philosophers: From Thales to Aristotle*. London: Methuen, 1950. Paperback, Harper & Row, 1960.

Hammond, Nicholas, G. L. *A History of Greece to 322* B.C. 2nd ed. Oxford: Clarendon, 1967.
Indispensable.

Harsh, Philip W. *A Handbook of Classical Drama*. Palo Alto: Stanford University Press, 1944.
Full of detailed information about the Greek and Roman drama.

Janson, Horst W. *Key Monuments of the History of Art*. Evanston: Prentice-Hall, 1959.

Janson, Horst W. *The Picture History of Painting*. New York: Abrams, 1957.

Jones, Arnold H. M. *Athenian Democracy*. Oxford: Blackwell, 1957.
Practical and informative essays on Athenian life and government.

Lawrence, A. W. *Greek Architecture*. Baltimore: Penguin, 1957.

Lord, Albert B. *The Singer of Tales*. Cambridge: Harvard University Press, 1960. Paperback, Atheneum, 1965.
An account of the modern illiterate bard and his methods, with an application of these investigations to Homeric problems.

MacKendrick, Paul. *The Greek Stones Speak*. New York: St. Martin's, 1962. Paperback, Mentor Books, 1966.

*Mongait, A. L. *Archaeology in the USSR*. Baltimore: Pelican, 1961.
An interesting account of the investigations of Russian scholars into the archaeology of the very early and medieval periods of their country as well as that of the Greek and Roman periods.

Mylonas, G. E. *Mycenae and the Mycenaean Age*. Princeton: Princeton University Press, 1966.

Neugebauer, O. *The Exact Sciences in Antiquity*. Providence: Brown University Press, 1957.

Parke, H. W., and Wormell, D. E. W. *The Delphic Oracle*. Oxford: Blackwell, 1956.

Pendlebury, J. D. S. *The Archaeology of Crete*. London: Methuen, 1939. Paperback, Norton, 1965.

Richter, Gisela M. A. *The Sculpture and Scultptors of the Greeks*. New Haven: Yale University Press, 1929.

*Rose, H. J. *Handbook of Greek Literature*. New York: Dutton, 1965.

*Seltman, Charles. *Approach to Greek Art*. New York: Dutton, 1960.
Fresh and stimulating.

*Snell, Bruno. *The Discovery of the Mind*. New York: Harper, 1960.
A study of the growth of self-consciousness among the Greeks; very modern in the questions it asks and the techniques it uses to answer them.

Starr, Chester G. *The Origins of Greek Civilization*. New York: Knopf, 1961.
A useful detailed study of the emergence of the Greeks from their Dark Age.

Wace, A. J. B., and Stubbings, F. A., eds. *A Companion to Homer*. New York: St. Martin's, 1962.
Essays by competent scholars on every aspect of the study of Homer.

Woodhead, A. G. *The Greeks in the West*. London: Thames & Hudson, 1962.

Zimmern, Alfred. *The Greek Commonwealth*. 5th ed. Oxford: Clarendon, 1931.
An excellent attempt to make Greek life intelligible in modern terms. There is a new edition in the Modern Library and a revision of the 5th edition in the Galaxy Books of the Oxford University Press.

THE ROMAN WORLD

Bailey, Cyril, ed. *The Legacy of Rome*. Oxford: Clarendon, 1924.

Balsdon, J. P. V. D., ed. *The Romans*. London: Watts, Ltd., 1965.

Baynes, N. H., and Moss, H. St. L. B. *Byzantium*. London: Oxford University Press (Oxford Paperbacks) 1948.

Bradford, J. S. P. *Ancient Landscapes*. London: Bell, 1957.
A description of some of the brilliant results of aerial photography applied to archaeology.

The Cambridge Economic History of Europe. Vol. 2. Cambridge: Cambridge University Press, 1952.
In this volume can be found a factual account of economic conditions in late Roman times.

Carcopino, J. *Daily Life in Ancient Rome*. Translated by Edith Lorimer. New Haven: Yale University Press, 1940. Paperback, 1960.

Drachmann, A. G. *The Mechanical Techniques of Greek and Roman Antiquity*. Madison: University of Wisconsin Press, 1963.
An interesting discussion of mechanical devices in a civilization that had not become mechanically minded.

*Duff, J. Wight. *A Literary History of Rome from the Origins to the Close of the Golden Age*. 3rd ed. Edited by A. M. Duff. New York: Barnes & Noble, 1963.
A revised paperback edition of the most popular history of Latin literature.

Duff, J. Wight. *A Literary History of Rome in the Silver Age*. New York: Scribner's, 1927.

Frank, Tenney. *An Economic Survey of Ancient Rome*. 5 vols. and Index Volume. Baltimore: The Johns Hopkins Press, 1933–40.
A collection of economic facts with commentary and with translations where necessary.

Grousset, René. *The Rise and Splendor of the Chinese Empire*. Berkeley: University of California Paperbacks, 1953.

Haywood, R. M. *The Myth of Rome's Fall*. New York: Crowell: 1958. Paperback, Apollo, 1962.
An analysis of the so-called decline and fall of the Roman Empire as seen in modern scholarship.

Heurgon, Jacques. *The Daily Life of the Etruscans*. New York: Macmillan, 1964.

Hubert, Henri. *The Greatness and Decline of the Celts*. London: Kegan Paul, 1934.

Johnston, Mary. *Roman Life*. Chicago: Scott Foresman, 1957.
This very useful book is a complete revision of *Private Life of the Romans*.

Jones, Arnold H. M. *The Later Roman Empire: 284–602* A.D. Norman: University of Oklahoma Press, 1964.
Full of exact information about society, economic conditions, and government in the late Empire.

Lot, Ferdinand. *The End of the Ancient World and the Beginning of the Middle Ages*. New York: Harper & Row, 1961.
A paperback edition with an introduction and bibliography by Glanville Downey.

*MacKendrick, Paul. *The Mute Stones Speak*. New York: St. Martin's, 1960. Paperback, Mentor Books.

Marrou, H. I. *A History of Education in Antiquity*. Translated by G. Lamb. New York: Sheed & Ward, 1956.

Moss, Henry St. L. B. *The Birth of the Middle Ages: 395–814*. London: Oxford University Press (Oxford Paperbacks), 1963.

Nock, A. D. *Conversion*. London: Oxford University Press, 1933.
A discussion of changes in the religious belief of individuals by a great authority on ancient religion.

Otis, Brooks. *Virgil*. London: Oxford University Press, 1963.
The volumes of Otis and Poeschl are good examples of modern criticism of Roman literature.

Paoli, U. E. *Rome, Its People and Customs*. New York: McKay, 1963.

Poeschl, V. *The Art of Virgil*. Translated by G. Seligson. Ann Arbor: University of Michigan Press, 1962.

Powell, Terence. *The Celts*. London: Thames & Hudson, 1959.

Richardson, Emeline H. *The Etruscans, Their Art and Civilization*. Chicago: University of Chicago Press, 1964.

Rostovtzeff, Michael I. *Social and Economic History of the Roman Empire*. 2d ed., revised by P. M. Fraser. Oxford: Oxford University Press, 1956.

Rostovtzeff, Michael I. *Social and Economic History of the Hellenistic World*. 3 vols. Oxford: Oxford University Press, 1941.

Rowell, Henry T. *Rome in the Augustan Age*. Norman: University of Oklahoma Press, 1962.

Scullard, Howard H. *The Etruscan Cities and Rome*. Ithaca: Cornell University Press, 1967.

Smith, Richard E. *The Failure of the Roman Republic*. Cambridge: Cambridge University Press, 1955.

Syme, Ronald. *The Roman Revolution*. London: Oxford University Press, 1939. Paperback, 1960.
A useful restudy of the end of the Republic and the beginning of the Empire.

Taylor, Lily Ross. *Party Politics in the Age of Caesar*. Berkeley: University of California Press, 1949. Paperback, 1961.

Thompson, E. A. *The Early Germans*. Oxford: Clarendon, 1965.

Warmington, B. H. *Carthage*. Baltimore: Penguin, 1965.

Wheeler, Robert E. Mortimer. *Rome Beyond the Imperial Frontiers*. London: Bell, 1965.
The archaeological story of trade with people outside the Empire, especially in Germany and India.

INDEX

INDEX

651

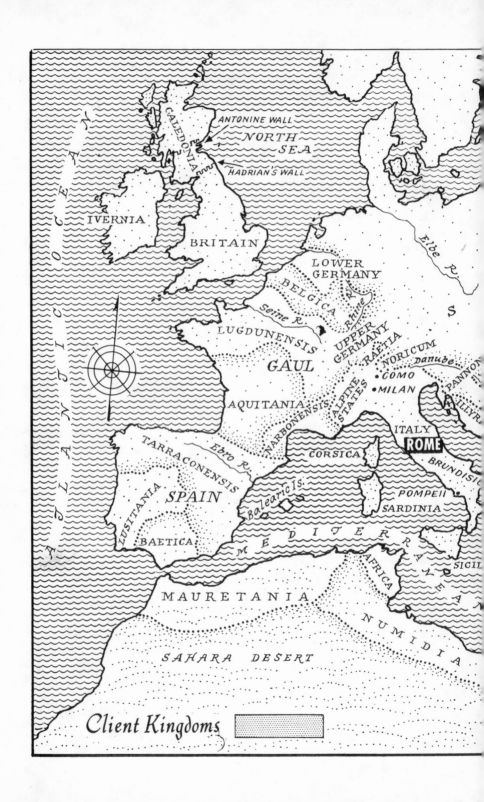